MILITARY AIRCRAFT
VISUAL ENCYCLOPEDIA

MILITARY AIRCRAFT
VISUAL ENCYCLOPEDIA

amber
BOOKS

First published in 2009 by
Amber Books Ltd
Bradley's Close
74–77 White Lion Street
London N1 9PF
United Kingdom
www.amberbooks.co.uk

Reprinted in 2010

ISBN: 978-1-906626-71-6

Project Editor: Sarah Uttridge
Editorial Assistant: Kieron Connolly
Design: Andrew Easton

Printed in China

CONTENTS

INTRODUCTION

Less than 10 years after the Wright Brothers' first flight in December 1903, the first aircraft was used for military purposes. Balloons had long been recognized as ideal for spotting on the battlefield, and the advantages of aircraft as spotters for the military were plain to see. But it was an Italian aircraft that first acted as a weapon in its own right, dropping explosives on the enemy during the Italian–Libyan War of 1911. Then, with the outbreak of World War I three years later, military aircraft development was given a massive boost.

By 1918, the frail reconnaissance aircraft of 1914 had developed into faster and stronger machines, armed with machine guns and capable of dramatic air manoeuvres while dogfighting the enemy. Bombers, too, appeared; large, lumbering beasts with a small bombload but with sufficient range to attack strategic targets such as London.

The end of the war saw the rate of technological advancement slowed, and there were few advances in military aircraft design until German rearmament began in the early 1930s. At this point there was a change in aircraft design, as fabric-covered biplanes were replaced in civil and then military service by monoplanes with light alloy skinning. The potential of these new aircraft against ground targets was shown in the German 'Blitzkrieg' campaigns of 1939–41.

The Emergence of Jet Propulsion

World War II demonstrated that command of the air was vital for any offensive employment of air assets for strategic bombing and ground support, and was also significant in protecting assets against an enemy's bombers, and safeguarding surface forces against enemy air attacks. World War II also saw the emergence of jet propulsion, although it was during the Korean War that the military jet earned its spurs.

The late 1950s was the heyday of the strategic bomber: large, multi-engined aircraft designed to deliver nuclear or conventional weapons to targets across thousands of miles of ocean. The US and Soviet Union fielded jet bombers early in the 1950s and to counter the threat of these, both East and West were forced to build a new generation of fast-climbing, radar-equipped aircraft that matched the bombers in complexity. During the 1950s and early 1960s, the vast majority of military jets were manufactured by the US, Soviet Union, Britain and France. Aircraft produced by these countries were also widely exported.

Revolutionary Advances

The 1960s saw the Soviet Union produce more advanced types and the late 1960s also heralded the arrival of a revolutionary new form of aircraft, the Vertical/Short TakeOff and Landing (V/STOL) Hawker Siddley Harrier. But the experience of the Vietnam War caused another rethink: instances of air-to-air combat were few and far between and by far the greatest threat faced by American pilots were the surface to-air missiles (SAMs), leading many analysts to predict the end of manned fighter aircraft.

Since the 1990s, the end of the Cold War has changed strategic considerations and emphasized the need for rapidly deployable forces and multi-role combat aircraft to police trouble spots. Stealth technology has emerged as the by-word of modern aviation, but as was demonstrated during the 2003 Iraq War, the military jet continues to be the most potent and important symbol of military might.

Above: The Harrier is one of the few truly successful aircraft that emerged from the V/STOL aircraft designs of the 1960s.

THE BIPLANE ERA

The first fighting aeroplanes were employed as a tool of the army, flying over enemy lines and observing enemy fire. Bombing and fighting were missions that only came later.

Between 1914 and 1918 air combat developed from airman firing small arms at passing opponents to vicious battles involving dozens of aircraft. The strategic potential of aircraft began to be realised with long-range raids by bombers and airships on cities. The basic aircraft construction materials remained wood, fabric and wire, with a handful of metal-skinned machines appearing at the war's end.

Left: The Sopwith Pup was a fine example of the mid-war fighting scout.
It was light and manoeuvrable, but armed with a single gun.

Early Birds

Before 1914, the few squadrons of the Royal Flying Corps and the Royal Naval Air Service operated a wide range of aircraft, few of them armed in any way. Even individual squadrons were often equipped with craft of several types from different manufacturers. On the outbreak of war, things became more standardized, and devices for mounting light bombs and machine guns were soon fitted. Until 1915, the main roles for aircraft remained reconnaissance and spotting the fall of artillery, for which stability was more important than agility.

British Army Aeroplane No I

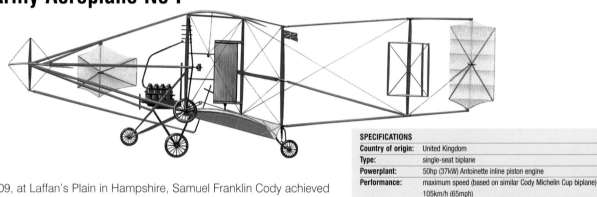

On 14 May 1909, at Laffan's Plain in Hampshire, Samuel Franklin Cody achieved the first aeroplane flight in Europe of more than 1.6km (1 mile) in his British Army Aeroplane No 1. The aircraft was built in great secrecy in 1907 at the Army Balloon Factory at Farnborough, where Cody was engaged as the chief kiting instructor to the Royal Engineers' Balloon Corps.

SPECIFICATIONS	
Country of origin:	United Kingdom
Type:	single-seat biplane
Powerplant:	50hp (37kW) Antoinette inline piston engine
Performance:	maximum speed (based on similar Cody Michelin Cup biplane) 105km/h (65mph)
Weights:	maximum take-off weight 1338kg (2950lb)
Dimensions:	span 15.85m (52ft 4in); length 11.73m (38ft 6in); height 3.96m (13ft); wing area 59.46 sq m (640 sq ft)

Royal Aircraft Factory B.E.2c

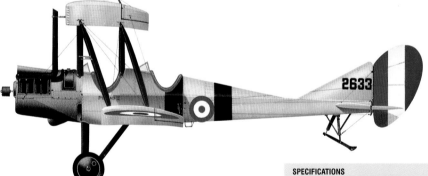

His Majesty's Balloon Factory at Farnborough diversified into heavier-than-air machines in 1909. The B.E.2c (Blériot Experimental) introduced the 90hp (66kW) RAF 1a engine and was the first to be armed with a machine gun. In wartime service, the B.E.2 was a fine reconnaissance platform, but its stability proved lethal in aerial combat and many were lost during the 'Fokker Scourge' of 1915–16. Production certainly exceeded the 3535 for which records survive.

SPECIFICATIONS	
Country of origin:	United Kingdom
Type:	two-seat reconnaissance/light bomber aircraft
Powerplant:	one 90hp (67kW) RAF 1a inline piston engine
Performance:	maximum speed 145km/h (90mph); service ceiling 2745m (9000ft); endurance 4hrs
Weights:	empty 649kg (1431lb); maximum take-off weight 953kg (2100lb)
Dimensions:	span 12.42m (40ft 9in); length 8.31m (27ft 3in); height 3.66m (12ft); wing area 33.44 sq m (360 sq ft)
Armament:	one .303in Vickers machine gun capable of being mounted on various upper centre wing and fuselage points

EARLY BIRDS TIMELINE

1909 May	1910	1911

Sopwith Tabloid

One of the first aircraft from Sopwith was a racing biplane, so small it was called the Tabloid. At Farnborough, it astonished everyone by reaching 148km/h (92mph) with a passenger and reaching 647m (1200ft) in one minute after leaving the ground. Thirty-six were subsequently built for the RFC and RNAS; RNAS machines mounted a series of famous attacks on the Zeppelin sheds in winter 1914. A float-equipped version was built as the Sopwith Schneider.

SPECIFICATIONS	
Country of origin:	United Kingdom
Type:	single-seat maritime patrol and attack seaplane
Powerplant:	one 100hp (74.5kW) Gnow Monosoupape 9-cylinder rotary piston engine
Performance:	maximum speed 148km/h (92mph); service ceiling 4600m (15,000ft); range 510km (315 miles)
Weights:	empty 545kg (1200lb); maximum take-off weight 717kg (1580lb)
Dimensions:	span 7.77m (25ft 6in); length 7.02m (23ft); height 3.05m (10ft)
Armament:	Royal Naval Air Service seaplanes had one .303in Lewis machine gun

Avro 504K

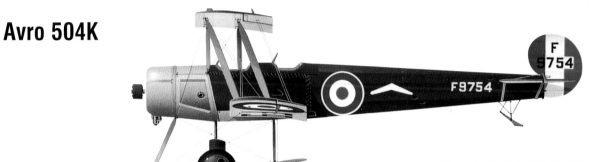

Production of the Avro 504K during World War I totalled around 8340 aircraft, but it remained in production until 1933, 20 years after the first models were ordered. Sixty-three of the basic version were produced and although these saw limited active service, including the raid on the Zeppelin sheds at Friedrichshafen in November 1914, the type saw more widespread use in the training role.

SPECIFICATIONS	
Country of origin:	United Kingdom
Type:	two-seat elementary trainer
Powerplant:	one 110hp (82kW) Le Rhône rotary piston engine
Performance:	maximum speed 153km/h (95mph); service ceiling 4875m (16,000ft); range 402km (250 miles)
Weights:	empty 558kg (1230lb); maximum take-off weight 830kg (1829lb)
Dimensions:	span 10.97m (36ft); length 8.97m (29ft 5in); height 3.17m (10ft 5in); wing area 30.66 sq m (330 sq ft)

Royal Aircraft Factory F.E.2b

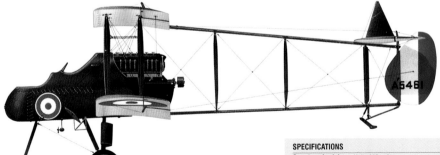

The layout of the F.E.2b was due to the need to fire a machine gun, since in 1913 there was no way of safely firing ahead through a tractor propeller. The pilot therefore occupied the rear cockpit, although for night operations this was reversed. The first order for 12 F.E.2as was placed in August 1914, followed by the more powerful F.E.2b and F.E.2c. In total, 1939 of these were built.

SPECIFICATIONS	
Country of origin:	United Kingdom
Type:	two-seat fighter
Powerplant:	one 120hp (89kW) Beardmore inline piston engine
Performance:	maximum speed 129km/h (80mph); service ceiling 2745m (9000ft); endurance 3hrs
Weights:	empty 904kg (1993lb); maximum take-off weight 1347kg (2970lb)
Dimensions:	span 14.55m (47ft 9in); length 9.83m (32ft 3in); height 3.85m (12ft 7in); wing area 45.89 sq m (494 sq ft)
Armament:	one or two .303in Lewis machine guns; plus up to 159kg (350lb) of bombs

1912 1913 1914 1915

Fighters and Scouts

Before long, reconnaissance aircraft encountered each other over the lines. The first known victim of an armed aerial combat was a German Aviatik two-seater, shot down by a French observer's rifle in October 1914. Deflector plates on propellers allowing forward-facing machine-guns followed by April 1915, but the real revolution came with the Fokker Eindecker and its interrupter gear. The stately BE.2s and RE.8s fell in large numbers to the 'Fokker Scourge', prompting many Allied countermeasures, including 'pusher' scouts like the DH.2 with its propeller behind the pilot.

Albatros B.III

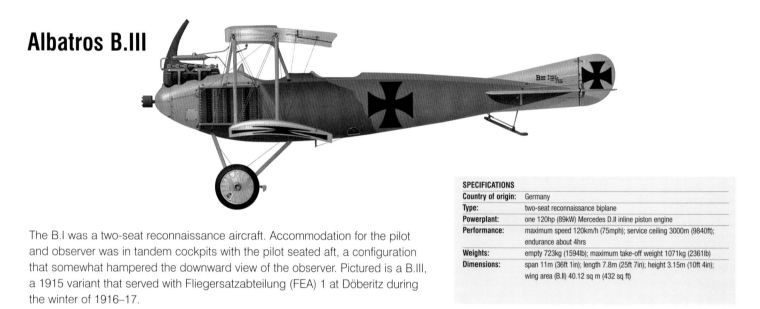

The B.I was a two-seat reconnaissance aircraft. Accommodation for the pilot and observer was in tandem cockpits with the pilot seated aft, a configuration that somewhat hampered the downward view of the observer. Pictured is a B.III, a 1915 variant that served with Fliegersatzabteilung (FEA) 1 at Döberitz during the winter of 1916–17.

SPECIFICATIONS	
Country of origin:	Germany
Type:	two-seat reconnaissance biplane
Powerplant:	one 120hp (89kW) Mercedes D.II inline piston engine
Performance:	maximum speed 120km/h (75mph); service ceiling 3000m (9840ft); endurance about 4hrs
Weights:	empty 723kg (1594lb); maximum take-off weight 1071kg (2361lb)
Dimensions:	span 11m (36ft 1in); length 7.8m (25ft 7in); height 3.15m (10ft 4in); wing area (B.II) 40.12 sq m (432 sq ft)

Aviatik B.II

The B.I two-seat reconnaissance aircraft appeared in service in 1914, and in common with contemporary unarmed reconnaissance machines, the observer was accommodated in the forward cockpit. The B.II appeared in 1915 and had a lightened and stronger rudder and elevator structure, as well as a more powerful Mercedes engine. Pictured is an Aviatik B.II of the Beobachterschule (Observers' School) based at Köln-Butzweilerhof in 1916.

SPECIFICATIONS	
Country of origin:	Germany
Type:	two-seat reconnaissance biplane
Powerplant:	one 120hp (89kW) Mercedes D.III 6-cylinder inline piston engine
Performance:	maximum speed 100km/h (62mph); endurance 4hrs
Weights:	1088kg (2400lb)
Dimensions:	span 13.97m (45ft 10in); length 7.97m (26ft 2in); height 3.3m (10ft 10in)

FIGHTERS AND SCOUTS TIMELINE
1915

Fokker E.III

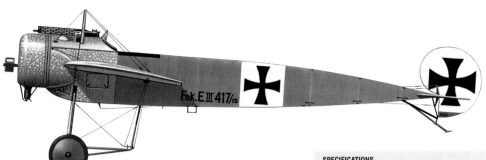

In April 1915, Roland Garros' aircraft, with his self-designed bullet deflector gear, fell into German hands, prompting them to develop a more effective interrupter gear. This was fitted to a short-span M.5k scout to produce the E.I, and from April until the end of December 1915 the Fokker monoplane was the scourge of Allied pilots on the Western Front. The E.III was the definitive model, with 300 aircraft produced, and was the favourite of the German aces Böelcke and Immelmann.

SPECIFICATIONS	
Country of origin:	France
Type:	two-seat observation biplane
Powerplant:	one 135hp (101kW) Renault 12-cylinder Vee piston engine
Performance:	maximum speed 135km/h (84mph); service ceiling 4000m (13,125ft); endurance 2hrs 20mins
Weights:	empty 748kg (1649lb); maximum take-off weight 1120kg (2469lb)
Dimensions:	span 17.6m (57ft 9in); length 9.25m (30ft 4in); height 3.9m (12ft 9in); wing area 52 sq m (560 sq ft)
Armament:	one or two .303 Lewis guns on flexible mount in nose position; light bombs and (F.40P) Le Prieur rockets

Royal Aircraft Factory R.E.8

A two-seat reconnaissance/artillery spotting aircraft, the R.E.8 resembled a scaled-up version of the B.E.2 and shared the same staggered biplane wing configuration. As a result of mysterious accidents in 1916, the tail was redesigned and the production of an eventual 4077 aircraft was resumed. However, like the B.E.2, the aircraft's inherent stability proved a major handicap in aerial combat, and it was never a really popular machine.

SPECIFICATIONS	
Country of origin:	United Kingdom
Type:	two-seat reconnaissance/artillery spotting aircraft
Powerplant:	one 150hp (112kW) RAF 4a 12-cylinder Vee piston engine
Performance:	maximum speed 164km/h (102mph); service ceiling 4115m (13,500ft); endurance 4hrs 15mins
Weights:	empty 717kg (1580lb); maximum take-off weight 1301kg (2869lb)
Dimensions:	span 12.98m (42ft 7in); length 6.38m (20ft 11in); height 2.9m (9ft 6in); wing area 22.67 sq m (444 sq ft)
Armament:	one fixed forward-firing .303in Vickers machine gun; one .303in Lewis machine gun on pivoted mounting over rear cockpit; plus a bomb load of up to 102kg (224lb)

Airco D.H.2

With no interrupter gear available to British aircraft designers, the unusual pusher layout was considered essential for the D.H.2, mounting a Lewis gun in the front cockpit, its field of fire unencumbered by the need to avoid the propeller. Controlling the aircraft while operating the gun was tricky, but the D.H.2 was the best fighter available to the British in mid-1916.

SPECIFICATIONS	
Country of origin:	United Kingdom
Type:	single-seat scout fighter biplane
Powerplant:	one 100hp (75kW) Gnome Monosoupape rotary piston engine; later examples had 110hp (82kW) Le Rhône rotary
Performance:	maximum speed 150km/h (93mph); service ceiling 1300m (4265ft); endurance 2hrs 45mins
Weights:	empty 428kg (943lb); maximum take-off weight 654kg (1441lb)
Dimensions:	span 8.61m (28ft 3in); length 7.68m (25ft 2in); height 2.91m (9ft 6¼in); wing area 23.13 sq m (249 sq ft)
Armament:	one forward-firing .303in Lewis gun on flexible mounting

1916

Nieuports

The famous Nieuport fighters designed by Gustave Délage had the lower wing much narrower than the upper wing, thus making them 'sesquiplanes'. This, and a slight wing sweepback on most models, gave a good view downwards, but structural strength suffered. The Nieuports were used by French, British, Italian and American units and were the mounts of many aces. The distinctive 'V' struts were replaced in the totally revised Nieuport 28 with parallel struts and a streamlined fuselage.

Nieuport 11

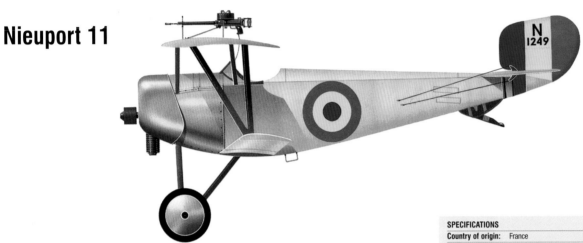

Gustave Délage's Nieuport 10 was a small two-seat reconnaissance sesquiplane (with the lower wing much smaller than the upper). However, it proved underpowered, and most of the two-seaters were converted to single-seat scouts. Délage also designed the Nieuport Bébé and developed this into the Type 11 scout. Hundreds were built for the RFC, RNAS, French and Belgian Aviation Militaire, and the Imperial Russian Air Service.

SPECIFICATIONS	
Country of origin:	France
Type:	single-seat fighting scout
Powerplant:	one 80hp (60kW) Le Rhône 9C 9-cylinder rotary engine
Performance:	maximum speed 155km/h (97mph); service ceiling 4500m (14,765ft); endurance 2hrs 30mins
Weights:	empty 350kg (772lb); maximum take-off weight 480kg (1058lb)
Dimensions:	span 7.55m (24ft 9in); length 5.8m (19ft); height 2.45m (8ft); wing area 13 sq m (140 sq ft)
Armament:	one fixed forward-firing .303in Vickers machine gun

Nieuport 17

The Nieuport 17 was unquestionably one of the finest Allied combat aircraft of World War I. The aircraft first flew in January 1916 and the first deliveries were made in May, helping to end the 'Fokker Scourge' of the previous months. The aircraft was highly manoeuvrable for its time, with a high rate of climb and good performance.

SPECIFICATIONS	
Country of origin:	France
Type:	single-seat fighting scout
Powerplant:	110hp (82kW) Le Rhône 9J rotary piston engine
Performance:	maximum speed 170km/h (106mph); service ceiling 1980m (6500ft); range 250km (155 miles)
Weights:	empty 374kg (825lb); maximum take-off weight 560kg (1235lb)
Dimensions:	span 8.2m (26ft 11in); length 5.96m (19ft 7in); height 2.44m (8ft); wing area 14.75 sq m (159 sq ft)
Armament:	one fixed forward-firing .303in Vickers machine gun

Nieuport 27

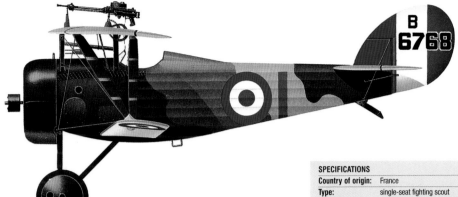

SPECIFICATIONS	
Country of origin:	France
Type:	single-seat fighting scout
Powerplant:	120hp (89kW) Le Rhône rotary piston engine
Performance:	maximum speed 185km/h (115mph); service ceiling 5550m
	(18,210ft); range 250km (155 miles)
Weights:	empty 380kg (838lb); maximum take-off weight 585kg (1289lb)
Dimensions:	span 8.2m (26ft 11in); length 5.85m (19ft 2in); height 2.42m
	(7ft 11in); wing area 14.75 sq m (159 sq ft)
Armament:	one fixed forward-firing .303in Vickers machine gun; one fixed
	forward-firing .303in Lewis machine gun

The most successful offshoot of the Type 17 was the Type 21, produced by substituting an 80hp (60kW) Le Rhône engine and enlarging the ailerons. Nearly 200 of these were produced, mostly for Russia and the United States, and in the years after the war it was the mount of a number of the barnstormers. Pictured is a Nieuport 27 of No 1 Squadron, RFC, with French-style two-tone camouflage.

Nieuport 28

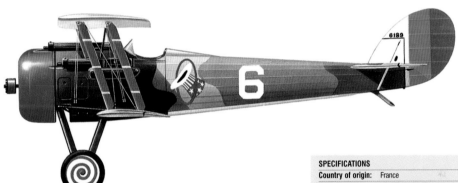

SPECIFICATIONS	
Country of origin:	France
Type:	single-seat fighter
Powerplant:	one 160hp (119kW) Gnome-Le Rhône 9N rotary piston engine
Performance:	maximum speed 195km/h (121mph); service ceiling 5200m
	(17,060ft); range 400km (248 miles)
Weights:	empty 532kg (1172lb); maximum take-off weight 740kg (1631lb)
Dimensions:	span 8m (26ft 3in); length 6.2m (20ft 4in); height 2.48m (8ft 2in);
	wing area 20 sq m (215 sq ft)
Armament:	two fixed forward-firing .303in Vickers machine guns

Unlike the Type 17, the Type 28 had wings of almost equal proportion, braced by parallel struts and a fuselage of circular section. In service from March 1918, the new Gnome engine proved totally unreliable, and at high speed any violent manoeuvre tended to rip the fabric from the upper wing. However, the Type 28 was the only fighter readily available to the US Expeditionary Force in 1918.

Nieuport-Délage Ni-D 29

SPECIFICATIONS	
Country of origin:	France
Type:	single-seat fighter
Powerplant:	one 300hp (224kW) Hispano-Suiza 8Fb 8-cylinder Vee piston engine
Performance:	maximum speed 235km/h (146mph); service ceiling 8500m
	(27,885ft); range 580km (360 miles)
Weights:	empty 760kg (1675lb); maximum take-off weight 1150kg (2535lb)
Dimensions:	span 9.7m (31ft 10in); length 6.49m (21ft 3in); height 2.56m
	(8ft 5in); wing area 26.7 sq m (287 sq ft)
Armament:	two fixed forward-firing .303in Vickers machine guns

The Nieuport Ni-D 29 was ordered into quantity production at the beginning of 1920. Initial deliveries of an eventual 250 aircraft to the French Aviation Militaire were made in 1922, followed by orders from Spain and Belgium. Japan was by far the biggest customer, with 608 built for the Japanese Army as the Ko-4.

Naval Aircraft

The first maritime aircraft, as opposed to airships or landplanes operated by naval services, were floatplanes and flying boats. These were used for coastal and anti-submarine patrol, naval gunfire spotting and other duties. The Short 184 had some success as a torpedo bomber. Camels were used by the RNAS in France and also towed on platforms (lighters) behind warships to intercept Zeppelins crossing the North Sea. Recovery involved ditching in the sea near the ship. Beardmore's W.B.III was one of the first aircraft designed specifically for operations from aboard ships.

Hansa-Brandenburg W.12

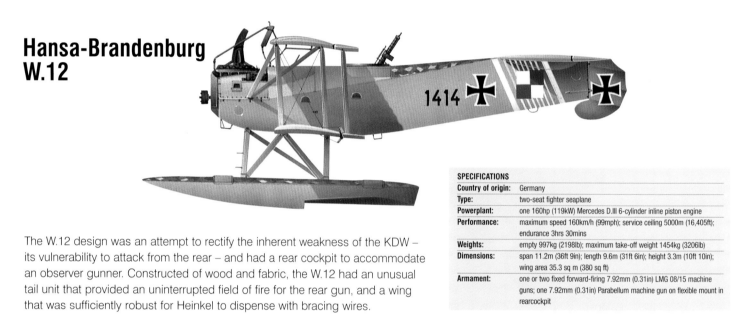

The W.12 design was an attempt to rectify the inherent weakness of the KDW – its vulnerability to attack from the rear – and had a rear cockpit to accommodate an observer gunner. Constructed of wood and fabric, the W.12 had an unusual tail unit that provided an uninterrupted field of fire for the rear gun, and a wing that was sufficiently robust for Heinkel to dispense with bracing wires.

SPECIFICATIONS	
Country of origin:	Germany
Type:	two-seat fighter seaplane
Powerplant:	one 160hp (119kW) Mercedes D.III 6-cylinder inline piston engine
Performance:	maximum speed 160km/h (99mph); service ceiling 5000m (16,405ft); endurance 3hrs 30mins
Weights:	empty 997kg (2198lb); maximum take-off weight 1454kg (3206lb)
Dimensions:	span 11.2m (36ft 9in); length 9.6m (31ft 6in); height 3.3m (10ft 10in); wing area 35.3 sq m (380 sq ft)
Armament:	one or two fixed forward-firing 7.92mm (0.31in) LMG 08/15 machine guns; one 7.92mm (0.31in) Parabellum machine gun on flexible mount in rear cockpit

Short 184

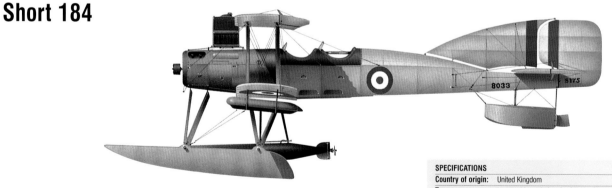

The Type 184 was built in response to an Admiralty requirement for a torpedo-carrying seaplane and gave sterling service during World War I. Some 900 aircraft were built, but after achieving some spectacular early successes the Type 184 was most commonly used for reconnaissance. The aircraft served in many theatres, from the Arctic Circle to the Indian Ocean. This is one of three aircraft attached to the famous seaplane-carrier HMS *Vindex*

SPECIFICATIONS	
Country of origin:	United Kingdom
Type:	two-seat torpedo-bomber/reconnaissance floatplane
Powerplant:	one 260hp (194kW) Sunbeam Maori Vee piston engine
Performance:	maximum speed 142km/h (88mph); service ceiling 2745m (9000ft); endurance 2hrs 45mins
Weights:	empty 1680kg (3703lb); maximum take-off weight 2433kg (5363lb)
Dimensions:	span 19.36m (63ft 6in); length 12.38m (40ft 7in); height 4.11m (13ft 6in); wing area 63.92 sq m (688 sq ft)
Armament:	one .303in Lewis machine gun on pivoted mount in rear cockpit; plus one 14in torpedo or up to 236kg (520lb) of bombs

NAVAL AIRCRAFT TIMELINE

1915　　　　1916　　　　1917

Sopwith Camel 2F.1

The final production version of the Camel was the 2F.1, a shipboard fighter with slightly reduced wingspan, jettisonable steel-tube landing gear and detachable rear fuselage (for compact carrier stowage). At the time of the Armistice, the Royal Air Force had 129 2F.1 Camels on charge, 112 of which were with the Grand Fleet. As well as being flown from aircraft carriers, they were catapulted from platforms erected on the gun turrets and forecastles of many warships.

SPECIFICATIONS	
Country of origin:	United Kingdom
Type:	single-seat fighting scout
Powerplant:	one 130hp (97kW) Clerget rotary piston engine
Performance:	maximum speed 185km/h (115mph); service ceiling 5790m (19,000ft); endurance 2hrs 30mins
Weights:	empty 421kg (929lb); maximum take-off weight 659kg (1453lb)
Dimensions:	span 8.2m (26ft 11in); length 5.72m (18ft 9in); height 2.59m (8ft 6in)
Armament:	one fixed forward-firing .303in Vickers machine gun; one .303in Lewis machine gun; plus (on some) two 22.7kg (50lb) bombs carried on fuselage sides

Beardmore W.B.III

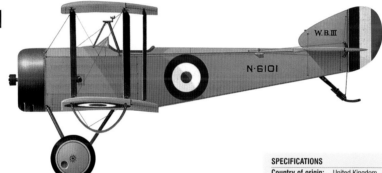

One of the many licensed wartime manufacturers of the Sopwith Pup was William Beardmore and Co Ltd of Balmuir, which developed a prototype version, the Beardmore W.B.III, for carrier operations. This had folding landing gear; folding, unstaggered wings; a lengthened fuselage carrying emergency flotation gear; a modified interplane strut configuration; and rod-operated ailerons with inter-aileron struts fitted to the upper and lower mainplanes.

SPECIFICATIONS	
Country of origin:	United Kingdom
Type:	single-seat shipboard fighter
Powerplant:	one 80hp (60kW) Le Rhône 9C or Clerget rotary piston engine
Performance:	maximum speed 166km/h (103mph); service ceiling 3780m (12,400ft); endurance 2hrs 45mins
Weights:	empty 404kg (890lb); maximum take-off weight 585kg (1289lb)
Dimensions:	span 7.62m (25ft); length 6.16m (20ft); height 2.47m (8ft 1in); wing area 22.57 sq m (243 sq ft)
Armament:	one .303in Lewis machine gun

Felixstowe F.5

Commander John C. Porte's F.2A was the standard RNAS flying-boat of World War I. The completely redesigned F.5 was the standard RAF flying-boat from 1918 until it was replaced by the Supermarine Southampton in August 1925. In 1918, the US Navy adopted a variant of the F.5 powered by the Liberty engine, which was built by Curtiss, Canadian Aeroplanes of Toronto and the US Naval Aircraft Factory.

SPECIFICATIONS	
Country of origin:	United Kingdom
Type:	reconnaissance flying-boat
Powerplant:	two 350hp (261kW) Rolls-Royce Eagle VIII 12-cylinder Vee piston engines
Performance:	maximum speed 142km/h (88mph); service ceiling 2075m (6800ft); endurance 7hrs
Weights:	empty 4128kg (9100lb); maximum take-off weight 5752kg (12,682lb)
Dimensions:	span 31.6m (103ft 8in); length 15.01m (49ft 3in); height 5.72m (18ft 9in); wing area 130.9 sq m (1409 sq ft)
Armament:	one .303in Lewis machine gun on flexible mount in nose position; one .303in Lewis machine gun on flexible mount in each midship position; underwing racks with provision for four 104kg (230lb) bombs

| 1918 | 1919 | 1920 | 1921 |

D.H.4s and 9s

Designed by Geoffrey de Havilland for the Aircraft Manufacturing Company (Airco), the D.H.4 was the first purpose-designed light day bomber and in service proved suitable for many other roles. The poorly located fuel tank between the crew positions caused difficulties in communication and led to the nickname 'flaming coffin'. The D.H.9A with the Liberty engine had a successful war career and a post-war career that stretched into the 1930s and around the globe.

Airco D.H.4

De Havilland designed the Airco D.H.4 around the 200 BHP (Beardmore-Halford-Pullinger) engine in response to an Air Ministry request for a new day bomber. In this role, the D.H.4 was the best aircraft in its class during the war. The wide separation between pilot and observer was a controversial and potentially dangerous feature, as it hampered communication in the air. Pictured is a Rolls-Royce Eagle VI-engined aircraft of No 5 (Naval) Squadron, RNAS.

SPECIFICATIONS	
Country of origin:	United Kingdom
Type:	two-seat day bomber biplane (Westland-built, Eagle VI engine)
Powerplant:	one 250hp (186kW) Rolls-Royce Eagle VI inline piston engine
Performance:	maximum speed 230km/h (143mph); service ceiling 6705m (22,000ft); endurance 3hrs 45mins
Weights:	empty 1083kg (2387lb); maximum take-off weight 1575kg (3742lb)
Dimensions:	span 12.92m (42ft 4in); length 9.35m (30ft 8in); height 3.35m (11ft); wing area 40.32 sq m (434 sq ft)
Armament:	four .303in Vickers MGs (two fixed forward-firing and two in rear cockpit); external pylons; provision for 209kg (460lb) of bombs

Airco D.H.4

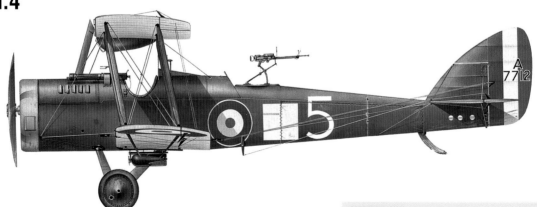

Seven different engines of between 200hp (149kW) and 275hp (205kW) output were fitted to production D.H.4 aircraft. The best D.H.4s had a 375hp (280kW) Eagle VIII from Rolls-Royce, but this was expensive to produce and, because of its larger propeller, needed longer landing gears. The Airco-built example pictured has the RAF 3a engine, distinguishable by the single exhaust stack and the frontal radiator, which is tapered slightly from top to bottom.

SPECIFICATIONS	
Country of origin:	United Kingdom
Type:	two-seat day bomber biplane (early RAF 3a engine)
Powerplant:	one 200hp (149kW) RAF 3a inline piston engine
Performance:	maximum speed 230km/h (143mph); service ceiling 5000m (17,400ft); endurance 3hrs 45mins
Weights:	empty 1083kg (2387lb); maximum take-off weight 1575kg (3742lb)
Dimensions:	span 12.92m (42ft 4in); length 9.35m (30ft 8in); height 3.35m (11ft); wing area 40.32 sq m (434 sq ft)
Armament:	one fixed forward-firing .303in Vickers MG and one .303in Lewis MG in rear cockpit; provision for 209kg (460lb) of bombs

Airco D.H.4 'Liberty Plane'

America showed great interest in the D.H.4, and from mid-1917 licensed manufacture of the aircraft was undertaken by US companies. Many of the aircraft passed to civilian operators after the war, when the D.H.4 flourished in the United States. No fewer than 60 separate versions were evolved for roles as diverse as crop-dusting and aerial mapping. Pictured is a D.H.4B.

SPECIFICATIONS	
Country of origin:	USA (United Kingdom)
Type:	two-seat day bomber biplane (US-built American Liberty engine)
Powerplant:	one 400hp (298kW) Packard Liberty 12 inline piston engine
Performance:	maximum speed 230km/h (143mph); service ceiling 5000m (17,400ft); endurance 3hrs 45mins
Weights:	empty 1083kg (2387lb); maximum take-off weight 1575kg (3742lb)
Dimensions:	span 12.92m (42ft 4in); length 9.35m (30ft 8in); height 3.35m (11ft); wing area 40.32 sq m (434 sq ft)
Armament:	one fixed forward-firing .303in Vickers machine gun and one .303in Lewis machine gun in rear cockpit; external pylons with provision for 209kg (460lb) of bombs

Airco D.H.9

The D.H.4 had a new fuselage and an unreliable low-powered engine, which contributed to heavy losses when it entered combat in early 1918 on the Western Front. It had more success where there was less air opposition, such as over Russia during the Civil War. Estonia operated D.H.9s from 1919–33 (an Estonian plane is pictured here).

SPECIFICATIONS	
Country of origin:	France
Type:	two-seat day bomber
Powerplant:	one 172kW (230hp) Armstrong Siddeley Puma inline piston engine
Performance:	maximum speed 182km/h (113mph); endurance: 4hrs 30 minutes; service ceiling: 4730m (15,500ft)
Weights:	empty 1014kg (2360lb); maximum 1723kg (3790lb)
Dimensions:	span 19.92m (42ft 5in); length 9.27m (30ft 5in); height 3.44m (11ft 4in); wing area 40.3 sq m (434 sq ft)
Armament:	one .303in Vickers machine gun, one or two .303in Lewis machine guns; up to 209kg (460lb) of bombs

Airco D.H.9A

German raids on Britain during World War I prompted a doubling in the size of the Royal Flying Corps. The D.H.9 attempted to rectify a weakness of the D.H.4 by placing the pilot and observer in back-to-back seating. In service from December 1917, the D.H.9's Puma engine was unreliable and the aircraft had a much-reduced ceiling of 3960m (13,000ft). The improved D.H.9A with a 400hp (298kW) Liberty engine was produced after the war.

SPECIFICATIONS	
Country of origin:	United Kingdom
Type:	two-seat day bomber biplane (American Liberty engine)
Powerplant:	one 420hp (313kW) Packard Liberty 12 vee-12 piston engine
Performance:	maximum speed 198km/h (123mph); service ceiling 5105m (16,750ft); endurance 5hrs 15mins
Weights:	empty 1270kg (2800lb); maximum take-off weight 2107kg (4645lb)
Dimensions:	span 14.01m (45ft 11in); length 9.22m (30ft 3in); height 3.45m (11ft 4in); wing area 45.22 sq m (487 sq ft)
Armament:	one fixed forward-firing .303in Vickers machine gun and one or two .303in Lewis machine guns on Scarff ring in rear cockpit; external pylons with provision for 299kg (660lb) of bombs

Big Bombers

Multi-engined aircraft were a rarity before 1914, as were aircraft that could carry much of a load beyond a crew. As the war progressed, the front lines became more static and fortified, and air forces called for bombers capable of striking at the enemy's rear areas, lines of communications and cities. The German Army Air Service in particular developed large and then 'giant' aircraft to complement the navy Zeppelins. Striking at Britain, they caused alarm and diverted resources from the front to anti-aircraft defence despite causing relatively little material damage.

Caproni Ca.3

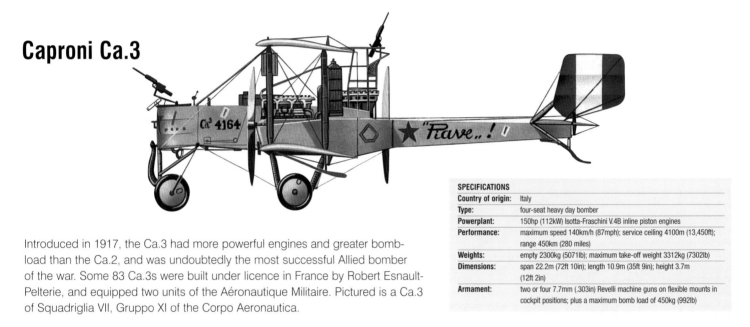

Introduced in 1917, the Ca.3 had more powerful engines and greater bomb-load than the Ca.2, and was undoubtedly the most successful Allied bomber of the war. Some 83 Ca.3s were built under licence in France by Robert Esnault-Pelterie, and equipped two units of the Aéronautique Militaire. Pictured is a Ca.3 of Squadriglia VII, Gruppo XI of the Corpo Aeronautica.

SPECIFICATIONS	
Country of origin:	Italy
Type:	four-seat heavy day bomber
Powerplant:	150hp (112kW) Isotta-Fraschini V.4B inline piston engines
Performance:	maximum speed 140km/h (87mph); service ceiling 4100m (13,450ft); range 450km (280 miles)
Weights:	empty 2300kg (5071lb); maximum take-off weight 3312kg (7302lb)
Dimensions:	span 22.2m (72ft 10in); length 10.9m (35ft 9in); height 3.7m (12ft 2in)
Armament:	two or four 7.7mm (.303in) Revelli machine guns on flexible mounts in cockpit positions; plus a maximum bomb load of 450kg (992lb)

Gotha G.V

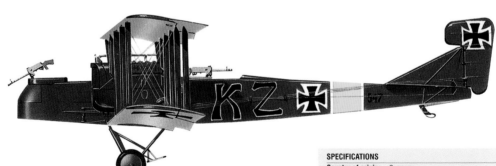

Alongside the airships and 'R' series from the Zeppelin works, the series of 'G' (Grossflugzeug, large aeroplane) designs from Gothaer Wagonfabrik played a major role in German strategic bombing in World War I. From the G.IV onwards, the major production version, there was a tunnel extending to a rear gunner's cockpit. There were a limited number of G.V and G.Va aircraft built before night-bombing was abandoned by the German Air Service in April 1918.

SPECIFICATIONS	
Country of origin:	Germany
Type:	three-seat long-range biplane bomber
Powerplant:	two 260hp (194kW) Mercedes D.IVa 6-cylinder inline piston engines
Performance:	maximum speed 140km/h (87mph); service ceiling 6500m (21,325ft); range 500km (500 km)
Weights:	empty 2740kg (6041lb); maximum take-off weight 3975kg (8763lb)
Dimensions:	span 23.7m (77ft 9in); length 11.86m (38ft 11in); height 4.3m (14ft 1in); wing area 89.5 sq m (963 sq ft)
Armament:	four 7.92mm (.31in) Parabellum MGs (two on flexible mount in nose; two on flexible mount dorsally); maximum bomb load of 500kg (1102lb)

BIG BOMBERS TIMELINE

1914

1916

Breguet Bre.14 A.2

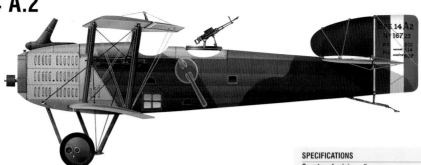

In the summer of 1916, Louis Breguet's chief engineer Louis Vullierme began the design of Breguet's most successful wartime product, the Bre.14. The prototype of this two-seat reconnaissance/light bomber aircraft made its first flight barely five months later, and the first Bre.14 A.2 production aircraft entered service with the Aéronautique Militaire the following spring. The Bre.14 quickly established a reputation for toughness and reliability.

SPECIFICATIONS	
Country of origin:	France
Type:	two-seat reconnaissance/light bomber biplane
Powerplant:	one 300hp (224kW) Renault 12Fe inline piston engine
Performance:	maximum speed 184km/h (114mph); service ceiling 6000m (19,690ft); endurance 3hrs
Weights:	empty 1030kg (2271lb); maximum take-off weight 1565kg (3450lb)
Dimensions:	span 14.36m (47ft 1in); length 8.87m (29ft 1in); height 3.3m (10ft 10in); wing area 47.50 sq m (530 sq ft)
Armament:	one fixed forward-firing .303 machine gun; twin .303in Lewis machine guns in rear cockpit; racks for up to 40kg (88lb) of bombs

Zeppelin-Staaken R-series

The largest aircraft used in World War I was the sluggish but capable Riesenflugzeug (giant aeroplane) series produced by the Zeppelin Werke Staaken. Via several one-off bombers, with three to five engines and different schemes of defensive armament, the design team of Baumann, Hirth and Klein eventually produced R.VI. Except for the V.G.O.I, which was lost in a crash, all the giant bombers were used on the Eastern Front or against Britain.

SPECIFICATIONS	
Country of origin:	Germany
Type:	heavy bomber
Powerplant:	four 245hp Maybach Mb.IV 6-cylinder inline piston engines
Performance:	maximum speed 130km/h (81mph); service ceiling 3800m (12,500ft); range 800km (500 miles)
Weights:	empty 7350kg (16,200lb); max take-off weight 11,460kg (25,265lb)
Dimensions:	span 42.2m (138ft 6in); length 22.1m (72ft 6in); height 6.3m (20ft 8in)
Armament:	one or two 7.92mm (.31in) Parabellum machine guns in nose position; one or two 7.92mm (.31in) Parabellum machine guns in dorsal cockpit; one 7.92mm (.31in) Parabellum machine gun in rear position; internal bay with provision for up to 18 100kg (220lb) or one 1000kg (2205lb) bomb carried in semi-recessed position, up to a maximum load of 2000kg (4409lb)

AEG G.IV

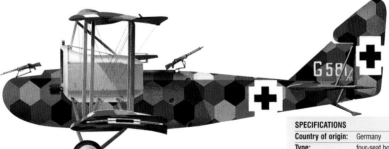

The G.IV did not enter service until the end of 1916. The four crew positions within the steel tube, fabric- and plywood-skinned aircraft were interconnected, enabling crew members to change position in flight as necessary. However, with a maximum bomb load and a crew of three, range was limited. Pictured is a G.IV of Bogohl 4, Staffel 19, stationed at Bazuel in the summer of 1918.

SPECIFICATIONS	
Country of origin:	Germany
Type:	four-seat bomber/reconnaissance biplane
Powerplant:	two 260hp (194kW) Mercedes D.IVa inline engines
Performance:	maximum speed 165km/h (103mph); service ceiling 4500m (14,765ft); endurance 5hrs
Weights:	empty 2400kg (5291lb); maximum take-off weight 3630kg (8003lb)
Dimensions:	span 18.40m (60ft 3in); length 9.7m (31 8in); height 3.9m (12ft 8in); wing area 67 sq m (721 sq ft)
Armament:	one 7.92mm (.31in) Parabellum MG on ring mounting in forward cockpit; one 7.92mm (.31in) Parabellum MG on rail mounting in aft cockpit; underwing pylons for maximum bomb load of 400kg (882lb)

Royal Aircraft Factory S.E.5a

Undoubtedly the best warplane to come from the Royal Aircraft Factory at Farnborough, the S.E.5 (Scout Experimental) was one of the great combat aircraft of World War I. It was designed around a new Hispano-Suiza engine (which, somewhat ironically, proved to be its lingering curse) by H. P. Folland with J. Kenworthy, and the first of three prototypes flew in November 1916.

Royal Aircraft Factory S.E.5a

Major Edward 'Mick' Mannock, Britain's top ace of World War I, flew this S.E.5a when leader of A Flight in No 74 Squadron, although he is not known to have scored any of his 61 victories in it. All but 16 of Mannock's victories were scored in S.E.5as, the rest in a variety of Nieuports.

SPECIFICATIONS	
Country of origin:	United Kingdom
Type:	single-seat fighting scout
Powerplant:	one 200hp (149kW) Wolseley (licence-built) Hispano-Suiza 8a 8-cylinder Vee piston engine
Performance:	maximum speed 222km/h (138mph); service ceiling 5185m (17,000ft); range 483km (300 miles)
Weights:	empty 639kg (1410lb); maximum take-off weight 902kg (1988lb)
Dimensions:	span 8.11m (26ft 7in); length 6.38m (20ft 11in); height 2.89m (9ft 6in); wing area 22.67 sq m (444 sq ft)
Armament:	one fixed forward-firing .303in Vickers machine gun; one .303in Lewis machine gun on Foster mount on upper wing

Royal Aircraft Factory S.E.5a

No 56 Squadron was the first unit to receive the S.E.5a in March 1917. The squadron's pilots, particularly ace Albert Ball, were instrumental in refining the design to the point where it became the most successful RFC fighter of the war. One important change was to remove a cumbersome windscreen the pilots called the 'greenhouse'.

SPECIFICATIONS	
Country of origin:	United Kingdom
Type:	single-seat fighting scout
Powerplant:	one 150hp (112kW) Hispano-Suiza 8a 8-cylinder inline piston engine
Performance:	maximum speed 177km/h (110mph); service ceiling 5185m (17,000ft); range 483km (300 miles)
Weights:	empty 639kg (1410lb); maximum take-off weight 902kg (1988lb)
Dimensions:	span 8.11m (26ft 7in); length 6.38m (20ft 11in); height 2.89m (9ft 6in); wing area 22.67 sq m (444 sq ft)
Armament:	one fixed forward-firing .303in Vickers machine gun, one .303in Lewis machine gun on Foster mount on upper wing

Royal Aircraft Factory S.E.5a

SPECIFICATIONS	
Country of origin:	United Kingdom
Type:	single-seat fighting scout
Powerplant:	one 180hp (134kw) Wolseley Viper 1 V-8
Performance:	maximum speed 177km/h (110mph); service ceiling 5185m (17,000ft); range 483km (300 miles)
Weights:	empty 639kg (1410lb); maximum take-off weight 902kg (1988lb)
Dimensions:	span 8.11m (26ft 7in); length 6.38m (20ft 11in); height 2.89m (9ft 6in); wing area 22.67 sq m (444 sq ft)
Armament:	one fixed forward-firing .303in Vickers machine gun, one .303in Lewis machine gun on Foster mount on upper wing

Another 56 Squadron machine, this S.E.5a survived the war and was sold to a civilian company in 1923, which used it for 'skywriting' advertisements over British cities using smoke trails. Following this second career, it was fortunate enough to be preserved and later put on display at the Royal Air Force Museum.

Royal Aircraft Factory S.E.5a

SPECIFICATIONS	
Country of origin:	United Kingdom
Type:	single-seat fighting scout
Powerplant:	one 200hp (149kW) Wolseley W.4a 8-cylinder Vee piston engine
Performance:	maximum speed 222km/h (138mph); service ceiling 5185m (17,000ft); range 483km (300 miles)
Weights:	empty 639kg (1410lb); maximum take-off weight 902kg (1988lb)
Dimensions:	span 8.11m (26ft 7in); length 6.38m (20ft 11in); height 2.89m (9ft 6in); wing area 22.67 sq m (444 sq ft)
Armament:	one fixed forward-firing .303in Vickers machine gun; one .303in Lewis machine gun on Foster mount on upper wing

The United States Army Air Service was a major user of the S.E.5a and the S.E.5e, a modified version built by Eberhart Aeroplane of New York with 180hp Wright-Hispano E engines. This S.E.5a wears the roundel of the USAS used in 1917–18.

Royal Aircraft Factory S.E.5a

SPECIFICATIONS	
Country of origin:	United Kingdom
Type:	single-seat fighting scout
Powerplant:	one 200hp (149kW) Wolseley W.4a 8-cylinder Vee piston engine
Performance:	maximum speed 222km/h (138mph); service ceiling 5185m (17,000ft); range 483km (300 miles)
Weights:	empty 639kg (1410lb); maximum take-off weight 902kg (1988lb)
Dimensions:	span 8.11m (26ft 7in); length 6.38m (20ft 11in); height 2.89m (9ft 6in); wing area 22.67 sq m (444 sq ft)
Armament:	one fixed forward-firing .303in Vickers machine gun; one .303in Lewis machine gun on Foster mount on upper wing

S.E.5s went on to serve with a number of Empire air arms, including the Royal Australian Air Force, which used 35 examples that remained in use into the late 1920s. One was converted to carry a second seat.

Albatros

Albatros Flugzeugwerke was one of the first successful aircraft manufacturers, and was established in 1909–10 at Johannisthal, Berlin. Its most notable early creation was the Albatros B.I two-seat reconnaissance aircraft, in which the pilot was seated in the aft cockpit and the observer forward. The 'D' series single-seat scouts had a wooden monocoque fuselage and V wing struts, which were a weak point. Albatros fighters were agile and fast, but mostly appeared slightly after superior Allied scouts.

Albatros C.III

The C.III, which first entered service in late 1916, was Albatros's most prolific two-seater. It followed a generally similar configuration to the C.I, with the observer aft of the pilot, but had a redesigned tail. Later aircraft were equipped with a synchronized forward-firing machine gun, and had a bay between the two crew for the stowage of small bombs. Pictured is the C.III of Lieutenant Bruno Maas of Fliegerabteilung 14, flying on the Eastern Front in January 1917.

SPECIFICATIONS	
Country of origin:	Germany
Type:	two-seat general purpose biplane
Powerplant:	one 150hp (112kW) Benz Bz.III or 160hp (119kW) Mercedes D.III inline piston engine
Performance:	maximum speed 140km/h (87mph); service ceiling 3350m (11,000ft); endurance about 4hrs
Weights:	empty 851kg (1876lb); maximum take-off weight 1353kg (2983lb)
Dimensions:	span 11.69m (38ft 4in); length 8.0m (26ft 3in); height with Benz engine 3.07m (10ft); Mercedes engine 3.10m (10ft 2in); wing area 36.91 sq m (397.31 sq ft)
Armament:	one 7.92mm (.31in) Parabellum machine gun on flexible mount in rear cockpit; later aircraft had one 7.92mm (.31in) LMG 08/15 fixed forward-firing machine gun, plus a small internal bomb bay

Albatros D.V

The D.V was one of the most colourful aircraft types in the German Air Service. This Jasta 5 example was flown by an unknown pilot and decorated in the colours of Bavaria, with a stylized version of that state's lion motif.

SPECIFICATIONS	
Country of origin:	Germany
Type:	single-seat scout fighter
Powerplant:	one 180/200hp (134/149kW) Mercedes D.II inline piston engine
Performance:	maximum speed 186km/h (116mph); service ceiling 5700m (18,700ft); endurance about 2hrs
Weights:	empty 687kg (1515lb); maximum take-off weight 937kg (2066lb)
Dimensions:	span 9.05m (29ft 7in); length 7.33m (24ft); height 2.70m (8ft 10in); wing area 21.20 sq m (228 sq ft)
Armament:	two fixed forward-firing 7.92mm (.31in) LMG 08/15 machine guns

Albatros D.V

SPECIFICATIONS	
Country of origin:	Germany
Type:	single-seat scout biplane
Powerplant:	one 180hp/200hp (134/149kW) Mercedes D.II inline piston engine
Performance:	maximum speed 186km/h (116mph); service ceiling 5700m (18,700ft); endurance about 2hrs
Weights:	empty 687kg (1515lb); maximum take-off weight 937kg (2066lb)
Dimensions:	span 9.05m (29ft 7in); length 7.33m (24ft); height 2.70m (8ft 10in); wing area 21.20 sq m (228 sq ft)
Armament:	two fixed forward-firing 7.92mm (.31in) LMG 08/15 machine guns

Introduced in early 1917, the 'D' series was for some time the best fighter scout aircraft. Following a familiar pattern of single-bay, staggered biplane wing planform, but with elliptical fuselage of monocoque structure, the 'D' series saw modifications through D.II and D.III with adjustments to the wing positions. Rapid improvements in Allied fighter capability prompted the development of the D.V.

Albatros D.Va

SPECIFICATIONS	
Country of origin:	Germany
Type:	single-seat scout fighter
Powerplant:	one 180/200hp (134/149kW) Mercedes D.II inline piston engine
Performance:	maximum speed 186km/h (116mph); service ceiling 5700m (18,700ft); endurance about 2hrs
Weights:	empty 687kg (1515lb); maximum take-off weight 937kg (2066lb)
Dimensions:	span 9.05m (29ft 8in); length 7.33m (24ft); height 2.70m (8ft 10in); wing area 21.20 sq m (228 sq ft)
Armament:	two fixed forward-firing 7.92mm (.31in) LMG 08/15 machine guns

The D.Va reverted to the the upper wing and aileron control system of the D.III. Production of the D.V and D.Va exceeded 3000 aircraft, with 1512 in service on the Western Front in May 1918, by which time they had been outclassed by the latest scout aircraft of both sides.

Albatros J.I

SPECIFICATIONS	
Country of origin:	Germany
Type:	two-seat close-support biplane
Powerplant:	one 200hp (149kW) Benz Bz.IV inline piston engine
Performance:	maximum speed 140km/h (87mph); service ceiling 4000m (13,120ft); endurance about 2hrs 30mins
Weights:	empty 1398kg (3082lb); maximum take-off weight 1808kg (3986lb)
Dimensions:	span 14.14m (46ft 4in); length 8.83m (28ft 11in); height 3.37m (11ft); wing area 42.82 sq m (461 sq ft)
Armament:	two fixed downward-firing 7.92mm (.31in) LMG 08/15 machine guns; one 7.92mm (.31in) Parabellum machine gun on movable mount in rear cockpit

For the new role of infantry close support, Albatros developed the J.I Amoured protection for low-level flying. This added weight (490kg/1080lb) and, coupled with a weaker engine, had a detrimental effect on performance. Entering service in late 1917, the J.I enjoyed some measure of success despite its shortcomings. Pictured is a J.I of the post-war Polish Air Force.

British Bombers

The desire to retaliate against German raids on Britain and strike against German cities led in late 1917 to the creation of an Independent Air Striking Force, with tasks separated from the tactical needs of the Army in the field. This was an important precursor to the establishment of the Royal Air Force in 1918. The most successful British maker of large aircraft was Handley Page, which built most of the wartime heavy bombers, including the massive V/1500 – just too late to see wartime action.

Handley Page 0/400

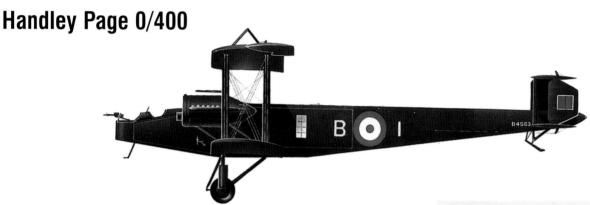

The US Air Service was eager to acquire the 0/400, and a production licence was negotiated for Standard Aircraft Corporation to build the aircraft with Packard Liberty 12 engines. A total of 33 were built by Standard, although only 13 actually went into US Army service. Pictured here is one of the first aircraft, No 62447, which was given the name Langley. No 62448 was used in Billy Mitchell's trials to demonstrate the potential of aircraft in an anti-shipping role.

SPECIFICATIONS

Country of origin:	United Kingdom
Type:	three-seat heavy bomber biplane
Powerplant:	two 350hp (261kW) Packard Liberty 12 inline piston engines
Performance:	maximum speed 122km/h (76mph); service ceiling 2590m (8500ft); range with bomb load 724km (450 miles)
Weights:	empty 3629kg (8000lb); loaded 6350kg (14,000lb)
Dimensions:	span 30.48m (100ft); length 19.16m (62ft 10in); height 6.7m (22ft); wing area 153.1 sq m (1648 sq ft)
Armament:	four .303in Lewis guns (twin ones in nose cockpit; one in dorsal position; one in ventral position); internal bomb bay for up to 1814kg (4000lb)

Handley Page 0/10

During 1919, Handley Page modified some surplus aircraft that it bought back from the government, with seated accommodation for 12–16 passengers, as the 0/10. Some 25 of these were operated from the company facility at Cricklewood for joyriding and on routes linking London to Paris, Brussels and Amsterdam. G-EATN was one of the last HP-built 0/400s, and was converted after the war to 0/10 standard, with accommodation for 12 passengers.

SPECIFICATIONS

Country of origin:	United Kingdom
Type:	12-seat passenger transport biplane
Powerplant:	two 360hp (268kW) Rolls-Royce Eagle VIII Vee-12 piston engines
Performance:	maximum speed 122km/h (76mph); service ceiling 2590m (8500ft); range 724km (450 miles)
Weights:	empty 3629kg (8000lb); maximum take-off weight 6350kg (14,000lb)
Dimensions:	span 30.48m (100ft); length 19.16m (62ft 10in); height 6.7m (22ft); wing area 153.1 sq m (1648 sq ft)

Handley Page 0/400

SPECIFICATIONS	
Country of origin:	United Kingdom
Type:	three-seat heavy bomber biplane
Powerplant:	two 360hp (268kW) Rolls-Royce Eagle VIII Vee-12 piston engines
Performance:	maximum speed 122km/h (76mph); service ceiling 2590m (8500ft); range with bomb load 724km (450 miles)
Weights:	empty 3629kg (8000lb); loaded 6350kg (14,000lb)
Dimensions:	span 30.48m (100ft); length 19.16m (62ft 10in); height 6.7m (22ft); wing area 153.1sq m (1648 sq ft)
Armament:	four .303in Lewis guns (twin ones in nose cockpit; one in dorsal position; one in ventral position); internal bomb bay for eight 113kg (250lb) or 16 51kg (112lb) bombs

In 1916, George Volkert modified the 0/100 into the 0/400 by moving the fuel tanks from the nacelles into the fuselage and fitting Rolls-Royce Eagle VIII engines. In the summer of 1918, the 0/400 was the backbone of the newly formed Independent Bombing Force. Large formations of up to 40 aircraft mounted night attacks on German industrial areas and communications centres.

Avro 529A

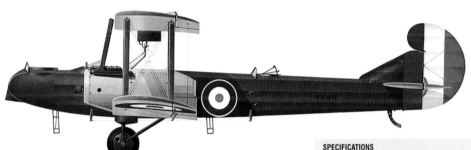

SPECIFICATIONS	
Country of origin:	United Kingdom
Type:	three-seat long-range bomber
Powerplant:	two 230hp (172kW) BHP inline piston engines
Performance:	maximum speed 153km/h (95mph); service ceiling 4115m (13,500ft); endurance 5hrs
Weights:	empty 2148kg (4736lb); maximum take-off weight 2862kg (6309lb)
Dimensions:	span 19.2m (63ft); length 12.09m (39ft 8in); height 3.96m (13ft); wing area 85.7 sq m (922 sq ft)
Armament:	two .303in Lewis guns on Scarff ring mounting (one in front cockpit; one in rear cockpit); internal bay for up to twenty 23kg (50lb) bombs

A prototype was created for the Avro 529, by stretching the dimensions of the original design. Other changes were wings that hinged outboard of the engines, a revised tail unit, and twin Rolls-Royce Falcon engines in a tractor rather than pusher installation. The second prototype substituted 230hp (172kW) BHP engines and had a revised fuel system. Communication between the crew positions by the Gosport tube system was an innovative feature, but no production order was made.

Vickers Vimy Mk II

SPECIFICATIONS	
Country of origin:	United Kingdom
Type:	twin-engined heavy bomber
Powerplant:	two 360hp (269kW) Rolls-Royce Eagle VIII Vee-12 piston engines
Performance:	maximum speed 166km/h (103mph); service ceiling 3048m (10,000ft); range 1464km (910 miles)
Weights:	empty 3222kg (7104lb); maximum 5647kg (12,450lb)
Dimensions:	span 20.47m (67ft 2in); length 13.27m (43ft 6.5in); height 4.65m (15ft 3in); wing area 123.56 sq m (1330 sq ft)
Armament:	two .303in Lewis machine guns; up to 1124kg (2476kg) bombs

The Vickers Vimy arrived on the Western Front just before the Armistice, but went on to be one of the most important interwar bombers and a long-range record breaker. The Mk II version seen here was originally intended to have American Liberty engines.

Two-Seaters

As the war progressed, two-seat reconnaissance aircraft and light bombers became more powerful and robust. Several types were armed with forward-firing guns and became 'fighting scouts', able to engage enemy fighters on better terms. When the Bristol F.2B was introduced in 1918, it was used like previous two-seaters, flying in formation with the gunners supplying mutual support. Albatroses of von Richthofen's 'Flying Circus' tore them to pieces, but soon it was realized that the F.2B was very effective when used aggressively as a fighter.

AEG C.IV

The Allgemeine Elektrizitäts Gesellschaft (AEG) 'C' series began with the C.I, introduced in March 1915 as a two-seat armed reconnaissance aircraft. Most important of the series was the C.IV. Development of the aircraft included the IV.N night bomber with increased span wings. Pictured is a C.IV of Fliegerabteilung 'A' (Artillery Cooperation) 224, from the spring of 1917.

SPECIFICATIONS	
Country of origin:	Germany
Type:	two-seat armed reconnaissance biplane
Powerplant:	one 160hp (119kw) Mercedes D.III inline piston engine
Performance:	maximum speed 115km/h (71mph); service ceiling 5000m (16,400ft); endurance 4hrs
Weights:	empty 800kg (1764lb); maximum take-off weight 1120kg (2469lb)
Dimensions:	span 13.45m (44ft 1in); length 7.15m (23ft 5in); height 3.35m (10ft 10in); wing area 39 sq m (420 sq ft)
Armament:	one fixed forward-firing 7.92mm (.31in) LMG 08/15 machine gun; one 7.92mm (.31in) Parabellum machine gun on ring mounting for observer in rear cockpit

Armstrong Whitworth F.K.8

The increasing importance of the army co-operation role from 1916 prompted development of a larger version of the F.K.3, designated the F.K.8. Koolhoven designed this with a sturdier fuselage to accommodate a more powerful engine. The 'Big Ack' gained a reputation for being strong and reliable, and undertook every kind of reconnaissance, bombing and strafing mission on the Western Front, in Macedonia and in Palestine.

SPECIFICATIONS	
Country of origin:	United Kingdom
Type:	two-seat general-purpose aircraft
Powerplant:	one 160hp (119kW) Beardmore, 150hp (112kW) Lorraine-Dietrich or 150hp (112kW) Royal Aircraft Factory.4A inline piston engine
Performance:	maximum speed 153km/h (95mph); service ceiling 3690m (13,000ft); endurance 3hrs
Weights:	empty 869kg (1916lb); maximum take-off weight 1275kg (2811lb)
Dimensions:	span 13.26m (43ft 6in); length 9.58m (31ft 5in); height 3.33m (10ft 11in); wing area 50.17 sq m (540 sq ft)
Armament:	one fixed forward-firing .303in Vickers machine gun; one .303in Lewis machine gun on flexible mount in rear cockpit

TWO-SEATERS TIMELINE
1916

Dorand Ar.I

In 1916, the French Government issued a specification for a biplane with a tractor engine to replace the Farman F.20. Colonel Dorand, Commander of the French Army's Technical Section, submitted an updated version of one of his (unsuccessful) 1914 biplanes, the D.O I. Redesignated as the Dorand AR.I, this aircraft completed trials in September 1916 and was produced in large numbers for Aviation Militaire for service over the Western and Italian Fronts.

SPECIFICATIONS	
Country of origin:	France
Type:	two-seat observation biplane
Powerplant:	(AR.I) one 200hp (149kW) Renault 8Gdy inline piston engine
Performance:	maximum speed 148km/h (92mph); service ceiling 5500m (18,045ft); endurance 3hrs
Weights:	maximum take-off weight 1315kg (2900lb)
Dimensions:	span 13.29m (43ft 7in); length 9.14m (30ft); height 3.3m (10ft 10in); wing area 50.17 sq m (540 sq ft)
Armament:	one fixed forward-firing .303in Vickers machine gun; plus one or two .303in Lewis guns on flexible mount in rear cockpit

Fokker C.I

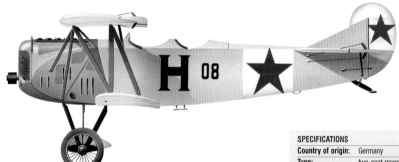

The C.I was, in effect, an enlarged version of the earlier D.VII. The prototype was tested as the V.38 at Schwerin in 1918, but none had been completed by the time of the Armistice. Fokker smuggled the uncompleted C.I airframes out of Germany into the Netherlands, where production continued. In total, some 250 aircraft were produced. The Dutch military was the largest customer, taking 62 C.Is for use in the reconnaissance role, while the Soviet Union purchased 42.

SPECIFICATIONS	
Country of origin:	Germany
Type:	two-seat reconnaissance aircraft
Powerplant:	one 185hp (138kW) B.M.W IIIa 6-cylinder inline piston engine
Performance:	maximum speed 175km/h (109mph); service ceiling 4000m (13,125ft); range 620km (385 miles)
Weights:	empty 855kg (1885lb); maximum take-off weight 1255kg (2767lb)
Dimensions:	span 10.5m (34ft 5½in); length 7.23m (23ft 8¼in); height 2.87m (9ft 5in); wing area 26.25 sq m (282.56 sq ft)
Armament:	one fixed forward-firing .303in machine gun, one .303in machine gun on ring mount over rear cockpit, underwing racks with provision for four 12.5kg (27.5lb) bombs

Bristol F.2B Fighter

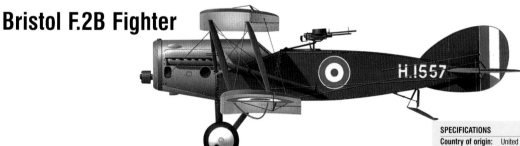

Frank Barnwell designed the Type 9 R.2A as a two-seat reconnaissance aircraft, but by August 1916 this had been re-engined and redesignated as the Type 12 F.2A, to denote its new fighter role. The F.2B was the main production variant and incorporated modified upper longerons for improved pilot visibility, enlarged fuel tank and a variety of engines. Production total was 5308 aircraft. It remained in service with the RAF until 1932.

SPECIFICATIONS	
Country of origin:	United Kingdom
Type:	two-seat fighter/army cooperation aircraft
Powerplant:	one 275hp (205kW) Rolls-Royce Falcon III inline piston engine
Performance:	maximum speed 198km/h (123mph); service ceiling 5485m (18,000ft); endurance 3hrs
Weights:	empty 975kg (2150lb); maximum take-off weight 1474kg (3250lb)
Dimensions:	span 11.96m (39ft 3in); length 7.87m (25ft 10in); height 2.97m (9ft 9in); wing area 37.62 sq m (405 sq ft)
Armament:	one fixed forward-firing .303in Vickers machine gun, plus one or two .303in Lewis guns on flexible mount in rear cockpit; underwing racks with provision for up to 12 9kg (28lb) of bombs

1917   1918

SPADs

An acronym standing for Société Pour L'Aviation et ses Dérivés, SPAD was a company founded in 1911 by Armand Deperdussin. The company's wartime fighters, designed by Louis Bécherau, were used by French, British, Belgian and American air arms during the war and as far afield as China afterwards. The SPAD series was noted for its speed and climbing ability, although the aircraft were tricky to handle at low speeds and generally less manoeuvrable than their competitors. They were also built strongly and were a particular favourite of the American pilots serving in France, and the mount of their top aces, including Eddie Rickenbacker.

S.XIII

The S.XIII was similar in appearance but larger in all dimensions than previous SPADs and first flew in April 1917. In all, nearly 8500 S.XIIIs were built and they served with at least 85 French Escadrilles (squadrons), which were designated 'Spa', a tradition that continued into the modern era. This example from Spa 48 features the unit's famous crowing cockerel insignia.

SPECIFICATIONS	
Country of origin:	France
Type:	single-seat fighter
Powerplant:	one 164.1kW (220hp) Hispano 8Bc 8-cylinder inline piston engine
Performance:	maximum speed 218km/h (135mph); endurance 1hr 40mins; service ceiling 6650m (21,815ft)
Weights:	empty 601kg (1326lb); maximum 856kg (1888lb)
Dimensions:	span 8.1m (26ft 7in); length 6.3m (20ft 8in); height 2.35m (7ft 8in); wing area 21.11 sq m (227.23 sq ft)
Armament:	two Vickers .303in machine guns

S.VII

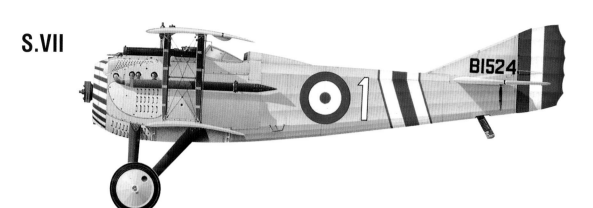

The SPAD S.VII proved to be a nimble and rugged fighter, with a respectable rate of climb and turn and the stability essential for accurate gun-laying. Pictured is an RFC S.VII of No 23 Squadron, flying from La Lovie aerodrome in France in the summer of 1917.

SPECIFICATIONS	
Country of origin:	France
Type:	single-seat fighting scout
Powerplant:	one 150hp (112kW) Hispano-Suiza 8Aa 8-cylinder Vee piston engine
Performance:	maximum speed 192km/h (119mph); service ceiling 5334m (17,500ft); range 360km (225 miles)
Weights:	empty 510kg (1124lb); maximum take-off weight 740kg (1632lb)
Dimensions:	span 7.81m (25ft 8in); length 6.08m (19ft 11in); height 2.20m (7ft 2in); wing area 17.85 sq m (192 sq ft)
Armament:	one fixed forward-firing .303in Vickers machine gun

S.VII

During World War I, the SPAD S.VII was supplied in large numbers to the Allied forces. This is the personal mount of the Commanding Officer of the XXIII Gruppo of the Italian Regia Aeronautica, stationed at Lonade Pozzolo in 1924.

SPECIFICATIONS	
Country of origin:	France
Type:	single-seat fighting scout
Powerplant:	one 180hp (134kW) Hispano-Suiza 8Ac 8-cylinder Vee piston engine
Performance:	maximum speed 192km/h (119mph); service ceiling 5334m (17,500ft); range 360km (225 miles)
Weights:	empty 510kg (1124lb); maximum take-off weight 740kg (1632lb)
Dimensions:	span 7.81m (25ft 8in); length 6.08m (19ft 11in); height 2.20m (7ft 2in); wing area 17.85 sq m (192 sq ft)
Armament:	one fixed forward-firing .303in Vickers machine gun

Sopwiths

T.O.M. 'Tommy' Sopwith created some of the most famous fighters of all time, notably the Camel, so named because of the 'hump' of structure around the guns. With its short wingspan and powerful rotary engine, the Camel was extremely sensitive in roll, a trait that could be exploited by experienced pilots to gain the advantage over an enemy. Its successor, the Snipe, saw limited war service but remained with RAF squadrons until 1926.

Sopwith 1½ Strutter

Deriving its nickname from the '1½' sets of struts attaching the upper wing, the 1½ Strutter was the first military aircraft to be designed from the outset with a synchronized gun, and (apart from the Russian Sikorsky IM series) the first to equip a strategic bombing force. It included such unexpected features as a variable-incidence tailplane and airbrakes on the lower wing.

SPECIFICATIONS	
Country of origin:	United Kingdom
Type:	two-seat multi-role combat aircraft
Powerplant:	one 130hp (97kW) Clerget rotary piston engine
Performance:	maximum speed 164km/h (102mph); service ceiling 3960m (13,000ft); range 565km (350 miles)
Weights:	empty 570kg (1260lb); maximum take-off weight 975kg (2149lb)
Dimensions:	span 10.21m (33ft 6in); length 7.7m (25ft 3in); height 3.12m (10ft 3in); wing area 32.14 sq m (346 sq ft)
Armament:	one fixed forward-firing .303in Vickers machine gun; plus up to four 25kg (56lb) bombs or an equivalent weight of smaller bombs

Sopwith Pup

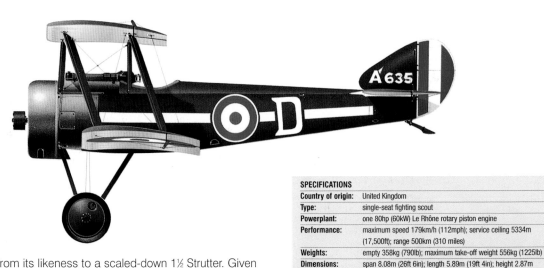

The Pup got its nickname from its likeness to a scaled-down 1½ Strutter. Given the relatively small power output, the fact that the Pup was such a pleasure to fly speaks volumes of its design and construction. It was very small, simple and reliable, and its generous wing area gave it excellent performance at height. Compared with an Albatros, it could turn twice for a single turn by the enemy.

SPECIFICATIONS	
Country of origin:	United Kingdom
Type:	single-seat fighting scout
Powerplant:	one 80hp (60kW) Le Rhône rotary piston engine
Performance:	maximum speed 179km/h (112mph); service ceiling 5334m (17,500ft); range 500km (310 miles)
Weights:	empty 358kg (790lb); maximum take-off weight 556kg (1225lb)
Dimensions:	span 8.08m (26ft 6in); length 5.89m (19ft 4in); height 2.87m (9ft 5in); wing area 23.60 sq m (254 sq ft)
Armament:	one fixed forward-firing .303in Vickers machine gun or one .303in Lewis aimed obliquely through cut-out in centre section of upper wing; anti-airship armament usually eight Le Prieur rockets launched from interplane struts

Sopwith Camel F.1

Perhaps the most famous aircraft of World War I, the Camel was so-called because of its distinctive 'humped' back, and between June 1917 and November 1918 it destroyed at least 3000 enemy aircraft – more than any other plane. In inexperienced hands, the Camel could bite, and the engine's torque was such that it had a nasty tendency to flip suddenly to the left on take-off. Casualties among trainee pilots were high.

SPECIFICATIONS	
Country of origin:	United Kingdom
Type:	single-seat fighting scout
Powerplant:	one 130hp (97kW) Clerget rotary piston engine
Performance:	maximum speed 185km/h (115mph); service ceiling 5790m (19,000ft); endurance 2hrs 30mins
Weights:	empty 421kg (929lb); maximum take-off weight 659kg (1453lb)
Dimensions:	span 8.53m (28ft); length 5.72m (18ft 9in); height 2.59m (8ft 6in); wing area 21.46 sq m (231 sq ft)
Armament:	two fixed forward-firing .303in Vickers machine guns; plus up to four 11.3kg (25lb) bombs carried on fuselage sides

Sopwith Camel F.1

The designation F.1 covered Camels fitted with numerous different engine and armament fits. There was also a night-fighter version with a pair of Lewis guns on a double Foster mounting above the top-wing centre section. Pictured is a Camel F.1, in post-war markings, built by Boulton & Paul.

SPECIFICATIONS	
Country of origin:	United Kingdom
Type:	single-seat fighting scout
Powerplant:	one 130hp (97kW) Clerget rotary piston engine
Performance:	maximum speed 185km/h (115mph); service ceiling 5790m (19,000ft); endurance 2hrs 30mins
Weights:	empty 421kg (929lb); maximum take-off weight 659kg (1453lb)
Dimensions:	span 8.53m (28ft); length 5.72m (18ft 9in); height 2.59m (8ft 6in); wing area 21.46 sq m (231 sq ft)
Armament:	two fixed forward-firing .303in Vickers machine guns; plus up to four 11.3kg (25lb) bombs carried on fuselage sides

Sopwith Snipe

Designed as a successor to the Camel, deliveries of the Snipe to units in France began only eight weeks before the Armistice, but in the few aerial combats the Snipe gave ample demonstration of its quality. Of the 4515 ordered, only 100 were delivered by the Armistice; post-war production brought the total to 497.

SPECIFICATIONS	
Country of origin:	United Kingdom
Type:	single-seat fighting scout
Powerplant:	one 230hp (172kW) Bentley B.R.2 rotary piston engine
Performance:	maximum speed 195km/h (121mph); service ceiling 5945m (19,500ft); endurance 3 hours
Weights:	empty 595kg (1312lb); maximum take-off weight 916kg (2020lb)
Dimensions:	span 9.17m (30ft 1in); length 6.02m (19ft 9in); height 2.67m (8ft 9in); wing area 25.08 sq m (270 sq ft)
Armament:	two fixed forward-firing synchronized .303in Vickers machine-guns, plus up to four 11.3kg (25lb) of bombs on external racks

Fokker Triplanes

When the Sopwith Triplane first appeared over the Western Front in late 1916, its performance far outshone any of the current German scouts, and the authorities immediately issued a request for triplane fighters. No fewer than 14 submissions were received, although they were all beaten to the mark by the Fokker Flugzeugwerke Dr.I (Dreidecker), because Fokker had seen the aircraft in action in April 1917 and did not have to wait for the example captured in July.

Fokker Dr.I

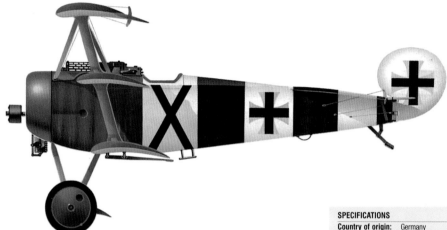

Dr.Is were delivered in a factory finish of streaky olive sides and upper surfaces with light blue on the undersides. Very few remained so plain, and personal schemes and markings abounded. The original colours and markings on this Jasta 26 example just show beneath the stripes and 1918-style national insignia.

SPECIFICATIONS	
Country of origin:	Germany
Type:	single-seat fighting scout
Powerplant:	one 110hp (82kW) Oberusel Ur.II 9-cylinder rotary piston engine
Performance:	maximum speed 185km/h (115mph); service ceiling 6100m (20,015ft); endurance 1hr 30mins
Weights:	empty 406kg (894lb); maximum take-off weight 586kg (1 291lb)
Dimensions:	span 7.19m (23ft 7in); length 5.77m (18ft 11in); height 2.95m (9ft 8in); wing area 18.66 sq m (201 sq ft)
Armament:	two fixed forward-firing 7.92mm (.31in) LMG 08/15 machine guns

Fokker Dr.I

This striking Dr.I is believed to have been the personal mount of August Raben, commander of Jasta 18. Raben had the only Triplane in the unit, which otherwise flew Albatros D.Vs before converting to Fokker D.VIIs. This Dr.I eventually fell into French hands.

SPECIFICATIONS	
Country of origin:	Germany
Type:	single-seat fighting scout
Powerplant:	one 110hp (82kW) Oberusel Ur.II 9-cylinder rotary piston engine
Performance:	maximum speed 185km/h (115mph); service ceiling 6100m (20,015ft); endurance 1hr 30mins
Weights:	empty 406kg (894lb); maximum take-off weight 586kg (1291lb)
Dimensions:	span 7.19m (23ft 7in); length 5.77m (18ft 11in); height 2.95m (9ft 8in); wing area 18.66 sq m (201 sq ft)
Armament:	two fixed forward-firing 7.92mm (.31in) LMG 08/15 machine guns

Fokker Dr.I

With its all-black colour and non-standard white crosses, the Dr.I of Leutnant Josef Jacobs of Jasta 7 was as distinctive in its own way as von Richthofen's red aircraft. Jacobs flew the Triplane from early 1918 until the Armistice and became Germany's fourth-ranked ace, claiming 48 enemy aircraft and balloons destroyed.

SPECIFICATIONS	
Country of origin:	Germany
Type:	single-seat fighting scout
Powerplant:	one 110hp (82kW) Oberusel Ur.II 9-cylinder rotary piston engine
Performance:	maximum speed 185km/h (115mph); service ceiling 6100m (20,015ft); endurance 1hr 30mins
Weights:	empty 406kg (894lb); maximum take-off weight 586kg (1291lb)
Dimensions:	span 7.19m (23ft 7in); length 5.77m (18ft 11in); height 2.95m (9ft 8in); wing area 18.66 sq m (201 sq ft)
Armament:	two fixed forward-firing 7.92mm (.31in) LMG 08/15 machine guns

Fokker Dr.I

Probably the most famous military pilot of all time, Manfred Albrecht Freiherr von Richthofen was the top scoring ace of World War I, claiming 80 Allied aircraft while flying a variety of Albatros and Fokker types. The 'Red Baron' flew at least six Triplanes, including this one in which he scored three victories.

SPECIFICATIONS	
Country of origin:	Germany
Type:	single-seat fighting scout
Powerplant:	one 110hp (82kW) Oberusel Ur.II 9-cylinder rotary piston engine
Performance:	maximum speed 185km/h (115mph); service ceiling 6100m (20,015ft); endurance 1hr 30mins
Weights:	empty 406kg (894lb); maximum take-off weight 586kg (1291lb)
Dimensions:	span 7.19m (23ft 7in); length 5.77m (18ft 11in); height 2.95m (9ft 8in); wing area 18.66 sq m (201 sq ft)
Armament:	two fixed forward-firing 7.92mm (.31in) LMG 08/15 machine guns

Fokker Dr.I

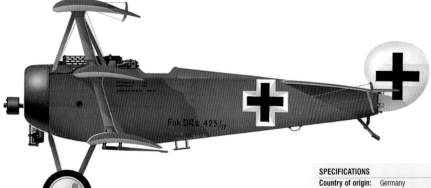

The last aircraft flown by von Richthofen is the all-red machine most associated with his name. Flying this Dr.I, he was killed during a combat with Sopwith Camels on 21 April 1918, although controversy persists to this day as to whether he was shot down by a pursuing Sopwith Camel or by gunners on the ground.

SPECIFICATIONS	
Country of origin:	Germany
Type:	single-seat fighting scout
Powerplant:	one 110hp (82kW) Oberusel Ur.II 9-cylinder rotary piston engine
Performance:	maximum speed 185km/h (115mph); service ceiling 6100m (20,015ft); endurance 1hr 30mins
Weights:	empty 406kg (894lb); maximum take-off weight 586kg (1291lb)
Dimensions:	span 7.19m (23ft 7in); length 5.77m (18ft 11in); height 2.95m (9ft 8in); wing area 18.66 sq m (201 sq ft)
Armament:	two fixed forward-firing 7.92mm (.31in) LMG 08/15 machine guns

1918 Fighters

By early 1918, the German Air Service had lost air superiority over the Western Front to the improved Sopwith, Nieuport and SPAD types that entered service the previous year. German industry raced to the rescue with several excellent aircraft, including the Fokker D.VII, regarded as the best fighter of the war, and the D.VIII 'razor' parasol, but it was too late to delay the inevitable defeat. The French Hanriot was another late-war fighter that saw limited service on the Western Front.

Hanriot HD.1

The French *Aviation Militare* rejected the HD.1 for its own use when it standardized on SPADs and Nieuports, and they were used mainly by the Belgian and Italian air arms. Sixteen HD.1s were used post-war by Switzerland, in whose markings this example is shown.

SPECIFICATIONS

Country of origin:	France
Type:	single-seat fighter
Powerplant:	one 110hp (81kW) Le Rhône 9J rotary piston engine
Performance:	maximum speed 184km/h (114mph); service ceiling 6400m (21,000ft); range 550km (342m)
Weights:	empty 407kg (895lb); maximum take-off weight 605kg (1331lb)
Dimensions:	span 8.70m (25ft 6in); length 5.85m (19ft 2in); height 2.94m (9ft 7.5in); wing area 18 sq m (193.7 sq ft)
Armament:	one or two Vickers .303in machine guns

Pfalz D.XII

Not as well regarded by pilots as the similar-looking D.VII, the Pfalz D.XII entered service in July 1918. Its climb performance was inferior to the Fokker's, but sturdier construction gave it the edge in the dive.

SPECIFICATIONS

Country of origin:	Germany
Type:	single-seat fighter plane
Powerplant:	one 180hp (134kW) Mercedes D.III inline piston engine
Performance:	maximum speed 170km/h (106mph); service ceiling 5640m (18,500ft); combat radius 370km (230miles)
Weights:	empty 717kg (1580lb); maximum take-off weight 902kg (1989lb)
Dimensions:	span 9.0m (29ft 6in); length 6.35m (21ft); height 2.7m (8ft 10in); wing area 21.70 sq m (233.6 sq ft)
Armament:	two 7.92mm (.31in) LMG 08/15 machine guns

1918 FIGHTERS TIMELINE

1923   1924   1925   19

Siemens-Schukert D.III

In 1916, Siemens-Schukert Werke built small numbers of the D.I, a copy of the French Nieuport 17. Service deliveries began in 1918 of the D.III and it demonstrated outstanding speed, climb and manoeuvrability. However, the Sh.IIIa engine proved to be so troublesome that the entire fleet was withdrawn and re-engined with the Sh.IIIa, with the lower cowl cut away to improve cooling.

SPECIFICATIONS	
Country of origin:	Germany
Type:	single-seat fighting scout
Powerplant:	one 200hp (150kW) Siemens und Halske Sh.IIIa rotary piston engine
Performance:	maximum speed 180km/h (112mph); service ceiling 8000m (26,245ft); endurance 2hrs
Weights:	empty 534kg (1177lb); maximum take-off weight 725kg (1598lb)
Dimensions:	span 8.43m (27ft 8in); length 6.7m (18ft 8in); height 2.8m (9ft 2in); wing area 203.44 sq m (19 sq ft)
Armament:	two fixed forward-firing 7.92mm (0.31in) LMG 08/15 machine guns

Fokker D.VII

The early 'D' series scouts (D.I to D.VI) were unremarkable aircraft with undistinguished service careers. They were eclipsed by the D.VII, designed in late 1917. The first unit to receive the type was Manfred von Richtofen's JG I, which was commanded by Hermann Göring after the death of the Red Baron in April 1918. Approximately 1000 of this extremely capable aircraft were completed by the time of the Armistice.

SPECIFICATIONS	
Country of origin:	Germany
Type:	single-seat fighting scout
Powerplant:	one 185hp (138kW) B.M.W III 6-cylinder inline piston engine
Performance:	maximum speed 200km/h (124mph); service ceiling 7000m (22,965ft); endurance 1hr 30mins
Weights:	empty 735kg (1620lb); maximum take-off weight 880kg (1940lb)
Dimensions:	span 8.9m (29ft 2in); length 6.95m (22ft 9in); height 2.75m (9ft); wing area 20.5 sq m (221 sq ft)
Armament:	two fixed forward-firing 7.92mm (.31in) LMG 08/15 machine guns

Fokker D.VIII

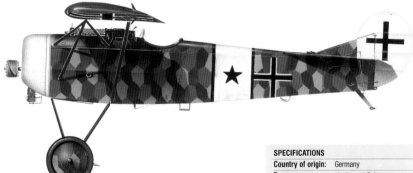

The parasol-wing D.VIII showed much promise with its lightweight ply construction and steel tube struts, but the early examples were shoddily built and service entry was delayed by crashes and production changes. Only one D.VIII victory was recorded before the Armistice.

SPECIFICATIONS	
Country of origin:	Germany
Type:	single-seat fighter
Powerplant:	one 110hp (82kW) Oberursel UR.II rotary piston engine
Performance:	maximum speed 204km/h (127mph); service ceiling 6300m (20,670ft); endurance 2hrs
Weights:	empty 384kg (848lb); maximum take-off weight 562kg (1238lb)
Dimensions:	span 8.40m (27ft 6.5in); length 5.86m (19ft 4in); height 2.8m (9ft 2in); wing area 10.7 sq m (115.5 sq ft)
Armament:	two 7.92mm (.31in) LMG 08/15 machine guns

1927

1928

1929

1930

1931

Early Interwar Bombers

The 1920s were a time of experimentation in the field of strategic bombing. New monoplanes with metal construction offered greater speed and strength, but senior officers did not entirely trust them, and biplane bombers remained in use into the next decade, particularly in Britain. In the United States, aircraft like the B-9 showed the way to the future, and it was the first in a long line of Boeing heavy bombers.

Barling XNBL-1

This enormous, curiously formed machine was designed by Walter Barling in response to a request for a strategic bomber. The XNBL-1 (Experimental Night Bomber Long-range), which first flew in August 1923, was at that time the world's largest aircraft with triplane wings, 10-wheel main gear and positions for seven machine guns in five locations around the fuselage. All this made it too heavy an aircraft for its six engines. Development was abandoned in 1925.

SPECIFICATIONS	
Country of origin:	United States
Type:	experimental long-range bomber
Powerplant:	six 420hp (313kW) Liberty inline piston engines
Performance:	maximum speed 154km/h (96mph); service ceiling 2355m (7725ft); range with 2268kg (5000lb) 274km (170 miles)
Weights:	empty 12,566kg (27,703lb); maximum take-off weight 19,309kg (42,569lb)
Dimensions:	span 36.58m (120ft); length 19.81m (65ft); height 8.23m (27ft); wing area 390.18 sq m (4200 sq ft)
Armament:	seven .3in machine guns on flexible mountings, plus up to 2268kg (5000lb) of bombs

Vickers Virginia Mk VII

Designed to replace the Vimy, the Vickers Virginia was the standard heavy bomber of the Royal Air Force from 1924 until 1937. It was large and heavy, and was constructed in much the same way as its predecessor, but in the event this proved something of a blessing because the aircraft's service career was progressively stretched far beyond its expected retirement date.

SPECIFICATIONS	
Country of origin:	United Kingdom
Type:	heavy night-bomber
Powerplant:	two 580hp Napier Lion VB W-12 piston engines
Performance:	maximum speed 174km/h (108mph); service ceiling 4725m (15,500ft); range 1585km (985 miles)
Weights:	empty 4377kg (9650lb); maximum take-off weight 7983kg (17,600lb)
Dimensions:	span 26.72m (87ft 8in); length 18.97m (62ft 3in); height 5.54m (18ft 2in); wing area 202.34 sq m (2178 sq ft)
Armament:	one .303in Lewis machine gun in nose position; twin .303in Lewis machine guns in dorsal position; plus up to 1361kg (93,000lb) of bombs

Beardmore Inflexible

With its stressed Duralumin construction and steel fittings, the Inflexible was indeed strong, but also too heavy to carry any useful load, and it remained an experimental type. Only one was built and the RAF continued with biplanes for several more years.

SPECIFICATIONS	
Country of origin:	United Kingdom
Type:	Experimental monoplane bomber
Powerplant:	three 650hp (485kW) Rolls-Royce Condor inline piston engines
Performance:	maximum speed 175km/h (109mph)
Weights:	loaded 16,783kg (37,000lb)
Dimensions:	span 48.01m (157ft 6in); length 23.01m (75 ft 6in); height 6.40m (21ft 2in)
Armament:	none

Lioré-et-Olivier LeO 20

In 1916, the company of Fernand Lioré and Henri Olivier produced its first independent design, the LeO 4 reconnaissance biplane. The later Leo 12 was a two-seat night-bomber, which spawned the LeO 20, the standard French heavy night-bomber between 1928 and 1939. Some 320 of these four-seat aircraft were produced, and despite its antiquated appearance the aircraft remained in production up until the start of the World War II.

SPECIFICATIONS	
Country of origin:	France
Type:	three/four-seat night-bomber
Powerplant:	two 420hp (313kW) Gnome-Rhône 9Ady (licence-built Bristol Jupiter) radial piston engines
Performance:	maximum speed 198km/h (123mph); service ceiling 5760m (18,900ft); range 1000km (621 miles)
Weights:	empty equipped 2725kg (6008lb); maximum take-off weight 5460kg (12,037lb)
Dimensions:	span 22.25m (73ft); length 13.81m (45ft 4in); height 4.26m (13ft 12in); wing area 105 sq m (1130 sq ft)
Armament:	two 7.7mm (0.303in) machine guns on pivoted mount in nose; two 7.7mm (0.303in) machine guns in dorsal position; one 7.7mm (0.303in) machine gun in ventral bin; bomb racks for up to 500kg (1102lb) of bombs

Martin B-10

Faster than the P-26 fighter, the B-10 bomber was the first mass-produced American bomber of all-metal construction. The prototype flew in 1932 and over 100 were built for the USAAC. Nearly 200 were built for export and were sold to the Netherlands East Indies, China and Turkey.

SPECIFICATIONS	
Country of origin:	United States
Type: (B-10B)	monoplane heavy bomber
Powerplant:	two 522kW (700hp) Wright R-1820-33 Cyclone radial piston engine
Performance:	Maximum speed 343 km/h (213 mph); service ceiling 7406 m (24,300 ft); range 771km (1240 miles)
Weights:	empty 4,391 kg (9,681 lb); maximum 7,439 kg (16,400 lb)
Dimensions:	span 23.4m (76ft 10in); length 15.7m (51ft 6in); height 4.70 m (15 ft 5 in); wing area 63.0 m2 (678 sqft)
Armament:	three 0.30in (7.62 mm) Browning machine-guns, 1000 kg (2200 lb) of bombs

Boeing Peashooters

Boeing's all-metal P-26 was one of the first low-wing monoplane fighters. Most previous fighters had parasol or gull wings, which had been regarded as stronger. Designed to be faster than contemporary bombers, the P-26A, nicknamed the 'Peashooter', was first flown in March 1932. It proved slower than the Martin B-10 bomber, but was well liked and considered a 'hot ship' compared to biplanes. It served into the early war years with the USAAF, and longer elsewhere.

P-26A

The US Army Air Corps adopted chrome yellow as the colouring for aircraft wings and tails in 1937 as a safety measure to prevent aerial collisions. Olive drab fuselages gave way in turn to light blue with coloured squadron identification bands. This colourful state of affairs lasted a decade until drab markings began their return.

SPECIFICATIONS	
Country of origin:	United States
Type:	single-engined monoplane fighter
Powerplant:	one 600hp (440kW) Pratt & Whitney R-1340-7 Wasp radial piston engine
Performance:	maximum speed 377km/h (234mph); range 580km (360 miles); service ceiling 8350m (27,400ft)
Weights:	empty 996kg (2196lb); loaded 1524kg (3360lb)
Dimensions:	span 8.50m (28ft); length 7.18m (23ft 7in); height 3.04m (10ft); wing area 13.89 sq m (149.5 sq ft)
Armament:	two 0.3in (7.62mm) M1919 Browning machine guns; five 14kg (30lb) or two 50kg (112lb) bombs

P-26A

The 34th Pursuit Squadron of the 17th Pursuit Group conducted camouflage experiments in 1935. This P-26A was painted in desert sand with mottles of olive drab and neutral grey, although it retained yellow under the wings.

SPECIFICATIONS	
Country of origin:	United States
Type:	single-engined monoplane fighter
Powerplant:	one 600hp (440kW) Pratt & Whitney R-1340-7 Wasp radial piston engine
Performance:	maximum speed 377km/h (234mph); range 580km (360 miles); service ceiling 8350m (27,400ft)
Weights:	empty 996kg (2196lb); loaded 1524kg (3360lb)
Dimensions:	span 8.50m (28ft); length 7.18m (23ft 7in); height 3.04m (10ft); wing area 13.89 sq m (149.5 sq ft)
Armament:	two .3in (7.62mm) M1919 Browning machine guns; five 14kg (30lb) or two 50kg (112lb) bombs

P-26A

A few Peashooters were in use as trainers and 'hacks' at Wheeler Field, Hawaii at the time of the Pearl Harbor attack in December 1941. By this time, the pre-war colours had fully given way to olive drab with neutral grey undersides on USAAF fighters.

SPECIFICATIONS	
Country of origin:	United States
Type:	single-engined monoplane fighter
Powerplant:	one 600hp (440kW) Pratt & Whitney R-1340-7 Wasp radial piston engine
Performance:	maximum speed 377km/h (234mph); range 580km (360 miles); service ceiling 8350m (27,400ft)
Weights:	empty 996kg (2196lb); loaded 1524kg (3360lb)
Dimensions:	span 8.50m (28ft); length 7.18m (23ft 7in); height 3.04m (10ft); wing area 13.89 sq m (149.5 sq ft)
Armament:	two .3in (7.62mm) M1919 Browning machine guns; five 14kg (30lb) or two 50kg (112lb) bombs

P-26A

When the P-26 appeared, the standard USAAC colour scheme was a mix of olive drab and chrome yellow, as seen on this P-26A of the 95th Pursuit Squadron. The 95th's kicking mule insignia is one of the oldest in US military aviation, and is still used today.

SPECIFICATIONS	
Country of origin:	United States
Type:	single-engined monoplane fighter
Powerplant:	one 600hp (440kW) Pratt & Whitney R-1340-7 Wasp radial piston engine
Performance:	maximum speed 377km/h (234mph); range 580km (360 miles); service ceiling 8350m (27,400ft)
Weights:	empty 996kg (2196lb); loaded 1524kg (3360lb)
Dimensions:	span 8.50m (28ft); length 7.18m (23ft 7in); height 3.04m (10ft); wing area 13.89 sq m (149.5 sq ft)
Armament:	two .3in (7.62mm) M1919 Browning machine guns; five 14kg (30lb) or two 50kg (112lb) bombs

P-26A

Guatemala purchased seven Peashooters from the United States in 1937, and during the war obtained some more that had been used by the USAAF in Panama. The P-26 remained in service with the Fuerza Aérea de Guatemalteca until as late as 1956, and even saw action in a 1954 coup attempt.

SPECIFICATIONS	
Country of origin:	United States
Type:	single-engined monoplane fighter
Powerplant:	one 600hp (440kW) Pratt & Whitney R-1340-7 Wasp radial piston engine
Performance:	maximum speed 377km/h (234mph); range 580km (360 miles); service ceiling 8350m (27,400ft)
Weights:	empty 996kg (2196lb); loaded 1524kg (3360lb)
Dimensions:	span 8.50m (28ft); length 7.18m (23ft 7in); height 3.04m (10ft); wing area 13.89 sq m (149.5 sq ft)
Armament:	two .3in (7.62mm) M1919 Browning machine guns; five 14kg (30lb) or two 50kg (112lb) bombs

Interwar Fleet Air Arm

Between 1918 and 1937, British naval aviation was the responsibility of the Royal Air Force, formed by the amalgamation of the RFC and RNAS. Until 1922, the Royal Navy had only one aircraft carrier, and the Fleet Air Arm a handful of squadrons flying a collection of elderly types. Development of carrier-borne types trailed that of land-based aircraft, and the only enduring FAA type of the period was the Swordfish, which remained in production and service until 1945.

Avro 555 Bison

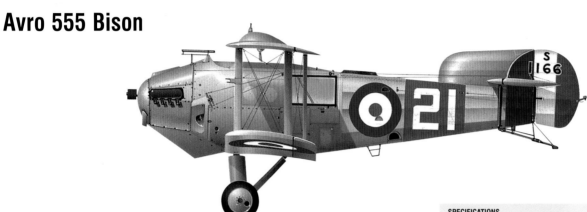

Avro produced very few naval aircraft, a notable exception being the Type 555 Bison. Designed as a spotter for naval gunfire and for general reconnaissance duties, the ungainly Bison was first flown in 1921 and delivered at a slow rate until 1927. Its career was brief, with retirement coming in 1929. It was replaced by the more streamlined Fairey IIIF. An attempted seaplane conversion was not a success.

SPECIFICATIONS	
Country of origin:	United Kingdom
Type:	four-seat carrier-based fleet spotter/reconnaissance aircraft
Powerplant:	one 450hp (366kW) Napier Lion II piston engine
Performance:	maximum speed 177km/h (110mph); service ceiling 4265m (14,000ft); range 547km (340 miles)
Weights:	empty 1887kg (4160lb); maximum take-off weight 2631kg (5800lb)
Dimensions:	span 14.02m (46ft); length 10.97m (36ft); height 4.22m (13ft 10in); wing area 57.6 sq m (620 sq ft)
Armament:	one .303 Lewis machine gun on flexible mount in aft cockpit

Fairey Flycatcher

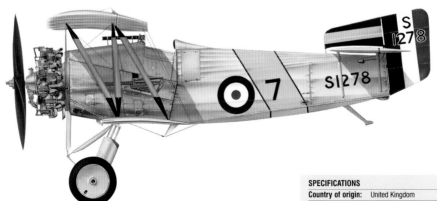

The Flycatcher was the FAA's main fighter for most of the 1920s, and some remained in service as late as 1934. This particular aircraft served with No 405 Flight on HMS Glorious. A prototype for an all-metal derivative, the Flycatcher II, was produced but not adopted.

SPECIFICATIONS	
Country of origin:	United Kingdom
Type:	single-seat biplane carrier fighter
Powerplant:	one 480hp (358kW) Bristol Mercury IIA 9-cylinder radial piston engine
Performance:	maximum speed 247km/h (153mph); service ceiling 5791m (19,000ft); range 500km (311 miles)
Weights:	empty 955kg (2106lb); loaded 1481kg (3266lb)
Dimensions:	span 10.67m (35ft); length 7.55m (24ft 9in); height 3.28m (10ft 9in); wing area 26.76 sq m (288 sq ft)
Armament:	two .303in Vickers Mk II machine guns; four 20lb (9kg) bombs

Fairey Swordfish Mk I

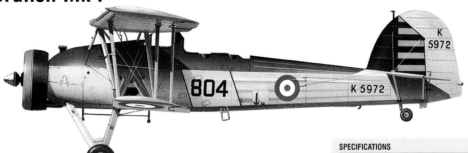

The Swordfish emerged from a 1930 requirement for a torpedo, strike and reconnaissance aircraft. The Fairey TSR.I prototype flew in 1933, and the TSR.II, which was the true predecessor of the Swordfish, in April 1934. The Swordfish Mk I illustrated was assigned to No 823 Squadron on HMS *Glorious*.

SPECIFICATIONS	
Country of origin:	United Kingdom
Type:	2–3-seat carrier-based torpedo bomber
Powerplant:	one 775hp (578kW) Bristol Pegasus IIIM.3 radial piston engine
Performance:	maximum speed 224km/h (139mph); service ceiling 3780m (12,400ft); range with torpedo 1658km (1030 miles)
Weights:	empty 2132kg (4700lb); maximum 3946kg (8700lb)
Dimensions:	span 13.87m (45ft 6in); length 11.07m (36ft 1in); height 3.92m (12ft 11in); wing area 56.39 sq m (607 sq ft)
Armament:	two .303in machine guns; one 726kg (1600lb) torpedo or up to 680kg (1500lb) bombs

Hawker Nimrod

The Nimrod was a naval adaptation of the Fury with a stronger undercarriage and longer wingspan. Introduced in 1933, the Nimrod replaced the Flycatcher. The Nimrod II, introduced a year later, had an arrestor hook and more powerful engine. Nimrods served with seven FAA squadrons.

SPECIFICATIONS	
Country of origin:	United Kingdom
Type:	single-engined carrier-based biplane fighter
Powerplant:	one 525hp (391kW) Rolls-Royce Kestrel VFP inline piston engine
Performance:	maximum speed 311km/h (194mph); service ceiling 8535m (28,000ft); endurance 1hr 40mins
Weights:	1413kg (3110lb); maximum 1841kg (4050lb)
Dimensions:	span 10.23m (33ft 7in); length 8.09m (26ft 6in); height 3.0m (9ft 10in); wing area 27.96 sq m (301 sq ft)
Armament:	two .303in Vickers machine guns; four 20lb (9kg) bombs

Blackburn B-5 Baffin

The Baffin was a naval development of the land-based Ripon and was introduced in 1934, but retired in 1936. This Baffin served with No 810 Squadron on HMS *Courageous* and was later sold to New Zealand.

SPECIFICATIONS	
Country of origin:	United Kingdom
Type:	two-seat carrier-based torpedo bomber
Powerplant:	one 565hp (421kW) Bristol Pegasus I.M3 9-cylinder radial piston engine
Performance:	maximum speed 219km/h (136mph); service ceiling 4570m (15,000ft); range 789km (490 miles)
Weights:	empty 1447kg (3184lb); loaded 3459kg (7610lb)
Dimensions:	span 13.67m (44ft 10in); length 11.68m (38ft 4in); height 3.91m (12ft 10in); wing area 6 sq m (683 sq ft)
Armament:	one .303in Vickers machine gun and one .303in Lewis machine gun; one 816kg (1800lb) torpedo or 726kg (1600lb) bombs

FIAT's Biplanes

Celestino Rosatelli of FIAT designed some of the best biplane fighters of the interwar era, and they took his initials as part of their designation. The later models were widely exported.The CR.32 saw a great deal of combat over Spain and the CR.42 had an extensive war career. Although obsolete in Western Europe, it performed usefully in the North African theatre.

FIAT CR.1

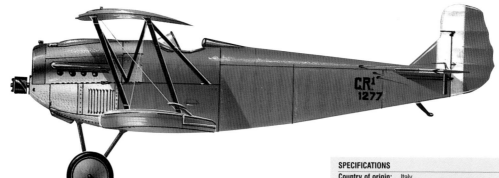

FIAT established an aircraft manufacturing subsidiary during World War I. After trials, first deliveries of an eventual 240 machines of the CR.1 aircraft began in 1925. During the 1930s, many Italian CR.1s were modified to take the 44hp (328kW) Isotta Fraschini Asso Caccia engine, and these served until 1937. The aircraft was exported to Latvia and was tested with different engines.

SPECIFICATIONS	
Country of origin:	Italy
Type:	single-seat fighter biplane
Powerplant:	one 300hp (224kW) Hispano-Suiza 42 8-cylinder radial engine
Performance:	maximum speed 272km/h (169mph); service ceiling 7450m (24,440ft); endurance 2hrs 35mins
Weights:	empty equipped 839kg (1850lb); maximum take-off weight 1154kg (2544lb)
Dimensions:	span 8.95m (29ft 4in); length 6.16m (20ft 2in); height 2.4m (7ft 10in); wing area 23 sq m (248 sq ft)
Armament:	two fixed forward-firing .303in Vickers machine guns

FIAT CR.20

The CR.20 was an unequal-span biplane of steel tube and fabric construction. Production for the Regia Aeronautica began in 1927, with the CR.20 swiftly becoming its standard fighter aircraft. It took part in the Italian conquest of Libya and Abyssinia as a ground attack aircraft. Pictured is a CR.20 of the Magyar Királyi Légierő (Royal Hungarian Air Force) in 1936.

SPECIFICATIONS	
Country of origin:	Italy
Type:	single-seat fighter biplane
Powerplant:	one 410hp (306kW) Fiat A.20 12-cylinder Vee piston engine
Performance:	maximum speed 260km/h (161mph); service ceiling 8500m (27,885ft); endurance 2hrs 30mins
Weights:	empty 970kg (2138lb); maximum take-off weight 1390kg (3064lb)
Dimensions:	span 9.8m (32ft 1in); length 6.71m (22ft); height 2.79m (9ft 1in); wing area 25.5 sq m (274 sq ft)
Armament:	two fixed forward-firing .303in Vickers machine guns

FIAT'S BIPLANES TIMELINE

 1922

 1924

 1925

FIAT CR.20bis

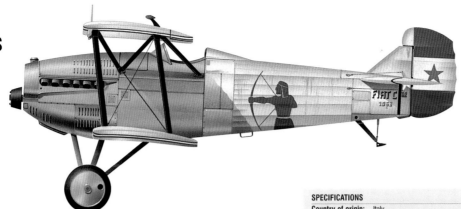

The fragile cross-axle rubber-sprung landing gear of the CR.20 proved to be an Achilles heel, and FIAT set about improving the arrangement. The CR.20bis of 1930 had oleo-pneumatic shock absorbers and wheel brakes, and was built in numbers totalling 232 aircraft. Some were bought by Austria, Hungary, Lithuania, Paraguay (pictured here), Poland and the Soviet Union. After the Anschluss with Austria in 1938, a number were repainted in Luftwaffe colours.

SPECIFICATIONS	
Country of origin:	Italy
Type:	single-seat fighter biplane
Powerplant:	one 410hp (306kW) Fiat A.20 12-cylinder Vee piston engine
Performance:	maximum speed 260km/h (161mph); service ceiling 8500m (27,885ft); endurance 2hrs 30mins
Weights:	empty 970kg (2138lb); maximum take-off weight 1390kg (3064lb)
Dimensions:	span 9.8m (32ft 1in); length 6.71m (22ft); height 2.79m (9ft 1in); wing area 25.5 sq m (274 sq ft)
Armament:	two fixed forward-firing .303in Vickers machine guns

FIAT CR.32quater

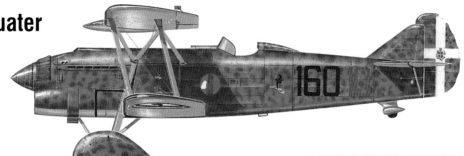

The CR.32 was the most important biplane fighter of the 1930s, certainly in terms of the number built (1712). It stemmed from the CR.30, designed by Chief Engineer Rosatelli in 1931 as a single-seat fighter and bearing many of his hallmarks, such as W-form interplane bracing. Its performance in the Spanish Civil War lulled the Italian Air Ministry into the false belief that the fighter biplane was a viable weapon of war, despite soon being outclassed by monoplanes.

SPECIFICATIONS	
Country of origin:	Italy
Type:	single-seat fighter biplane
Powerplant:	one 600hp (447kW) Fiat A.30 RA bis 12-cylinder Vee piston engine
Performance:	maximum speed 375km/h (233mph); service ceiling 8800m (28,870ft); range 680km (422 miles)
Weights:	empty 1325kg (2921lb); maximum take-off weight 1850kg (4079lb)
Dimensions:	span 9.5m (31ft 2in); length 7.45m (24ft 5in); height 2.63m (8ft 7in); wing area 22.10 sq m (238 sq ft)
Armament:	two fixed forward-firing .303in Breda-SAFAT machine guns

FIAT CR.42 Falco

Sweden bought 72 CR.42s in 1940, which they designated J.11s. They equipped the F.9 wing at Gothenburg and remained in service until 1945 when fully replaced by SAAB J.21s. The type was also used by Italy, Hungary, Germany and Belgium.

SPECIFICATIONS	
Country of origin:	Italy
Type:	single-engined biplane fighter
Powerplant:	one 840hp (627kW) Fiat A.74 RIC38 14-cylinder radial piston engine
Performance:	maximum speed 441km/h (274mph); combat radius 780km (485 miles); service ceiling 10,210m (33,500ft)
Weights:	empty 1782kg (3929lb); loaded 2295kg (5060lb)
Dimensions:	span 9.7m (31ft 10in); length 8.25m (27ft 1in); height 3.06m (10ft); wing area 22.4 sq m (241 sq ft)
Armament:	two 12.7mm (.5in) Breda SAFAT machine guns; 200kg (440lb) bombs

1931

Curtiss Army Biplanes

The Curtiss company was an active participant in the inter-war craze for air racing, and with prize-winning aircraft like the R-6 they advanced the state of aeronautical technology, particularly for engine cooling, and won US Army Air Corps orders. The PW-8 racer led to the famous Hawk biplane fighter series for the Army and to related radial-engine designs for the Navy.

Curtiss R-6

During the 1920s, competition provided the greatest spur for aircraft development. The first Curtiss racing machines were developed for the James Gordon Bennett Trophy race at Etampes in September 1920. Pictured is the R-6, one of two built for the US Army, which was flown into second place by Lester Maitland at Selfridge Field in 1922.

SPECIFICATIONS	
Country of origin:	United States
Type:	single-seat racing biplane
Powerplant:	one 465hp (347kW) Curtiss D-12 12-cylinder Vee piston engine
Performance:	maximum speed 380km/h (236mph); range 455km (283 miles)
Weights:	loaded 884kg (1950lb)
Dimensions:	span 5.79m (19ft); length 5.75m (18ft 11in); height 2.41m (7ft 11in)

Curtiss Model 33/34 (PW-8)

The inspiration that Curtiss gained from the company's racing activities is visible in the designs of its fighters. In 1922, Curtiss began to develop a new fighter design, the L-18-1. By the end of the year, this had become the prototype PW-8. It was a two-bay biplane with considerable wing stagger and a streamlined fuselage of metal construction. The second prototype was modified with tapered wings for the 1924 Pulitzer Trophy, and took third place in this competition.

SPECIFICATIONS	
Country of origin:	United States
Type:	single-seat fighter biplane
Powerplant:	one 440hp (328kW) Curtiss D-12 12-cylinder Vee piston engine
Performance:	maximum speed 275km/h (171mph); service ceiling 6205m (20,350ft); range 875km (544 miles)
Weights:	empty 991kg (2185lb); maximum take-off weight 1431kg (3155lb)
Dimensions:	span 9.75m (32ft); length 7.03m (23ft 1in); height 2.76m (9ft 1in); wing area 25.94 sq m (279 sq ft)
Armament:	two fixed forward-firing .3in Browning machine guns

CURTISS BIPLANES TIMELINE
1923 1925 1926

Curtiss P-1B

During testing of the XPW-8B with redesigned wings, problems associated with wing flutter prompted Curtiss to revert to the single-bay wing of the R-6 for production of the P-1 Hawk. Initial P-1s in 1925 had extra centre-section bracing and a modified rudder. Continued development of the P-1 resulted in the P-1A, with a lengthened fuselage, modified cowling and Curtiss D-12C engine, followed by 23 P-1Bs (pictured) and 33 P-1Cs with a V-1150 engine.

SPECIFICATIONS	
Country of origin:	United States
Type:	single-seat pursuit aircraft
Powerplant:	one 435hp (324kW) Curtiss V-1150-3 piston engine
Performance:	maximum speed 248km/h (154mph); service ceiling 6344m (20,800ft); range 1046km (650 miles)
Weights:	empty 970kg (2136lb); all-up weight 1349kg (2973lb)
Dimensions:	span 9.6m (31ft 6in); length 7.06m (23ft 2in); height 2.72m (8ft 11in); wing area 23.41 sq m (252 sq ft)
Armament:	two fixed forward-firing .3in machine guns

Curtiss P-6D Hawk

To produce the prototype XP-6 Hawk, Curtiss took the airframe of a P-1 and installed a Curtiss V-1570 Conqueror engine. This was flown into second place at the 1927 National Air Races at Skopane, Washington. The US Army contracted Curtiss for 18 P-6s for evaluation, which had modified cowl and deeper fuselage. In the spring of 1932, all the P-6s were re-engined with the Prestone cooling system, becoming P-6Ds.

SPECIFICATIONS	
Country of origin:	United States
Type:	single-seat pursuit aircraft
Powerplant:	one 700hp (522kW) Curtiss V-1570C Conqueror inline piston engine
Performance:	maximum speed 319km/h (198mph); service ceiling 7530m (24,700ft); range 459km (285 miles)
Weights:	empty equipped 1224kg (2669lb); maximum take-off weight 1559kg (3436lb)
Dimensions:	span 9.6m (31ft 6in); length 7.06m (23ft 2in); height 2.72m (8ft 11in); wing area 23.41 sq m (252 sq ft)
Armament:	two fixed forward-firing .3in machine guns

Curtiss P-6E Hawk

Most prolific and impressive of the P-6 Hawk family was the P-6E, the last biplane fighter to be delivered to the United States Army Air Corps. Generally similar to the P-6D, it had a slimmer forward fuselage, with the engine radiator mounted slightly forward of the landing gear, which comprised single-strut main legs with spat-type wheel fairings. Forty-six were ordered in July 1931.

SPECIFICATIONS	
Country of origin:	United States
Type:	single-seat pursuit aircraft
Powerplant:	one 600hp (448kW) Curtiss V-1570-23 Conqueror inline piston
Performance:	maximum speed 319km/h (198mph); service ceiling 7530m (24,700ft); range 917km (570 miles)
Weights:	empty equipped 1224kg (2669lb); maximum take-off weight 1539kg (3392lb)
Dimensions:	span 9.6m (31ft 6in); length 7.06m (23ft 2in); height 2.72m (8ft 11in); wing area 23.41 sq m (252 sq ft)
Armament:	two fixed forward-firing .3in machine guns

1927

1933

1936

Czech Biplanes

Czechoslovakia had a thriving aircraft industry between the wars. Following Germany's occupation in 1938–39, their output served the Nazis and their allies. Of the many national manufacturers, Avia and the smaller Aero company, both founded in 1919, were the most successful, equipping many of Germany's allies with biplane fighters and bombers. The B.534 biplane fighter saw action on the Eastern Front as late as 1944.

Aero A.18

The A.18 was Aero Tovarna Letadel Dr Kabes's successful submission to a Czech Air Force competition for a new single-seat fighter aircraft. The A.18 was a smaller version of the A.11, and followed that aircraft's single-bay, unequal-span biplane wing planform. The twin machine guns, synchronized to fire through the propeller disc, came from Vickers.

SPECIFICATIONS

Country of origin:	Czechoslovakia
Type:	single-seat fighter biplane
Powerplant:	one 185hp (138kW) BMW IIIa inline piston engine
Performance:	maximum speed 229km/h (142mph); service ceiling 9000m (29,530ft); range 400km (249 miles)
Weights:	empty 637kg (1404lb); maximum take-off weight 862kg (1900lb)
Dimensions:	span 7.6m (24ft 11in); length 5.9m (19ft 4in); height 2.9m (9ft 6in); wing area 15.9 sq m (171 sq ft)
Armament:	two fixed forward-firing synchronized machine guns

Avia BH.21

The Avia company was founded in 1919 and established workshops near Cakovice in the newly formed republic of Czechoslovakia. The BH.21 traced its lineage to the BH-17 biplane fighter of 1924, and had revised forward upper fuselage for improved pilot view, single underfuselage radiator to replace the twin mainwheel leg mounted units of the BH.17, and single-bay 'N' interplane struts. The Czech Air Force acquired 137 aircraft, which served until the 1930s.

SPECIFICATIONS

Country of origin:	Czechoslovakia
Type:	single-seat fighter biplane
Powerplant:	one 310hp (231kW) Avia (licence-built Hispano-Suiza) 8Fb inline piston engine
Performance:	maximum speed 245km/h (152mph); service ceiling 5500m (18,045ft); range 550km (342 miles)
Weights:	empty 720kg (1587lb); maximum take-off weight 1084kg (2390lb)
Dimensions:	span 8.9m (29ft 2in); length 6.87m (22ft 6in); height 2.74m (8ft 11in); wing area 21.96 sq m (236 sq ft)
Armament:	two fixed forward-firing .303in Vickers machine guns in forward fuselage

CZECHS TIMELINE

1923

1927

Avia BH.26

The prototype for the BH.26 two-seat fighter reconnaissance aircraft first flew in 1927. The aircraft had a slab-sided fuselage, single-bay unequal-span biplane wing planform, a rudder but no fixed vertical tail fin. Early flight testing revealed the inadequacy of this configuration and the design was revised to include the fin and rudder assembly that appeared on production aircraft. Only a very limited production run of eight aircraft was completed for the Czech Air Force.

SPECIFICATIONS	
Country of origin:	Czechoslovakia
Type:	two-seater fighter reconnaissance biplane
Powerplant:	one 450hp (336kW) Walter (licence-built Bristol Jupiter IV) 9-cylinder radial piston engine
Performance:	maximum speed 242km/h (150mph); service ceiling 8500m (27,885ft); range 530km (329 miles)
Weights:	empty 1030kg (2721lb); maximum take-off weight 1630kg (3594lb)
Dimensions:	span 10.8m (35ft 5in); length 8.85m (29ft); height 3.35m (10ft 11in); wing area 31 sq m (334 sq ft)
Armament:	two fixed forward-firing .303in Vickers MGs in forward fuselage; two .303in Lewis MGs on Skoda mount over rear cockpit

Aero A.100

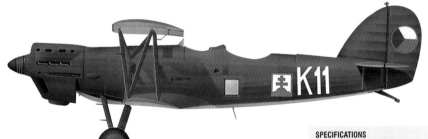

The success of its A.11 encouraged Aero to fund further development of the basic airframe. From the A.30 was spawned the A.430 prototype, a single example of which was built with a 650hp (485kW) Avia engine and oleo-pneumatic shock-struts for the main landing-gear units. This aircraft offered improved performance over the A.30. Redesignated as the A.100, some 44 aircraft were produced for the Czech Air Force, including two bomber versions.

SPECIFICATIONS	
Country of origin:	Czechoslovakia
Type:	two-seat long-range reconnaissance biplane
Powerplant:	one 650hp (485kW) Avia Vr-36 inline piston engine
Performance:	maximum speed 270km/h (168mph); service ceiling 6500m (21,325ft); endurance 4hrs
Weights:	empty 2040kg (4497lb); maximum take-off weight 3220kg (7099lb)
Dimensions:	span 14.7m (48ft 2in); length 10.6m (34ft 9in); height 3.5m (11ft 5in); wing area 44.3 sq m (477 sq ft)
Armament:	two fixed forward-firing .303in Vickers machine guns; two Lewis guns on flexible mount in rear cockpit; external pylons for a maximum bomb load of 600kg (1322lb)

Avia B.534-IV

The first production model of this outstanding fighter was the B.534-I, which had a wooden screw to replace the metal unit of the prototype and an open cockpit. The definitive B.536-IV variant had an enclosed cockpit and revised aft fuselage decking. Pictured is one of the three B.534-IVs used during the Slovak National Uprising of September 1944. The aircraft operated from the airfield at Tri Duby.

SPECIFICATIONS	
Country of origin:	Czechoslovakia
Type:	single-seat fighter biplane
Powerplant:	one 850hp (634kW) Hispano-Suiza HS 12Ydrs inline piston engine
Performance:	maximum speed 394km/h (245mph); service ceiling 10,600m (34,775ft); range 580km (360 miles)
Weights:	empty 1460kg (3219lb); maximum take-off weight 2120kg (4674lb)
Dimensions:	span 9.4m (30ft 10in); length 8.2m (26ft 10in); height 3.1m (10ft 2in); wing area 23.56 sq m (254 sq ft)
Armament:	four fixed forward-firing 7.7mm (.303in) Model 30 machine guns in forward fuselage; underwing Pantof racks with provision for six 20kg (44lb) bombs

1933

1934

Dive Bombers

The technique of dive-bombing offered surprise and accuracy, and was particularly suitable for smaller carrier-based aircraft. The Curtiss biplane dive-bombers, most of which were named 'Helldiver', inspired German and Japanese developments, which proved devastating in the early war years. Of the aircraft illustrated below, only the Henschel Hs 123 saw much – if any – service in the world war to come, as a second generation of monoplane dive-bombers had by then entered widespread service.

Curtiss BF2C-1

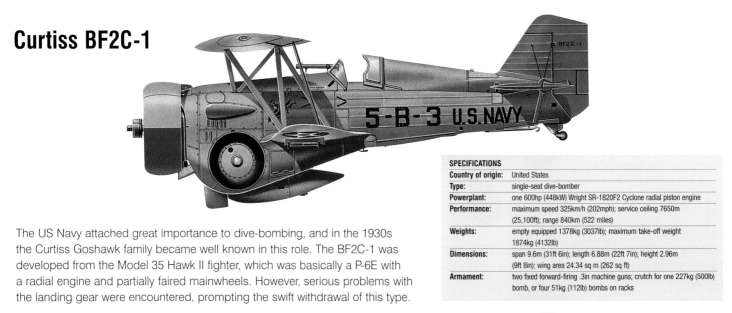

The US Navy attached great importance to dive-bombing, and in the 1930s the Curtiss Goshawk family became well known in this role. The BF2C-1 was developed from the Model 35 Hawk II fighter, which was basically a P-6E with a radial engine and partially faired mainwheels. However, serious problems with the landing gear were encountered, prompting the swift withdrawal of this type.

SPECIFICATIONS

Country of origin:	United States
Type:	single-seat dive-bomber
Powerplant:	one 600hp (448kW) Wright SR-1820F2 Cyclone radial piston engine
Performance:	maximum speed 325km/h (202mph); service ceiling 7650m (25,100ft); range 840km (522 miles)
Weights:	empty equipped 1378kg (3037lb); maximum take-off weight 1874kg (4132lb)
Dimensions:	span 9.6m (31ft 6in); length 6.88m (22ft 7in); height 2.96m (9ft 8in); wing area 24.34 sq m (262 sq ft)
Armament:	two fixed forward-firing .3in machine guns; crutch for one 227kg (500lb) bomb, or four 51kg (112lb) bombs on racks

Henschel Hs 123A-1

One of the first designs of Henschel Flugzeugwerke was the Hs 123, a sesquiplane dive-bomber. The first of four prototypes was tested in August 1935, two being destroyed in high-speed dives due to wing structural failure. The fourth was extensively modified to correct these problems and went into production. In 1936, five Hs 123A-1s were sent to Spain, where many of the ground-support tactics used in the later Blitzkrieg campaigns were pioneered.

SPECIFICATIONS

Country of origin:	Germany
Type:	single-seat dive bomber and close-support aircraft
Powerplant:	one 880hp (656kW) BMW 132Dc 9-cylinder radial engine
Performance:	maximum speed 340km/h (211mph); service ceiling 9000m (29,530ft); range 855km (531 miles)
Weights:	empty 1500kg (3307lb); maximum take-off weight 2215kg (4884lb)
Dimensions:	span 10.5m (34ft 5in); length 8.33m (27ft 4in); height 3.2m (10ft 6in); wing area 24.85 sq m (267 sq ft)
Armament:	two fixed forward-firing 7.92mm (.31in) MG 17 machine guns; underwing racks with provision for up to 450kg (992lb) of bombs

DIVE BOMBERS TIMELINE

1924

1927

1928

Curtiss Model 77 (SBC-3 Helldiver)

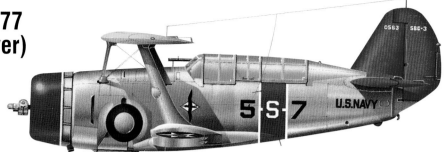

In prototype, the XSBC-2 (Model 77) had staggered biplane wings and a Wright R-1510-12 engine. In 1936, this was changed to the Pratt & Whitney R-1535-82, and the new designation XSBC-3 was adopted. In this form, the aircraft was ordered by the US Navy as the SBC-3 Helldiver. A late production SBC-3 was used as a prototype for the SBC-4, of which 174 examples were ordered for the US Navy, the first arriving in March 1939.

SPECIFICATIONS	
Country of origin:	United States
Type:	two-seat carrier-based scout bomber
Powerplant:	one 700hp (522kW) Pratt & Whitney R-1535-82 Twin Wasp radial engine
Performance:	maximum speed 377km/h (234mph); service ceiling 7315m (24,000ft); range with 227kg (500lb) bomb 652km (405 miles)
Weights:	empty 2065kg (4552lb); maximum take-off weight 3211kg (7080lb)
Dimensions:	span 10.36m (34ft); length 8.57m (28ft 1in); height 3.17m (10ft 5in); wing area 29.45 sq m (317 sq ft)
Armament:	one fixed forward-firing .3in machine gun; one .3in machine gun on flexible mount, underfuselage rack for one 227kg (500lb) bomb

Aichi D1A2 'Susie'

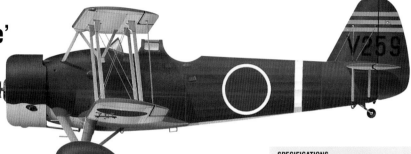

Ernst Heinkel's design staff produced a prototype carrier-based dive bomber (the He 66) for Aichi in 1931. Under Japanese manufacture with a Nakajima engine, this became the Aichi D1A1. From it was developed the Aichi D1A2, which appeared in 1936 with a more powerful Nakajima Hikari engine, spatted wheels and more streamlined windscreens. Production totalled 428, but by the time of Japan's entry into World War II, it was relegated to second-line duties.

SPECIFICATIONS	
Country of origin:	Japan
Type:	two-seat carrier-based biplane dive bomber
Powerplant:	one 730hp (544kW) Nakajima Hikari 1 radial piston engine
Performance:	maximum speed 310km/h (193mph); climb to 3000m (9845ft) in 7mins 50secs; service ceiling 7000m (22,965ft); range 930km (578 miles)
Weights:	empty 1516kg (3342lb); maximum take-off weight 2610kg (5754lb)
Dimensions:	span 11.4m (37ft 4in); length 9.3m (30ft 6in); height 3.41m (11ft 2in); wing area 34.7 sq m (373 sq ft)
Armament:	two fixed forward-firing 7.7mm (.303in) Type 97 machine guns and one 7.7mm (.303in) Type 92 machine gun on flexible mount in rear cockpit; plus external pylons for one 250kg (551lb) and two 30kg (66lb) bombs

Curtiss SBC Cleveland

France ordered a large number of SBC-4s, but none actually entered service before their forces capitulated. Five found their way to the RAF and were named Cleveland Mk Is, although they never saw active service and were used as ground trainers.

SPECIFICATIONS	
Country of origin:	United States
Type:	two-seat carrier-based dive bomber
Powerplant:	one 950hp (709kW) Wright R-1820-34 Cyclone radial piston engine
Performance:	maximum speed 381km/h (237mph); combat radius 950km (590 miles); service ceiling 8320m (27,300ft)
Weights:	empty 2196kg (4841lb); maximum 3462kg (7632lb)
Dimensions:	span 1036m (34ft 0in); length 8.64m (28ft 4in); height 3.84m (12ft 7in); wing area 29.5 sq m (317 sq ft)
Armament:	two .3in M1919 Browning machine guns; one bomb up to 1000lb (450kg)

1930

1934

RAF Biplane Bombers

The RAF was late to adopt the monoplane configuration for bombers or fighters. Its main requirement in the 1920s and 1930s was for rugged general-purpose types, such as the Wapiti and Vildebeest, which were suitable for the colonial policing role in India, Africa and the Far East. Home-based bombers evolved more slowly. The Overstrand introduced enclosed gun turrets and a covered cockpit, deemed necessary because of its then-scorching top speed of around 225km/h (140mph).

Hawker Horsley Mk II

Pictured in the colours of No 33 (Bomber) Squadron, the Hawker Horsley was a two-seat medium day-bomber developed as a replacement for the Airco D.H.9. Hawker began the construction of the prototype in 1924, this having unequal-span, slightly swept, biplane wings; a conventionally braced tail unit; and tailskid landing gear. Early examples of the Horsley Mk II were of mixed wood and fabric construction, while the later aircraft had an all-metal basic structure.

SPECIFICATIONS

Country of origin:	United Kingdom
Type:	two-seat day-bomber
Powerplant:	one 665hp (496kW) Rolls-Royce Condor IIIA 12-cylinder Vee-piston engine
Performance:	maximum speed 201km/h (125mph); service ceiling 4265m (14,000ft); endurance 10hrs
Weights:	empty 2159kg (4760lb); maximum take-off weight 3538kg (7800lb)
Dimensions:	span 17.21m (56ft 6in); length 11.84m (38ft 10in); height 4.17m (13ft 8in); wing area 64.38 sq m (693 sq ft)
Armament:	one fixed-forward firing .303in Vickers Mk II machine gun; one .303in Lewis machine gun on pivoted mount in rear cockpit; external racks with provision for 680kg (1500lb) of bombs or one 46cm (18in) torpedo

Westland Wapiti IIA

The Wapiti was employed in a variety of roles, including reconnaissance, bombing and army cooperation. It was used in Afghanistan, India and licence-produced in South Africa. This Wapiti II was used by one of the five Coastal Defence Flights of the Indian Air Force Volunteer Reserve, who used the type up to 1939.

SPECIFICATIONS

Country of origin:	United Kingdom
Type:	general-purpose two-seat biplane
Powerplant:	one 1420hp (313kW) Bristol Jupiter VI radial piston engine
Performance:	maximum speed 208km/h (112mph); combat radius 580km (360 miles); service ceiling 5730m (18,800ft)
Weights:	empty 1732kg (3810lb); loaded 2459kg (5410lb)
Dimensions:	span 14.15m (46ft 5in); length 9.65m (31ft 8in); height 3.96m (13ft); wing area 45 sq m (488 sq ft)
Armament:	one .303in Vickers and one .303in Lewis machine guns; up to 264kg (580lb) of bombs

Vickers Vildebeest Mk III

In 1927, the British Air Ministry began its search for a new light bomber to replace the Hawker Horsley torpedo/day bomber. The Vickers Vildebeest was designed to this requirement, and was flown as the Type 132 prototype in April 1928. The Mk III had a revised rear cockpit for a third crew member. In December 1937, the last of 57 Mk IVs, the last production series, was delivered.

SPECIFICATIONS	
Country of origin:	United Kingdom
Type:	three-seat general-purpose aircraft
Powerplant:	one 660hp (492kW) Bristol Pegasus IIM3 sleeve-valve radial piston engine
Performance:	maximum speed 230km/h (142mph); service ceiling 5182m (17,000ft); range 2500km (1553 miles)
Weights:	empty 1918kg (4229lb); maximum take-off weight 3674kg (8100lb)
Dimensions:	span 14.94m (49ft in); length 11.17m (36ft 8in); height 5.42m (17ft 9in)
Armament:	one fixed forward-firing .303in Vickers machine gun; one.303in Lewis machine gun on pivoted mount in rear cockpit

Boulton Paul P.75 Overstrand

The Boulton Paul P.75 Overstrand was developed from the airframe of the eighth production P.29 Sidestrand, a twin-engined medium bomber. The P.75 had a power-operated nose turret, one of the first to be fitted to a production aircraft; an enclosed cockpit; three-axis autopilot; and a heating system.

SPECIFICATIONS	
Country of origin:	United Kingdom
Type:	five-seat medium bomber
Powerplant:	two 580hp (433kW) Bristol Pegasus IIM.3 radial piston engines
Performance:	maximum speed 246km/h (153mph); service ceiling 6860m (22,500ft); range 877km (545 miles)
Weights:	empty 3600kg (7936lb); maximum take-off weight 5443kg (12,000lb)
Dimensions:	span 21.95m (72ft); length 14.02m (46ft); height 4.72m (15ft 6in); wing area 91.04 sq m (980 sq ft)
Armament:	one .303in Lewis gun in nose turret; one .303in Lewis gun in each of the two dorsal ventral positions; internal bay with provision for up to 726kg (1600lb) of bombs

Handley Page H.P.50 Heyford Mk IA

When it first appeared in 1930, the ungainly appearance of the H.P.50 was roundly derided, yet this aircraft formed the backbone of Britain's so-called strategic bombing fleet in the 1930s and soldiered on until more capable types were introduced. The RAF took delivery of 124 H.P.50s.

SPECIFICATIONS	
Country of origin:	United Kingdom
Type:	heavy night-bomber
Powerplant:	two 575hp (429kW) Rolls Royce Kestrel IIIS 12-cylinder Vee-piston engine
Performance:	maximum speed 229km/h (142mph); service ceiling 6400m (21,000ft); range with 726kg (1600lb) bomb load 1481kg (920 miles)
Weights:	empty 4173kg (9200lb); maximum take-off weight 7666kg (16,900lb)
Dimensions:	span 22.86m (75ft); length 17.68m (58ft); height 5.33m (17ft 6in); wing area 136.56 sq m (1470 sq ft)
Armament:	one .303in Lewis machine gun on flexible mount each in nose position, dorsal position and ventral turret; internal bay with provision for up to 1588kg (3500lb) of bombs

Rebirth of the Luftwaffe

German military aviation was officially reborn with the establishment of the Luftwaffe in 1935, although by then pilots had been secretly training in the Soviet Union and with the civil airlines for over a decade. Gliding became a popular inter-war sport encouraged by the Nazis, introducing thousands of youths to the principles of flight. The Luftwaffe's first aircraft were mostly developed under the guise of 'sport planes' or converted from airliner designs.

Heinkel He 51A-1

The Treaty of Versailles forbade German manufacturers from building military aircraft and so Heinkel, like many other German designers, formed partnerships and subsidiaries in other countries. As the likelihood of Allied legal action receded, Heinkel dared to build the prototype of an aircraft that blatantly disregarded the Treaty – the He 37 – which first flew in 1928. This was followed by He 49 prototypes, which formed the basis for the He 51, delivered in 1934.

SPECIFICATIONS

Country of origin:	Germany
Type:	single-seat fighter biplane
Powerplant:	one 750hp (559kW) BMW V1 7,3Z 12-cylinder Vee piston engine
Performance:	maximum speed 330km/h (205mph); service ceiling 7700m (25,260ft); range 570km (354 miles)
Weights:	empty 1460kg (3219lb); maximum take-off weight 1895kg (4178lb)
Dimensions:	span 11m (36ft 1in); length 8.4m (27ft 7in); height 3.2m (10ft 6in); wing area 27.2 sq m (293 sq ft)
Armament:	two fixed forward-firing 7.92mm (.31in) MG 17 machine guns

Arado Ar 68F

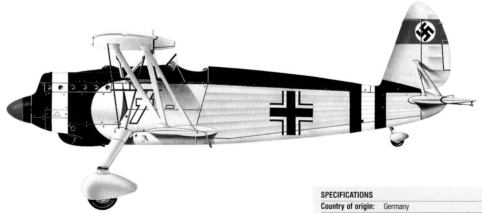

Despite its good engines, the Ar 68 was never an outstanding machine, and ran second in both timing and performance to the Heinkel He 51 that was its great rival. Almost as soon as it had entered service, it was made obsolete by the Messerschmitt Bf 109, and almost all had been relegated to advanced fighter-trainer status by the outbreak of the war.

SPECIFICATIONS

Country of origin:	Germany
Type:	single-seat fighter
Powerplant:	one 750hp (570kW) BMW VI Vee-12- piston engine
Performance:	maximum speed 305km/h (190mph); service ceiling 8100m (26,575ft)
Weights:	empty 1840kg (4057lb); maximum take-off weight 2475kg (5457lb)
Dimensions:	span 11m (36ft 1in); length 9.5m (31ft 2in); height 3.28m (10ft 9in)
Armament:	two fixed forward-firing 7.92mm (.31in) MG 17 machine guns

Junkers Ju 52

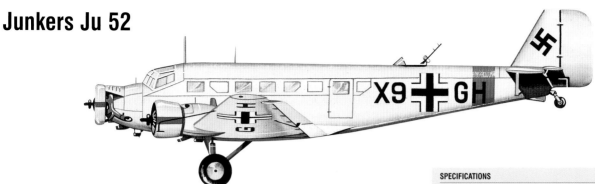

Derived from the single-engined Ju 52, the trimotor Ju 52/3m became one of the most important transport aircraft of all time. Notable for its corrugated metal skin, the Ju 52/3m was used as a bomber over Spain as well as a transport. This one served with a training school.

SPECIFICATIONS	
Country of origin:	Germany
Type:	three-engined transport aircraft and bomber
Powerplant:	three 533kW (715hp) BMW 132T radial piston engines
Performance:	maximum speed 265km/h (165mph)); service ceiling 5490m (18,000 ft); range 870km (540 miles)
Weights:	empty 6510kg (14,325lb); maximum 10,990kg (24,200lb)
Dimensions:	span 29.25m (95ft 10in); length 18.90m (62ft 0in); height 4.5m (14ft 10in); wing area 110.5 sq m (1190 sq ft)
Armament:	one 13mm (.5in) MG 131 machine-gun or two 7.92mm (.31in) MG 15 machine-guns

Junkers Ju 86D-1

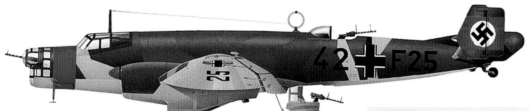

The Junkers Ju 86 was planned as a medium bomber. The first two production variants were the Ju 86D and Ju 86E, which entered service in spring 1936. They differed in their powerplants, the latter type having 810hp (655kW) BMW 132 radial engines. Operational service revealed that performance was poor, so the type was then developed as civil transports and the Ju 86G bomber trainer.

SPECIFICATIONS	
Country of origin:	Germany
Type:	(Ju 86D-1) four-seat medium bomber
Powerplant:	two 600hp (447kW) Junkers Jumo 205C-4 vertically opposed Diesel engines
Performance:	maximum speed 325km/h (202mph); service ceiling 5900m (19,360ft); range 1140km (708 miles) with maximum bomb load
Weights:	empty 5800kg (12,786lb); maximum take-off weight 8200kg (18,078lb)
Dimensions:	span 22.50m (73ft 9.75in); length 17.57m (58ft 7.13in); height 5.06m (16ft 7.25in)
Armament:	one 7.92mm (.31in) trainable forward-firing machine gun in the nose position, one 7.92mm (.31in) trainable rearward-firing machine gun each in the dorsal position retractable ventral 'dustbin', plus an internal bomb load of 1000kg (2205lb)

HE 100

The He 100 was a streamlined and fast fighter first flown in 1938. Only about 25 were built before Heinkel was ordered to concentrate on bomber production. Some He 100Ds were extensively photographed in spurious markings to convince the world that it was a new type in service.

SPECIFICATIONS	
Country of origin:	Germany
Type:	(HE 100D) single-engined monoplane fighter
Powerplant:	one 1175hp (876kW) Daimler-Benz DB 601M liquid-cooled supercharged V12 piston engine
Performance:	maximum speed 668km/h (416mph); service ceiling 11,000m (36,090ft); range 900km (460 miles)
Weights:	empty 1617kg (3565lb); maximum 2248kg (4957lb)
Dimensions:	span 8.20m (26ft 11in); length 8.20m (26ft 11in); height 3.60m (11ft 10in); wing area 14.5 sq m (156 sq ft)
Armament:	two 7.92mm (.31in) MG 17 machine guns and one 20mm (.78in) MG FF cannons

Spanish Civil War Part One

The Spanish Civil War of 1936–38 was in many ways a precursor of the global conflict to come. General Franco's fascist allies, Germany and Italy, equipped the Nationalist Air Force and sent their own air contingents. The German Condor Legion and the Italian Aviazione Legionaria contributed to the eventual Nationalist victory and provided air crews with experience that would become invaluable in 1939–40.

Savoia-Marchetti S.M.81 Pipistrello

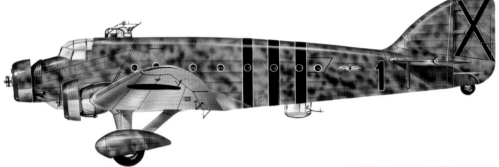

The Pipestrello, or 'Bat', was the main bomber used by Italy's Aviazione Legionaria in Spain. This one was based at Talavera de la Reina in October 1936. Several engine choices were available for the S.M.81, one of many Italian trimotor designs.

SPECIFICATIONS	
Country of origin:	Italy
Type:	six-crew medium bomber
Powerplant:	three 670hp (522kW) Piaggio P.X RC.15 radial piston engines
Performance:	maximum speed 320km/h (211mph); service ceiling 7000m (23,000ft); range 1500km (1240 miles)
Weights:	empty 6800kg (13,900lb); maximum 10,505kg (20,500lb)
Dimensions:	span 24m (78ft 9in); length 18.3m (58ft 5in); height 4.3m (14ft 7in); wing area 92.2 sq m (1001 sq ft)
Armament:	six 7.7mm (.303in) Breda-SAFAT machine guns; up to 2000kg (4415lb) bombs

Heinkel He 112

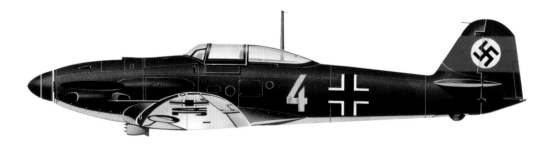

Like the He 100, the He 112 saw limited production, although many of the 100 or so examples built saw combat in Spain and later with German allies, such as Romania and Hungary. About 17 He 112Bs were supplied to the Nationalist Air Force.

SPECIFICATIONS	
Country of origin:	Germany
Type:	single-engined fighter
Powerplant:	one 522kW (700hp) Junkers Jumo 210Ga inverted V-12 piston engine
Performance:	maximum speed 510km/h (317mph); service ceiling 9500m (31,200ft); range 1150km (715 miles)
Weights:	empty 1617kg (3565lb); maximum 2248 kg (4957lb)
Dimensions:	span 9.09m (29ft 10in); length 9.22m (31ft 0in); height 3.82m (12ft 7in); wing area 17sq m (183sq ft)
Armament:	two 7.92mm (.31in) MG 17 machine-guns and two 20mm (.78in) MG FF cannon

Heinkel He 70

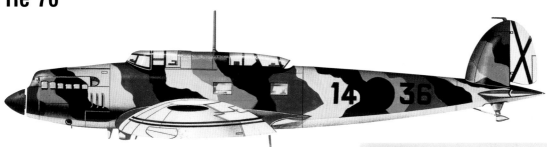

SPECIFICATIONS	
Country of origin:	Germany
Type:	(He 70F-2) single-engined light bomber
Powerplant:	one 750hp (559kW) BMW VI 7.3 12-cylinder piston engine
Performance:	maximum speed 360km/h (224mph); combat radius 900km (559 miles); service ceiling 5350m (17,552ft)
Weights:	empty 2360kg (5203lb); maximum 3460kg (7630lb)
Dimensions:	span 14.80m (48ft 7in); length 12m (39ft 5in); height 3.1m (10ft 2in); wing area 36.5 sq m (392.89 sq ft)
Armament:	one 7.92mm (.3in) MG 15 machine gun; six 110lb (50kg) or 24 22lb (10kg) bombs

With its origins as a high-speed mailplane, the He 70 was faster than most contemporary fighters, but carried a limited bomb load and was prone to catching fire when hit. This one served with Grupo 7-G-14 in the winter of 1937–38.

Fiat G.50 Freccia

SPECIFICATIONS	
Country of origin:	Italy
Type:	single-engined fighter
Powerplant:	one 838hp (625kW) Fiat A.74 RC38 radial piston engine
Performance:	maximum speed 484km/h (301mph); service ceiling 9835m (32,258ft); range 670km (418 miles)
Weights:	empty 1975kg (4354lb); maximum 2706kg (5965lb)
Dimensions:	span 10.96m (35ft 11in); length 7.79m (25ft 7in); height 2.96m (9ft 9in); wing area 18.2 sq m (196 sq ft)
Armament:	two 12.7mm (.5in) Breda-SAFAT machine guns

The G.50 entered Italian service in early 1938 and was rushed to Spain to take part in operational trials. It proved one of the best fighters of the war, but was not much faster than the CR.42 biplane and was soon obsolescent.

Messerschmitt Bf 109B

SPECIFICATIONS	
Country of origin:	Germany
Type:	(Bf 109C) single-engined fighter
Powerplant:	one 700hp (522kW) Junkers Jumo 210Ga inverted V-12 piston engine
Performance:	maximum speed 470km/h (292mph); service ceiling 8400m (27,600ft); range 650km (450 miles)
Weights:	empty 1597kg (3522lb); maximum 2296kg (5062lb)
Dimensions:	span 9.85m (32ft 5in); length 8.55m (28ft 1in); height 2.45m (8ft); wing area 16.40 sq m (176.53 sq ft)
Armament:	four 7.9mm (.31in) MG 17 machine guns

The Bf 109 made its combat debut in Spain, mainly in Jumo-powered Bf 109B and C forms. About 130 Bf 109s served in the Nationalist Air Force and with the Condor Legion. Several of the Luftwaffe's future top aces had their first victories over Spain in these aircraft.

Spanish Civil War Part Two

The Republicans entered the war operating most of the pre-war equipment of the government air force, or Aviación Militar. Like the Nationalists, they received help from sympathetic nations, especially the Soviet Union, and quantities of the latest Soviet aircraft served on the Republican side, sometimes with Soviet pilots.

Hawker Fury

Only three Hispano-engined Hawker Spanish Furies reached the Republican government before the outbreak of war. At least one was captured and used by the Nationalists and later recaptured by the Republicans.

SPECIFICATIONS	
Country of origin:	United Kingdom
Type:	(Fury 1) single-engined biplane fighter
Powerplant:	one 700hp (522kW) Hispano-Suiza 12 Xbrs piston engine
Performance:	maximum speed 333km/h (207mph); service ceiling 8534m (28,000ft); range 490km (305 miles)
Weights:	empty 1189kg (2623lb); maximum 1583kg (3490lb)
Dimensions:	span 9.14m (30ft); length 8.12m (26ft 8in); height 3.09m (10ft 2in); wing area 76.80 sq m (252 sq ft)
Armament:	two .303in (7.62mm) Vickers machine guns

Nieuport Delage Ni-D 52

At the 1924 Paris Salon de l'Aéronautique, Nieuport-Delage unveiled no less than three new designs at a time when the military fighter market was severely depressed. Stemming from these aircraft, the Ni-D 52 of 1927 (pictured in the Spanish Republican Air Force colours) closely resembled the Ni-D 42, but was constructed of metal instead of wood. It won the 1928 Spanish fighter competition and was built under licence by Hispano until 1936.

SPECIFICATIONS	
Country of origin:	France
Type:	single-seat fighter
Powerplant:	one 580hp (433kW) Hispano-Suiza 12Hb 12-cylinder Vee piston engine
Performance:	maximum speed 255km/h (158mph); service ceiling 7000m (2965ft); range 400km (249 miles)
Weights:	empty 1368kg (3016lb); maximum take-off weight 1837kg (4050lb)
Dimensions:	span 12m (39ft 4in); length 7.5m (24ft 7in); height 3m (9ft 10in); wing area 30.90 sq m (333 sq ft)
Armament:	two fixed forward-firing 7.62mm (.29in) Vickers machine guns

Douglas DC-2

SPECIFICATIONS	
Country of origin:	United Kingdom
Type:	twin-engined transport
Powerplant:	two 730hp (540kW) Wright Cyclone GR-F53 9-cylinder radial piston engines
Performance:	maximum speed 338km/h (210mph); service ceiling 6930m (22,750ft); range 1448km (900 miles)
Weights:	empty 5650kg (12,455lb); loaded 8420kg (18,560lb)
Dimensions:	span 25.9m (85ft); length 19.1m (62ft 6in); height 4.8 (15ft 10in); wing area 87.3 sq m (940 sq ft)
Armament:	none

Both sides used Douglas DC-2s as transports during the war, including this ex-Swissair example used by the Republicans. It was one of five DC-2s that had been in civilian use with Lineas Aeroeas Postales Espanolas.

Polikarpov I-16

SPECIFICATIONS	
Country of origin:	Russia
Type:	(I-16 Type 10) single-engined fighter
Powerplant:	one 1100hp (820kW) Shvetsov M-25V radial piston engine
Performance:	maximum speed 447km/h (278mph); service ceiling 8320m (27,000ft); range 700km (435 miles)
Weights:	empty 1336kg (2945lb); loaded 1726kg (3805lb)
Dimensions:	span 8.95m (29ft 6in); length 6.13m (20ft 1in); height 3.25m (10ft 1in); wing area 14.5 sq m (156.1 sq ft)
Armament:	four .3in ShKAS machine guns

The Republicans called the I-16 the 'Mosca' (fly) and the Nationalists called it the 'Rata' (rat). The Soviet-built Polikarpov was the first monoplane fighter with a retractable undercarriage. Although fast and easy to manoeuvre, the I-16 usually lost in combats with the Bf 109.

Tupelov SB-2

SPECIFICATIONS	
Country of origin:	USSR
Type:	(SB 2M) medium bomber
Powerplant:	two 860hp (641kW) Klimov M-100A V-12 piston engines
Performance:	maximum speed 423km/h (244mph); service ceiling 9571m (31,400ft); range 1250km (777 miles)
Weights:	empty 4060kg (8951lb); maximum 5628kg (12,407lb)
Dimensions:	span 20.33m (66ft 9in); length 20.33m (66ft 9in); height 3.25m (10ft 8in); wing area 56.67 sq m (610 sq ft)
Armament:	four .3in ShKAS machine guns; up to 600kg (1322lb) bombs

Also known as the ANT-40 – after design bureau head Alexi N. Tupolev – the SB 2 was one of the fastest and most advanced bombers of the 1930s. It was sometimes called the 'Martin' because it was mistaken for the American B-10, which did not participate in the Spanish war.

Silver Wings RAF Fighters

The late 1920s and early 1930s were something of a golden age for RAF Fighter Command, which was much in the public eye with its regular aerobatic displays and its polished and painted silver biplanes. Bomber design was advancing, however, and before long the RAF's biplane fighters were struggling to keep up with the RAF's bombers, let alone those of any potential adversary. The biplane had reached the peak of its development and the next generation of fighters would be monoplanes.

British 105 Bulldog IIA

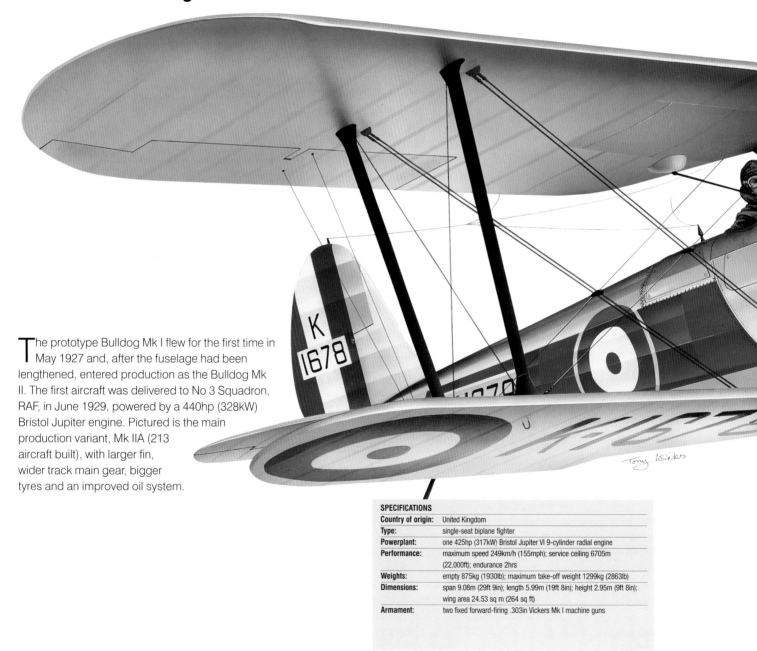

The prototype Bulldog Mk I flew for the first time in May 1927 and, after the fuselage had been lengthened, entered production as the Bulldog Mk II. The first aircraft was delivered to No 3 Squadron, RAF, in June 1929, powered by a 440hp (328kW) Bristol Jupiter engine. Pictured is the main production variant, Mk IIA (213 aircraft built), with larger fin, wider track main gear, bigger tyres and an improved oil system.

SPECIFICATIONS	
Country of origin:	United Kingdom
Type:	single-seat biplane fighter
Powerplant:	one 425hp (317kW) Bristol Jupiter VI 9-cylinder radial engine
Performance:	maximum speed 249km/h (155mph); service ceiling 6705m (22,000ft); endurance 2hrs
Weights:	empty 875kg (1930lb); maximum take-off weight 1299kg (2863lb)
Dimensions:	span 9.08m (29ft 9in); length 5.99m (19ft 8in); height 2.95m (9ft 8in); wing area 24.53 sq m (264 sq ft)
Armament:	two fixed forward-firing .303in Vickers Mk I machine guns

Armstrong Whitworth Siskin IIIA

SPECIFICATIONS	
Country of origin:	United Kingdom
Type:	single-seat fighter biplane
Powerplant:	one 420hp (313kW) Armstrong Siddeley Jaguar IV radial engine
Performance:	maximum speed 251km/h (156mph); service ceiling 8230m (27,000ft); endurance 3hrs
Weights:	empty 935kg (2061lb); maximum take-off weight 1366kg (3012lb)
Dimensions:	span 10.11m (33ft 2in); length 7.72m (25ft 4in); height 3.10m (10ft 2in); wing area 27.22 sq m (293 sq ft)
Armament:	two fixed forward-firing .303in Vickers machine guns in forward fuselage; underwing racks with provision for up to four 9kg (20lb) Cooper practice bombs

This superbly aerobatic airircraft formed the vanguard of Britian's home-defence squadrons from March 1927 but faded swiftly in the 1930s as technology developed and newer types such as the Bristol Bulldog. Pictured is a Siskin IIIA of No 43 Squadron in 1929.

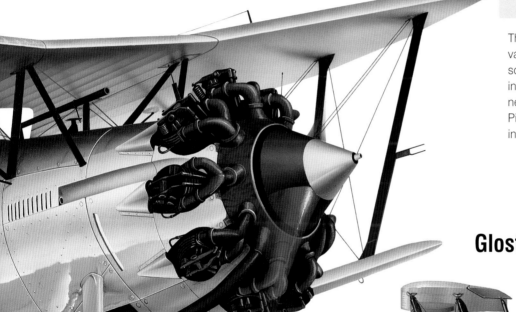

Gloster Gamecock Mk I

The Gloster Gamecock was first flown in February 1925, and 100 were acquired by the RAF, remaining in service until 1931. Pictured is a Gamecck Mk I of No 32 Squadron, based at RAF Kenley.

SPECIFICATIONS	
Country of origin:	United Kingdom
Type:	single-seat biplane fighter
Powerplant:	one 490hp (365kW) Bristol Jupiter VIIF radial piston engine
Performance:	maximum speed 280km/h (174mph); service ceiling 8940m (29,300ft); range 482km (300 miles)
Weights:	empty 1008kg (2222lb); maximum take-off weight 1583kg (3490lb)
Dimensions:	span 10.3m (33ft 10in); length 7.7m (25ft 2in); height 2.7m (8ft 9in); wing area 28.47 sq m (307 sq ft)
Armament:	two fixed forward-firing .303in Vickers machine guns; underwing racks with provision for up to four 9kg (20lb) bombs

Hawker Hart Family

The Hawker Hart light bomber proved adaptable to a variety of roles and spawned over 70 variants, including the Demon two-seat fighter, Audax army cooperation aircraft and the Hind light bomber, which was the Hart's replacement. The series was widely exported, with many versions having a variety of radial and inline engines in place of the Kestrels of most RAF models. Surplus Hinds were passed on to Empire air forces as trainers and general-purpose aircraft, serving into the 1940s.

Hawker Hart Mk I

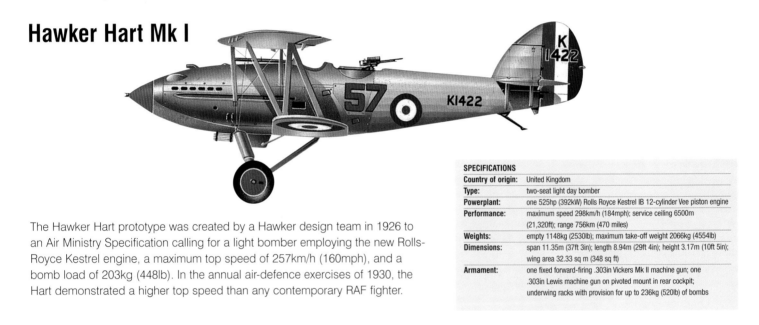

The Hawker Hart prototype was created by a Hawker design team in 1926 to an Air Ministry Specification calling for a light bomber employing the new Rolls-Royce Kestrel engine, a maximum top speed of 257km/h (160mph), and a bomb load of 203kg (448lb). In the annual air-defence exercises of 1930, the Hart demonstrated a higher top speed than any contemporary RAF fighter.

SPECIFICATIONS	
Country of origin:	United Kingdom
Type:	two-seat light day bomber
Powerplant:	one 525hp (392kW) Rolls Royce Kestrel IB 12-cylinder Vee piston engine
Performance:	maximum speed 298km/h (184mph); service ceiling 6500m (21,320ft); range 756km (470 miles)
Weights:	empty 1148kg (2530lb); maximum take-off weight 2066kg (4554lb)
Dimensions:	span 11.35m (37ft 3in); length 8.94m (29ft 4in); height 3.17m (10ft 5in); wing area 32.33 sq m (348 sq ft)
Armament:	one fixed forward-firing .303in Vickers Mk II machine gun; one .303in Lewis machine gun on pivoted mount in rear cockpit; underwing racks with provision for up to 236kg (520lb) of bombs

Hawker Demon Mk I

The performance of the Hawker Hart caused great consternation among the Air Staff, hastening the development of a two-seat fighter version as an interim measure before the Hawker Fury became available. Hawker Demons differed from the Hart by having a revised rear cockpit to improve the field of fire, radio communications equipment and, in some later models, a tailwheel.

SPECIFICATIONS	
Country of origin	United Kingdom
Type:	two-seat fighter biplane
Powerplant:	one 584hp (392kW) Rolls Royce Kestrel IIS 12-cylinder Vee piston engine
Performance:	maximum speed 303km/h (188mph); service ceiling 6500m (21,320ft); range 756km (470 miles)
Weights:	empty 1148kg (2530lb); maximum take-off weight 2066kg (4554lb)
Dimensions:	span 11.35m (37ft 3in); length 8.94m (29ft 4in); height 3.17m (10ft 5in); wing area 32.33 sq m (348 sq ft)
Armament:	two fixed forward-firing .303in Vickers Mk II machine guns; one .303in Lewis Mk machine gun on pivoted mount in rear cockpit

HAWKER HART FAMILY TIMELINE
1928   1929

Hawker Audax

The Hawker Audax was developed as an army cooperation aircraft to replace the Armstrong Whitworth Atlas, primarily for service in the Middle East and the North West Frontier of India. The prototype Audax was created by modifying the airframe of an early Hart (K1438) with a message pick-up hook, and first flew in December 1931. A distinguishing feature was the long exhaust pipe, which extended to the fuselage mid-point. Production for the RAF totalled 624.

SPECIFICATIONS	
Country of origin:	United Kingdom
Type:	two-seat army cooperation aircraft
Powerplant:	one 580hp (433kW) Bristol Pegasus II.M2 radial piston engine
Performance:	maximum speed 274km/h (170mph); service ceiling 6555m (21,500ft); endurance 3hrs 30mins
Weights:	empty 1333kg (2938lb); maximum take-off weight 1989kg (4386lb)
Dimensions:	span 11.35m (37ft 3in); length 9.02m (29ft 7in); height 3.17m (10ft 5in); wing area 32.33 sq m (348 sq ft)
Armament:	one fixed forward-firing .303in Vickers Mk II machine gun; one .303in Lewis machine gun on pivoted mount in rear cockpit; underwing racks with provision for four 9kg (20lb) or two 51kg (112lb) stores

Hawker Hart
Trainer Series 2A

The Hart was built in a great number of variants, including 57 Hart (India) and 72 Hart (Special) aircraft with tropical equipment and Kestrel IB, V or X engines (the latter fitted to late 77 Specials only). The most prolific of the family were the dual-control trainers, 507 of which were built in four main batches between 1934 and 1936. Pictured is the restored Series 2A example in the collection of the RAF Museum at Hendon.

SPECIFICATIONS	
Country of origin:	United Kingdom
Type:	two-seat advanced trainer
Powerplant:	one 510hp (300kW) Rolls Royce Kestrel XDR 12-cylinder Vee piston engine
Performance:	maximum speed 298km/h (184mph); service ceiling 6500m (21,320ft); range 756km (470 miles)
Weights:	empty 1148kg (2530lb); maximum take-off weight 2066kg (4554lb)
Dimensions:	span 11.35m (37ft 3in); length 8.94m (29ft 4in); height 3.17m (10ft 5in); wing area 32.33 sq m (348 sq ft)

Hawker Hind

As an interim light bomber after the Hart, the Hind was powered by a 640hp (477kW) Kestrel V engine, had a cut-down rear cockpit that afforded a better field of fire, and a tailwheel in place of the skid. The prototype Hind was flown in September 1934 and was followed by 527 production aircraft.

SPECIFICATIONS	
Country of origin:	United Kingdom
Type:	two-seat light day-bomber
Powerplant:	one 640hp (477kW) Rolls-Royce Kestrel V 12-cylinder Vee piston engine
Performance:	maximum speed 298km/h (184mph); service ceiling 8045m (26,400ft); range 692km (430 miles)
Weights:	empty 1475kg (3251lb); maximum take-off weight 2403kg (5298lb)
Dimensions:	span 11.35m (37ft 3in); length 9.02m (29ft 7in); height 3.23m (10ft 7in); wing area 32.33 sq m (348 sq ft)
Armament:	one fixed-forward firing .303in Vickers Mk II machine gun; one .303in Lewis machine gun on pivoted mount in rear cockpit; underwing racks with provision for up to 227kg (500lb) of bombs

1934

1937

Hawker Furies

One of a number of successful types derived from the Hart bomber of 1928, the Fury was selected as the RAF's first dedicated interceptor fighter in 1930. Powered by a water-cooled V-12 Kestrel engine, Furies were more streamlined and faster than contemporary RAF fighters, but also more expensive, and only three squadrons were equipped with Fury Is, and four with the improved Fury II. It also served as the basis for the Nimrod naval fighter.

Hawker Fury Mk I

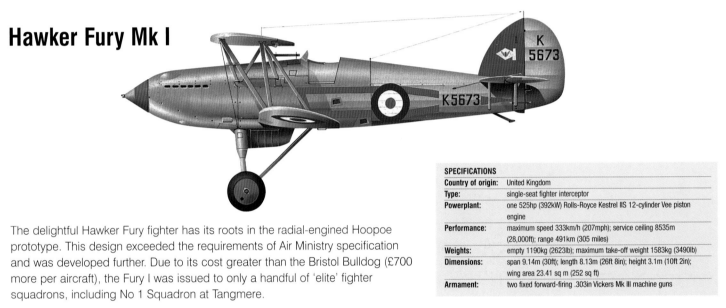

The delightful Hawker Fury fighter has its roots in the radial-engined Hoopoe prototype. This design exceeded the requirements of Air Ministry specification and was developed further. Due to its cost greater than the Bristol Bulldog (£700 more per aircraft), the Fury I was issued to only a handful of 'elite' fighter squadrons, including No 1 Squadron at Tangmere.

SPECIFICATIONS	
Country of origin:	United Kingdom
Type:	single-seat fighter interceptor
Powerplant:	one 525hp (392kW) Rolls-Royce Kestrel IIS 12-cylinder Vee piston engine
Performance:	maximum speed 333km/h (207mph); service ceiling 8535m (28,000ft); range 491km (305 miles)
Weights:	empty 1190kg (2623lb); maximum take-off weight 1583kg (3490lb)
Dimensions:	span 9.14m (30ft); length 8.13m (26ft 8in); height 3.1m (10ft 2in); wing area 23.41 sq m (252 sq ft)
Armament:	two fixed forward-firing .303in Vickers Mk III machine guns

Hawker Fury Mk II

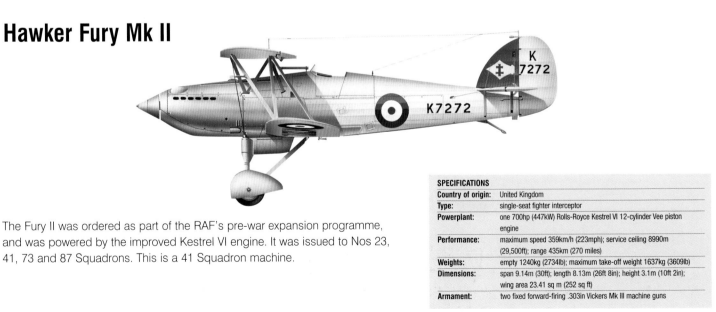

The Fury II was ordered as part of the RAF's pre-war expansion programme, and was powered by the improved Kestrel VI engine. It was issued to Nos 23, 41, 73 and 87 Squadrons. This is a 41 Squadron machine.

SPECIFICATIONS	
Country of origin:	United Kingdom
Type:	single-seat fighter interceptor
Powerplant:	one 700hp (447kW) Rolls-Royce Kestrel VI 12-cylinder Vee piston engine
Performance:	maximum speed 359km/h (223mph); service ceiling 8990m (29,500ft); range 435km (270 miles)
Weights:	empty 1240kg (2734lb); maximum take-off weight 1637kg (3609lb)
Dimensions:	span 9.14m (30ft); length 8.13m (26ft 8in); height 3.1m (10ft 2in); wing area 23.41 sq m (252 sq ft)
Armament:	two fixed forward-firing .303in Vickers Mk III machine guns

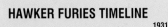 **HAWKER FURIES TIMELINE** 1931 1933

Hawker Fury Mk II

South Africa received a batch of surplus RAF Fury IIs in 1935 and more in 1940. They saw some action in 1940–41 in East Africa, shooting down a number of Italian bombers. This one was assigned to home-based No 43 Squadron SAAF in 1942.

SPECIFICATIONS	
Country of origin:	United Kingdom
Type:	single-seat fighter interceptor
Powerplant:	one 700hp (447kW) Rolls-Royce Kestrel VI 12-cylinder Vee piston engine
Performance:	maximum speed 359km/h (223mph); service ceiling 8990m (29,500ft); range 435km (270 miles)
Weights:	empty 1240kg (2734lb); maximum take-off weight 1637kg (3609lb)
Dimensions:	span 9.14m (30ft); length 8.13m (26ft 8in); height 3.1m (10ft 2in); wing area 23.41 sq m (252 sq ft)
Armament:	two fixed forward-firing .303in Vickers Mk III machine guns

Hawker Fury Mk I

The Fury had limited export success, particularly in comparison with the two-seat Hawker biplanes. One minor user was the Portuguese Arma de Aeronautica, who purchased just three Furies from Britain in 1935.

SPECIFICATIONS	
Country of origin:	United Kingdom
Type:	single-seat fighter interceptor
Powerplant:	one 525hp (392kW) Rolls-Royce Kestrel IIS 12-cylinder Vee piston engine
Performance:	maximum speed 333km/h (207mph); service ceiling 8535m (28,000ft); range 491km (305 miles)
Weights:	empty 1190kg (2623lb); maximum take-off weight 1583kg (3490lb)
Dimensions:	span 9.14m (30ft); length 8.13m (26ft 8in); height 3.1m (10ft 2in); wing area 23.41 sq m (252 sq ft)
Armament:	two fixed forward-firing .303in Vickers Mk III machine guns provision for four 12.5kg (27.5lb) bombs

Hawker Fury Mk II

The Fury II had the distinction of being the last biplane fighter produced for the RAF, although the Gladiator remained in service longer. The Munich crisis in 1938 saw Furies such as this No 43 Squadron example exchange their polished and silver doped finish for camouflage.

SPECIFICATIONS	
Country of origin:	United Kingdom
Type:	single-seat fighter interceptor
Powerplant:	one 700hp (447kW) Rolls-Royce Kestrel VI 12-cylinder Vee piston engine
Performance:	maximum speed 359km/h (223mph); service ceiling 8990m (29,500ft); range 435km (270 miles)
Weights:	empty 1240kg (2734lb); maximum take-off weight 1637kg (3609lb)
Dimensions:	span 9.14m (30ft); length 8.13m (26ft 8in); height 3.1m (10ft 2in); wing area 23.41 sq m (252 sq ft)
Armament:	two fixed forward-firing .303in Vickers Mk III machine guns

1934

Flying Boats

Large land-planes need long runways, which were rare commodities until the 1940s. For long-range maritime patrol and anti-submarine attack, flying boats were ideal, and particularly appealed to naval air arms who wanted a stake in large aircraft development. Construction methods evolved from wooden boatbuilding to modern aluminium and stressed-skin airframes. Lighter structure, combined with powerful radial engines, greatly increased range and patrol endurance in flying boats.

Supermarine Southampton Mk I

Developed from the commercial Supermarine Swan, the elegant Southampton five-crew biplane flying boat first flew in March 1925 and deliveries to the RAF began a few months later. The Mk II had a Duralumin hull, which represented a considerable weight saving over the wooden-hulled Mk I. Production total was 68 aircraft.

SPECIFICATIONS	
Country of origin:	United Kingdom
Type:	(Mk II) general reconnaissance flying-boat
Powerplant:	two 500hp (373kW) Napier Lion VA W-12 piston engines
Performance:	maximum speed 174km/h (108mph); service ceiling 4265m (14,000ft); range 1497km (930 miles)
Weights:	empty 4082kg (9000lb); maximum take-off weight 6895kg (15,200lb)
Dimensions:	span 22.86m (75ft); length 15.58m (51ft 1in); height 6.82m (22ft 4in); wing area 134.61 sq m (1449 sq ft)
Armament:	one .303in Lewis gun on pivoted mount in nose position; one .303in Lewis gun on pivoted mount in each of two midships positions, plus up to 499kg (1100lb) of bombs

CAMS 55/2

Chantiers Aéro-Maritimes de la Seine (CAMS) employed Maurice Hurel to design the twin-engine biplane CAMS 51 flying boat in 1926, from which the CAMS 45 GR (Grand Raid), CAMS 53 and CAMS 55 were developed. The CAMS 53 was the most successful French commercial flying boat of its era. The military CAMS 55 made its maiden flight in 1928. Production orders followed for 29 55/2s and 32 55/10s with greater fuel capacity.

SPECIFICATIONS	
Country of origin:	France
Type:	long-range maritime reconnaissance flying-boat
Powerplant:	two 480hp (358kW) Gnome-Rhône Jupiter 9Akx radial piston engines
Performance:	maximum speed 195km/h (121mph); service ceiling 3400m (11,155ft); maximum range 1875km (1165 miles)
Weights:	empty 4590kg (10,119lb); maximum take-off weight 6900kg (15,212lb)
Dimensions:	span 20.4m (66ft 11in); length 15.03m (49ft 3in); height 5.41m (17ft 9in); wing area 113.45 sq m (1221 sq ft)
Armament:	two .303in Lewis machine guns in bow cockpit and two in midships cockpit; underwing racks with provision for two 75kg (165lb) bombs

FLYING BOATS TIMELINE

1922

Blackburn R.B.1 Iris

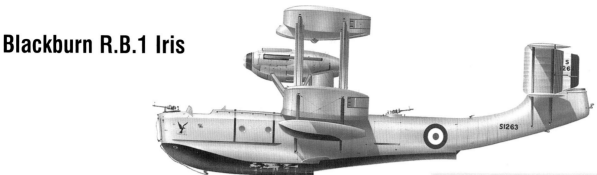

Robert Blackburn was among the first generation of British aviation pioneers. The wooden-hulled R.B.1 prototype first flew in June 1926. Refitted with a metal hull and Rolls-Royce Condor IIIA engines, the aircraft undertook a successful overseas tour; in this form it was ordered as the Blackburn R.B.1B Iris Mk III. The first of three aircraft was delivered in November 1929, and all three served with No 209 Squadron.

SPECIFICATIONS	
Country of origin:	United Kingdom
Type:	five-seat long-range reconnaissance flying-boat
Powerplant:	three 675hp (503kW) Rolls Royce Condor IIIB inline piston engines
Performance:	maximum speed 190km/h (118mph); service ceiling 3230m (10,600ft); range 1287km (800 miles)
Weights:	empty 8640kg (19,048lb); maximum take-off weight 13,376kg (29,489lb)
Dimensions:	span 29.57m (97ft); length 20.54m (67ft 4in); height 7.77m (25ft 6in); wing area 207.07 sq m (2229 sq ft)
Armament:	one .303in Lewis machine gun each in nose position, mid-ships position and tail position; underwing racks with provision for up to 907kg (2000lb) of bombs

Beriev MBR-2

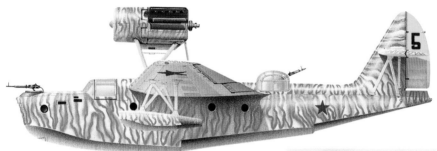

Georgi M. Beriev's first design, Aircraft No 25, was for a reconnaissance flying boat that went on to achieve production success as the MBR-2. Deliveries of this aircraft began in 1934. It was a shoulder-wing cantilever monoplane with a two-step plywood fuselage, overwing strut-mounted engine and partly enclosed cockpit. The definitive MBR-2AM-34 had a fully enclosed cockpit, glazed mid-ship gunners position, and a redesigned fin and rudder. Some 1300 were built.

SPECIFICATIONS	
Country of origin:	USSR
Type:	short-range reconnaissance/patrol flying-boat
Powerplant:	one 680hp (507kW) M-17B inline piston engine
Performance:	maximum speed 200km/h (124mph); service ceiling 4400m (14,435ft); normal range 650km (404 miles)
Weights:	empty 2475kg (5456lb); maximum take-off weight 4100kg (9039lb)
Dimensions:	span 19m (62ft 4in); length 13.5m (44ft 3in); wing area 55 sq m (592 sq ft)
Armament:	one 7.62mm (.29in) ShKAS machine gun on ring mount in bow cockpit and one on flexible mount in mid-ship cockpit; underwing racks with provision for up to 500kg (1102lb) of bombs or depth charge

Martin PBM Mariner

Designed in 1936, Martin PBM Mariner was of huge importance to the Allied war effort. It was of a very advanced design, with high wing loading and retractable stabilizing floats built into the wing tips. The most prolific variant was the PBM-3, which had its own subvariants. The PBM-3B (32 built) was supplied to the RAF under the Lend Lease Act as the Mariner Gr Mk I.

SPECIFICATIONS	
Country of origin:	United States
Type:	nine-seat maritime patrol and anti-submarine flying-boat
Powerplant:	two 1900hp (1417kW) Wright R-2600-22 Cyclone radial piston engine
Performance:	maximum speed 340km/h (211mph); service ceiling 6035m (19,800ft); range 3605km (2240 miles)
Weights:	empty 15,048kg (33,175lb); maximum take-off weight 26,308kg (58,000lb)
Dimensions:	span 35.97m (118ft); length 24.33m (79ft 10in); height 8.38m (27ft 6in); wing area 130.80 sq m (1408 sq ft)
Armament:	two .5in Browning machine guns each in nose turret, dorsal turret and tail turret; one .5in Browning machine gun in two ventral positions; provision for up to 3628kg (8000lb) of bombs or depth charges

1923

1934

Vickers Bombers and Transports

Vickers dominated British bomber production between the wars. The Vimy was used for record-breaking flights and, like the Virginia, the type was frequently rebuilt and re-engined to create new marks. Although little remembered today, the Virginia was the main RAF heavy bomber for many years. Derivatives of the Virginia with new fuselages, the Vernon and Valentia, became the first purpose-built troop transports and air ambulances.

Vickers Virginia Mk VII

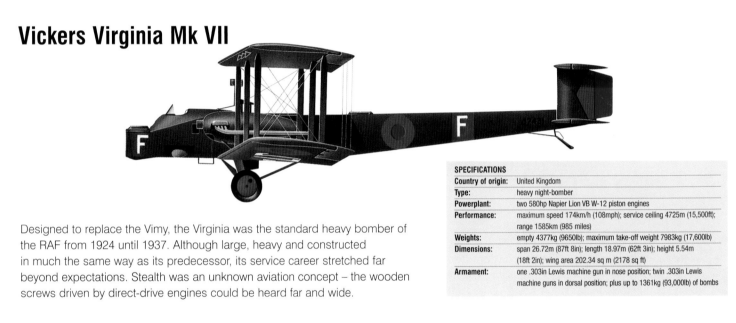

Designed to replace the Vimy, the Virginia was the standard heavy bomber of the RAF from 1924 until 1937. Although large, heavy and constructed in much the same way as its predecessor, its service career stretched far beyond expectations. Stealth was an unknown aviation concept – the wooden screws driven by direct-drive engines could be heard far and wide.

SPECIFICATIONS	
Country of origin:	United Kingdom
Type:	heavy night-bomber
Powerplant:	two 580hp Napier Lion VB W-12 piston engines
Performance:	maximum speed 174km/h (108mph); service ceiling 4725m (15,500ft); range 1585km (985 miles)
Weights:	empty 4377kg (9650lb); maximum take-off weight 7983kg (17,600lb)
Dimensions:	span 26.72m (87ft 8in); length 18.97m (62ft 3in); height 5.54m (18ft 2in); wing area 202.34 sq m (2178 sq ft)
Armament:	one .303in Lewis machine gun in nose position; twin .303in Lewis machine guns in dorsal position; plus up to 1361kg (93,000lb) of bombs

Vickers Valentia

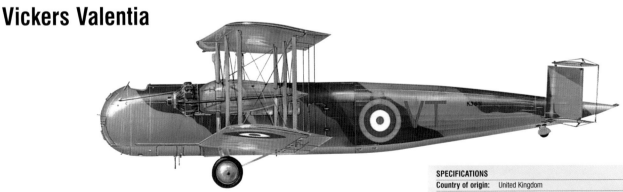

Vickers derived a military transport aircraft for the Royal Air Force from the Vickers Virginia bomber. The new aircraft, which first flew in 1922, shared the biplane wing and tail unit of its predecessor, but had a completely new large-capacity fuselage with accommodation for two crew in an open cockpit and up to 23 fully equipped troops in an enclosed cabin. The Valentia served with the RAF in the Middle East until 1944.

SPECIFICATIONS	
Country of origin:	United Kingdom
Type:	troop transport
Powerplant:	two 622hp (464kW) Bristol Pegasus IIL3 radial piston engine
Performance:	maximum speed 193km/h (120mph); service ceiling 4955m (16,250ft); range 1287km (800 miles)
Weights:	empty 4964kg (10,944lb); maximum take-off weight 8845kg (19,500lb)
Dimensions:	span 26.62m (87ft 4in); length 18.14m (59ft 6in); height 5.41m (17ft 9in); wing area 202.34 sq m (2178 sq ft)
Armament:	provision to fit underwing racks for 998kg (2200lb) bomb load

VICKERS TIMELINE

 1933

 1934

Vickers Vimy Ambulance

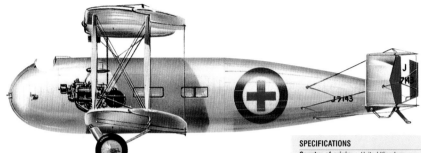

The final two versions in the Vimy family were the Napier-Lion-powered Vimy Ambulance and the Vickers Vernon bomber/transport. The Vimy Ambulance was generally similar to the Commercial but with a nose-loading door to provide access for the four stretchers or eight sitting patients, plus two medical attendants. The Vimy Ambulance was built to the extent of four aircraft. All Vernons served with Nos 45 and 70 Squadrons in the Middle East in the 1920s.

SPECIFICATIONS	
Country of origin:	United Kingdom
Type:	air ambulance
Powerplant:	two 450hp (336kW) Napier Lion inline piston engines
Performance:	cruising speed 135km/h (84mph); service ceiling 3200m (10,500ft); range 724km (450 miles)
Weights:	take-off weight 5670kg (12,500lb)
Dimensions:	span 20.47m (67ft 2in); length 13m (42ft 8in); height 4.76m (15ft 7in); wing area 123.56 sq m (1330 sq ft)

Vickers Vimy Mk II

Some 158 Vimys were completed to Mk I standard and there followed 74 other variants. The designation Vimy Mk II is confusing, as it appears to have been given to many different types. To complicate matters further, the Mk III and Mk IV were redesignated Mk II in 1923, in an attempt to introduce some clarity! What is certain is that the Vimy was the standard heavy bomber of the RAF from 1919 to 1930, after which it began to be replaced by the Vickers Victoria.

SPECIFICATIONS	
Country of origin:	United Kingdom
Type:	heavy bomber
Powerplant:	two 360hp (269kW) Rolls-Royce Eagle VIII 12-cylinder Vee piston engines
Performance:	maximum speed 166km/h (103mph); service ceiling 2135m (7000ft); range 1464km (910 miles)
Weights:	empty 3221kg (7101lb); maximum take-off weight 5670kg (12,500lb)
Dimensions:	span 20.75m (68ft 1in); length 13.27m (43ft 6in); height 4.76m (15ft 7in); wing area 123.56 sq m (1330 sq ft)
Armament:	one .303in Lewis Mk III machine gun each on pivoted mount in nose, on pivoted mount in dorsal position and on pivoted mount in ventral or each of two beam positions; internal bomb cells and underwing racks with provision for up to 2179kg (4804lb) of bombs

Vickers Vincent

The RAF selected a modified version of the Vildebeest, which it called the Type 266 Vincent, to supersede the Fairey IIIF and Westland Wapiti in the army cooperation role. The prototype was a converted Mk I Vildebeest; and although derived directly from the Mk III Vildebeest, the Vincent differed by having an extra fuel tank in place of a torpedo as well as message-retrieval equipment.

SPECIFICATIONS	
Country of origin:	United Kingdom
Type:	three-seat general purpose aircraft
Powerplant:	one 825hp (615kW) Bristol Perseus VIII sleeve-valve radial piston engine
Performance:	maximum speed 230km/h (142mph); service ceiling 5182m (17,000ft); range 2500km (1553 miles)
Weights:	empty 1918kg (4229lb); maximum take-off weight 3674kg (8100lb)
Dimensions:	span 14.94m (49ft 0in); length 11.17m (36ft 8in); height 5.42m (17ft 9in)
Armament:	one fixed forward-firing .303in Vickers machine gun; one.303in Lewis machine gun on pivoted mount in rear cockpit

1935

1936

French Creations

The French aero industry went through a seemingly constant process of reorganization in the 1930s, and failed to produce many worthwhile aircraft at a time when its neighbours were rearming at a furious rate. In French bombers, concepts such as retractable undercarriage and streamlining came late – if at all. A year before the Spitfire flew, France was still producing fighters with fixed gear and open cockpits like the D.510.

Amiot 143M

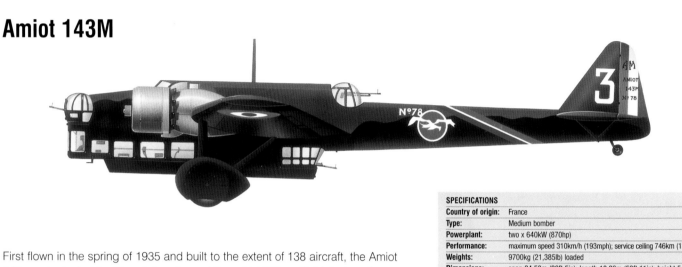

First flown in the spring of 1935 and built to the extent of 138 aircraft, the Amiot 143 was typical of the French bombers of the mid-1930s, with high-drag lines, fixed landing gear and large ventral gondola.

SPECIFICATIONS	
Country of origin:	France
Type:	Medium bomber
Powerplant:	two x 640kW (870hp)
Performance:	maximum speed 310km/h (193mph); service ceiling 746km (1200 miles)
Weights:	9700kg (21,385lb) loaded
Dimensions:	span 24.53m (80ft 5in); length 18.26m (59ft 11in); height 5.68m (18ft 8in)
Armament:	four 7.5mm (.295in) MGs in nose turret, dorsal turret, forward-fuselage floor hatch and rear of ventral gondola; up to 1600kg (3527lb) bombs

Dewoitine D.510C.1

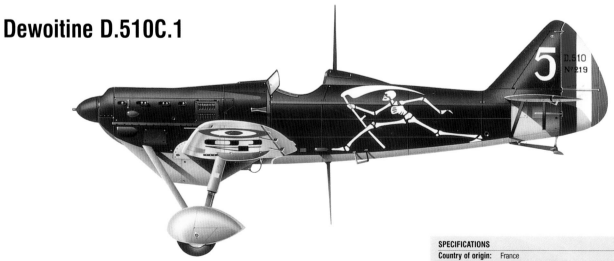

The D.510 was an interim fighter with fixed landing gear and open accommodation, but it had moderately good armament in the form of one 20mm (.79in) fixed forward-firing cannon (between the cylinder banks to fire through the hollow propeller shaft) and two 7.5mm (.295in) machine guns.

SPECIFICATIONS	
Country of origin:	France
Type:	monoplane fighter
Powerplant:	one 860hp (641kW) hispano-Suiza liquid-cooled V-12 engine
Performance:	maximum speed 402km/h (250mph); combat radius 700km (435 miles); service ceiling 11,000m (36,090ft)
Weights:	loaded 1929kg (4244lb)
Dimensions:	span 12.09m (39ft 8in); length 7.94m (26ft 0.5in); height 2.42m (7ft 11in); wing area 16.50 sq m (177.61 sq ft)
Armament:	one 20mm (.79in) HS9 cannon and two 7.5mm (.295in) MGs

Bloch MB.200B.4

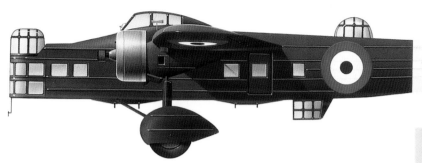

Entering service late in 1934, the MB.200B.4 was a medium bomber wholly typical of French designers' angular approach to the creation of large aircraft at this time. Deliveries eventually totalled 208 aircraft, all used for training by May 1940.

SPECIFICATIONS	
Country of origin:	France
Type:	medium bomber
Powerplant:	two 870hp (649kW) engines
Performance:	maximum speed 285km/h (177mph); service ceiling 8000m (26,245ft); range 1000km (621 miles)
Weights:	loaded 7480kg (16,490lb)
Dimensions:	span 22.45m (73ft 8in); length 16m (52ft 6in); height 3.9m (12ft 10in)
Armament:	single 7.5mm (.295in) trainable machine guns in nose, dorsal and ventral positions; up to 1200kg (2646lb) of bombs

Farman F.222.1Bn.5

Some 35 F.222 heavy night-bombers were delivered to the French Air Force: 11 F.222.1s with a short nose and flat outer wing panels, and 24 F.222.2s with a longer nose and dihedralled outer wing panels. These were the only four-engined heavy bombers in French service during 1939.

SPECIFICATIONS	
Country of origin:	France
Type:	heavy night-bomber
Powerplant:	four 970hp (723kW) engines
Performance:	maximum speed 360km/h (224mph); service ceiling 8000m (26,245ft); range 2000km (1243 miles)
Weights:	loaded 18,700kg (41,226lb)
Dimensions:	span 36m (118ft 1in); length 21.45m (70ft 5in); height 5.19m (17ft 1in); wing area 188 sq m (2023 sq ft)
Armament:	three 7.5mm (.295in) MGs, one in the nose turret, one in dorsal turret and one in ventral 'dustbin' position; up to 4000kg (8800lb) of either 20 200kg (440lb) or 40 100kg (220lb) bombs, or a mix of these with 50kg (110lb) bombs

LN (Loire-Nieuport) .40

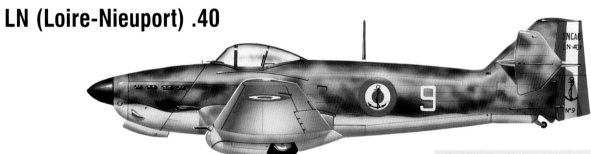

First flown in LN.40.01 prototype form in June 1938, the LN.40 was schemed as a carrierborne dive-bomber for the French naval air arm. The aircraft pictured here is an LN.401 that formed part of Escadrille AB.2 of the Aéronavale, based at Berck in France in May 1940.

SPECIFICATIONS	
Country of origin:	France
Type:	(LN.401BP.1) single-seat carrierborne and land-based dive-bomber
Powerplant:	one 690hp (514kW) Hispano-Suiza 12Xcrs 12-cylinder Vee engine
Performance:	maximum speed 380km/h (236mph); service ceiling 9500m (31,170ft); range 1200km (746 miles)
Weights:	empty 2135kg (4707lb); maximum take-off weight 2823kg (6224lb)
Dimensions:	span 14.00m (45ft 11.25in); length 9.75m (31ft 11.75in); height 3.50m (11ft 5.75in)
Armament:	one 20mm (.78in) fixed forward-firing cannon in an engine installation; two 7.5mm (.29in) fixed forward-firing machine guns in the leading edges of the wing, plus an external bomb load of 225kg (496lb)

USAAC

The United States Army Air Corps was ahead of its European contemporaries in the 1930s in replacing biplane designs with all-metal monoplanes with enclosed cockpits and retractable undercarriages. By 1939, the United States had one of the most modern air forces in the world, but such was the pace of aeronautical development that many of their aircraft were found wanting when they first saw combat in World War II in 1941–42.

Seversky P-35

Designed by Alexander Seversky, the P-35 was the first truly modern American fighter, although it was underarmed and lacked armour protection. This example from the 27th Pursuit Squadron wore temporary camouflage for 1940 war games.

SPECIFICATIONS	
Country of origin:	United States
Type:	(P-35A) single-seat fighter
Powerplant:	one 1050hp (783kW) Pratt & Whitney R-1830-45 14-cylinder radial piston engine
Performance:	maximum speed 499km/h (310mph); service ceiling 9571m (31,400 ft); range 1529km (910 miles)
Weights:	empty 2075kg (4475lb); maximum 3050kg (6723 lb)
Dimensions:	span 10.97m (36ft); length 8.18m (26ft 10in); height 2.97m (9ft 9in); wing area 20.44 sq m (220 sq ft)
Armament:	two .5in and two .3in machine guns; up to 158kg (350lb) of bombs

P-36A Hawk

The P-36 was similar to the P-35 but more refined and more stable. The P-36A was very lightly armed and had lower performance than the contemporary Spitfire I and Bf 109D. The 1937 order for 210 aircraft was the largest US fighter order since 1918. This P-36A flew with the 79th Pursuit Squadron of the 20th Pursuit Group.

SPECIFICATIONS	
Country of origin:	United States
Type:	(P-36A) single-seat fighter
Powerplant:	one 1050hp (783kW) Pratt & Whitney R-1830-13 14-cylinder radial piston engine
Performance:	maximum speed 480km/h (298 mph); service ceiling 10,000m (32,808ft); range 1300 km (807 miles)
Weights:	empty 2070kg (4565lb); loaded 2700kg (5952lb)
Dimensions:	span 11.4m (37ft 5in); length 8.7m (28ft 6in); height 3.7m (12ft 2in); wing area 21.92 sq m (236 sq ft)
Armament:	two .3in machine guns

Martin B-10

SPECIFICATIONS	
Country of origin:	United States
Type:	(Model 139W) four-seat medium bomber
Powerplant:	two 775hp (578kW) Wright R-1820 G-102 Cyclone 9-cylinder single-row radial engines
Performance:	maximum speed 322km/h (200mph); initial climb rate 567m (1860ft) per minute; service ceiling 7680m (25,200ft); range 950km (590 miles) with maximum bomb load
Weights:	empty 4682kg (10,322lb); maximum take-off weight 7210kg (15,894lb)
Dimensions:	span 21.60 m (70ft 10.5in); length 13.46m (44ft 2in); height 3.53m (11ft 7in) 63 sq m (678sq ft)
Armament:	one .3in trainable forward-firing machine gun in nose turret; one .3in trainable rearward-firing machine gun in dorsal position, and one in the ventral position; internal and external bomb load of 1025kg (2260lb)

The first American-designed bomber to be flown in combat, the B-10 bomber series was obsolete by the beginning of World War II, but in its time it was a pioneering type. This was the first American bomber of all-metal construction to enter large-scale production, the first American warplane with turreted armament, and the US Army Air Corps' first cantilever low-wing monoplane.

B-17D Flying Fortress

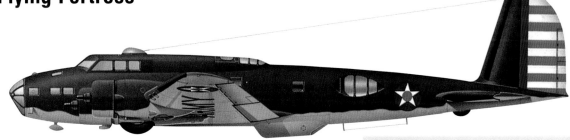

SPECIFICATIONS	
Country of origin:	United States
Type:	(B-17D) four-engined heavy bomber
Powerplant:	four 1200hp (895kW) Wright R-1820 G-205A Cyclone radial piston engines
Performance:	maximum speed 515km/h (320mph); range 5086km (3160 miles)
Weights:	empty 14,129kg (31,150lb); loaded 20,625kg (45,470lb)
Dimensions:	span 31.65m (103ft 10in); length 20.68m (67ft 11in); height 4.69m (15ft 5in); wing area 138 sq m (1,486 sq ft)
Armament:	one .3in (7.62mm) and four .5in (12.7mm) machine guns; up to 1134kg (2500lb) of bombs

The original 'sharks-fin' B-17s were among very few four-engined combat aircraft produced before the war. Although nicknamed 'Flying Fortress' by a reporter in 1935, they actually lacked adequate defences against modern fighters of the types being developed in Japan and Germany.

P-38 Lightning

SPECIFICATIONS	
Country of origin:	United States
Type:	(P-38E) twin-engined fighter
Powerplant:	two 1225hp (913kW) Allison V-1710-49/52 piston engines
Performance:	maximum speed 636km/h (395mph); service ceiling 11,887m (39,000ft); range 3367km (2260 miles)
Weights:	empty (P-38F) 5563kg (12,264lb); maximum (P-38E) 7022kg (15,482lb)
Dimensions:	span 15.86m (52ft); length 11.53m (37ft 10in); height 3.9m (9ft 10in); wing area 36.39 sq m (327.5 sq ft)
Armament:	one 20mm (.78in) Hispano M1 cannon, four .5in Colt-Browning MG 53-2 machine guns

Lockheed's P-38 was a radical design for its time, built for high speed at high altitude with long endurance. The twin-engined layout allowed for heavy weapons to be mounted in the nose, unaffected by propellers. The first production models entered service in August 1941, but fewer than 50 were in service by the time of the Pearl Harbor attack.

Grumman Barrels

With the FF-1, the first fighter with a retractable undercarriage in US Navy service, Grumman started a line of Navy fighters that would remain in service for over 70 years until the retirement of the F-14 Tomcat. The basic fuselage shape and many other features – such as the hand-cranked undercarriage that retracted into the fuselage with wheels exposed – carried through from the biplane fighters to the monoplane F4F Wildcat, one of the most important fighters of the early war years.

Grumman FF-1

The FF-1, sometimes nicknamed 'Fifi', was a two-seat fighter used aboard American carriers from 1933 to 1936. This one is illustrated in the colours of the USS *Lexington*. A small number of FF-1s were purchased by Canada and used as the Goblin Mk I.

SPECIFICATIONS	
Country of origin:	United States
Type:	(Model FF-1) two-seat fighter
Powerplant:	one 700hp (520kW) Wright R-1820-78 Cyclone radial piston engine
Performance:	maximum speed 333km/h (207mph); service ceiling 6735m (22,100ft); range 1100km (685 miles)
Weights:	empty 1405kg (3098lb); maximum 2121kg (4677lb)
Dimensions:	span 10.52m (34ft 6in); length 7.47m (24ft 6in); height 3.38m (11ft 1in); wing area 28.8 sq m (310sq ft)
Armament:	two .3in (7.7mm) M1919 Browning machine guns; one 100lb (45kg) bomb

Grumman SF-1

The Grumman Aircraft Engineering Corporation began its long association with the US Navy in 1931, when it was contracted to build seaplane floats incorporating retracting land wheels. The SF-1 followed the FF-1 into service from February 1934, with increased fuel capacity at the expense of one of the machine guns and a 700hp (522kW) R-1820-78 radial engine.

SPECIFICATIONS	
Country of origin:	United States
Type:	two-seat carrierborne scouting biplane
Powerplant:	one 700hp (522kW) Wright R-1820-78 9-cylinder radial piston engine
Performance:	maximum speed 333km/h (207mph); service ceiling 6400m (21,000ft); range 1428km (921 miles)
Weights:	empty 1474kg (3250lb); maximum take-off weight 2190kg (4828lb)
Dimensions:	span 10.52m (34ft 6in); length 7.47m (24ft 6in); height 3.38m (11ft 1in); wing area 28.8 sq m (310 sq ft)
Armament:	one fixed forward-firing .3in Browning machine gun; two .3in Browning machine guns on a gimballed mounting attached to observer's seat

Grumman F2F-1

Encouraged by the success of the FF/SF-1 aircraft, Grumman design staff drew up a proposal for a single-seat version, and in June 1932 offered it to the US Navy, which ordered a prototype in November. This was slightly smaller than its predecessor, and had ailerons on the upper wing only. The aircraft served with VF-2B on USS *Lexington* until September 1940.

SPECIFICATIONS

Country of origin:	United States
Type:	single-seat carrierborne biplane fighter
Powerplant:	one 650hp (522kW) Pratt & Whitney R-1535-72 Twin Wasp Junior radial piston engine
Performance:	maximum speed 383km/h (238mph); service ceiling 8380m (27,500ft); range 1585km (985 miles)
Weights:	empty 1221kg (2691lb); maximum take-off weight 1745kg (3847lb)
Dimensions:	span 8.69m (28ft 6in); length 6.53m (21ft 5in); height 2.77m (9ft 1in); wing area 21.37 sq m (230 sq ft)
Armament:	two fixed forward-firing .3in Browning machine guns; underwing racks for two 53kg (116lb) bombs

Grumman F3F-1

The F3F stemmed from the G-11 design evolved by Grumman as a slightly enlarged version of the F2F-1 fighter, with changes to correct the earlier warplane's lack of directional stability and tendency to spin. The production version differed from the third XF3F-1 prototype only in a slight increase in fuselage length. They were delivered between January and September 1936.

SPECIFICATIONS

Country of origin:	United States
Type:	single-seat carrierborne and land-based fighter and fighter-bomber
Powerplant:	one 700hp (522kW) Pratt & Whitney R-1535-84 Twin Wasp Junior 14-cylinder radial engine
Performance:	maximum speed 372km/h (231mph); service ceiling 8685m (28,500ft); range 1609km (1000 miles)
Weights:	empty 1339kg (2952lb); maximum take-off weight 1997kg (4403lb)
Dimensions:	span 9.75m (32ft); length 7.09m (23ft 3in); height 2.77m (9ft 1in); wing area 24.15 sq m (260 sq ft)
Armament:	one .5in fixed forward-firing machine gun; one .3in fixed forward-firing machine gun in upper part of forward fuselage; plus external bomb load of 232lb (105kg)

Grumman F4F Wildcat

The F4F was the US Navy's most important fighter at the time of the United States' entry into World War II in December 1941 after the Japanese attack on Pearl Harbor, and it remained in production right through the war. The aircraft was originally schemed as the XF4F-1 biplane, before being revised as the XF4F-2 monoplane that first flew in September 1937.

SPECIFICATIONS

Country of origin:	United States
Type:	(F4F-4 and Wildcat Mk II) single-seat carrierborne fighter and fighter-bomber
Powerplant:	one 1200hp (895kW) Pratt & Whitney R-1830-86 Twin Wasp 14-cylinder two-row radial engine
Performance:	maximum speed 512km/h (318mph); initial climb rate 594m (1950ft) per minute; service ceiling 10,365m (34,000ft); range 2012km (1250 miles)
Weights:	empty 2612kg (5758lb); maximum take-off weight 3607kg (7952lb)
Dimensions:	span 11.58m (38ft); length 8.76m (28ft 9in); height 2.81m (9ft 2.5in)
Armament:	six .5in fixed forward-firing machine guns in the leading edges of the wing; plus an external bomb load of 91kg (200lb)

Rising Sun

Japan expanded its influence in the Far East in the 1930s through a series of territorial conquests in China and fighting a brief war with the Soviet Union. These operations gave Japan the chance to evaluate its aircraft and tactics in combat, and to train an experienced core of aviators. In Europe and America, Japanese military aircraft were dismissed as Western copies and their pilots as short-sighted. Such misconceptions proved critical in 1941.

Mitsubishi G3M 'Nell'

Although it was already obsolescent when Japan entered World War II in 1941, the G3M belied its technical limitations by scoring a number of stunning successes in the opening phases of Japan's offensive onslaught. First flown in July 1935, the G3M was designed to provide the Imperial Japanese Navy Air Force with the means to project its air power deep into the Pacific.

SPECIFICATIONS	
Country of origin:	Japan
Type:	(G3M2) seven-seat medium attack bomber
Powerplant:	two 1075hp (801.5kW) Mitsubishi Kinsei 41, 42 or 45 14-cylinder two-row radial engines
Performance:	maximum speed 373km/h (232mph); climb to 3000m (9845ft) in 8 mins 19 secs; service ceiling 9130m (29,950ft); range 4380km (2722 miles)
Weights:	empty 4965kg (10,936lb); maximum take-off weight 8000kg (17,637lb)
Dimensions:	span 25m (82ft 0.25in); length 16.45m (53ft 11in); height 3.69m (12ft 1in)
Armament:	one 20mm (.78in) trainable rearward-firing cannon in dorsal turret, one 7.7mm (.303in) trainable machine gun in retractable dorsal turret, one 7.7mm (.303in) machine gun in beam positions, provision for one 7.7mm (.303in) machine gun in cockpit, plus a bomb load of 800kg (1764lb)

Nakajima Ki-27 'Nate'

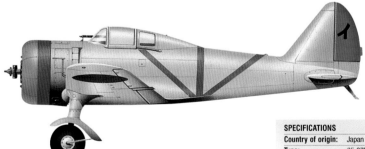

The Japanese counterpart to the naval A5M, the Ki-27 was a cantilever low-wing fighter with fixed landing gear but advanced features such as an enclosed cockpit, and offered creditable performance and a high level of agility. The type first flew in October 1936 and was the army's standard fighter between 1937 and mid-1942. Production totalled some 3495 aircraft; the Ki-27b was the definitive type, with a clear-view canopy and provision for underwing bombs.

SPECIFICATIONS	
Country of origin:	Japan
Type:	(Ki-97b) single-seat fighter and fighter-bomber
Powerplant:	one 780hp (581.5kW) Nakajima Ha-1b (Army Type 97) nine-cylinder single-row radial engine
Performance:	maximum speed 470km/h (292mph); climb to 5000m (16,405ft) in 5 mins 22 secs; service ceiling 12,250m (40,190ft); range 1710km (1063 miles)
Weights:	empty 1110kg (2447lb); maximum take-off weight 1790kg (3946lb)
Dimensions:	span 11.31m (37ft 1.25in); length 7.53m (24ft 8.5in); height 3.25m (10ft 8in)
Armament:	two 7.7mm (.303in) fixed forward-firing machine guns in the upper part of the forward fuselage, plus an external bomb load of 100kg (220lb)

RISING SUN TIMELINE

1935

1936

Mitsubishi A5M 'Claude'

SPECIFICATIONS	
Country of origin:	Japan
Type:	(A5M4) single-seat carrierborne and land-based fighter
Powerplant:	one 785hp (585kW) Nakajima Kotobuki 41 or Kotobuki 41 Kai nine-cylinder single-row radial engine
Performance:	maximum speed 435km/h (270mph); climb to 3000m (9845ft) in 3 mins 35 secs; service ceiling 9800m (32,150ft); range 1400km (870 miles)
Weights:	empty 1263kg (2874lb); maximum take-off weight 1822kg (4017lb)
Dimensions:	span 11.00m (36ft 1.13in); length 7.57m (4ft 9.88in); height 3.27m (10ft 8.75in)
Armament:	two 7.7mm (.303in) fixed forward-firing machine guns in the upper part of the forward fuselage, plus an external bomb load of 60kg (132lb)

It is impossible to overstate the importance of the A5M carrierborne fighter in the development of Japanese industry and military capabilities in the mid-1930s. With this type, Japan moved from dependence on Western imports and thinking to an indigenous product that became its first carrierborne monoplane fighter – one that was comparable with the best of its Western equivalents in terms of performance and capabilities. It is estimated that nearly 1000 A5Ms were built.

Mitsubishi Ki-15-I

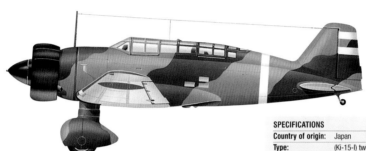

SPECIFICATIONS	
Country of origin:	Japan
Type:	(Ki-15-I) two-seat reconnaissance aircraft
Powerplant:	one 640hp (477kW) Nakajima Ha-8 radial piston engine
Performance:	maximum speed 480km/h (298mph); service ceiling 11,400m (37,400ft); range 2400km (1491 miles)
Weights:	empty 1400kg (3086lb); maximum 2300kg (5071lb)
Dimensions:	span 12.00m (39 ft 5in); length 8.70m (28ft 7in); height 3.35m (11ft); wing area 20.36 sq m (219.16 sq ft)
Armament:	one 7.7mm (.303in) machine gun

Designed for high-speed reconnaissance and communications roles, the Ki-15 first flew in May 1936 and entered Imperial Japanese Army Air Force service in the late 1930s as the Ki-15-I. Production of the Ki-15 series totalled 435 aircraft, the later craft completed to Ki-15-II standard with an uprated engine. Pictured is a Ki-15-I, operated by the 1sr Chuitai, 15th Hikosentai.

Nakajima Ki 43 Hayabusa 'Oscar'

SPECIFICATIONS	
Country of origin:	Japan
Type:	(Ki-43-II) single-seat fighter
Powerplant:	one 1130hp (890kW) Nakajima Ha-115 radial piston engine
Performance:	maximum speed 530km/h (329mph); service ceiling 11,200m (36,750ft); range 1610km (1000 miles)
Weights:	empty 1975kg (4355lb); loaded 2590kg (5710lb)
Dimensions:	span 10.84m (29ft 3in); length 8.92m (29ft 3in); height 3.37m (10ft 8in); wing area 21.40 sq m (230.35 sq ft)
Armament:	two 12.7mm (.5in) Ho-103 machine guns; 250kg (550lb) bombs observer's seat

Nakajima's Hayabusa (Peregrine Falcon) later became known to the Allies as 'Oscar' and was the main Imperial Japanese Air Force (IJAAF) fighter of the war. This one is shown in the colours of the air force of the puppet Manchukuo government in northeastern China.

1940

China

Faced with aggression from Japan and internal political strife, the Chinese Nationalist Government sought aid from the Soviet Union and the United States to build a modern air force. Full-scale war between China and Japan broke out in 1937, and despite fighting valiantly the Chinese Air Force had to withdraw to regroup in late 1938. By late 1941, it was reduced to very little capability, when American support – both official and unofficial – began to arrive in large quantities.

Polikarpov I-15

From 1933, Nikolai Nikolayevich Polikarpov planned the I-15 as successor to his I-5 biplane fighter, with a gulled upper wing (intended to improve the pilot's forward field of vision) and a powerplant of an imported US radial piston engine. The I-15 entered service in 1934, at first complemented and later supplanted by the I-15bis (or I-152), which had improved M-25V engine in a longer-chord cowling, a conventional upper wing and doubled firepower.

SPECIFICATIONS	
Country of origin:	USSR
Type:	(I-15bis) single-seat fighter
Powerplant:	one 750hp (559kW) M-25B nine-cylinder single-row radial engine
Performance:	maximum speed 370km/h (230mph); climb to 1000m (3280ft) in 1 min 6 secs; service ceiling 9000m (29,530ft); range about 530km (329 miles)
Weights:	empty 1310kg (2888lb); maximum take-off weight 1730kg (3814lb)
Dimensions:	span 10.20m (33ft 5.5in); length 6.33m (20ft 9.25in); height 2.19m (7ft 2.25in)
Armament:	four 7.62mm (.29in) fixed forward-firing machine guns in the upper part of the forward fuselage, plus an external bomb load of 100kg (220lb)

Polikarpov I-153

Experience in Spain taught the Soviets that there was still a place for the biplane because of its superior manoeuvrability. The I-153 'Chaika' (Gull) first flew in 1938, was used by Soviets units against Japan in 1939, and was supplied to China in 1940. It reverted to the type of gulled upper wing used on the I-15 and introduced manually operated retractable main landing gear units.

SPECIFICATIONS	
Country of origin:	USSR
Type:	(I-153) single-engined biplane fighter
Powerplant:	one 800hp (597kW) Shvetsov M-62 radial piston engine
Performance:	maximum speed 426km/h (265mph); service ceiling 11,000m (36,080ft); range 740km (460 miles)
Weights:	empty 1348kg (2966lb) loaded 1765kg (3883lb)
Dimensions:	span 10.0m (32ft 10in); length 6.18m (20ft 3in); height 3.0m (9ft 10in); wing area 22.1 sq m (237.8 sq ft)
Armament:	four 7.62mm (.29in) ShKAS machine guns

Curtiss BF2C Hawk III

SPECIFICATIONS	
Country of origin:	United States
Type:	(Curtiss BF2C Hawk III) single-seat biplane fighter
Powerplant:	one 770hp (574kW) Wright R-1820-04 Cyclone radial piston engine
Performance:	maximum speed 362 km/h (225mph); service ceiling 8230m (27,000ft); range 1617km (725 miles)
Weights:	empty 1509kg (3326lb); maximum 2065kg (4552lb)
Dimensions:	span 9.6m (31ft 6in); length 7.41m (24ft 4in); height 3.03m (12ft); wing area 24.34 sq m (262 sq ft)
Armament:	two .3in Browning machine guns; 227kg (500lb) of bombs

The Curtiss Goshawk, or Hawk III, was the last carrier-based fighter this company produced and had a fairly short US Navy career. Just over 100 export models were supplied to the Chinese Nationalists. This one served with their No 25 Squadron at Shanghai in 1937.

Curtiss 75A-5 Hawk

SPECIFICATIONS	
Country of origin:	United States
Type:	(75A-5) single-seat fighter
Powerplant:	one 1200hp (895kW) Wright R-1820-G205A Cyclone piston engine
Performance:	maximum speed 486km/h (302mph); service ceiling 9967m (32,700ft); range 970km (603 miles)
Weights:	empty 2019kg (4451lb); maximum 3022kg (6662lb)
Dimensions:	span 11.38m (37ft 4in); length 8.7m (28ft 8in); height 3.56m (11ft 8in); wing area 21.92 sq m (236 sq ft)
Armament:	six .3in (7.62mm) Browning machine guns

The Hawk 75 was the export designation of the P-36. China's Model 75A-5s had Wright Cyclone engines and were intended for Chinese production. Only a few were assembled there before production was moved to India. Many were completed as Mohawk IVs for the RAF.

Curtiss BT-32 Condor

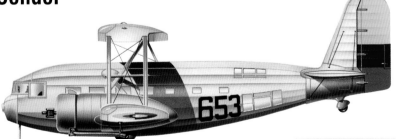

SPECIFICATIONS	
Country of origin:	United States
Type:	(BT-32) twin-engined biplane transport and bomber
Powerplant:	two 710hp (529kW) SCR-1820-F3 Cyclone radial piston engines
Performance:	maximum speed 283km/h (176mph); service ceiling 6705m (22,000ft); range 1352km (840 miles)
Weights:	empty 5095kg (11,233lb); maximum 7938kg (17,500lb)
Dimensions:	span 24.99m (82ft); length 15.09m (49ft 6in); height 4.98m (16ft 4in); wing area 118.54 sq m (1276 sq ft)
Armament:	five .3in (7.62mm) M1919 Browning machine guns; 762kg (1680lb) of bombs

A rare example of a large biplane with retractable undercarriage, the BT-32 was a bomber-transport version of the T-32 airliner first flown in 1933. This BT-32 was delivered to China in 1934 and used mainly as a personal transport by Generalissimo Chang Kai Shek, as well as for some bombing missions.

RAF on the Eve of World War II

By 1939, the Royal Air Force had replaced the majority of its biplanes with modern types. The Hurricane and Spitfire flew in 1935 and 1936 respectively. The Spitfire and Battle were of all-metal construction, but fabric covering over a wood and metal structure was still used on many types, including the Hurricane, Anson and Wellesley. Damage repair and general maintenance of traditionally constructed airframes was easier for a generation of airmen trained on biplanes.

Avro Anson GR Mk I

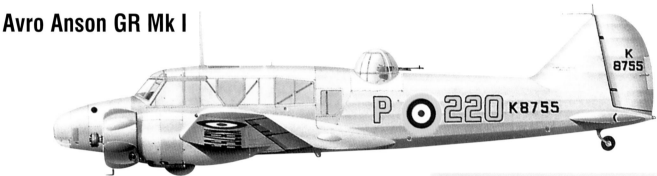

This Anson is seen in Coastal Command's standard finish and markings of the period immediately before World War II, namely an overall silver dope finish with yellow-outlined roundels, black serials and yellow squadron markings.

SPECIFICATIONS

Country of origin:	United Kingdom
Type:	(GR.Mk I) coastal patrol
Powerplant:	two 350hp (261kW) Armstrong Siddeley Cheetah IX radial piston engines
Performance:	maximum speed 303km/h (188mph); service ceiling 5791m (19,000ft); range 1271km (790 miles)
Weights:	loaded 3629kg (8000lb)
Dimensions:	span 17.22m (56ft 6in); length 12.88m (39ft 7in); height 3.99m (13ft 1in)
Armament:	two 7.7mm (.303in) machine guns; provision to carry up to 163kg (360lb) of bombs

Vickers Wellesley

Designed for a general-purpose role but technically and tactically obsolete by the start of World War II, the Wellesley nonetheless saw limited but useful operational service in North Africa and, more importantly, in the Middle East and East Africa during the first part of the war.

SPECIFICATIONS

Country of origin:	United Kingdom
Type:	light bomber
Powerplant:	one 950hp (708kW) Bristol Pegasus radial piston engine
Performance:	maximum speed 367km/h (228mph); service ceiling 10,058m (33,000ft); range 1786km (1110 miles)
Weights:	loaded 5035kg (11,100lb)
Dimensions:	span 22.73m (74ft 7in); length 11.96m (39ft 3in); height 3.76m (12ft 4in)
Armament:	one 7.7mm (.303in) machine gun and one Vickers machine gun in rear cockpit; up to 907kg (2000lb) bombs

RAF TIMELINE

1935

Fairey Battle Mk I

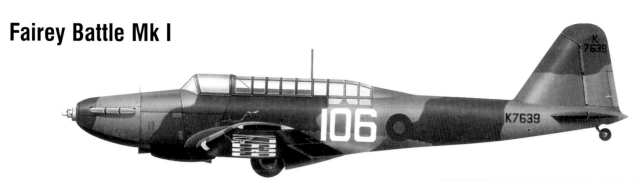

The Battle remained in production long after it was understood to be too slow, too lightly armed (both offensively and defensively) and too lacking in agility for a battlefield bombing role. Such persistence was mainly due to the fact that it had no suitable successor, and production could not be interrupted.

SPECIFICATIONS	
Country of origin:	United Kingdom
Type:	light bomber
Powerplant:	one 1030hp (768kW) Rolls-Royce Merlin II liquid-cooled V-12 piston engine
Performance:	maximum speed 388km/h (241mph); service ceiling 7620m (25,000ft); range 1450km (900 miles)
Weights:	loaded 4895kg (10,792lb)
Dimensions:	span 16.46m (54ft); length 12.9m (42ft 4in); height 4.72m (15ft 6in)
Armament:	two 7.7mm (0.303in) machine guns; 113kg (250lb) bomb load

Hawker Hurricane MK I

This early Hurricane Mk I of No. 87 Squadron has a two-bladed wooden fixed-pitch propeller, and undersides painted black and white for recognition purposes. The squadron was part of the British Expeditionary Force sent to France in late 1939.

SPECIFICATIONS	
Country of origin:	United Kingdom
Type:	(Mk I) single-seat fighter
Powerplant:	one 1030hp (768KW) Rolls-Royce Merlin II liquid-oooled V-12
Performance:	maximum speed 496km/h (308mph); service ceiling 10,180m (33,400ft); range 845km (525 miles)
Weights:	loaded 2820kg (6218lb)
Dimensions:	span 12.19m (40ft); length 9.55m (31ft 4in); height 4.07m (13ft 4.5in)
Armament:	eight 7.7mm (.303in) Browning machine guns

Supermarine Spitfire Mk IA

Edinburgh-based No 603 Squadron exchanged its Gloster Gladiators for Spitfires within two weeks of the outbreak of war, and shot down the first enemy aircraft to fall over Britain since 1918 – a Junkers Ju 88 bomber – in mid-October 1939.

SPECIFICATIONS	
Country of origin:	United Kingdom
Type:	(Mk Ia) single-seat fighter
Powerplant:	one 1030hp (768kW) Rolls-Royce Merlin III liquid-cooled V-12 engine
Performance:	maximum speed 582km/h (362mph); service ceiling 9725m (31,900ft); range 636km (395 miles)
Weights:	loaded about 2624kg (5784lb)
Dimensions:	span 11.22m (36ft 10in); length 9.11m (29ft 115in); height 2.69m (8ft 10in)
Armament:	two 20mm (.79in) Hispano cannon and four 7.7mm (.303in) Browning machine guns

1936

WORLD WAR II

The greatest armed conflict in history saw the biplane era end and the jet age begin. Aircraft were developed to meet a range of tactical and strategic roles, with air power playing a vital part in the Allied victory.

Aluminium alloy structures and monoplane configuration swept away fabric coverings and biplanes in all but a few specialist roles, although a few wooden aircraft built with modern methods still had their place. America alone built over 100,000 fighter aircraft during the war years and by 1944 it was not uncommon for 3000 Allied aircraft to enter enemy airspace over Europe in a single day.

Left: A Heinkel He 111 over London, England on 7th September 1940 – 'Black Saturday' – the first day of the offensive against the capital.

Blitzkrieg on Poland

On 1 September 1939, German forces rolled into Poland, beginning World War II in Europe. Polish Air Force squadrons were equipped mainly with products of the divisions of the PZL (Panstwowe Zaklady Lotnicze, State Aviation Works). Despite their qualities, most of Poland's aircraft were half a generation behind those of their opponents, who had learned from their Spanish experiences. Concentrating on Polish airfields, the Luftwaffe quickly won air superiority.

Messerschmitt Bf 109E-1

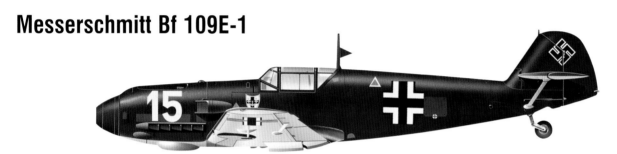

Based at Schippenbeil in East Prussia in August 1939, and detached from the rest of JG 1 – which was located at Heiligenbeil – these fighters saw little air combat: most of the Polish Air Force was destroyed on the ground.

SPECIFICATIONS	
Country of origin:	Germany
Type:	single-seat fighter
Powerplant:	1200hp (895kW) DB 601N 12-cylinder inverted V
Performance:	maximum speed 570km/h (354mph): range 700km (435 miles); service ceiling 10,500m (34,450ft)
Weights:	2505kg (5523lb) max loaded
Dimensions:	span 9.87m (32ft 4in); length 8.64m (28ft 4in); height 2.28m (7ft 5.5in)
Armament:	Early E-1: four 7.92mm (.31in) MGs plus four 50kg (110lb) or one 250kg (551lb) bombs

Dornier Do 17Z-2

The staff flight of III Gruppe, KG 3, was based in Heiligenbeil in East Prussia in August 1939, from where the Geschwader flew against Polish targets at the outbreak of war. KG 3 had originally been known as KG 153.

SPECIFICATIONS	
Country of origin:	Germany
Type:	light bomber
Powerplant:	2 x 1000hp (746kW) BMW Bramo 323P Fafnir nine-cylinder radials
Performance:	maximum speed 425km/h (263mph); range 1160km (721 miles) with light load; service ceiling 8150m (26,740ft)
Weights:	9000kg (19,841lb) loaded
Dimensions:	span 18m (59ft); length 15.79m (51ft 9in); height 4.56m (14ft 11.5in)
Armament:	six 7.92mm (.31in) MGs; 1000kg (2205lb) bomb load

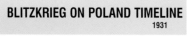 **BLITZKRIEG ON POLAND TIMELINE** 1931    1934

PZL P.11c

In 1939, the Polish Air Force was only just moving into the era of 'modern' monoplane design and was outclassed by a Luftwaffe equipped with more advanced aircraft. The Polish fighter arm was poorly served with gull-winged fighters with fixed landing gear. Similar to the P.7 but with a more powerful engine, the P.11 was much liked by its pilots for good handling in the air. It claimed 125 victories in the air before the defeat of Poland.

SPECIFICATIONS	
Country of origin:	Poland
Type:	single-seat fighter
Powerplant:	one 630hp (470kW) Bristol Mercury V S2 radial engine
Performance:	maximum speed 375km/h (233mph); service ceiling 8000m (26,246ft); range 550km (341 miles)
Weights:	loaded 1650kg (3638lb)
Dimensions:	span 10.72m (35ft 2in); length 7.55m (24ft 9in); height 2.85m (9ft 4in)
Armament:	two to four 7.92mm (.31in) machine guns, plus 50kg (110lb) bomb load

PZL P.23 Karas

Stemming from the P.13 project for a six-passenger transport, the P.23 Karas (Crucian Carp) was a light bomber and army cooperation warplane. The P.23/I Karas was the first of three prototypes and flew in August 1934. With their fixed landing gear, indifferent performance, poor armament and cramped accommodation, the aircraft suffered very heavy losses in the German invasion of September 1939. Pictured is a P.23B operated by No 42 Squadron.

SPECIFICATIONS	
Country of origin:	Poland
Type:	(P.23B Karas) three-seat light reconnaissance bomber
Powerplant:	one 680hp (507kW) PZL (Bristol) Pegasus VIII nine-cylinder single-row radial engine
Performance:	maximum speed 300km/h (186mph); climb to 2000m (6560ft) in 4 mins 45 secs; service ceiling 7300m (23,950ft); range 1400km (870 miles)
Weights:	empty 1928kg (4250lb); maximum take-off weight 3526kg (7773lb)
Dimensions:	span 13.95m (45ft 9.25in); length 9.68m (31ft 9.25in); height 3.30m (10ft 10in)
Armament:	one 7.7mm (.303in) fixed forward-firing machine gun in the forward fuselage, one 7.7mm (.303in) trainable rearward-firing machine gun with 600 rounds in the rear cockpit, and one 7.7mm (.303in) machine gun in the ventral position, plus an external bomb load of 700kg (1543lb)

Lublin R.XIIId

The R-XIII liaison and observation aeroplane was produced in a complex series of variants with wheeled landing gear and float alighting gear. The prototype first flew in July 1931, and total manufacture of 273 aircraft included major variants. Although already obsolescent by the outbreak of war in 1939, the type equipped seven observation squadrons and suffered heavy losses.

SPECIFICATIONS	
Country of origin:	Poland
Type:	(R-XIIID) two-seat observation and liaison aeroplane
Powerplant:	one 220hp (164kW) Skoda-built Wright Whirlwind J-5 seven-cylinder single-row radial engine
Performance:	maximum speed 195km/h (121mph); climb to 3000m (9845ft) in 15 mins 50 secs; service ceiling 4450m (14,600ft); range 600km (373 miles)
Weights:	empty 887kg (1956lb); normal take-off weight 1330kg (2932lb)
Dimensions:	span 13.20m (43ft 4in); length 8.46m (27ft 9.25in); height 2.76m (9ft 0.25in)
Armament:	one or two 7.7mm (.303in) trainable rearward-firing machine guns in the rear cockpit

1935

Invasion of the Low Countries

On 10 May 1940, after months of what Britain called the 'Phoney War' – in which hostilities had been declared but few actions had taken place between British and German forces – the Germans invaded France, Belgium and the Netherlands. The Dutch had small numbers of Fokker-built fighters and bombers, as well as some American aircraft, while Belgium's equipment was mainly British in origin, including Hurricanes and the outwardly modern but ultimately useless Battle light bombers.

Fokker T.V

First flown in October 1937 and built to the extent of 16 aircraft intended for long-range fighter as well as medium bomber roles, the T.V operated only as a bomber. The nine serviceable aircraft flown by the Bomber Squadron on 10 May 1940 were all destroyed over the following five days. This aircraft shown was part of Bomber Squadron / 1st Air Regiment, Schiphol, Netherlands, May 1940.

SPECIFICATIONS	
Country of origin:	Netherlands
Type:	Medium bomber
Powerplant:	2 x 925hp (690kW) Bristol Pegasus XXVI air-cooled radial engines
Performance:	maximum speed 417km/h (257mph); range 1550km (956 miles); service ceiling 7700m (25,256ft)
Weights:	7250kg (15,950lb) loaded
Dimensions:	span 21m (68ft 11in); length 16m (60ft 10in); height 5m (16ft 5in)
Armament:	one 20mm (.79in) cannon in nose; five 7.9mm (.295in) MGs in dorsal, ventral, both lateral positions and tail cupola; 1000kg (2205lb) of bombs

Douglas (Northrop) DB-8A-3N

The Dutch Air Force received 18 of these planes between August and November 1939, and 12 of them were operational at the time of the German invasion. This one – part of 3rd Fighter Squadron / 2nd Air Regiment, Ypenburg, Netherlands, May 1940 – was lost on the ground, and of the 11 that took off, seven were shot down and the surviving four were later destroyed on the ground.

SPECIFICATIONS	
Country of origin:	United States
Type:	fighter
Powerplant:	746kW (1000hp) Wright XR-1820-32 piston engine
Performance:	maximum speed 410km/h (255mph); range 1240km (773 miles); service ceiling 7780m (25,530ft)
Weights:	2905kg (6404lb)
Dimensions:	span 12.65m (41ft 6in); length 10.08m (33ft 1in); height 4.14m (13ft 7in)
Armament:	two 12.7mm (.5in) forward-firing MGs

LOW COUNTRIES TIMELINE

1934

1936

1937

Fokker G.IB

During the mid-1930s, there was considerable interest in the concept of a twin-engined heavy fighter that would offer speed and climb performance comparable with that of single-engined fighters, together with longer range and heavier firepower. Among the countries that essayed such a type was the Netherlands, and the G.I first flew as a two-seat prototype in March 1937. Orders were placed by six countries for the G.IB export model.

SPECIFICATIONS	
Country of origin:	Netherlands
Type:	(G.IA) two/three-seat heavy fighter and close-support warplane
Powerplant:	two 830hp (619kW) Bristol Mercury VIII nine-cylinder single-row radial engines
Performance:	maximum speed 475km/h (295mph); climb to 6000m (19,685ft) in 8 mins 54 secs; service ceiling 9300m (30,510ft); range 1500km (932 miles)
Weights:	empty 3330kg (7341lb); maximum take-off weight 5000kg (11,023lb)
Dimensions:	span 17.16m (56ft 3.6in); length 10.87m (35ft 7.9in); height 3.80m (12ft 5.6in)
Armament:	eight 7.92mm (.31in) fixed forward-firing machine guns in the nose, and one 7.92mm (.31in) trainable rearward-firing machine gun in the nacelle tailcone position, plus an external bomb load of 400kg (882lb)

Gloster Gladiator I

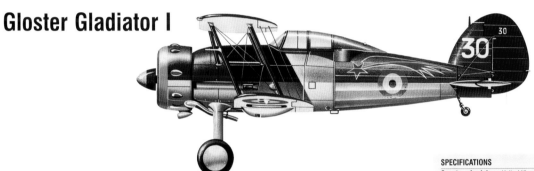

The Gloster Gladiator was the last British biplane fighter to enter service. At the time of the German invasion, the Belgians had received 22 Gladiators, 15 of which were operational in one squadron in May 1940.

SPECIFICATIONS	
Country of origin:	United Kingdom
Type:	single-seat biplane fighter
Powerplant:	one 619kW (830hp) Bristol Mercury VIIIAS air-cooled 9-cylinder radial
Performance:	maximum speed 407km/h (253mph); service ceiling 9845m (32,300ft); normal range 684km (425 miles)
Weights:	loaded 2272kg (5020lb)
Dimensions:	span 9.83m (32ft 3in); length 8.36m (27ft 5in); height 3.52m (11ft 7in)
Armament:	four 7.7mm (.303in) Browning machine guns

Fairey Battle Mk I

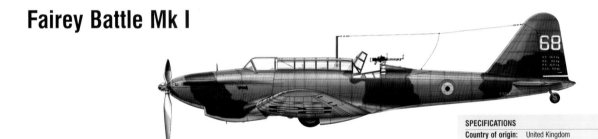

Pictured is a Fairey Battle Mk I from 5/III /3rd Air Regiment, Belgium, Evere, May 1940. All 18 Battle Mk I light bombers delivered to Belgium served with this squadron, which had 14 aircraft on strength at the time of the German invasion. Six out of nine were shot down while attacking a bridge over the Albert Canal on 11 May, and the others were also soon lost.

SPECIFICATIONS	
Country of origin:	United Kingdom
Type:	light bomber
Powerplant:	2 x 1030hp (768kW) Rolls-Royce Merlin I Vee piston engines
Performance:	maximum speed 414km/h (257mph); range 1609km (1000 miles); service ceiling 7620m (25,000ft)
Weights:	4895kg (10,792lb) loaded
Dimensions:	span 16.46m (54ft); length 12.9m (42ft 4in); height 4.72m (15ft 6in)
Armament:	two 7.7mm (.303in) Vickers MGs: one fixed-forward firing in the leading edge of the starboard wing; one Vickers 'K' trainable rearward-firing in the rear of the cockpit; up to 113kg (250lb) bombs carried internally, two 113kg (250lb) carried externally

1939

Gauntlets and Gladiators

Although only just remaining in RAF Fighter Command service by 1940, the Gladiator had been widely exported before the war and saw considerable action in its early years. Its predecessor, the Gauntlet, had been obsolescent as soon as it appeared. It saw some action in East Africa with the South African Air Force, but Denmark's 13 or so examples were destroyed on the ground during the German invasion.

Gauntlet II

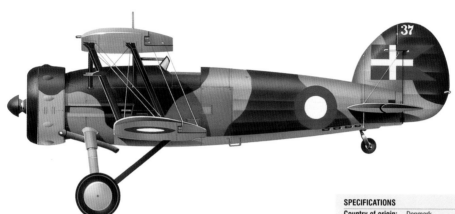

Denmark built the Gauntlet under licence, as well as buying British-built examples. This one served with 1 Eskadrille of the Danish Army Aviation Troops (Hærens Flyvertropper) and is painted in the camouflage adopted in 1939.

SPECIFICATIONS	
Country of origin:	Denmark
Type:	single-seat biplane fighter
Powerplant:	one 645hp (481kW) Bristol Mercury VI S2 9-cylinder radial piston engine
Performance:	maximum speed 370km/h (230mph); service ceiling 10,210m (33,500ft); 740km (460 miles)
Weights:	1259kg (2770lb); loaded 1805kg (3970lb)
Dimensions:	span 10.0m (32ft 9.5in); length 8.05m (26ft 5in); height 3.13m (10ft 3in); wing area 29.3 sq m (315 sq ft)
Armament:	two .303in (7.7mm) Vickers machine guns

Gladiator I

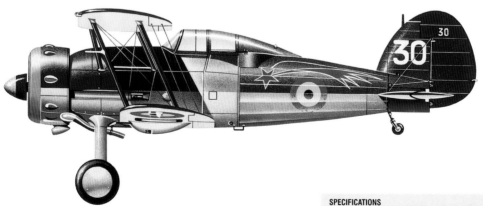

Belgium was one of 17 nations to fly the Gladiator, operating 22 Mk Is from 1937. All those still in service when the German invasion began were wiped out or abandoned by the end of 11 May 1940, including this one from La Comete squadron at Diest-Schaffen.

SPECIFICATIONS	
Country of origin:	United Kingdom
Type:	single-seat fighter
Powerplant:	one 830hp (619kW) Bristol Mercury VIIIAS air-cooled 9-cylinder radial engine
Performance:	maximum speed 407km/h (253mph); range 684km (425 miles); service ceiling 9845m (32,300ft)
Weights:	loaded 2272kg (5020lb)
Dimensions:	span 9.83m (32ft 3in); length 8.36m (27ft 5in); height 3.52m (11ft 7in)
Armament:	four 7.7mm (.303in) Browning machine guns

Gladiator II

The pilots of Norway's 12 Gladiators made eight claims against Luftwaffe aircraft on 9 April 1940, one of them by Sergeant Kristian Schye in this aircraft. Schye himself was shot down by future ace Helmut Lent in a Bf 110, but survived.

SPECIFICATIONS	
Country of origin:	United Kingdom
Type:	single-seat fighter biplane
Powerplant:	one 830hp (619kW) Bristol Mercury VIIIA 9-cylinder radial piston engine
Performance:	maximum speed 414km/h (257mph); service ceiling 10,120m (33,500ft); range 708km (440 miles)
Weights:	empty 1562kg (3444lb); maximum take-off weight 2206kg (4864lb)
Dimensions:	span 9.83m (32ft 3in); length 8.36m (27ft 5in); height 3.53m (11ft 7in); wing area 30.01 sq m (323 sq ft)
Armament:	four fixed forward-firing .303in Colt Browning machine guns

J8 Gladiator I

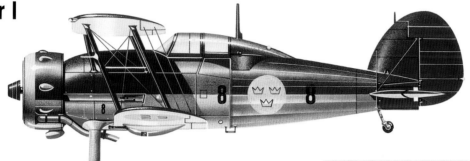

Sweden purchased 45 Gladiators in 1937, which equipped Flygflottilj (Wing) 8 (F8) at Barkaby. Their 37 Mk Is were designated J 8s and the 18 Mk IIs, J 8As, with J standing for Jaktplan (fighter). Gladiators used in Scandinavia were often fitted with skis for operation off snow and ice.

SPECIFICATIONS	
Country of origin:	United Kingdom
Type:	single-seat fighter biplane
Powerplant:	one 645hp (481kW) Bristol Mercury VIS2 radial piston engine
Performance:	maximum speed 414km/h (257mph); service ceiling 10,120m (33,500ft); range 708km (440 miles)
Weights:	empty 1562kg (3444lb); maximum take-off weight 2206kg (4864lb)
Dimensions:	span 9.83m (32ft 3in); length 8.36m (27ft 5in); height 3.53m (11ft 7in); wing area 30.01 sq m (323 sq ft)
Armament:	four fixed forward-firing .303in Colt Browning machine guns

J8 A Gladiator

Although neutral, Sweden sent a unit (F19) of volunteer pilots with Gladiators to help Finland in its 1939–40 war with the Soviet Union. Wearing Finnish markings, these Gladiators had a number of successes against Russian bombers before returning to Sweden.

SPECIFICATIONS	
Country of origin:	United Kingdom
Type:	single-seat fighter biplane
Powerplant:	one 840hp (626kW) Bristol Mercury VIII radial piston engine
Performance:	maximum speed 414km/h (257mph); service ceiling 10,120m (33,500ft); range 708km (440 miles)
Weights:	empty 1562kg (3444lb); maximum take-off weight 2206kg (4864lb)
Dimensions:	span 9.83m (32ft 3in); length 8.36m (27ft 5in); height 3.53m (11ft 7in); wing area 30.01 sq m (323 sq ft)
Armament:	four fixed forward-firing .303in Colt Browning machine guns

Battle of France: Luftwaffe

On 10 May 1940, German forces began an attack on France from three directions, bypassing the Maginot Line defences and driving the British Expeditionary Force to the Channel. Germany's tactics of Blitzkrieg, or 'Lightning War', emphasized speed through motorization of forces, concentration of attacks and good communications between units. Their fighters were faster and better armed, and their bombers – particularly dive bombers – destroyed many French aircraft on their airfields.

Henschel Hs 123A

This aircraft of the (Schlacht)/Lehrgeschwader 2 was based at St Trond in Belgium in May 1940. Hs 123 aircraft supported Guderian's Panzers, which smashed through the Ardennes and into France, operating from advance bases to considerable effect.

SPECIFICATIONS	
Country of Origin:	Germany
Crew:	1
Powerplant:	880hp (656kW) BMW 132Dc nine-cylinder radial
Performance:	Maximum speed 341km/h (212mph); Range: 860km (534 miles); service ceiling: 9000m (29,525ft)
Dimensions:	Span 10.5m (34ft 5.5in); length 8.33m (27ft 4in); height 3.22m (10ft 7in)
Weight:	2217kg (4888lb) loaded
Armament:	two 7.92mm (.31in) MGs; racks for four 50kg (110lb) bombs or bomblet dispensers

Junkers Ju 87B

Aircraft of 7./StG 51 (soon to be redesignated as 4./StG 1) carried the unit's charging bison insignia and a bold yellow shooting star along the fuselage.

SPECIFICATIONS	
Country of Origin:	Germany
Crew:	2
Powerplant:	895kW (1200hp) Junkers Jumo 211
Performance:	maximum speed: 350km/hr (217mph); service ceiling: 8100m (26,570ft); range: 600km (373 miles)
Dimensions:	length 11m (36ft 1.1in); span 13.2m (43ft 4in); height 3.77m (12ft 4in)
Weight:	4400kg (9700lb) max take-off
Armament:	three 7.92mm (.31in) MGs plus a single 500kg (1102lb) bomb

BATTLE OF FRANCE TIMELINE

1934

1935

Messerschmitt Bf 110C-2

I/ZG 52 operated from Charleville in Belgium as the battle for France reached its climax. As an escort fighter, the Bf 110 proved less than effective, and attrition rates grew rapidly over France and later over England.

SPECIFICATIONS	
Country of Origin:	Germany
Crew:	2
Powerplant:	2 x 820kW (1100hp) DB 601A 12-cylinder inverted V
Maximum speed:	560km/hr (349mph); range: 775km (482 miles)
Dimensions:	span 16.27m (50ft 3in); length 12.65m (41ft 6in); height 3.5m (11ft 6in)
Weight:	6750kg (14,881lb) max take-off
Armament:	two 20mm (.78in) and four 7.92mm (.31in) plus twin 7.92mm (.31in) in rear cockpit

Dornier Do 17Z-2

Sometimes referred to as the 'flying pencil' because of its sleek and thin airframe, which made it a difficult target to hit. It was based at Cormeilles-en-Vexin in July 1940 for attacks on RAF airfields.

SPECIFICATIONS	
Country of Origin:	Germany
Crew:	4
Powerplant:	2 x 746kW (1000hp) BMW Bramo 323P Fafnir nine-cylinder radials
Maximum speed:	425km/hr (263mph)
Range:	1160km (721 miles) with light load
Service ceiling:	8150m (26,740ft)
Dimensions:	span 18m (59ft); length 15.79m (51ft 9in); height 4.56m (14ft 11.5in)
Weight:	9000kg (19,841lb) loaded
Armament:	six 7.92mm (.31in) MGs; 1000kg (2205lb) bombload

Heinkel He 111H-1

This was often described as 'The Wolf in sheep's clothing' because it masqueraded as a transport aircraft, but its duty was to provide the Luftwaffe with a fast medium bomber.

SPECIFICATIONS	
Country of Origin:	Germany
Crew:	4/5
Powerplant:	2 x 895kW (1200hp) Junkers Jumo 211D 12-cylinder
Maximum speed:	415km/hr (258mph); range: 1200km (745 miles) with max load; service ceiling: 7800m (25,590ft)
Dimensions:	span 22.6m (74ft 2in); length 16.4m (53ft 9.5in); height 4m (13ft 1.5in)
Weight:	14,000kg (30,864lb) max loaded
Armament:	up to seven MG; one 20mm (.78in) cannon; up to 2000kg (4410lb) bombload internal or external

1936

Battle of France: Armée de L'air

In May 1940, Germany fielded a third more aircraft on the Western Front than all its opponents combined. The Armée de l'Air was equipped with a variety of fighters and medium bombers, few of which could be considered modern. The D.520 was the best French fighter of 1940, but many of those ordered were still at the factory awaiting propellers when the Germans arrived. D.520 pilots claimed more than two enemy aircraft for each loss, but it was not enough.

Bloch MB.174A.3

Entering service only in the later part of March 1940, the MB.174 was planned as a reconnaissance attack-bomber, but the 56 aircraft completed were used only in the reconnaissance role, more than half of the 49 operational aircraft being lost by the time of France's capitulation in June 1940.

SPECIFICATIONS	
Crew:	3
Powerplant:	2 x 820kW (1100hp)
Maximum speed:	530km/h (329mph); range: 1650km (1025 miles); service ceiling: 11,000m (36,090ft)
Dimensions:	span 17.9m (58ft 9in); length 12.25m (40ft 3in); height 3.55m (11ft 8in)
Weight:	7160kg (15,784lb) loaded
Armament:	seven 7.5mm (.295in) MGs: two fixed on leading edge of wing, two trainable rearward ones in dorsal position, three trainable rearward ones on ventral wobble mounts; up to 500kg (1102lb) bombs

Breguet Bre.693.AB.2

Making its combat debut on 12 May 1940, the Bre.693 had a disastrous beginning, 10 out of the 11 aircraft being lost or damaged beyond repair. This aircraft was part of the 4e Escadrille, Groupe de Bombardement d'Assaut II/54, based in Roy, May 1940.

SPECIFICATIONS	
Crew:	2
Powerplant:	2 x 522kW (700hp)
Maximum speed:	490km/h (304mph); range: 1350km (839 miles); service ceiling: 4000m (13,125ft)
Dimensions:	span 15.37m (50ft 5in); length 9.67m (31ft 9in); height 3.19m (10ft 6in)
Weight:	4900kg (10,803lb) loaded
Armament:	one 20mm (.78in) forward-firing cannon and four 7.5mm (.295in) MGs in nose (two), rear cockpit and ventral position; up to 400kg (882lb) of bombs carried internally

BATTLE OF FRANCE TIMELINE 1937 1938

Bloch MB.152C.1

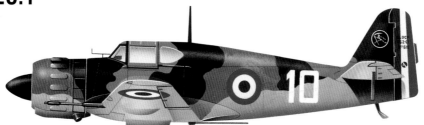

This aircraft was part of the 3e Escadrille, based at Buc in May 1940, facing the main German offensive. Of some 300 aircraft delivered by January 1940, about two-thirds were non-operational for lack of the required propeller.

SPECIFICATIONS	
Crew:	1
Powerplant:	746kW (1000hp) Gnome-Rhone 14N-25 air-cooled 14-cylinder radial
Maximum speed:	509km/h (316mph); range:540km (335 miles); service ceiling: not available
Dimensions:	span 10.54m (34ft 7in); length 9.10m (29ft 10.25in); height 3.03m (9ft 11.33in)
Weight:	2800kg (6160lb) loaded
Armament:	two 20mm (.78in) Hispano-Suiza HS-404 cannon and four 7.5mm (.295in) MAC1934 MGs

Morane-Saulnier MS.406C.1

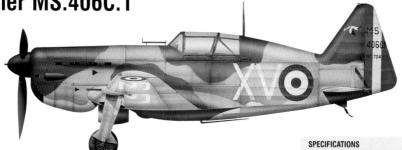

The MS.406 was France's first 'modern' monoplane fighter, but was in all major respects – except firepower – an indifferent warplane with little to commend it except ease of manufacture and availability. Based at Nimes, this aircraft was part of the 1e Escadrille, Groupement de Chasse 12.

SPECIFICATIONS	
Crew:	1
Powerplant:	641kW (860hp) Hispano-Suiza liquid-cooled V-12
Maximum speed:	490km/h (304mph); range:750km (466 miles); service ceiling: 9400m (30,840ft)
Dimensions:	span 10.62m (34ft 9.5in); length 8.17m (26ft 9.33in); height 3.25m (10ft 8in)
Weight:	2471kg (5448lb) loaded
Armament:	one 20mm (.78in) HS9 or HS404 cannon and two 7.5mm (.295in) MAC1934 MGs

Dewoitine D.520C.1

The D.520 was without doubt the best single-seat fighter available to the French in the first part of World War II, but was at that time delivered in only small numbers, and its pilots could therefore exercise no real impact on events. This aircraft was part of the GC II/7.

SPECIFICATIONS	
Crew:	1
Powerplant:	686kW (920hp) Hispano-Suiza 12Y-45 liquid-cooled V-12
Maximum speed:	535km/h (332mph)
Range:	900km (553 miles)
Service ceiling:	11,000m (36,090ft)
Dimensions:	span 10.20m (33ft 5.5in); length 8.76m (28ft 8.75in); height 2.57m (8ft 5.25in)
Weight:	2783kg (6134lb) loaded
Armament:	one 20mm (.78in) Hispano-Suiza HS-404 cannon and four 7.5mm (.295in) MAC1934 MGs

1939

Early WWII British Bombers

RAF Bomber Command began the war with a force of twin-engined bombers of limited bomb loads and armed with only a handful of rifle-calibre machine guns. Crews on early missions over Germany were ordered to avoid damage to private (as opposed to state) property. There were many leaflet-dropping raids, which were just as dangerous to fly as bombing missions but had little military effect. Daylight raids soon proved too costly in terms of aircraft lost.

Armstrong Whitworth Whitley Mk I

This aeroplane is depicted in the standard camouflage and markings of the period, with yellow-ringed fuselage roundels, black under surfaces, and dark-green and dark-earth upper surfaces. It was part of No 10 Squadron, based at RAF Dishforth, Yorkshire, in 1939–40.

SPECIFICATIONS	
Crew:	5
Powerplant:	2 x 593kW (795hp) Tiger IX
Maximum speed:	362km/h (225mph); range: 2414km (1315 miles); service ceiling: 7925m (26,001ft)
Dimensions:	span 25.6m (84ft); length 21.1m (69ft 3in); height 4.57m (15ft)
Weight:	15,196kg (33,501lb) loaded
Armament:	one 7.7mm (.303in) Lewis gun mounted in front and rear turrets; 1135kg (2500lb) bomb load

Handley Page Hampden Mk I

The Hampden Mk I was operated by a four-man crew all located in the 'pod' section of the fuselage. This was so narrow that it was impossible for anyone to exchange seats and so a badly wounded pilot could not be replaced. It was part of No 106 Squadron, No 5 Group, RAF Bomber Command, Finningley, Yorkshire, April 1940.

SPECIFICATIONS	
Crew:	4
Powerplant:	two 746kW (1000hp) Bristol Pegasus XVIII radial piston engines
Maximum speed:	409km/h (254mph); range:3034km (1885 miles); service ceiling: 5791m (19,000ft)
Dimensions:	span 21.08m (69ft 2in); length 16.33m (53ft 7in); height 4.55m (14ft 11in)
Weight:	8508kg (18,756lb) loaded
Armament:	two forward-firing and twin 7.7mm (.303in) MGs; 1814kg (4000lb) bombs

BRITISH BOMBERS TIMELINE
1936

Vickers Wellington Mk IC

Features of the Wellington Mk IC were two beam guns in place of one ventral gun, and larger main wheels that extended below the engine nacelle when retracted. This aircraft flew with No 99 Squadron, No 3 Group, RAF Bomber Command, Newmarket, Cambridgeshire, in 1940.

SPECIFICATIONS	
Crew:	6
Powerplant:	2 x 783kW (1050hp) Bristol Pegasus XVIII 9 cylinder radial engines
Maximum speed:	378km/h (235mph); range: 2905km (805 miles); service ceiling: 5486m (18,000ft)
Dimensions:	span 26.26m (86ft 2in); length 18.54m (60ft 10in); height 5.33m (17ft 6in)
Weight:	12,927kg (28,500lb) loaded
Armament:	two 7.7mm (.303in) Browning MGs in both nose and tail; two 7.7mm (.303in) beam guns; 2041kg (4500lb) bomb load

Bristol Blenheim Mk I

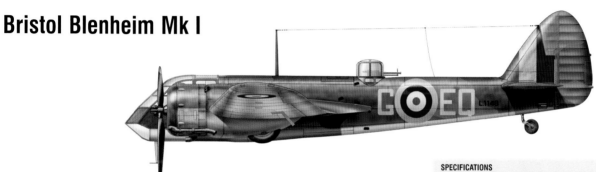

This Blenheim Mk I flew with No 57 Squadron, which re-equipped from the Hawker Hind single-engined biplane to the Blenheim twin-engined monoplane in 1938, and was transferred to France in September 1939. The unit suffered heavy losses in the first 10 days of the German advance into France, as it attacked troop and transport columns. It was then withdrawn to England to recuperate and rebuild.

SPECIFICATIONS	
Crew:	3
Powerplant:	627kW (840hp) Bristol Mercury VIII 9-cylinder single-row radial engines
Maximum speed:	459km/h (285mph); range: 1810km (1125 miles); service ceiling: 8315m (27,280ft)
Dimensions:	span 17.17m (56ft 4in); length 12.12m (39ft 9in); height 3m (9ft 10in)
Weight:	4031kg (8839lb) loaded
	Armament: two 7.7mm (.3in) MGs; 454kg (1000lb) bomb load

Short Stirling Mk I Series I

No 7 Squadron was the first unit to receive the Stirling, the squadron getting its first aircraft at Leeming in Yorkshire during August 1940. MG-D was the first of the aircraft to be delivered.

SPECIFICATIONS	
Country of origin:	United Kingdom
Type:	heavy bomber
Powerplant:	4 x 1375hp (1030kW) Bristol Hercules radial engines
Performance:	maximum speed 410km/h (255mph); range 3750km (2330 miles); service ceiling 5030m (16,500ft)
Weights:	31,750kg (70,000lb) loaded
Dimensions:	span 30.2m (99ft 1in); length 26.6m (87ft 3in); height 8.8m (28ft 10in)
Armament:	eight 7.7mm (.303in) Browning machine guns (two in the nose, four in the tail, two in dorsal position); up to 8164kg (18,000lb) of bombs

1937

1939

Battle of Britain: Spitfires

The Supermarine Spitfire is the icon of RAF Fighter Command and the Battle of Britain, which officially lasted from July to November 1940. Nineteen squadrons flew Spitfires during this time, mostly Mk IAs with eight machine guns, but also a small number of Mk IBs with a pair of 20mm (.79in) cannon. In August and September 1940, the RAF lost 147 Spitfires, but production of replacements was just able to keep pace with this rate of attrition.

Supermarine Spitfire Mk IA

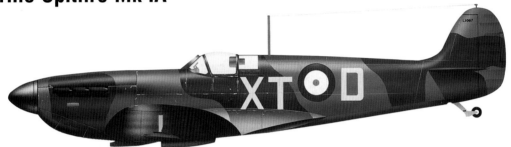

Within two weeks of the outbreak of war in September 1939, No 603 'City of Edinburgh' Squadron began to receive Spitfires. It was operational with the aircraft in time to intercept the first German air raid on the British Isles on 16 October, when it destroyed the first enemy aircraft to be shot down over Britain in World War II.

SPECIFICATIONS

Country of origin:	United Kingdom
Type:	Single-seat fighter
Powerplant:	1030hp (768kW) Rolls-Royce Merlin III liquid-cooled V-12
Performance:	maximum speed 582km/h (362mph); range 636km (395 miles); service ceiling 9725m (31,900ft)
Weights:	2624kg (5784lb) loaded
Dimensions:	span 11.22m (36ft 10in); length 9.11m (29ft 11in); height 2.69m (8ft 10in)
Armament:	eight 7.7mm (.303in) Browning MGs

Supermarine Spitfire Mk IA

Led by Squadron Leader F. L. White, No 74 Squadron was one of the three Spitfire units operating in No 11 Group's Hornchurch sector. The squadron had 15 aircraft at this time, 12 of them serviceable. Spitfire Mk I K9953 was flown by one of the most famous Battle of Britain aces and leaders, Flight Lieutenant Adolphus 'Sailor' Malan.

SPECIFICATIONS

Country of origin:	United Kingdom
Type:	Single-seat fighter
Powerplant:	1030hp (768kW) Rolls-Royce Merlin III liquid-cooled V-12
Performance:	maximum speed 582km/h (362mph); range 636km (395 miles); service ceiling 9725m (31,900ft)
Weights:	2624kg (5784lb) loaded
Dimensions:	span 11.22m (36ft 10in); length 9.11m (29ft 11in); height 2.69m (8ft 10in)
Armament:	eight 7.7mm (.303in) Browning MGs

Supermarine Spitfire Mk IA

With 12 serviceable and four unserviceable aircraft on 1 July 1940, No 66 Squadron was part of No 12 Group RAF Fighter Command, based at Coltishall in East Anglia. Flying this Spitfire, Sergeant F. N. Robertson scored the first aerial victory against the Luftwaffe in the Battle of Britain, when he shot down a Dornier Do 17 on 23 June 1940.

SPECIFICATIONS	
Country of origin:	United Kingdom
Type:	Single-seat fighter
Powerplant:	1030hp (768kW) Rolls-Royce Merlin III liquid-cooled V-12
Performance:	maximum speed 582km/h (362mph); range 636km (395 miles); service ceiling 9725m (31,900ft)
Weights:	2624kg (5784lb) loaded
Dimensions:	span 11.22m (36ft 10in); length 9.11m (29ft 11in); height 2.69m (8ft 10in)
Armament:	eight 7.7mm (.303in) Browning MGs

Supermarine Spitfire Mk IA

With 12 serviceable and four unserviceable aircraft on 1 July 1940, No 602 Squadron was part of No 13 Group, based at Drem in Scotland. Mk IA L1004 was the mount of Squadron Leader 'Sandy' Johnstone, who scored several kills in it. This Spitfire survived the battle and was later converted to the prototype Mk V.

SPECIFICATIONS	
Country of origin:	United Kingdom
Powerplant:	1030hp (768kW) Rolls-Royce Merlin III liquid-cooled V-12
Performance:	maximum speed 582km/h (362mph); range 636km (395 miles); service ceiling 9725m (31,900ft)
Weights:	2624kg (5784lb) loaded
Dimensions:	span 11.22m (36ft 10in); length 9.11m (29ft 11in); height 2.69m (8ft 10in)
Armament:	eight 7.7mm (.303in) Browning MGs

Supermarine Spitfire Mk IB

The Spitfire Mk IB of No 92 Squadron RAF Fighter Command marked an important evolutionary step in the firepower of the Spitfire family, as it was one of a few Spitfire Mk IAs in which four of the the eight 7.7mm (.303in) machine guns of were replaced by two 20mm (.78in) cannon.

SPECIFICATIONS	
Country of origin:	United Kingdom
Powerplant:	1030hp (768kW) Rolls-Royce Merlin III liquid-cooled V-12
Performance:	maximum speed 582km/h (362mph); range 636km (395 miles); service ceiling 9725m (31,900ft)
Weights:	about 2624kg (5784lb) loaded
Dimensions:	span 11.22m (36ft 10in); length 9.11m (29ft 11in); height 2.69m (8ft 10in)
Armament:	two 20mm (.78in) Hispano cannon; four 7.7mm (.303in) Browning MGs

Battle of Britain: Bombers

In 1940, the Luftwaffe was able to field 4000 aircraft against Britain from bases in France, Belgium, the Netherlands and Norway. From October, Italy committed a contingent of the Regia Aeronautica, to little effect. By striking airfields and radar stations, the Luftwaffe came close to neutralizing the defences, but a switch to raids on London gave the RAF breathing space to replace its losses and refine its tactics. The Luftwaffe failed to achieve air superiority and called off its invasion plans.

Dornier Do 17Z

Dornier 17s were used for several low-level raids on RAF airfields, which were relatively effective but very costly for the attackers and soon discontinued. This Do 17Z of 9. Staffel KG 76 was based at Cormeilles-en-Vexin, and took part in these raids.

SPECIFICATIONS	
Country of origin:	Germany
Type:	four-man bomber
Powerplant:	2 x 1000hp (746kW) BMW Bramo 323P Fafnir nine-cylinder radials
Performance:	maximum speed 425km/hr (263mph); range 1160km (721 miles) with light load; service ceiling 8150m (26,740ft)
Weights:	9000kg (19,841lb) loaded
Dimensions:	span 18m (59ft); length 15.79m (51ft 9in); height 4.56m (14ft 11.5in)
Armament:	six 7.92mm (.31in) MGs; 1000kg (2205lb) bomb load

Messerschmitt Bf 110C

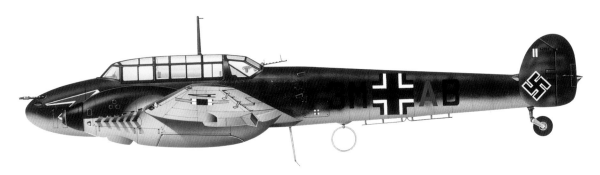

The Bf 110 was a heavy Zerstorer (destroyer) fighter. Used as a high-speed light bomber, Bf 110s made some notable precision raids on targets on England's south coast, but as an escort fighter it proved vulnerable to the RAF's single-engined fighters.

SPECIFICATIONS	
Country of origin:	Germany
Type:	two-man heavy fighter/light bomber
Powerplant:	two 820kW (1100hp) DB 601A 12-cylinder inverted V engines
Performance:	maximum speed 560km/h (349mph); range 775km (482 miles); service ceiling 10,500m (34,450ft)
Weights:	maximum take-off weight 6750kg (14,881lb)
Dimensions:	span 16.27m (50ft 3in); length 12.65m (41ft 6in); height 3.5m (11ft 6in)
Armament:	two 20mm (.78in) cannon; four 7.92mm (.31in) machine guns; plus twin 7.92mm (.31in) machine guns in rear cockpit

Heinkel III H-2

SPECIFICATIONS	
Country of origin:	Germany
Type:	five-crew medium bomber
Powerplant:	two 1100hp (820kW) Junkers Jumo 211A-3 piston engines
Performance:	maximum speed 435km/h (270mph); range 2000km (1243 miles); service ceiling 6500m (21,340ft)
Weights:	empty 6740kg (14,859lb); maximum 12600kg (27,778lb)
Dimensions:	span 22.6m (74ft 6in); length 16.60m (54ft 6in); height 4.0m (13ft 1in); wing area 87.6 sq m (943 sq ft)
Armament:	one 20mm (.78in) cannon; up to seven machine guns; up to 2000kg (4410lb) bomb load, internal or external

Attacking London on 15 September 1940, this He III came under fire from Spitfires. Badly damaged, it force-landed at Armentières. The He III was the most numerous of the Luftwaffe's bombers in the Battle of Britain, but also the slowest. The main bomb load was stored vertically in racks and tumbled when dropped, affecting accuracy.

Heinkel III H-3

SPECIFICATIONS	
Country of origin:	Germany
Type:	five-crew medium bomber
Powerplant:	two 1200hp (894kW) Junkers Jumo 211D-1 inverted V-12 piston engines
Performance:	maximum speed 435km/h (270mph); range 2000km (1243 miles); service ceiling 6500 m (21,340 ft)
Weights:	empty 7720kg (17,000lb); maximum 14,000kg (30,865lb)
Dimensions:	span 22.6m (74ft 6in); length 16.60m (54ft 6in); height 4.0m (13ft 1in); wing area 87.6 sq m (943 sq ft)
Armament:	four 7.92mm (.31in) MG 15 machine guns; one 20mm (.78in) cannon; up to 2000kg (4410lb) of bombs

The He III H-3 differed in powerplant and armament from previous versions. The example pictured, from Kampfgeschwader 1, wears temporary formation markings. KG 1 was a mixed unit: two of its Gruppen flew He IIIs and one Do 17Zs.

Junkers Ju 88A-1

SPECIFICATIONS	
Country of origin:	Germany
Type:	four-crew medium bomber
Powerplant:	two 1200hp (895kW) Junkers Jumo 211B-1 inverted V-12 piston engines
Performance:	maximum speed 450km/h (280mph); range 1700km (1056 miles); service ceiling 9800m (32,150ft)
Weights:	empty 7700kg (16,975lb); maximum 10,360kg (22,840lb)
Dimensions:	span 18.26m (59ft 11in); length 8.43m (47ft 2in); height 4.85m (15ft 11in); wing area 47.8 sq m (515 sq ft)
Armament:	three 7.92mm (.31in) MG 15 machine guns; 2400kg (5290lb) of bombs

Once the Luftwaffe switched mainly to attacks on cities and precision became less important, the 'Night Blitz' began. This Ju 88A-1 of KG 51 'Edelweiss', based at Melun-Villaroche, wears the night camouflage scheme adopted in late 1940.

Junkers Ju 88

The Ju 88 was the most versatile Luftwaffe aircraft of the war and was adapted into dozens of variants for many roles, including dive-bomber, missile carrier and night fighter. Its bomber variants could carry 2400kg (5290lb) for short missions, but the bomb bays were usually filled with auxiliary fuel tanks and the bombs carried on external racks. The crew positions were more concentrated together than on its Heinkel and Dornier contemporaries, making for good inter-crew communications.

Junkers Ju 88A-4

The A-4 was the main bomber variant of the Ju 88 series. This example of I Gruppe, KG 30 – based in the Netherlands in 1940 – is depicted dropping a 1000kg (2200lb) parachute mine, a munition often used as a blast weapon against urban targets.

SPECIFICATIONS	
Country of origin:	Germany
Type:	Ju 88G-7a four-crew heavy night bomber
Powerplant:	two 1725hp (1286kW) Junkers Jumo 213E inverted V-12 piston engine
Performance:	maximum speed 636km/h (389mph); range 2253km (1400 miles); service ceiling 10,000m (32,808ft)
Weights:	empty 13,109kg (28,900lb); loaded 14,674kg (32,350lb)
Dimensions:	span 20.0m (65ft 8in); length 16.5m (54ft 2in); height 4.85m (15ft 11in); wing area 54.5 sq m (587 sq ft)
Armament:	six 20mm (.78in) MG 151 cannon and one 13mm (.5in) MG 131 machine gun

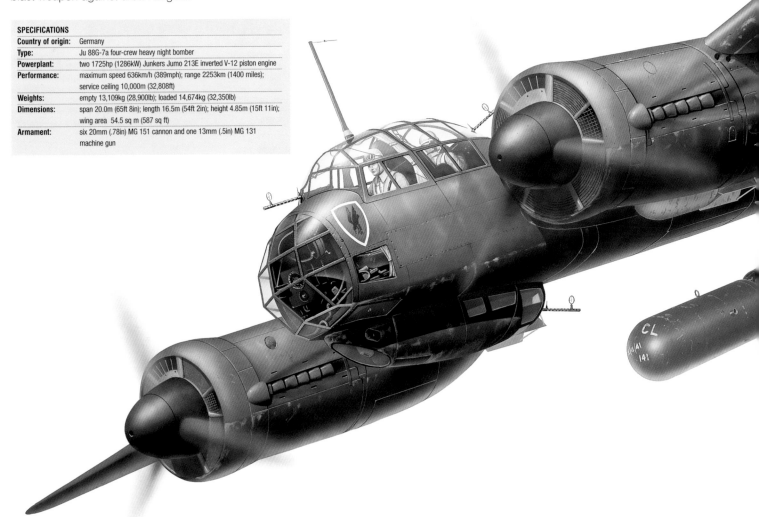

Junkers Ju 88G-7a

Equipped with radar and heavy cannon, the Ju 88 made one of the best night fighters of the war. This Ju 88G-7, a model of IV/NJG 6 in the winter of 1944–45, has its fin painted to resemble that of the older Ju 88C, probably to conceal the fact that a new model had entered service.

SPECIFICATIONS	
Country of origin:	Germany
Type:	four-crew heavy night fighter
Powerplant:	two 1725hp (1286kW) Junkers Jumo 213E inverted V-12 piston engines
Performance:	maximum speed 636km/h (389 mph); range 2253km (1400 miles); service ceiling 10,000m (32,808ft)
Weights:	empty 13,109kg (28,900lb); loaded 14,674kg (32,350lb)
Dimensions:	20.0m (65ft 8in); length 16.5m (54ft 2in); height 4.85m (15ft 11in); wing area 54.5 sq m (587 sq ft)
Armament:	six 20mm (.78in) MG 151 cannon and one 13mm (.5in) MG 131 machine gun

Junkers Ju 88A-4

The Ju 88As were often used in an anti-shipping role.1./KG 54 'Totenkopf' (Death's Head) operated against the Allied landings on Sicily in September 1943. It sports a 'scribble' pattern over the standard Mediterranean theatre colour scheme.

SPECIFICATIONS	
Country of origin:	Germany
Type:	four-crew medium bomber
Powerplant:	two 1340hp (999kW) Junkers Jumo 211J-1/2 inverted V-12 piston engines
Performance:	maximum speed 470km/h (292mph); range 1790km (1112 miles); service ceiling 9800m (32,150ft)
Weights:	empty 9860kg (21,737lb); maximum 14,000kg (30,865lb)
Dimensions:	span 20m (65ft 8in); length 8.43m (47ft 2in); height 4.85m (15ft 11in); wing area 54.5 sq m (587 sq ft)
Armament:	three 7.92mm (.31in) MG 15 machine guns; 2400kg (5290lb) bombs

Battle of Britain: Hurricanes

The Hurricane was less technologically sophisticated than the Spitfire, slower and less manoeuvrable, but it was a more stable gun platform and more resistant to battle damage. Most importantly, it was more numerous, with 1715 in service between July and November 1940. Hurricanes destroyed more Luftwaffe aircraft than all other defences combined, including fighters, anti-aircraft guns and barrage balloons. Fuselages were fabric covering over a metal tube and wooden structure.

Hawker Hurricane Mk IA

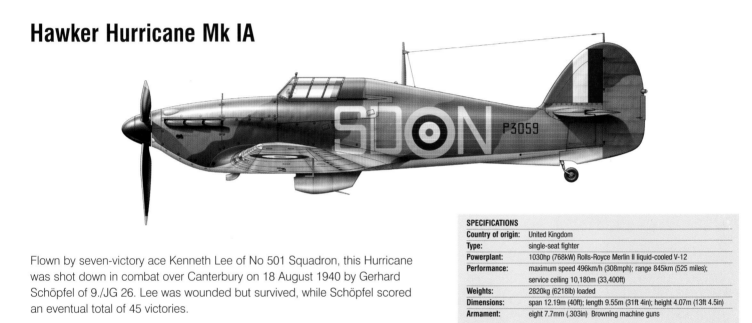

Flown by seven-victory ace Kenneth Lee of No 501 Squadron, this Hurricane was shot down in combat over Canterbury on 18 August 1940 by Gerhard Schöpfel of 9./JG 26. Lee was wounded but survived, while Schöpfel scored an eventual total of 45 victories.

SPECIFICATIONS	
Country of origin:	United Kingdom
Type:	single-seat fighter
Powerplant:	1030hp (768kW) Rolls-Royce Merlin II liquid-cooled V-12
Performance:	maximum speed 496km/h (308mph); range 845km (525 miles); service ceiling 10,180m (33,400ft)
Weights:	2820kg (6218lb) loaded
Dimensions:	span 12.19m (40ft); length 9.55m (31ft 4in); height 4.07m (13ft 4.5in)
Armament:	eight 7.7mm (.303in) Browning machine guns

Hawker Hurricane Mk I

P3120 was one of several aircraft of the Polish-manned No 303 Squadron to wear a diagonal red band around the fuselage, probably denoting a flight leader's aircraft. It was destroyed on the ground at Northolt on 6 October 1940. The Hurricane was an excellent blend of the old (steel tube in the structure and largely fabric covering) and the new (low-set cantilever wing, enclosed cockpit).

SPECIFICATIONS	
Country of origin:	United Kingdom
Type:	single-seat fighter
Powerplant:	1030hp (768kW) Rolls-Royce Merlin II liquid-cooled V-12
Performance:	maximum speed 496km/h (308mph); range 845km (525 miles); service ceiling 10,180m (33,400ft)
Weight:	2820kg (6218lb) loaded
Dimensions:	span 12.19m (40ft); length 9.55m (31ft 4in); height 4.07m (13ft 4.5in)
Armament:	eight 7.7mm (.303in) Browning MGs

Hawker Hurricane Mk IA

For each victory scored by Flight Lieutenant A. V. Clowes of No 1 Squadron, he had his ground crew paint another yellow stripe on the wasp insignia on the cowl. Clowes scored nine confirmed victories and several 'probables' before P3395 was passed on to a training unit.

SPECIFICATIONS	
Country of origin:	United Kingdom
Type:	single-seat fighter
Powerplant:	1030hp (768kW) Rolls-Royce Merlin II liquid-cooled V-12
Performance:	maximum speed 46km/h (308mph); range 845km (525 miles); service ceiling 10,180m (33,400ft)
Weights:	2820kg (6218lb) loaded
Dimensions:	span 12.19m (40ft); length 9.55m (31ft 4in); height 4.07m (13ft 4.5in)
Armament:	eight 7.7mm (.303in) Browning MGs

Hawker Hurricane Mk IA

Wearing the famous hexagon insignia of No 85 Squadron, this Hurricane was normally flown by Squadron Leader Peter Townsend, the unit's commanding officer. Townsend was wounded during the Battle of Britain and the squadron suffered heavy losses in August 1940.

SPECIFICATIONS	
Country of origin:	United Kingdom
Type:	single-seat fighter
Powerplant:	1030hp (768kW) Rolls-Royce Merlin II liquid-cooled V-12
Performance:	maximum speed 496km/h (308mph); range 845km (525 miles); service ceiling 10,180m (33,400ft)
Weights:	2820kg (6218lb) loaded
Dimensions:	span 12.19m (40ft); length 9.55m (31ft 4in); height 4.07m (13ft 4.5in)
Armament:	eight 7.7mm (.303in) Browning MGs

Hawker Hurricane Mk I

This Hurricane was flown by Pilot Officer R. G. A. Barclay of No 249 Squadron at Church Fenton in July 1940. Squadron mate James Nicholson was the only fighter pilot to be awarded the Victoria Cross during the Battle of Britain.

SPECIFICATIONS	
Country of origin:	United Kingdom
Type:	single-seat fighter
Powerplant:	1030hp (768kW) Rolls-Royce Merlin II liquid-cooled V-12
Performance:	maximum speed 496km/h (308mph); range 845km (525 miles); service ceiling 10,180m (33,400ft)
Weights:	2820kg (6218lb) loaded
Dimensions:	span 12.19m (40ft); length 9.55m (31ft 4in); height 4.07m (13ft 4.5in)
Armament:	eight 7.7mm (.303in) Browning MGs

Battle of Britain: Bf 109s

The Bf 109E was comparable to the Spitfire Mk I in speed and manoeuvrability. Its fuel-injected Daimler-Benz engine had the advantage of not cutting out when subjected to negative g-forces (unlike the Merlin) and its 20mm (.78in) cannon packed a powerful punch. Operating over southeast England, however, the 'Emil' was at the extremes of its range and could spend only about 20 minutes in combat. The radios fitted to Luftwaffe fighters were not compatible with those in bombers.

Messerschmitt Bf 109E

The Bf 109E-4 was the definitive version of the 'Emil' series. The 4/N sub-variant had the DB 601 engine with water-methanol boost and the engine-mounted cannon removed. This E-4 was flown by Gerhard Schöpfel of 9./JG 26.

SPECIFICATIONS	
Country of origin:	Germany
Type:	(Bf 109E-4/N) single-seat fighter
Powerplant:	1200hp (895kW) Daimler-Benz DB 601N inverted V-12 piston engine
Performance:	maximum speed 560km/h (348mph); range 660km (410 miles); service ceiling 10,500m (34,449ft)
Weights:	2505kg (5523lb) max loaded
Dimensions:	span 9.87m (32ft 5in); length 8.64m (28ft 4in); height 2.50m (8ft 2in); wing area 16.17 sq m (179.97 sq ft)
Armament:	two 20mm (.78in) MG-FF/M cannon; two 7.9mm (.31in) MG 13 machine guns

Messerschmitt Bf 109E-3

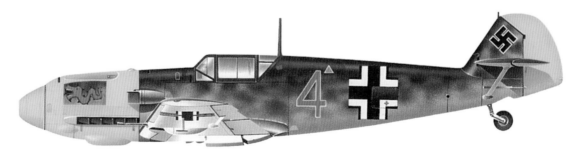

The Bf 109E-3 was designed with a 20mm (.78in) cannon mounted between the engine cylinders and firing through the propeller hub, but this proved inaccurate and prone to jamming and was usually deactivated. This E-3 served with JG 3.

SPECIFICATIONS	
Country of origin:	Germany
Type:	single-seat fighter
Powerplant:	1160hp (865kW) Daimler-Benz DB601Aa inverted V-12 piston engine
Performance:	maximum speed 560 km/h (348 mph); range: 660km (410 miles); service ceiling: 10,500m (34,449ft)
Weights:	empty 1900kg (4189lb); maximum 2665kg (5875lb)
Dimensions:	span 9.87m (32ft 5in); length 8.64m (28ft 4in); height 2.50m (8ft 2in); wing area 16.17 sq m (179.97 sq ft)
Armament:	two 20mm (.78in) MG-FF cannon; two 7.9mm (.31in) MG 13 machine guns

Messerschmitt Bf 109E-3

This Bf 109E-3 of JG 53 'Pik As' (Ace of Spades) was based at Wissant, France, in the early stages of the battle. The commander of III Gruppe JG 53, Werner Mölders, was the first pilot to score 100 aerial victories.

SPECIFICATIONS	
Country of origin:	Germany
Type:	single-seat fighter
Powerplant:	1200hp (895kW) DB 601N 12-cylinder inverted V
Performance:	maximum speed 570km/h (354mph); range 700km (435 miles); service ceiling 10,500m (34,450ft)
Weights:	2505kg (5523lb) maximum loaded
Dimensions:	span 9.87m (32ft 4in); length 8.64m (28ft 4in); height 2.28m (7ft 5.5in)
Armament:	one 20mm (.78in) cannon; four 7.92mm (.31in) MGs

Messerschmitt Bf 109E

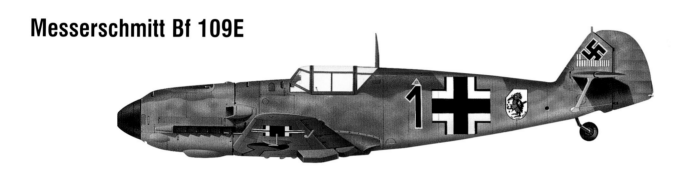

Horst 'Jakob' Tietzen of 5./JG 51 scored 27 victories, seven of them in Spain. He was killed on 18 August 1940 in combat over the Thames Estuary with Hurricanes of No 85 Squadron, possibly the victim of Peter Townsend.

SPECIFICATIONS	
Country of origin:	Germany
Type:	single-seat fighter
Powerplant:	1200hp (895kW) DB 601N 12-cylinder inverted V
Performance:	maximum speed 570km/h (354mph); range 700km (435 miles); service ceiling 10,500m (34,450ft)
Weights:	2505kg (5523lb) maximum loaded
Dimensions:	span 9.87m (32ft 4in); length 8.64m (28ft 4in); height 2.28m (7ft 5.5in)
Armament:	two 20mm (.78in) cannon; two 7.92mm (.31in) MGs

Messerschmitt Bf 109E-4

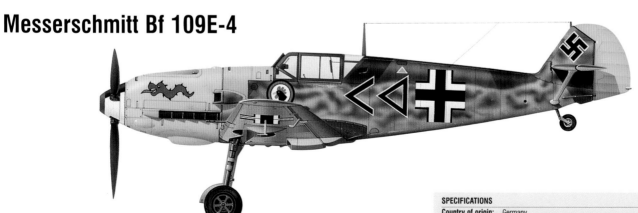

This Bf 109E-4 was flown by Hans von Hahn, the Gruppenkommodore of JG 3. Von Hahn scored 31 wartime victories, most of them over the Eastern Front, but he also shot down five RAF fighters in the Battle of Britain. The cockerel motif was his personal insignia.

SPECIFICATIONS	
Country of origin:	Germany
Type:	single-seat fighter
Powerplant:	1200hp (895kW) DB 601N 12-cylinder inverted V
Performance:	maximum speed 570km/h (354mph); range 700km (435 miles); service ceiling 10,500m (34,450ft)
Weights:	2505kg (5523lb) maximum loaded
Dimensions:	span 9.87m (32ft 4in); length 8.64m (28ft 4in); height 2.28m (7ft 5.5in)
Armament:	two 20mm (.78in) cannon; two 7.92mm (.31in) machine guns

Battle of Britain: Other Players

As well as the Spitfires and Messerschmitts, Hurricanes and Heinkels, the epic air battle of the summer of 1940 was also fought by a variety of second-line types. The Regia Aeronautica created the Corpo Aereo Italiano with about 200 aircraft to make a (largely unwelcome) contribution to the Luftwaffe campaign against Britain. Arriving at the tail end of the battle, the Italians had little impact, losing most of their aircraft in combat and accidents.

Boulton Paul Defiant

The Defiant was designed as a bomber destroyer with a four-gun powered turret, but no forward-facing armament. It was heavier than a Spitfire or Hurricane but had much the same engine. Defiants were withdrawn as day fighters after suffering heavy losses in August 1940.

SPECIFICATIONS	
Country of origin:	United Kingdom
Type:	(Defiant Mk I) two-seat fighter
Powerplant:	1030hp (768kW) Rolls-Royce Merlin III V-12 piston engine
Performance:	maximum speed 504km/h (302mph); range 748km (465 miles); service ceiling 8565m (28,100ft)
Weights:	empty 2757kg (6078lb); maximum 3900kg (8600lb)
Dimensions:	span 11.99m (39ft 4in); length 10.77m (35ft 4in); height 3.45m (11ft 4in); wing area 23.23 sq m (250 sq ft)
Armament:	Four .303in (7.7 mm) Browning machine guns

Bristol Blenheim Mk IF

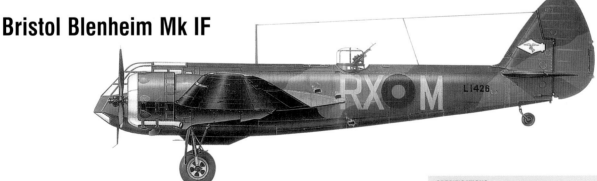

An interim fighter created by adding a four-gun ventral pack to the Blenheim Mk I light bomber, the Blenheim IF served with eight squadrons of Fighter Command in July 1940, including No 25 at North Weald, depicted here.

SPECIFICATIONS	
Country of origin:	United Kingdom
Type:	two-seat fighter
Powerplant:	two 840hp (626kW) Bristol Mercury VIII air-cooled 9-cylinder radial
Performance:	maximum speed 447km/h (278mph); range 1690km (1050 miles); service ceiling 8315m (27,280ft)
Weights:	5534kg (12,200lb) loaded
Dimensions:	span 17.17m (56ft 4in); length 12.12m (39ft 9in); height 3m (9ft 10in)
Armament:	five 7.7mm (.303in) Browning MGs; one 7.7mm (.303in) Vickers 'K' machine gun

OTHER PLAYERS TIMELINE

1935
1937

Bristol Beaufighter Mk IF

No 25 Squadron at North Weald began to replace its Blenheims with Beaufighter Mk Is in August 1940. Although initially painted in standard day camouflage, they acted as night fighters with early airborne radar. Beaufighters scored their first victory in November 1940.

SPECIFICATIONS	
Country of origin:	United Kingdom
Type:	two-seat fighter
Powerplant:	two 1500hp (1119kW) Bristol Hercules XI air-cooled engines
Performance:	maximum speed 492km/h (306mph); range 2414km (1500 miles); service ceiling 8810m (28,900ft)
Weights:	9435kg (21,100lb) loaded
Dimensions:	span 17.63m (57ft 10in); length 12.60m (41ft 4in); height 4.82m (15ft 10in)
Armament:	four 20mm (.78in) cannon; six 7.7mm (.303in) MGs

Fiat CR 42LW

The Italian contribution included Fiat's CR.42 and G.50 fighters and BR.20 bombers. Without oxygen, radios or instrument flying skills, the Italian fighter pilots were at a disadvantage from the beginning, despite the superior agility of their aircraft.

SPECIFICATIONS	
Country of origin:	Italy
Type:	single-seat fighter 1
Powerplant:	840hp (626kW) Fiat A74 14-cylinder radial engine
Performance:	maximum speed 438km/h (272mph); range 775km (482 miles); service ceiling 10,000m (33,000ft)
Weights:	2295kg (5060lb)
Dimensions:	span 8.7m (28ft 6in); length 8.26m (27ft 1in); height 3.58m (11ft 8in)
Armament:	two Breda Safat 12.7mm (.5in) MGs in wings

Fiat G.50bis

The open-cockpit Fiat G.50 with its two guns was something of an anachronism by 1940. It was barely faster than the biplane CR.42 and it played no significant part in the battle. This G.50bis was with 20° Gruppo, 51° Stormo, based at Ursel, Belgium, in late 1940.

SPECIFICATIONS	
Country of origin:	Italy
Type:	Single-seat fighter
Powerplant:	838hp (625kW) piston engine Fiat A.74 RC38 radial piston engine
Performance:	maximum speed 484km/h (301mph); range 980km (609 miles); service ceiling 9835m (32,258ft)
Weights:	empty 2077kg (4579lb); maximum 2706kg (5986lb)
Dimensions:	10.96m (35ft 11in); length 7.79m (25ft 7in); height 2.96m (9ft 9in); wing area 18.2 sq m (196 sq ft)
Armament:	two 12.7mm (.5in) Breda-SAFAT machine guns

1939

Battle over the Balkans

Italy began attacks on Albania in October 1940, prompting Greece to seek British help in defending its air space. Aware that Greek airfields could be used to attack Germany's oil fields in Romania, Hitler ordered his forces to attack Yugoslavia and Greece in April 1941. Within a month, both countries were defeated and British and Allied forces were concentrated on Crete. A massed German parachute assault forced a British retreat to North Africa, but not without heavy German losses.

PZL P.24F

Greece had three squadrons of Polish-built P.24F and P.24G fighters when German forces invaded. A refinement of the open-cockpit P.11, the P.24 was no match for the Luftwaffe's fighters and they were soon eliminated. This P.11F served with 22 Mira Dioxeos (Fighter Squadron).

SPECIFICATIONS	
Country of origin:	Greece
Type:	(PZL P.24F) single-seat fighter
Powerplant:	970hp (723kW) Gnome-Rhône 14N.07 14-cylinder radial piston engine
Performance:	maximum speed 430km/h (267mph); range 700km (435 miles); service ceiling 10,500m (34,450ft)
Weights:	empty 1332kg (2937lb); maximum 2000kg (4409lb)
Dimensions:	span 10.7m (32ft 11in); length 7.6m (24ft 11in); height 2.7m (35ft 1in); wing area 17.9 sq m (192.67 sq ft)
Armament:	four .303in (7.7mm) machine guns

Hawker Hurricane Mk I

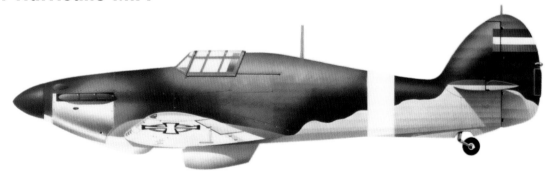

The Yugoslav Royal Air Force had some of the most modern aircraft in the Balkans theatre, with 24 Hurricanes bought from the United Kingdom and another 20 produced under licence by local firm Zmaj. Nonetheless, Belgrade fell to German forces in less than two weeks.

SPECIFICATIONS	
Country:	Yugoslavia
Type:	Single-seat fighter
Powerplant:	1030hp (768kW) Rolls-Royce Merlin II liquid-cooled V-12
Performance:	maximum speed 496km/h (308mph); range 845km (525 miles); service ceiling 10,180m (33,400ft)
Weights:	2820kg (6218lb) loaded
Dimensions:	span 12.19m (40ft); length 9.55m (31ft 4in); height 4.07m (13ft 4.5in)
Armament:	eight 7.7mm (.303in) Browning MGs

Messerschmitt Bf 110C

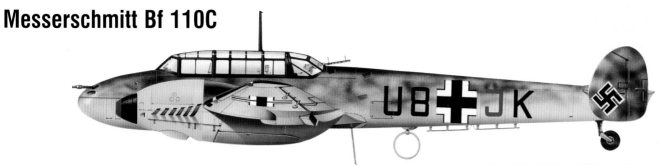

The long-range Bf 110 helped secure air superiority for the repeated parachute assaults on Crete's airfields. This Bf 110C-4 served with 2./ZG 26, which operated from Argos in Greece during the Cretan operation.

SPECIFICATIONS	
Country of origin:	Germany
Type:	single-seat fighter
Powerplant:	1200hp (895kW) DB 601N 12-cylinder inverted V
Performance:	maximum speed 570km/h (354mph); range 700km (435 miles);
	service ceiling 10,500m (34,450ft)
Weights:	2505kg (5523lb) maximum loaded
Dimensions:	span 9.87m (32ft 4in); length 8.64m (28ft 4in); height 2.28m (7ft 5.5in)
Armament:	one 20mm (.78in) cannon; four 7.92mm (.31in) MGs

Junkers Ju 87B-2

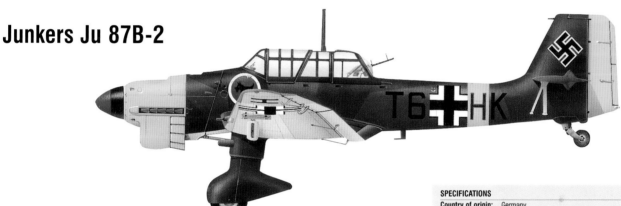

Two Gruppen of Stukageschwader 2 were assigned to Fliegerkorps VII to provide support to the Fallschirmjäger attacking Crete in May 1941. This aircraft is from the 1st Gruppe.

SPECIFICATIONS	
Country of origin:	Germany
Type:	two-seat fighter
Powerplant:	1200hp (895kW) Junkers Jumo 211
Performance:	maximum speed 350km/hr (217mph); range 600km (373 miles);
	service ceiling 8100m (26,570ft)
Weights:	maximum take-off weight 4400kg (9700lb)
Dimensions:	span 13.2m (43ft 3.7in); length 11m (36ft 1.1in); height 3.77m
	(12ft 4.4in)
Armament:	three 7.92mm (.31in) MGs; plus a single 1000kg (2205lb) bomb

Junkers Ju 52/3mg4e

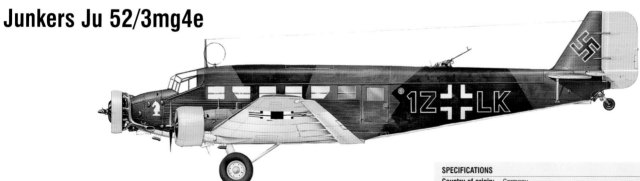

Carrying 16 paratroopers at a time, the Ju 52 squadrons based in mainland Greece made repeated missions to drop over 10,000 paratroopers and then land thousands more troops on Crete's airfields. Nearly 150 Ju 52s were lost and as many damaged during the assault.

SPECIFICATIONS	
Country of origin:	Germany
Type:	(Ju 52/3mg7e) three-seat transport with accommodation for 18 troops
Powerplant:	three 730hp (544kW) BMW 132T-2 nine-cylinder radial engines
Performance:	maximum speed 286km/h (178mph); range 1305km (811 miles);
	service ceiling 5900m (19,360ft)
Weights:	empty 6500kg (14,328lb); maximum take-off weight 11,030kg (24,317lb)
Dimensions:	span 29.20m (95ft 10in); length 18.90m (62ft); height 4.52m (14ft 10in)
Armament:	one 13mm (.5in) or 7.92mm (.31in) trainable rearward-firing machine
	gun in rear dorsal position; provision for 7.92mm (.31in) MG in forward
	dorsal and both beam positions

Finland's Winter War

On 30 November 1939, Soviet forces invaded Finland. The Finnish Air Force (Ilmavoimat) was small with few modern aircraft, but kept fighting with clever tactics. By dispersing their aircraft to frozen lakes and forest airstrips, and by using decoys, they avoided losing aircraft to attacks on airfields. New aircraft of many diverse types were quickly acquired, and captured aircraft were used against their former owners. In March 1941, Stalin abandoned the campaign against Finland.

Fokker C.X

The C.X was used as a dive bomber, reconnaissance aircraft and general utility aircraft by the Finns, who built 35 under licence. This C.X of LLv12 survived the Winter War, but ran out of fuel and crashed later in 1941.

SPECIFICATIONS	
Country of origin:	Germany
Type:	two-seat dive-bomber
Powerplant:	one 850hp (634kW) Bristol Pegasus XII nine-cylinder radial piston engine
Performance:	maximum speed 356km/h (211mph); range 841km (522 miles); service ceiling 8400m (27,560ft)
Dimensions:	span 12.00m (39ft 4.5in); length 9.1m (29ft 9in); height 3.30m (10ft 10in)
Weight:	empty 1400kg (3086lb); maximum 2900kg (6393lb)
Armament:	two 7.7mm and one 7.62mm machine guns; 400kg of bombs

Polikarpov I-16 Type 24

This I-16 Type 24 was on strength with the 4th IAP (fighter regiment) in the Lake Ladoga region near Leningrad during the Winter War. The later model I-16s could carry bombs or rockets for ground attack.

SPECIFICATIONS	
Country of origin:	USSR
Type:	(I-16 Type 24) single-seat fighter
Powerplant:	one 1000hp (746kW) Shvetsov M-62R 9-cylinder radial piston engine
Performance:	maximum speed 490km/h (304mph); range 600km (373 miles); service ceiling 9470m (31,070ft)
Dimensions:	span 8.9 m (29ft 6in); length 6.13m (20ft 1in); height 3.25m (10ft 1in); wing area 14.5 sq m (156.1 sq ft)
Weight:	empty 1475kg (3252lb); maximum 2060kg (4542lb)
Armament:	four 7.62mm (.3in) ShKAS machine guns; up to 200kg (440lb) of bombs or six RS-82 rockets

FINLAND TIMELINE

1933

1934

Brewster B-239 Buffalo

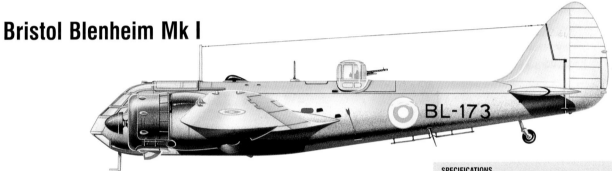

In US, Dutch and Commonwealth hands, the Buffalo gained a reputation as one of the worst fighters ever built, but the Finns had considerable success with the 'Brewster'. This Buffalo was flown by 13.5 victory ace Heimo Lampi at Tiiksjarvi.

SPECIFICATIONS	
Country of origin:	United States
Type:	single-seat fighter
Powerplant:	one 940hp (701kW) Wright R-1820-34 Cyclone 9 radial piston engine
Performance:	maximum speed 478km/h (297mph); range 1600km (1000 miles); service ceiling 10,100 m (33,000ft)
Dimensions:	span 10.7m (35ft); length 7.9m (26ft); height 3.63m (11ft 11in); wing area 19.41 sq m (208.9 sq ft)
Weights:	empty 1717kg (3875lb); loaded 2640kg (5820lb)
Armament:	four .5in machine guns

Bristol Blenheim Mk I

Finland had bought 41 Blenheims and had built another 15 by the time the war started. BL-173 was one of the 75 Mk Is eventually operated by Finland alongside 22 Mk IVs. Blenheims flew more than 400 missions in the Winter War.

SPECIFICATIONS	
Country of origin:	United Kingdom
Type:	(Blenheim Mk IV) three-crew bomber
Powerplant:	905hp (675kW) Bristol Mercury XV radial piston engines
Performance:	maximum speed 428km/hr (266 mph); range 2350km (1460 miles); service ceiling 8310m (27,260ft)
Dimensions:	span 17.17m (56ft 4in); length 12.98m (42ft 7in); height 3m (9ft 10in)
Weight:	6532kg (14,400lb)
Armament:	five 7.7mm (.303in) machine guns, up to 454kg (1000lb) of bombs internally and 145kg (320lb) externally

Tupolev SB-2

The SB-2, usually known as just the 'SB', was the most numerous bomber in Soviet service in 1940–41. The Soviet Union began the war with a bombing raid on Helsinki that killed over 90 people, the most destructive of the short war.

SPECIFICATIONS	
Country of origin:	USSR
Type:	(SB 2M-100) medium bomber
Powerplant:	two 860hp (641kW) Klimov M-100A V-12 piston engines
Performance:	maximum speed 423km/h (244mph); range 1250km (777 miles); service ceiling 9571m (31,400ft)
Dimensions:	span 20.33m (66ft 9in); length 20.33m (66ft 9in); height 3.25m (10ft 8in); wing area 56.67 sq m (610 sq ft)
Weights:	4060kg (8951lb); maximum 5628kg (12,407lb)
Armament:	four .3in ShKAS machine guns; up to 1322lb of bombs

1936

1937

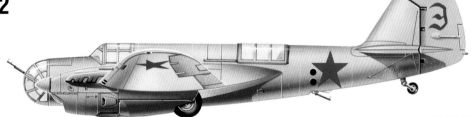

Fairey Swordfish

The Swordfish first flew in 1934, outlasted its successor and was still in production in 1945. In all, around 2300 were built for the Fleet Air Arm, RAF and RCAF by Fairey and Blackburn. The lumbering 'Stringbag' played a pivotal role in the destruction of the battleship *Bismarck* and destroyed the major surface units of the Italian fleet at Taranto. Fitted with Air to Surface Vessel (ASV) radar, the Swordfish protected convoys and hunted submarines from the smallest escort carriers.

Fairey Swordfish I Floatplane

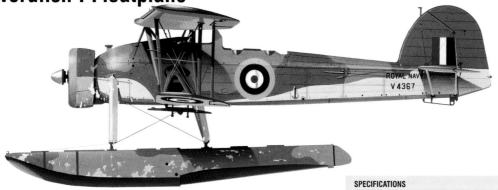

The Swordfish could be operated as a landplane or a floatplane. Before the war, two units were established to supply Swordfish for the Royal Navy's larger warships. This Mk I floatplane was assigned to No 701 Catapult Flight aboard the Battleship HMS *Malaya* in 1940. The main wartime version of the Swordfish was the Mk I, which served in some of the most famous actions of World War II, two of the most notable being the attack on the Italian fleet at Taranto in 1940.

SPECIFICATIONS	
Country of origin:	United Kingdom
Type:	Swordfish I (wheeled) 2-3-seat carrier-based torpedo bomber
Powerplant:	one 775hp (578kW) Bristol Pegasus IIIM.3 radial piston engine
Performance:	maximum speed 224km/h (139mph); service ceiling 3780m (12,400ft); range 1658km (1030 miles)
Weights:	empty 2132kg (4700lb); maximum 3946kg (8700lb)
Dimensions:	span 13.87m (45ft 6in); length 11.07m (36ft 1in); height 3.92m (12ft 11in); wing area 56.39 sq m (607 sq ft)
Armament:	two .303in (7.62mm) machine guns; one 726kg (1600lb) torpedo or up to 680kg (1500lb) of bombs

Fairey Swordfish Mk II

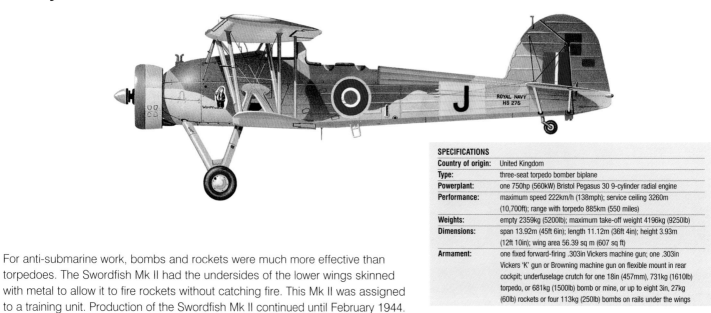

For anti-submarine work, bombs and rockets were much more effective than torpedoes. The Swordfish Mk II had the undersides of the lower wings skinned with metal to allow it to fire rockets without catching fire. This Mk II was assigned to a training unit. Production of the Swordfish Mk II continued until February 1944.

SPECIFICATIONS	
Country of origin:	United Kingdom
Type:	three-seat torpedo bomber biplane
Powerplant:	one 750hp (560kW) Bristol Pegasus 30 9-cylinder radial engine
Performance:	maximum speed 222km/h (138mph); service ceiling 3260m (10,700ft); range with torpedo 885km (550 miles)
Weights:	empty 2359kg (5200lb); maximum take-off weight 4196kg (9250lb)
Dimensions:	span 13.92m (45ft 6in); length 11.12m (36ft 4in); height 3.93m (12ft 10in); wing area 56.39 sq m (607 sq ft)
Armament:	one fixed forward-firing .303in Vickers machine gun; one .303in Vickers 'K' gun or Browning machine gun on flexible mount in rear cockpit; underfuselage crutch for one 18in (457mm), 731kg (1610lb) torpedo, or 681kg (1500lb) bomb or mine, or up to eight 3in, 27kg (60lb) rockets or four 113kg (250lb) bombs on rails under the wings

Fairey Swordfish Mk III

The Swordfish Mk III was equipped with ASV Mk X search radar in a pod between the undercarriage legs. This prevented the carriage of underfuselage stores, and so it became normal practice for Swordfish units to operate in packs, one Mk III in the search role, accompanied by Mk IIs carrying bombs and torpedoes. In all, 327 Mk IIIs were built.

SPECIFICATIONS	
Country of origin:	United Kingdom
Type:	three-seat anti-submarine biplane
Powerplant:	one 750hp (560kW) Bristol Pegasus 30 9-cylinder radial engine
Performance:	maximum speed 222km/h (138mph); service ceiling 3260m (10,700ft); range with torpedo 885km (550 miles)
Weights:	empty 2359kg (5200lb); maximum take-off weight 4196kg (9250lb)
Dimensions:	span 13.92m (45ft 6in); length 11.12m (36ft 4in); height 3.93m (12ft 10in); wing area 56.39 sq m (607 sq ft)
Armament:	one fixed forward-firing .303in Vickers machine gun; one .303in Vickers 'K' gun or Browning machine gun on flexible mount in rear cockpit; up to eight 3in 27kg (60lb) rockets or four 113kg (250lb) bombs on rails under wings

Fairey Swordfish Mk IV

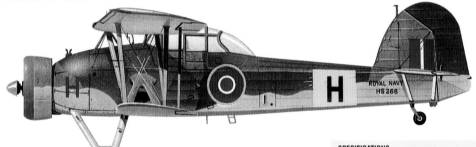

This 'Blackfish' was a Swordfish MK IV, the final version of the Swordfish, which had a rudimentary enclosed cockpit for winter operations. This modification was no doubt welcomed by the Swordfish crews, who were often called upon to mount patrols over the Atlantic. Most Mk IVs were used by training schools in Canada, like this one from No 1 Naval Air Gunnery School, Nova Scotia.

SPECIFICATIONS	
Country of origin:	United Kingdom
Type:	Swordfish IV 2-3 seat trainer/escort plane
Powerplant:	one 560hp (750W) Bristol Pegasus IIIM.3 radial piston engine
Performance:	maximum speed 222km/h (139mph); service ceiling 3260m (10,700ft); range 885km (550 miles)
Weights:	empty 2359kg (5200lb); maximum 4196kg (9250lb)
Dimensions:	span 13.92m (45ft 6in); length 11.12m (36ft 4in); height 3.93m (12ft 10in); wing area 56.39 sq m (607 sq ft)
Armament:	one .303in Vickers forward firing MG, one Browning machine gun in rear cockpit; bombload of four 113kg (250lb) under wings

Fairey Albacore

The Albacore was intended as the Swordfish's more refined successor, but was less agile and initially suffered from an unreliable engine. The Albacore failed to live up to expectations and the 'Stringbag' soldiered on. Until it was replaced in 1943 by the Fairey Barracuda, the Albacore was involved in sea and land actions in the Western Desert, the Arctic, the Mediterranean and the Indian Ocean.

SPECIFICATIONS	
Country of origin:	United Kingdom
Type:	three-seat torpedo bomber
Powerplant:	one 1130hp (843kW) Bristol Taurus XII 14-cylinder radial piston engine
Performance:	maximum speed 259km/h (161mph); service ceiling 6310m (20,700ft); range 1497km (930 miles)
Weights:	empty 3289kg (7250lb); maximum take-off weight 4745kg (10,460lb)
Dimensions:	span 15.24m (50ft); length 12.14m (39ft 10in); height 4.32m (14ft 2in); wing area 57.88 sq m (623 sq ft)
Armament:	one .303in Vickers MG in starboard wing, two .303in Vickers 'K' MGs in rear cockpit; one 730kg (1610lb) torpedo or 227kg (500lb) bombs

North Africa: Axis

Italy entered the war in late 1940 and the balance of power in the Mediterranean shifted against Britain. Italian colonial forces overran British Somaliland and threatened the Suez Canal. A decisive victory eluded them, however, and the Germans sent a fighter wing and then bombers to help the Italians, followed by the establishment of the Afrika Korps. By November 1941, there were 600 German and 1200 Italian first-line aircraft ranged against 1000 of the RAF and its allies.

BR.20M Cicogna

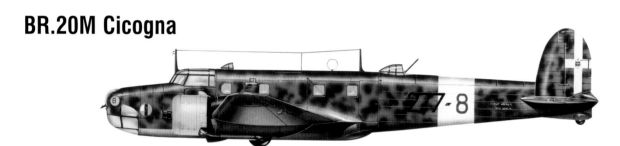

The BR.20M (M standing for Modificato, or modified) was the main version of the Fiat Cicogna (Stork) medium bomber in service in 1941. Although it had more armour and a stronger structure than the original BR.20, its performance remained the same because of aerodynamic refinements.

SPECIFICATIONS	
Country of origin:	Italy
Type:	(BR.20M) five-crew medium bomber
Powerplant:	two 1030hp (788kW) Fiat A.80 RC.41 radials piston engines
Performance:	maximum speed 343 km/h (267 mph); range 1329km (770 miles); service ceiling 7199m (23,620ft)
Dimensions:	span 21.56m (70ft 9in); length 17.4m (57ft 9in); height 4.75m (15ft 7in); wing area 74 sq m (796.56 sq ft)
Weight:	empty 6850kg (15,102lb); maximum 10,450kg (23,038lb)
Armament:	two .303in (7.7m) and one .5in (12.7mm) machine guns; up to 1600kg (3527lb) of bombs

Fieseler Storch

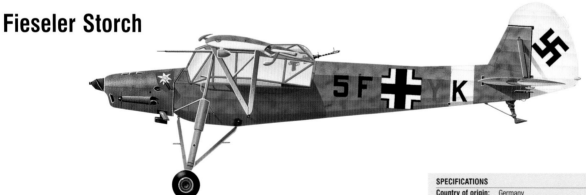

The Fieseler Fi.156 Storch (Stork) was found wherever Germany's land forces operated. With its low speed and large windows. it made an ideal observation platform, and with its extreme short landing capability it could deliver people and orders to any battlefield. This Fi.156C-3 was used by General Erwin Rommel in North Africa.

SPECIFICATIONS	
Country of origin:	Germany
Type:	three-seat liaison aircraft
Powerplant:	240hp (179kW) Argus As-10 eight-cylinder inverted V
Performance:	maximum speed 175km/h (109mph); range 467km (290 miles)
Dimensions:	span 14.25m (46ft 9in); length 9.9m (32ft 6in); height 3m (10ft)
Weight:	empty 1325kg (2921lb) normal loaded
Armament:	provision for one 7.92mm (.3in) machine gun

NORTH AFRICA TIMELINE

1935

1936

Messerschmitt Bf 109F-4Z/Trop

With a good balance of armour and armament, the Bf 109F was regarded as the nicest of the 109 series to fly. This Bf 109F-4Z/Trop variant was assigned to Hans-Arnold Stahlschmidt of 2./JG 27, who shot down 59 British and Commonwealth aircraft in more than 400 combat missions over the desert before going missing in action in September 1942.

SPECIFICATIONS	
Country of origin:	Germany
Type:	single-seat fighter
Powerplant:	1300hp (969kW) DB 601E
Performance:	maximum speed 628km/h (390mph); range 700km (435 miles); service ceiling 11,600m (38,000ft)
Dimensions:	span 9.92m (32ft 6.5in); length 8.85m (29ft 0.5in); height 2.59m (8ft 6in)
Weight:	2746kg (6054lb) max loaded
Armament:	1 x 20mm (.8in) cannon; 2 x 7.92mm (.3in) MGs

Junkers Ju 87B-2 Stuka

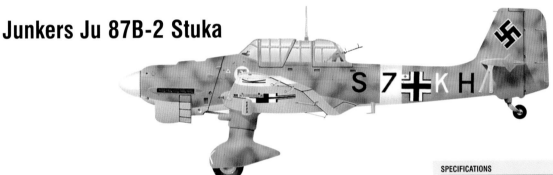

Wearing theatre markings of a white fuselage band and wingtips, this Ju 87B-2/Trop served with *Stukageschwader* 3 in early 1942. The Trop (tropicalized) versions of the Ju 87 had a sand/dust filter for the engine and a desert survival kit stowed in the fuselage. This Ju 87B-2 flew from a variety of front-line fields after the fall of Tobruk and during the German advance towards Egypt in 1942.

SPECIFICATIONS	
Country of origin:	Germany
Type:	two-seat fighter
Powerplant:	1200hp (895kW) Junkers Jumo 211
Performance:	maximum speed 350km/h (217mph); range 600km (373 miles); service ceiling 8100m (26,570ft)
Dimensions:	span 13.2m (43ft 3.7in); length 11m (36ft 1.1in); height 3.8m (12ft 4in)
Weight:	4400kg (9700lb) max take-off
Armament:	3 x 7.92mm (.3in) MGs plus a single 1000kg (2205lb) bomb

Messerschmitt Bf 110D-3

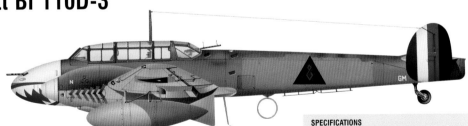

Iraqi nationalist leader Rashid Ali launched an uprising against the British in May 1941, supported by Germany. This Bf 110D-3 of ZG 76 was repainted in Iraqi markings for the assault on RAF Habbaniya. The Bf 110s quickly became unserviceable. due to poor-quality fuel and the harsh conditions.

SPECIFICATIONS	
Country of origin:	Germany
Type:	(Bf 110C-4) twin-engined long-range fighter
Powerplant:	two 1100hp (809kW) Daimler-Benz inverted V-12 piston engines
Performance:	maximum speed 560km/h (348mph); range 2410km (1500 miles); service ceiling 10,500m (35,000ft)
Dimensions:	span 16.3m (53ft 4in); length 12.3m (40ft 6in); height 3.3m (10ft 9in); wing area 38.8 sq m (414 sq ft)
Weight:	empty 4500kg (9900lb); maximum 6700kg (14,800lb)
Armament:	two 20mm MG FF/M cannon, four 7.92mm MG 17 and one 7.92mm MG 15 machine gun

North Africa: Allies

When Italy entered the war in late 1940, its forces in Africa were numerically superior and technically comparable with Britain's. The RAF presence was increased by several means, including shipping aircraft to West Africa and flying them on the Takoradi Route to the combat zone. The RAF and South African Air Force helped defeat Italy in East Africa before the Greek campaign.

Curtiss P-40 Tomahawk Mk IIB

Tomahawk Mk IIB was the designation that the Royal Air Force applied to the British-ordered version of the Hawk 81A-2, ordered by France but delivered to the United Kingdom after the fall of France, for service with the designation Tomahawk Mk IIA. This aircraft flew with No 112 Squadron, Western Desert Air Force, Sidi Haneich, October 1941.

SPECIFICATIONS	
Country of origin:	United States
Type:	single-seat fighter
Powerplant:	1150hp (860kW)
Performance:	maximum speed 580km/h (360mph); range 1100km (650 miles); service ceiling 8800m (29,000ft)
Dimensions:	span 11.38m (37ft 4in); length 9.66m (31ft 8in); height 3.76m (12ft 4in)
Weight:	3760kg (8280lb) loaded
Armament:	6 x 12.7mm (.5in) M2 Browning MGs in wings

Curtiss P-40 Kittyhawk Mk I

Like the closely related Tomahawk, the Kittyhawk was a member of the tactical fighter family known to the US Army Air Forces as the P-40. The type operated almost exclusively in the low-level fighter-bomber role, with weapons such as a 227kg (500lb) bomb under the fuselage. The aircraft pictured flew as part of No 112 Squadron, Western Desert Air Force in 1942.

SPECIFICATIONS	
Country of origin:	United States
Type:	single-seat low-level fighter bomber
Powerplant:	1200hp (895kW) Allison piston engine
Performance:	maximum speed 563km/h (350mph); range 1738km (1080 miles); service ceiling 9450m (31,000ft)
Dimensions:	span 11.36m (37ft 4in); length 10.16m (33ft 4in); height 3.76m (12ft 4in)
Weight:	3511kg (7740lb) loaded
Armament:	4 x 12.7mm (.5in) Browning MGs in wings; 227kg (500lb) bomb under fuselage

NORTH AFRICA TIMELINE
1935

Hawker Hurricane IIB

This Hurricane Mk IIB has visible desert equipment in the form of the duct under the nose for the Vokes air filter. It flew as part of No 73 Squadron in the Western Desert in 1942.

SPECIFICATIONS	
Country of origin:	United Kingdom
Type:	single-seat fighter
Powerplant:	1280hp (954kW) Rolls-Royce Merlin XX liquid-cooled V-12
Performance:	maximum speed 529km/h (329mph); range 1480km (920 miles); service ceiling 10,850m (35,600ft)
Dimensions:	span 12.19m (40ft 0in); length 9.81m (32ft 2.25in); height 3.98m (13ft 1in)
Weight:	about 3649kg (8044lb) loaded
Armament:	12 x 7.7mm (.303in) Browning MGs and up to 454kg (1000lb) of bombs

Martin Baltimore Mk V

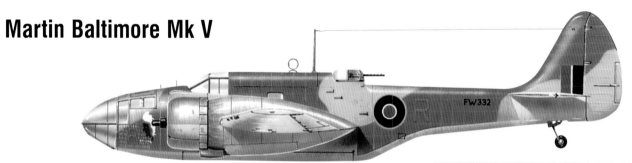

A development of the concept embodied in the Maryland, the Baltimore was designed to European standards. Production totalled 1575 aircraft – used mostly in the Mediterranean theatre – with a 907kg (2000lb) bomb load and up to 14 7.7mm (.303in) fixed and trainable machine guns. This aircraft flew as part of No 232 Wing in 1944.

SPECIFICATIONS	
Country of origin:	United States
Type:	four-crew attack-bomber
Powerplant:	2 x 1660hp (1238kW) Wright Cyclone radial piston engines
Performance:	maximum speed 486km/h (302mph); range 1529km (950 miles); service ceiling 7315m (24,000ft)
Dimensions:	span 18.59m (61ft 4in); length 14.78m (48ft 6in); height 5.41m (17ft 9in)
Weight:	6895kg (15,200lb) loaded
Armament:	14 x 7.7mm (.303in) machine guns; bomb load of 907kg (2000lb)

Bristol Blenheim Mk IV

The Free French Air Force (*Forces Aériennes Françaises Libres*, or FAFL) was equipped mainly with British and American aircraft. Blenheims of Groupe de Bombardement (GRB) 1 'Lorraine' supported Allied ground forces in North Africa. This Mk IV was based at Abu Sueir, Egypt in October 1941.

SPECIFICATIONS	
Country of origin:	United Kingdom
Type:	twin-engined light bomber
Powerplant:	two 920hp (690kW) Bristol Mercury XV radial piston engines
Performance:	maximum speed 428km/h (266mph); range 2351km (1460 miles); service ceiling 8310m (27,260ft)
Dimensions:	span 17.17m (56ft 4in); length 12.98m (42ft 7in); height 3.0m (9ft 10in); wing area 43.6 sq m (469 sq ft)
Weight:	empty 4450kg (9790lb); loaded 6545kg (14,400lb)
Armament:	three or four .303in machine guns; up to 598kg (1320lb) of bombs

1938

1941

Coastal Command

Formed in 1936 with a mix of hand-me-down aircraft, Coastal Command became increasingly important during the war as the threat from U-boats to Britain's trade grew. In 1939, there were no specialized anti-shipping or anti-submarine weapons in the RAF inventory. The development of depth charges and the introduction of long-range aircraft with radar helped clear the U-boats from British coastal waters and severely disrupted German merchant shipping.

Supermarine Stranraer

This aircraft flew as part of No 240 Squadron operating from Pembroke Dock, South Wales in 1940. The Stranraer flying boat remained in a general reconnaissance role until 1941.

SPECIFICATIONS

Country of origin:	United Kingdom
Type:	seven-crew flying boat
Powerplant:	2 x 920hp (686kW) Bristol Pegasus X 9 cylinder air-cooled radial engines
Performance:	maximum speed 241km/h (150mph); range 1609km (1000 miles); service ceiling 5640m (18,500ft)
Dimensions:	span 25.91m (85ft); length 16.71m (54ft 10in); height 6.63m (21ft 9in)
Weight:	8618kg (19,000lb) loaded
Armament:	3 x 7.7mm (.303in) MGs; up to 454kg (1000lb) of bombs, mines or depth charges

Avro Anson GR. Mk I

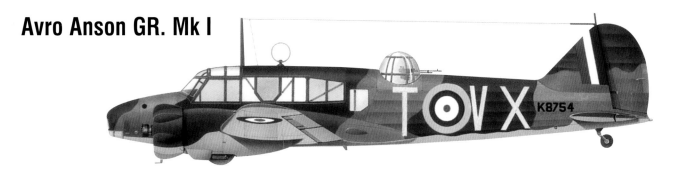

No 206 Squadron received this Anson in 1937, and flew it over the North Sea until 1940 before passing the aeroplane to No 1 Operational Training Unit. The machine crashed and was lost on 29 August 1940.

SPECIFICATIONS

Country of origin:	United Kingdom
Type:	twin-engine multi-role aircraft
Powerplant:	2 x 350hp (261kW) Armstrong Siddeley Cheetah IX radial piston engines
Performance:	maximum speed 303km/h (188mph); range 1271km (790 miles); service ceiling 5790m (19,000ft)
Dimensions:	span 17.2m (56ft 5in); length 12.88m (42ft 3in); height 3.99m (13ft 1in)
Weight:	3629kg (8000lb) loaded
Armament:	2 x 7.7mm (.303in) MGs; up to 163kg (360lb) of bombs

COASTAL COMMAND TIMELINE

 1934    1935    1936

Handley Page Hampden TB Mk I

A machine manufactured in Canada and operated in the torpedo-bomber role, this aeroplane flew anti-ship operations over the northern North Sea and Norwegian Sea in Coastal Command's standard finish of sea-grey upper surfaces and sky-blue under surfaces. It was part of No 489 Squadron, Royal New Zealand Air Force, RAF Coastal Command, based in Wick, Scotland, 1942.

SPECIFICATIONS	
Country of origin:	United Kingdom
Type:	four-crew torpedo-bomber
Powerplant:	2 x 1000hp (746kW) Bristol Pegasus XVII radial piston engines
Performance:	maximum speed 409km/h (254mph); range 3034km (1885 miles); service ceiling 5791m (19,000ft)
Dimensions:	span 21.08m (69ft 2in); length 16.33m (53ft 7in); height 4.55m (14ft 11in)
Weight:	8508kg (18,756lb) loaded
Armament:	2 x 7.7mm (.303in) forward-firing twin MGs in dorsal and ventral positions; up to 1814kg (4000lb) of bombs

Bristol Beaufort Mk I

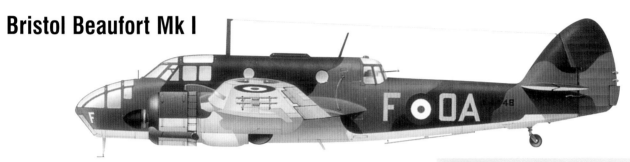

Initially based in the UK, No 22 Squadron and its Beaufort aircraft were shipped to Ceylon during March 1942. The squadron remained in the Far East for the rest of World War II, but transitioned to the Bristol Beaufighter during June 1944.

SPECIFICATIONS	
Country of origin:	United Kingdom
Type:	four-crew twin-engined torpedo-bomber
Powerplant:	2 x 1130hp (843kW) Bristol Taurus VI, XII or XVI radial piston engines
Performance:	maximum speed 418km/h (260mph); range 1666km (1035 miles); service ceiling 5030m (16,500ft)
Dimensions:	span 17.63m (57ft 10in); length 13.59m (44ft 7in); height 13.59m (44ft 7in)
Weight:	9630kg (21,230lb) loaded
Armament:	4 x 7.7mm (.303in) MGs (two each in nose and dorsal turrets) and, in some aircraft, three additional 7.7mm (.303in) MGs (one in blister beneath the nose and two in beam positions); up to 1680kg (1500lb) of bombs or mines, or 1 x 728kg (1605lb) torpedo

Lockheed Hudson GR. Mk III

Developed from an American civil transport (the Lockheed Model 14) to meet a British requirement for a successor to the Avro Anson, the Hudson proved notably successful in the shorter-range coastal and maritime reconnaissance roles. The aircraft pictured flew with No 233 Squadron, RAF Coastal Command, based at Aldergrove and St Eval in 1942.

SPECIFICATIONS	
Country of origin:	United Kingdom
Type:	six-crew coastal reconnaissance
Powerplant:	2 x 1200hp (890kW) Wright Cyclone 9-cylinder radial engines
Performance:	maximum speed 397km/h (246mph); range 3150km (1960 miles); service ceiling 7470m (24,500ft)
Dimensions:	span 19.96m (65ft 4in); length 13.50m (44ft 4in); height 3.62m (11ft 10in)
Weight:	7930kg (17,500lb) loaded
Armament:	7 x 7.7mm (.303in) Browning MGs (two in nose, two in dorsal turret, two in beam and one ventral); 340kg (750lb) of bombs or depth charges

1938

Coastal Command Part Two

Arthur Harris, the commander of Bomber Command, was reluctant to let any resources, particularly four-engined bombers, be allocated to Coastal Command instead of his campaign against German cities. In 1942, B-17E Flying Fortresses – a type rejected for daylight bombing raids by Bomber Command – were made available to Coastal Command, followed by B-24s. These so-called Very Long Range Liberators closed the Atlantic Gap and kept U-boats at bay.

Lockheed Hudson GR. Mk IV

During August 1941, RAF Coastal Command introduced a revised colour scheme for its aircraft: the upper surfaces remained dark green and ocean grey, but the under surfaces were gloss white and the vertical surface matt white.

SPECIFICATIONS

Country of origin:	United Kingdom
Type:	five-crew reconnaissance aircraft
Powerplant:	2 x 1200hp (895kW) Pratt & Whitney Twin Wasp radial piston engines
Performance:	maximum speed 420km/h (261mph); range 3476km (2160 miles); service ceiling 8230m (27,000ft)
Dimensions:	span 19.96m (65ft 6in); length 13.51m (44ft 4in); height 3.63m (11ft 11in)
Weight:	8391kg (18,500lb) loaded
Armament:	2 x 7.7mm (.303in) MGs in fixed forward and dorsal turret; 1 x 7.7mm (.303n) MG in ventral position; option of 2 x 7.7mm (.303in) MGs in beam positions; up to 454kg (1000lb) of bombs or underwing rockets

Short Sunderland Mk III

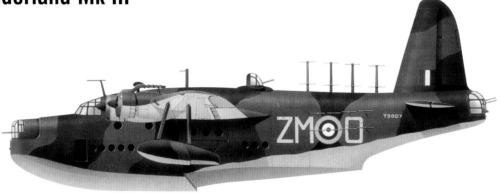

Remaining in service to 1944, this flying boat carries the early type of over-fuselage antennae associated with air-to-surface search radar. Operating from No 201 Squadron, RAF Coastal Command, Castle Archdale, Co Fermanagh, Northern Ireland, in 1941, the squadron's aircraft could range deep into the Atlantic Ocean.

SPECIFICATIONS

Country of origin:	United Kingdom
Type:	10 crew flying boat
Powerplant:	4x 1010hp (753kW) Bristol Pegasus XXII 9 cylinder single-row radial engines
Performance:	maximum speed 336km/h (209mph); range 4023km (2500 miles); service ceiling 4570m (15,000ft)
Dimensions:	span 34.38m (11ft 9.5in); length 26m (85ft 3.5in); height 10.52m (34ft 6in)
Weight:	22,226kg (49,000lb) loaded
Armament:	8 x 7.7mm (.303in) MGs; internal bomb, depth charge and mine load of 907kg (2000lb)

Consolidated Coronado GR. Mk I

The RAF received 10 examples of the Coronado flying boat, with this aircraft flying from RAF Coastal Command, Beaumaris, in 1943. However, they found the type unsuitable for a long-range reconnaissance/anti-submarine role, and passed the aircraft to No 231 Squadron of No 45 Group, based at Boucherville, Toronto, as transports with accommodation for VIPs and 44 passengers.

SPECIFICATIONS	
Country of origin:	United States
Type:	nine-crew heavy bomber
Powerplant:	4 x 1200hp (895kW) Pratt & Whitney Twin Wasp radial piston engines
Performance:	maximum speed 359km/h (223mph); range 3814km (2370 miles); service ceiling 6250m (20,500ft)
Dimensions:	span 35.05m (115ft); length 24.16m (79ft 3in); height 8.38m (27ft 6in)
Weight:	30,844kg (68,000lb) loaded
Armament:	2 x 12.7mm (.5in) MGs in bow, dorsal and tail turrets, and 1 x 12.7mm (.5in) machine gun in two beam positions; up to 5443kg (12,000lb) of bombs, depth charges or torpedoes

Consolidated Liberator GR. Mk I

This aircraft flew as part of No 120 Squadron, Aldergrove, Northern Ireland, in 1942. The Liberator's long range made it a natural choice for the maritime role, and this machine carries ASV Mk II air-to-surface search radar as well as a ventral pack with four 20mm (.79in) cannon for additional anti-submarine punch.

SPECIFICATIONS	
Country of origin:	United Kingdom
Type:	10-crew heavy bomber
Powerplant:	4 x 1200hp (895kW) Pratt & Whitney Twin wasp radial piston engines
Performance:	maximum speed 488km/h (303mph); range 1730km (1080 miles); service ceiling 8540m (28,000ft)
Dimensions:	span 33.53m (110ft); length 20.22m (66ft 4in); height 5.49m (18ft)
Weight:	32,296kg (71,200lb) loaded
Armament:	4 x 20mm (.79in) in ventral position, plus 2 x 12.7mm (.5in) guns each in dorsal, tail and retractable ball turrets; up to 3629kg (8000lb) of bombs

Boeing Fortress Mk IIA

A development of the USAAF's B-17F Flying Fortress heavy bomber for British service, the Fortress Mk II was deemed unsuitable for RAF Bomber Command and passed to RAF Coastal Command for the very-long-range maritime role.

SPECIFICATIONS	
Country of origin:	United States
Type:	eight-crew long range maritime bomber
Powerplant:	4 x 1200hp (894kW) Wright Cyclone air-cooled radial piston engines
Performance:	maximum speed 480km/h (298mph); range 1835km (1140 miles); service ceiling 10,363m (34,000ft)
Dimensions:	span 31.62m (103ft 9in); length 22.5m (73ft 10in); height 5.84m (19ft 2in)
Weight:	12,542kg (27,650lb) loaded
Armament:	10 x 12.7mm (.5in) MGs in nose, dorsal, ventral, tail and beam; normal bomb load of up to 2722kg (6000lb) of bombs and/or depth charges

1938

1941

Operation Barbarossa

On 22 June 1941, Hitler launched the invasion of the Soviet Union under the codename Operation Barbarossa. The invasion came as a complete surprise to Stalin, whose purges of the Red Army officer corps had robbed the high command of good intelligence. With the VVS (*Voenno-Vosdushniye Sili* – Soviet Air Force) on a peacetime footing, their aircraft were not dispersed and were destroyed in great numbers on the ground. Most aircraft were obsolete with inadequate radios, if any.

Polikarpov I-16 Type 24

The I-16 was very tricky to fly as a result of its short and tubby fuselage, and nearly all pilots preferred an open cockpit.

SPECIFICATIONS

Country of origin:	USSR
Type:	single-seat monoplane fighter
Powerplant:	1100hp (820kW) M-63 radial piston engine
Performance:	maximum speed 2490km/h (304mph); range 600km (373 miles); service ceiling 9470m (31,070ft)
Dimensions:	span 8.88m (29ft 2in); length 6.04m (19ft 10in); weight 2060kg (4542lb) loaded
Armament:	4 x 7.62mm (3in) ShKAS MGs (sometimes 2 x 20mm [.8in] replacing 2 x ShKAS MGs in wings); up to 200kg (441lb) bomb load

Polikarpov I-153

The I-153 was first flown in 1938 as an attempt to modernise the I-15bis by reducing drag. The aircraft was flown with some degree of success by experienced pilots, but in the hands of less experienced aviators it could be a handful.

SPECIFICATIONS

Country of origin:	USSR
Type:	single-seat fighter and fighter-bomber
Powerplant:	one 1000hp (746kW) Shvetsov M-62 nine-cylinder single-row radial engine
Performance:	maximum speed 444km/h (276mph); climb to 300m (9845ft) in three minutes; range 880km (547 miles); service ceiling 10,700m (35,105ft)
Dimensions:	span 10m (32ft 9.5in); length 6.17m (20ft 2.9in); weight 1348kg (2972lb) empty, 2110kg (4652lb) max. take-off
Armament:	4 x 12.7mm fixed forward-firing machine guns in the forward fuselage, plus an external bomb and racket load of 200g (441lb)

BARBAROSSA TIMELINE

1933　　　　　1935　　　　　1937

Hawker Hurricane Mk IIB

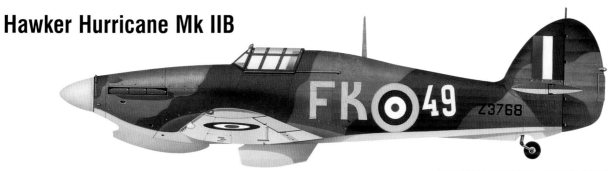

In response to a call for British assistance, a wing of Hurricane IIBs was sent by sea to Murmansk in August 1941. No 151 Wing, consisting of 81 and 134 Squadrons, flew missions and trained Soviet personnel before handing its aircraft over, the first of over 3000 Hurricanes eventually supplied to the Soviet Union.

SPECIFICATIONS	
Country of origin:	United Kingdom
Type:	single-seat fighter
Powerplant:	91280hp (54kW) Rolls-Royce Merlin XX liquid-cooled V-12
Performance:	maximum speed 529km/h (329mph); range 1480km (920 miles); service ceiling 10,850m (35,600ft)
Dimensions:	span 12.19m (40ft); length 9.81m (32ft 2.25in); height 3.98m (13ft 1in)
Weight:	3629kg (8044lb) loaded
Armament:	8 x 7.7mm (.303in) Browning MGs

Sukhoi Su-2

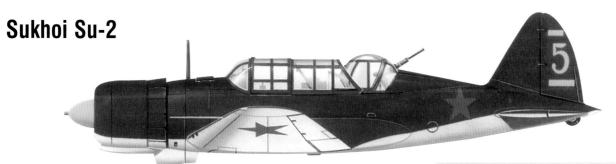

Designed as a light reconnaissance bomber with ground-attack capability, the Su-2 was built to the extent of 500 or slightly more aircraft in 1940–42. Early operational experience against German fighters revealed that the Su-2 lacked the performance, agility, armament and protection for battlefield survival.

SPECIFICATIONS	
Country of origin:	USSR
Type:	two-seat reconnaissance bomber
Powerplant:	1 x 1520hp (1134kW)
Performance:	maximum speed 486km/h (302mph); range 1100km (683 miles); service ceiling 8800m (28,870ft)
Dimensions:	span 14.30m (46ft 11in); length 10.46m (34ft 4in); height 3.80m (12ft 6in)
Weight:	3273kg (7216lb) loaded
Armament:	4 x 7.62mm (.3in) fixed wing MGs and 1 x 7.62mm (.3in) MG in dorsal turret; 400kg (880lb) of bombs

Mikoyan-Gurevich MiG-3

'Za Stalina' (For Stalin) was a common legend on Soviet aircraft of the period. The aircraft pictured was part of the 34th IAP (Fighter Aviation Regiment) in the 6th IAK (Fighter Aviation Corps), in Moscow, winter 1941–42.

SPECIFICATIONS	
Country of origin:	USSR
Type:	single-seat fighter
Powerplant:	1350hp (1007kW) Mikuli AM-35A V12 piston engine
Performance:	maximum speed 640km/h (398mph); range 1195km (743 miles); service ceiling 12,000m (39,370ft)
Dimensions:	span 10.20m (33ft 6in); length 8.26m (27ft 1in); height 3.50m (11ft 6in)
Weight:	3350kg (7385lb) loaded
Armament:	1 x 12.7mm (.5in) Beresin and 2 x 7.62mm (.3in) ShKAS MGs; up to 200kg (441lb) bomb load or 6 x RS-82 rockets on underwing racks

1938

1940

Operation Barbarossa Part Two

With air superiority at least temporarily won, the Luftwaffe could concentrate on supporting the army with ground attack, observation and reconnaissance and transport units. The Luftwaffe fielded 4389 aircraft against the Soviet Union in the opening days of Operation Barbarossa, and lost over 2000 of them by December when the campaign came to a halt outside Moscow.

Henschel Hs 123A-1

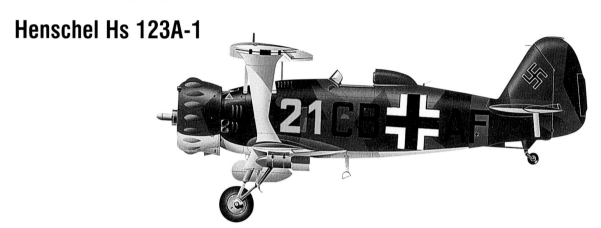

Although relegated to a training role before the invasion of Russia, the obsolescent Hs 123 was returned to combat use to try to meet the demands of the operational close-support units serving on the Eastern Front.

SPECIFICATIONS

Country of origin:	Germany
Type:	single-seat close-support biplane
Powerplant:	880hp (656kW) BMW 132Dc nine-cylinder radial
Performance:	maximum speed 341km/hr (212mph); range 860km (534 miles); service ceiling 9000m (29,525ft)
Dimensions:	span 10.5m (34ft 5.5in); length 8.33m (27ft 4in); height 3.22m (10ft 7in)
Weight:	2217kg (4888lb) loaded
Armament:	2 x 7.92mm (.3in) MGs; racks for 4 x 50kg (110lb) bombs, bomblets or 20mm (.8in) cannon pods

Focke-Wulf Fw 189A-1

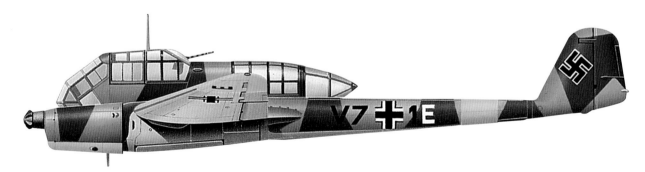

Bearing the brown and green splinter camouflage more common over the forested terrain of the northern sector of the Eastern Front, this Fw 189 Eule (Owl) flew out of a base at Kemi in Finland.

SPECIFICATIONS

Country of origin:	Germany
Type:	three-seat, twin-boom reconnaissance aircraft
Powerplant:	2 x 465hp (347kW) Argus As 410
Performance:	maximum speed 350km/hr (217mph); range 670km (416 miles); service ceiling 7300m (23,950ft)
Dimensions:	span 18.4m (60ft 4in); length 12.03m (39ft 5in); height 3.1m (10ft 2in)
Weight:	4170kg (9193lb) max. loaded
Armament:	4 x 7.92mm (.3in) MGs; 4 x 50kg (110lb) bombs

BARBAROSSA TIMELINE

1934 1935

Dornier Do 17Z-2

This Dornier Do 17, which was flown as part of a German Luftwaffe unit by volunteers from Croatia, was operating out of Vitebsk at the end of 1941. Early operations by these volunteer formations were not successful.

SPECIFICATIONS	
Country of origin:	Germany
Type:	four-seat light bomber
Powerplant:	2 x 1000hp (746kW) Bramo 323P Fafnir nine-cylinder radials
Performance:	maximum speed 425km/h (263mph); range 1160km (721 miles) with light load; service ceiling 8150m (26,740ft)
Dimensions:	span 18m (59ft); length 15.79m (51ft 9in); height 4.56m (14ft 11.5in)
Weight:	9000kg (19,841lb) loaded
Armament:	6 x 7.92mm (.3in) MGs; 1000kg (2205lb) bombload

Heinkel He 111H-8/R-2

One of a number of glider-towing variants of the He 111, this aircraft was based at Pskov-South in the northern sector early in 1942. After Crete, the Luftwaffe rarely used gliders in assaults or as anything but non-combat transports.

SPECIFICATIONS	
Country of origin:	Germany
Type:	four-five seat medium bomber
Powerplant:	2 x 1200hp (895kW) Junkers Jumo 211D 12-cylinder
Performance:	maximum speed 415km/hr (258mph); range 1200km (745 miles) with max. load; service ceiling 7800m (25,590ft)
Dimensions:	span 22.6m (74ft 2in); length 16.4m (53ft 9.5in); height 4m (13ft 1.5in)
Weight:	14,000kg max. loaded
Armament:	up to 7 x MGs; 1 x 20mm (.8in) cannon could be fitted to ventral gondola

Messerschmitt Bf 109 F-2

This Bf 109F was in operation on the northern sector of the Eastern Front during the fighting around Leningrad early in 1942. The winter camouflage was produced by overpainting large areas with white distemper.

SPECIFICATIONS	
Country of origin:	Germany
Type:	single-seat fighter
Powerplant:	1300hp (969kW) DB 601E
Performamce:	maximum speed 628km/hr (390mph); range 700km (435 miles); service ceiling 11,600m (38,000ft)
Dimensions:	span 9.92m (32ft 6.5in); length 8.85m (29ft 0.5in); height 2.59m (8ft 6in)
Weight:	2746kg (6054lb) max loaded
Armament:	1 x 20mm (.8in) cannon; 2 x 7.92mm (.3in) MGs

1938

Junkers Ju 52

The Junkers company pioneered a type of corrugated-skin metal construction for aircraft that was almost exclusively used by their aircraft. Although it had a high strength-to-weight ratio, it was high drag and suitable only for roles such as transport, where speed was not essential. The 'Tante Ju' (Auntie Ju), or Ju 52/3m, was a trimotor version of the single-engined Ju 52 first flown in 1930. Also built post-war in Spain and France, three Ju 52/3ms remained in Swiss service until 1982.

Junkers Ju 52/3mg4e

Pending deliveries of purpose-built bomber designs, the new Luftwaffe adapted the Ju 52 for bombing, with its passenger compartment filled with bomb racks. A gun position was added in a precarious 'dustbin' turret. This Ju 52/3m3ge saw action with the Spanish Nationalists in 1938.

SPECIFICATIONS	
Country of origin:	Germany
Type:	three-engined bomber
Powerplant:	three 748hp (558kW) BMW 132A nine-cylinder radial piston engines
Performance:	Maximum speed: 265 km/h (165 miles); range: 1100 km (684 miles); range 1305km (811 miles)
Weights:	empty unknown; loaded 9,500 kg (20,943 lb)
Dimensions:	span 29.20m (95ft 10in); length 18.90m (62ft); height 4.52m (14ft 10in)
Armament:	one 7.92mm machine gun in dorsal position and one 7.92mm machine gun in ventral 'dustbin' turret; up to 32 50kg (110lb) bombs in modified cabin

Junkers Ju 52/3mg6e

From 1941, the Ju 52 was produced with the more powerful BMW 132T-2 engine. It was still slow and vulnerable, however, and some – like this Ju 52/3m6ge sub-variant serving in the Mediterranean in 1942 – were fitted with an additional gun position.

SPECIFICATIONS	
Country of origin:	Germany
Type:	three-engined bomber
Powerplant:	three 830hp (619kW) BMW 132T-2 nine-cylinder radial piston engines
Performance:	Maximum speed: 265 km/h (165 miles); range: 1100 km (684 miles); range 1305km (811 miles)
Weights:	empty unknown; loaded 9500 kg (20,943 lb)
Dimensions:	span 29.20m (95ft 10in); length 18.90m (62ft); height 4.52m (14ft 10in)
Armament:	one 7.92mm machine gun in dorsal position and one 7.92mm machine gun in mount above cockpit

Junkers Ju 52/3mg6e

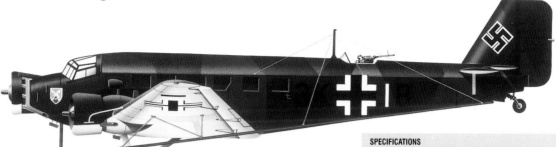

SPECIFICATIONS	
Country of origin:	Germany
Type:	three-engined anti-mine aircraft
Powerplant:	three 730hp (544kW) BMW 132T-2 nine-cylinder radial engines
Performance:	maximum speed 286km/h (178mph); service ceiling 5900m (19,360ft); range 1305km (811 miles)
Weights:	empty 6500kg (14,328lb); maximum take-off weight 11,030kg (24,317lb)
Dimensions:	span 29.20m (95ft 10in); length 18.90m (62ft); height 4.52m (14ft 10in)
Armament:	one 13mm or 7.92mm trainable rearward-firing machine gun in rear dorsal position, provision for one 7.92mm trainable machine gun in forward dorsal position, and one 7.92mm trainable lateral-firing machine gun in each of the two beam positions

Magnetically triggered sea mines were among the biggest threats to shipping. One counter was to fly over a mined area while generating a magnetic field to trigger them. Fitted with a huge charged duralumin hoop, the Ju 52 was ideal for this work. The RAF also fitted Wellingtons with a similar system.

Junkers Ju 52/3mg4e

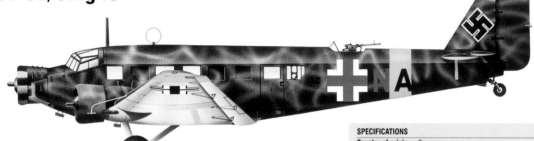

SPECIFICATIONS	
Country of origin:	Germany
Type:	(Ju 52/3m g7e) three-seat transport with accommodation for 18 troops, or 12 litters, or freight
Powerplant:	three 730hp (544kW) BMW 132T-2 nine-cylinder radial engines
Performance:	maximum speed 286km/h (178mph); climb to 3000m (9845ft) in 17 minutes 30 seconds; service ceiling 5900m (19,360ft); range 1305km (811 miles)
Weights:	empty 6500kg (14,328lb); maximum take-off 11,030kg (24,317lb)
Dimensions:	span 29.20m (95ft 10in); length 18.90m (62ft); height 4.52m (14ft 10in)
Armament:	one 13mm or 7.92mm trainable rearward-firing machine gun in rear dorsal position, provision for one 7.92mm trainable machine gun in forward dorsal position, and one 7.92mm trainable lateral-firing machine gun in each of the two beam positions

The Ju 52/3m served initially as a bomber as well as transport, but in World War II was a transport and airborne forces aeroplane that saw operational use in every German theatre right up to May 1945.

Amiot AAC.1

SPECIFICATIONS	
Country of origin:	France
Type:	(Ju 52/3m g7e) three-seat transport with accommodation for 18 troops, or 12 litters, or freight
Powerplant:	three 730hp (544kW) BMW 132T-2 nine-cylinder radial engines
Performance:	maximum speed 286km/h (178mph); climb to 3000m (9845ft) in 17 minutes 30 seconds; service ceiling 5900m (19,360ft); range 1305km (811 miles)
Weights:	empty 6500kg (14,328lb); maximum take-off 11,030kg (24,317lb)
Dimensions:	span 29.20m (95ft 10in); length 18.90m (62ft); height 4.52m (14ft 10in)
Armament:	none

The Amiot factory in France turned out Ju 52s for the Luftwaffe until 1944. After the war, production continued under the designation AAC.1 Toucan for the Armée de l'Air and amounted to 415 aircraft. Spain also built 170 as the CASA 352. Most surviving aircraft are from Spanish production.

Continuation War

Although not part of the Nazi orbit, Finland received help from Germany when the Soviet Union attacked again in June 1941, and allowed German bases and operations from its soil. This helped it recover much of the territory ceded to Moscow in 1940. In the period called the Interim Peace, the Ilmavoimat had built up its strength with aircraft from a variety of sources. It supplemented these with captured aircraft supplied by Germany. The short Lapland War of 1944–45 saw Finland chase out its former German allies.

Polikarpov I-15

The Finns made great use of aircraft captured from the Soviets, either directly or supplied via Germany. Five of the elderly fixed-gear Polikarpov I-15 fighters were captured during the Winter War and put into Ilmavoimat service then or during the Interim Peace.

SPECIFICATIONS	
Country of origin:	USSR
Type:	single-seat biplane fighter
Powerplant:	one 473hp (353kW) M-22 radial piston engine
Maximum speed:	350km/h (220mph); range 500km (310 miles); service ceiling 7250m (23,800ft)
Dimensions:	span 9.75m (32ft 0in); length 6.10m (20ft); height 2.20m (7ft 3in); wing area 21.9 sq m (236 sq ft)
Weight:	empty 1012kg (2226lb); maximum 1415kg (3113lb)
Armament:	two 12.7mm BS machine guns; up to 100kg (220lb) bombs or six RS-82 rockets

MS.406 Mörkö Morane

Finland supplemented its French-supplied Morane-Saulnier MS.406 fighters with examples from Germany, which also provided a stock of Russian Klimov M-105 engines. These the Finns fitted to 41 MS.406s, creating the Mörkö-Morane. The type remained in service until 1948; this one wears post-1945 markings.

SPECIFICATIONS	
Country of origin:	France
Type:	single-seat fighter
Powerplant:	one 1100hp (820kW) Klimov M-105PP V-12 piston engine
Performance:	maximum speed 510km/h (317mph); range 840km (522 miles); service ceiling 8500m (27,887ft)
Dimensions:	span 10.62m (34ft 10in); length 8.17m (26ft 10in); height 3.26m (10ft 8in); wing area 17 sq m (183 sq ft)
Weight:	empty 1940kg (4277lb); maximum 2750kg (6063lb)
Armament:	one 20mm Mauser MG 151 cannon and two 7.5mm MAC 1934 machine guns

CONTINUATION WAR TIMELINE

 1933   1934   1935

Petlyakov Pe-2 'Buck'

The Petlyakov Pe-2 was a sophisticated light bomber and one of the best early-war Soviet aircraft. Finland acquired seven Pe-2s from German stocks between 1941–44 and flew them against their former owners. Of this handful of aircraft, four were lost on operations.

SPECIFICATIONS	
Country of origin:	USSR
Type:	three-seat light bomber
Powerplant:	two 1210hp (903kW) Klimov M-105PF piston engines
Performance:	maximum speed 580km/h (360mph); range 1160km (721 miles); service ceiling 8800m (28,870ft)
Dimensions:	span 17.16m (56ft 3in); length 12.66m (41ft 6in); height 3.5m (11ft 6in); wing area 40.5 sq m (436 sq ft)
Weight:	empty 5875kg (12,952lb); loaded 7563kg (16,639lb)
Armament:	four 7.62mm ShKAS machine guns; 1600kg (3520lb) of bombs

Dornier Do 17Z-3

A squadron of Dornier Do 17Z bombers was supplied to Finland in January 1942. Do 17Z-3 DN-58 of PLeLv43 was used in the photographic reconnaissance role, survived the war and served into the 1950s on mapping duties.

SPECIFICATIONS	
Country of origin:	Germany
Type:	four-seat light bomber
Powerplant:	2 x 1000hp (746kW) Bramo 323P Fafnir nine-cylinder radials
Performance:	maximum speed 425km/h (263mph); range 1160km (721 miles) with light load; service ceiling 8150m (26,740ft)
Dimensions:	span 18m (59ft); length 15.79m (51ft 9in); height 4.56m (14ft 11.5in)
Weight:	9000kg (19,841lb) loaded
Armament:	6 x 7.92mm (.3in) MGs; 1000kg (2205lb) bombload

Junkers Ju 88

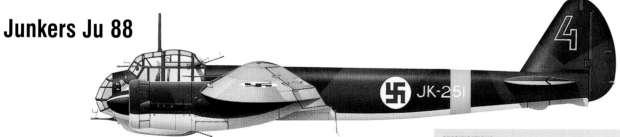

In April 1943, Finland took delivery of 24 Ju 88A-4s. The bombers flew over 550 missions in the Continuation War and 115 in the Lapland War, losing only three of their number on operations, although another crashed in Latvia on its delivery flight to Finland.

SPECIFICATIONS	
Country of origin:	Germany
Type:	four-seat high speed, level and dive bomber
Powerplant:	two 340hp (1000kW) Junkers Jumo 12 cylinder inverted V
Performance:	maximum speed 433km/hr (269mph); range 700km (435 miles); service ceiling 10,500m (34,450ft)
Dimensions:	span 20.13m (65ft 10in); length 14.4m (47ft 2in); height 4.85m (15ft 11in)
Weight:	14,000kg (30,865lb) max. loaded
Armament:	up to eight 7.92mm (.3in) MGs, 500kg (1102lb) internal bombload, external racks to maximum bombload of 3000kg (6615lb)

1939

Night Blitz

Although the Battle of Britain officially ended in late October 1940, the heaviest period of air attacks on Britain was just beginning. Night raids on industrial targets within cities had begun in August. During one of these, bombs were mistakenly dropped on London, an event followed by an RAF retaliatory raid on Berlin. Outraged, Hitler ordered all-out attacks on London and other cities. Over 40,000 civilians had died by the time the Luftwaffe turned its attention to Barbarossa in May 1941.

Heinkel He 111H-3

The Luftwaffe used the intersection of radio beams to navigate to a target. Specially equipped He 111s of KG 100 like this one were used as pathfinders to lead other bombers to cities like Coventry, which was largely destroyed in raids in late 1940 and early 1941.

SPECIFICATIONS	
Country of origin:	Germany
Type:	five-crew medium bomber
Powerplant:	two 1200hp (894kW) Junkers Jumo 211D-1 inverted V-12 piston engines
Performance:	maximum speed 435km/h (270mph); range 2000km (1243 miles); service ceiling 6500 m (21,340 ft)
Weights:	empty 7720kg (17,000lb); maximum 14,000kg (30,865lb)
Dimensions:	span 22.6m (74ft 6in); length 16.6m (54ft 6in); height 4m (13ft 1in); wing area 87.6 sq m (943 sq ft)
Armament:	four 7.92mm (.31in) MG 15 machine guns; one 20mm (.78in) cannon; up to 2000kg (4410lb) of bombs

Dornier Do 17Z-10

The last Do 17s off the production line were converted to night fighters and intruders under the designation Do 17Z-10 Kauz II (Screeching Owl). Based at Gilze-Rijen in the Netherlands, this aircraft of 2./NJG 2 flew intruder missions over British airfields in 1941.

SPECIFICATIONS	
Country of origin:	Germany
Type:	twin-engined night fighter
Powerplant:	two 1200hp (895kW) BMW-Bramo Fafnir 323R-2 radial piston engines
Performance:	maximum speed 425km/h (264mph); range 3000km (1864 miles); service ceiling 8050m (26,410ft)
Dimensions:	span 17.99m (59ft); length 16.25m (53ft 4in); height 4.56m (15ft); wing area 55 sq m (592 sq ft)
Weight:	(approx) empty 5962kg (13,145lb); maximum 8590kg (18,937lb)
Armament:	six 7.62mm MG 17, two 20mm cannon

Boulton Paul Defiant Mk II

Although a failure as a day fighter, the Defiant had considerably more success at night. The Defiant II had a larger fin and more powerful Merlin engine, but most importantly, AI Mk IV air intercept radar. This example served with No 151 Squadron at Wittering, Cambridgeshire.

SPECIFICATIONS	
Country of origin:	United Kingdom
Type:	two-seat night fighter
Powerplant:	one 1280hp (954kW) Rolls-Royce Merlin XX V-12 piston engine
Performance:	504km/h (313mph); range 748km (465 miles); service ceiling: 10,242m (33,600ft)
Dimensions:	span 11.99m (39ft 4in); length 10.77m (35ft 4in); height 4.39m (14ft 5in); wing area 23.23 sq m (250 sq ft)
Weight:	empty 2849kg (6282lb); maximum 3900kg (8600lb)
Armament:	Four .303in (7.7mm) Browning machine guns

Bristol Blenheim Mk IF

The Blenheim fighter was another aircraft that worked better at night against bomber targets. Early AI radar was very short-ranged and the interceptor was guided near to the target by ground controllers before the onboard operator was able to pick it up on his primitive screen. This Blenheim IF was with a training unit, No 51 OTU, based at Church Fenton.

SPECIFICATIONS	
Country of origin:	United Kingdom
Type:	three-seater light bomber
Powerplant:	two 840hp (627kW) Bristol Mercury VIII nine-cylinder single-row radial engines
Performance:	maximum speed 459km/h (285mph); range 1810km (1125 miles); service ceiling: 8315m (27,280ft)
Dimensions:	span 17.17m (56ft 4in); length 12.12m (39ft 9in); height 3m (9ft 10in)
Weight:	empty 4013kg (6282lb); maximum 5947kg (13,100lb)
Armament:	Ventral pack containing four .303-in machine guns and one .303-in machine-gun in dorsal turret

Bristol Beaufighter Mk IF

The Blenheim was barely fast enough to catch most German bombers, so the next platform was the more powerful Beaufighter, which entered service in November 1940. This Mk IF belonged to No 604 Squadron at Middle Wallop, the unit of night ace John 'Cat-Eyes' Cunningham.

SPECIFICATIONS	
Country of origin:	United Kingdom
Type:	twin-engined night fighter
Powerplant:	two 1650hp (1230kW) Bristol Hercules III radial piston engines
Maximum speed:	528km/h (330mph); range 2478km (1540 miles); service ceiling 8077m (26,500ft)
Dimensions:	span 17.63m (57ft 10in); length 12.6m (41ft 8in); height 4.84m (15ft 10in); wing area 46.73 sq m (503 sq ft)
Weight:	empty 6260kg (13,800lb); loaded 9525kg (21,000lb)
Armament:	four 20mm cannon and six .303in (7.7mm) machine guns

Malta

Situated between Sicily and North Africa, the island of Malta gained a reputation as the most bombed place on Earth between 1940 and 1943. Home to a vital British naval base and several airfields, Malta was initially defended by a handful of Gladiators and other obsolete types. The Axis forces failed to neutralize or invade it, and heroic efforts to resupply the island with aircraft, weapons and fuel cost the Allies many ships but allowed offensive operations from the island to continue.

Junkers Ju 87B-2 Stuka

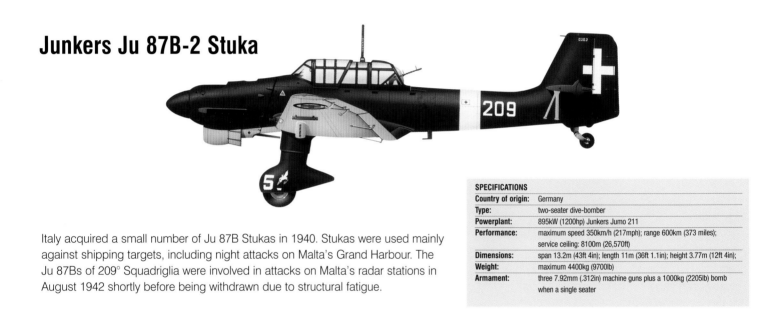

Italy acquired a small number of Ju 87B Stukas in 1940. Stukas were used mainly against shipping targets, including night attacks on Malta's Grand Harbour. The Ju 87Bs of 209° Squadriglia were involved in attacks on Malta's radar stations in August 1942 shortly before being withdrawn due to structural fatigue.

SPECIFICATIONS	
Country of origin:	Germany
Type:	two-seater dive-bomber
Powerplant:	895kW (1200hp) Junkers Jumo 211
Performance:	maximum speed 350km/h (217mph); range 600km (373 miles); service ceiling: 8100m (26,570ft)
Dimensions:	span 13.2m (43ft 4in); length 11m (36ft 1.1in); height 3.77m (12ft 4in);
Weight:	maximum 4400kg (9700lb)
Armament:	three 7.92mm (.312in) machine guns plus a 1000kg (2205lb) bomb when a single seater

Junkers Ju 88A-5

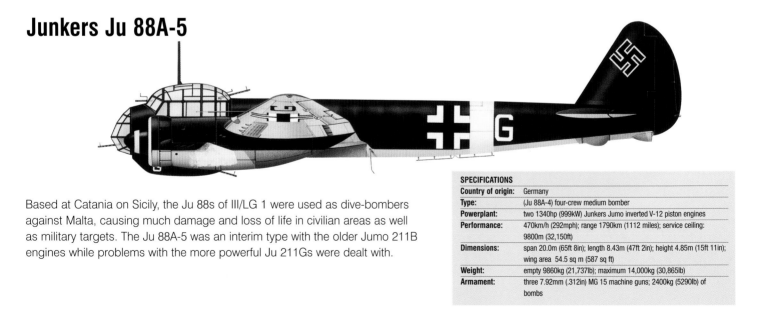

Based at Catania on Sicily, the Ju 88s of III/LG 1 were used as dive-bombers against Malta, causing much damage and loss of life in civilian areas as well as military targets. The Ju 88A-5 was an interim type with the older Jumo 211B engines while problems with the more powerful Ju 211Gs were dealt with.

SPECIFICATIONS	
Country of origin:	Germany
Type:	(Ju 88A-4) four-crew medium bomber
Powerplant:	two 1340hp (999kW) Junkers Jumo inverted V-12 piston engines
Performance:	470km/h (292mph); range 1790km (1112 miles); service ceiling: 9800m (32,150ft)
Dimensions:	span 20.0m (65ft 8in); length 8.43m (47ft 2in); height 4.85m (15ft 11in); wing area 54.5 sq m (587 sq ft)
Weight:	empty 9860kg (21,737lb); maximum 14,000kg (30,865lb)
Armament:	three 7.92mm (.312in) MG 15 machine guns; 2400kg (5290lb) of bombs

MALTA TIMELINE

1934

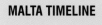

Savoia Marchetti S.M.79 Sparviero

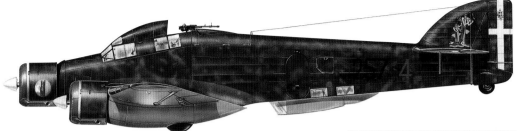

The Savoia Marchetti S.M.79 Sparviero (Sparrowhawk) was one of the best anti-shipping aircraft of the war, not least because it could carry two torpedoes. This S.M.79 of the 283° Squadriglia of the 130° Gruppo Autonomo was used against the Malta convoys in 1942.

SPECIFICATIONS	
Country of origin:	Italy
Type:	three-engined medium torpedo-bomber
Powerplant:	three 860hp (642kW) Alfa Romeo 128-RC18 radial piston engines
Performance:	maximum speed 460km/h (286mph); range 2600km (1615 miles); service ceiling 7500m (24,600ft)
Dimensions:	span 20.2m (66ft 3in); length 16.2m (53ft 2in); height 4.1m (13ft 6in); wing area 61.7 sq m (664 sq ft)
Weight:	7700kg (16,975lb); loaded 10,050kg (25,132lb)
Armament:	one 20mm MG 151 cannon; one 12.7mm (.50in) dorsal Breda-SAFAT and two 7.7mm (.303in) machine guns; up to 1200kg (2645lb) of bombs or two 450mm (17.72in) torpedoes

Gloster Sea Gladiator

The Sea Gladiator Mk I was the full-standard carrierborne fighter derived closely from the Gladiator, which was the UK's last land-based biplane fighter.

SPECIFICATIONS	
Country of origin:	United Kingdom
Type:	single-seat biplane fighter
Powerplant:	830hp (619kW) Bristol Mercury VIIIAS air-cooled 9-cylinder radial
Performance:	maximum speed 407km/h (253mph); range 684km (425 miles); service ceiling 9845m (32,300ft)
Dimensions:	span 9.83m (32ft 3in); length 8.36m (27ft 5in); height 3.52m (11ft 7in)
Weight:	2272kg (5020lb) loaded
Armament:	4 x 7.7mm (.303in) Browning MGs

Martin Maryland Mk I

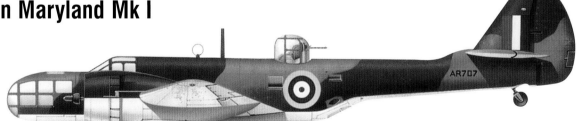

Delivered to US standard but fitted with an Armstong Whitworth dorsal turret, the Maryland Mk I was operated from Malta primarily in the long-range reconnaissance role, deep into the Mediterranean and around Italy's coast.

SPECIFICATIONS	
Country of origin:	United Kingdom
Type:	four-crew reconnaissance bomber
Powerplant:	2 x 1200hp (895kW) Pratt & Whitney twin Wasp radial piston engines
Performance:	maximum speed: 447km/h (278mph); range 2897km (1800 miles); service ceiling: 9449m (31,000ft)
Dimensions:	span 18.69m (61ft 4in); length 14.22m (46ft 8in); height 4.57m (15ft)
Weight:	7624kg (16,809lb) loaded
Armament:	4 x 7.7mm (.303in) Browning MGs; 2 x single Vickers K MGs; up to 907kg (2000lb) of bombs

1939

Macchi Fighters

The MC.200 was the second Italian monoplane fighter, following the Fiat G.50 into the air by 11 months. It appeared with a radial engine because the air force preferred their reliability, and armament of only two machine guns was specified. Thus underpowered and underarmed, the MC.200 was no match for most Allied fighters. The decision was made to convert the design to an inline engine, using the Daimler-Benz DB 601 (as used in the Bf 109E) built under licence by Alfa Romeo.

Macchi MC.202 Folgore

The Folgore (Thunderbolt) was a fairly straightforward conversion of the MC.200 with a DB 601 engine, although availability of these engines was always a problem. The type entered service in the summer of 1941 and this MC.205 of 151° Squadriglia was flown by eight-victory ace Ennio Tarantola.

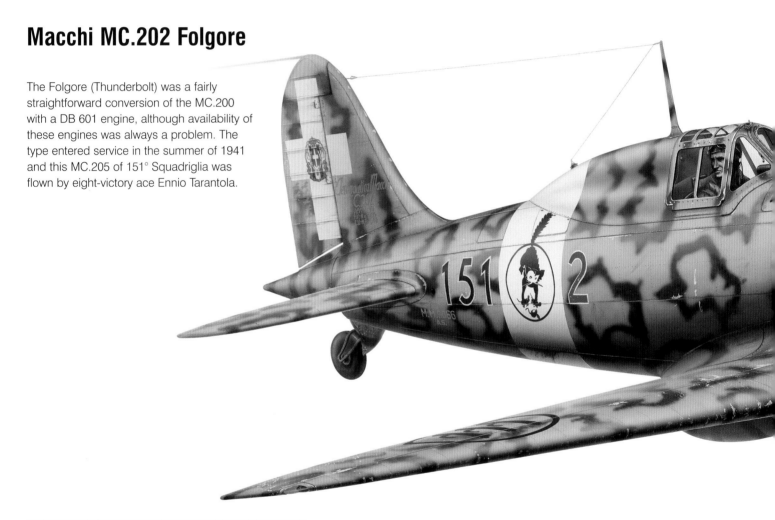

SPECIFICATIONS	
Country of origin:	Italy
Type:	(MC.202 Series VII) single-seat fighter
Powerplant:	one 1175hp (864kW) Alfa Romeo R.A.1000 R.C.41I inverted V-12 piston engine
Performance:	maximum speed 600km/h (372mph); range 765km (475 miles); service ceiling 11,500m (37,730ft)
Dimensions:	span 10.58m (34ft 8.5in); length 8.85m (29ft 1in); 3.49m (11ft 5in); wing area 16.82 m sq (181.04 sq ft)
Weight:	empty 2491kg (5492lb); maximum 2930kg (6460lb)
Armament:	two 12.7mm Breda-SAFAT machine guns; two 7.7mm Breda-SAFAT machine guns; up to 160kg (350lb) of bombs

Macchi MC.205V Veltro

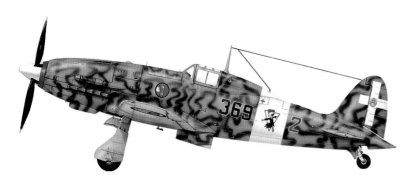

SPECIFICATIONS	
Country of origin:	Italy
Type:	(MC.205V) single-seat fighter and fighter-bomber
Powerplant:	one 1475hp (1100kW) Fiat RA.1050 RC.58 Tifone 12-cylinder inverted-Vee engine
Performance:	maximum speed 642km/h (399mph); climb to 5000m (16,405ft) in 4 minutes 47 seconds; service ceiling 11,000m (36,090ft); range 1040km (646 miles)
Weights:	empty 2581kg (5691lb); normal take-off 3224kg (7108lb); maximum take-off 3408kg (7514lb)
Dimensions:	span 10.58m (34ft 8.5in); length 8.85m (29ft 0.5in); height 3.04m (9ft 11.5in)
Armament:	two 12.7mm fixed forward-firing machine guns in the upper part of the forward fuselage, and two 20mm forward-firing cannon in the leading edges of the wing, plus bomb load of 320kg (705lb)

The MC.205 prototype was an MC.202 conversion that first flew in April 1942 with the new engine as well as larger outer wing panels. The new fighter entered production and was built to the extent of 262 MC.205V Veltro (greyhound) aircraft that were committed to combat from July 1943.

Macchi MC.200 Saetta

SPECIFICATIONS	
Country of origin:	Italy
Type:	(MC.200CB) single-seat fighter and fighter-bomber
Powerplant:	one 870hp (649kW) Fiat A.74 RC.38 14-cylinder two-row radial engine
Performance:	maximum speed 503km/h (312mph); climb to 5000m (16,405ft) in 5 minutes 51 seconds; service ceiling 8900m (29,200ft); range 870km (541 miles)
Weights:	empty 2019kg (4451lb); normal take-off 2339kg (5597lb)
Dimensions:	span 10.58m (34ft 8.5in); length 8.19m (26ft 10.4in); height 3.51m (11ft 5.75in)
Armament:	two 12.7mm fixed forward-firing machine guns in the upper part of the forward fuselage, plus an external bomb load of 320kg (705lb)

Designed from 1936 and first flown in prototype form during December 1937, the MC.200 won the fighter contest held in 1938 and entered service in October 1939. The original type of enclosed cockpit was initially altered to an open and finally a semi-enclosed type, ostensibly because Italian pilots preferred this layout!

RAF Intruders

With the immediate threat of an invasion of England passed, but no prospect either of an Allied invasion of Europe, RAF Fighter Command was tasked with taking the war to the enemy. Intruder bombing missions codenamed 'Ramrods', and 'Rhubarb' fighter sweeps, set out to destroy precision targets, stir up the Luftwaffe and engage it in combat. These missions proved costly, and it is debatable whether they were worth the loss of aircraft and crews.

Westland Whirlwind

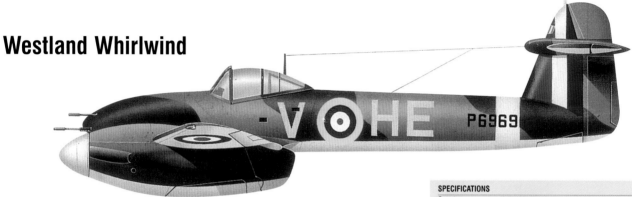

No 263 Squadron was one of only two squadrons equipped with the Whirlwind twin-engined long-range fighter and fighter-bomber. With its good range and considerable firepower, the Whirlwind was well suited to the coastal role, in defence as well as offence.

SPECIFICATIONS	
Country:	United Kingdom
Type:	single-seat fighter
Powerplant:	2 x 885hp (659kW) Peregrine engines
Performance:	maximum speed 580km/h (360mph); range 1300km (808 miles); service ceiling 9240m (30,315ft)
Dimensions:	span 13.72m (45ft); length 9.83m (32ft 3in); height 3.53m (11ft 7in)
Weight:	4697kg (10,356lb) loaded
Armament:	4 x Hispano 20mm (.8in) cannon in nose (60 rounds per gun, 240 rounds total)

Lockheed Ventura Mk II

A high-speed light bomber of US design and manufacture, the Ventura saw limited British service, primarily for daylight operations over German-occupied Europe. No 21 Squadron received its first Ventura bombers in mid-1942. This aircraft flew with No 21 Squadron, RAF Bomber Command, Methwold, in mid-1943.

SPECIFICATIONS	
Country of origin:	United States
Type:	five-man bomber
Powerplant:	two 2000hp (1491kW) Pratt & Whitney GR-2800-S1A4-G Double Wasp radial piston engines
Performance:	maximum speed 483km/h (300mph); range 1529km (950 miles); service ceiling 7620m (25,000ft)
Dimensions:	span 19.96m (65ft 6in); length 15.62m (51ft 3in); height 3.63m (11ft 11in)
Weight:	11,793kg (26,000lb) loaded
Armament:	4 x 12.7mm (.5in) MGs; 2 x 7.62mm (.3in) MGs; 1400kg (3000lb) general ordnance or 6 x 147kg (325lb) depth charges or 1 x torpedo

RAF INTRUDERS TIMELINE

1935

1936

1938

Hawker Hurricane IIC

The Hurricane IIC was a version well-suited to the intruder role, with cannon armament and bombs. No 1 Squadron flew IICs on night intruder raids from Lympne, Kent, during the spring of 1943.

SPECIFICATIONS	
Country of origin:	United Kingdom
Type:	single-seat fighter-bomber
Powerplant:	one 1850hp (954kW) Rolls-Royce Merlin XX V-12 piston engine
Performance:	maximum speed 547 km/h (340 mph); range 740 km (460 miles); service ceiling 12,192m (40,000ft)
Dimensions:	span 12.19m (40ft 0in); length 9.82m (32ft 3in); Height 2.66m (8ft 9in); wing area 24 sq m (257.5 sq ft)
Weight:	empty 2624kg (5785lb); maximum 3951kg (8710lb)
Armament:	four 20mm Hispano cannon; 230kg (500lb) of bombs

North American Mustang I

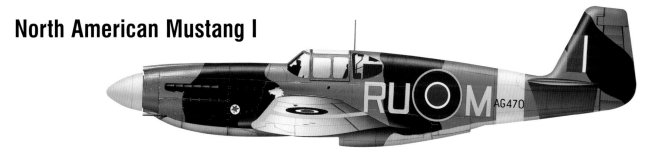

The RAF commissioned the Mustang but was disappointed with its high-altitude performance and relegated it to low-level ground attack and photo-reconnaissance missions. This Mustang I of No 414 (RCAF) Squadron was flown by Hollis Hills, who scored the first aerial victory made with the Mustang.

SPECIFICATIONS	
Country:	Canada
Type:	single-seat reconnaissance fighter
Powerplant:	one 1150hp (858kW) Allison V-1710-39 V-12 piston engine
Maximum speed:	628km/h (390mph); range 1207km (810 miles); service ceiling: 9555m (31,350ft)
Dimensions:	span 11.28m (37ft); length 9.83m (32ft 3in); height 3.71m (12ft 2in); wing area 21.65 sq m (233 sq ft)
Weight:	empty 2971kg (6550lb); maximum 3992kg (8880lb)
Armament:	four .50in (12.7mm) and four .303in (7.7mm) Browning machine-guns

Spitfire Mk VB

The Polish-manned No 303 Squadron, temporarily based at Redhill, flew Spitfire VBs on sweeps over northern France to cover the Dieppe Raid amphibious landing in August 1942. Over 100 RAF aircraft were lost covering the operation, including many Spitfire Vs.

SPECIFICATIONS	
Country of origin:	United Kingdom
Type:	single-engined fighter
Powerplant:	one 1470hp (1096kW) Rolls-Royce Merlin 45 V-12 piston engine
Performance:	maximum speed 602km/h (375mph); range 756km (470 miles); service ceiling: 11,278m (37,000ft)
Dimensions:	span 11.23m (36ft); length 9.12m (29ft 11in); height 3.47m (11ft 5in); wing area 22.48 sq m (242 sq ft)
Weight:	empty 2251kg (4963lb); loaded 3071kg (6525lb)
Armament:	two 20mm Hispano cannon; four .303in (7.7mm) Browning machine guns; up to 227kg (500lb) bombs

1940

1941

Pearl Harbor

On 7 December 1941, Imperial Japan attempted to eliminate the naval power of the United States, its main rival in the Pacific, by launching a raid from six aircraft carriers against the base at Pearl Harbor, Hawaii. Taken by surprise, the US Army had parked most of its Hawaiian-based aircraft in rows, and B-17s coming from the mainland found they were not fitted with guns. By chance, the Navy's carriers were at sea on manoeuvres and survived to play a decisive role later in the Pacific War.

Mitsubishi A6M2

A total of 126 of the 441 aircraft aboard the Japanese carriers were Mitsubishi A6M2 Type '0' fighters. The carrier *Hiryu* launched six Zeroes on the first wave of attacks and eight on the second. This A6M2 Model 21 belonged to the 1st Koku Kantai (Air Fleet), 2nd Koku Sentai (Carrier Air Group) and embarked on *Hiryu* for the Pearl Harbor attack.

SPECIFICATIONS	
Country of origin:	Japan
Type:	single-seat carrier-based fighter
Powerplant:	one 950hp (709kW) Nakajima Sakae 12 radial piston engine
Performance:	maximum speed 533km/h (331mph); range: 3105 km (1929 miles); service ceiling: 10,000m (33,000ft)
Dimensions:	span 12.0m (39ft 4in); length 9.06m (29ft 9in); height 3.05m (10ft 0in); wing area 22.44 sq m (241.5 sq ft)
Weight:	empty 1680kg (3704lb); maximum 2410kg (5313lb)
Armament:	two 7.7mm (.303in) Type 97 machine guns; two 20mm Type 99 cannon

Aichi D3A1 'Val'

The fixed-gear Type 99 dive-bomber carried a fairly small load not very fast, but in the opening campaigns of the Pacific War, particularly at Pearl Harbor, it was used to devastating effect. Of the 135 D3A1s (known as 'Vals' to the Allies) used on 7 December, 15 were shot down, but they caused great destruction at Wheeler Field air base as well as to the US battleships.

SPECIFICATIONS	
Country of origin:	Japan
Type:	two-seat carrier-based dive-bomber
Powerplant:	one 1300hp (969kW) Mitsubishi Kinsei 54 radial piston engine
Performance:	maximum speed 430km/h (267mph); range: 1352km (840 miles); service ceiling 10,500m (34,450ft)
Dimensions:	span 14.37m (47ft 2in); length 10.2m (33ft 5in); height 3.8m (12ft 8in); wing area 34.9 sq m (375.6 sq ft)
Weight:	empty 2570kg (5666lb); maximum 4122kg (9100lb)
Armament:	two 7.7mm (.303in) Type 97 machine guns and one 7.7mm (.303in) Type 92 machine-gun; up to 250kg (550lb) bombs

PEARL HARBOR TIMELINE

1935

1936

1937

Nakajima B5N 'Kate'

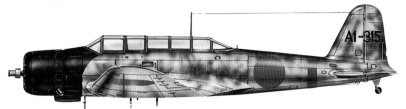

The B5N 'Kate' was used as both a high-level bomber and as a torpedo bomber during the Pearl Harbor attack. The carrier *Akagi* launched 15 'Kate' bombers and 12 armed with torpedoes in the first wave. The leader of the raid flew in an *Akagi* 'Kate'. The B5Ns suffered only five losses, all torpedo bombers, for the 144 launched from all six carriers.

SPECIFICATIONS	
Country of origin:	Japan
Type:	(Type 97, model 3) three-seat carrier-based bomber/torpedo-bomber
Powerplant:	one 1000hp (750kW) Nakajima Sakae 11 radial piston engine
Performance:	maximum speed 378km/h (235mph); range 1992km (1237 miles); service ceiling 8260m (27,100ft)
Dimensions:	span 15.52m (50ft 11in); length 10.30m (33ft 10in); height 3.70m (12ft 2in); wing area 37.7 sq m (406sq ft)
Weight:	empty 2279kg (5024lb); loaded 3800kg (8380lb)
Armament:	one 7.7mm (.303in) Type 92 machine gun; one 800kg (1760lb) Type 91 torpedo or up to 250kg (550lb) of bombs

Curtiss P-36C Mohawk

Although in the process of being replaced by P-40s, there were over 40 P-36 Mohawks in Hawaii on 7 December 1941. Five got airborne from Wheeler Field and shot down two Zeroes, and another one joined with P-40s from an outlying field to destroy seven Vals. One P-36 was lost in air combat and another shot down by American ground fire.

SPECIFICATIONS	
Country of origin:	United States
Type:	single-seat fighter
Powerplant:	2 x 2000hp (1491kW) Pratt & Whitney GR-2800-S1A4-G Double Wasp radial piston engines
Performance:	maximum speed 483km/h (300mph); range 1529km (950 miles); service ceiling 7620m (25,000ft)
Dimensions:	span 19.96m (65ft 6in); length 15.62m (51ft 3in); height 3.63m (11ft 11in)
Weight:	11,793kg (26,000lb) loaded
Armament:	4 x 12.7mm (.5in) MGs; 2 x 7.62mm (.3in) MGs; 1400kg (3000lb) general ordnance or 6 x 147kg (325lb) depth charges or 1 x torpedo

Grumman F4F-3A Wildcat

The Japanese failed to destroy the US carrier fleet because it was engaged in various tasks on the day. *Enterprise* had been ferrying F4F Wildcats to reinforce Wake Island and was returning to Pearl Harbor when the Japanese struck. Several of its own F4Fs were destroyed by ground fire when they arrived over the scene shortly after the attack. This is an F4F-3 from VF-6 on *Enterprise*.

SPECIFICATIONS	
Country of origin:	United States
Type:	single-seat carrier-based fighter
Powerplant:	one 1200hp (900kW) Pratt & Whitney R-1830-76 radial piston engine
Performance:	maximum speed 531km/h (331mph); range 1360km (845 miles); service ceiling 12,000m (39,500ft)
Dimensions:	span 11.58m (38ft); length 8.76m (28ft 9in); height 3.60m (11ft 10in); wing area 24.15 sq m (260 sq ft)
Weight:	empty 2422kg (5342lb); loaded 7000kg (3176kg)
Armament:	four .5in (12.7mm) Browning M2 machine guns; up to 90kg (200lb) of bombs

1938

1939

East Indies and Malaya

With the attack on Pearl Harbor, Japan struck against US forces in the Philippines and the British and Dutch in Malaya and the Netherlands East Indies. In each of these assaults, Japanese airpower was crucial and Allied air defence largely ineffective. The long range and quality of Japanese aircraft surprised their opponents, who had dismissed Japanese pilots as short-sighted and poor aviators. The colonial powers were largely driven out of Southeast Asia by March 1942.

Curtiss Hawk 75A-7

The semi-independent government of the Netherlands East Indies ordered 24 H-75A-7s, a variant of the P-36 Mohawk in late 1939. Aircraft such as the Hawk 75 were the best that most Western nations could obtain on the eve of war. In December 1941, aircraft C-332 was assigned to 1st Lt W. Boxman at Maospati airfield, Madioen, Java.

SPECIFICATIONS	
Country of origin:	Netherlands East Indies
Type:	single-seat fighter
Powerplant:	one 1200hp (895kW) Wright R-1820-G205A Cyclone piston engine
Performance:	486km/h (302mph); range 970km (603 miles); service ceiling: 9967m (32,700ft)
Dimensions:	span 11.38m (37ft 4in); length 8.8m (28ft 8in); height 3.56m (11ft 8in); wing area 21.92 sq m (236 sq ft)
Weights:	empty 2019kg (4451lb); maximum 3022kg (6662lb)
Armament:	four .5in (12.7mm) Browning machine guns

Brewster B-239 Buffalo

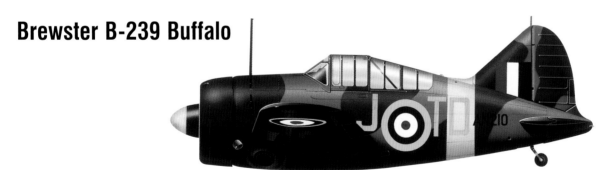

No 453 Squadron RAAF was one of two Australian units to fly the Brewster Buffalo in Malaysia and Singapore alongside squadrons from the RAF and RNZAF. Although the Finns had been successful with their lighter versions of the 'Buff', the Commonwealth units found themselves completely outclassed by the Zeroes of the Japanese Navy, and in early February 1942, 453 became the last Buffalo unit to abandon its few remaining aircraft and withdraw to Java.

SPECIFICATIONS	
Country of origin:	Australia
Type:	single-seat fighter
Powerplant:	one 940hp (701kW) Wright R-1820-34 Cyclone 9 radial piston engine
Performance:	maximum speed 457km/h (284mph); range 1600km (1000 miles); service ceiling: 9144m (30,000ft)
Dimensions:	span 10.7m (35ft); length 7.9m (26ft); Height 3.63m (11ft 11in); wing area 19.41 sq m (208.9 sq ft)
Weights:	empty 4732lb (2146kg); maximum 6321lb (2867kg)
Armament:	provision for 1 x 7.92mm (.3in) MG

EAST INDIES TIMELINE

 1935 1936  1937

Mitsubishi G32M 'Nell'

This G3M2 of the Genzan Kokutai was one of those that took part of the sinking of the British battlecruisers *Repulse* and *Prince of Wales*. Based in Saigon, Indochina, 27 'Nells' dropped bombs from 2500m (8202ft) while 56 G4M 'Betty' torpedo bombers attacked from low level. Buffalos from Malaya arrived only after the attack was over.

SPECIFICATIONS	
Country of origin:	Japan
Type:	twin-engined medium bomber
Powerplant:	two 1075hp (791kW) Mitsubishi Kinsei 45 radial piston engines
Performance:	maximum speed 375km/h (233mph); range 4400km (2730 miles); service ceiling 9200m (30,200ft)
Dimensions:	span 25m (82ft); length 16.45m (54ft); height 3.68m (12ft 1in); wing area 75 sq m (800 sq ft)
Weights:	empty 4965kg (10,923lb); loaded 8000kg (17,600lb)
Armament:	one Type 99 20mm cannon; four Type 92 7.7mm machine guns; up to 800kg (1764lb) bombs or one torpedo

Nakajima Ki-27b 'Nate'

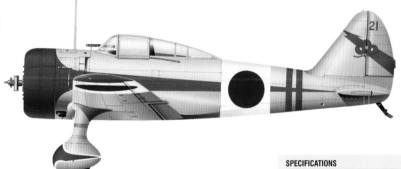

The most numerous IJAAF fighter in 1941 was the Ki-27b 'Nate', of which 4000 were built by the end of 1942. Having been in combat over China since early 1938, the Ki-27 units were extremely proficient with the type, which was widely used in the invasion of Burma, Malaya, the Netherlands East Indies and Thailand, where this example from the 64th Sentai was based in March 1942.

SPECIFICATIONS	
Country of origin:	Japan
Type:	single-seat fighter
Powerplant:	one 650hp (485kW) Nakajima Ha-1 Otsu air-cooled radial piston engine
Performance:	maximum speed 444 km/h (275 mph); range 630km (390 miles); service ceiling 10,040m (32,940ft)
Dimensions:	span 11.30m (37ft 1in); length 7.53m (24ft 8in); height 3.35m (11ft 7in); wing area 18.61 sq m (200.3 sq ft)
Weights:	empty 1174kg (2588lb); maximum 1790kg (3946lb)
Armament:	two 7.7mm (.303in) Type 89 machine guns; up to 100kg (220lb) bombs

Nakajima Ki-43-Ic 'Oscar'

The Nakajima Ki-43 Hayabusa (Peregrine Falcon) was a single-engine land-based fighter used by the Imperial Japanese Army Air Force in World War II. It was one of the most mass produced aircraft (5900 up until the end of World War II). The main variants were the Ki-43-I, the Ki-43-II and the Ki-43-III.

SPECIFICATIONS	
Country of origin:	Japan
Type:	single-engined fighter
Powerplant:	one 980hp (731kW) Nakajima Ha-25 Army Type 99 radial piston engine
Performance:	maximum speed 496km/h (308mph); range 1199km (745 miles); service ceiling 11,735m (38,500ft)
Dimensions:	span 11.44m (37ft 6in); length 8.83m (28ft 11in); height 3.27m (10ft 9in); wing area 22 sq m (236.8 sq ft)
Weights:	empty 1580kg (3483lb); maximum 2583kg (5695lb)
Armament:	two12.7mm (.50in) Type 1 (Ho-103) machine guns

1938

1939

Flying Tigers

Formed by a former US Army Captain named Clare Chennault, the American Volunteer Group (AVG) was a band of pilots and ground crew recruited in early 1941 to operate fighters against the Japanese on behalf of Chinese Nationalist leader Chiang Kai-shek. Contrary to legend, the AVG – nicknamed the 'Flying Tigers' by the Chinese – did not engage the Japanese before 7 December 1941, but became among the first Americans to fly offensive missions in the Pacific War.

Curtiss Hawk 81A-2

The Flying Tigers' aircraft was an export model similar to the RAF's Tomahawk Mk II, officially designated Hawk 81A-2, but usually referred to as 'P-40s' by the pilots. The 1st Pursuit Squadron of the AVG marked their aircraft with this apple and Adam and Eve insignia, commemorating the 'first pursuit' in history.

SPECIFICATIONS	
Country of origin:	United States
Type:	single-engined fighter
Powerplant:	one 1150hp (858kW) Allison V-1710-33 V-12 piston engine
Performance:	maximum speed: 571km/h (355mph); range: 1450km (900 miles); 467km (290 miles); service ceiling: 8800m (29,000ft)
Dimensions:	11.38m (37ft 4in); length 9.68m (31ft 9in); height 3.76m (12ft 4in); wing area 21.9 sq m (236 sq ft)
Weights:	empty 2880kg (6350lb); maximum 4200kg (9200lb)
Armament:	two .5in and four .303in Browning machine guns; various small bombs

Curtiss Hawk 81A-2 Tomahawk

The AVG's 2nd Pursuit Squadron was nicknamed the 'Panda Bears'. Aircraft 38 was usually flown by Henry Geselbracht, who was not one of the Flying Tigers' aces, of whom there were about 25. The AVG claimed 286 Japanese aircraft destroyed, but the real figure is probably closer to 115.

SPECIFICATIONS	
Country of origin:	Germany
Type:	two-seater dive-bomber
Powerplant:	895kW (1200hp) Junkers Jumo 211
Performance:	maximum speed 350km/h (217mph); range 600km (373 miles); service ceiling: 8100m (26,570ft)
Dimensions:	span 13.2m (43ft 4in); length 11m (36ft 1.1in); height 3.77m (12ft 4in);
Weight:	maximum 4400kg (9700lb)
Armament:	three 7.92mm (.312in) machine guns plus a 1000kg (2205lb) bomb when a single seater

Curtiss Hawk 81-A2

With the build-up of official American units in Burma and China, the volunteer Tigers were disbanded in July 1942. The majority of its members did not stay on to join the 14th Air Force's 23rd Fighter Group, which adopted the Flying Tigers aircraft and famous sharksmouth marking, as seen in this 3rd Squadron aircraft.

SPECIFICATIONS	
Country of origin:	United States
Type:	single-engined fighter
Powerplant:	one 1150hp (858kW) Allison V-1710-33 V-12 piston engine
Performance:	maximum speed: 571km/h (355mph); range: 1450km (900 miles); 467km (290 miles); service ceiling: 8800m (29,000ft)
Dimensions:	11.38m (37ft 4in); length 9.68m (31ft 9in); height 3.76m (12ft 4in); wing area 21.9 sq m (236 sq ft)
Weights:	empty 2880kg (6350lb); maximum 4200kg (9200lb)
Armament:	two .5in and four .303in Browning machine guns; various small bombs

Curtiss Hawk 75

By 1941, China's own air force had been fighting Japan for over three years, and many of its best pilots and aircraft had been lost. With the help of Chennault, the Chinese were able to acquire more modern fighters from Curtiss, including the simplified Hawk 75M and the Hawk 75A-5 seen here, which was built for a time under licence in China.

SPECIFICATIONS	
Country of origin:	United States
Type:	(75A-5) single-seat fighter
Powerplant:	one 1200hp (895kW) Wright R-1820-G205A Cyclone piston engine
Performance:	maximum speed 486km/h (302mph); service ceiling 9967m (32,700ft); range 970km (603 miles)
Weights:	empty 2019kg (4451lb); maximum 3022kg (6662lb)
Dimensions:	span 11.38m (37ft 4in); length 8.7m (28ft 8in); height 3.56m (11ft 8in); wing area 21.92 sq m (236 sq ft)
Armament:	six .3in (7.62mm) Browning machine guns

Mitsubishi K-46 II

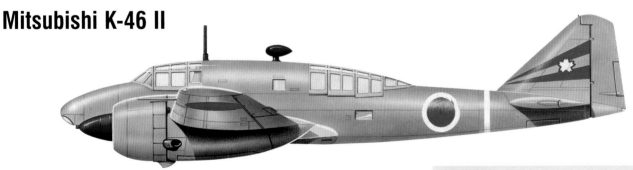

The Mitsubishi Ki-46, or Type 100 Command Reconnaissance Aircraft, was frequently used to photograph the bases of the AVG and Chinese Air Force in preparation for attack. Its high speed, long range and high operating altitude made it almost immune from interception by the fighters operating in China in 1941–42.

SPECIFICATIONS	
Country of origin:	Japan
Type:	two-seat reconnaissance aircraft
Powerplant:	two 1080hp (807kW) Mitsubishi 14-cylinder radial piston engines
Performance:	maximum speed 604km/h (375mph); 4000km (2485 miles); service ceiling: 10,000m (32,800ft)
Dimensions:	span 14.70m (48ft 3in); length 11.00m (36ft 1in); height 3.88m (12ft 9in); wing area 32.0 sq m (344 sq ft)
Weights:	empty 3830kg (8444lb); maximum 6500kg (14,330lb)
Armament:	one 7.7mm (.303in) Type 89 machine-gun

Grumman Wildcats

The ultimate development of a line of carrier-based biplane fighters stretching back to 1931, the Wildcat emerged as the underpowered XF4F-2 in 1937, but later evolved into the most important US fighter of the early Pacific War for both the Navy and Marine Corps. It also proved to be eminently suitable for operation from the small escort carriers used in the North Atlantic and elsewhere by both the US and Royal navies. Nearly 8000 Wildcats were built, two-thirds by a division of General Motors.

Grumman F4F-3 Wildcat

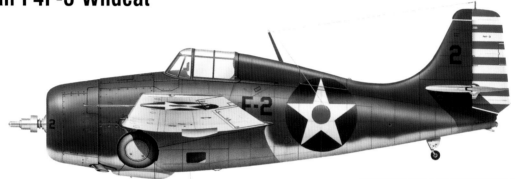

The initial production version of the Wildcat was the F4F-3, ordered in 1939. The F4F-3 had four guns and fixed (non-folding) wings. At the Battle of the Coral Sea in May 1942, Ensign Scott McCuskey flew this Wildcat from the USS *Yorktown* and destroyed one A6M, the first of his 13.5 recorded aerial victories.

SPECIFICATIONS	
Country of origin:	United States
Type:	single-engined carrier-based fighter
Powerplant:	one 1200hp (895kW) Pratt & Whitney R-1830-86 radial piston engine
Performance:	maximum speed 528km/h (328mph); range 1360km (845 miles);
Dimensions:	span 11.58m (38ft); length 8.76m (28ft 9in); height 2.81m (9ft 3in); wing area 24.15 sq m (260 sq ft)
Weights:	empty 2423kg (5342lb); maximum 3698kg (8152lb)
Armament:	four .5in (12.7mm) Browning machine guns

Grumman F4F-4 Wildcat

The F4F-4 introduced wing folding and an extra pair of guns in the outer wings. Performance suffered slightly due to the extra weight, but range increased with the addition of drop tanks. Ace Edwin 'Whitey' Feightner flew this F4F-4 from *Enterprise* in 1942–43.

SPECIFICATIONS	
Country of origin:	United States
Type:	single-engined carrier-based fighter
Powerplant:	one 1200hp (895kW) Pratt & Whitney R-1830-76 radial piston engine
Performance:	maximum speed: 512km/h (318mph); range: 1464km (910 miles); service ceiling: 10,363 m (34,000ft)
Dimensions:	span 11.58m (38ft 0in); length 8.76m (28ft 9in); height 2.81m (9ft 3in); wing area 24.15 sq m (260 sq ft)
Weights:	empty 2674kg (5895lb); loaded 3607kg (7952lb)
Armament:	six .5in (12.7mm) Browning machine guns; up to (200lb) bombs

Grumman F4F-3S Wildcat Floatplane

Built as a response to the Nakajima 'Rufe' floatplane version of the Mitsubishi 'Zero', the F4F-3S 'Wildcatfish' was not a great success. Top speed and range suffered greatly due to the weight and drag of the floats. Construction of more carriers and island airfields reduced the need for floatplanes, and only a single prototype was built.

SPECIFICATIONS	
Country of origin:	United States
Type:	single-engined carrier-based fighter
Powerplant:	one 1200hp (895kW) Pratt & Whitney R-1830-86 radial piston engine
Performance:	maximum speed 409km/h (254mph); range unknown; service ceiling unknown
Dimensions:	span 11.58m (38ft); height unknown; length unknown
Weights:	unknown
Armament:	four .5in (12.7mm) Browning machine guns

Grumman F4F-4 Wildcat

The early-model Wildcats were inferior in manoeuvrability to the Zero, but through the development of better formation tactics and their inherent strength and self-protection, they acquitted themselves well in air combat. Enlisted pilot Machinist Donald Runyon scored eight Wildcat kills in the Solomons Campaign of 1942.

SPECIFICATIONS	
Country of origin:	United States
Type:	single-engined carrier-based fighter
Powerplant:	one 1200hp (895kW) Pratt & Whitney R-1830-76 radial piston engine
Performance:	maximum speed: 512km/h (318mph); range: 1464km (910 miles); service ceiling: 10,363m (34,000ft)
Dimensions:	span 11.58m (38ft); length 8.76m (28ft 9in); height 2.81m (9ft 3in); wing area 24.15 sq m (260 sq ft)
Weights:	empty 2674kg (5895lb); loaded 3607kg (7952lb)
Armament:	six .5in (12.7mm) Browning machine guns; up to 200lb bombs

Grumman FM-2 Wildcat

The majority of Wildcats (4777) were built by Eastern Aircraft as FM-2s, with a Wright Cyclone engine and a taller fin. The Wildcat remained in use on 'jeep' carriers until late in the war. FM-2 'Mah Baby' was flown by Bruce Allen McGraw of VC-99 on USS *Gambier Bay* in October 1944.

SPECIFICATIONS	
Country of origin:	United States
Type:	single-engined carrier-based fighter
Powerplant:	one 1350hp (1007kW) Wright R-1820-56 Cyclone piston engine
Maximum speed:	maximum speed 534km/h (332mph); range 1448km (900 miles); service ceiling: 10,575m (34,700ft)
Dimensions:	span 11.58m (38ft); length 8.76m (28ft 9in); height 3.02m (9ft 11in); wing area 24.15 sq m (260 sq ft)
Weight:	empty 2471kg (5448lb); maximum 3752kg (8721lb)
Armament:	four .5in (12.7mm) Browning machine guns; two 113kg (250lb) bombs or six 5in (12.7cm) rockets

US Carrier Strike Power

By late 1941, the US Navy had replaced all the colourful biplanes on its few carrier decks with blue-grey monoplanes. Faced with war against a technologically sophisticated enemy, some of the Navy's concepts and equipment proved lacking. The Buffalo fighter and Vought Vindicator bomber were verging on obsolescence and were replaced, while the lumbering Devastator was removed from service by Japan at Coral Sea and Midway. Also, American torpedoes were terribly unreliable.

Douglas SBD Dauntless

SPECIFICATIONS	
Country of origin:	United States
Type:	carrierborne dive-bomber
Performance:	maximum speed 427km/h (266mph); service ceiling 9175m (31,000ft); range: 972km (604 miles)
Dimensions:	span 12.65m (41ft 6in); length 9.68m (31ft 9in); height 3.91m (12ft 10in)
Weight:	3183kg (7018lb) loaded
Armament:	two 12.7mm (.5in) Browning machine guns in the nose and one 7.62mm (.3in) in the rear cockpit; bomb load of one 454kg (1000lb) bomb under centre fuselage and two 45kg (100lb) bombs under wings

Illustrated here in pre-war Marine Corps colours, the SBD ('slow but deadly') Dauntless dive-bomber proved crucial to victory at the Battle of Midway, and sank many thousands of tons of Japanese shipping before retirement from frontline service in 1944.

Grumman TBF-1 Avenger

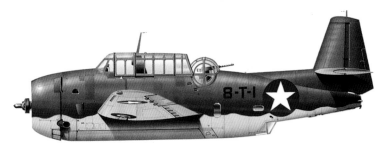

SPECIFICATIONS	
Country of origin:	United States
Type:	three-seat carrierborne and land-based torpedo bomber
Powerplant:	one 1700hp (1268kW) Wright Cyclone 14-cylinder two-row radial engine
Performance:	414km/h (257mph); service ceiling 6525m (21,400ft); range 4321km (2685 miles)
Dimensions:	span 16.51m (54ft 2in); length 12.42m (40ft 9in); height 4.19m (13ft 9in)
Weights:	empty 4788kg (10,555lb); maximum take-off weight 7876kg (17,364lb)
Armament:	four machine guns: two .5in forward-firing in the wing, one .5in trainable rearward-firing in the dorsal turret, and one .3in rearward ventral firing; torpedo, bomb and rocket load of 1134kg (2500lb)

Named Avenger on its public debut just after Pearl Harbor, the Grumman TBF had a disastrous debut at the Battle of Midway. Torpedo Squadron Eight (VT-8) lost all but one of the six aircraft it launched from Midway Island, but the Avenger went on to have a long and successful career.

Douglas TBD Devastator

Introduced in 1937, the TBD-1 Devastator was then the most modern torpedo-bomber in the world, but by the Battle of Midway in June 1942, the Devastators of VT-8 and VT-6 (illustrated here) were all but wiped out by fighters and anti-aircraft fire, and did no damage to the Japanese carriers.

SPECIFICATIONS	
Country of origin:	United States
Type:	Three-seat carrier-based torpedo-bomber
Powerplant:	one 900hp (671kW) Pratt & Whitney Twin Wasp radial piston engine
Performance:	Maximum speed: 331km/h (206mph); service ceiling 6000m (19,700ft); range 1152km (716 miles)
Dimensions:	15.24m (50ft); length 10.67m (35ft 0in); height 4.60m (15ft 1in); wing area 39.2 sq m (422 sq ft)
Weights:	empty 2804kg (6182lb); maximum 4623kg (10,194lb)
Armament:	two or three .3in (7.62mm) machine guns; one 1000lb (453kg) bomb or one 1200lb (544kg) torpedo

Early Island Campaign

The Japanese quickly captured Wake Island and Guam, but were checked at Coral Sea and Midway. In August 1942, the Marines landed in the Solomon Islands to deny Japan a base from which to attack supply lines to Australia and New Zealand. They soon faced counterattacks from the Japanese fortress of Rabaul on New Britain, including land, sea and air engagements. Rabaul was constantly bombed by the Allies, but never invaded. It surrendered only in August 1945.

Mitsubishi G4M1 'Betty'

The G4M 'Betty' was the most important Japanese bomber of the war, with extremely long range and good defensive armament. Its Achilles' heel was poor damage tolerance and a tendency to catch fire when hit. This G4M1 model 11 was based on Rabaul at the time of the US landings in 1942.

SPECIFICATIONS	
Country of origin:	Japan
Type:	twin-engined medium bomber
Powerplant:	two 1530hp (1141kW) Mitsubishi Kasei Type 11 piston engines
Performance:	maximum speed 426km/h (265mph); range 4335km (2694 miles); service ceiling 8500m (27,890ft)
Dimensions:	span 24.9m (81ft 7in); length 19.98m (65ft 6in); height 4.90m (16ft 1in); wing area 78.13 sq m (840.9 sq ft)
Weight:	empty 7000kg (15,430lb); loaded 9500kg (20,940lb)
Armament:	four 7.7mm machine-guns, one 20mm Type 99 cannon; up to 1000kg (2403b) of bombs or one 800kg (1764lb) of bombs

Mitsubishi A6M Zero

Over 60 A6M2 Zeroes (Allied codename 'Zeke') of the Tainan kokutai were based at Lakunai Field on Rabaul from August 1942. Among their pilots was Ensign Saburo Sakai, who was wounded over Guadalcanal, but eventually went on be Japan's fourth-ranking ace, with over 60 kills.

SPECIFICATIONS	
Country of origin:	Japan
Type:	single-seat carrierborne and land-based fighter and fighter-bomber
Powerplant:	one 950hp (708kW) Nakajima 12 14-cylinder two-row radial engine
Performance:	maximum speed 534km/h (332mph); service ceiling 10,000m (32,810ft); range 3104km (1929 miles)
Dimensions:	span 12.00m (39ft 4.5in); length 9.06m (29ft 8.75in); height 3.05m (10ft)
Weight:	empty 1680kg (3704lb); maximum take-off weight 2796kg (6164lb)
Armament:	two 20mm forward-firing cannon in the wing, two 7.7mm forward-firing MGs in the forward fuselage, external bomb load of 120kg (265lb)

EARLY ISLAND TIMELINE

 1937   1938    1939

Nakajima (Mitsubishi) A6M2-N 'Rufe'

In 1940, the IJN commissioned Nakajima to build a floatplane version of its rival Mitsubishi's Type 0 fighter, which became the A6M2-N 'Rufe'. For the island campaigns, where airfields were few and far between, floatplanes and flying boats allowed remote outposts to be defended and supplied.

SPECIFICATIONS	
Country of origin:	Japan
Type:	single-seat floatplane fighter
Powerplant:	one 940hp (701kW) Nakajima NK1C Sakae 12 radial piston engine
Performance:	maximum speed 436 km/h (271 mph); range 1780km (1106 miles); service ceiling: 10,000m (32,810ft)
Dimensions:	span 12m (39ft 5in); length 10.1m (33ft 2in); height 4.30m (14ft 1in); wing area 22.44 sq m (241.55 sq ft)
Weights:	empty 1912kg (4215lb); maximum 2880kg (6349lb)
Armament:	two .303in (7.7mm) machine guns and two 20mm cannon; two 132lb (60kg) bombs

Grumman F4F-4 Wildcat

The Marine squadrons on Guadalcanal operated under the most primitive conditions, under regular artillery bombardment as well as air attack and ground assault. Joe Foss of VMF-121, whose F4F-4 is shown, was one of the most successful 'Cactus Air Force' pilots, scoring 23 victories over the Solomons.

SPECIFICATIONS	
Country of origin:	United States
Type:	single-engined carrier-based fighter
Powerplant:	one 1200hp (895kW) Pratt & Whitney R-1830-76 radial piston engine
Performance:	maximum speed: 512km/h (318mph); range: 1464km (910 miles); service ceiling: 10,363m (34,000ft)
Dimensions:	span 11.58m (38ft); length 8.76m (28ft 9in); height 2.81m (9ft 3in); wing area 24.15 sq m (260 sq ft)
Weights:	empty 2674kg (5895lb); loaded 3607kg (7952lb)
Armament:	six .5in (12.7mm) Browning machine guns; up to 200lb of bombs

Curtiss Kittyhawk III

From April 1943, the Royal New Zealand Air Force contributed fighter squadrons to the Pacific Islands campaign. No 15 Squadron RNZAF flew P-40K Kittyhawks from Guadalcanal, Espiritu Santos and other islands, later receiving F4U-1D Corsairs.

SPECIFICATIONS	
Country of origin:	United States
Type:	single-engined fighter
Powerplant:	one 1325hp (989kW) Allison V-1710-73 (F4R) V-12 piston engine
Performance:	maximum speed 583km/h (362mph); range 2575km (1600 miles); service ceiling 8534m (28,000ft)
Dimensions:	span 11.37m (37ft 4in); length 10.15m (33ft 4in); height 3.75m (12ft 4in); wing area 21.93 sq m (236 sq ft)
Weights:	empty 2903kg (6400lb); maximum 4536kg (10,000lb)
Armament:	six .5in (12.7mm) Browning machine guns; one 500b (227kg) bomb

1942

The Americans Arrive in Europe

Americans had served in the European Theatre of Operations (ETO) since the Battle of Britain and with the 'Eagle Squadrons', composed of volunteers who crossed into Canada to join the RCAF. They were absorbed into the newly formed Eighth Air Force from early 1942. Confident that they could mount precision raids, the USAAF flew daylight missions, leaving the night to RAF Bomber Command, who had switched to the hours of darkness out of bitter experience.

Supermarine Spitfire Mk VB

The three Eagle Squadrons of the RAF (Nos 71, 121 and 133) were reformed as the 4th Fighter Group's 334th (illustrated), 335th and 336th Squadrons when the United States formally entered the war. They flew Spitfire Vs until conversion to the P-47 was complete in April 1943.

SPECIFICATIONS	
Country of origin:	United Kingdom
Type:	single-seat fighter and fighter-bomber
Powerplant:	one 1470hp (1096kW) Merlin 50 engine
Performance:	maximum speed 594km/h (369mph); range 1827km (1135 miles); service ceiling 11,125m (36,500ft)
Dimensions:	span 11.23m (36ft 10in); length 9.12m (29ft 11in); height 3.02m (9ft 11in)
Weight:	2911kg (6417lb) loaded
Armament:	4 x 7.7mm (.303in) MGs; 2 x 20mm (.8in) cannons in wings

Republic P-47C Thunderbolt

The P-47 was fast and long-ranged – and heavy. It was nicknamed the 'Jug' (either for 'juggernaut' or its resemblance to a milk jug). The 334th Squadron of the 4th Fighter Group took the Thunderbolt into combat for the first time in March 1943 from Debden, Essex.

SPECIFICATIONS	
Country of origin:	United States
Type:	single-engined fighter
Powerplant:	one 2300hp (1715kW) Pratt & Whitney Double Wasp radial piston engine
Performance:	maximum speed 697km/h (433mph); range 2012km (1250 miles); service ceiling 12,810m (42,000ft)
Dimensions:	span 12.44m (40ft 10in); length 11.02m (36ft 2in); height 4.31m (14ft 2in); wing area 27.87 sq m (300 sq ft)
Weights:	empty 4491kg (9900lb); maximum 6770kg (14,925lb)
Armament:	eight .5in (12.7mm) machine guns

AMERICANS TIMELINE
1935

1939

Boeing B-17E Flying Fortress

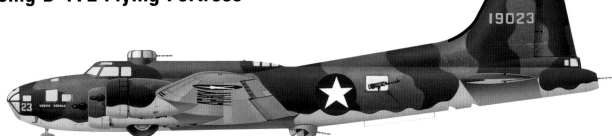

The Flying Fortress was the iconic aircraft of the Eighth Air Force. As German defences improved, early models like the B-17E were found to lack defensive armament and armour plate. 'Yankee Doodle', of the 97th Bomb Group, led the first USAAF B-17 mission over Germany in August 1942.

SPECIFICATIONS	
Country of origin:	United States
Type:	8-10 seat medium bomber
Powerplant:	4 x 1200hp (895kW) Wright turbo-supercharged engines
Performance:	maximum speed 510km/h (317mph); range 5150km (3200 miles); service ceiling 10,973m (36,000ft)
Dimensions:	span 31.6m (103ft 9in); length 22.5m (73ft 10in); height 6.3m (19ft 2in)
Weight:	23,133kg (51,000lb) loaded
Armament:	1 x 7.62mm (.3in) MG in nose; 2 x 12.7mm (.5in) waist MGs; nose, ventral and tail turrets each with 2 x 12.7mm (.5in) MGs; 1905kg (4200lb) of bombs

Consolidated B-24D Liberator

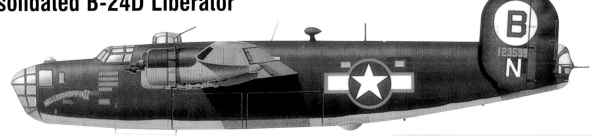

The B-24 was faster than the B-17 and had greater maximum range, but was less resistant to battle damage. B-24Ds of the 93rd Bomb Group, like 'Hellzapoppin II', flew several 'shuttle' missions from England to North Africa, returning via strikes on Romanian oil fields.

SPECIFICATIONS	
Country of origin:	United States
Type:	10 seat long-range heavy bomber
Powerplant:	4 x 1200hp (895kW) Pratt & Whitney radial piston engines
Performance:	maximum speed 488km/h (303mph); range 1730km (1080 miles); service ceiling 8540m (28,000ft)
Dimensions:	span 33.52m (110ft); length 20.22m (66ft 4in); height 5.46m (17ft 11in)
Weight:	27216kg (60,000lb) loaded
Armament:	1 (or 3) x 12.7mm (.5in) nose MGs; 6 x 12.7mm (.5in) MGs: two in dorsal turret, two in retractable ball turret, two in waist positions; 3629kg (8000lb) of bombs

Lockheed P-38J Lightning

The twin-boomed P-38 was the most distinctive of the Allied fighters. Early P-38s suffered from engine supercharger problems and unreliable heating, reducing their altitude potential, but by 1944 and the P-38J, the Lightning was mature.

SPECIFICATIONS	
Country of origin:	United States
Type:	twin-engined fighter
Powerplant:	two 1426hp (1063kW) Allison V-1719-89/91 V-12 piston engines
Performance:	maximum speed 663km/h (411mph); range 1529km (950 miles); service ceiling 13,350m (43,800ft)
Dimensions:	span 15.85m (52ft); length 11.53m (37ft 10in); height 3m (9ft 10in) wing area 30.42 sq m (327.44 sq ft)
Weights:	empty 5797kg (12,870lb); maximum 9798kg (21,601lb)
Armament:	one 20mm cannon, four .5in MGs; up to 1814kg (4000lb) of bombs

1941

Focke-Wulf Fw 190

Illustrating the gap between German and Allied aircraft production capabilities, the Focke-Wulf Fw 190 was the only truly mass-produced combat aircraft developed, flown and put into *Luftwaffe* service after the outbreak of war. The outstanding 190 was a huge surprise to the RAF when it was first encountered in August 1941, and inflicted heavy losses against their fighter sweeps. Dozens of sub-variants were built, with the late-model Fw 190D interceptor retaining only the wing of the original.

Focke-Wulf Fw 190A-2

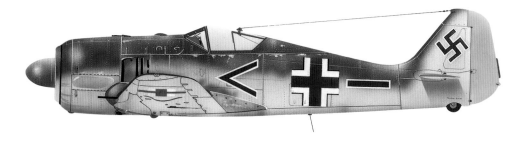

The first major operation for the Fw 190 came early in 1942, when JG 26 was part of the force used by Adolf Galland to provide 24-hour cover to the battlecruisers *Scharnhorst* and *Gneisenau* as they dashed up the English Channel.

SPECIFICATIONS	
Country of origin:	Germany
Type:	Single-seat fighter-bomber
Powerplant:	1600hp (1193kW) BMW 801C-2 14-cylinder two-row radial
Performance:	maximum speed 624km/h (388mph); range 900km (560 miles); service ceiling 11,410m (37,400ft)
Dimensions:	span 10.49m (34ft 5.5in); length 8.84m (29ft); height 3.96m (13ft)
Weight:	4900kg (10,800lb) loaded
Armament:	4 x 7.92mm (.3in) MGs, two on wing root and two above engine, 2 x 20mm (.8in) cannon in wing roots

Focke-Wulf Fw 190A-6/R11

Based at Abbeville in May 1943, this aircraft saw action against British cross-Channel raiders and against the bombers of the 8th US Army Air Force, which were now beginning to mount large-scale raids.

SPECIFICATIONS	
Country of origin:	Germany
Type:	single-seat fighter-bomber
Powerplant:	1268kW (1700hp) BMW 801D-2 water-injected 18-cylinder two-row radial
Performance:	maximum speed 670km/hr (416mph); range 900km (560 miles); service ceiling 11,410m (37,400ft)
Dimensions:	span 10.49m (34ft 5.5in); length 8.84m (29ft); height 3.96m (13ft)
Weight:	4900kg (10,800lb) loaded
Armament:	4 x 20mm (.8in) cannon; 2 x 7.92mm (.3in) MGs; 1 x 500kg (1102lb) bomb

Focke-Wulf Fw 190A-5/U8

SPECIFICATIONS

Country of origin:	Germany
Type:	single-engined fighter-bomber
Powerplant:	one 1730hp (1272kW) BMW 801D-2 radial piston engine
Performance:	maximum speed 656km/h (408mph); range 656km/h (408mph); service ceiling 11,410m (37,430ft)
Dimensions:	span 10.51m (34ft 5in); length 8.95m (29ft 4in); height 3.95m (12ft 12in); wing area 18.3 sq m (196.99 sq ft)
Weights:	empty 3200kg (7060lb); maximum 4300kg (9480lb)
Armament:	two 20mm MG 151/20 E cannon; one 1102lb (500kg) SC-500 bomb

The Fw 190A-5/U8 was a long-range fighter-bomber variant. The U stood for Umrüst-Bausätze, or factory conversion set. The U8 kit added a centreline bomb rack. This example wears subdued camouflage for dawn and dusk 'tip and run' raids on the United Kingdom.

Focke-Wulf Fw 190D-9

SPECIFICATIONS

Country of origin:	Germany
Type:	single-engined fighter
Powerplant:	one 1580hp (1287kW) Junkers Jumo inverted-V-12 piston engine
Performance:	maximum speed 685km/h (426mph); range 935km (519 miles); service ceiling 12,000m (39,370ft)
Dimensions:	span 19.96m (65ft 6in); length 15.62m (51ft 3in); height 3.63m (11ft 11in)
Weights:	empty 3490kg (7694lb); maximum 4840kg (10,670lb)
Armament:	two 13mm MG 131 machine guns, two 20mm MG 151 cannon; one 500kg (1102lb) SC 500 bomb

The 'Dora 9' version married the Fw 190A wing with an elongated fuselage and a Jumo 213 inverted V-12 version instead of the BMW 801 radial. Entering service in October 1944, it was a match for the P-51D Mustang, but relatively few were completed by the war's end.

Focke-Wulf Ta 152

SPECIFICATIONS

Country of origin:	Germany
Type:	single-engined interceptor fighter
Powerplant:	one 1287kW (1750hp) Jumo 213E inverted V-12 piston engine
Performance:	maximum speed 483km/h (300mph); range 2000km (1240 miles); service ceiling 14,800m (48,550ft)
Dimensions:	length 10.82m (33ft 11in); height 3.36m (13ft 1in); wing area 23.5 sq m (253.0 sq ft)
Weights:	empty 4031kg (8640lb); maximum 5217kg (11,501lb)
Armament:	one MK 108 30mm cannon and two MG 151/20 20mm cannon

Given the designation Ta 152 (in honour of designer Kurt Tank), this final version of the Focke-Wulf 190 series was intended for production in versions for high- and low-altitude use, but in the end only a small number of the long-winged Ta 152H high-altitude version entered service.

Trainers

To meet the enormous demand for aircrew, particularly pilots and navigators, all the major nations employed large numbers of training aircraft. Aircrew training could be as dangerous as combat flying, with nearly half of the Canadian airmen who died in the war killed while in training – a statistic mirrored in other air forces. Whereas Allied airmen had the United States and Canada to train over, for much of the war the training airspace for German aircrew was the battlefield.

Bucker Bü 131B Jungmann

The Jungmann was Germany's primary pre-war and wartime trainer, and was supplied to several European countries. Kyushu in Japan built over 1200 for their army and navy training schools. The Bü 131B was also used on the Eastern Front as a light ground-attack aircraft.

SPECIFICATIONS	
Country of origin:	Germany
Type:	two-seat biplane trainer
Powerplant:	one 105hp (78kW) Hirth HM 504A-2 inverted inline piston engine
Performance:	maximum speed 183km/h (114mph); service ceiling 3000m (9840ft); range 650km (404 miles)
Weights:	empty 390kg (860lb); maximum 680kg (1499lb)
Dimensions:	span 7.40m (24ft 4in); length 6.60m (21ft 8in); height 2.25m (7ft 5in); wing area 13.5 sq m (145.32 sq ft)

De Havilland Tiger Moth

The greatest number of Tiger Moths were built to Air Ministry Specification T.26/33 as Tiger Moth Mk IIs, with a rear fuselage decking in plywood rather than fabric and stringers, and provision for a blind flying hood over the rear cockpit (for instrument-only flying training). Most of Britain's wartime pilots were trained on the Moth, and after the conflict many of the 7290 aircraft produced became available to civilian customers at a knockdown price.

SPECIFICATIONS	
Country of origin:	United Kingdom
Type:	two-seat elementary trainer biplane
Powerplant:	one 130hp (89kW) de Havilland Gipsy Major I inline piston engine
Performance:	maximum speed 167km/h (104mph); service ceiling 4145m (13,600ft); range 483km (300 miles)
Weights:	empty 506kg (1115lb); maximum take-off weight 828kg (1825lb)
Dimensions:	span 8.94m (29ft 4in); length 7.29m (23ft 11in); height 2.69m (8ft 1in); wing area 22.2 sq m (239 sq ft)

TRAINERS TIMELINE

 1931

 1934

Airspeed AS.10 Oxford

In various guises, the humble Airspeed Oxford was used to train pilots, navigators, gunners, radio operators and camera operators. Between 1937 and 1945, over 8500 were built, many of them used as part of the British Commonwealth Air Training Plan in Canada.

SPECIFICATIONS	
Country of origin:	United Kingdom
Type:	twin-engined trainer
Powerplant:	Two 265hp (355kW) Armstrong Siddeley Cheetah X radial piston engines
Performance:	maximum speed: 300km/h (185mph); range 1500km (960 miles); service ceiling: 5850m (19,200ft)
Dimensions:	span 53ft 4in (16.26m); length 34ft 6in (10.52m); height 11ft 1in (3.38m); wing area 32.3 sq m (348 sq ft)
Weights:	empty 5380lb (2440kg); maximum 7600lb (3450kg)

Heinkel He 51

Once its frontline career as a fighter was over, the Heinkel He 51 was relegated to the training role. Its relatively high performance suited it to training pilots in fighter tactics. This He 51B served with A/B Schule 123 at Zagreb, Yugoslavia, in spring 1942.

SPECIFICATIONS	
Country of origin:	Germany
Type:	single-seat fighter biplane
Powerplant:	one 750hp (559kW) BMW V1 7,3Z 12-cylinder Vee piston engine
Performance:	maximum speed 330km/h (205mph); range 570km (354 miles); service ceiling 7700m (25,260ft)
Dimensions:	span 11m (36ft 1in); length 8.4m (27ft 7in); height 3.2m (10ft 6in); wing area 27.2 sq m (293 sq ft)
Weights:	empty 1460kg (3219lb); maximum take-off weight 1895kg (4178lb)

Boeing N2S-5 Kaydet

Designed by the Stearman Aircraft Company in 1933, the Kaydet trainer became a Boeing product following a takeover in 1939. Under various designations, including PT-13, PT-17 and N2S, over 10,000 of the rugged and dependable 'Stearmans were built for the USAAF, USN and RCAF.

SPECIFICATIONS	
Country of origin:	United States
Type:	(N2S-5) two-seat primary trainer
Powerplant:	one 220hp (165kW) Lycoming R-680-17 radial piston engine
Performance:	maximum speed 200km/h (124mph); range 813km (505mph); service ceiling 3415m (11,200ft)
Dimensions:	span 9.8m (32ft 2in); length 7.5m (24ft 10in); height 2.7m (9ft 2in); wing area 27.6 sq m (297.4 sq ft)
Weight:	empty 878kg (1936lb); maximum 1232kg (2717lb)

1937

1942

RAF 'Heavies'

RAF Bomber Command pounded Germany's cities and other targets in occupied Europe from 1939–45 in the longest battle of the war. The RAF was able to mount a number of 'thousand-bomber' raids beginning in May 1942. From February 1941 and the operational debut of the Stirling, Bomber Command began the shift to four-engined 'heavies' for the campaign. Alongside the triad of Stirling, Halifax and Lancaster, specialist units used American-built Liberators and Fortresses.

Short Stirling III

The Stirling was a worthy rather than genuinely capable bomber, and throughout its first-line bomber career suffered from poor payload/range figures and a low service ceiling. By 1943, the type was being relegated to the transport role.

SPECIFICATIONS	
Country of origin:	United Kingdom
Type:	seven-seat heavy bomber
Powerplant:	4 x 1375hp 1030kW() Bristol Hercules radial engines
Performance:	maximum speed 410km/h (255mph); range 3750km (2330 miles); service ceiling 5030m (16,500ft)
Dimensions:	span 30.2m (99ft 1in) length 26.6m (87ft 3in); height 8.8m (28ft 10in)
Weight:	31,750kg (70,000lb) loaded
Armament:	8 x 7.7mm (.303in) Browning MGs: two in the nose, four in the tail, two dorsal; up to 8164kg (18,000lb) of bombs

Handley Page Halifax Mk III

Carrying the nickname 'Friday the 13th', this was the first Halifax to complete 100 operational sorties, and survived World War II with a total of 128 sorties, the largest number recorded by any Halifax bomber. This aircraft was part of No 158 Squadron, RAF Bomber Command, Lissett, in 1945.

SPECIFICATIONS	
Country of origin:	United Kingdom
Type:	seven-seat heavy bomber
Powerplant:	1615hp (1204kW) Bristol Hercules XVI radial piston engines
Performance:	maximum speed 454km/h (282mph); range 1658km (1030 miles); service ceiling 7315m (24,000ft)
Dimensions:	span 31.75m (104ft 2in); length 21.36m (70ft 1in); height 6.32m (20ft 9in)
Weight:	29,484kg (65,000lb) loaded
Armament:	9 x 7.7mm (.303in) MGs; up to 5897kg (13,000lb) bomb load

Avro Lancaster B.Mk I

This aircraft flew as part of No 467 Squadron, Royal Australian Air Force, RAF Bomber Command, in 1945. No 467 Squadron was one of four bomber squadrons of the RAAF to serve with RAF Bomber Command, the others being Nos 460, 463 and 466 Squadrons. However, there were insufficient squadrons to allow the creation of an Australian group like the Canadian No 6 Group.

SPECIFICATIONS

Country of origin:	Australia
Type:	seven-seat heavy bomber
Powerplant:	4 x 1640hp (1223kW) Rolls-Royce Merlin XXIV V-12 piston engines
Performance:	462km/h (287mph); range 4070km (2530 miles); service ceiling 7470m (24,500ft)
Dimensions:	span 31.09m (102ft); length 21.18m (69ft 6in); height 6.10m (20ft)
Weight:	16738kg (36,900lb) loaded
Armament:	8 x 7.7mm (.303in) MGs; bomb load of either one 9979kg (22,000lb) or up to 6350kg (4000lb) of smaller bombs

Boeing Fortress Mk III

This aeroplane was operated in the electronic jamming and intelligence-gathering roles in the later stages of World War II. It flew as part of No 223 (Special Duties) Squadron, No 100 Group, RAF Bomber Command, Oulton, Norfolk, 1944–45.

SPECIFICATIONS

Country of origin:	United Kingdom
Type:	eight-seat heay bomber (reconnaissance & electronic countermeasures)
Powerplant:	4 x 1200hp (895kW) Wright Cyclone GR-1820 radial piston engines
Performance:	maximum speed 451km/h (280mph); range 4410km (2740 miles); service ceiling 9601m (31,500ft)
Dimensions:	span 31.62m (103ft 9in); length 22.25m (73ft); height 4.72m (15ft 6in)
Weight:	29,030kg (64,000lb) loaded
Armament:	13 x 12.7mm (.5in) MGs in nose, turrets, waist and tail; up to 5806kg (12,800lb) bomb load

Consolidated Liberator B.Mk IV

With its long range, the Liberator was used mostly in the maritime reconnaissance bomber role by RAF Coastal Command, but its speed and large fuselage also led to its use by Bomber Command's No 100 Group in the special duties support role. This aircraft flew with No 223 Squadron, No 100 Group, RAF Bomber Command, Oulton, in August 1944.

SPECIFICATIONS

Country of origin:	United Kingdom
Type:	eight-seat special duties heavy bomber
Powerplant:	4 x 1200hp (895kW) Pratt & Whitney Twin Wasp radial piston engines
Performance:	maximum speed 435km/h (270mph); range 2366km (1470 miles); service ceiling 8534m (28,000ft)
Dimensions:	span 17.63m (57ft 10in); length 12.7m (41ft 8in); height 4.83m (15ft 10in)
Weight:	11,431kg (25,200lb) loaded
Armament:	4 x 20mm (.79in) cannon, 7 x 7.7mm (.303in) MGs; 1 x torpedo and 2 x 113kg (250lb) bombs or 8 x 41kg (90lb) rocket projectiles

De Havilland Mosquito

Built as a private venture, and allowed to go ahead only because it used mainly 'non-strategic' materials (spruce and balsawood), the Mosquito was one of the most versatile aircraft of the war. The bomber and reconnaissance variants used their speed rather than armament for self-protection, while the night-fighter, fighter-bomber and anti-shipping models packed a heavy punch with machine guns, cannon and rockets. The Mosquito was licence-built in Canada and Australia.

De Havilland Mosquito PR.1

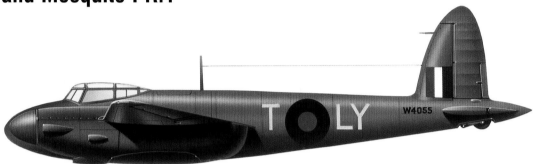

The PR.I was the first Mosquito variant to enter service, and W4055 was the first to fly an operational sortie when it flew a photo mission over Brest on 17 September 1941. Assigned to 1 Photo Reconnaissance Unit (1 PRU), it later failed to return from a flight over Norway.

SPECIFICATIONS

Country of origin:	United Kingdom
Type:	twin-engined reconnaissance aircraft
Powerplant:	Two 1280hp (954kW) Rolls-Royce Merlin 21 V-12 piston engines
Performance:	maximum speed 612km/h (380mph); service ceiling 9144m (30,000ft); range 2990km (1860 miles)
Weights:	empty 6396kg (14,100lb); maximum 7938kg (17,500lb)
Dimensions:	span 16.5m (54ft 2in); length 40ft 10in); height 4.66m (15ft 4in); wing area 42.18 sq m (454 sq ft)
Armament:	none

De Havilland Mosquito IV

The Mosquito bomber could carry the same bombload to Berlin as a Lancaster, but with two crew rather than seven. No 105 Squadron began making low-level raids in the spring of 1942, striking at rail yards, factories, airfields and other precision targets.

SPECIFICATIONS

Country of origin:	United Kingdom
Type:	(B.IV Series 2) twin-engined bomber
Powerplant:	Two 1280hp (954kW) Rolls-Royce Merlin 23 V-12 piston engines
Performance:	maximum speed 612km/h (380mph); service ceiling 9144m (30,000ft); range 3384km (2040 miles)
Weights:	empty 6396kg (14,100lb); loaded 10,151kg (22,380lb)
Dimensions:	span 16.5m (54ft 2in); length 12.35m (40ft 10in); height 4.66m (15ft 4in); wing area 42.18 sq m (454 sq ft)
Armament:	up to 4000lb of bombs

De Havilland Sea Mosquito T.33

Having used Mosquitoes from land bases, the Fleet Air Arm ordered a navalized version with wing folding and a nose-mounted sea search radar. Although a Mosquito was the first twin-engined aircraft to fly from carriers, the Sea Mosquito had a very short frontline career.

SPECIFICATIONS	
Country of origin:	United Kingdom
Type:	twin-engined carrier-based torpedo bomber
Powerplant:	two 1620hp (1208kW) Rolls-Royce Merlin 25 V-12 piston engines
Performance:	maximum speed 612km/h (380mph); service ceiling 10,058m (33,000 ft); range 2415km (1500 miles)
Weights:	empty 6486kg (14,300lb); maximum take-off 10,115kg (22,300lb)
Dimensions:	16.5m (54ft 2in) length 12.44m (40ft 2in); height 4.66m (15ft 4in); wing area 42.18 sq m (454 sq ft)
Armament:	four 20mm Hispano cannon; 454kg (1000lb) of bombs or one 18in (46cm) torpedo

De Havilland Mosquito PR.XVI

Based on the B.IX bomber version, the PR.XVI reconnaissance Mosquito had a pressurized cockpit and Merlins with a two-stage supercharger for high-altitude work. PR.XVI NS777 flew with No 140 Squadron at Melsbroek, Belgium in December 1944.

SPECIFICATIONS	
Country of origin:	United Kingdom
Type:	twin-engined reconnaissance aircraft
Powerplant:	two 1680hp (1253kW) Rolls-Royce Merlin 72/73 piston engines
Performance:	maximum speed 668km/h (415mph); service ceiling 10,516m (34,500ft); range 3943km (2450 miles)
Weights:	empty 6638kg (14,635lb); maximum 10,719kg (23,630lb)
Dimensions:	16.5m (54ft 2in); length 13.56m (44ft 6in); height 3.81m (12ft 6in); wing area 42.18 sq m (454sq ft)
Armament:	none

De Havilland Mosquito T.3

The sometimes-tricky handling of the Mosquito, particularly with one engine out, brought a requirement that resulted in the T.III trainer version painted a vivid yellow. Wartime examples were converted from F.II night fighters, but more were built post-war with the revised designation T.3.

SPECIFICATIONS	
Country of origin:	United Kingdom
Type:	twin-engined trainer
Powerplant:	two 1620hp (1208kW) Rolls-Royce Merlin 25 V-12 piston engines
Performance:	maximum speed 618km/h (384mph); service ceiling 11,430m (37,500ft); range 2511km (1560 miles)
Weights:	empty 6486kg (14,300lb); loaded 9072kg (20,000lb)
Dimensions:	16.5m (54ft 2in); length 12.44m (40ft 10in); height 4.65m (15ft 3in); wing area 42.18 sq m (454 sq ft)
Armament:	none

Luftwaffe Night Fighters

As the RAF night raids grew heavier, the Luftwaffe adopted an efficient system of ground-controlled interception, dividing air space into operating 'boxes' for night fighters and equipping its aircraft with high-quality radar. Most sorts of combat aircraft were adapted for night fighting, from single-engined fighters to twin-engined bombers, but only one purpose-designed night fighter, the He 219, entered service during the war. The Luftwaffe's night squadrons claimed 7308 kills.

Messerschmitt Bf 110G-4

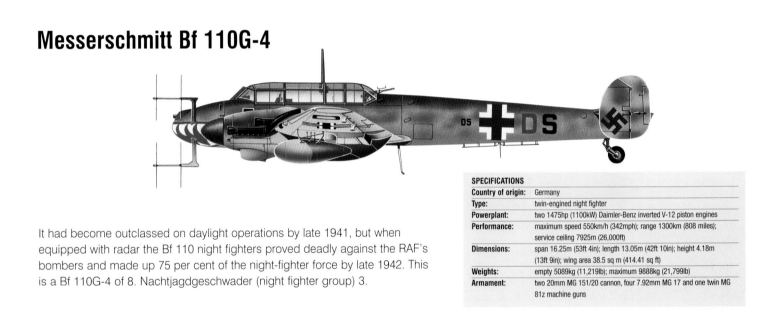

It had become outclassed on daylight operations by late 1941, but when equipped with radar the Bf 110 night fighters proved deadly against the RAF's bombers and made up 75 per cent of the night-fighter force by late 1942. This is a Bf 110G-4 of 8. Nachtjagdgeschwader (night fighter group) 3.

SPECIFICATIONS	
Country of origin:	Germany
Type:	twin-engined night fighter
Powerplant:	two 1475hp (1100kW) Daimler-Benz inverted V-12 piston engines
Performance:	maximum speed 550km/h (342mph); range 1300km (808 miles); service ceiling 7925m (26,000ft)
Dimensions:	span 16.25m (53ft 4in); length 13.05m (42ft 10in); height 4.18m (13ft 9in); wing area 38.5 sq m (414.41 sq ft)
Weights:	empty 5089kg (11,219lb); maximum 9888kg (21,799lb)
Armament:	two 20mm MG 151/20 cannon, four 7.92mm MG 17 and one twin MG 81z machine guns

Junkers Ju 88G-6

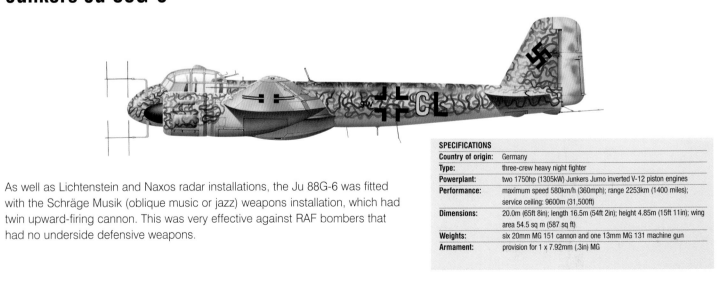

As well as Lichtenstein and Naxos radar installations, the Ju 88G-6 was fitted with the Schräge Musik (oblique music or jazz) weapons installation, which had twin upward-firing cannon. This was very effective against RAF bombers that had no underside defensive weapons.

SPECIFICATIONS	
Country of origin:	Germany
Type:	three-crew heavy night fighter
Powerplant:	two 1750hp (1305kW) Junkers Jumo inverted V-12 piston engines
Performance:	maximum speed 580km/h (360mph); range 2253km (1400 miles); service ceiling 9600m (31,500ft)
Dimensions:	20.0m (65ft 8in); length 16.5m (54ft 2in); height 4.85m (15ft 11in); wing area 54.5 sq m (587 sq ft)
Weights:	six 20mm MG 151 cannon and one 13mm MG 131 machine gun
Armament:	provision for 1 x 7.92mm (.3in) MG

LUFTWAFFE TIMELINE

1938   1939   1942

Focke-Wulf 189 Uhu

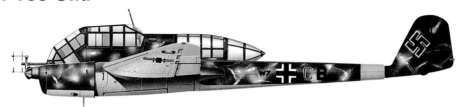

The unusual Focke Wulf 189 Uhu (Owl) observation aircraft found an additional role as a night interceptor of Soviet Po-2s and other night-harassment aircraft. This Fw 189A-4 with Lichtenstein C-1 radar was based at Griefswald, Germany, in February 1945.

SPECIFICATIONS	
Country of origin:	Germany
Type:	twin-engined night fighter
Powerplant:	two 465hp (347kW) Argus As 410A-1 inline piston engines
Performance:	maximum speed 350km/h (217mph); range 1340km (832 miles); service ceiling 7300m (23,950ft)
Dimensions:	18.40m (60ft 5in); length 12.03m (39ft 6in); height 3.1m (10ft 2in); wing area 38 sq m (409 sq ft)
Weights:	empty 2680kg (5920lb); maximum 4170kg (9193lb)
Armament:	three 20mm MG 151/20 cannon

Focke-Wulf Fw 190A-6/r11

British counter-measures, such as the use of 'Window', often negated the effect of the night-fighter boxes. In 1943, Major Hajo Hermann introduced the successful *Wilde Sau* (Wild Boar) tactics that allowed certain units (including 1. Nachtjagdgeschwader 10 with the Fw 190A-6) to roam free, hunting for their own targets.

SPECIFICATIONS	
Country of origin:	Germany
Type:	single-engined night fighter
Powerplant:	one 1730hp (1272kW) BMW 801D-2 radial piston engine
Performance:	maximum speed 656km/h (408mph); range 800km (500 miles); service ceiling 11,410m (37,430ft)
Dimensions:	span 10.51m (34ft 5in); length 8.95m (29ft 4in); height 3.95m (12ft 12in); wing area 18.3 sq m (196.99 sq ft)
Weights:	empty 3200kg (7060lb); maximum 3900kg (8598lb)
Armament:	six 20mm MG 151/20 E cannon; two 7.92mm MG 17 machine guns

Heinkel He 219-0 Uhu

Built from the outset as a night fighter, the He 219 Uhu (Owl) was made in relatively small numbers (288) despite its sensational operational debut. On the night of 11–12 June 1943, Werner Streib, flying a pre-production He 219A-0 (illustrated), destroyed five Lancasters.

SPECIFICATIONS	
Country of origin:	Germany
Type:	(He 219A-7/R-1) two-seat twin-engined night fighter
Powerplant:	two 1800hp (1324kW) Daimler-Benz V-12 piston engines
Performance:	maximum speed 616km/h (385mph); range: 1540km (960 miles); service ceiling 9300m (30,500ft)
Dimensions:	span 18.5m (60ft 8in); length 15.5m (51ft); height 4.4m (14ft 5in); wing area 44.4 sq m (478 sq ft)
Weights:	empty 11,200kg (24,692lb); maximum 13,580g (29,900lb)
Armament:	four 30mm MK 108, two 30mm MK 103, two 20mm MG 151/20 cannon

1943

Consolidated Catalina

In 1933, Douglas and Consolidated entered the battle to supply the US Navy with its first cantilever monoplane flying-boat to replace the P2Y-2s and Y-3s. Isaac B. Landon's design for Consolidated beat Douglas' admirable entry, and the Consolidated XP3Y-1 prototype evolved into one of the greatest aircraft in history. Six hundred and fifty Catalinas – the British service designation for the aircraft – were delivered to the RAF Coastal Command during World War II.

Consolidated PBY-5

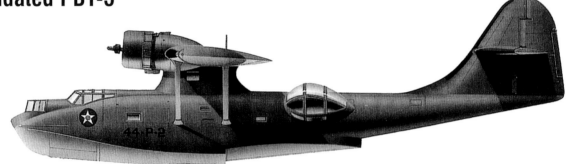

The Catalina served across the Pacific from Alaska to the Solomons, where Patrol Squadron 44 (illustrated) operated in early 1943. VP-44 later became one of the 'Black Cat' squadrons flying night anti-shipping missions against Japanese supply convoys.

SPECIFICATIONS

Country of origin:	United States
Type:	nine-seat maritime reconnaissance and bomber flying boat
Powerplant:	two 1200hp (895kW) Pratt & Whitney R-1830-82 Twin Wasp 14-cylinder two-row radial engines
Performance:	maximum speed 322km/h (200mph); range 3050km (1895 miles); service ceiling 6585m (21,600ft)
Dimensions:	span 31.7m (104ft); length 19.45m (63ft 10in); height 5.76m (18ft 11in)
Weights:	empty 7893kg (17,400lb); maximum take-off weight 15,145kg (33,389lb)
Armament:	three .3in MGs (two in bow turret, one in ventral tunnel), one .5in MG in each 'blister' beam position, external; bomb load of 2041kg (4500lb)

Consolidated Catalina GR.IIA

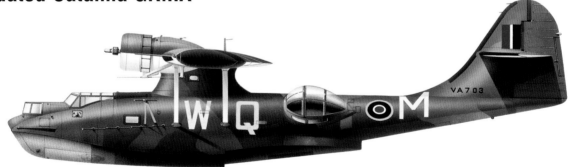

Canadian Vickers built a large number of Catalinas under licence, and the name Canso was often applied to them. The RAF's 36 Catalina GR.IIa models were originally ordered for the RCAF. This one served with No 209 Squadron at Pembroke Dock in mid-1942.

SPECIFICATIONS

Country of origin:	United States
Type:	nine-seat maritime reconnaissance and bomber flying boat
Powerplant:	two 1200hp (895kW) Pratt & Whitney R-1830-82 Twin Wasp 14-cylinder two-row radial engines
Performance:	maximum speed 322km/h (200mph); range 3050km (1895 miles); service ceiling 6585m (21,600ft)
Dimensions:	span 31.7m (104ft); length 19.45m (63ft 10in); height 5.76m (18ft 11in)
Weights:	empty 7893kg (17,400lb); maximum take-off weight 15,145kg (33,389lb)
Armament:	three .3in MGs (two in bow turret, one in ventral tunnel), one .5in MG in each 'blister' beam position, external; bomb load of 2041kg (4500lb)

Consolidated PBY-5

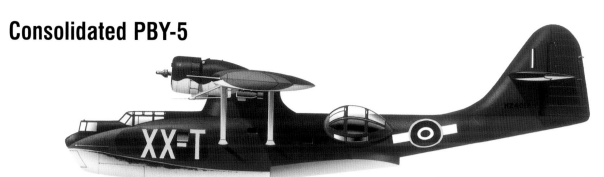

The Royal New Zealand Air Force operated 56 Catalinas, all flying-boat versions, from 1943 to 1953. About half of them were Boeing-built P2B-1 Nomads. This is a PBY-5 of No 6 Squadron RNZAF, based at Halavo Bay, Florida Island in the Solomons, in 1943.

Consolidated OA-10A Catalina

The USAAF operated 58 PBY-5A amphibians under the designation OA-10 for air sea-rescue duties, and another 252 Canadian-built PBV-1As as OA-10As. They featured air-surface radar in a podded installation above the cockpit.

Consolidated PBY-6A Canso

The Royal Danish Air Force operated both Canadian-built Cansos and USN-surplus PBY-6A Catalinas in the post-war years. This is one of the latter, acquired in 1957 and used for patrol in Danish waters, the Baltic and from bases in Greenland.

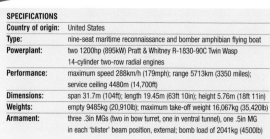

Sink the *Tirpitz*

The German battleship *Tirpitz*, sister ship to *Bismarck*, was a thorn in the side of the Royal Navy for most of the war. Although she made few forays out of the Norwegian fjords in which she was based, she posed such a potential threat to Russian-bound convoys that she tied up a large proportion of the British Home Fleet. Damaged by a midget submarine attack and then by carrier-based raids, *Tirpitz* was moved to northern Norway in late 1944, where she was in range of RAF bombers.

Fairey Barracuda TB Mk II

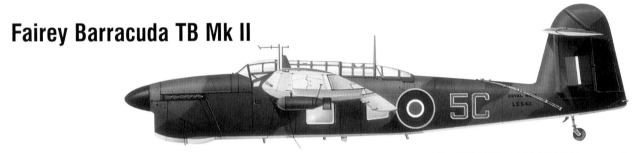

The first air attack to do serious harm to the *Tirpitz* was Operation Tungsten in April 1944. Six British carriers and many escorting destroyers were involved. Two waves of Fairey Barracuda dive-bombers caused serious damage to the battleship, with 14 direct hits.

SPECIFICATIONS	
Country of origin:	United Kingdom
Type:	single-engined carrier-based dive/torpedo-bomber
Powerplant:	one 1640hp (1225kW) Rolls-Royce Merlin 32 V-12 piston engine
Performance:	maximum speed 340km/h (210mph); service ceiling 6585m (21,600ft); range 1165km (725 miles)
Weights:	empty 4445kg (9800lb); maximum take-off weight 6385kg (14,080lb)
Dimensions:	span 14.49m (47ft 6in); length 12.18m (40ft); height 4.6m (15ft); wing area 37.62 sq m (404.94 sq ft)
Armament:	two .303in (7.7mm) Vickers K machine guns; one torpedo or 735kg (1620lb) of bombs

Grumman F6F Hellcat

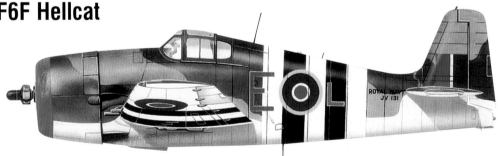

No 800 Squadron's Hellcat F Mk I fighters embarked on HMS *Emperor*-escorted Fleet Air Arm attacks on the *Tirpitz* in April 1944, shooting down three Luftwaffe fighters. This 800 Squadron Hellcat is depicted at the time of the D-Day landings.

SPECIFICATIONS	
Country of origin:	United States
Type:	single-seat carrierborne fighter and fighter-bomber
Powerplant:	one 2000hp (1491kW) Pratt & Whitney R-2800-10 or 10W Double Wasp 18-cylinder two-row radial engine
Performance:	maximum speed 603km/h (375mph); service ceiling 11,705m (38,400ft); range 2559km (1590 miles)
Weights:	empty 4128kg (9101lb); maximum take-off weight 7025kg (15,487lb)
Dimensions:	span 13.06m (42ft 10in); length 10.24m (33ft 7in); height 3.99m (13ft 1in)

TIRPITZ TIMELINE

1937

1938

1942

Avro Lancaster

In late 1944, several special missions were launched by Nos 9 and 617 Squadrons, using modified Lancasters armed with 5443kg (12,000lb) Tallboy bombs. Operations Paravane and Obviate caused some damage, but Operation Catechism on 12 November struck three fatal blows.

SPECIFICATIONS	
Country of origin:	United Kingdom
Type:	five-seat special mission bomber
Powerplant:	four 1640hp (1223kW) Rolls-Royce Merlin 24 12-cylinder Vee engines
Performance:	maximum speed 462km/h (287mph); range 2494km (1550 miles); service ceiling 5790m (19,0000ft)
Dimensions:	span 31.09m (10ft); length 21.18m (69ft 6in); height 6.25m (20ft 6in)
Weights:	empty 16,083kg (35,457lb) loaded; maximum take-off weight 32,659kg (72,000lb)
Armament:	four .303in trainable MGs in the tail turret, plus a semi-internal bomb load of one 9979kg (22,000lb) 'Grand Slam' bomb

Arado Ar.196

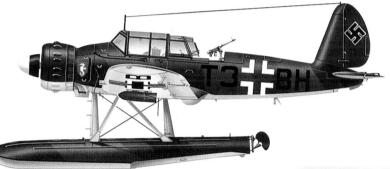

The Arado Ar.196 was the Kriegsmarine's main ship-borne aircraft. The *Tirpitz* could carry four, but its own aircraft were based elsewhere when the ship was confined to the fjords. This Ar.196A-3 of 1./Bordfliegergruppe flew from the Lofoten Islands near Stavanger, Norway, in 1944.

SPECIFICATIONS	
Country of origin:	Germany
Type:	two-seat reconnaissance and light attack floatplane
Powerplant:	one 970hp (723kW) BMW 132K nine-cylinder single-row radial engine
Performance:	maximum speed 320km/h (199mph); service ceiling 7000m (22,960ft); range 1070km (665 miles)
Dimensions:	span 12.40m (50ft 9.5in); length 11m (36ft); height 4.45m (14ft 7in)
Weights:	empty 2572kg (5670lb); maximum take-off weight 3730kg (8223lb)
Armament:	two 20mm fixed forward-firing cannon in wing, one 7.92mm fixed forward-firing machine gun in starboard side of forward fuselage, and one 7.92mm trainable rearward-firing MG in rear of cockpit, plus external bomb load of 100kg (220lb)

Messerschmitt Bf 109G-10

Jadgeschwader (fighter group) 5 'Eismeer' was the Luftwaffe wing assigned to the northern flank of 'Fortress Europe'. Its BF 109s failed to intercept the final raid on the *Tirpitz,* and Major Ehrler, the Geschwaderkommodore, was court-martialled and sentenced to death, although this was later commuted to a lesser punishment.

SPECIFICATIONS	
Country of origin:	Germany
Type:	single-seat fighter and fighter-bomber
Powerplant:	one 1475hp (1100kW) Daimler-Benz 605
Performance:	maximum speed 653km/h (400mph); range 700km (435 miles); service ceiling 11,600m (38,000ft)
Dimensions:	span 9.92m (32ft 6.5in); length 9.04m (29ft 8in); height 2.59m (8ft 6in)
Weights:	3400kg (7496lb) loaded
Armament:	one 20mm (.8in) cannon; two 7.92mm (.3in) or 13mm (.5in) MGs

1943

Battle of the Atlantic

The long-range Focke Wulf Condors based on the Bay of Biscay coast not only found targets for the U-boat 'Wolf Packs' but also struck them with bombs and strafed them with machine guns and cannon. Lone merchantmen sailing to and from Africa or South America without protection of the convoy system were frequent victims of the 'Scourge of the Atlantic'. However, the Condor had serious structural weaknesses and many simply broke in half on landing.

Focke Wulf Fw 200C-Condor

Initially designed as an airliner, the Focke Wulf Condor first flew in July 1937. In the spring of 1939, a new unit was established to attack ships in the Bay of Biscay, and the Condor was adapted for this role as the Fw 200C-0. The Condor was not stressed for the extra weight of carrying armaments, and many suffered structural failure on landing.

SPECIFICATIONS	
Country of origin:	Germany
Type:	four-engined, five-seat maritime patrol bomber
Powerplant:	four 830hp (619kW) BMW 132H radial piston engines
Performance:	maximum speed 360km/h (224mph); service ceiling 6000m (19,685ft); range 4440km (2795 miles)
Weights:	22,700kg (50,045lb) loaded
Dimensions:	span 32.82m (107ft 8in); length 23.46m (76ft 11.5in); height 6.3m (20ft 8in)
Armament:	three 7.92mm (.31in) MG 15 machine guns and one 20mm MG FF cannon, bomb load of up to four 250kg (551lb) bombs or two 1000kg (2205lb) mines

Junkers Ju 188

By 1941, delays in the Ju 288 programme – intended as the successor to the Ju 88 – meant that an interim aircraft was required. Consequently the Ju 188, which had emerged from the Ju 88B prototype, entered service in 1942 and production of about 110 aircraft included bomber, reconnaissance, high-altitude and intruder variants, among others.

SPECIFICATIONS	
Country of origin:	Germany
Type:	(Ju 188E-1) four-seat medium bomber
Powerplant:	one 1677hp (1250kW) BMW 14-cylinder two-row radial engines
Performance:	maximum speed 544km/h (338mph); service ceiling 10,100m (33,135ft); range 2480km (1541 miles)
Weights:	empty 9410kg (20,745lb); maximum take-off weight 14,570kg (32,121lb)
Dimensions:	span 22m (72ft 2in); length 15.06m (49ft 5in); height 4.46m (14ft 7in)
Armament:	one 20mm trainable forward-firing cannon in nose position, one 13mm machine gun in dorsal turret, one 13mm rearward-firing machine gun in rear of cockpit, and one 7.92mm two-barrel machine gun in undernose gondola, plus a bomb load of 3000kg (6613lb)

Dornier Do 217E-2

The Do 217 was Dornier's response to a 1937 requirement for a long-range warplane optimized for the heavy level and dive-bombing roles. Some 800 Do 217Es were built, before being succeeded by 950 Do 217Ks. Variants included bombers, anti-shipping bombers, high-altitude reconnaissance aircraft and a missile-launching aircraft.

SPECIFICATIONS	
Country of origin:	Germany
Type:	four-seat heavy bomber
Powerplant:	two 1178kW (1580hp) BMW 14-cylinder piston engine
Performance:	maximum speed 515km/h (320mph); service ceiling 9000m (29,530ft); range 2800km (1740 miles)
Weights:	empty 10,535kg (23,225lb); maximum take-off weight 16,465kg (36,299lb)
Dimensions:	span 19m (62ft 4in); length 18.2m (59ft 8.5in); height 5.03m (16ft 6in)
Armament:	one 15mm cannon in lower port nose, one 13mm MG in dorsal turret, one 13mm MG in ventral step position, 7.92mm MG in nose, one 7.92mm MG in each cockpit side window; bombload of 4000kg (8818lb)

American Transports

The United States built more transport aircraft than any other nation during the war. In fact, the British let the Americans supply all their airlifter needs, thus enabling their own industry to focus on combat aircraft. The major American transports had their origins in pre-war airliner designs. The most famous is the C-47, or Dakota, of which over 10,000 were built in various guises. The C-46 had twice the cargo capacity of the C-47 and was especially suited to flying the 'Hump' over the Himalayas.

Curtiss C-46A Commando

Although designed with the civil market in mind, few Curtiss CW-20 transports were built before the USAAF took on the design in 1940 and ordered production as the C-46 Commando. In total, 3181 were built and they had a long post-war career with several air forces.

SPECIFICATIONS	
Country of origin:	United States
Type:	twin-engine transport aircraft
Powerplant:	two 2000hp (1500kW) Pratt & Whitney R-2800-51 radial piston engines
Performance:	maximum speed 433km/h (269mph); range 4750km (2950 miles); service ceiling 8410m (27,600ft)
Dimensions:	span 32.9m (108ft 1in); length 23.27m (76ft 4in); height 6.63m (21ft 9in); wing area 126.8 sq m (1360 sq ft)
Weights:	14,700kg (32,400lb); maximum 22,000kg (48,000lb)
Armament:	none

Douglas C-49K Skytrooper

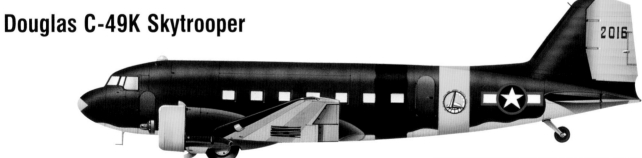

As well as thousands of C-47s built to military specifications, the USAAF impressed numerous civil DC-3s from airlines under various designations. The 23 C-49K Skytroopers came directly off the production line, and many were leased back to airlines flying routes deemed important to the war effort.

SPECIFICATIONS	
Country of origin:	United States
Type:	four-engined passenger transport
Powerplant:	two 1100hp (820kW) Wright R-1820-G105A Cyclone radial piston engines
Performance:	maximum speed 396km/h (246mph); range 4350km (2700 miles); service ceiling 8000m (26,200ft)
Dimensions:	span 32.69m (107ft 3in); length 22.66m (74ft 4in); height 6.32m (20ft 9in); wing area 138.1 sq m (1,486 sq ft)
Weights:	empty 13,700kg (30,300lb); maximum 25,400kg (56,000lb)
Armament:	none

TRANSPORTS TIMELINE

1935

1938

1940

Boeing C-75 Stratoliner (Model 307)

Only 10 of the Boeing 307 pressurized airliner were sold to airlines before the war. TWA's five Stratoliners were impressed into Air Transport Command service as C-75s and were among the first landplanes to fly regular (VIP) services across the Atlantic, carrying many top generals.

SPECIFICATIONS	
Country of origin:	United States
Type:	four-engined passenger transport
Powerplant:	two 1100hp (820kW) Wright R-1820-G105A Cyclone radial piston engines
Performance:	maximum speed 396km/h (246mph); range 4350km (2700 miles); service ceiling 8000m (26,200ft)
Dimensions:	span 32.69m (107ft 3in); length 22.66m (74ft 4in); height 6.32m (20ft 9in); wing area 138.1 sq m (1486 sq ft)
Weights:	empty 13,700kg (30,300lb); maximum 25,400kg (56,000lb)
Armament:	none

Douglas C-54A

Douglas' C-54 Skymaster transport was ordered straight into production without a prototype in early 1942. War Department needs superseded orders for the civilian DC-4, and over 1200 were built – for the Army as C-54s and the Navy as R5Ds – mainly for use in the Pacific.

SPECIFICATIONS	
Country of origin:	United States
Type:	four-engined military transport
Powerplant:	four 1450hp (1080kW) Pratt & Whitney R-2000-9 radial piston engines
Performance:	maximum speed 442km/h (275mph); range 6400km (4000 miles); service ceiling 6800m (22,300ft)
Dimensions:	span 35.8m (117ft 6in); length 28.6m (93ft 10in); height 8.38m (27ft 6in); wing area 136 sq m (1,460 sq ft)
Weights:	empty 17,660kg (38,930lb); maximum 33,000kg (73,000lb)
Armament:	none

Lockheed L-749 Constellation

The USAAF took over the first L-749 Constellations as C-69s and used them as personnel transports within the United States. Howard Hughes, owner of TWA, managed to keep some in airline markings, which proved good publicity when the war was over and they returned to civil service.

SPECIFICATIONS	
Country of origin:	United States
Type:	four-engined transport
Powerplant:	four 2200hp (1641kW) Wright R-3350-35 Cyclone radial piston engine
Performance:	maximum speed 531km/h (330mph); range 3862km (2400 miles); service ceiling 7620m (25,000ft)
Dimensions:	span 37.49m (123ft); length 29.01m (95ft 2n); height 7.21m (23ft 8in); wing area 153.29 sq m (1640 sq ft)
Weights:	empty 22,906kg (50,500lb); maximum 32,659kg (72,000lb)
Armament:	none

1942

1943

Lockheed Lightning

Designed by Clarence L. 'Kelly' Johnson, the P-38 Lightning was a radical design for 1938. Its unusual layout allowed the mounting of engines and superchargers with long ducts in the booms, and heavy armament in the cockpit nacelle. Unlike many contemporary twin-engined aircraft, the propellers counter-rotated, eliminating the directional problems often experienced on take-off due to engine torque. The P-38 was most successful in the Pacific theatre.

P-38 Lightning I

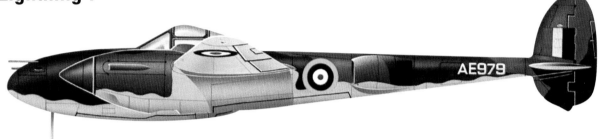

The RAF ordered nearly 700 Lightnings, but after evaluating three examples in 1942, it cancelled the order. The RAF's version was ordered without turbocharged engines for compatibility with their Curtiss Hawk 81s, but the result had extremely disappointing performance.

SPECIFICATIONS	
Country of origin:	United States
Type:	twin-engined fighter
Powerplant:	two 1090hp (813kW) Allison V-1710-C15 V-12 piston engines
Performance:	maximum speed 575km/h (357mph); service ceiling unknown; range unknown
Weights:	loaded 6133kg (13,500lb)
Dimensions:	span 15.86m (52 ft) length 11.53 m (37 ft 10 in); height 3.9m (9ft 10in); wing area 36.39 sq m (327.5 sq ft)
Armament:	one 20mm Hispano M1 cannon, four .303in Browning machine guns

F-5B Lightning

Under the designation F-5, many Lightnings were produced or converted for photoreconnaissance missions, with the nose filled with cameras. The Free French Air Force unit GR II/33 flew F-5s from Corsica. Antoine de Saint-Exupery, aviator and author of *The Little Prince,* was lost in an F-5B in July 1944.

SPECIFICATIONS	
Country of origin:	United States
Type:	two-seat elementary trainer biplane
Powerplant:	one 89kW (130hp) de Havilland Gipsy Major I inline piston engine
Performance:	maximum speed 167km/h (104mph); service ceiling 4145m (13,600ft); range 483km (300 miles)
Weights:	empty 506kg (1115lb); maximum take-off weight 828kg (1825lb)
Dimensions:	span 8.94m (29ft 4in); length 7.29m (23ft 11in); height 2.69m (8ft 10in); wing area 22.20 sq m (239 sq ft)

P-38E Lightning

This P-38E was captured intact and reused by a Luftwaffe unit called Zirkus Rosarius, which toured airfields demonstrating the strengths and weaknesses of Allied aircraft. There is evidence that, on occasion, captured P-38s were used to infiltrate Allied formations and shoot down bombers.

SPECIFICATIONS	
Country of origin:	United States
Type:	twin-engined fighter
Powerplant:	two 1225hp (913kW) Allison V-1710-49/52 piston engines
Performance:	maximum speed 636km/h (395mph); service ceiling 11,887m (39,000ft); range 3367km (2260miles)
Weights:	empty (P-38F): 5563kg (12,264lb); maximum (P-38E) 7022kg (15,482lb)
Dimensions:	span 15.86m (52 ft) length 11.53m (37ft 10in); height 3.9m (9ft 10in); wing area 36.39 sq m (327.5 sq ft)
Armament:	one 20mm Hispano M1 cannon, four .5in Colt-Browning MG 53-2 machine guns

P-38L Lightning

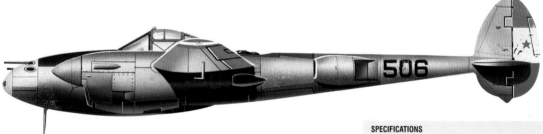

The Central American nation of Honduras acquired 12 P-38Ls in the late 1940s. As well as the Fuerza Aerea Hondurena, Latin American countries that flew Lightnings post-war included Cuba, the Dominican Republic and Colombia.

SPECIFICATIONS	
Country of origin:	United States
Type:	two-engined fighter
Powerplant:	two 1600hp (1194kW) Allison V-1710-111/113 engine
Performance:	maximum speed 666km/h (414mph); service ceiling 13,410m (20,000ft); range 4184km (2600 miles)
Weights:	maximum take-off weight 9798kg (21,600lb)
Dimensions:	span 15.85m (52ft); length 11.53m (37ft 10in); height 2.99m (9ft 10in)
Armament:	one 20mm (.8in) cannon and four 12.7mm (.5in) MGs in nose, plus two 907kg (2000lb) bombs

P-38L Lightning

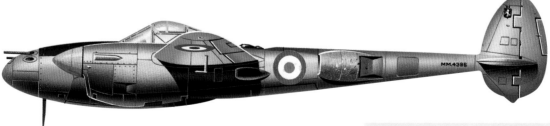

When Italy joined NATO in 1949, the United States supplied 50 Lightnings to the Aeonautica Militare Italiana, a mix of P-38Ls, Js and F-5Es. These helped the air arm re-establish itself before jets became widely available in the mid-1950s. This is a P-38L of 4 Stormo.

SPECIFICATIONS	
Country of origin:	United States
Type:	two-engined fighter
Powerplant:	two 1600hp (1194kW) Allison V-1710-111/113 engine
Performance:	maximum speed 666km/h (414mph); service ceiling 13,410m (20,000ft); range 4184km (2600 miles)
Weights:	maximum take-off weight 9798kg (21,600lb)
Dimensions:	span 15.85m (52ft); length 11.53m (37ft 10in); height 2.99m (9ft 10in)
Armament:	one 20mm (.8in) cannon and four 12.7mm (.5in) MGs in nose, plus two 907kg (2000lb) bombs

Operation Torch

In November 1942, the Allies followed up the British victory at El Alamein in Egypt with landings in Morocco and Algeria, codenamed Operation Torch. The landings were opposed by Vichy French forces, and most of the French fleet had to be sunk by the Royal Navy. US Navy aircraft and Vichy French fighters met in combat several times. Supported by USAAF and RAF aircraft, Allied ground forces finally pushed the Afrika Korps out of Tunisia in May 1943.

Grumman Martlet II

The British landings were supported by seven Royal Navy carriers. For Operation Torch, the FAA aircraft involved wore US insignia. This Martlet II was one of 12 assigned to No 888 Squadron on HMS *Formidable* for the Torch landings.

SPECIFICATIONS	
Country of origin:	United States
Type:	single-engined carrier-based fighter
Powerplant:	one 1200hp (895kW) Pratt & Whitney Whitney R-1830-S3C4-G radial piston engine
Performance:	maximum speed 512km/h (318mph); range 1464km (910 miles); service ceiling 10,363m (34,000ft)
Dimensions:	span 11.58m (38ft); length 8.76m (28ft 9in); height 2.81m (9ft 3in); wing area 24.15 sq m (260 sq ft)
Weights:	empty 2674kg (5895lb); loaded 3607kg (7952lb)
Armament:	six .5in (12.7mm) Browning machine-guns; up to 200lb of bombs

Douglas SBD-3 Dauntless

USS *Ranger* was the main US fleet carrier in the landings. Nine of its SBD-3 Dauntlesses were lost during the operation, but they struck the final blow against the French battleship *Jean Bart* in Casablanca harbour, knocking out her one remaining functional turret.

SPECIFICATIONS	
Country of origin:	United States
Type:	single-engined carrier-based dive bomber
Powerplant:	one 1000hp (746kW) Wright R-1820-52 Cyclone piston engine
Performance:	402km/h (250mph); range 2165km (1345 miles); service ceiling 8260m (27,100ft)
Dimensions:	span 12.66m (41ft 6in); length 9.96m (38ft 8in); height 4.14m (13ft 7in)
Weights:	empty 2878kg (6345lb); maximum 4717kg (10,400lb)
Armament:	two .5in (12.7mm) and two .3in (7.62mm) Browning machine guns

Douglas A-20B Havoc

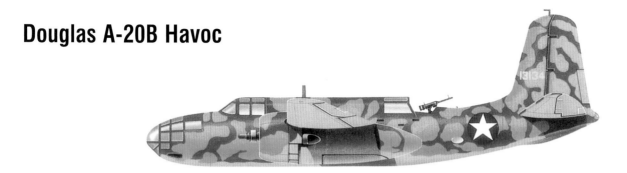

The A-20B light attack bomber was the USAAF's counterpart of the DB-7A delivered by Douglas to the French Air Force. The aeroplane could carry 1179kg (2600lb) of bombs internally, and had two fixed forward-firing machine guns. This aircraft flew as part of the 84th Bomb Squadron, 47th Bomb Group, US Twelfth AAF, Medioun, in Morocco in December 1942.

SPECIFICATIONS	
Country of origin:	United States
Type:	two-three seat light attack bomber
Powerplant:	two 1690hp (1260kW) Wright R-2600-11 radial piston engines
Performance:	maximum speed 515km/h (320mph); range 1996km (1240 miles); service ceiling 7470m (24,500ft)
Dimensions:	span 18.69m (61ft 4in); length 14.48m (47ft 6in); height 5.36m (17ft 7in)
Weights:	empty 5534kg (12,200lb); maximum take-off weight 9789kg (21,580lb)
Armament:	three 12.7mm (.5in) and one 7.62mm (.3in) Browning machine guns; up to 2400lb (1089kg) of bombs

Curtiss P-40L

The P-40L was a lightened version of the P-40F, sharing that model's Packard-built Merlin engine but usually having only four guns. 'Lighthouse Louie' was flown by Colonel G. H. Austin of the HQ Flight of the 325th Fighter Group in Tunisia in early 1943.

SPECIFICATIONS	
Country of origin:	United States
Type:	single-engined fighter
Powerplant:	one 969kW (1300hp) Packard Merlin 28 V-12 piston engine
Performance:	maximum speed 595km/h (370mph); range 2213km (1375 miles); service ceiling 10,973m (36,000ft)
Dimensions:	span 11.35m (37ft 4in); length 9.49m (31ft 2in); height 3.32m (10ft 11in); wing area 21.92 sq m (235.94 sq ft)
Weights:	empty 2939kg (6480lb); maximum 4037kg (8900lb)
Armament:	four .5in (12.7mm) Browning machine-guns

Consolidated B-24D Liberator

Once established in Tunisia, the bombers of the 15th Air Force struck against Sicily, Italy and the Romanian oil refineries that were so important to the Axis war effort. 'Teggie Ann' was a B-24D of the 376th Bomb Group 'The Liberandos', based in Cyrenacia, Libya, in 1943.

SPECIFICATIONS	
Country of origin:	United States
Type:	ten-seat heavy bomber
Powerplant:	4 x 1200hp (895kW) Pratt & Whitney radial piston engines
Performance:	maximum speed 488km/h (303mph); range 1730km (1080 miles); service ceiling 8540m (28,000ft)
Dimensions:	span 33.53m (110ft); length 20.22m (66ft 4in); height 5.46m (17ft 11in)
Weights:	27,216kg (60,000lb) loaded
Armament:	one (or three) 12.7mm (.5in) nose MGs, six 12.7mm (.5in) MGs: two in dorsal turret, two in retractable ball turret and two in waist positions, 3629kg (8000lb) of bombs

Invasion of Sicily

Following the ousting of the Afrika Korps, the next step for the Allies was to strike at the soft underbelly of Europe. Operation Husky was launched to invade Sicily in July 1943. It was hoped that Italy could be knocked out of the war without an invasion of the mainland, but at the very least it aimed to eliminate most of the threat to Mediterranean shipping by destroying Axis bases on Sicily. The invasion saw the first mass use of US paratroopers and British glider forces.

CANT Z.1007bis

Italy's aircraft designers had a particular penchant for the trimotor. One of the most important bombers in Italian service was the three-engined CANT Z.1007. This Z.1007bis wears night camouflage for attacks against Allied ports and targets on the North African coast in early 1943.

SPECIFICATIONS	
Country of origin:	Italy
Type:	five-seat medium bomber
Powerplant:	three 1000hp (746kW) Piaggio P.XI 14-cylinder two-row radial engines
Performance:	maximum speed 466km/h (290mph); service ceiling 8200m (26,900ft); range 1750km (1087 miles)
Weights:	empty 9396kg (20,715lb); maximum take-off weight 13,621g (30,029lb)
Dimensions:	span 24.8m (81ft 4.33in); length 18.35m (60ft 2.5in); height 5.22m (17ft 5in)
Armament:	one 12.7mm trainable MG in dorsal turret, one 12.7mm trainable rearward-firing MG in ventral step position, one 7.7mm lateral-firing MG in each of the two beam positions, internal bomb load 1200kg (2646lb)

Messerschmitt Bf 109G-2

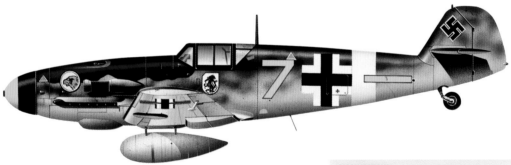

The Bf 109G was the definitive version of the series, and was fitted with a wide variety of factory or field conversion sets to give different armament configurations. This Bf 109G-2 was on the strength of II/JG 51 'Molders' at Casa Zeppera, Sardinia, in 1943.

SPECIFICATIONS	
Country of origin:	Germany
Type:	single-seat fighter and fighter-bomber
Powerplant:	one 1250hp (932kW) DB 605A-1 inverted V12 piston engine
Performance:	maximum speed 621km/h (386mph); range 1000km (621 miles); service ceiling 11,550m (37,890ft)
Dimensions:	span 9.92m (32ft 6.5in); length 8.85m (29ft 0.5in); height 2.5m (8ft 2.5in)
Weights:	empty 2673kg (5893lb); maximum take-off weight 3400kg (7496lb)
Armament:	one 20mm or 30mm fixed forward-firing cannon in engine installation, two 13mm fixed forward-firing MGs in upper forward fuselage, external bomb load of 250kg (551lb)

North American A-36A Apache

SPECIFICATIONS	
Country of origin:	United States
Type:	single-engined fighter bomber
Powerplant:	one 1325hp (1988kW) Allison 87 liquid-cooled piston V12 engine
Performance:	maximum speed 590km/h (365mph); service ceiling 7650m (25,100ft); range 885km (550 miles)
Weights:	4535kg (1000lb) loaded
Dimensions:	span 11.28m (37ft 1in); length 9.83m (32ft 3in); height 3.71m (12ft 2in)
Armament:	six 12.7mm (.5in) M2 Browning machine guns in wings

The original Allison engine in the P-51 Mustang proved disappointing at high altitudes, but was ideal for a low-level ground-attack aircraft. The Allison-powered A-36 Apache had dive-brakes in the wings and cannon armament. This A-36A was with the 27th Fighter Bomber Group on Corsica.

Martin Marauder Mk IA

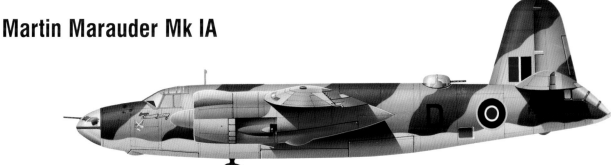

SPECIFICATIONS	
Country of origin:	United Kingdom
Type:	(B-26B (Marauder 1A))twin-engined medium bomber
Powerplant:	two 1920hp (1423kW) R-2800-41 piston engines
Performance:	maximum speed 491km/h (305mph); service ceiling 8534m (28,000ft); range 1931km (1200 miles)
Weights:	empty 7712kg (17,000lb); maximum 16,556kg (36,500lb)
Dimensions:	span 21.64m (71ft); length 17.53m (57ft 6in); height 6.1m (20ft); wing area 61.7 sq m (664 sq ft)
Armament:	six .5in (12.7mm) Browning machine-gun; up to 1814kg (4000lb) of bombs

The RAF's B-26s were exclusively used by the Desert Air Force in the North African and Italian campaigns. The type first entered service with No 14 Squadron in Egypt in August 1942. This is a 14 Squadron Marauder MK IA, equivalent to the USAAF's B-26B.

Curtiss Kittyhawk III

SPECIFICATIONS	
Country of origin:	United States
Type:	single-seat fighter
Powerplant:	1200hp (895kW) Allison V-1710-81 (F20R) engine
Performance:	maximum speed 563km/h (350mph); range 1738km (1080 miles); service ceiling 9450m (31,000ft)
Dimensions:	span 11.36m (37ft 4in); length 10.16m (33ft 4in); height 3.76m (12ft 4in)
Weights:	3511kg (7740lb) loaded
Armament:	4 x 12.7mm (.5in) Browning MGs in wings

The P-40 (known as the Tomahawk or Kittyhawk to the British) was the main RAF fighter in the desert war. By late 1943, it was obsolescent in Europe, but it soldiered on in the Italian campaign. This Kittyhawk III (P-40M) belonged to No 240 Squadron.

Fieseler Storch

One of the most remarkable aircraft produced by the German aero industry during the Nazi regime, the Storch (Stork) remains a vivid example of Gerhard Fieseler's interest in STOL aircraft. The Storch could take off in 65m (71yd), land in 20m (22yd) and virtually hover in a 40km/h (25mph) wind without any loss of control. It entered service in 1937, and production totalled 2900 aircraft. The main variants were the unarmed A, the armed model C and the air ambulance model D.

Fi 156-3 Storch

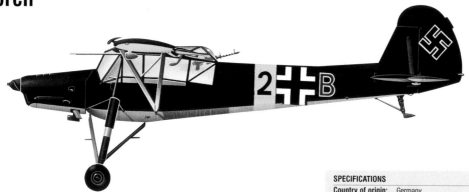

Pictured is a Fi 156C Storch of the Kurierstaffel Oberkommando de Luftwaffe, operating in the Don section of the Eastern Front in August 1942.The Storch was the result of a 1935 requirement for an army co-operation, casualty evacuation and liaison aircraft, and first flew in 1936.

SPECIFICATIONS	
Country of origin:	Germany
Type:	three-seat army co-operation, battlefield reconnaissance, liaison and casualty evacuation aeroplane
Powerplant:	one 240hp (179kW) Argus As 10C-3 eight-cylinder inverted-Vee engine
Performance:	maximum speed 175km/h (109mph); range 1015km (631 miles); service ceiling 5200m (17,060ft)
Dimensions:	span 14.25m (46ft 9in) length 9.9m (32ft 5.75in); height 3.05m (10ft)
Weights:	empty 940kg (2072lb); maximum take-off weight 1320kg (2910lb)
Armament:	one 7.92mm trainable rearward-firing machine gun in the rear of the cockpit

Fi 156-3 Trop Storch

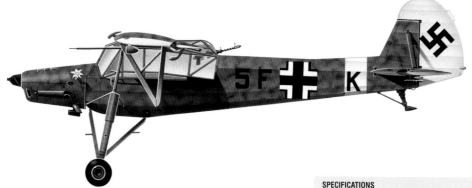

The Fi 156C-3/Trop was a tropicalized version with filtered intakes for use in desert conditions. Amongst other roles, it was used to spot enemy armoured formations and vehicles, which could be detected when on the move by the dust clouds they kicked up.

SPECIFICATIONS	
Country of origin:	Germany
Type:	three-seat army co-operation, battlefield reconnaissance, liaison and casualty evacuation aeroplane
Powerplant:	one 240hp (179kW) Argus As 10C-3 eight-cylinder inverted-Vee engine
Performance:	maximum speed 175km/h (109mph); range 1015km (631 miles); service ceiling 5200m (17,060ft)
Dimensions:	span 14.25m (46ft 9in) length 9.9m (32ft 5.75in); height 3.05m (10ft)
Weights:	empty 940kg (2072lb); maximum take-off weight 1320kg (2910lb)
Armament:	one 7.92mm trainable rearward-firing machine gun in the rear of the cockpit

Fi 156C Storch

Although information on Italian Storch operations is sparse, the type became famous in Italy when it was used to recover the dictator Mussolini from his prison in the mountains of central Italy in September 1943. This Italian Storch was based at Tirana in Albania.

SPECIFICATIONS	
Country of origin:	Germany
Type:	three-seat army co-operation, battlefield reconnaissance, liaison and casualty evacuation aeroplane
Powerplant:	one 240hp (179kW) Argus As 10C-3 eight-cylinder inverted-Vee engine
Performance:	maximum speed 175km/h (109mph); range 1015km (631 miles); service ceiling 5200m (17,060ft)
Dimensions:	span 14.25m (46ft 9in) length 9.9m (32ft 5.75in); height 3.05m (10ft)
Weights:	empty 940kg (2072lb); maximum take-off weight 1320kg (2910lb)
Armament:	one 7.92mm trainable rearward-firing machine gun in the rear of the cockpit

Fi 156D Storch

Spain used around 10 Fi 156D models, which were configured as air ambulances. The Storch was produced under licence in France as the MS.500 Criquet, and in Czechoslovakia as the K-65 Cap. The Soviet Union also began production of a copy before the war.

SPECIFICATIONS	
Country of origin:	Germany
Type:	(Fi 156C-2) three-seat army co-operation, battlefield reconnaissance, liaison and casualty evacuation aeroplane
Powerplant:	one 179kW2 (40hp) Argus As 10C-3 eight-cylinder inverted-Vee engine
Performance:	maximum speed 175km/h (109mph); climb to 1000m (3280ft) in 3 mins 24 secs; service ceiling 5200m (17,060ft); range 1015km (631 miles)
Weights:	empty 940kg (2072lb); maximum take-off weight 1320kg (2910lb)
Dimensions:	span 14.25m (46ft 9in); length 9.9m (32ft 5.75in); height 3.05m (10ft)
Armament:	one 7.92mm trainable rearward-firing machine gun in the rear of the cockpit

Fi 156C Storch

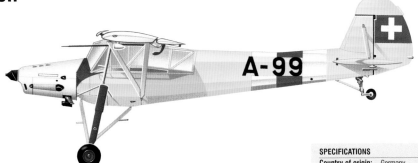

The Swiss found the Storch extremely useful as a rescue aircraft that could operate on high meadows or glaciers. Switzerland acquired a number of Storches post-war and used them until at least 1963.

SPECIFICATIONS	
Country of origin:	Germany
Type:	(Fi 156C-2) three-seat army co-operation, battlefield reconnaissance, liaison and casualty evacuation aeroplane
Powerplant:	one 240hp (179kW) Argus As 10C-3 eight-cylinder inverted-Vee engine
Performance:	maximum speed 175km/h (109mph); service ceiling 5200m (17,060ft); range 1015km (631 miles)
Weights:	empty 940kg (2072lb); maximum take-off weight 1320kg (2910lb)
Dimensions:	span 14.25m (46ft 9in); length 9.9m (32ft 5.75in); height 3.05m (10ft)

The Italian Campaign

In early September 1943, using Sicily as a springboard, the Allies landed in Italy. They quickly gained a foothold, not least because the Italian Government announced an armistice. German forces, however, continued resistance and the Allied advance was bogged down in the mountains. The mountaintop monastery of Monte Cassino became a particular obstacle, and was the subject of heavy bombing raids by B-25s and other Allied aircraft.

North American P-51B Mustang

The 332nd Fighter Group was manned by black pilots, who began training at Tuskegee, Alabama. Edward Toppins of the 99th FS was the group's second-highest-scoring pilot. The 'Red Tails' group flew bomber escort and ground attack missions from Italian bases.

SPECIFICATIONS	
Country of origin:	United States
Type:	single-seat fighter
Powerplant:	one 1044hp (1400kW) Packard V-1650 Rolls-Royce Merlin engine
Performance:	maximum speed 690km/h (430mph); service ceiling 12,649m (41,500ft); range 3540km (2200 miles)
Weights:	4173kg (9200lb) loaded
Dimensions:	span 11.27m (37ft); length 9.84m (32ft 4in); height 4.15m (13ft 8in)
Armament:	six 12.7mm (.5in) machine guns

North American B-25 Mitchell

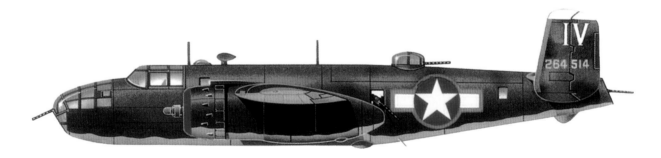

Southern Italy and Sicily soon became bases for Allied bombers flying against targets in the north. The main Allied tactical bomber was the B-25 Mitchell, as illustrated by this B-25C of the 81st BS, 21st BG, which was based at Gerbini, Sicily, in the autumn of 1943.

SPECIFICATIONS	
Country of origin:	United States
Type:	five-seat medium bomber
Powerplant:	2 x 1700hp (1268kW)
Performance:	maximum weight 457km/h (284mph); range 3219km (2000 miles); service ceiling 7163m (23,500ft)
Dimensions:	span 20.7m (68ft); length 16.2m (53ft); height 4.8m (15ft 9in)
Weights:	18,960kg (41,800lb) loaded
Armament:	two 12.7mm (.5in) nose-mounted MGs; 4 x 12.7mm (.5in) MGs (pair in top and pair in bottom turret); 2359kg (5200lb) of bombs

Macchi MC.205V Veltro

SPECIFICATIONS

Country of origin:	Italy
Type:	single-seat fighter and fighter-bomber
Powerplant:	one 1475hp (1100kW) Fiat RA.1050 RC.58 Tifone 12-cylinder engine
Performance:	maximum speed 642km/h (399mph); service ceiling 11,000m (36,090ft); range 1040km (646 miles)
Weights:	empty 2581kg (5691lb); maximum take-off weight 3408kg (7514lb)
Dimensions:	span 10.58m (34ft 8.5in); length 8.85m (29ft 0.5in); height 3.04m (9ft 11.5in)
Armament:	two 12.7mm fixed forward-firing MGs in the upper part of the forward fuselage, and two 20mm forward-firing cannon in the leading edges of the wing, plus bomb load of 320kg (705lb)

Becoming operational in mid-1943 in time to support the Sicily campaign, the MC.205V Veltro (Greyhound) was Italy's best wartime fighter. When the Italian Government made peace with the Allies, only 96 had been delivered. Total production was only 265 MC.205Vs.

Messerschmitt Bf 109G-6

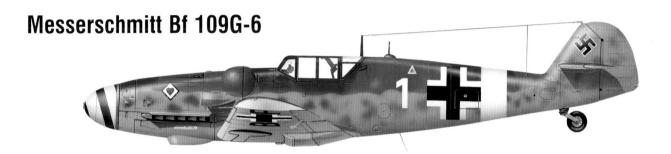

The Bf 109G-6 could be distinguished from earlier marks by the bulges for cannon ammunition ahead of the cockpit. The pilot of this Bf 109G-6 of 1./JG 77, Ernst Reinert, scored a total of 174 wartime kills, 51 of them in the Mediterranean theatre.

SPECIFICATIONS

Country of origin:	Germany
Type:	single-seat fighter and fighter-bomber
Powerplant:	1475hp (1100kW) DB 605
Performance:	maximum speed 653km/hr (400mph); range 700km (435 miles); service ceiling 11,600m (38,000ft)
Dimensions:	span 9.92m (32ft 6.5in); length 9.04m (29ft 8in); height 2.59m (8ft 6in)
Weights:	3400kg (7496lb) maximum loaded
Armament:	1 x 20mm (.8in) cannon; 2 x 13mm (.5in) MGs over engine

Messerschmitt Me 410A Hornisse

SPECIFICATIONS

Country of origin:	Germany
Type:	two-seat heavy fighter
Powerplant:	two 1750hp (1305kW) DB 12-cylinder inverted-Vee engine
Performance:	maximum speed 624km/h (388mph); service ceiling 10,000m (32,810ft); range 1670km (1050 miles)
Weights:	empty 7518kg (16,574lb); normal take-off weight 9651kg (21,276lb)
Dimensions:	span 16.35m (53ft 7.75in); length 12.48m (40ft 11.5in); height 4.28m (14ft 0.5in)
Armament:	four 20mm cannon (two in nose, two in ventral tray), two 7.92mm MGs in nose and one 13mm MG in each of two barbettes on side

Developed from the unsuccessful Me 210, the Me 410 was a fast and powerful twin-engined fighter and reconnaissance platform, although it was not built in great numbers. This Me 410A of 9./ ZG 1 was based at Gerbini, Sicily, before the German withdrawal.

The Italian Campaign Part Two

Landings at Anzio behind the German defensive line failed to break the deadlock on the Italian peninsula. Rome fell in June 1944, but in diverting forces to capture it, the Americans missed the chance to cut off a major German retreat. The Italian Co-Belligerent Army (and Air Force) fought alongside the Allies against the Germans and Mussolini's rump fascist state, the Italian Social Republic, which operated its own air arm. Considerable partisan activity added to the confusion.

Republic P-47D Thunderbolt

The P-47D appeared in both 'razorback' and 'bubbletop' forms, the latter having far superior pilot visibility. In February 1945, the 12th Air Force's 86th Fighter Squadron of the 79th Fighter Group operated this P-47D from Fano, on the Adriatic Coast near Rimini.

SPECIFICATIONS	
Country of origin:	United States
Type:	single-seat fighter and fighter-bomber
Powerplant:	2535hp (1891kW) Pratt & Whitney R-2800-59W Double Wasp
Performance:	maximum speed 697km/h (433mph); range 3060km (1900 miles) with drop tanks; service ceiling 12,495m (41,000ft)
Dimensions:	span 12.42m (40ft 9in); length 11.02m (36ft 2in); height 4.47m (14ft 8in)
Weights:	maximum take-off weight 7938kg (17,500lb)
Armament:	eight 12.7mm (.5in) MGs in wings, plus provision for 1134kg (2500lb) external bombs or rockets

Martin B-26B Marauder

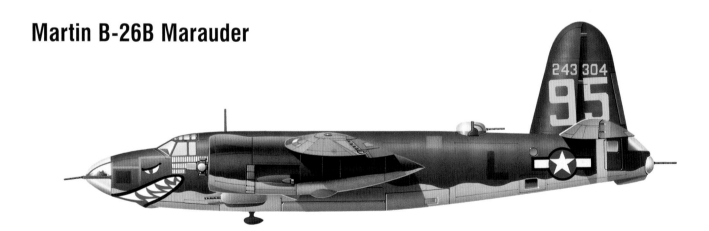

The island of Sardinia fell into Allied hands without the need for an invasion. Former Axis airfields were turned over to new management, including Decimomannu near Cagliari, where the 444th Bomb Squadron of the 320th Bomb Group flew B-26B Marauders in early 1945.

SPECIFICATIONS	
Country of origin:	United Kingdom
Type:	B-26B (Marauder 1A) twin-engined medium bomber
Powerplant:	two 1920hp (1423kW) R-2800-41 piston engines
Performance:	maximum speed 491km/h (305mph); service ceiling 8534m (28,000ft); range 1931km (1200 miles)
Weights:	empty 7712kg (17,000lb); maximum 16,556kg (36,500lb)
Dimensions:	span 21.64m (71ft); length 17.53m (57ft 6in); height 6.10m (20ft); wing area 61.7 sq m (664 sq ft)
Armament:	six .5in (12.7mm) Browning machine gun; up to 1814kg (4000lb) of bombs

Macchi MC.205 Veltro

The Facist Aeronautica Nazionale Repubblicana acquired the majority of MC.205Vs extant in mid-1943 and continued production. This MC 205V Serie III was flown by Vittorio Satta of 1° Squadriglia, 1° Gruppo in early 1944, and wears the ANR's 'postage stamp' national insignia.

SPECIFICATIONS	
Country of origin:	Italy
Type:	single-seat fighter and fighter-bomber
Powerplant:	one 1475hp (1100kW) Fiat RA.1050 RC.58 Tifone 12-cylinder engine
Performance:	maximum speed 642km/h (399mph); service ceiling 11,000m (36,090ft); range 1040km (646 miles)
Weights:	empty 2581kg (5691lb); maximum take-off weight 3408kg (7514lb)
Dimensions:	span 10.58m (34ft 8.5in); length 8.85m (29ft 0.5in); height 3.04m (9ft 11.5in)
Armament:	two 12.7mm fixed forward-firing MGs in the upper part of the forward fuselage, and two 20mm forward-firing cannon in the leading edges of the wing, plus bomb load of 320kg (705lb)

Reggiane Re.2001

The Re.2000's potential could not initially be realized for lack of adequate power, Italy having ignored the advisability of developing potent Vee engines. The solution was found in the licensed production of German engines, and an early development was the Re.2001 Falco II, first flown in June 1940. The aircraft pictured flew in the 362 Squadriglia, 22 Gruppo Autonomo.

SPECIFICATIONS	
Country of origin:	Italy
Type:	single-seat night-fighter
Powerplant:	one 1175hp (876kW) Alfa Romeo 12-cylinder inverted Vee engine
Performance:	maximum speed 545km/h (339mph); service ceiling 11,000m (36,090ft); range 1100km (684 miles)
Weights:	empty 2460kg (5423lb); maximum take-off weight 3280kg (7231lb)
Dimensions:	span 11m (36ft 1in); length 8.36m (27ft 5in); height 3.15m (10ft 4in)
Armament:	two 12.7mm MGs in upper part of forward fuselage and two 7.7mm forward-firing guns in leading edges of wing

Bell P-39N-1 Airacobra

The unusual mid-engined Bell Airacobra saw little combat in Europe, but the USA supplied the Italian Co-Belligerent Air Force with 150 of them in June 1944. P-39Ns like this example were mainly used for training and P-39Qs for ground-attack missions, mainly against targets in Albania.

SPECIFICATIONS	
Country of origin:	United States
Type:	single-seat fighter and fighter-bomber
Powerplant:	one 1125hp (839kW) Alison V 12-cylinder Vee engine
Performance:	maximum speed 605km/h (376mph); service ceiling 11,665m (38,270ft); range 1569km (975 miles)
Weights:	empty 2903kg (6400lb); maximum take-off weight 3992kg (8800lb)
Dimensions:	span 10.36m (34ft); length 9.2m (30ft 2in); height 3.79m (12ft 5in)
Armament:	one 37mm fixed forward-firing cannon and two .5in fixed forward-firing MGs in nose; four .3in fixed forward-firing MGs in leading edges of wing, plus external bomb load of 227kg (500lb)

Eyes in the Skies

Photographic reconnaissance aircraft played a vital part in most military operations in World War II. They were used for both pre-strike reconnaissance and post-strike battle-damage assessment. The Allies modified existing fighter and bomber types as photoreconnaissance platforms. Most US fighter and bomber types had a camera-equipped version with an 'F' designation. Germany and Japan had a few purpose-built reconnaissance aircraft in their inventories.

Blohm und Voss BV 141

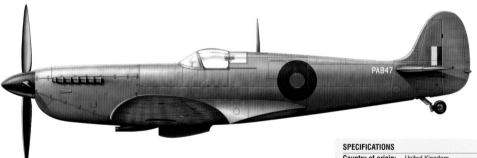

The BV 141 had a highly unusual asymmetric layout, with the fully glazed crew nacelle offset to starboard of the centreline, a boom carrying the engine at its front and a tail unit at its rear offset to port. The first of three protypes flew in February 1938. Used on operational trials from 1941, the BV 141 suffered development delays and the programme was terminated in 1943.

SPECIFICATIONS	
Country of origin:	Germany
Type:	three-seat tactical reconnaissance and observation aeroplane with limitied close support capability
Powerplant:	one 1560hp (1163kW) BMW 14-cylinder two-row radial engine
Performance:	maximum speed 438km/hr (272mph); range 1900km (1181 miles); service ceiling 10,000m (32,810ft)
Dimensions:	span 17.46m (57ft 3.5in); length 13.95m (45ft 9.25in); height 3.6m (11ft 9.75in)
Weights:	empty 4700kg (10,362lb); maximum take-off weight 6100kg (13,448lb)
Armament:	two 7.92mm fixed forward-firing MGs in the front crew nacelle, one 7.92mm trainable rearward firing MG in dorsal position, one 7.92mm trainable rearward-firing MG in rotating tailcone position, plus external bomb load of 200kg (441lb)

Spitfire PR.Mk XI

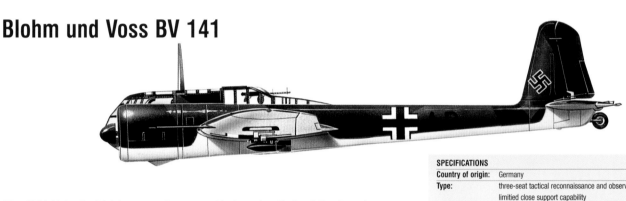

The PR. Mk XI Spitfire was a modification of the basic Mk XI fighter with armament and armour removed. A larger oil tank was fitted, which changed the undernose profile, and cameras were fitted under the rear fuselage. In all, 471 PR XIs were built.

SPECIFICATIONS	
Country of origin:	United Kingdom
Type:	Photo reconnaissance
Powerplant:	1565hp (1170kW) 12-cylinder Rolls-Royce Merlin 61 engine
Performance:	maximum speed 642km/h (410mph); range 698km (435 miles) on internal fuel tanks; service ceiling 12,650m (41,500ft)
Dimensions:	span 11.23m (36ft 10in); length 9.47m (31ft 1in); height 3.86m (12ft 8in)
Weights:	3343kg (7370lb) loaded
Armament:	None

EYES IN THE SKIES TIMELINE
1938 1942  1943

North American F-6D Mustang

The F-6D was a camera-equipped version of the P-51D Mustang, with oblique cameras mounted in the rear fuselage. They retained the armament of the fighter Mustangs, and a number of F-6 pilots became aces.

SPECIFICATIONS	
Country of origin:	United States
Type:	photo reconnaissance
Powerplant:	1695hp (1264kW) Packard Merlin V-1650-7 V-12 piston engine
Performance:	maximum speed 703km/h (437mph); range 3347km (2080 miles); service ceiling 12,770m (41,900ft)
Dimensions:	span 11.28m (37ft); length 9.83m (32ft 3in); height 4.17m (13ft 8in)
Weights:	5488kg (12,100lb) loaded
Armament:	6 x 12.7mm (.5in) MGs in wings

Lockheed F-5E Lightning

The F-5E was a reconnaissance version of the late-model P-38J or L Lightning, with four camera positions in the nose rather than guns. About 15 F-5Es were supplied to Nationalist China after the war to supplement Lightning fighters already in service.

SPECIFICATIONS	
Country of origin:	United States
Type:	photo reconnaissance
Powerplant:	two 1600hp (1193kW) Allison V-1710-111/113 engine
Performance:	maximum speed 666km/h (414mph); service ceiling 13,410m (20,000ft); range 4184km (2600 miles)
Weights:	loaded 9798kg (21,600lb)
Dimensions:	span 15.85m (52ft) length 11.53m (37ft 10in); height 3.9m (9ft 10in); wing area 36.39 sq m (327.5 sq ft)
Armament:	none

Mitsubishi Ki-46 III Dinah

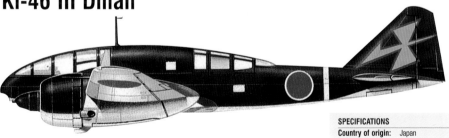

Anticipating that Allied fighters capable of intercepting the Ki-46-II would appear in the later part of 1942, the Imperial Japanese Army Air Force had ordered an improved version. The Ki-46-III was without doubt the best strategic reconnaissance aeroplane used in significant numbers in World War II, offering long range as well as high speed and a good service ceiling.

SPECIFICATIONS	
Country of origin:	Japan
Type:	(Ki-46-III) two-seat high-altitude reconnaissance aeroplane
Powerplant:	two 1500hp (1118kW) Mitsubishi Ha-112-II (Army Type 4) 14-cylinder two-row radial engines
Performance:	maximum speed 630km/h (391mph); climb to 8000m (26,245ft) in 20 mins 15 secs; service ceiling 10,500m (34,450ft); range 4000km (2486 miles)
Weights:	empty 3831kg (8446lb); maximum take-off 6500kg (14,330lb)
Dimensions:	span 14.7m (48ft 2.75in); length 11m (36ft 1in); height 3.88m (12ft 8.75in)
Armament:	one 7.7mm trainable rearward-firing machine gun in the rear cockpit

1944

The Mighty Eighth

The Eighth Air Force was the most powerful air formation of the war. Based mainly in eastern England, 8AF Bomber Command was established in mid-1942, using borrowed RAF aircraft. From these humble beginnings, it grew to over 40 heavy bomber groups. On some of its missions, over 2000 bombers and 1000 fighters plus support aircraft were in the air at a time. The 'Mighty Eighth' also initially operated medium bomber and transport groups, but these were detached to the Ninth Air Force in preparation for the D-Day landings.

De Havilland Mosquito PR Mk XVI

The aeroplane was completed in PRU blue with black/white 'invasion stripes' on its under-surfaces, and its USAAF association was revealed by the national markings, the red tail unit and the 653rd Bomb Squadron's marking on the fin. The USAAF acquired 40 Canadian-built Mosquitoes, mostly photoreconnaissance versions, and a further 100 from the RAF under the designation F-8. UK-based 'Mossies' were used for photo missions, weather reconnaissance and dispensing Window or chaff.

SPECIFICATIONS	
Country of origin:	United Kingdom
Type:	twin-engined reconnaissance aircraft
Powerplant:	2 x 1680hp (1253kW) Merlin 72 engines
Performance:	maximum speed 668km/h (415mph); range 2400km (1300 miles); service ceiling 11,000m (37,000ft)
Dimensions:	span 16.52m (54ft 2in); length 12.43m (44ft 6in); height 5.3m (17ft 5in)
Weights:	6490kg (14,300lb) empty
Armament:	none

Consolidated B-24 Liberator

The 406th Squadron specialized in dropping supplies to the French Resistance and agents into occupied Europe. They were responsible for the nocturnal delivery of leaflet 'bombs', which were laminated paper cylinders, each holding 80,000 leaflets and designed to burst in the air at an altitude between 305m (1000ft) and 610m (2000ft). For these clandestine 'Carpetbagger' missions, a black colour scheme was applied.

SPECIFICATIONS

Country of origin:	United States
Type:	four-engined heavy bomber
Powerplant:	four 1184hp (1120kW) Pratt & Whitney R 1830-65 radial piston engines
Performance:	maximum speed 467km/h (290mph); range 3380km (1825 miles); service ceiling 8535m (28,000ft)
Dimensions:	span 33.53m (110ft); length 20.47m (67ft 2in); height 5.49m (18ft)
Weights:	empty 16,556kg (36,506lb); maximum 32,296kg (71,213lb)
Armament:	ten 12.7mm (.5in) machine guns; up to 5806kg (12,800lb)

Boeing B-17G

With a twin-gun chin turret and other defensive improvements, the B-17G was the definitive version of the Flying Fortress. 'Chow-Hound' of the 322nd BS, 91st BG flew 43 missions before it was shot down by anti-aircraft fire over France in August 1944.

SPECIFICATIONS

Country of origin:	United States
Type:	four-engined heavy bomber
Powerplant:	four 1200hp (895kW) Wright R Cyclone nine-cylinder radial engines
Performance:	maximum speed 475km/h (295mph); range 5085km (3160 miles); service ceiling 10,850m (35,600ft)
Dimensions:	span 31.62m (103ft 9in); length 22.8m (74ft 9in); height 5.85m (19ft 2in)
Weights:	maximum 29,710kg (65,500lb)
Armament:	13 x 12.7mm (.5in) machine guns; up to 6169kg (13,600lb) bomb load

The Mighty Eighth Part Two

The capability of the Eighth Air Force's bombers to strike at targets deep in Germany without prohibitive losses was largely a function of the range of its escort fighters. The Spitfires initially used could provide escort only about as far as Paris. The Mustang had the range to reach Hamburg, and the P-38 could take the bombers nearly all the way to Berlin. Development of disposable drop tanks and finally the P-51D version of the Mustang put almost all of Germany within reach.

North American P-51B Mustang

The P-51B was the first Merlin-engined Mustang in service. Its arrival in late 1943 began to tip the balance against the Luftwaffe, and soon its pilots racked up impressive scores. Henry Brown, pilot of 'The Hun Hunter From Texas' of the 336th Fighter Squadron, 4th Fighter Group, was credited with 17 victories.

SPECIFICATIONS	
Country of origin:	United States
Type:	single-seat fighter and fighter bomber
Powerplant:	1400hp (1044kW) Packard V-1650-3 Rolls-Royce Merlin engine
Performance:	maximum speed 690km/h (430mph); range 3540km (2200 miles); service ceiling 12,649m (41,500ft)
Dimensions:	span 11.27m (37ft); length 9.84m (32ft 4in); height 4.15m (13ft 8in)
Weights:	4173kg (9200lb) loaded
Armament:	six 12.7mm (.5in) MGs

Supermarine Spitfire PR.Mk XI

The 7th Photo Group was the Eighth Air Force's main tactical reconnaissance unit. It flew F-5 Lightnings, F-6 Mustangs and Spitfire PR.XIs. The latter was a version of the Mk XI fighter converted by removing armament and installing two vertically mounted cameras to obtain information about bombardment targets and damage inflicted by bombardment operations.

SPECIFICATIONS	
Country of origin:	United Kingdom
Type:	single-seat photoreconnaissance
Powerplant:	1565hp (1170kW) 12-cylinder Rolls-Royce Merlin 61 engine
Performance:	maximum speed 642km/h (410mph); range 698km (435 miles) on internal fuel tanks; service ceiling 12,650m (41,500ft)
Dimensions:	span 11.23m (36ft 10in); length 9.47m (31ft 1in); height 3.86m (12ft 8in)
Weights:	3343kg (7370lb) loaded
Armament:	none

Lockheed P-38L Lightning

The P-38 had greater range than its contemporaries in 1942–43, but took longer to produce and was needed in the Pacific and North Africa. Teething troubles with its engines meant that it failed to live up to its potential in Europe. This is a P-38L of the 20th Fighter Group at King's Cliffe.

SPECIFICATIONS	
Country of origin:	United States
Type:	single-seat long range fighter and fighter-bomber
Powerplant:	2 x 1600hp (1194kW) Allison V-1710-111/113
Performance:	maximum speed 666km/h (414mph); range 4184km (2600 miles); service ceiling 13,410m (20,000ft)
Dimensions:	span 15.85m (52ft); length 11.53m (37ft 10in); height 2.99m (9ft 10in)
Weights:	maximum take-off weight 9798kg (21,600lb)
Armament:	1 x 20mm (.8in) cannon and 4 x 12.7mm (.5in) MGs in nose, plus 2 x 907kg (2000lb) bombs

Republic P-47D Thunderbolt

'Butch II' was a late P-47D of the 352nd FS, 353rd FG, which replaced its Thunderbolts with Mustangs from October 1944. One Eighth AF fighter group, the 56th FG, became masters of the P-47 and managed to retain them until the war's end.

SPECIFICATIONS	
Country of origin:	United States
Type:	single-seat fighter and fighter-bomber
Powerplant:	2535hp (1891kW) Pratt & Whitney R-2800-59W Double Wasp
Performance:	maximum speed 697km/h (433mph); range 3060km (1900 miles) with drop tanks; service ceiling 12,495m (41,000ft)
Dimensions:	span 12.42m (40ft 9in); length 11.02m (36ft 2in); height 4.47m (14ft 8in)
Weights:	maximum take-off weight 7938kg (17,500lb)
Armament:	8 x 12.7mm (.5in) MGs in wings, plus provision for 1134kg (2500lb) external bombs or rockets

North American P-51D Mustang

The bubble-canopy P-51D arrived in Europe soon after D-Day. By the end of the war, all but one of the Eighth's fighter groups flew them. 'Louisiana Heat Wave' was flown by seven-victory ace Claude Crenshaw of the 487th FS, 352nd FG, at East Wretham in late 1944.

SPECIFICATIONS	
Country of origin:	United States
Type:	single-seat fighter and fighter-bomber
Powerplant:	1695hp (1264kW) Packard Merlin V-1650-7 V-12 piston engine
Performance:	maximum speed 703km/h (437mph); range 3347km (2080 miles); service ceiling 12,770m (41,900ft)
Dimensions:	span 11.28m (37ft); length 9.83m (32ft 3in); height 4.17m (13ft 8in)
Weights:	5488kg (12,100lb) loaded
Armament:	6 x 12.7mm (.5in) MGs in wings, plus up to 2 x 454kg (1000lb) bombs

Messerschmitt Bf 109

Designed by Willi Messerschmitt, the Bf 109 was in production in Germany from before the war until its end. Spain and Czechoslovakia continued making modified versions even after that, and the last examples of the breed were retired only in the late 1960s. Nearly 34,000 were built by 1945, making it the most numerous fighter aircraft ever produced. Germany's top aces continued to fly 109s even when the superior Fw 190 came along, and the 109 became the highest-scoring fighter.

Messerschmitt Bf 109B

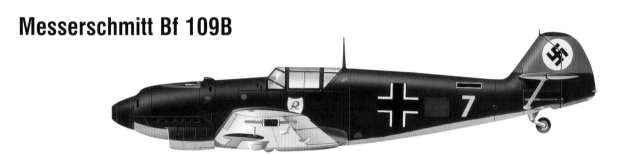

The Jumo-engined 'Bertha' was the first mass-produced model of the series. Like the earliest Spitfires, it featured a fixed-pitch two-bladed propeller, which limited its potential performance. This Bf 109B-1 was with 6./JG 132 'Richthofen' at Juterbog-Damm in the autumn of 1937.

SPECIFICATIONS	
Country of origin:	Germany
Type:	single-seat fighter and fighter-bomber
Powerplant:	635hp (474kW) Junkers Jumo 210D 12-cylinder inverted V
Performance:	maximum speed approx 470km/h (292mph); range 650km (450 miles); service ceiling 10,500m (34,450ft)
Dimensions:	span 9.87m (32ft 4.5in); length 8.51m (27ft 11in); height 2.28m (7ft 5in)
Armament:	3 x 7.92mm (.3in) Rheinmetall-Borsig MG 17 above engine and through propeller hub

Messerschmitt Bf 109E

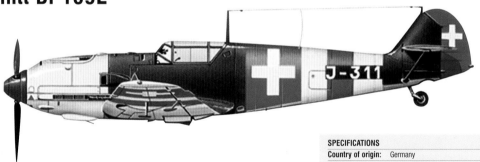

The main early-war version was the Bf 109E, or 'Emil'. Switzerland purchased 80 Bf 109E-3s in April 1939 and various later models, some of which landed in Switzerland and were interned. Swiss 109s fought Luftwaffe aircraft that violated their airspace on several occasions.

SPECIFICATIONS	
Country of origin:	Germany
Type:	single-seat fighter
Powerplant:	one 1160hp (865kW) Daimler-Benz DB601Aa inverted V-12 piston engine
Performance:	maximum speed 560 km/h (348 mph); range 660km (410 miles); service ceiling 10,500m (34,449ft)
Dimensions:	span 9.87m (32ft 5in); length 8.64m (28ft 4in); height 2.5m (8ft 2in); wing area 16.17 sq m (179.97 sq ft)
Weights:	empty 1900kg (4189lb); maximum 2665kg (5875lb)
Armament:	two 20mm MG-FF cannon, two 7.9mm MG 13 machine guns

MESSERSCHMITT 109 TIMELINE  1937   1938   1940

Messerschmitt Bf 109F

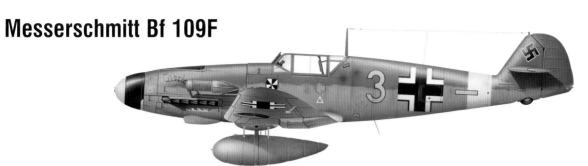

The Bf 109F was regarded as the best of the series to fly, its handling uncompromised by the additional weapons, ammunition and armour plate that were to encumber some of the later versions. The 'Friedrich' is especially associated with the units fighting in the Mediterranean campaign such as JG 3.

SPECIFICATIONS	
Country of origin:	Germany
Type:	single-seat fighter
Powerplant:	1300hp (969kW) DB 601E
Performance:	maximum speed 628km/hr (390mph); range 700km (435 miles); service ceiling 11,600m (38,000ft)
Dimensions:	span 9.92m (32ft 6.5in); length 8.85m (29ft 0.5in); height 2.59m (8ft 6in)
Weights:	2746kg (6054lb) maximum loaded
Armament:	1 x 20mm (.8in) cannon; 2 x 7.92mm (.3in) MGs

Messerschmitt Bf 109G-2

Jadgeschwader 54 'Grunhertz' (green hearts) was famed for its exploits on the Eastern Front, and for its unique colour schemes. This 'Gustav' was with II/JG 54 when it was operating from Siverskaya, near St Petersburg in 1942. Bf 109Gs had the so-called 'Galland' hood, with less framing.

SPECIFICATIONS	
Country of origin:	Germany
Type:	single-seat fighter
Powerplant:	one 1100kW (1475hp) DB 605 engine
Performance:	maximum speed 653km/h (400mph); range 700km (435 miles); service ceiling 11,600m (38,000ft)
Dimensions:	span 14.3m (46ft 11in); length 10.46m (34ft 4in); height 3.8m (12ft 6in)
Weights:	3273kg (7216lb) loaded
Armament:	4 x 7.62mm (.3in) fixed wing MGs and 1 x 7.62mm (.3in) MG in dorsal turret; 400kg (880lb) of bombs

Messerschmitt Bf 109K-4

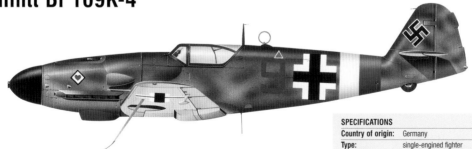

Appearing in late 1944, the final wartime variant of the 109 to be built in quantity was the K-4. One distinguishing feature was its taller wooden fin. Armament was concentrated in the fuselage, and the simplified 'Kurfurst' was the fastest of all 109 variants.

SPECIFICATIONS	
Country of origin:	Germany
Type:	single-engined fighter
Powerplant:	one 2000hp (1491kW) Daimler-Benz inverted-V-12 piston engine
Performance:	maximum speed 700km/h (435mph); range 573km/h (356 miles); service ceiling 12,500 m (41,010ft)
Dimensions:	span 9.9m (32ft 9in); length 8.85m (29ft 1in); height 2.5m (8ft 3in); wing area 16.1 sq m (173 sq ft)
Weights:	empty 2725kg (6008lb); maximum 3375kg (7441lb)
Armament:	one 30mm MK 108 cannon and two 15mm MG 151/15 machine-guns

1941 1942

D-Day

After many months of build-up, the Allies were ready to launch Operation Overlord, the invasion of occupied France, in June 1944. An important part of Overlord was deceiving the enemy as to where and when the invasion would occur. Raids and reconnaissance missions on targets outside Normandy were as important as those in the area of the planned landings. The Allied air forces had around 12,000 aircraft available to support Overlord.

Martin B-26B Marauder

Tactical bombers like this B-26B Marauder of the 598th BS, 397th BG were vital in striking transportation targets such as rail yards, bridges and tunnels to prevent or delay German reinforcement. Bombing the Normandy beach fortifications was less successful, due in part to cloud cover on 6 June.

SPECIFICATIONS	
Country of origin:	United Kingdom
Type:	two-seat elementary trainer biplane
Powerplant:	one 130hp (89kW) de Havilland Gipsy Major I inline piston engine
Performance:	maximum speed 167km/h (104mph); service ceiling 4145m (13,600ft); range 483km (300 miles)
Weights:	empty 506kg (1115lb); maximum take-off weight 828kg (1825lb)
Dimensions:	span 8.94m (29ft 4in); length 7.29m (23ft 11in); height 2.69m (8ft 10in); wing area 22.2 sq m (239 sq ft)

De Havilland Mosquito FB.VI

The RAF established the 2nd Tactical Air Force in June 1943 in preparation for the invasion. Its fighter-bomber units, including No 138 Wing with the Mosquito FB.VI, struck at precision targets, airfields, river traffic and trains. With a low-drag airframe built largely of a plywood/balsa/plywood sandwich material for low weight and considerable strength, the Mosquito was very adaptable and fast.

SPECIFICATIONS	
Country of origin:	United Kingdom
Type:	twin-engined fighter-bomber
Powerplant:	two 1103kW (1480hp) Rolls-Royce Merlin 23 V-12 piston engines
Performance:	maximum speed 612km/h (380mph); range 2655km (1650 miles); service ceiling 11,430m (37,500ft)
Dimensions:	span 16.5m (54ft 2in); length 12.47m (40ft 11in); height 4.65m (15ft 3in); wing area 42.18 sq m (454 sq ft)
Weights:	empty 6486kg (14,300lb); maximum 10,569kg (22,300lb)
Armament:	four .303in (7.7mm) Browning machine guns and four 20mm Hispano machine-guns; up to 1361kg (3000lb) of bombs or eight rockets

Supermarine Spitfire Mk IX

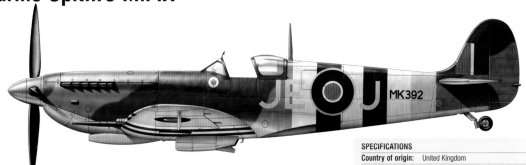

SPECIFICATIONS	
Country of origin:	United Kingdom
Type:	single-seat fighter
Powerplant:	1565hp (1170kW) 12-cylinder Rolls-Royce Merlin 61 engine
Performance:	maximum speed 642km/h (410mph); range 698km (435 miles) on internal fuel tanks; service ceiling 12,650m (41,500ft)
Dimensions:	span 11.23m (36ft 10in); length 9.47m (31ft 1in); height 3.86m (12ft 8in)
Weights:	3343kg (7370lb) loaded
Armament:	4 x 7.7mm (.303in) MGs and 2 x 20mm (.8in) cannons

Wing Commander James 'Johnnie' Johnson flew this Spitfire Mk IX in his role as leader of No 127 (Canadian) Wing when it moved to the Continent. With a final total of 38 kills, Johnson was the RAF's top surviving ace of the war.

Douglas C-47A Skytrain

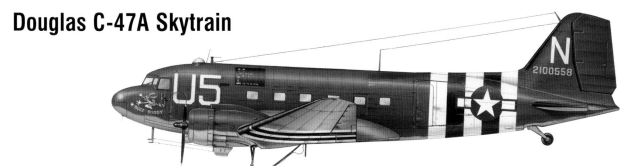

Around 1000 USAAF C-47 Skytrains, C-53 Skytroopers and RAF Dakotas took part in D-Day, dropping two divisions of paratroopers and towing hundreds of gliders into Normandy. Normal capacity was 28 fully equipped paratroopers.

SPECIFICATIONS	
Country of origin:	United Kingdom
Type:	twin-engined military transport
Powerplant:	two 1200hp (895kW) Pratt & Whitney R-1830-92 radial piston engines
Performance:	maximum speed 370km/h (230mph); service ceiling 7315m (24,000ft); range 2600km (1600 miles)
Weights:	empty 8250kg (18,190lb); loaded 10,841kg (29,300lb)
Dimensions:	span 28.96m (95ft); length 19.66m (64ft 6in); height 5.18m (17ft); wing area 91.69 sq m (987 sq ft)
Armament:	none

Focke-Wulf Fw 190

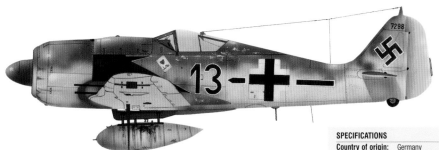

SPECIFICATIONS	
Country of origin:	Germany
Type:	single-engined fighter-bomber
Powerplant:	one 1730hp (1272kW) BMW 801D-2 radial piston engine
Performance:	maximum speed 656km/h (408mph); range 656km/h (408mph); service ceiling 11,410m (37,430ft)
Dimensions:	span 10.51m (34ft 5in); length 8.95m (29ft 4in); height 3.95m (12ft 12in); wing area 18.3 sq m (196.99 sq ft)
Weights:	empty 3200kg (7060lb); maximum 4300kg (9480lb)
Armament:	two 20mm MG 151/20 E cannon; one 1102lb (500kg) SC-500 bomb

Confused by the deception operations, the Luftwaffe put up a minimal response on D-Day itself. Josef 'Pips' Priller, Geschwaderkommodore of JG 26, and a wingman made a sweep over the Normandy beaches in Fw 190A-5s, one of the few retaliatory missions of the day.

Hawker Typhoon and Tempest

The Typhoon was both the Western Allies' finest ground-attack fighter and also a distinct failure, as it had been designed not for ground attacks but as a heavily armed interceptor. It was planned in two forms, one with a liquid-cooled engine, which became the Typhoon, the other with an air-cooled radial engine, which became the Tempest. Structural weaknesses in the Typhoon's tail and indifferent performance at altitude failed it as an interceptor, before its ground-attack role was recognized.

Hawker Typhoon Mk 1B

The first Typhoons had relatively good visibility but a 'car-door' arrangement for cockpit entry and exit, which was hard to use in emergencies. Structural failures of the tail section were cured by adding strengthening plates forward of the tailplane, as seen on this No 247 Squadron Mk IB.

SPECIFICATIONS	
Country of origin:	United Kingdom
Type:	single-seat ground attack aircraft
Powerplant:	2260hp (1685kW) Napier Sabre II liquid cooled H-24 in-line piston engine
Performance:	maximum speed 650km/h (405mph); range 980km (610 miles); service ceiling 10,400m (34,000ft)
Dimensions:	span 12.67m (41ft 7in); length 9.73m (31ft 11in); height 4.66m (15ft 4in)
Weights:	5170kg (11,400lb) loaded
Armament:	4 x 20mm (.8in) Hispano-Suiza HS.404 cannons, 2 x454 kg (1000lb) bombs

Hawker Typhoon Mk 1B

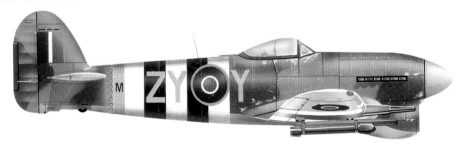

During Typhoon production, the car door was replaced by a sliding teardrop canopy. Weapons racks were added, allowing the carriage of rockets or bombs, which proved devastating against German troops and armour in Normandy. This 'Bombphoon' was used by No 193 Squadron.

SPECIFICATIONS	
Country of origin:	United Kingdom
Type:	close air support fighter-bomber
Powerplant:	2260hp (1685kW) Napier Sabre II piston engine
Performance:	maximum speed 650km/h (405mph); range 980km (610 miles); service ceiling 10,400m (34,000ft)
Dimensions:	span 12.67m (41ft 7in); length 9.73m (31ft 11in); height 4.66m (15ft 4in)
Weights:	5170kg (11,400lb) loaded
Armament:	four 20mm (.8in) Hispano-Suiza HS.404 cannons, eight 27kg (60lb) rockets for ground-attack purposes

TYPHOON & TEMPEST TIMELINE
1940 1942 1943

Hawker Tempest Mk V

The Tempest was developed as a refined version of the Typhoon, with a thinner wing and longer fuselage. It was one of the fastest fighters of the war, and entered service with No 486 (NZ) Squadron (illustrated) in January 1944. It was one of the few fighters able to chase down V-1 flying bombs.

SPECIFICATIONS	
Country of origin:	United Kingdom
Type:	single-seat fighter and fighter-bomber
Powerplant:	2180hp (1626kW) Napier Sabre IIA H-type piston engine
Performance:	maximum speed 686km/h (426mph); range 2092km (1300 miles); service ceiling 10,975m (36,000ft)
Dimensions:	span 12.5m (41ft); length 10.26m (33ft 8in); height 4.9m (16ft 1in)
Weights:	6142kg (13,540lb) loaded
Armament:	4 x 20mm (.8in) Hispano cannon in wings, plus up to 907kg (2000lb) disposable stores consisting of either 2 bombs or 8 rockets for ground attack role

Hawker Tempest Mk VI

The Tempest Mk VI was a tropicalized version of the Mk V. Its oil cooler and carburettor intakes were moved to the wing roots and the radiator was larger. The Mk VI appeared after the war and was exported to India and Pakistan. This one served with No 213 Squadron RAF in Cyprus.

SPECIFICATIONS	
Country of origin:	United Kingdom
Type:	single-seat fighter and fighter-bomber
Powerplant:	one 2340hp (1745kW) Napier Sabre VA H-24 piston engine
Performance:	maximum speed 686km/h (426mph); range 2092km (1300 miles); service ceiling 10,975m (36,000ft)
Dimensions:	span 12.5m (41ft); length 10.26m (33ft 8in); height 4.9m (16ft 1in)
Weights:	6142kg (13,540lb) loaded
Armament:	4 x 20mm (.8in) Hispano cannon in wings, plus up to 907kg (2000lb) disposable stores consisting of either 2 bombs or 8 rockets for ground attack role

Hawker Tempest Mk II

The Tempest was tested with a variety of engines. The Mk V could be brought into service quickest and so became the main production version. The Mk II with the sleeve-valved Centaurus radial engine began production only as the war ended. It was used by some RAF squadrons and Pakistan.

SPECIFICATIONS	
Country of origin:	United Kingdom
Type:	single-seat fighter and fighter bomber
Powerplant:	one 2590hp (1931kW) Bristol Centaurus V 17-cylinder radial engine
Performance:	maximum speed 708km/h (440mph); service ceiling 11,430m (37,500ft); range 2736km (1700 miles)
Weights:	empty 4218kg (9300lb); maximum take-off weight 5352kg (11,800lb)
Dimensions:	span 12.49m (41ft); length 10.49m (34ft 5in); height 4.42m (14ft 6in); wing area 22.2 sq m (239 sq ft)
Armament:	four 20mm fixed forward-firing cannon in the leading edges of the wing, external bomb and rocket load of 907kg (2000lb)

1944

Fleet Air Arm

At the outset of war, the Fleet Air Arm was hampered by Admiralty specifications for its aircraft, including a requirement for multiple crew members. Having a fleet of mostly obsolete types in 1940, the FAA adapted land-based RAF fighters for aircraft carrier use, with varying degrees of success. They had more luck with American-built naval fighters and torpedo bombers. British fleet carriers had armoured flight decks, which made them less vulnerable to Kamikaze attacks and bomb hits.

Blackburn Skua Mk II

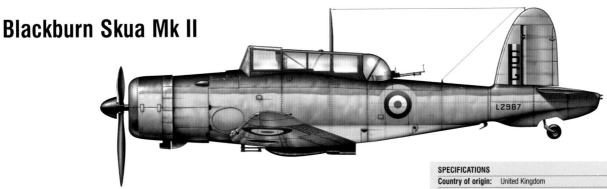

Typifying the flawed concepts prevalent in pre-war naval aircraft, the Skua was a fighter and dive bomber derived from the Roc fighter. Although it had forward-firing wing guns, unlike the Roc, the engine was the same and so the power-weight ratio was even worse. Skuas were mostly withdrawn by 1941.

SPECIFICATIONS	
Country of origin:	United Kingdom
Type:	Two-seat carrier-based fighter and dive-bomber
Powerplant:	890hp (664kW) Bristol Perseus XII radial engine
Maximum speed:	maximum speed 362km/h (225mph); range 1223km (760 miles); service ceiling 6160m (20,200ft)
Dimensions:	span 14.07m (46ft 2in); length 10.85m (35ft 7in); height 3.81m (12ft 6in)
Weights:	3732kg (8228lb) loaded
Armament:	4 x 7.7mm (.303in) MGs in wings; Lewis rear gun; 1 x 227kg (500lb) bomb beneath fuselage

Hawker Sea Hurricane Mk 1A

The Sea Hurricane was a fairly simple conversion from the land-based fighter, with an arrestor hook mounted to its tubular structure. Its wide-track undercarriage gave it better landing and deck-handling characteristics than the Seafire. About 800 Sea Hurricanes were converted.

SPECIFICATIONS	
Country of origin:	United Kingdom
Type:	single-engined carrier-based fighter
Powerplant:	one 1460hp (1088kW) Rolls-Royce Merlin XXII V-12 piston engine
Performance:	maximum speed 550km/h (342mph); range 1545km (960 miles); service ceiling 10,851m (35,600ft)
Dimensions:	12.19m (40ft); length 9.83m (32ft 3in); height 4.04m (13ft 3in); wing area 23.97 sq m (258 sq ft)
Weights:	empty 2631kg (5800lb); maximum 3538 kg (7800lb)
Armament:	four 20mm Hispano cannon

FLEET AIR ARM TIMELINE

1937

1940

Fairey Fulmar

The Fulmar entered FAA service in June 1940, with the same powerplant and armament as the Hurricane, but a larger airframe and second crewman. This reduced its performance to below that of most adversary fighters, but it had reasonable success in the Mediterranean against German and Italian bombers.

SPECIFICATIONS	
Country of origin:	United Kingdom
Type:	single-engined carrier-based fighter
Powerplant:	one 1300hp (969kW) Rolls-Royce Merlin 30 V-12 piston engine
Performance:	maximum speed 440km/h (273mph); range 1255km (780 miles); service ceiling 8300m (27,230ft)
Dimensions:	span 14.14m (46ft 4in); length 12.24m (40ft 2in); height 3.25m (10ft 8in); wing area 31.77 sq m (342 sq ft)
Weights:	empty 3182kg (7015lb); maximum 4627kg (10,200lb)
Armament:	eight .303in (7.7mm) Browning machine guns; two 113kg (350lb) bombs

Vought Corsair Mk I

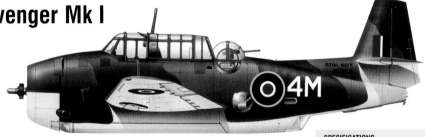

The US Navy initially rejected the Corsair for carrier use due to its poor landing characteristics. Through modifications to the undercarriage and adoption of new landing techniques, the FAA approved it for service at sea. This early 'birdcage' canopy Corsair Mk I served with No 1835 Squadron in late 1943.

SPECIFICATIONS	
Country of origin:	United States
Type:	single-engined carrier-based fighter
Powerplant:	one 2000hp (1490kW) Pratt & Whitney R-2800-8(B) radial piston engine
Performance:	maximum speed 671 km/h (417 mph); range 2425km (1507 miles); service ceiling 11,308m (37,100ft)
Dimensions:	10.16m (41ft); length 10.2m (33ft 4in); height 4.58m (15ft); wing area 29.17 sq m (314 sq ft)
Weights:	empty 4025kg (8873lb); maximum 6281kg (13,846lb)
Armament:	six .5in (12.7mm) Browning machine guns

Grumman Avenger Mk I

Just over 620 Avengers served with the Fleet Air Arm from January 1943 to 1947. They were Initially operated from shore bases against U-boats and German shipping, but later saw much use in the Far East, where they struck oil refineries in Java and targets in the Japanese home islands.

SPECIFICATIONS	
Country of origin:	United States
Type:	three-seat carrierborne bomber
Powerplant:	one 1700hp (1268kW) Wright Cyclone 14-cylinder two-row engine
Performance:	maximum speed 414km/h (257mph); service ceiling 6525m (21,400ft); range 4321km (2685 miles)
Weights:	empty 4788kg (10,555lb); maximum take-off weight 7876kg (17,364lb)
Dimensions:	span 16.51m (54ft 2in); length 12.42m (40ft 9in); height 4.19m (13ft 9in)
Armament:	three .5in MGs (two in leading edges of wing, one in dorsal turret), one .3in MG in ventral position, bomb load of 1134kg (2500lb)

1941

Long-Range Luftwaffe

The area of the Bay of Biscay was the hunting ground for the Luftwaffe's long-range squadrons based around Bordeaux on France's Atlantic coast, which spotted for U-boats and attacked Allied shipping bound for the Mediterranean. Maritime patrol aircraft were also based in the Baltic Sea and Norway to interdict ships supplying Russia. Germany built relatively few four-engined landplanes. Flying boats and seaplanes had their places in all theatres right up until the war's end.

Heinkel He 115C-1

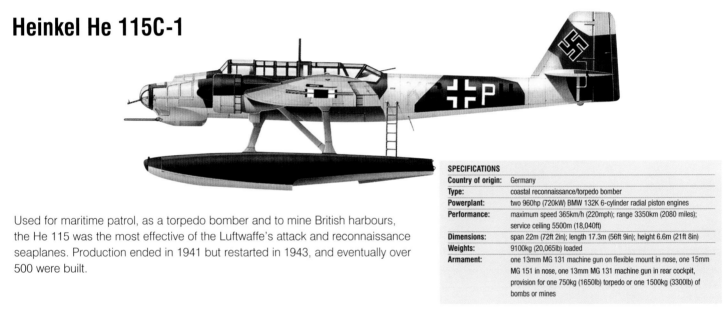

Used for maritime patrol, as a torpedo bomber and to mine British harbours, the He 115 was the most effective of the Luftwaffe's attack and reconnaissance seaplanes. Production ended in 1941 but restarted in 1943, and eventually over 500 were built.

SPECIFICATIONS	
Country of origin:	Germany
Type:	coastal reconnaissance/torpedo bomber
Powerplant:	two 960hp (720kW) BMW 132K 6-cylinder radial piston engines
Performance:	maximum speed 365km/h (220mph); range 3350km (2080 miles); service ceiling 5500m (18,040ft)
Dimensions:	span 22m (72ft 2in); length 17.3m (56ft 9in); height 6.6m (21ft 8in)
Weights:	9100kg (20,065lb) loaded
Armament:	one 13mm MG 131 machine gun on flexible mount in nose, one 15mm MG 151 in nose, one 13mm MG 131 machine gun in rear cockpit, provision for one 750kg (1650lb) torpedo or one 1500kg (3300lb) of bombs or mines

Blohm und Voss BV 138C-1/U1

The aircraft subsidiary of the Blohm und Voss shipyard, Hamburger Flugzeugbau, was founded in 1933. First designed for twin engines, development problems necessitated a redesign to accept three engines. First prototypes flew in July 1937, but the Ha 138 proved unstable both on water and in the air, and main production variants were not delivered until March 1941.

SPECIFICATIONS	
Country of origin:	Germany
Type:	five-man reconnaissance flying boat
Powerplant:	three 880hp (656kW) Junkers Juno inline diesel piston engines
Performance:	maximum speed 275km/h (171mph); range 5000km (3107 miles); service ceiling 5000m (16,405ft)
Dimensions:	span 27m (88ft 7in); length 19.9m (65ft 3in); height 6.6m (21ft 8in)
Weights:	empty 8100kg (17,857lb); max take-off 14,700kg (32,408lb)
Armament:	two 20mm (.8in) cannons (in bow and rear hull); one 13mm MG in centre nacelle; provision for six 50kg (110lb) bombs

LONG-RANGE TIMELINE			
 1937		 1941	

Dornier Do 24T

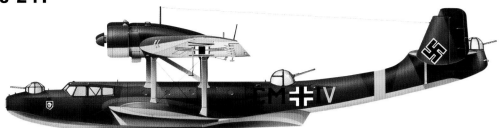

The Dornier 24 originated with a 1935 Dutch specification for an aircraft to patrol the East Indies. Production continued in the Netherlands and France after the German occupation. In Luftwaffe service, its main function was as an air-sea rescue craft for recovering downed aircrew.

SPECIFICATIONS	
Country of origin:	Netherlands
Type:	air-sea rescue and transport flying boat
Powerplant:	three 1000hp (746kW) BMW-Bramo Fafnir radial piston engines
Performance:	maximum speed 340km/h (211mph); range 2900km (1802 miles); service ceiling 5900m (19,355ft)
Dimensions:	span 27m (88ft 7in); length 22.05m (72ft 4in); height 5.75m (18ft 10in)
Weights:	empty 9200kg (20,286lb) maximum take-off weight 18,400kg (40,565lb)
Armament:	one 20mm trainable cannon, one 7.92mm MG in bow, another in rear turret

Blohm und Voss BV 222 Wiking

The BV 222 was designed before World War II for a proposed transatlantic service. The prototype's first flight was in September 1940, when it was seconded for military transport operations in Norway and the Mediterranean. Armament was fitted to all subsequent prototypes.

SPECIFICATIONS	
Country of origin:	Germany
Type:	transport and military reconnaissance flying boat
Powerplant:	six 71000hp (46kW) Junkers Jumo 12-cylinder diesel engines
Performance:	maximum speed 390km/h (242mph); range 6100km (3790 miles); service ceiling 7300m (23,950ft)
Dimensions:	span 46m (150ft 11in); length 37m (121ft 5in); height 10.9m (35ft 9in)
Weights:	empty 30,650kg (67,572lb); maximum take-off 49,000kg (108,025lb)
Armament:	three 20mm cannon (in dorsal turret and in each power-operated wing turret), one 13mm MG in bow position, one 13mm MG in each of four lateral hull positions

Junkers Ju 290A-5

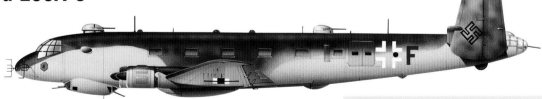

Built in tiny numbers in numerous versions, the Ju 290 failed to live up to its potential. With 11 built, the Ju 290A-5 was the main version to enter service. A derivative of the 290, the Ju 390 flew from France to within sight of the US coast and back, but no raids on America were carried out.

SPECIFICATIONS	
Country of origin:	Germany
Type:	nine-seat long-range maritime reconnaissance aircraft
Powerplant:	four 1268kW (1700hp) BMW 14-cylinder radial engines
Performance:	maximum speed 440km/h (273mph); service ceiling 6000m (19,685ft); range 6150km (3821 miles)
Weights:	40,970kg (90,322lb) normal loaded; 50,500kg (111,332lb) max overload
Dimensions:	span 42m (137ft 9in); length 28.64m (93ft 11in); height 6.83m (22ft 5in)
Armament:	six 20mm (.8in) MGs in dorsal turret, aft waist, tailcone and front of ventral gondola positions; one 13mm (.6in) in rear of ventral gondola

1942

1943

Lavochkin Fighters

Designed by the trio of Lavochkin, Gorbunov and Gudkov, the LaGG-1 fighter first flew in March 1940. The structure was a novel type of plastic-impregnated wood, leading to jokes that LaGG stood for 'varnished, guaranteed coffin' in Russian. In general, the inline-engined LaGGs were inadequate, and the series was saved only by installation of more powerful boosted radials under Lavochkin's direction. The La-5 and La-7 were equal to their German adversaries in the hands of good pilots.

LaGG-3

The LaGG-3 was a development of the LaGG-1 with lighter armament and more power, but it was still inferior to the Polikarpov I-16. Due to the war situation in 1941–42, production continued at a high rate nonetheless, and over 6500 were produced before replacement by the radial-engine models.

SPECIFICATIONS	
Country of origin:	USSR
Type:	single-seat fighter and fighter-bomber
Powerplant:	one 1260hp (939.5kW) Klimov VK-105PF-1 12-cylinder Vee engine
Performance:	maximum speed 575km/h (357mph); service ceiling 9700m (31,825ft); range 1000km (621 miles)
Weights:	empty 2620kg (5776lb); maximum take-off weight 3190kg (7032lb)
Dimensions:	span 9.8m (32ft 1.75in); length 8.81m (28ft 11in); height 2.54m (8ft 4in)
Armament:	one 20mm forward-firing cannon in engine installation, two 7.62mm machine guns in upper part of forward fuselage, plus external bomb load and rocket load of 20kg (441lb)

La-5UTI

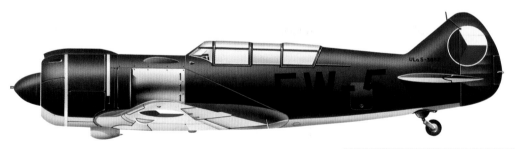

During the war, the Russians utilized two-seat conversions of fighters as trainers more than most other nations. The La-5FN-UTI appeared in August 1943. This one was used post-war by the 1st Czechoslovak Fighter Regiment under the designation CS.95.

SPECIFICATIONS	
Country of origin:	USSR
Type:	single-seat fighter and fighter-bomber
Powerplant:	one 1630hp (1215kW) Shvetsov 14-cylinder two-row radial engine
Performance:	maximum speed unknown; service ceiling unknown; range unknown
Weights:	uninown
Dimensions:	span 9.8m (32ft 1.75in); length unknown; height 2.54m (8ft 4in)
Armament:	one 20mm ShVAK cannon

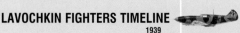

LAVOCHKIN FIGHTERS TIMELINE
1939   1943

La-5FN

Installing the Shvetsov M-82FN engine in the basic airframe of the LaGG-3 proved tricky, not least because of its width, but it transformed the fighter's performance. Over 5700 La-5FNs were built, this one serving with a Czech-manned unit in the Ukraine in 1944.

SPECIFICATIONS	
Country of origin:	USSR
Type:	single-seat fighter and fighter-bomber
Powerplant:	one 1630hp (1215kW) Shvetsov 14-cylinder two-row radial engine
Performance:	maximum speed 648km/h (403mph); service ceiling 11,000m (36,090ft); range 765km (475 miles)
Weights:	empty 2605kg (5743lb); maximum take-off weight 3402kg (7500lb)
Dimensions:	span 9.8m (32ft 1.75in); length 8.67m (28ft 5.33in); height 2.54m (8ft 4in)
Armament:	two 20mm forward-firing cannon in upper part of forward fuselage, plus external bomb and rocket load of 500kg (1102lb)

La-7

The La-7 was a strengthened derivative of the La-5FN, with metal rather than wooden wing spars and other improvements. The aircraft shown was flown by Ivan Kozhedub, who was awarded the title Hero of the Soviet Union three times. He shot down 62 German aircraft, including an Me 262 jet.

SPECIFICATIONS	
Country of origin:	USSR
Type:	single-seat fighter
Powerplant:	one 1850hp (1380kW) Shvetsov M-82FN radial piston engine
Performance:	maximum speed 680km/h (425mph); service ceiling 9500m (31,160ft); range 990km (618 miles)
Weight:	loaded 3280kg (7231lb)
Dimensions:	span 9.8m (32ft 2in); length 8.6m (28ft 3in)
Armament:	two 20mm (.8in) ShVAK cannon or three 20mm (.8in) Berezin B-20 cannon in nose; plus up to 200kg (441lb) bomb load

La-11

The La-11 was the last of the piston-engined Lavochkins, as jet fighters were clearly the way of the future. By 1947, however, the technology was not fully proven, and the La-11 offered a reliable design, plus a longer range. Nearly 1200 were built, many of them supplied to China and North Korea.

SPECIFICATIONS	
Country of origin:	USSR
Type:	single-engined fighter
Powerplant:	one 1850hp (1380kW) Shvetsov ASh-82FN radial piston engine gine
Performance:	maximum speed 674km/h (419mph); service ceiling 10,250m (33,628ft); range 2235km (1388 miles)
Weights:	empty 2770kg (6107lb); maximum 3996kg (8810lb)
Dimensions:	span 9.8m (32ft 2in); length 8.62m (28ft 3in); height 3.47m (11ft 5in); wing area 17.6 sq m (189 sq ft)
Armament:	three 23mm Nudelman-Suranov NS-23 cannon

1947

Soviet Ground Attack

The Great Patriotic War (as the Soviets termed it) was characterized by great distances and vast use of armour over open terrain. Once the Soviet Union got over the initial shock of the invasion and stopped the Germans at the gates of Moscow, its industry (largely relocated east of the Urals) recovered to supply its air forces with modern ground-attack aircraft, supplemented by the United States and United Kingdom under the Lend-Lease programme.

Ilyushin Il-2

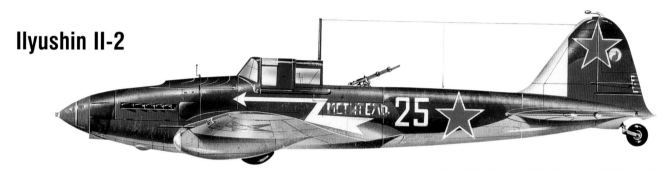

With around 36,180 built, the Il-2 Sturmovik was the most numerous combat aircraft ever produced. Initially fielded as a single-seater, it proved vulnerable to fighter attack, and some were fitted with makeshift rear gunners' positions before the factory-built, two-seat Il-2M3 was developed. The inscription reads 'The Avenger'.

SPECIFICATIONS	
Country of origin:	USSR
Type:	two-seat ground attack aircraft
Powerplant:	1 x 1770hp (1320kW) Mikulin Am-38F liquid-cooled inline piston engine
Performance:	maximum speed 404km/h (251mph); range 600km (375 miles); service ceiling 5945m (19,500ft)
Dimensions:	span 14.6m (47ft 11in); length 11.6m (38ft 0.5in); height 3.4m (11ft 1in)
Weights:	6360kg (14,021lb) loaded
Armament:	2 x 23mm (.9in) VYa-23 cannon, 2 x 7.62mm (.3in) MGs, 1 x 12.7mm (.5in) rear-mounted MG; and 8 x 82mm (3.2in) RS-82 or 132mm (5.2in) RS-132 rocket projectiles

Polikarpov Po-2

Production of the Polikarpov Po-2, mostly for use as a trainer and utility aircraft, exceeded even that of the Il-2, with over 40,000 made. Also called the U-2, it pioneered night-harassment missions on the Eastern Front, flying over enemy encampments, making noise and dropping light bombs to deprive soldiers of rest.

SPECIFICATIONS	
Country of origin:	USSR
Type:	two-seat trainer and ground attack biplane
Powerplant:	one 100hp (75kW) engine
Performance:	maximum speed 156km/h (97mph); range 400km (249 miles); service ceiling 4000m (13,125ft)
Dimensions:	span 11.4m (37ft 5in); length 8.17m (26ft 10in); height 3.1m (10ft 2in)
Weights:	890kg (1962lb) loaded
Armament:	one 7.62mm (.3in) rear-facing machine gun and up to 250kg (551lb) of bombs under the lower wing.

SOVIET GROUND ATTACK TIMELINE 1928   1936    1938

Petlyakov Pe-2FT

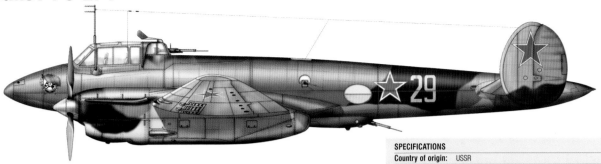

The vane above the forward edge of the turret immediately to the rear of the cockpit was an aerodynamic balance area to offset the drag of the 12.7mm (.5in) machine gun as the turret was traversed, and so obviate the need for the turret to be power-operated.

SPECIFICATIONS	
Country of origin:	USSR
Type:	three-seat dive bomber
Powerplant:	two 1100hp (820kW) Klimov
Performance:	maximum speed 540km/h (336mph); range 1500km (932 miles); service ceiling 8800m (28,870ft)
Dimensions:	span 17.16m (56ft 4in); length 12.66m (41ft 7in); height 4m (13ft 2in)
Weights:	8496kg (12,943lb) loaded
Armament:	two 7.62mm (.3in) ShKAS MGs in nose and one 7.62mm (.3in) ShKAS MG in ventral or dorsal station; maximum bomb load 1200kg (2646lb)

Douglas A-20G

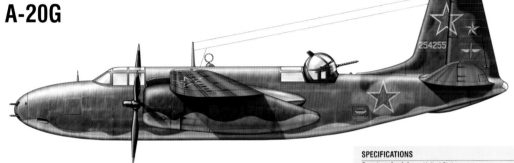

The Soviet Union received 3125 aircraft of the DB-7 series as part of US Lend-Lease deliveries, many of them receiving a number of local modifications, such as the Soviet dorsal turret evident here. The Soviet Naval Air Force operated its aircraft in the anti-shipping role from the Arctic Ocean to the Black Sea. This A-20G served with Soviet Naval Air Forces in the Tula area in 1944.

SPECIFICATIONS	
Country of origin:	United States
Type:	three-seat light attack bomber
Powerplant:	2 x 1600hp (1193kW) Wright radial piston engines
Performance:	maximum speed 510km/h (217mph); range 1521km (945 miles); service ceiling 7225m (23,700ft)
Dimensions:	span 18.69m (61ft 4in); length 14.63m (48ft); height 5.36m (17ft 7in)
Weights:	10,964kg (24,127lb) loaded
Armament:	six 12.7mm (.5in) Browning M2 fixed forward-firing MGs, and 2 x similar weapons in power-operated dorsal turret, and one rearward-firing through ventral tunnel; up to 1814kg (4000lb) of bombs

Ilyushin Il-4/DB-3F

Initially known as the DB-3F, the Il-4 was built to the extent of 5256 aircraft in a programme extending from 1941 to 1945. Differentiated from predecessor variants by its more streamlined and glazed nose, the Il-4 provided the backbone of the Soviet Union's longer-range bomber capability throughout World War II.

SPECIFICATIONS	
Country of origin:	USSR
Type:	four-seat long-range medium bomber
Powerplant:	two 1100hp (821kW) 88B radial piston engines
Performance:	maximum speed 410km/h (255mph); range 2600km (1616 miles); service ceiling 10,000m (32,810ft)
Dimensions:	span 21.44m (70ft 4in); length 14.8m (48ft 6in); height 4.1m (13ft 6in)
Weights:	10,000kg (22,046lb) loaded
Armament:	12.7mm (.5in) MGs in nose, dorsal turret and ventral positions; maximum bomb load 1000kg (2205lb)

1939

Luftwaffe on the Eastern Front

The winter of 1941–42 brought the German advance to a halt, but gave the Soviets the chance to rearm. When mobile fighting resumed in the spring, the Luftwaffe racked up enormous scores against Russian aircraft and armour, but found its own supply lines stretched by the huge distances. Fighting on multiple fronts, a situation Hitler had hoped to avoid, reduced the flow of replacement equipment. Despite its mostly superior pilots and equipment, the Luftwaffe was drawn into a war of attrition.

Focke-Wulf Fw 190A-4

JG 54 was the second highest-scoring fighter *Geschwader* in the *Luftwaffe*, claiming over 9600 kills by war's end. Its bases in the east ranged from the Baltic Sea in the north to the Caspian in the south. This 190A-4 of I Gruppe, JG 54, was flown by Anton Doebele, who scored 94 victories.

SPECIFICATIONS	
Country of origin:	Germany
Type:	single-seat ground attack and close-support fighter
Powerplant:	one 1700hp (1268kW) BMW water-injected 18-cylinder radial engine
Performance:	maximum speed 670km/h (416mph); service ceiling 11,410m (37,400ft); range 900km (560 miles)
Weights:	loaded 4900kg (10,800lb)
Dimensions:	span 10.49m (34ft 5.5in); length 8.84m (29ft); height 3.96m (13ft)
Armament:	four 20mm (.8in) cannon, two 7.92mm (.3in) machine guns, one 500kg (1102lb) bomb

Henschel Hs 123A

Despite its apparent obsolescence and production stopping in 1937, the tough and accurate Hs 123 found plenty of employment on the steppes of Russia and the Ukraine in 1941–44. The black triangle marking was the emblem of the *Schlacht* (literally 'slaughter') close-support units on the Eastern Front.

SPECIFICATIONS	
Country of origin:	Germany
Type:	single-seat dive-bomber and close-support aircraft
Powerplant:	one 880hp (656W) BMW 9-cylinder radial engine
Performance:	maximum speed 340km/h (211mph); range 855km (531 miles); service ceiling 9000m (29,530ft)
Dimensions:	span 10.5m (34ft 5in); length 8.33m (27ft 4in); height 3.2m (10ft 6in); wing area 24.85 sq m (267 sq ft)
Weights:	empty 1500kg (3307lb); maximum take-off weight 2215kg (4884lb)
Armament:	two fixed forward-firing 7.92mm MG 17 machine guns; underwing racks with provision for up to 450kg (992lb) of bombs

Henschel Hs 129B-3

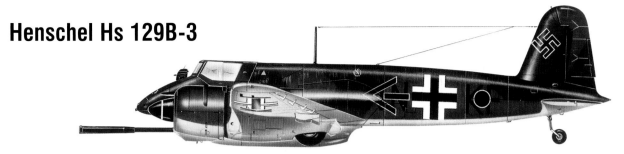

The Hs 129 was one of fairly few single-seat twin-engined wartime aircraft. Although underpowered, with poor handling and terrible pilot vision, the HS 129 was heavily armoured and well armed. Improved Soviet tank armour led to development of a version with a long-barrelled 75mm cannon, although few were built.

SPECIFICATIONS	
Country of origin:	Germany
Type:	single-seat close support and anti-tank aircraft
Powerplant:	two 700hp (522kW) Gnome-Rhône 14-cylinder two-row radial engines
Performance:	maximum speed 407km/h (253mph); service ceiling 9000m (29,530ft); range 560km (348 miles)
Dimensions:	span 14.2m (46ft 7in); length 9.75m (31ft 11.75in); height 3.25m (10ft 10in)
Weights:	empty 4020kg (8862lb); maximum take-off weight 5250kg (11,574lb)
Armament:	two 20mm fixed forward-firing cannon and two 13mm fixed forward-firing machine guns in the upper and lower sides of the fuselage, provision under the forward-firing cannon or four 7.92mm forward-firing machine guns, bomb load of 450kg (992lb)

Messerschmitt Bf 109E-7/B

Although not ideal in the role, the Bf 109E was one of the many types used by the close-support squadrons in Russia. The Bf 109E-7 was the fighter-bomber version of the Bf 109E, able to carry a single 250kg (551lb) bomb. This E-7 of II/SG.1 was used at Stalingrad in the autumn of 1942. The rifle and laurel leaf symbol beneath the cockpit is the Infantry Assault award, which was often carried by *Schlacht* aircraft.

SPECIFICATIONS	
Country of origin:	Germany
Type:	single-seat fighter
Powerplant:	one 1175hp (876kW) DB 601N 12-cylinder inverted V
Performance:	maximum speed 570km/hr (354mph); range 700km (435 miles); service ceiling 10,500m (34,450ft)
Dimensions:	span 9.87m (32ft 4in); length 8.64m (28ft 4in); height 2.28m (7ft 5.5in)
Weights:	2505kg (5523lb) maximum loaded
Armament:	two 20mm (.8in) cannon; two 7.92mm (.3in) MGs; one 250kg (551lb) bomb

Messerschmitt Bf 110C-4

The Bf 110 became obsolescent as a day fighter in Western Europe fairly quickly, but its long range and good armament gave it a useful role in the East. Wearing the famous *Wespe* (wasp) insignia of Zerstorergeschwader 1, this Bf 110C-4 operated in the Caucasus region in the autumn of 1942.

SPECIFICATIONS	
Country of origin:	Germany
Type:	two-seat heavy fighter
Powerplant:	two 1100hp (820kW) Daimler-Benz cylinder inverted V
Performance:	maximum speed 560km/h (349mph); range 775km (483 miles); service ceiling 10,000m (32,810ft)
Weights:	maximum take-off weight 6750kg (14,881lb)
Dimensions:	span 16.27m (50ft 3in); length 12.67m (41ft 6in); height 3.5m (11ft 6in)
Armament:	two 20mm (.8in) cannon and four 7.92mm (.3in) machine guns, twin 7.92mm (.3in) machine guns in rear cockpit, 900kg (1984lb) bomb load

Luftwaffe on the Eastern Front Part Two

The Battle of Stalingrad that began in August 1942 was the turning point for Germany's fortunes on the Eastern Front. The Luftwaffe attempted to resupply the encircled 6th Army from the air using transport aircraft. The Red Army targeted all the landing grounds with artillery, and nearly 500 multi-engined aircraft were lost. The Luftwaffe failed to bring in sufficient supplies and the 6th Army surrendered in February 1943, having lost 290,000 troops killed or captured.

Junkers Ju 86E-2

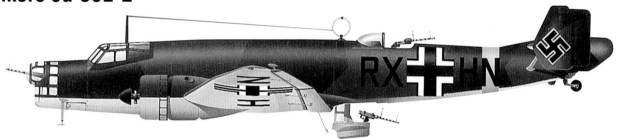

The Junkers 86 bomber had numerous faults and was mainly assigned to training schools by 1939, but was brought out of retirement for frontline duties on several occasions for emergency use, including acting as an auxiliary transport at Stalingrad.

SPECIFICATIONS	
Country of origin:	Germany
Crew:	five-six-seat transport plane
Powerplant:	two 800hp (597kW) BMW 132 nine-cylinder radials
Performance:	maximum speed 325km/h (202mph); range 1200km (746 miles); service ceiling 6800m (22,310ft)
Dimensions:	span 22.6m (73ft 10in); length 17.9m (58ft 8in); height 4.7m (15ft 5in)
Weights:	8200kg (18,080lb)
Armament:	three 7.92mm (.3in) MGs

Messerschmitt Me 323D-2

The six-engined Me 323 Gigant transport was derived from the Me 321 glider and was one of the largest aircraft of the war. Its metal tube structure covered in fabric allowed it to survive a fair deal of battle damage, but did not offer much protection for the 120 troops or 80 stretcher patients it could carry.

SPECIFICATIONS	
Country of origin:	Germany
Type:	six-ten seat transport plane
Powerplant:	6 x 1140hp (851kW) Gnome-Rhone 14-cylinder radials
Performance:	cruising speed 190km/h (118mph); range 1100km (684 miles)
Dimensions:	span 55m (180ft 5in); length 28.5m (93ft 6in); height 9.6m (31ft 6in)
Weights:	45,000kg (99,210lb) maximum
Payload:	up to 120 troops or 60 stretchers with attendants or 11,500kg (25,353lb) of cargo

Focke-Wulf Fw 200C-0 Condor

Although known as a patrol aircraft, the early model Fw 200C Condors were delivered as passenger transports. This was one of those used in January 1943 in the vain effort to relieve Stalingrad. Nine Condors are known to have been lost at Stalingrad.

SPECIFICATIONS	
Country of origin:	Germany
Type:	four-seat transport aircraft
Powerplant:	4 x 850hp (634kW) BMW 132D nine-cylinder radials
Performance:	maximum speed 360km/h (224mph); range 3560km (2212 miles); service ceiling 6000m (19,685ft)
Dimensions:	span 32.85m (107ft 9in); length 23.45m (76ft 11in); height 6.3m (20ft 8in)
Weights:	17,000kg (37,490lbs) empty; 24,520kg (50,057lb) max

Junkers Ju 88C-6

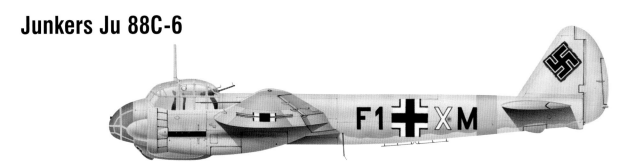

The Ju 88C heavy fighter was used as a ground-attack aircraft on the Eastern Front and was particularly effective against trains.This C-6 of 4./KG 76 was based at Taganrog on the Black Sea, and has its solid fighter nose painted to disguise it as a lower-performance Ju 88A bomber.

SPECIFICATIONS	
Country of origin:	Germany
Type:	two-seat ground attack fighter
Powerplant:	two 1340hp (1000kW) Junkers Jumo 211J 12-cylinder inverted V
Performance:	maximum speed 480km/h (300mph); range 1980km (1230 miles) service ceiling 9900m (32,480ft)
Dimensions:	span 20.13m (65ft 10in); length 14.4m (47ft 2in); height 5m (16ft 7.5in)
Weights:	12,485kg (27,500lb) maximum loaded
Armament:	typically 2/3 x 7.92mm (.3in) MGs plus 1/2 x 20mm (.8in) cannon

Heinkel He 177A-1 Greif

The troubled Heinkel He 177 bomber was initially used as a transport at Stalingrad by KG 20. After the battle, some of its aircraft were fitted with a huge 30mm MK 101 cannon installation and used to suppress Russian flak batteries.

SPECIFICATIONS	
Country of origin:	Germany
Type:	five-crew transport plane and ground attack aircraft and heavy bomber
Powerplant:	two 2950hp 2200kW() DB 610 paired 12-cylinder inverted V
Performance:	maximum speed 462km/h (295mph); range 1200km (746 miles); service ceiling 7000m (22,965ft)
Dimensions:	span 31.44m (103ft 2in); length 22m (72ft 2in); height 6.4m (21ft)
Weights:	empty 18,040kg (39,771lb); maximum take-off weight 30,000kg (66,139lb)
Armament:	1 x 30mm (1.2in) cannon; 1/3 x 7.92mm (.3in) MGs; 2/4 13mm (.5in) MGs; 2 x 20mm (.8in) cannon; 6000kg (13,228lb) bombload

Ninth Air Force

The USAAF's Ninth Air Force was formed in late 1942 and initially served in North Africa. In August 1943, it was reestablished in the United Kingdom as the tactical counterpart to the Eighth Air Force in preparation for the invasion of France. Its role was largely to gain superiority by destroying the Luftwaffe in the air and on the ground. Following the invasion, most of its squadrons moved to the Continent and followed the front lines as they moved into Belgium, Holland and Germany.

North American P-51D Mustang

The 370th FG was one of the Ninth AF's Mustang groups based in France in late 1944. 'Sierra Sue II' was flown by the 402nd FS's Robert Bohna. It survived the war, was sold to Sweden and then Nicaragua, and is still airworthy today.

SPECIFICATIONS	
Country of origin:	United States
Type:	single-seat fighter and fighter-bomber
Powerplant:	one 1695hp (1264kW) Packard 12-cylinder Vee engine
Performance:	maximum speed 703km/h (437mph); service ceiling 12,770m (41,900ft); range 3703km (2301 miles)
Weights:	empty 3103kg (6840lb); maximum take-off weight 5493kg (12,100lb)
Dimensions:	span 11.28m (37ft 0.25in); length 9.84m (32ft 3in); height 4.16m (13ft 8in) with the tail down

Republic P-47D Thunderbolt

'Tarheel Hal' was a late-model P-47D of the 366th FS, 358th FG. The Thunderbolts of the Ninth AF wreaked havoc on trains, airfields, tanks and troops. When the weather cleared in late January 1945, the Thunderbolts helped destroy the last mobile tank units in the Ardennes.

SPECIFICATIONS	
Country of origin:	United States
Type:	single-seat fighter and fighter-bomber
Powerplant:	2535hp (1891kW) Pratt & Whitney R-2800-59W Double Wasp
Performance:	maximum speed 697km/h (433mph); range 3060km (1900 miles) with drop tanks; service ceiling 12,495m (41,000ft)
Dimensions:	span 12.42m (40ft 9in); length 11.02m (36ft 2in); height 4.47m (14ft 8in)
Weights:	maximum take-off weight 7938kg (17,500lb)
Armament:	eight 12.7mm (.5in) MGs in wings, plus provision for 1134kg (2500lb) external bombs or rockets

Northrop P-61A Black Widow

SPECIFICATIONS	
Country of origin:	United States
Type:	two/three-seat night-fighter
Powerplant:	two 2250hp (1678kW) Pratt & Whitney R-2800-65 18 cylinder radial engines
Performance:	maximum speed 594km/h (369mph); range 3058km (1900 miles); service ceiling 10.090m (33,100ft)
Dimensions:	span 20.12m (66ft); length 14.91m (48ft 11in); height 4.46m (14ft 8in)
Weights:	maximum take-off weight 15,513kg (34,200lb)
Armament:	4 x 20mm (.8in) cannon in underside of forward fuselage

The USAAF's only purpose-designed night-fighter, the P-61 was used by the Ninth AF from July 1944. The first Black Widows were, in fact, delivered in olive drab and grey colours, and lacked the intended top turret – as seen on this P-61A of the 422nd Night Fighter Squadon at Hurn.

Martin B-26G Marauder

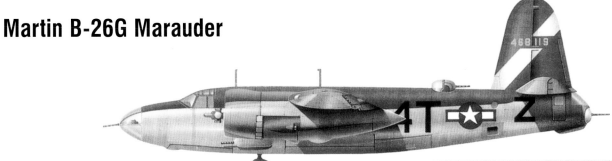

SPECIFICATIONS	
Country of origin:	United States
Type:	seven-seat medium attack bomber
Powerplant:	two 1850hp (1379kW) Pratt & Whitney 18-cylinder two-row radials
Performance:	maximum speed 507km/h (315mph); service ceiling 7620m (25,000ft); range 1609km (1000 miles)
Weights:	empty 9696kg (21,375lb); maximum take-off weight 14,515kg (32,000lb)
Dimensions:	span 18.81m (65ft); length 17.07m (56ft); height 6.05m (19ft 10in)
Armament:	one trainable forward-firing machine gun in nose, two .5in trainable machine guns in dorsal turret, one .5in trainable rearward-firing machine gun in tail position, plus bomb load of 2177kg (4800lb)

The early model Marauders gained a terrible reputation for accidents, in part due to the type's relatively short wings and tail surfaces, which caused long take-off runs. Later variants like the 'big wing' B-26G reversed this trend and the Marauder eventually had the lowest overall loss rate of any US bomber.

Douglas A-26B Invader

SPECIFICATIONS	
Country of origin:	United States
Type:	three-seat light attack and reconnaissance bomber
Powerplant:	two 2000hp (1491kW) Pratt & Whitney radial piston engines
Performance:	maximum speed 600km/h (373mph); range 2253km (1400 miles); service ceiling 6735m (22,100ft)
Dimensions:	span 21.34m (70ft); length 15.62m (51ft 3in); height 5.56m (18ft 3in)
Weights:	15,876kg (35,000lb) loaded
Armament:	6 x 12.7mm (.5in) MGs: two each in nose, dorsal and ventral positions; up to 1814kg (4000lb) of bombs

The A-26 Invader was conceived by Douglas as a replacement for the DB-7 (A-20) series. Similar in configuration to its predecessor, but more streamlined, powerful and better armed, the Invader reached the European theatre in late 1944. This particular aircraft, 'Stinky', was based in eastern France in April 1945.

North American B-25 Mitchell

The B-25 was the principal American medium bomber of the war, seeing service on all fronts. It gained early war fame when B-25Bs led the first bombing raid on Japan from the carrier *Hornet*. With the addition of extra guns, armour and bomb capacity – but only modest improvements in engine power – later models were slower than their predecessors. Gun armament grew to be the heaviest of any US bomber, and the Mitchell excelled in the anti-shipping and low-level attack roles.

B-25A

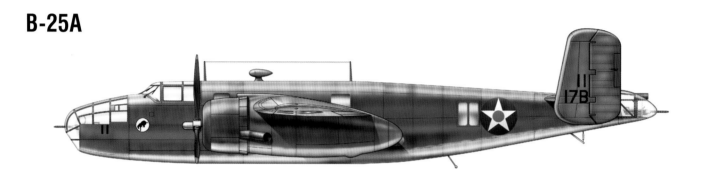

The original B-25 (no suffix) and the B-25A, which varied in having self-sealing fuel tanks, were built in relatively small numbers. Both of these early versions were used by the 17th Bomb Group at McChord, Washington, in September 1941.

SPECIFICATIONS	
Country of origin:	Germany
Type:	twin-engined medium bomber
Powerplant:	two 1700hp (1267kW) Wright R-2600-13 radial piston engines
Performance:	maximum speed 507km/h (315mph); range 2172km (1350 miles); service ceiling 8230m (27,000ft)
Dimensions:	span 16.13m (67ft 7in); length 16.49m (54ft 1in); height 4.75m (15ft 9in); wing area 56.67 sq m (610 sq ft)
Weights:	empty 8105kg (17,870lb); maximum 12,293kg (27,100lb)
Armament:	one .5in (12.7mm) and three .3in (7.62mm) machine guns; up to 1452kg (3200lb) of bombs

B-25C

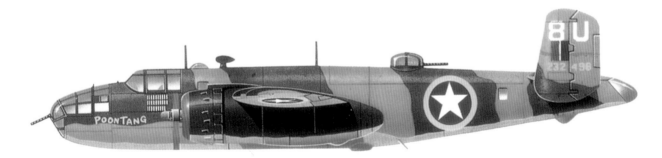

Combat experience showed the need for more armament on the B-25. The B-25C had a twin-gun turret mounted at the rear of the fuselage and a retractable ventral turret. 'Poontang' was a Tunisian-based B-25C of the 488th BS, 340th BG, in April 1943.

SPECIFICATIONS	
Country of origin:	United States
Type:	twin-engined medium bomber
Powerplant:	two 1700hp (1267kW) Wright R-2600-9 radial piston engines
Performance:	maximum speed 483km/h (300mph); range 2172km (1350 miles); service ceiling 7163m (23,500ft)
Dimensions:	span 16.13m (67ft 7in); length 16.13m (52ft 11in); height 4.75m (15ft 9in); wing area 56.67 sq m (610 sq ft)
Weights:	empty 9072kg (20,000lb); maximum 12,909kg (28,460lb)
Armament:	four .5in (12.7mm) and three .3in (7.62mm) machine guns; up to 1452kg (3200lb) of bombs

Mitchell Mk. II

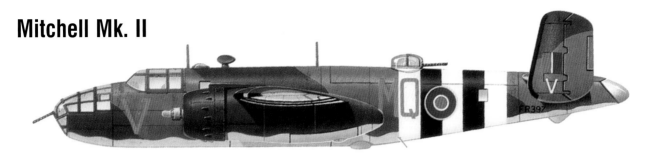

The RAF's equivalent of the B-25C was the Mitchell Mk. II, used mainly by the 2nd Tactical Air Force, the British equivalent of the US Ninth AF. No 320 Squadron was manned by Dutch aircrew, and this example was written off due to damage it received during a mission over Venlo airfield in October 1944.

SPECIFICATIONS	
Country of origin:	United States
Type:	twin-engined medium bomber
Powerplant:	two 1700hp (1267kW) Wright R-2600-9 radial piston engines
Performance:	maximum speed 483km/h (300mph); range 2172km (1350 miles); service ceiling 7163m (23,500ft)
Dimensions:	span 16.13m (67ft 7in); length 16.13m (52ft 11in); height 4.75m (15ft 9in); wing area 56.67 sq m (610 sq ft)
Weights:	empty 9072kg (20,000lb); maximum 12,909kg (28,460lb)
Armament:	four .5in (12.7mm) and three .3in (7.62mm) machine guns; up to 1452kg (3200lb) of bombs

B-25J

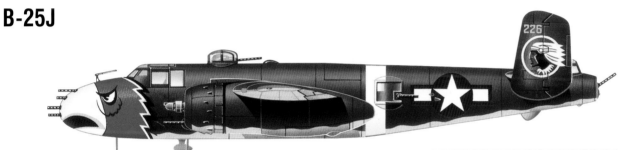

The major production version was the B-25J. Its main distinctive feature was the relocation of the top turret to a position behind the cockpit. For strafing attacks, a solid gun nose was fitted, supplemented by 'package' guns on the fuselage sides – as seen on this Philippines-based 345th BG B-25J.

SPECIFICATIONS	
Country of origin:	United States
Type:	twin-engined medium bomber
Powerplant:	two 1850hp (1380kW) Wright R-2600-29 radial piston engines
Performance:	maximum speed 442km/h (275mph); service ceiling 7600m (25,000ft); range 2172km (1350 miles)
Weights:	empty 9580kg (21,120lb); maximum 19,000kg (28,460lb)
Dimensions:	span 16.13m (67ft 7in); length 16.13m (52ft 11in); height 4.8m (17ft 7in); wing area 56.67 sq m (610 sq ft)
Armament:	nine 12.7mm (.5in) machine guns and one 7.62mm (.303in) machine gun; up to 2700kg (6000lb) of bombs

B-25J

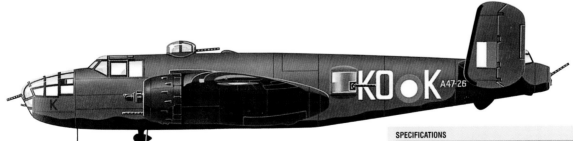

In 1944, the RAAF received some B-25s from the Netherlands East Indies Air Force based in Australia, and others directly from the United States. This glass-nose B-25J flew with No 2 Squadron alongside Mitchells of No 18 Squadron NEIAF on missions against Japanese shipping.

SPECIFICATIONS	
Country of origin:	United States
Type:	twin-engined medium bomber
Powerplant:	two 1850hp (1380kW) Wright R-2600-29 radial piston engines
Performance:	maximum speed 442km/h (275mph); service ceiling 7600m (25,000ft); range 2172km (1350 miles)
Weights:	empty 9580kg (21,120lb); maximum 19,000kg (28,460lb)
Dimensions:	span 16.13m (67ft 7in); length 16.13m (52ft 11in); height 4.8m (17ft 7in); wing area 56.67 sq m (610 sq ft)
Armament:	16 12.7mm (.5in) machine guns; up to 2700kg (6000lb) of bombs

The Luftwaffe's Last Strikes

In the last 11 months of the war, following the Normandy invasion, the Luftwaffe moved to a largely defensive footing, but was still able to mount token raids on the United Kingdom and elsewhere. Operation Steinbock, the so-called 'Baby Blitz' from January to May 1945, cost the Luftwaffe's bomber arm more than 300 aircraft and had little effect on the Allied war effort. Hitler's obsession with 'wonder weapon' jets and missiles was another of his delusions, wasting essential resources.

Junkers Ju 88S-1

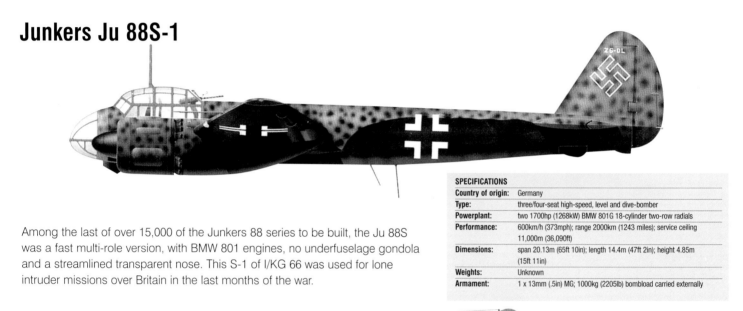

Among the last of over 15,000 of the Junkers 88 series to be built, the Ju 88S was a fast multi-role version, with BMW 801 engines, no underfuselage gondola and a streamlined transparent nose. This S-1 of I/KG 66 was used for lone intruder missions over Britain in the last months of the war.

SPECIFICATIONS	
Country of origin:	Germany
Type:	three/four-seat high-speed, level and dive-bomber
Powerplant:	two 1700hp (1268kW) BMW 801G 18-cylinder two-row radials
Performance:	600km/h (373mph); range 2000km (1243 miles); service ceiling 11,000m (36,090ft)
Dimensions:	span 20.13m (65ft 10in); length 14.4m (47ft 2in); height 4.85m (15ft 11in)
Weights:	Unknown
Armament:	1 x 13mm (.5in) MG; 1000kg (2205lb) bombload carried externally

Junkers Ju 88A-4 Mistel

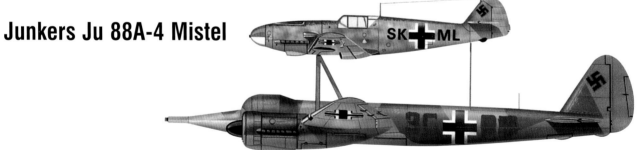

The Mistel (Mistletoe) was a composite aircraft consisting of an explosives-packed surplus bomber flown to a launch point by a fighter mounted on top. The version shown combined a Ju 88A-4 with a Bf 109F-4. Mistels were inaccurate and caused negligible damage on the few occasions they were used.

SPECIFICATIONS	
Country of origin:	Germany
Crew:	fighter/flying bomb combination
Powerplant:	one 1325hp (988kW) Daimler Benz DB-601E-1and two 999kW (1340hp) Junkers Jumo 211J-1/2 inverted V-12 piston engines
Performance:	maximum speed unknown; range unknown; service ceiling unknown
Dimensions:	span 20m (65ft 8in); length 8.43m (47ft 2in); height unknown; wing area 54.5 sq m (587 sq ft)
Weights:	unknown
Armament:	two 7.9mm MG 17 machine guns, one 20mm MG 151/20 cannon; one 7716lb (3500kg) warhead

LUFTWAFFE TIMELINE
1939  1943

Heinkel He 111H-22

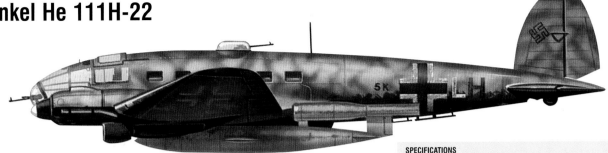

In July 1944, the Luftwaffe made the first-ever attacks with air-launched cruise missiles, mounting V-1 (Fieseler Fi.103) flying bombs beneath the He 111H-23 bomber. Up to January 1945, 1176 were launched, of which about 40 per cent failed, the remainder doing little significant damage.

SPECIFICATIONS	
Country of origin:	Germany
Type:	twin-engined missile carrier
Powerplant:	two 1750hp (1305kW) Junkers Jumo inverted-V-12 piston engines
Performance:	480km/h (298mph); range: 2800km (1740 miles); service ceiling: 8500m (27,890ft)
Dimensions:	span 22.6m (74ft 2in); length 16.4m (53ft 10in); height 4.01m (13ft 2in); wing area 86.5 sq m (932 sq ft)
Weights:	empty 8680kg (19,136lb); maximum 16,000kg (35,273lb)
Armament:	one 13mm (.51in) and four .792mm machine guns, on Fi.103 missile with an 800kg (1760lb) warhead

Arado Ar 234

The Arado Ar 234 was the world's first jet bomber. Entering service in the reconnaissance role in July 1944, the Blitz made flights over Britain and France almost undetected. As a bomber it was also quite successful, but operations were hampered by attacks on airfields and fuel supplies.

SPECIFICATIONS	
Country of origin:	Germany
Type:	single-seat reconnaissance plane and bomber
Powerplant:	two Junkers Jumo 004B turbojets, each delivering 900kg (1984lb) of thrust
Performance:	maximum speed 742km/h (461mph); range 1556km (967 miles); service ceiling 10,000m (32,810ft)
Dimensions:	span 14.41m (46ft 3in); length 12.64m (41ft 5in); height 4.29m (14ft 1in)
Armament:	2 x 20mm (.8in) MG 151 in belly pod; 2 x rearward-firing 20mm (.8in) cannon

Heinkel He 177

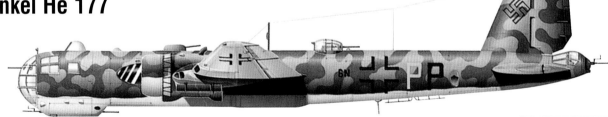

The Heinkel He 177 had a pair of coupled DB 601 engines in each nacelle, which proved tremendously difficult to prevent from catching fire. He 177s, including this A-5 from I/KG 4, were used for the 'Little Blitz' against Britain in the spring of 1944.

SPECIFICATIONS	
Country of origin:	Germany
Type:	six-seat heavy bomber
Powerplant:	two 2950hp (2200kW) DB 610 paired 12-cylinder inverted V
Performance:	maximum speed 462km/h (295mph); range 5000km (3107 miles); service ceiling 7000m (22, 965ft)
Dimensions:	span 31.44m (103ft 2in); length 22m (72ft 2in); height 6.4m (21ft)
Weights:	31,000kg (68,343lb) loaded
Armament:	1/3 x 7.92mm (.3in) MGs; 2/4 13mm (.5in) MGs; 2 x 20mm (.8in) cannon; 6000kg (13,228lb) bombload

1944

Avro Lancaster

The Lancaster was the best of the RAF's four-engined 'heavies', and the best remembered. Derived from the Manchester, which had twin engines (neither of them reliable), the Lancaster entered service early in 1942. Able to fly higher and further than the Halifax or Stirling, it became the mainstay of Bomber Command. It proved adaptable to various special weapons, including the Upkeep 'bouncing bomb', and post-war was used by the United Kingdom, Canada and France.

Avro Manchester B.I

The Avro Manchester first flew in July 1939, becoming operational in November 1940. The Manchester heavy bomber was not successful in itself, largely because of the chronic unreliability of its two under-developed Rolls-Royce Vulture engines, but it paved the way for the Lancaster with four Rolls-Royce Merlin engines.

SPECIFICATIONS

Country of origin:	United Kingdom
Type:	seven-seat medium bomber
Powerplant:	two 1760hp (1312kW) Rolls-Royce Vulture inline piston engines
Performance:	maximum speed 426km/h (265mph); range 2623km (1630 miles); service ceiling 5850m (19,200ft)
Dimensions:	span 27.46m (90ft 1in); length 21.13m (69ft 4in); height 5.94m (19ft 6in)
Weights:	25,401kg (56,000lb) loaded
Armament:	8 x 7.7mm (.3i03n) MGs (two each in nose and dorsal turrets, four in tail turret); up to 4695kg (10,350lb) of bombs

Avro Lancaster B.III

A specially adapted 'dams raid' aircraft, this machine was otherwise a standard Lancaster Mk III, of which 3020 were built to a different standard from the Lancaster Mk I, with Packard rather than Roll-Royce Merlin engines. No 617 Squadron was created for the task of smashing the Ruhr Valley dams. The mission was carried out by 19 Lancasters in May 1943, targeting five dams.

SPECIFICATIONS

Country of origin:	United Kingdom
Type:	six-seat special mission bomber
Powerplant:	four 1460hp (1089kW) Packard (Rolls-Royce) Merlin piston engines
Performance:	maximum speed 462km/h (287mph); range 2784km (1730 miles); service ceiling 5790m (19,000ft)
Dimensions:	span 31.09m (102ft); length 20.98m (68ft 10in); height 6.19m (20ft 4in)
Weights:	empty 16,783kg (37,000lb); maximum take-off weight 29,484kg (65,000lb)
Armament:	seven 7.7mm (.303in) machine guns; plus a 3900kg (8599lb) 'bouncing bomb' semi-recessed under the fuselage

AVRO LANCASTER TIMELINE

 1939  1941  1942

Avro Lancaster B.I Special

To carry the enormous Grand Slam and Tallboy bombs, Lancasters of Nos 9 and 617 (illustrated) were modified by removing bomb doors and other equipment, including guns. They were used in several precision attacks against canals, bridges and U-boat pens.

SPECIFICATIONS	
Country of origin:	United Kingdom
Type:	five-seat special mission bomber
Powerplant:	four 1640hp (1223kW) Rolls-Royce Merlin XXIV inline piston engines
Performance:	maximum speed 462km/h (287mph); range 4072km (2530 miles); service ceiling 7470m (24,500ft)
Dimensions:	span 31.09m (102ft); length 21.18m (69ft 6in); height 6.1m (20ft)
Weights:	31,751kg (70,000lb) loaded
Armament:	8 x 7.7mm (.303in) MGs; 1 x 'Grand Slam' 9979kg (22,000lb) bomb

Avro Lancaster B.VI

To perform the role of electronic countermeasures and electronic counter-countermeasures for the Pathfinder Force, a total of nine Lancaster bombers were converted from Mk I and Mk III aircraft. Re-engined and with all armaments removed except for the tail turret, Mk VI's had tremendous performance. This example served with No 635 Squadron, a dedicated Pathfinder unit.

SPECIFICATIONS	
Country of origin:	United Kingdom
Type:	five-seat special mission bomber
Powerplant:	one 1640hp (1223kW) Packard Merlin 85/87 12-cylinder Vee engines
Performance:	maximum speed 555km/h (345mph); service ceiling 6500m (21,418ft); range 2949km (1550 miles)
Weights:	empty 16,083kg (35,457lb); maximum take-off weight 32,659kg (72,000lb)
Dimensions:	span 31.09m (102ft); length 21.18m (69ft 6in); height 6.25m (20ft 6in)
Armament:	four .303in trainable machine guns in tail turret

Avro Lancaster GR.III

With H2S radar in a ventral dome and superfluous equipment removed, the Lancaster made a good long-range patrol aircraft before the purpose-built Shackleton entered service. This Lancaster GR.III served with the School of Maritime Reconnaissance at St Mawgan, Cornwall, in the 1950s.

SPECIFICATIONS	
Country of origin:	United Kingdom
Type:	long-range patrol aircraft
Powerplant:	4 x 1640hp (1223kW) Packard Merlin 224 piston engines
Performance:	maximum speed 452km/h (281mph); range 4313km (2680 miles); service ceiling 7460m (24,500ft)
Dimensions:	span 31.09m (102ft); length 20.98m (68ft 10in); height 6.19m (20ft 4in)
Weights:	18,598kg (41,000lb) loaded

1943

1944

The First Jets

Frank Whittle in Britain and Hans von Ohain in Germany independently developed working turbojet engines in the late 1930s. Germany was first in the air with the He 178 in 1939, while the Gloster E.28/39 (the Gloster Whittle) flew in May 1941. Neither was a suitable basis for a combat aircraft. The Bell XP-59, the first American jet, saw limited production, but did not enter service. Germany was again ahead with the first operational jet, the Me 262, but Britain's Meteor saw decades of service.

Heinkel He 178

Developed as a private venture in conjunction with the He 176 rocket-powered aircraft, the He 178 was powered by Heinkel's HeS 3b turbojet. The aircraft was intended only as an experimental test bed, although it made its mark at a test flight in August 1939. Officials took little interest and the project was discontinued in favour of the larger He 280. Note the fabric-covered tail and high-set wing in the example illustrated.

SPECIFICATIONS	
Country of origin:	Germany
Type:	single-engined experimental jet aircraft
Powerplant:	one 4.4kN (992lb) thrust HeS 3 turbojet engine
Performance:	maximum speed 598km/h (375mph); range 200km (125 miles); service ceiling unknown
Weights:	empty 1620kg (3572lb); maximum 1998kg (4405lb)
Dimensions:	span 7.2m (23ft 3in); length 7.48m (24ft 6in); height 2.1m (6ft 10in); wing area 9.1 sq m (98 sq ft)

Heinkel He 280V-3

When work on the He 178 was discontinued in 1939, Heinkel redirected energies into the He 280 project. The aircraft was far more advanced, designed to be powered by pairs of HeS 8 and HeS 30. However, with limited thrust when launched, performance was hardly sparking. Although this was increased a little, the He 280 ultimately lost out to the Messerschmitt Me 262.

SPECIFICATIONS	
Country of origin:	Germany
Type:	two-seat elementary trainer biplane
Powerplant:	two 5.9kN (1323lb) Heinkel HeS 8A turbojets
Performance:	maximum speed 800km/h (497mph)
Weights:	loaded 4340kg (9550lb)
Dimensions:	span 12m (39ft 4in); length 10.4m (34ft 1in)

THE FIRST JETS TIMELINE
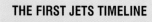 1939  1940 1942

Messerschmitt Me 262V3

The prototype of the Me 262 first flew with a piston engine and a tailwheel undercarriage in April 1941, but it was nearly a year before testing under jet power began using the third prototype seen here. The fifth prototype had a nosewheel undercarriage, as would be used on production models.

SPECIFICATIONS	
Country of origin:	Germany
Type:	twin-engined experimental jet aircraft
Powerplant:	two 5.40kN (1200lb) thrust BMW 003 turbo engines and one 515kW (690hp) Junkers Jumo 210G piston engine
Performance:	maximum speed unknown; service ceiling unknown; range unknown
Weights:	unknown
Dimensions:	12.6m (41ft 6in); length 10.6m (34ft 9in); height 3.5m (11ft 6in); wing area 21.7 sq m (234 sq ft)

Bell YP-59A Airacomet

Development work on jet aircraft began rather later in America than in Europe, and with considerable British assistance. In September 1941, Bell Aircraft was requested to design a jet fighter and, in October, a Whittle turbojet. Barely a year later, the Bell P-59A Airacomet was ready to fly.

SPECIFICATIONS	
Country of origin:	United States
Type:	single-seat jet fighter trainer
Powerplant:	two 8.9kN (2000lb) General Electric J31-GE-3 turbojets
Performance:	maximum speed 671km/h (413mph); service ceiling 14,080m (46,200ft); range 837km (520 miles)
Weights:	empty 3610kg (7950lb); maximum take-off weight 6214kg (13,700lb)
Dimensions:	span 13.87m (45ft 6in); length 11.63m (38ft 11.5in); height 3.66m (12ft); wing area 35.84 sq m (385.8 sq ft)

Gloster Meteor

Gloster's Meteor, at first known by its specification number F9/40, was delayed by problems with its intended Whittle W.2 engines. The fifth prototype (illustrated), flew in March 1943 with de Havilland (Hallford) engines. Apart from armament, it was close to the production Meteor F.I version.

SPECIFICATIONS	
Country of origin:	United Kingdom
Type:	twin-engined jet fighter prototype
Powerplant:	two 10.2kN (2300lb) thrust de Havilland Halford H.1 turbojet engines
Performance:	maximum speed unknown; range unknown; service ceiling unknown
Weights:	empty 3692kg (8140lb); maximum unknown
Dimensions:	span 13.11m (43ft); length 12.57m (41ft 3in); height 3.96m (13ft); wing area 34.74 sq m (374 sq ft)

1943

Yakovlev Fighters

Fighters of the Yakovlev Design Bureau, known universally as Yaks, were the most recognized and most numerous Soviet wartime fighters. From the roughly built, plywood and steel tube Yak-1 to the much heavier metal-clad Yak-9U, the series had its ups and downs. The Yak-1 spawned two distinct development paths – the Yak-3 lightweight dogfighter and the Yak-7 and -9 heavy fighters, including two-seat trainers, fighter-bombers, long-range fighters and tankbusters.

Yak-1

With 8720 built, the Yak-1 was the most numerous of the family. This aircraft was flown by Lilya Litvak, the most successful of the USSR's female fighter pilots, who scored 12 victories before her death in action in August 1943, aged just 22.

SPECIFICATIONS	
Country of origin:	USSR
Type:	single-seat fighter and fighter-bomber
Powerplant:	one 1100hp (820kW) Klimov M-105P 12-cylinder Vee engine
Performance:	maximum speed 600km/h (373mph); service ceiling 10,000m (32,810ft); range 700km (435 miles)
Weights:	empty 2347kg (5174lb); maximum take-off weight 2847kg (6276lb)
Dimensions:	span 10m (32ft 9.7in); length 8.48m (27ft 9.9in); height 2.64m (8ft 8in)

Yak-1M

The Yak-1M had a cut-down rear fuselage to aid visibility and a lighter structure, making it the lightest Allied monoplane fighter of the war. The inscription on this 31st Guards IAP Yak-1M is a dedication from the Stakhanov collective farm to the pilot, Major Yevemen.

SPECIFICATIONS	
Country of origin:	USSR
Type:	single-seat fighter and fighter-bomber
Powerplant:	one 1180hp (880kW) Klimov M-105PF V-12 liquid-cooled engine
Performance:	maximum speed 592km/h (368mph); service ceiling 10,050m (33,000ft); range 700km (435 miles)
Weights:	2883kg (6343lb) loaded
Dimensions:	span 10m (32ft 10in); length 8.5m (27ft 11in)
Armament:	one 20mm (.8in) ShVAK cannon, one 12.7mm (.5in) Berezin UBS machine gun

YAKS TIMELINE

1940

1942

Yak-3

Entering service in June 1944, the Yak-3 was the fastest of the series, and a formidable dogfighter at low level. This example was flown by ace Sergey Lugansky, who scored 37 victories, including two in Taran or ramming attacks. This aircraft was gifted by the city of Alma-Ata.

SPECIFICATIONS	
Country of origin:	USSR
Type:	single-seat fighter
Powerplant:	one 1290hp (962kW) Klimov VK-105PF V12 liquid-cooled piston engine
Performance:	maximum speed 646km/h (401mph); service ceiling 10,700m (35,000ft); range 650km (405 miles)
Weight:	loaded 2692kg (5864lb)
Dimensions:	span 9.2m (30ft 2in); length 8.5m (27ft 11in); height 2.39m (7ft 11in)
Armament:	one 20mm (.8in) ShVAK cannon, two 12.7mm (.5in) Berezin UBS machine gun

Yak-9

In 1941, the Free French Government offered Russia a squadron of pilots for service on the Eastern Front, which was later expanded to four squadrons and known as the Normandie-Niemen Régiment. This Yak-9 was the mount of eight-victory ace René Challe.

SPECIFICATIONS	
Country of origin:	USSR
Type:	single-seat fighter
Powerplant:	one 1180hp (880KW) Klimov V-12 liquid-cooled piston engine
Performance:	maximum speed 591km/h (367mph); service ceiling 9100m (30,000ft); range 884km (549 miles)
Weights:	maximum take-off weight 3117kg (6858lb)
Dimensions:	span 9.74m (31ft 11in); length 8.55m (28ft); height 3m (9ft 10in)
Armament:	one 20mm (.8in) ShVAK cannon, one 12.7mm (.5in) Berezin UBS machine gun

Yak-9D

Some versions of the Yak-9 could carry four light bombs in a bay behind the cockpit. The Yak-9D (illustrated) was designed for long range, with additional fuel capacity. The Yak-9DD was a version with even greater fuel capacity and radio-navigation equipment for long-range bomber escort missions.

SPECIFICATIONS	
Country of origin:	USSR
Type:	single-seat fighter
Powerplant:	one 1180hp (880kW) Klimov M-105 PF V-12 liquid-cooled piston engine
Performance:	maximum speed 591km/h (367mph); service ceiling 9100m (30,000ft); range 1360km (845 miles)
Weights:	loaded 3117kg (6858lb)
Dimensions:	span 9.74m (31ft 11in); length 8.55m (28ft); height 3m (9ft 10in)
Armament:	one 20mm (.8in) ShVAK cannon, one 12.7mm (.5in) Berezin UBS machine gun

Defence of the Reich

In the last year of the war, the Luftwaffe put three types of jet and two rocket-powered aircraft into service, and test flew several others. Built largely by slave labourers using poor-quality materials and without adequate testing, many of these last-ditch designs were more dangerous to their pilots than to the enemy. Only the Me 262 Schwalbe (Swallow) and Me 163 Komet scored a significant number of victories, while German blueprints greatly influenced post-war US and Soviet aircraft.

Me 163B-1A Komet

The Me 163 was perhaps the most radical and futuristic of World War II aircraft. The concept of the short-endurance, high-speed interceptor powered by a rocket engine was certainly valid. Bereft of a horizontal tail and with an extremely short fuselage, the Me 163 was propelled by two extremely volatile liquids. By May 1944, these tiny aircraft were devastating US bomber formations.

SPECIFICATIONS

Country of origin:	Germany
Type:	single-seat interceptor
Powerplant:	one 16.7kN (3750lb) Walter HWK 509A-2 bi-propellant rocket burning concentrated hydrogen peroxide and hydrazine/methanol
Performance:	maximum speed 960km/h (596mph); service ceiling 16,500m (54,000ft); range 100km (62 miles)
Weights:	empty 1905kg (4191lb); maximum take-off weight 4110kg (9042lb)
Dimensions:	span 9.3m (30ft 7in); length 5.69m (18ft 8in); height 2.74m (9ft)
Armament:	two 300mm MK 108 cannon with 60 rounds each

Horton Ho IX V2

As early as the 1920s, Reimar and Walter Horten were extolling the merits of tailless aircraft. The Horton Ho IX V2 bears more than a passing resemblance to the Northrop B2 Spirit. Only two prototypes were built and the second of these was lost after an engine flameout. Production had been planned on a large scale, but US forces captured the workshops.

SPECIFICATIONS

Country of origin:	Germany
Type:	single-seat experimental flying wing jet fighter
Powerplant:	two 8.8kN (1984lb) BMW 003 turbojets
Performance:	maximum speed about 800km/h (500mph)
Weights:	about 9080kg (20,000lb)
Dimensions:	span 16m (52ft 6in)
Armament:	(proposed) four 30mm MK 108 cannon for day fighter; provision for up to 908kg (2000lb) of bombs as fighter-bomber

DEFENCE OF THE REICH TIMELINE
1943   1944

Me 262B-1a/U1

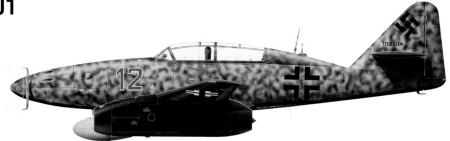

The 262B-1a/U1 was a modified B-1a conversion trainer, fitted with FuG 218 Neptun V radar with a Hirschgeweih (Antler) antenna and FuG 350 ZC Naxos, for homing in to emissions from British H2S radar equipment. The first unit to receive the aircraft was Kommando Welter, a specialized unit staffed by experienced Wilde Sau (night-fighting) personnel.

SPECIFICATIONS	
Country of origin:	United Kingdom
Type:	two-seat night fighter
Powerplant:	two 8.8kN (1984lb) Junkers Jumo 004B-1, -2, or -3 turbojets
Performance:	maximum speed 869km/h (540mph); service ceiling 12,190m (40,000ft); range 1050km (652 miles)
Weights:	empty 3795kg (8378lb); maximum take-off weight 6387kg (14,080lb)
Dimensions:	span 12.5m (40ft 11.5in); length 10.58m (34ft 9.5in); height 3.83m (12ftt 7in); wing area 21.73 sq m (234 sq ft)
Armament:	two 30mm Rheinmetall-Borsig Mk 108A-3 cannon with 100 rounds for upper pair and 80 rounds for lower

Heinkel He 162

Popularly known as the Volksjäger (People's Fighter), the He 162 was designed and produced by the war-torn German aviation industry in only six months. On 8 September 1944, the Reichsluftfahrtsministerium issued a specification for a 750km/h (466mph) fighter, and Heinkel won the competition with a tiny wooden machine with an engine perched on top. Deliveries began in January 1945.

SPECIFICATIONS	
Country of origin:	Germany
Type:	single-seat jet interceptor
Powerplant:	one 7.8kN (1764lb) BMW 003A-1 turbojet
Performance:	maximum speed 840km/h (522mph); service ceiling 12,040m (39,500ft); endurance 57 minutes at 10,970m (35,990ft)
Weights:	empty 2050kg (4250lb); maximum take-off weight 2695kg (5941lb)
Dimensions:	span 7.2m (23ft 7.5in); length 9.05m (29ft 8.25in); height 2.55m (8ft 4.25in); wing area 11.20 sq m (120,56 sq ft)

Dornier Do 335V-1

Dornier's unique Pfeil (Arrow) was the fastest piston-engined fighter to enter wartime service, although fewer than 40 were ever built. In an emergency, the Do 335's rear pusher propeller and tail fin would be blown off and the pilot could escape using an ejection seat.

SPECIFICATIONS	
Country of origin:	Germany
Type:	twin-engined fighter-bomber
Powerplant:	two 1287kW (1726hp) Daimler-Benz DB 603A inverted V-12 piston engines
Performance:	maximum speed 765km/h (474mph); service ceiling 11,400m (37,400ft); range 1380km (858 miles)
Weights:	empty 5210kg (11,484lb); maximum 8590kg (19,500lb)
Dimensions:	span 13.8m (45ft 1in); length 13.85m (45ft 5in); height 4.55m (15ft); wing area 55 sq m (592 sq ft)
Armament:	one 30mm MK 103 and two 20mm MG 151 cannon; up to 1000kg (2200lb) bombs

Vought F4U Corsair

Designed with an inverted gull wing to keep span and main landing gear lengths as short as possible, the F4U Corsair was planned as a carrierborne fighter, but matured as a superlative ground-attack and close-support fighter that saw service mainly in the Pacific theatre. First flying in 1940, it entered operational service in February 1943 in the land-based role, as the type's carrier-borne capabilities were initially thought suspect. It remained in production until after World War II.

F4U-2 Corsair

The F4U-2 was a night-fighter variant with an APS-4 airborne intercept radar mounted in a pod on the starboard wing, and an armament of only four machine guns. Only 12 were converted and they served in three squadrons, one scoring the first kill by a radar-equipped single-seat fighter.

SPECIFICATIONS	
Country of origin:	United States
Type:	single-engined night fighter
Powerplant:	one 2250hp (1678kW) Pratt & Whitney R-2800-8W radial engine
Performance:	maximum speed 684km/h (425 mph); service ceiling 11,200m (36,900ft); range 1634km (1015 miles)
Weights:	empty 4073kg (8982lb); maximum take-off weight 6300kg (14,000lb)
Dimensions:	span 12.5m (41ft); length 10.1m (33ft 4in); height 4.9m (16ft 1in); wing area 29.17 sq m (314 sq ft)
Armament:	four .5in (12.7mm) Browning machine guns

F4U-1D Corsair

Wearing the late-war geometric markings that identified aircraft of the USS *Essex* air group, this F4U-1D was used for ground-attack missions against Japanese-held islands in 1945. Late-model F4U-1Ds were able to carry a battery of 127mm (5in) high-velocity aerial rockets.

SPECIFICATIONS	
Country of origin:	United States
Type:	single-seat carrierborne and land-based fighter and fighter-bomber
Powerplant:	one 2250hp (1678kW) Pratt & Whitney 18-cylinder two-row radial engine
Performance:	maximum speed 718km/h (446mph); service ceiling 12,650m (41,500ft); range 2511km (1560 miles)
Weights:	empty 4175kg (9205lb); maximum take-off weight 6149kg (13,555lb) as a fighter, or 8845kg (19,500lb) as a fighter-bomber
Dimensions:	span 12.49m (40ft 11.75in); length 10.27m (33ft 8.25in); height 4.5m (14ft 9in)
Armament:	six 12.7mm (.5in) machine guns, eight 127mm (5in) HVAR rockets

F4U-1D Corsair

The first Corsairs built by Goodyear were designated FG-1, and in Fleet Air Arm service became the Corsair Mk IV, of which 977 were delivered. This example of No 1850 Squadron, on HMS *Vengeance* in the Pacific, wears a non-standard type of national insignia.

SPECIFICATIONS	
Country of origin:	United States
Type:	single-engined carrier-based fighter
Powerplant:	one 2250hp 1678kW() Pratt & Whitney R-2800-8W radial engine
Performance:	maximum speed 684km/h (425 mph); service ceiling 11,200m (36,900ft); range 1634km (1015 miles)
Weights:	empty 4073kg (8982lb); maximum take-off weight 6300kg (14,000lb)
Dimensions:	span 12.5m (41ft); length 10.1m (33ft 4in); height 4.9m (16ft 1in); wing area 29.17 sq m (314 sq ft)
Armament:	six 12.7mm (.5in) M2 Browning machine guns, plus bomb load of 910kg (2000lb)

F4U-4C Corsair

The C suffix to the model designation indicated a cannon-armed version. The F4U-4C mounted four 20mm cannon instead of six machine guns. The orange band marks this Corsair as belonging to a post-war reserve unit, in this case operating from NAS Glenview, Illinois.

SPECIFICATIONS	
Country of origin:	United States
Type:	single-engined carrier-based fighter
Powerplant:	one 1677kW (2250hp) Pratt & Whitney R-2800-18W radial piston engine
Performance:	maximum speed 167km/h (104mph); service ceiling 11,308m (41,500ft); range 2425 km (1507 miles)
Weights:	empty 4175kg (8873lb); maximum 6654kg (13,846lb)
Dimensions:	span 10.16m (41ft); length 10.27m (33ft 8in); height 4.5m (14ft 9in); wing area 29.17 sq m (314 sq ft)
Armament:	four 20mm M3 cannon

F4U-7 Corsair

Corsair development continued post-war with the F4U-5 and AU-1 ground-attack variant. France's Aéronavale commissioned a version of the latter with additional armour that entered service as the F4U-7 in 1952 and was used in Indochina and Algeria.

SPECIFICATIONS	
Country of origin:	United States
Type:	single-engined carrier-based fighter-bomber
Powerplant:	one 2300hp (1715kW) Pratt & Whitney R-2800-43W radial piston engine
Performance:	maximum speed 708km/h (440mph); service ceiling 11,308m (41,500ft); range 1802km (1120 miles)
Weights:	empty 4461kg (9835lb); maximum 8798kg (19,398lb)
Dimensions:	span 12.5m (41ft); length 10.1m (33ft 4in); height 4.5m (14ft 9in); wing area 29.17 sq m (314 sq ft)
Armament:	four 20mm M3 cannon; up to 2268kg (5000lb) bombs or rockets

Japanese Bombers

As with its early-war fighter aircraft, Japan's navy emphasized range over self-protection for most of its bombers. The Allies were frequently surprised by the appearance of Japanese aircraft at extreme distances from known bases, but soon learned of their vulnerabilities, such as the lack of self-sealing fuel tanks and often puny defensive armament. The IJN also made use of flying boats as long-range bombers.

Nakajima B6N2 Tenzan 'Jill'

The first B6N Tenzan (Heavenly Mountain) prototypes flew in spring 1941, but production aircraft entered service only in late 1943. The powerplant was changed to a Mitsubishi for the B6N2, of which 1133 were built, but they lacked capable aircrews.

SPECIFICATIONS	
Country of origin:	Japan
Type:	three-seat carrierborne and land-based torpedo bomber
Powerplant:	one 1850hp (1379kW) Mitsubishi MK4T Kasei 25 14-cylinder two-row radial engine
Performance:	maximum speed 481km/h (299mph); range 3045km (1892 miles); service ceiling 9040m (29,660ft);
Weights:	empty 3010kg (6636lb); maximum take-off weight 5650kg (12,456lb)
Dimensions:	span 14.89m (48ft 10.6in); length 10.87m (35ft 7.8in); height 3.8m (12ft 5.6in)

Mitsubishi G4M1 'Betty'

The G4M was the ultimate expression of the Imperial Japanese Navy Air Force's desire to project land-based air power from its island garrisons deep into the Pacific Ocean. However, this range came at the expense of crew protection. Entering service in 1941, production totalled 1200 G4M1 variants, such as Convoy Fighter escort, Model 11 attack bomber, trainers and transport aircraft.

SPECIFICATIONS	
Country of origin:	Japan
Type:	seven-seat medium attack bomber
Powerplant:	two 1530hp (1141kW) Mitsubishi 14-cylinder two-row radial engine
Performance:	maximum speed 428km/h (266mph); range 6033km (3749 miles); service ceiling 8500m (27,890ft)
Weights:	empty 6800kg (14,991lb); maximum take-off weight 9500kg (20,944lb)
Dimensions:	span 25m (83ft 0.25in); length 20m (65ft 7.25in); height 6m (19ft 8.25in)
Armament:	one 20mm cannon in tail; three 7.7mm MGs in dorsal position and each beam position, external bomb and torpedo load of 800kg (1764lb)

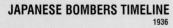 **JAPANESE BOMBERS TIMELINE**  1936  1939

Nakajima Ki-49 Donryu 'Helen'

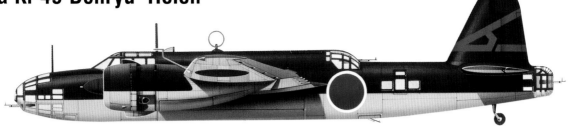

The Donryu (Storm Dragon) was planned from 1938 as a replacement for the Mitsubishi Ki-21, but it proved so indifferent that it supplemented rather than replaced the older type. The inability of the Ki-49 to fulfil its intended role as a heavy bomber meant that it was relegated to secondary roles in the later stages of the war.

SPECIFICATIONS	
Country of origin:	Japan
Type:	eight-seat 'heavy' (actually medium) bomber
Powerplant:	two 1500hp (1118kW) Nakajima 14-cylinder two-row radial engines
Performance:	maximum speed 492km/h (306mph); range 2950km (1833 miles); service ceiling 9300m (30,510ft)
Weights:	empty 6530kg (14,3965lb); maximum take-off weight 11,400kg (25,133lb)
Dimensions:	span 20.42m (67ft); length 16.5m (54ft 1.6in); height 4.25m (13ft 1.2in)
Armament:	one 20mm cannon in dorsal turret, one 12.7mm MG in nose, one 12.7mm MG in tail , one 12.7mm MG in ventral position, one 7.7mm MG in each beam position; bombload of 1000kg (2205lb)

Kawanishi H6K 'Mavis'

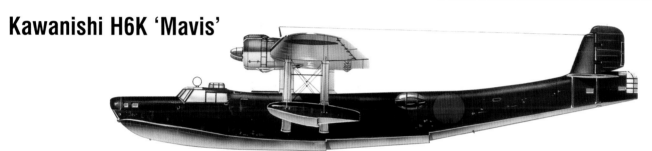

The H6K flying boat resulted from a 1933 requirement and was one of the best warplanes of the Imperial Japanese Navy at the start of World War II's Pacific campaign. The type remained in useful service throughout the war, as it was supplemented – although never really replaced – by the superb Kawanishi H8K 'Emily'. The first of four prototypes flew in July 1936.

SPECIFICATIONS	
Country of origin:	Japan
Type:	(H6K5) nine-seat maritime reconnaissance flying boat
Powerplant:	four 1300hp (969kW) Mitsubishi Kinsei 14-cylinder radial engines
Performance:	maximum speed 385km/h (239mph); service ceiling 9560m (31,365ft); range 6772 km (4208 miles)
Weights:	empty 12,380kg (27,117lb); maximum take-off 23,000kg (50,706lb)
Dimensions:	span 40m (131ft 2.75in); length 25.63m (84ft 0.75in); height 6.27m (20ft 6.75in)
Armament:	one 20mm trainable rearward-firing cannon in tail turret, one 7.7mm MG in bow turret, one 7.7mm rearward-firing MG in dorsal position, and two 7.7mm trainable lateral-firing MG in blister positions, plus a torpedo and bomb load of 3527lb (1600kg)

Kawanishi H8K1 'Emily'

Kawanishi's 'Emily' flying boat was an excellent large flying boat with particularly heavy armament and good armour and fire-fighting protection. Only 167 were produced, but they saw service until the end of the war, by which time only four were airworthy.

SPECIFICATIONS	
Country of origin:	Japan
Type:	four-engined flying boat
Powerplant:	four 1850hp (1380kW) Mitsubishi Kasei 22 radial piston engines
Performance:	maximum speed 465km/h (290mph); service ceiling 8760m (28,740ft); range 4440 miles (7150km)
Weights:	empty 18,380kg (40,436lb); maximum 32,500kg (71,500lb)
Dimensions:	span 38m (124ft 8in); length 28.15m (92ft 4in); height 9.15m (30ft); wing area 160 sq m (1721 sq ft)
Armament:	five 20mm Type 99 cannon, five 7.7mm Type 97 machine-guns; two 800kg (1760lb) torpedoes or 1000kg (2200lb) of bombs

1941

Japan's Homeland Defence

The capture of Japan's island bases and its oil refineries saw the ability of the IJAAF to protect the home islands shrink in 1944–45. Industry produced some outstanding late-war aircraft, but shortages of fuel and spare parts and, particularly, of trained pilots were to make them little more than an inconvenience to the B-29 raids that began devastating Japan's cities in July 1944. The situation called for desperate measures, including some jet and rocket aircraft, as well as kamikaze units.

Nakajima Ki-84-1a 'Frank'

Designed as the successor to the Ki-43, the Hayate (Gale) was one of the best fighters available to the Imperial Japanese Army Air Force in the closing stages of World War II. Entering service in the first half of 1944, the Ki-84 was built to the extent of 3512 aircraft in two primary variants, namely the Ki-84-I and the Ki-84-II derivative with wooden rear fuselage and fittings.

SPECIFICATIONS	
Country of origin:	Japan
Type:	(Ki-84-Ia) single-seat fighter and fighter-bomber
Powerplant:	one 1900hp (1417kW) Nakajima Ha-45 (Army Type 4) Model 23 18-cylinder two-row radial engine
Performance:	maximum speed 631km/h (392mph); service ceiling 10,500m (34,450ft); range 2168km (1347 miles)
Weights:	empty 2660kg (5864lb); maximum take-off 4170kg (9193lb)
Dimensions:	span 11.24m (36ft 10.5in); length 9.92m (32ft 6.5in); height 3.39m (11ft 1.25in)
Armament:	two 20mm cannon in the leading edges of the wing, two 12.7mm MGs in the forward fuselage, external bomb load of 500kg (1102lb)

Nakajima Ki-44 Shoki 'Tojo'

Entering service in 1942, the Shoki (Demon) was designed as a small and highly loaded fighter specifically for the interception role. The type was the only interceptor to serve with the Imperial Japanese Army Air Force, and after the start of strategic attacks on the Japanese home islands by American bombers, the Shoki proved its worth as the fastest-climbing Japanese fighter.

SPECIFICATIONS	
Country of origin:	Japan
Type:	(Ki-44-II) single-seat fighter
Powerplant:	one 1520hp (1133kW) Nakajima Ha-109 (Army Type 2) 14-cylinder
Performance:	maximum speed 605km/h (376mph); service ceiling 11,200m (36,745ft); range 1700km (1056 miles)
Weights:	empty 2106kg (4643lb); maximum take-off weight 2993kg (6598lb)
Dimensions:	span 9.45m (31ft); length 8.79m (28ft 9.9in); height 3.25m (10ft 8in)
Armament:	two 12.7mm MGs in the upper part of the forward fuselage, and two 12.7mm fixed forward-firing MGs in the leading edges of the wing, plus a bomb load of 200kg (441lb)

HOMELAND DEFENCE TIMELINE 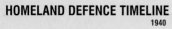 1940 1941 1942

Mitsubishi J2M Raiden

First flown in March 1942, the Raiden (Thunderbolt) was designed as the land-based successor to the A6M Reisen. It failed to live up to its initial promise, was very slow in development, and finally entered service with performance little better than that of its legendary predecessor, despite the use of a more potent engine. However, it had an excellent stability, handling and field performance.

SPECIFICATIONS	
Country of origin:	Japan
Type:	(J2M3) single-seat interceptor fighter
Powerplant:	one 1870hp (1394kW) Mitsubishi MK4R-A Kasei 23a 14-cylinder two-row radial engine
Performance:	maximum speed 587km/h (365mph); service ceiling 11,700m (38,385ft); range 1899km (1180 miles)
Weights:	empty 2460kg (5423lb); normal take-off 3435kg (7573lb); maximum take-off weight 3945kg (8697lb)
Dimensions:	span 10.8m (35ft 5.25in); length 9.95m (31ft 9.75in); height 3.95m (12ft 11.25in)
Armament:	four 20mm fixed forward-firing cannon in the leading edges of the wing, plus an external bomb load of 120kg (265lb)

Mitsubishi Ki-46-III Kai 'Dinah'

One of the finest machines of its type to see service in World War II – and one of the most elegant aircraft of all time – the Ki-46 was designed specifically as a high-altitude reconnaissance aeroplane to meet a 1937 requirement, and the prototype made its maiden flight in November 1939. With a strong powerplant, it was initially virtually impossible to intercept.

SPECIFICATIONS	
Country of origin:	Japan
Type:	(Ki-46-II) two-seat high-altitude reconnaissance aeroplane
Powerplant:	two 1055hp (787kW) Mitsubishi 14-cylinder two-row radial engines
Performance:	maximum speed 604km/h (375mph); service ceiling 10,720m (35,170ft); range 2474km (1537 miles)
Weights:	empty 3263kg (7194lb); maximum take-off weight 5800kg (12,787lb)
Dimensions:	span 14.7m (48ft 2.75in); length 11.m (36ft 1in); height 3.88m (12ft 8.75in)
Armament:	one 7.7mm trainable rearward-firing machine gun in the rear cockpit

Kawasaki Ki-45 KAI-c Toryu 'Nick'

Designed to a 1937 requirement, the Toryu (Dragon Killer) was a twin-engined heavy fighter that became one of the Imperial Japanese Army Air Force's most important warplanes. The type entered service in autumn 1942 with fighter, ground-attack/anti-shipping fighter and night-fighter models. Production of the Ki-45 KAI-c reached 477 aircraft, while the variants a, b and d totalled 1198.

SPECIFICATIONS	
Country of origin:	Japan
Type:	(Ki-45 Kai-c) two-seat night-fighter
Powerplant:	two 1080hp (805kW) Mitsubishi Ha-102 14-two-row radial engines
Performance:	maximum speed 540km/h (336mph); service ceiling 10,000m (32,810ft); range 2000km (1243 miles)
Weights:	empty 4000kg (8818lb); maximum take-off weight 5500kg (12,125lb)
Dimensions:	span 15.02m (49ft 3.25in); length 11m (36ft 1in); height 3.7m (12ft 1.75in)
Armament:	one 37mm cannon in forward fuselage, two 20mm cannon in central fuselage, one 7.92mm MG in rear cockpit, 500kg (1102lb) bomb load

1943

'Tony' and Ki-100

The only frontline Japanese combat aircraft to deviate from the radial engine for motive power, the Kawasaki Ki-61 Hien (Swallow) was dubbed the 'Tony' by the Allies. It was frequently mistaken for the Messerschmitt Me 109, although all it had in common was the (Kawasaki-built) DB 601 engine. Its service was hindered by poor engine reliability and availability. Later conversion of some to power by Mitsubishi HA-112 radials created one of the war's finest interceptors, the Ki-100, in early 1945.

Kawasaki Ki-61 Hien 'Tony'

Okinawa was the last opposed American landing of the Pacific War, and over 1500 Japanese aircraft were expended in suicide attacks. This Ki-61-I-KAIc, of the 23rd Independent Chutai, was captured at Yontan Airfield on Okinawa, which fell on 1 April 1945.

SPECIFICATIONS	
Country of origin:	Japan
Type:	Ki-61-I-KAIc single-seat fighter
Powerplant:	one 1175hp (876kW) Kawasaki Ha-40 (Army Type 2) 12-cylinder inverted-Vee engine
Performance:	maximum speed 592km/h (368mph); service ceiling 11,600m (37,730ft); range 1100km (684 miles)
Weights:	empty 2210kg (4872lb); maximum take-off weight 3250kg (7165lb)
Dimensions:	Span 12m (39ft 4.25in); length 8.75m (28ft 8.5in); height 3.7m (12ft 1.75in)
Armament:	two 20mm cannon and two 12.7mm (.5in) machine guns; up to 500kg (1102 lb) of bombs

Kawasaki Ki-61 Hien 'Tony'

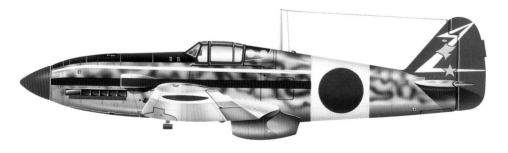

This Ki-61-I-KAIc wears the colours of the 3rd Chutai (squadron), 59th Sentai (group), at Ashiya, Japan, in August 1945. The Hien proved very maintenance-intensive and many were grounded for lack of parts. This one wears a rudder from another unit's aircraft.

SPECIFICATIONS	
Country of origin:	Japan
Type:	single-seat fighter
Powerplant:	one 1175hp (876kW) Kawasaki Ha-40 12-cylinder inverted-Vee engine
Performance:	maximum speed 592km/h (368mph); service ceiling 11,600m (37,730ft); range 1100km (684 miles)
Weights:	empty 2210kg (4872lb); maximum take-off weight 3250kg (7165lb)
Dimensions:	Span 12m (39ft 4.25in); length 8.75m (28ft 8.5in); height 3.7m (12ft 1.75in)
Armament:	two 12.7mm fixed forward-firing machine guns in the forward fuselage and two 12.7mm fixed forward-firing machine guns in the wing

Kawasaki Ki-61 Hien 'Tony'

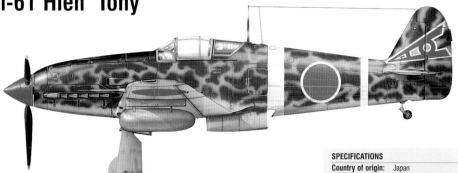

The second production variant was the Ki-61-1b or -1 Otsu. Armament was increased and the unreliable tailwheel mechanism locked down. This aircraft was flown by Shogo Tekuichi, commander of the 2nd Chutai, 68th Sentai, at Wewak Airfield, New Guinea, in late 1943.

SPECIFICATIONS	
Country of origin:	Japan
Type:	single-seat fighter
Powerplant:	one 1175hp (876kW) Kawasaki Ha-40 12-cylinder inverted-Vee engine
Performance:	maximum speed 592km/h (368mph); service ceiling 11,600m (37,730ft); range 1100km (684 miles)
Weights:	empty 2210kg (4872lb); maximum take-off weight 3250kg (7165lb)
Dimensions:	Span 12m (39ft 4.25in); length 8.75m (28ft 8.5in); height 3.7m (12ft 1.75in)
Armament:	two 12.7mm fixed forward-firing machine guns in the forward fuselage and two 12.7mm fixed forward-firing machine guns in the wing

Kawasaki Ki-100-1 Otsu

Problems with the Ki-61-II forced Kawasaki to store a number of airframes for lack of the appropriate engines and, in an inspired piece of improvisation, combined the Ki-61-II Kai airframe with the Mitsubishi Ha-112-II radial engine. From March 1945, there were two subvariants, including the Ki-100-Ib (Ki-100-1 Otsu) with an all-round vision canopy.

SPECIFICATIONS	
Country of origin:	Japan
Type:	single-seat fighter and fighter-bomber
Powerplant:	one 1500hp (1118kW) Mitsubishi Ha-112-II 14-cylinder two-row radial engine
Performance:	maximum speed 580km/h (360mph); service ceiling 11,000m (36,090ft); range 2000km (1367 miles)
Weights:	empty 2525kg (5567lb); maximum take-off weight 3495kg (7705lb)
Dimensions:	span 12m (39ft 4.5in); length 8.82m (28ft 11.25in); height 3.75m (12ft 3.63in)
Armament:	two 20mm forward-firing cannon in forward fuselage, two 12.7mm forward-firing MGs in wing, external bomb load of 500kg (1102lb)

Kawasaki Ki-100-1a

Entering service in March 1945, the Ki-100 was soon established as the Imperial Japanese Army Air Force's best fighter. Although the Mitsubishi engine was larger than the Kawasaki HA-140 it replaced, a remarkably neat installation was devised to combine the radial engine with the Ki-100's narrow fuselage.

SPECIFICATIONS	
Country of origin:	Japan
Type:	single-seat fighter and fighter-bomber
Powerplant:	one 1500hp (1118kW) Mitsubishi Ha-112-II two-row radial engine
Performance:	maximum speed 580km/h (360mph); service ceiling 11,000m (36,090ft); range 2000km (1367 miles)
Weights:	empty 2525kg (5567lb); maximum take-off weight 3495kg (7705lb)
Dimensions:	span 12m (39ft 4.5in); length 8.82m (28ft 11.25in); height 3.75m (12ft 3.63in)
Armament:	two 20mm forward-firing cannon in forward fuselage, two 12.7mm forward-firing MGs in wing, external bomb load of 500kg (1102lb)

The Last Bombs

The immense effort to develop and field the complex, pressurized B-29 Superfortress on conventional missions over Japan matched that to develop the atomic weapons that they would eventually use in the war's last act. Only a titanic industrial effort got the Superfortress operational for the final offensive against Japan. Conventional bombs, dropped mainly by B-29s, as well as B-24s and B-32s, did more damage than the two atomic bombs dropped in August 1945 on Japan.

Curtiss SB2C-3 Helldiver

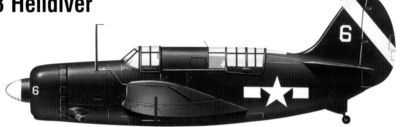

The SB2C replaced the Dauntless as the main carrier-based US Navy bomber during 1943. Despite its many faults, it was built in large numbers and made many strikes on ports and other targets on mainland Japan. This SB2C-3 was with VB-20 on the USS *Hancock* in early 1945.

SPECIFICATIONS	
Country of origin:	United States
Type:	(SB2C-1C) two-seat carrierborne and land-based scout and dive-bomber
Powerplant:	one 1268kW (1700hp) Wright R-2600-8 Cyclone 14-cylinder two-row radial engine
Performance:	maximum speed 452km/h (281mph); ceiling 7375m (24,200ft); range 2213 km (1375miles)
Weights:	empty 4588kg (10,114lb); maximum take-off 7626kg (16,812lb)
Dimensions:	span 15.15m (49ft 8.26in); length 11.18m (36ft 8in); height 4m (13ft 1.5in)
Armament:	two 20mm cannon in the wing, two .3in MGs in the rear of the cockpit, plus torpedo, bomb and depth charge load of 1361kg (3000lb)

Consolidated B-24J Liberator

The capture of islands in the Marianas and Ryuku island chains allowed USAF bombers to strike at the Japanese home islands, including the B-24Js of the 43rd Bomb Group, who flew from Ie Shima in the spring of 1945. 'The Dragon and his Tail' was a particularly colourful 43 BG Liberator.

SPECIFICATIONS	
Country of origin:	United States
Type:	(B-24J) eight/12-seat long-range heavy bomber
Powerplant:	four 1200hp (895kW) Pratt & Whitney R-1830-65 14-cylinder two-row radial
Performance:	maximum speed 483km/h (300mph); service ceiling 8535m (28,000ft); range 3380km (2100 miles)
Weights:	empty 16,556kg (36,500lb); maximum take-off 29,484kg (65,000lb)
Dimensions:	span 33.53m (110ft); length 20.47m (67ft 2in); height 5.49m (18ft)
Armament:	two .5in MGs in each of nose, dorsal, ventral and tail turrets, one .5in MG in each of waist positions; internal bomb load of 3992kg (8800lb)

LAST BOMBS TIMELINE

1940

1941

Consolidated B-32A Dominator

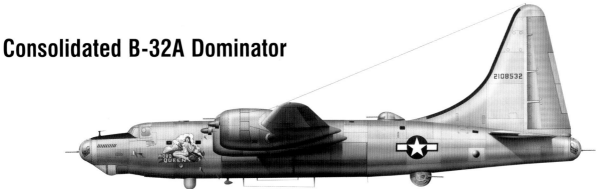

The B-32 Dominator was built as something of an insurance policy in case the B-29 programme failed. Only 74 production B-32s were built, with one squadron seeing combat from Okinawa. 'Hobo Queen II' was damaged by fighters on a photo mission after Japan announced its surrender.

SPECIFICATIONS	
Country of origin:	United States
Type:	four-engined heavy bomber and reconnaissance aircraft
Powerplant:	four 2200hp (1641kW) Wright R-3350-23 Duplex Cyclone radial piston engines
Performance:	maximum speed 575km/h (357mph); service ceiling 10,668m (35,000ft); range 4815km (3000 miles)
Weights:	empty 27,000kg (60,000lb); maximum 50,580kg (111,500lb)
Dimensions:	span 41.2m (135ft); length 25.3m (83ft 1in); height 10.1m (33ft); wing area 132.1 sq m (1422 sq ft)
Armament:	10 .5in machine guns; up to 9100kg (20,000lb) of bombs

Boeing B-29

B-29s brought the war home to Japan, initially flying from India and China before settling on bases like Tinian in the Marianas Islands, from where they could carry full bomb loads to Japan. This 444th Bomb Group B-29 had black undersides and bombing radar for night missions.

SPECIFICATIONS	
Country of origin:	United States
Type:	(B-29) nine-seat long-range heavy bomber
Powerplant:	four 2200hp (1640kW) Wright R-3350-23 18-cylinder two-row radial engines
Performance:	maximum speed 576km/h (358mph); service ceiling 9710m (31,850ft); range 9382km (5830 miles)
Weights:	empty 31,816kg (70,140lb); maximum take-off 56,246kg (124,000lb)
Dimensions:	span 43.05m (141ft 2.75in); length 30.18m (99ft); height 9.02m (29ft 7in)
Armament:	one 20mm rearward-firing cannon and two .5in rearward-firing MGs in tail, two .5in MGs in each of two dorsal and two ventral barbettes, plus an internal bomb load of 9072kg (20,000lb)

Boeing B-29

The specially formed 509th Bomb Group was equipped with stripped-down 'Silverplate' B-29s modified to carry single large bombs. On 6 August 1945, 'Enola Gay' dropped the 'Little Boy' atomic weapon on the city of Hiroshima, followed three days later by B-29 'Bockscar' destroying Nagasaki with 'Fat Man'.

SPECIFICATIONS	
Country of origin:	United States
Type:	(B-29) nine-seat long-range heavy bomber
Powerplant:	four 2200hp (1640kW) Wright 18-cylinder two-row radial engines
Performance:	maximum speed 576km/h (358mph); service ceiling 9710m (31,850ft); range 9382km (5830 miles)
Weights:	empty 31,816kg (70,140lb); maximum take-off 56,246kg (124,000lb)
Dimensions:	span 43.05m (141ft 2.75in); length 30.18m (99ft); height 9.02m (29ft 7in)
Armament:	two 12.7mm (.5in) machine guns; one 4630kg (10,200lb) 21-kiloton yield 'Fat Man' atomic bomb an internal bomb load of 9072kg (20,000lb)

1942

THE COLD WAR

A new conflict sprang up within a few years of the end of World War II as former allies the USSR and the Western powers competed for influence in Europe, Asia and elsewhere.

Atomic weapons threatened the end of civilization, but thankfully remained unused. Actual fighting in the Cold War years was largely constrained to proxy wars in countries like Vietnam and Afghanistan, although aerial spying reached new heights. Aircraft development was rapid, with new materials such as titanium needed to cope with the heat caused by supersonic speeds and afterburning jet engines.

Left: The F-4 Phantom II first entered service in 1960 and continued to form a major part of US military air power throughout the 1970s and 1980s.

Early Jets

The first generation of turbine-powered aircraft that entered service immediately after the war were essentially piston-engined aircraft with jets in them. This was literally true of the J 21R and Fireball, but in general early jets were quite conservative designs. British and German engine designs dominated this first generation. Although the Vampire's centrifugal flow design was almost universal initially, the German axial-flow engine design was to become dominant over time.

De Havilland Spider Crab (Vampire)

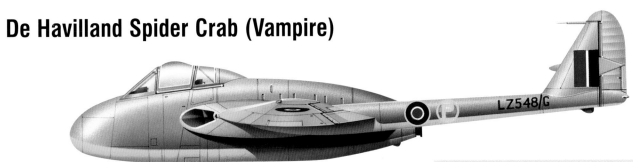

Originally named Spider Crab, but fortunately changed to Vampire in April 1944, the de Havilland DH.100 was designed around the Halford H.1 centrifugal-flow turbojet and had a relatively tubby fuselage. The Vampire entered squadron service until March 1946 and became a great export success.

SPECIFICATIONS	
Country of origin:	United Kingdom
Type:	single-engined jet fighter
Powerplant:	one 12kN (2700lb) thrust Halford H.1 turbojet engine
Performance:	maximum speed 915km/h (570mph); range unknown; service ceiling unknown
Weights:	(approx) empty 3290kg (7520lb); maximum 5620kg (12,390lb)
Dimensions:	span 11.6m (38ft); length 9.37m (30ft 9in); height 2.69m (8ft 10in); wing area 24.34 sq m (262 sq ft)
Armament:	none

Lockheed P-80 Shooting Star

The USAF's first operational jet fighter first flew as the XP-80 in January 1944. Crashes of early test and production aircraft killed several experienced pilots. Several P-80s were rushed to Europe in 1945 and two examples saw limited service in Italy before the war's end.

SPECIFICATIONS	
Country of origin:	United States
Type:	single-seat fighter bomber
Powerplant:	one 17.1kN (3850lb) Allison J33-GE-11 turbojet
Performance:	maximum speed at sea level 966km/h (594mph); service ceiling 14,265m (46,800ft); range 1328km (825 miles)
Weights:	empty 3819kg (8420lb); maximum take-off weight 7646kg (16,856lb)
Dimensions:	wingspan 11.81m (38ft 9in); length 10.49m (34ft 5in); height 3.43m (11ft 3in); wing area 22.07 sq m (237.6sq ft)
Armament:	six .5in machine guns, plus two 454kg (1000lb) bombs and eight rockets

EARLY JETS TIMELINE

1943    1944

Ryan FR-1 Fireball

The US Navy took a more cautious approach for its first jet-propelled aircraft, commissioning the mixed-powerplant Fireball in 1942. The jet engine was regarded as an adjunct to the radial to give the dash speed for catching Kamikazes, but the Fireball was too late for operational war service.

SPECIFICATIONS

Country of origin:	United States
Type:	mixed-powerplant carrier-based fighter
Powerplant:	one 7.1kN (1600lb) thrust General Electric J31-GE-3 turbojet engine and one 1060kW (1350hp) Wright R-1820-72W Cyclone radial piston engine
Performance:	maximum speed 686km/h (426mph); range 2100km (1300 miles); service ceiling 13,137m (43,100ft)
Weights:	empty 3590kg (7915mph); maximum 4806kg (10,595lb)
Dimensions:	span 12.19m (40ft); length 12.19m (32ft 4in); height 4.15m (13ft 8in); wing area 25.6 sq m (275 sq ft)
Armament:	four .5in (12.7mm) Browning M2 machine guns; up to 908kg (2000lb) of bombs or eight 127mm (5in) rockets

Mikoyan-Gurevich MiG-9 'Fargo'

The MiG-9 was the first Soviet jet to fly, powered by Russian copies of the German BMW 003 turbojet. It was built in relatively large numbers (610 examples) and received the reporting name 'Fargo', but was never regarded as a satisfactory fighter despite its heavy cannon armament.

SPECIFICATIONS

Country of origin:	USSR
Type:	twin-engined jet fighter
Powerplant:	two 7.8kN (1533lb) thrust Kolesov RD-20 afterburning turbojet engines
Performance:	maximum speed 909km/h (565mph); range 800km (495 miles); service ceiling 13,000m (42,650ft)
Weights:	empty 3420kg (7540lb); maximum 5500kg (12,125lb)
Dimensions:	span 10m (32ft 10in); length: 9.83m (32ft 3in); height 3.22m (10ft 7in); wing area 18.2 sq m (196 sq ft)
Armament:	one 37mm NL-37 37mm cannon, two NS-23 23mm cannon

Saab J 21R

Saab's J 21A fighter was a pusher-engined twin-boom fighter that entered service in 1945. Then, in 1947 and as a stepping-stone to new jet designs, Saab created the J 21R (R standing for *Reaktion* or jet) with a Goblin engine. The 64 built were used mainly as ground-attack aircraft.

SPECIFICATIONS

Country of origin:	Sweden
Type:	single-seat jet fighter-bomber
Powerplant:	one 13.8kN (3100lb) thrust De Havilland Goblin 2 turbojet engine
Performance:	maximum speed 800km/h (497mph); range 720km (450 miles); service ceiling 12,000m (39,400ft)
Weights:	empty 3200kg (7055lb); maximum 5000kg (11,023lb)
Dimensions:	span 11.37m (37ft 4in); length 10.45m (34ft 3in); height 2.9m (9ft 8in); wing area 22.3 sq m (240 sq ft)
Armament:	one 20mm Bofors cannon, four 13.2mm M/39A machine guns; 10 100mm or five 180mm rockets

1946

1947

US Carrier Air Power

In August 1945, the US Navy had several advanced piston-engined designs ready for introduction to the fleet, but none made it to the front before the war ended. Hellcats, Avengers and especially Helldivers were soon retired from frontline service and scrapped, converted to target drones or relegated to reserve units. The new aircraft replaced them in those squadrons that were not immediately disbanded.

Grumman F8F-1 Bearcat

Lightweight and powerful, the F8F Bearcat was one of the fastest single-seat piston-engined fighters ever built. Although in service by May 1945, it missed out on wartime combat. Highly regarded by pilots, the Bearcat had a short frontline career before its replacement by jets.

SPECIFICATIONS	
Country of origin:	United States
Type:	single-engined carrier-based fighter
Powerplant:	one 156kW (2100hp) Pratt & Whitney R-2800-34W Double Wasp radial piston engine
Performance:	maximum speed 678km/h (421mph); range 1778km (1105 miles); service ceiling 11,796m (38,700ft)
Weights:	empty 3207kg (7070lb); maximum 5873kg (12,947lb)
Dimensions:	span 10.92m (35ft 10in); length 8.61m (28ft 3in); height 4.21m (13ft 9in);
Armament:	four .5in (12.7mm) M2 machine guns; up to 454kg (1000lb) of bombs or four 5in (127mm) rockets

Grumman F7F-2N Tigercat

Designed for operation off the new 'Midway'-class carriers, the Tigercat was Grumman's first twin-engined combat aircraft. Marine units received some before the war's end, but it missed out on combat until Korea. The F7F-2N was a two-seat night-fighter variant, used mainly from land bases.

SPECIFICATIONS	
Country of origin:	United States
Type:	twin-engined night fighter
Powerplant:	two 1790kW (2400hp) Pratt & Whitney R-2800-22W radial piston engines
Performance:	maximum speed 582km/h (362mph); range 1545km (960 miles); service ceiling 12,131m (39,800ft)
Weights:	empty 7380kg (16,270lb); loaded 11,880kg (26,190lb)
Dimensions:	span 15.7m (51ft 6in); length 13.8m (45ft 4in); height 4.6m (15ft 2in); wing area 42.3 sq m (455 sq ft)
Armament:	four 20mm cannon and four .5in (12.7mm) Browning machine guns

North American FJ-1 Fury

Although it had a relatively undistinguished career, the Fury was the first aircraft to complete an operational tour at sea, and paved the way for the more aesthetically pleasing F-86 Sabre. For a brief period, it could also claim to be the fastest aircraft in US Navy service.

SPECIFICATIONS

Country of origin:	United States
Type:	single-seat carrier-borne fighter
Powerplant:	one 17.8kN (4000lb) Allison J35-A-2 turbojet
Performance:	maximum speed 880km/h (547mph); service ceiling 9754m (32,000ft); range 2414km (1500 miles)
Weights:	empty 4011kg (8843lb); maximum loaded 7076kg (15,600lb)
Dimensions:	wingspan 9.8m (38ft 2in); length 10.5m (34ft 5in); height 4.5m (14ft 10in); wing area 20.5 sq m (221sq ft)
Armament:	six .5in machine guns

McDonnell F2H-2 Banshee

The success of the FH-1 Phantom meant that it was almost inevitable that McDonnell would be asked to submit a design to succeed the Phantom in service. The new aircraft was larger, incorporating folding wings and a lengthened fuselage to accommodate more fuel and more powerful engines. The F2H-1 was delivered in 1948. The F2H-2 had wingtip fuel tanks.

SPECIFICATIONS

Country of origin:	United States
Type:	carrier-based all-weather fighter
Powerplant:	one 14.5kN (3250llb) Westinghouse turbojet
Performance:	maximum speed 933km/h (580mph); range 1883km (1170 miles); service ceiling 14,205m (46,600ft)
Weights:	empty 5980kg (13,183lb); maximum take-off weight 11,437kg (25,214lb)
Dimensions:	span 12.73m (41ft 9in); length 14.68m (48ft 2in); height 4.42m (14ft 6in); wing area 27.31 sq m (294sq ft)
Armament:	four 20mm cannon; underwing racks with provision for two 227kg (500lb) or four 113kg (250lb) bombs

Martin AM-1 Mauler

Able to carry a heavy load of bombs or torpedoes, the Mauler was intended to replace several types, including the Avenger and Helldiver. It proved difficult to operate from carriers and was passed to reserve units in favour of the smaller but more reliable Douglas AD Skyraider.

SPECIFICATIONS

Country of origin:	United States
Type:	single-engined carrier-based multi-purpose bomber
Powerplant:	one 2237kW (3000hp) Pratt & Whitney R-4360-4 Wasp Major radial piston engine
Performance:	maximum speed 591km/h (376mph); range 2885km (1800 miles); service ceiling 9296m (30,500ft)
Weights:	empty 6557kg (14,500lb); maximum 10,608kg (23,386lb)
Dimensions:	span 15.24m (50ft); length 12.55m (41ft 2in); height 5.13m (16ft 10in); wing area 46.1 sq m (496 sq ft)
Armament:	four 20mm cannon; up to 4488kg (10,698lb) of bombs

English Electric Canberra

First flown in 1949, the Canberra became one of the great post-war successes of the British aircraft industry, with 782 built for the RAF and RN, and another 120 for export customers. Canberras saw action in numerous wars in Africa, Southeast Asia and South America. Photoreconnaissance Canberras flew missions around (and sometimes inside) the borders of the Soviet Union and Warsaw Pact countries, and in conflicts with British involvement up to Afghanistan and Iraq in the 2000s.

Canberra B.2

To meet specification B.3/45, W.E.W. Petter planned a straightforward unswept jet bomber with a broad wing for good behaviour at high altitude. Like the Mosquito, the A.1 bomber was to be fast enough to escape interception, whilst carrying a 2727kg (6000lb) bomb load over a radius of 750 nautical miles. It was to have a radar sight for blind attacks in all conditions. The first B.2s, tactical day bombers, were delivered in May 1951.

SPECIFICATIONS	
Country of origin:	United Kingdom
Type:	two-seat interdictor aircraft
Powerplant:	two 28.9kN (6500lb) Rolls-Royce Avon Mk 101 turbojets
Performance:	maximum speed 917km/h (570mph); service ceiling 14,630m (48,000ft); range 4274km (2656 miles)
Weights:	empty not published approx. 11,790kg (26,000lb); maximum take-off weight 24,925kg (54,950lb)
Dimensions:	wingspan 29.49m (63ft 11in); length 19.96m (65ft 6in); height 4.78m (15ft 8in); wing area 97.08 sq m (1045 sq ft)
Armament:	internal bomb bay with provision for up to 2727kg (6000lb) of bombs, plus an additional 909kg (2000lb) of underwing pylons

Canberra PR.3

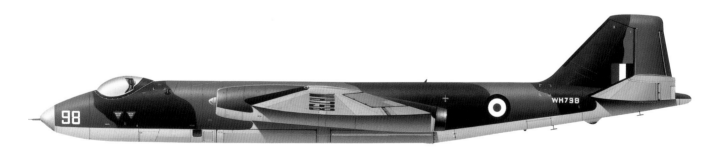

The PR.3 was a photographic reconnaissance version of the B.2 and entered service in late 1952. Instead of weapons, it had mounts for one vertical camera and six oblique cameras. The bomb bay itself was replaced by an extra fuel tank and flares for night photography.

SPECIFICATIONS	
Country of origin:	United Kingdom
Type:	twin-engined jet photoreconnaissance aircraft
Powerplant:	two 28.9kN (6500lb) Rolls-Royce Avon Mk 101 turbojets
Performance:	maximum speed 917km/h (570mph); service ceiling 14,630m (48,000ft); range 4274km (2656 miles)
Weights:	empty not published approx 11,790kg (26,000lb); maximum take-off weight 24,925kg (54,950lb)
Dimensions:	wingspan 29.49m (63ft 11in); length 20.3m (66ft 8in); height 4.78m (15ft 8in); wing area 97.08 sq m (1045 sq ft)
Armament:	none

Canberra B(I).8

The B(I).8 was an interdictor/strike variant and the first to have the offset fighter-style canopy. The bomb aimer was replaced by a low-altitude bombing system computer. For strike missions it could carry nuclear weapons, or a cannon pack in the interdictor role.

SPECIFICATIONS	
Country of origin:	United Kingdom
Type:	twin-engined jet bomber
Powerplant:	two 33.23kN (7490lb) thrust turbojet engine Avon R.A.7 turbojet engines
Performance:	maximum speed 933km/h (580mph); range 5440km (3380 miles); service ceiling 15,000m (48,000ft)
Weights:	9820kg (21,650lb); maximum 24,948kg (55,000lb)
Dimensions:	span 19.51m (65ft 6in); length 19.96m (65ft 6in); height 4.77m (15ft 3in); wing area 88.19 sq m (960 sq ft)
Armament:	four 20mm cannon

Canberra TT.18

The Royal Navy operated a number of Canberra variants for roles such as target towing. The TT.18 was converted from the B.2, with underwing winches allowing the streaming of target drogues for aerial or naval gunnery. It could also operate as a target itself to train radar operators.

SPECIFICATIONS	
Country of origin:	United Kingdom
Type:	twin-engined jet target tug
Powerplant:	two 28.9kN (6500lb) Rolls-Royce Avon Mk 101 turbojets
Performance:	maximum speed 917km/h (570mph); service ceiling 14,630m (48,000ft); range 4274km (2656 miles)
Weights:	empty not published approx. 11,790kg (26,000lb); maximum take-off weight 24,925kg (54,950lb)
Dimensions:	wingspan 29.49m (63ft 11in); length 19.96m (65ft 6in); height 4.78m (15ft 8in); wing area 97.08 sq m (1045 sq ft)
Armament:	none

Canberra PR.9

Longest-lived of the UK-built Canberras, the PR.9s were delivered in 1959 and were finally retired in 2006. During their career, they received many camera and sensor fits, including the Hycon B or System III camera used in the U-2 and an infrared line scan (IRLS) unit.

SPECIFICATIONS	
Country of origin:	United Kingdom
Type:	photoreconnaissance aircraft
Powerplant:	two 46.7kN (10,500lb) Rolls-Royce Avon Mk 206 turbojets
Performance:	maximum speed about 650mph (1050km/h) at medium altitude; service ceiling 14,630m (48,000ft); range 5842km (3630 miles)
Weights:	empty not published approx. 11,790kg (26,000lb); maximum take-off weight 24,925kg (54,950lb)
Dimensions:	wingspan 20.68m (67ft 10in); length 20.32m (66ft 8in); height 4.78m (15ft 8in); wing area 97.08 sq m (1045 sq ft)
Armament:	none

Israeli War of Independence

The state of Israel was formally created from the former British Mandate of Palestine in 1948. On the day of independence, Israel was attacked by Egypt, Iraq, Syria and Lebanon. The Israeli Air Force, Hel HaAvir, was quickly established in the face of an international arms embargo. Israel acquired aircraft by various means, and its pilots – many of them with much combat experience – also came from far and wide.

Boeing B-17G Fortress

Israel obtained four B-17Gs from a broker in Florida in early 1948 and flew them to Czechoslovakia for modification and refurbishment, although one was impounded en route. Targets in Egypt were bombed on the delivery flight to Israel in July 1949. They flew about 200 sorties in the following year.

SPECIFICATIONS	
Country of origin:	United States
Type:	(B-17G) 10-seat heavy bomber
Powerplant:	four 895kW (1200hp) Wright R-1820-97 nine-cylinder radial engines
Performance:	maximum speed 486km/h (302mph); service ceiling 10,850m (35,600ft); range 2897km (1800 miles)
Weights:	empty 20,212kg (44,560lb); maximum take-off weight 32,659kg (72,000lb)
Dimensions:	span 31.63m (103ft 9.4in); length 22.78m (74ft 9 in); height 5.82m (19ft 1in)
Armament:	12 .5in machine guns (in chin turret, cheek positions, in dorsal turret, in roof position, in ventral turret, in waist positions, in tail), plus a bomb load of 7983kg (17,600lb)

De Havilland Mosquito FB.VI

The French government sold Israel 67 surplus and rather worn Mosquitoes in 1951, among them 40 FB.VI fighter bombers as illustrated. More Mosquitoes later arrived from Britain. They flew mainly reconnaissance missions over Israel's neighbours before retirement in 1957.

SPECIFICATIONS	
Country of origin:	United Kingdom
Type:	(B.IV Series 2) twin-engined bomber
Powerplant:	Two 954kW (1280hp) Rolls-Royce Merlin 23 V-12 piston engines
Performance:	maximum speed 612km/h (380mph); service ceiling 9144m (30,000ft); range 3384km (2040 miles)
Weights:	empty 6396kg (14,100lb); loaded 10,151kg (22,380lb)
Dimensions:	span 16.5m (54ft 2in); length 12.35m (40ft 10in); height 4.66m (15ft 4in); wing area 42.18 sq m (454 sq ft)
Armament:	up to 1814kg (4000lb) of bombs

Supermarine Spitfire

Newly communist Czechoslovakia supplied Israel with 76 of its ex-RAF Spitfires in 1948–49. Serving alongside Avia S.199s in 101 Squadron, Israeli Spitfires claimed a number of Egyptian MC.205s and also three RAF Spitfires and a Tempest in incidents of mistaken identity.

SPECIFICATIONS	
Country of origin:	United Kingdom
Type:	(Spitfire F.Mk IX) single-seat fighter and fighter-bomber
Powerplant:	one 1167kW (1565hp) Rolls-Royce Merlin 61 or 1230kW (1650hp) Merlin 63 12-cylinder Vee engine
Performance:	maximum speed 655km/h (408mph); service ceiling 12,105m (43,000ft); range 1576km (980 miles)
Weights:	empty 2545kg (5610lb); maximum take-off weight 4309kg (9500lb)
Dimensions:	span 11.23m (36ft 10in); length 9.46m (31ft); height 3.85m (12ft 7.75in)
Armament:	two 20mm fixed forward-firing cannon and four .303in fixed forward-firing machine guns in the leading edges of the wing, plus an external bomb load of 454kg (1000lb)

Macchi MC.205 Veltro

Egypt bought 24 Macchi fighters from Italy in 1948. Some were MC.205 Veltros and others were older MC.202s rebuilt to MC.205V standard. This example served with 2 Squadron, Royal Egyptian Air Force, at Al Arish. Egyptian Macchis claimed three kills in 1948–49.

SPECIFICATIONS	
Country of origin:	Italy
Type:	(MC.205V) single-seat fighter and fighter-bomber
Powerplant:	one 1100kW (1475hp) Fiat RA.1050 RC.58 Tifone 12-cylinder inverted-Vee engine
Performance:	maximum speed 642km/h (399mph); service ceiling 11,000m (36,090ft); range 1040km (646 miles)
Weights:	empty 2581kg (5691lb); maximum take-off weight 3408kg (7514lb)
Dimensions:	span 10.58m (34ft 8.5in); length 8.85m (29ft 0.5in); height 3.04m (9ft 11.5in)
Armament:	two 12.7mm fixed forward-firing machine guns in the upper part of the forward fuselage, and two 20mm forward-firing cannon in the leading edges of the wing, plus bomb load of 320kg (705lb)

Supermarine Spitfire

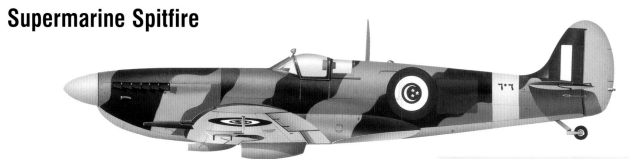

Egypt's Spitfire Mk Vs and IXs (illustrated) fought Israel's own Spitfires on several occasions. Although they are not believed to have won any engagements, they did destroy several Avias and other IAF aircraft. At least one crash-landed REAF Spitfire was captured and put into Israeli service.

SPECIFICATIONS	
Country of origin:	United Kingdom
Type:	(Spitfire F.Mk IX) single-seat fighter and fighter-bomber
Powerplant:	one 1167kW (1565hp) Rolls-Royce Merlin 61 or 1230kW (1650hp) Merlin 63 12-cylinder Vee engine
Performance:	maximum speed 655km/h (408mph); service ceiling 12,105m (43,000ft); range 1576km (980 miles)
Weights:	empty 2545kg (5610lb); maximum take-off weight 4309kg (9500lb)
Dimensions:	span 11.23m (36ft 10in); length 9.46m (31ft); height 3.85m (12ft 7.75in)
Armament:	two 20mm cannon and four .303in machine guns in the wing, plus an external bomb load of 454kg (1000lb)

Korean War

In June 1950, North Korea launched a surprise attack on its southern neighbour, with massive ground forces supported by air power. The North Korean Air Force had about 180 aircraft, the majority of them Yak fighters and Il-10 ground attackers. The nearest and strongest United Nations forces were those of the USAF in Japan, who had one wing of F-80 jets and various piston-engined aircraft. B-29s soon flattened most of North Korea's industry, and by November UN troops were nearing victory.

North American F-51D Mustang

Flown by Arnold 'Moon' Mullins, this F-51D Mustang of the 67th Fighter Bomber Squadron shot down at least one North Korean Yak-9 in February 1951. Mustangs were used mainly for ground-attack missions and proved more vulnerable to ground fire than radial-engined aircraft.

SPECIFICATIONS	
Country of origin:	United States
Type:	(F-51D) single-engined fighter-bomber
Powerplant:	one 1264kW (1695hp) Packard V-1650-7 12-cylinder Vee engine
Performance:	maximum speed 703km/h (437mph); service ceiling 12,770m (41,900ft); range 3703km (2301 miles)
Weights:	empty 3103kg (6840lb); maximum take-off weight 5493kg (12,100lb)
Dimensions:	span 11.28m (37ft 0.25in); length 9.84m (32ft 3.25in); height 4.16m (13ft 8in) with the tail down
Armament:	six .5in fixed forward-firing machine guns in the leading edges of the wing, plus an external bomb and rocket load of 907kg (2000lb)

Boeing B-29B Superfortress

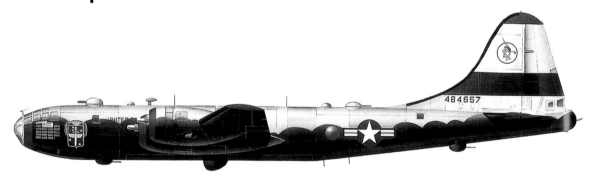

'Command Decision' was a B-29B Superfortress of the 19th Bomb Group, 28th Bomb Squadron, based on Okinawa. Its claim to fame is that its gunners shot down five North Korean fighters. In total, B-29 gunners were credited with 27 victories over North Korean aircraft.

SPECIFICATIONS	
Country of origin:	United States
Type:	(B-29) nine-seat long-range heavy bomber
Powerplant:	four 1640kW (2200hp) Wright 18-cylinder two-row radial engines
Performance:	maximum speed 576km/h (358mph); service ceiling 9710m (31,850ft); range 9382km (5830 miles)
Weights:	empty 31,816kg (70,140lb); maximum take-off 56,246kg (124,000lb)
Dimensions:	span 43.05m (141ft 2.75in); length 30.18m (99ft); height 9.02m (29ft 7in)
Armament:	one 20mm cannon and six .5in MGs (in tail, and dorsal and ventral barbettes), plus an internal bomb load of 9072kg (20,000lb)

Lockheed F-80C

SPECIFICATIONS	
Country of origin:	United States
Type:	single-engined fighter-bomber
Powerplant:	one 24.0kN (5400lb) thrust Allison J33-A-35 turbojet engine
Performance:	maximum speed 965 km/h (600 mph); service ceiling 14,000m (46,000ft); range 1930km (1200 miles)
Weights:	empty 3819kg (8420lb); maximum 7646kg (16,856lb)
Dimensions:	wingspan 11.81m (38ft 9in); length 10.49m (34ft 5in); height 3.43m (11ft 3in); wing area 22.07 sq m (237.6 sq ft)
Armament:	six .5in (12.7mm) machine guns; two 454kg (1000lb) bombs or eight 2.75in rockets

Jet squadrons were sent to South Korea as soon as North Korean troops were driven out. 'Eagle Eyed Fleagle/Miss Barbara Ann' was an F-80C of the 36th FBS based at Suwon. F-80s of this squadron claimed several Yak-9s in air combat in July 1950.

Republic F-84E Thunderjet

SPECIFICATIONS	
Country of origin:	United States
Type:	single-engined jet fighter-bomber
Powerplant:	one 21.8kN (4900lb) thrust Allison J35-A-17 turbojet engine
Performance:	maximum speed 986km/h (613mph); range 2390km (1485 miles); service ceiling 13,180m (43,240ft)
Weight:	loaded 10,185kg (22,455lb)
Dimensions:	span 11.1m (36ft 5in); length 11.41m (36ft 5in); height 3.91m (12ft 10in); wing area 214.8 sq m (260 sq ft)
Armament:	six .5in (12.7mm) machine guns; two 454kg (1000lb) bombs or eight 2.75in rockets

The F-84E was one of the stalwarts of the tactical ground-attack effort in Korea, attacking trains, convoys, artillery positions and other targets. It was not noted as a dogfighter, however, and this 9th FBS Thunderjet was shot down by North Korean MiGs in September 1952.

Gloster Meteor F.8

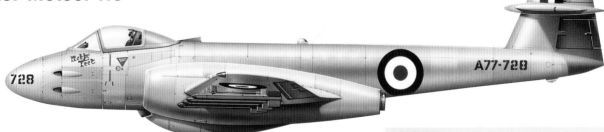

SPECIFICATIONS	
Country of origin:	United Kingdom
Type:	single-seat fighter
Powerplant:	two 16.0kN (3600lb) Rolls-Royce Derwent 8 turbojets
Performance:	maximum speed (33,000ft) 962km/h (598mph); service ceiling 13,106m (43,000ft); range 1580km (980 miles)
Weights:	empty 4820kg (10,626lb); loaded 8664kg (19,100lb)
Dimensions:	wingspan 11.32m (37ft 2in); length 13.58m (44ft 7in); height 3.96m (13ft)
Armament:	four 20mm Hispano cannon, foreign F.8s often modified to carry two iron bombs or eight rockets

Australia first committed Mustangs and then Meteor F.8s to Korea in July 1951. No 77 Squadron found its straight-wing jets inferior to the MiG-15 and lost more Meteors in combat than it claimed MiGs. Reassigned to ground-attack duties, the RAAF Meteors were much more successful.

Korean War: Later Types

Carrier-based air power played an important part in the Korean conflict from the start. Both Royal Navy prop-driven fighters and USN jets began strikes on the North in early July 1950. The situation changed in November 1950 with two events – the Chinese intervention in the land battle and the arrival of swept-wing MiG-15s supplied by the Soviet Union and largely flown by Soviet pilots.

Hawker Sea Fury FB.11

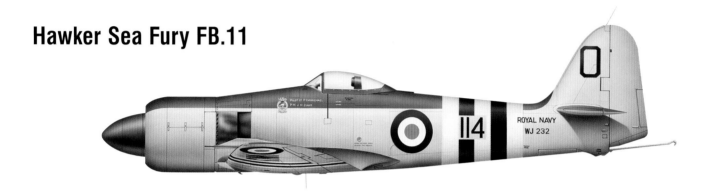

Despite its pioneering work introducing jets to carriers, the Fleet Air Arm deployed only piston-engined aircraft in Korea. Flown by Peter Carmichael of No 805 Squadron on HMS *Ocean*, this Sea Fury FB.11 destroyed a MiG-15 in air combat in August 1952.

SPECIFICATIONS	
Country of origin:	United Kingdom
Type:	single-engined carrier-based fighter-bomber
Powerplant:	one 1850kW (2480hp) Bristol Centaurus XVIIC radial piston engine
Performance:	maximum speed 740 km/h (460 mph); range 1127km (700 miles); service ceiling 10,900m (35,800ft)
Weights:	empty 4190kg (9240lb); maximum 5670kg (12,500lb)
Dimensions:	span 11.7m (38ft 4in); length 10.6m (34ft 8in); height 4.9m (16ft 1in); wing area 26 sq m (280 sq ft)
Armament:	four 20mm Hispano Mk V cannon; up to 908kg (2000 lb) of bombs or 12 3in rockets

Vought F4U-4B Corsair

The wartime-vintage Corsair was brought back into production for Korea, where its ruggedness and heavy warload were valuable. Marine units like VMA-312 used cannon-armed F4U-4Bs from land bases in their traditional close air-support role.

SPECIFICATIONS	
Country of origin:	United States
Type:	(F4U-4) single-seat carrierborne and land-based fighter and fighter-bomber
Powerplant:	one 1678kW (2250hp) Pratt & Whitney R-2800-18W Double Wasp 18-cylinder two-row radial engine
Performance:	maximum speed 718km/h (446mph); service ceiling 12,650m (41,500ft); range 2511km (1560 miles)
Weights:	empty 4175kg (9205lb); maximum take-off weight 6149kg (13,555lb) as fighter or 8845kg (19,500lb) as fighter-bomber
Dimensions:	span 12.49m (40ft 11.75in); length 10.27m (33ft 8.25in); height 4.50m (14ft 9in)
Armament:	six .5in MGs, external bomb and rocket load of 907kg (2000lb)

Grumman F9F-2 Panther

Grumman's Panther was the US Navy's primary strike jet of the war. Panthers had relatively few encounters with North Korean fighters. This F9F-2 of VF-781 on the USS *Bon Homme Richard*, however, shot down a MiG-15 flown by a Russian pilot in November 1952.

SPECIFICATIONS	
Country of origin:	United Kingdom
Type:	single-engined carrier-based jet fighter-bomber
Powerplant:	one 26.5kN (5950lb) thrust Pratt & Whitney J42-P-6/P-8 turbojet engine
Performance:	maximum speed 925 km/h (575 mph); range 2100km (1300 miles); service ceiling 13,600m (44,600ft)
Weights:	empty 4220kg (9303lb); maximum 7462kg (16,450lb)
Dimensions:	span 11.6m (38ft); length 11.3m (37ft 5in); height 3.8m (11ft 4in); wing area 23 sq m (250 sq ft)
Armament:	four 20mm M2 cannon; up to 910kg (2000lb) bombs, six 5in (127mm) rockets

Mikoyan-Gurevich MiG-15 'Fagot'

The MiG-15 was very much the equivalent of the F-86 Sabre with some advantages, such as heavy armament, and weaknesses, such as a poorer turn radius. This MiG-15bis was flown by a North Korean defector to Kimpo airfield near Seoul in September 1953 and later evaluated in the United States.

SPECIFICATIONS	
Country of origin:	USSR
Type:	single-seat fighter
Powerplant:	one 26.3kN (5952lb) Klimov VK-1 turbojet
Performance:	maximum speed 1100km/h (684 mph); service ceiling 15,545m (51,000ft); range at height with slipper tanks 1424km (885 miles)
Weights:	empty 4000kg (8820lb); maximum loaded 5700kg (12,566lb)
Dimensions:	wingspan 10.08m (33ft 0.75in); length 11.05m (36ft 3.75in); height 3.4m (11ft 1.75in); wing area 20.60 sq m (221.74 sq ft)
Armament:	one 37mm N-37 cannon and two 23mm NS-23 cannon, plus up to 500kg (1102lb) of mixed stores on underwing pylons

Ilyushin Il-28 'Beagle'

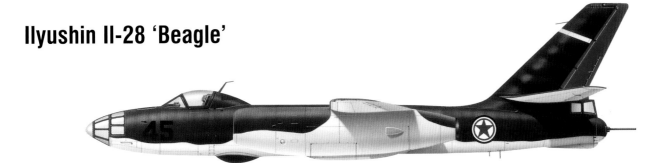

One of the most important early jet bombers, the Il-28 'Beagle' was supplied to North Korea late in the war. The threat of such bombers worried the UN commanders, but they flew no known bombing missions against the South. North Korea still uses the Il-28 in the form of the Chinese-built Harbin H-5.

SPECIFICATIONS	
Country of origin:	USSR
Type:	three seat bomber and ground attack/torpedo carrier
Powerplant:	two 26.3kN (5952lb) Klimov VK-1 turbojets
Performance:	max speed 902 km/h (560mph); service ceiling 12,300m (40,355ft); range 2180km (1355 miles); with bomb load 1100km (684 miles)
Weights:	empty 12890kg (28,418lb); maximum take-off 21,200kg (46,738lb)
Dimensions:	wingspan 21.45sq m (70ft 4.5in); length 17.65m (57ft 10.75in); height 6.70m (21ft 11.8in); wing area 60.80 sq m (654.47 sq ft)
Armament:	four 23mm cannon; internal bomb capacity 1000kg (2205lb), max bomb capacity 3000kg (6614lb); torpedo version: provision for two 400mm light torpedoes

Korean Sabres

Emblematic of the Korean War, the North American F-86 Sabre escorted bombers and flew ground-attack missions, but is best remembered for its duels with North Korean MiGs. The introduction of the MiGs saw a wing of F-86As shipped from the United States to Korea in November 1950, and the first victory against a MiG was recorded in mid-December. The Sabres were restricted by their modest endurance and rules that prevented them pursuing the enemy too close to Chinese airspace.

F-86A-5

Joseph E. Fields, 1st Lieutenant of the 336th Fighter Inceptor Squadron flew this F-86A. Fields scored a MIG-15 kill outright on 21 September 1952. In total, Sabre pilots claimed 792 MiGs destroyed for about 80 losses in air combat, but modern research suggests the kill-loss ratio was less favourable.

SPECIFICATIONS

Country of origin:	United States
Type:	single-engined jet fighter
Powerplant:	one 23.7kN (5340lb) thrust General Electric J47-GE-7 turbojet engine
Performance:	maximum speed 965km/h (600mph); range 530km (329 miles); service ceiling 14,600 m (48,000 ft)
Weights:	empty 4700kg (10,500lb); maximum 6300kg (13,791lb)
Dimensions:	span 11.3m (37ft 1in); length 11.4m (37ft 6in); height 4.4m (14ft 8in); wing area 26.76 sq m (288 sq ft)
Armament:	six .5in (12.7mm) machine guns

F-86A-5

The majority of Korean Sabres flew in an unpainted natural metal finish, but several aircraft flew in an experimental camouflage scheme, as seen on this F-86A of the 335th FIS. Another project included the fitting of 20mm cannon to Sabres. The cannon-armed Sabres claimed six MiGs before the war's end.

SPECIFICATIONS

Country of origin:	United States
Type:	single-engined jet fighter
Powerplant:	one 23.7kN (5340lb) thrust General Electric J47-GE-7 turbojet engine
Performance:	maximum speed 965km/h (600mph); range 530km (329 miles); service ceiling 14,600m (48,000 ft)
Weights:	empty 4700kg (10,500lb); maximum 6300kg (13,791lb)
Dimensions:	span 11.3m (37ft 1in); length 11.4m (37ft 6in); height 4.4m (14ft 8in); wing area 26.76 sq m (288 sq ft)
Armament:	six .5in (12.7mm) machine guns

F-86E-10

SPECIFICATIONS	
Country of origin:	United States
Type:	single-engined jet fighter
Powerplant:	one 23.1kN (5200lb) thrust General Electric J47-GE-13 turbojet engine
Performance:	maximum speed 965km/h (600mph); range 530km (329 miles); service ceiling 14,600 m (48,000 ft)
Weights:	empty 4700kg (10,500lb); maximum 6300kg (13,791lb)
Dimensions:	span 11.3m (37ft 1in); length 11.4m (37ft 6in); height 4.4m (14ft 8in); wing area 26.76 sq m (288 sq ft)
Armament:	six .5in (12.7mm) machine guns

The F-86E Sabre introduced an all-moving tailplane that improved handling as the Sabre neared the speed of sound. The pilot of F-86E 'Four Kings and a Queen', Cecil Foster, was 1st Lieutenant of the 16th Fighter Interceptor Squadron, he was the top-scoring 16th FIS pilot, with nine victories.

F-86E-10

SPECIFICATIONS	
Country of origin:	United States
Type:	single-engined jet fighter
Powerplant:	one 23.1kN (5200lb) thrust General Electric J47-GE-13 turbojet engine
Performance:	maximum speed 965km/h (600mph); range 530km (329 miles); service ceiling 14,600 m (48,000 ft)
Weights:	empty 4700kg (10,500lb); maximum 6300kg (13,791lb)
Dimensions:	span 11.3m (37ft 1in); length 11.4m (37ft 6in); height 4.4m (14ft 8in); wing area 26.76 sq m (288 sq ft)
Armament:	six .5in (12.7mm) machine guns

Walker 'Bud' Mahurin was a World War II ace and commander of the 4th Fighter Interceptor Group. His final score was 24.5, including 3.5 MiGs. 'Half' scores were credited for kills shared between pilots, each of whom damaged the target.

F-86F-30

SPECIFICATIONS	
Country of origin:	United States
Type:	single-engined jet fighter-bomber
Powerplant:	one 26.3kN (5910lb) thrust General Electric J47-GE-27 turbojet engine
Performance:	maximum speed at sea level 1091km/h (678mph); service ceiling 15,240m (50,000ft); range 914km (568 miles)
Weights:	empty 5045kg (11,125lb); maximum loaded 9350kg (20,611lb)
Dimensions:	wingspan 11.3m (37ft 1in); length 11.43m (37ft 6in); height 4.47m (14ft 8.75in); wing area 28.15 sq m (302.3 sq ft)
Armament:	six .5in (12.7mm) machine guns; 908kg (2000lb) of bombs

The first fighter-bomber variant of the Sabre was the F-86F. The F-86F-30 had a wider chord wing root and an extra pylon for bombs or drop tanks. This machine was flown by US Marine exchange pilot John Glenn, who shot down three MiGs and went on to later fame as an astronaut and politician.

Nightfighters Over Korea

As on the Eastern Front, the Po-2 biplane was used for night-harassment raids. Destroying these 'Bedcheck Charlies' consumed a lot of resources, including deployment of several types of night fighters. Some were soon more gainfully employed in the night-interdiction role, attacking North Korean truck convoys, trains and other nocturnal activities. Jet night fighters were also used as escorts for night B-29 raids, and there were a small number of night victories over MiGs.

F-82G Twin Mustang

One of the most unusual aircraft of the era, the F-82 was essentially two P-51 fuselages joined with a new wing and powered by Allison engines with counter-rotating propellers. F-82Gs of the 68th Fighter (All-Weather) Squadron scored the first three aerial victories of the war, all by daylight.

SPECIFICATIONS	
Country of origin:	United States
Type:	twin-engined night fighter
Powerplant:	two 1781kW (1380hp) Allison V-1710-143/145 V-12 piston engines
Performance:	maximum speed 740km/h (460mph); range 3605km (2520 miles); service ceiling 11,855m (38,900ft)
Weights:	empty 7271kg (15,997lb); maximum 11,632kg (25,591lb)
Dimensions:	span 15.62m (51ft 3in); length 12.93m (42ft 9in); height 4.22m (13ft 10in); wing area 37.9 sq m (408 sq ft)
Armament:	six .5in (12.7mm) Browning M2 machine guns; 25 127mm (5in) rockets or up to 1800kg (4000lb) of bombs

Lockheed F-94B Starfire

The F-94B, a much-changed derivative of the F-80, arrived in Korea in mid-1951 as a replacement for the F-82G. It struggled against the slower Po-2s and did not destroy one until January 1953, when this 319th FIS jet claimed one. Another was destroyed in a collision, which was fatal to all involved.

SPECIFICATIONS	
Country of origin:	United States
Type:	tandem-seat all-weather interceptor
Powerplant:	one 26.7kN (6000lb) Allison J33-A-33 turbojet
Performance:	maximum speed at 30,000ft, 933km/h (580mph); service ceiling 14,630m (48,000ft); range 1850km/h (1150 miles)
Weights:	empty 5030kg (11,090lb); maximum take-off weight 7125kg (15,710lb)
Dimensions:	wingspan not including tip tanks 11.85m (38ft 10.5in); length 12.2m (40ft 1in); height 3.89m (12ft 8in); wing area 22.13 sq m (238sq ft)
Armament:	four .5in machine guns

Douglas F3D-2 Skynight

The Douglas Skyknight replaced the Tigercat in Korea. Between November 1952 and the end of the war, Marine F3Ds shot down five MiG-15s and a Po-2. The first kill was scored by an aircraft of VMF-(N)-513, whose victim was credited as a Yak-15, although this type was not in the North's inventory.

SPECIFICATIONS	
Country of origin:	United States
Type:	twin-engined jet night fighter
Powerplant:	two 15.1kN (3400lb) thrust Westinghouse J34-WE-36 turbojet engines
Performance:	maximum speed 852km/h (460mph); range 2212km (1374 miles); service ceiling 11,200m (36,700ft)
Weights:	empty 6813kg (14,989lb); maximum 12,151kg (26,731lb)
Dimensions:	span 15.24m (50ft); length 13.85m (45ft 5in); height 4.9m (16ft 1in); wing area 37.2 sq m (400 sq ft)
Armament:	four 20mm Hispano-Suiza M2 cannon

Grumman F7F-3N Tigercat

Tigercats scored only two kills against Po-2s, partly because of their higher speed, which meant they quickly overtook the target once identified. With bombs, rockets and napalm, however, they proved effective at interdiction and night-attack missions.

SPECIFICATIONS	
Country of origin:	United States
Type:	twin-engined night fighter
Powerplant:	two 1566kW (21000hp) Pratt & Whitney R-2800-34W radial piston engines
Performance:	maximum speed 700km/h (435mph); range 1545km (960 miles); service ceiling 12,405m (40,700ft)
Weights:	empty 7380kg (16,270lb); loaded 11,880kg (26,190lb)
Dimensions:	span 15.7m (51ft 6in); length 13.8 (45ft 4in); height 4.6m (15ft 2in); wing area 42.3 sq m (455 sq ft)
Armament:	four 20mm cannon and four .5in (12.7mm) Browning machine guns; up to 1814kg (4000lb) of bombs

Vought F4U-5N Corsair

Marine Corps and Navy squadrons flew F4U-5N Corsairs from austere land bases in Korea. The most successful pilot was Guy Bordelon of the Navy's VC-3, who scored five kills. The AN/APS-6 radar of the F4U-5N had a range of about 8km (5 miles).

SPECIFICATIONS	
Country of origin:	United States
Type:	single-engined night fighter
Powerplant:	one 1827kW (2450hp) Pratt & Whitney radial piston engine
Performance:	maximum speed 718km/h (446mph); range 2425km (1507 miles); service ceiling 11,308m (41,500ft)
Weights:	empty 4175kg (8873lb); maximum 6654kg (13,846lb)
Dimensions:	10.16m (41ft); length 10.27m (33ft 8in); height 4.5m (14ft 9in); wing area 29.17 sq m (314 sq ft)
Armament:	four 20mm M3 cannon; 10 127mm (5in) rockets or up to 2390kg (5200lb) of bombs

British V-Bombers

Three manufacturers responded to a 1946 requirement for a new British heavy jet bomber, with three designs – the Valiant, Victor and Vulcan – entering service in that order from 1954 to 1956. The Valiant was the most conservative but was put into production partly in case the others failed. The crescent-winged Victor was futuristic in appearance, but still basically conventional, unlike the tailless delta Vulcan. All three saw action as conventional bombers and later use as aerial tankers.

Vickers Valiant B(K).1

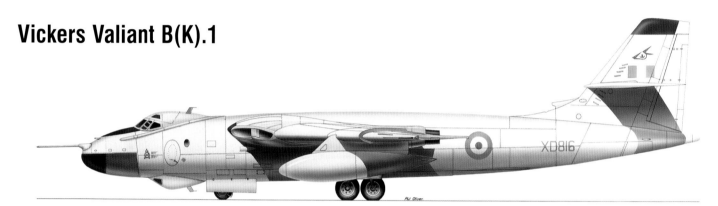

The Valiant was the first to enter service, the first to see action (in the Suez crisis in 1956) and the first to be retired. The introduction of Soviet surface-to-air-missiles (SAMs) saw a switch to low-level operations, which caused excessive fatigue, forcing its complete retirement by 1965.

SPECIFICATIONS	
Country of origin:	United Kingdom
Type:	strategic bomber
Powerplant:	four 44.7kN (10,050lb) Rolls-Royce Avon 204 turbojets
Performance:	maximum speed at high altitude 912km/h (567mph); service ceiling 16,460m (54,000ft); maximum range 7242km (4,500 miles)
Weights:	empty 34,4191kg (75,881lb); maximum loaded with drop tanks 79,378kg (175,000lb)
Dimensions:	wingspan 34.85m (114ft 4in); length 33m (108ft 3in); height 9.8m (32ft 2in); wing area 219.43 sq m (2,362 sq ft)
Armament:	internal weapons bay with provision for up to 9525kg (21,000lb) of conventional or nuclear weapons

Handley Page Victor B.2

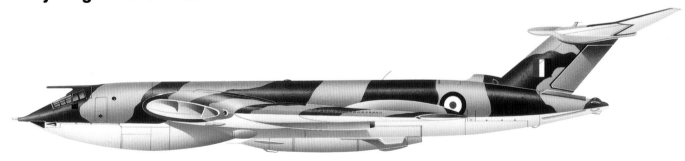

The initial Victor B.1 was replaced by the B.2 with revised wings, more powerful engines and a wider range of weapons options. Conventional bombs were dropped by Victors over Borneo on a single mission during the Confrontation with Indonesia in the early 1960s.

SPECIFICATIONS	
Country of origin:	United Kingdom
Type:	four-seat air-refuelling tanker
Powerplant:	four 91.6kN (20,600lb) Rolls-Royce Conway Mk 201 turbofans
Performance:	max speed 1030km/h (640mph); maximum cruising height 18,290m (60,000ft)
Weights:	empty 41,277kg (91,000lb); maximum take-off 105,687kg (233,000lb)
Dimensions:	wingspan 36.58m (120ft); length 35.05m (114ft 11in); height 9.2m (30ft 1.5in); wing area 223.52 sq m (2,406 sq ft)
Armament:	up to 35 1000lb (450kg) bombs

Handley Page Victor K.2

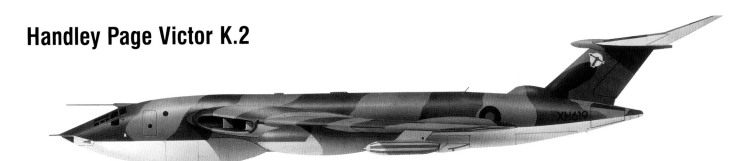

When the Victor B.1 was retired from the bombing role, a number were refitted as tankers. The same happened with the B.2, which became the K.2 tanker, with three refuelling points. Victor K.2s became the last V-bombers in service, retiring from RAF service in 1993.

SPECIFICATIONS	
Country of origin:	United Kingdom
Type:	four-seat air-refuelling tanker
Powerplant:	four 91.6kN (20,600lb) Rolls-Royce Conway Mk 201 turbofans
Performance:	max speed 1030km/h (640mph); maximum cruising height 18,290m (60,000ft); range with internal fuel 7,400km (4,600 miles)
Weights:	empty 41,277kg (91,000lb); maximum take-off 105,687kg (233,000lb)
Dimensions:	wingspan 36.58m (120ft); length 35.05m (114ft 11in); height 9.2m (30ft 1.5in); wing area 223.52 sq m (2406 sq ft)
Armament:	none

Avro Vulcan B.1

The Vulcan was the most distinctive of the V-bombers. The B.1 version entered service in 1957, and was used for a number of record-breaking long-range flights. Able to carry a range of British and American weapons, most B.1s were painted white to reflect the flash of a nuclear explosion.

SPECIFICATIONS	
Country of origin:	United Kingdom
Type:	Four-engined strategic bomber
Powerplant:	four 48.93kN (11,000lb) Bristol Siddeley Olympus 101 thrust turbojet engines
Performance:	maximum speed 1017km/h (632mph); range 6293km (3910 miles); service ceiling 17,000m (55,000ft)
Weights:	empty 37,909kg (83,573lb); maximum 86,000kg (190,00 lb)
Armament:	21,000lb (9500kg) of conventional bombs or single nuclear weapon
Dimensions:	span 30.3m (99ft 5in); length 30.5 m (97ft 1in); height 8.1m (26ft 6in); wing area 330.2 sq m (3554 sq ft)

Avro Vulcan B.2

The smoother leading edge identified the B.2 version of the Vulcan, which also had more powerful engines and strengthened structure. The Vulcan's only combat missions were flown in the Falklands War, including three by Vulcan B.2A XM607, illustrated here.

SPECIFICATIONS	
Country of origin:	United Kingdom
Type:	low-level strategic bomber
Powerplant:	four 88.9kN (20,000lb) Olympus Mk.301 turbojets
Performance:	maximum speed 1038km/h (645mph) at high altitude; service ceiling 19,810m (65,000ft); range with normal bomb load about 7403km/h (4600 miles)
Weights:	maximum take-off weight 113,398kg (250,000lb)
Dimensions:	wingspan 33.83m (111ft); length 30.45m (99ft 11in); height 8.28m (27ft 2in); wing area 368.26 sq m (3964 sq ft)
Armament:	internal weapon bay for up to 21,454kg (47,198lb) bombs

NORAD

North American Air Defense Command (NORAD) was established to counter the threat of Soviet bombers and missiles attacking over the North Pole. Its assets included Arctic radar stations, interceptors and missiles. Fighters were armed with barrages of unguided rockets or even nuclear-tipped rockets for destroying bomber formations. Canada's contribution included the CF-100. America convinced the Canadian government to abandon the much more sophisticated CF-105 Arrow in favour of Bomarc SAMs, which was then cancelled, and Canada was sold Voodoo fighters instead.

North American F-86D Sabre Dog

SPECIFICATIONS

Country of origin:	United States
Type:	single-seat night and all-weather interceptor
Powerplant:	one 33.3kN (7500lb) General Electric J47-GE-17B turbojet
Performance:	maximum speed 1138km/h (707mph); range 1344km (835 miles); service ceiling 16,640m (54,600ft)
Weight:	loaded 7756kg (17,100lb)
Dimensions:	span 11.3m (37ft 1in); length 12.29m (40ft 4in); height 4.57m (15ft);
Armament:	24 7mm (2.75in) 'Mighty Mouse' air-to-air unguided rocket projectiles

The most famous of the early generation jet fighters, the F-86 Sabre flew for the first time in October 1947, with the first operational aircraft delivered two years later. During the Korean War, Sabres claimed the destruction of 810 enemy aircraft, 792 of them MiG-15s. Numerous variants were built, with most made by Canadair destined for NATO airforces. It was also built under licence in Australia.

Avro Canada CF-100 Mk 4b

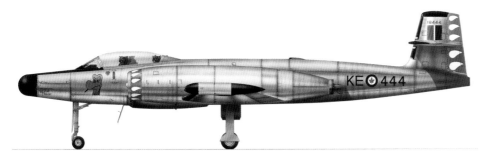

The CF-100 Canuck, usually called the 'Clunk', was Canada's main interceptor for most of the 1950s. Just under 700 were built in five marks. Some had an eight-gun pack under the fuselage, but the primary weapons were rocket pods, which were fired when the radar judged the target was in range.

SPECIFICATIONS	
Country of origin:	Canada
Type:	twin-engined all-weather fighter
Powerplant:	two 32.5kN (7300lb) thrust Avro Canada Orenda 11 turbojet engines
Performance:	maximum speed 888km/h (552mph) ;range 3200km (1988 miles); service ceiling 13,700m (45,000ft)
Weight:	loaded 15,170kg (33,450lb)
Dimensions:	span 17.4m (57ft 2 in); length 16.5m (54ft 2in); height 4.4m (14ft 6in); wing area 54.9 sq m (591 sq ft)
Armament:	58 70mm (2.75in) rockets

McDonnell F-101B Voodoo

The F-101B was a two-seat, all-weather, long-range interceptor version of the Voodoo, accommodating a pilot and radar operator to work the MG-13 fire-control system and more powerful engines. By fitting a tandem cockpit, internal fuel capacity was sacrificed. A total of 407 were built, with final delivery taking place in March 1961.

SPECIFICATIONS	
Country of origin:	United States
Type:	two-seat all-weather long-range interceptor
Powerplant:	two 75.1kN (16,900lb) Pratt & Whitney J57-P-55 turbojets
Performance:	maximum speed at 12190m (40,000ft) 1965km/h (1221mph); service ceiling 16,705m (54,800ft); range 2494km (1550 miles)
Weights:	empty 13,141kg (28,970lb); maximum take-off 23,768kg (52,400lb)
Dimensions:	wingspan 12.09m (39ft 8in); length 20.54m (67ft 4.75in); height 5.49m (18ft); wing area 34.19 sq m (368 sq ft)
Armament:	two Mb-1 Genie missiles with nuclear warheads and four AIM-4C,-4D, or 4G Falcon missiles, or six Falcon missiles

Air Sea Rescue

In an era before long-range helicopters, the only way to find and aid survivors of foundering vessels, downed military pilots and passengers of ditched airliners was to drop supplies or lifeboats, or land a flying boat nearby. The USAF Air Rescue Service built on its wartime experience by developing rescue versions of the B-29 and B-17. Flying boats and amphibians remained in service as rescue craft long after their replacement in other roles.

Boeing B-17H Fortress (later SB-17G)

First known as the SB-17G and later redesignated B-17H, surplus Flying Fortresses were converted to the ASR role with the addition of search radar and droppable A-1 lifeboat. This laminated mahogany vessel had twin engines and berths, and supplies for 20 survivors.

SPECIFICATIONS	
Country of origin:	United States
Type:	10-seat heavy bomber
Powerplant:	four 895kW (1200hp) Wright R-1820-97 nine-cylinder radial engines
Performance:	maximum speed 486km/h (302mph); service ceiling 10,850m (35,600ft); range 2897km (1800 miles)
Weights:	empty 20,212kg (44,560lb); maximum take-off 32,659kg (72,000lb)
Dimensions:	span 31.63m (103ft 9.4in); length 22.78m (74ft 9 in); height 5.82m (19ft 1in)
Armament:	none

Martin PBM-5 Mariner

The PBM Mariner was built as a patrol and bomber flying boat, but variants were created for the Coast Guard and surplus aircraft sold to several nations. The Uruguayan Navy obtained three PBM-5Es in the mid-1950s and used them for search-and-rescue duties.

SPECIFICATIONS	
Country of origin:	United States
Type:	nine-seat maritime patrol and anti-submarine flying-boat
Powerplant:	two 1566kW (2100hp) Wright Double Wasp radial piston engines
Performance:	maximum speed 340km/h (211mph); range 4345km (2700 miles); service ceiling 6160m (20,200ft)
Weights:	empty 15,422kg (34,000lb); maximum take-off 27,216kg (60,000lb)
Dimensions:	span 35.97m (118ft); length 24.33m (79ft 10in); height 8.38m (27ft 6in); wing area 130.8 sq m (1408 sq ft)
Armament:	nacelle bays and underwing racks with provision for up to 3628kg (8000lb) of bombs or depth charges

Grumman HU-16 Albatross

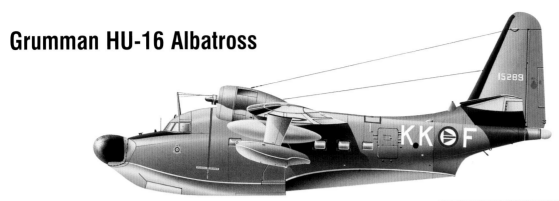

Norway was one of over 20 countries to use the Albatross. Two units, including 333 Skvadron at Andøya (illustrated), used the aircraft for SAR and other duties, including medical evacuation, postal delivery and polar-bear tracking. The Norwegian SA-16Bs were passed on to Greece in 1968.

SPECIFICATIONS	
Country of origin:	United States
Type:	twin-engined amphibian
Powerplant:	two 1063kW (1425hp) Wright R-1820-76 Cyclone radial piston engines
Performance:	maximum speed 380km/h (236mph); range 4587km (2850 miles); service ceiling 6553m (21,500ft)
Weights:	empty 9100kg (20,000lb); maximum 14,969lb (33,000kg)
Dimensions:	span 24.4m (80ft); length 19.16m (62ft 10in); height 7.8m (25ft 10in); wing area 82 sq m (883 sq ft)
Armament:	none

Dornier Do 24T-2

In autumn 1937, licensed production of 48 Do 24K-2 aircraft was started by Aviolanda in the Netherlands. Only 25 had been delivered before the German occupation of the Netherlands in May 1940. Manufacturing was re-established under German control, with 159 examples built and additional aircraft supplied by French production throughout and after the war.

SPECIFICATIONS	
Country of origin:	Germany
Type:	air-sea rescue and transport flying boat
Powerplant:	three 746kW (1000hp) BMW-Bramo 323R-2 Fafnir radial piston engines
Performance:	maximum speed 340km/h (211mph); range 2900km (1802 miles; service ceiling 5900m (19,355ft)
Weights:	empty 9200kg (20,286lb); maximim take-off weight 18,400kg (40,565lb)
Dimensions:	span 27m (88ft 7in); length 22.05m (72ft 4in); height 5.75m (18ft 10in); wing area 108 sq m (1163 sq ft)
Armament:	one 20mm MG 151 cannon in dorsal turret, two 7.92mm MG 15 machine guns (in bow turret and tail turret)

Douglas SC-54D Skymaster

Convair converted 38 Douglas C-54s for the USAF Air Rescue Service as the SC-54G. Most of the changes were internal, but a large transparent blister was added to the starboard rear fuselage to aid visual searches. Their main role was dropping supplies and rescuers to people lost in Arctic regions.

SPECIFICATIONS	
Country of origin:	United States
Type:	four-engined military search and rescue aircraft
Powerplant:	four 1014kW (1360hp) Pratt & Whitney R-2000-11 radial piston engines
Performance:	maximum speed 442km/h (275mph); range 6400km (4000 miles); service ceiling 6800m (22,300ft)
Dimensions:	span 35.8m (117ft 6in); length 28.6m (93ft 10in); height 8.38m (27ft 6in); wing area 136 sq m (1460 sq ft)
Weights:	empty 17,660kg (38,930lb); maximum 33,000kg (73,000lb)
Armament:	none

Hawker Hunter

The Hunter was one of the most successful British jet fighters, with nearly 2000 delivered to the RAF, FAA and 20 foreign users. Hunters were built under licence in Belgium and the Netherlands as well as by Hawker in the United Kingdom, who also refurbished and resold export aircraft to new customers. The Hunter saw action in numerous conflicts, in particular with India against Pakistan and with the RAF at Suez, in Aden and Borneo.

Hunter F.1

Without question the most successful post-war British fighter aircraft, the Hunter has a grace that complements its effectiveness as a warplane. Entering service in July 1954, the aircraft was produced in numerous guises and remained in service for 40 years. The F.1 was easily supersonic in a shallow dive.

SPECIFICATIONS	
Country of origin:	United Kingdom
Type:	single-seat fighter
Powerplant:	one 28.9kN (6500lb) Rolls-Royce Avon 100 turbojet
Performance:	maximum speed at sea level 1144km/h (710mph); service ceiling 15,240m (50,000ft); range on internal fuel 689km (490 miles)
Weights:	empty 5501kg (12,128lb); loaded 7347kg (16,200lb)
Dimensions:	wingspan 10.26m (33ft 8in); length 13.98m (45ft 10.5in);height 4.02m (13ft 2in); wing area 32.42 sq m (349 sq ft)
Armament:	four 30mm Aden cannon; underwing pylons with provision for two 1000lb bombs and 24 3in rockets

Hunter F.5

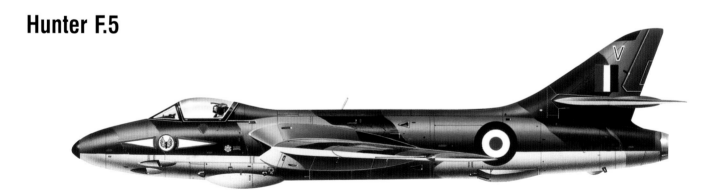

Unlike other Hunters, the F.5 was built with Armstrong-Siddeley Sapphire engines rather than Rolls-Royce Avons. It entered service in 1954, and only 45 were built. Like most subsequent models, they featured collectors for empty cannon shell cases under the fuselage, known as 'Sabrinas'.

SPECIFICATIONS	
Country of origin:	United Kingdom
Type:	single-seat fighter
Powerplant:	one 35.59kN (8000lb) Armstrong-Siddeley Sapphire turbojet engine
Performance:	maximum speed at sea level 1144km/h (710mph); service ceiling 15,240m (50,000ft); range on internal fuel 689km (490 miles)
Weights:	empty 5501kg (12,128lb); loaded 8501kg (18,742lb)
Dimensions:	wingspan 10.26m (33ft 8in); length 13.98m (45ft 10.5in);height 4.02m (13ft 2in); wing area 32.42 sq m (349 sq ft)
Armament:	four 30mm Aden cannon; up to 2722kg (6000lb) of bombs or rockets

Hunter F.58

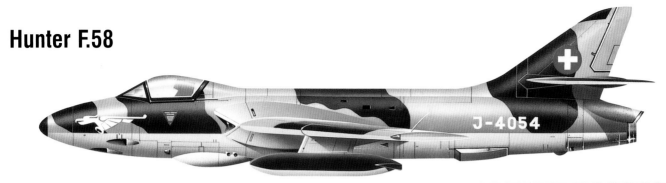

SPECIFICATIONS

Country of origin:	United Kingdom
Type:	single-seat fighter
Powerplant:	one 45.13kN (10,145lb) thrust Rolls-Royce Avon 207 turbojet engine
Performance:	maximum speed at sea level 1144km/h (710mph); service ceiling 15,240m (50,000ft); range on internal fuel 689km (490 miles)
Weights:	empty 6405kg (14,122lb) maximum 17,750kg (24,600lb)
Dimensions:	wingspan 10.26m (33ft 8in); length 13.98m (45ft 10.5in);height 4.02m (13ft 2in); wing area 32.42 sq m (349 sq ft)
Armament:	four 30mm Aden cannon; up to 2722kg (6000lb) of bombs or rockets; AIM-9 Sidewinder AAMs or AGM-65 ASMs

The Swiss Air Force was the last European user of the Hunter, retiring the type in 1994 after over 30 years of service. Switzerland's F.58s, which were a version of the RAF Hunter F.6, could be equipped with air-to-air and air-to-ground missiles. They also equipped the Patrouille Swiss aerobatic team.

Hunter T.8M

SPECIFICATIONS

Country of origin:	United Kingdom
Type:	dual-seat advanced trainer
Powerplant:	one 35.6kN (8000lb) Rolls-Royce Avon 122 turbojet
Performance:	maximum speed at sea level 1117km/h (694mph); service ceiling 14,325m (47,000ft); range on internal fuel 689km (429 miles)
Weights:	empty 6406kg (14,122lb); loaded 7802kg (17,200lb)
Dimensions:	wingspan 10.26m (33ft 8in); length 14.89m (48ft 10in); height 4.02m (13ft 2in); wing area 32.42 sq m (349 sq ft)
Armament:	two 30mm Aden cannon with 150 rounds

Production models of the Hunter T.7 trainer began entering service in 1958, with the T.8 derived for naval use. Common to all versions were the side-by-side seating and dual controls of the enlarged cockpit. Two-seat trainers were supplied to a number of countries.

Hunter T.75A

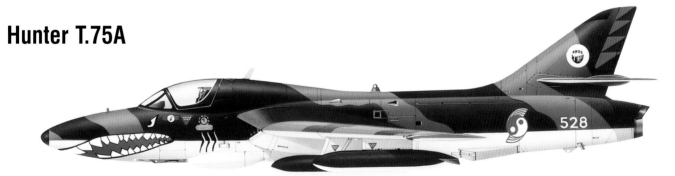

SPECIFICATIONS

Country of origin:	United Kingdom
Type:	dual-seat advanced trainer
Powerplant:	one 45.13kN (10,145lb) thrust Rolls-Royce Avon 207 turbojet engine
Performance:	maximum speed at sea level 1117km/h (694mph); service ceiling 14,325m (47,000ft); range on internal fuel 689km (429 miles)
Weights:	empty 6406kg (14,122lb); loaded 7802kg (17,200lb)
Dimensions:	wingspan 10.26m (33ft 8in); length 14.89m (48ft 10in); height 4.02m (13ft 2in); wing area 32.42 sq m (349 sq ft)
Armament:	four 30mm Aden cannon

Singapore ordered Hunters in 1968 and operated them into the early 1990s in the air defence role. Singapore's eight two-seat T.75s were converted from single-seat F.4 models before delivery, whereas its 38 single-seaters had mostly been FGA.9 models.

X-Planes

X stands for the unknown in mathematics and physics, and the US aircraft designated in the X series from the 1940s until the present day pushed the boundaries of flight to extremes of speed and altitude that had never before been achieved. Early successes of the programme, mainly conducted from Edwards Air Force Base in the Mojave Desert, included the first scientifically measured flights past the speed of sound and then double that speed, or Mach 2.

Bell X-1A

This development of the classic X-1 duplicated its predecessor's record-breaking achievements, but throughout its life lived under the shadow of accidents. The X-1A had a longer fuselage than the X-1, improved cockpit visibility and turbo-driven fuel pumps. In 1953, veteran high-speed test pilot Major Charles 'Chuck' Yeager flew the rocket plane to 2560km/h (1650mph) at a height of 21,350m (70,000ft), smashing the previous world record.

SPECIFICATIONS	
Country of origin:	United States
Type:	high-altitude high-speed research aircraft
Powerplant:	one 26.7kN (6000lb) thrust (at sea level) four-chamber Reaction Motors XLR11-RM-5 rocket engine
Performance:	maximum speed Mach 2.44 or 2655.4km/h (1646.35mph); endurance approximately 4 min 40 sec; service ceiling over 27432m (90,000ft)
Weights:	empty 3296kg (7251lb); loaded 7478kg (16,452lb)
Dimensions:	span 8.53m (28 ft); length 10.9m (35ft 8in); height 3.3m (10ft 10in); wing area 39.6 sq m (426 sq ft)
Armament:	none

Bell X-2

Bell began working on its X-2 in October 1945. The aircraft were rocket-powered, and designed for the analysis of structural and heating effects at speeds up to Mach 3.5 and altitudes up to 38,100m (125,000ft). Captive trials began in July 1951. The first aircraft exploded, while the second completed 12 very successful flights, before crashing on its thirteenth. Nonetheless, the type paved the way for future aircraft programmes.

SPECIFICATIONS	
Country of origin:	United States
Type:	single-seat supersonic research aircraft
Powerplant:	one 66.7kN (15,000lb) thrust Curtiss-Wright XLR25-CW-1 rocket engine
Performance:	maximum speed 3058km/h (1896mph); service ceiling 38405m (126,000ft); endurance 10 min 55 sec of powered flight; fuel capacity 2960 litres (782 gal) liquid oxygen; 3376 litres (892 gal) ethyl alcohol and water
Weights:	empty 5314kg (11,690lb); maximum take-off 11299kg (24,858lb)
Dimensions:	span 9.75m (32 ft); length 13.41m (44ft); height 4.11m (13ft 6in); wing area 24.19 sq m (260 sq ft)
Armament:	none

X-PLANES TIMELINE

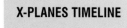 1948

 1951

 1952

Douglas X-3A Stiletto

First flying in 1952, the X-3 looked strange, with the pilot positioned in a pressurized cabin on a downwards-firing ejection seat. It was hard to handle when taxiing, tricky on take-off and very difficult to fly. Design of the X-3 was of unprecedented complexity because of the use of titanium and other advanced materials. Unfortunately, it was underpowered and offered little to researchers.

SPECIFICATIONS	
Coury of origin:	United States
Type:	single-seat research aircraft
Powerplant:	two 21.6kN (4860lb thrust) Westinghouse J34-WE-17 turbojet engines
Performance:	maximum speed 1136km/h (704mph); take-off speed 418 km/h (260mph); endurance one hour; range 805km (500 miles); service ceiling 11580m (38,000ft)
Weights:	empty 7312kg (16,086lb); maximum take-off 10813kg (23,788lb)
Dimensions:	span 6.91m (22ft 8in) length 20.35m (66ft 9in) height 3.81m (12ft 6in) wing area 15.47 sq m (166 sq ft)
Armament:	none

Bell X-4

The diminutive X-4 tested the tailless configuration at speeds of Mach 0.85 and higher. Drawing on experience gleaned from Northrop flying wings of the 1940s – and sharing some characteristics with today's B-2 stealth bomber – the two X-4s accumulated a wealth of data for the US Air Force and the National Advisory Committee for Aeronautics (NACA, the forerunner to NASA).

SPECIFICATIONS	
Coury of origin:	United States
Type:	single-seat experimental research aircraft
Powerplant:	two 7.12kN (1600lb thrust) Westinghouse XJ30-WE-7 turbojets; later two Westinghouse J30-W-9 turbojets, using standard JP-4 jet engine fuel
Performance:	Mach 0.92 or 1123km/h (630mph) at 10,000m (33,000 ft) under extreme test conditions; range 676km (420 miles); service ceiling 13906m (42,300 ft)
Weights:	empty 2294kg (5507lb); maximum loaded 3547kg (7803lb)
Dimensions:	span 8.18m (27ft) length 7.19m (23ft) height 4.58m (15ft) wing area 18.58 sq m (300 sq. ft)
Armament:	none

Bell X-5

US troops occupying the town of Oberammergau, Germany, in 1945, discovered an experimental facility with the almost complete Messerschmitt P.1101 prototype. The P.1101 was brought to the US and Bell won a contract to build two test machines based on the German design. The two X-5s were very similar in layout to the P.1101, but considerably more complex.

SPECIFICATIONS	
Coury of origin:	United States
Type:	single-seat experimental research aircraft
Powerplant:	one 21.8kN (4890lb-thrust) Allison J35-A-17 turbojet engine
Performance:	maximum speed approx. 1046km/h (650mph); range 1207km (750 miles); service ceiling 13000m (42,650ft)
Weights:	empty 2880kg (6336lb); maximum take-off weight 4536kg (9980lb)
Dimensions:	span unswept 9.39m (31ft) span swept 5.66m (19ft); length 10.16m (33ft); height 3.66m (12ft); wing area 16.26 sq m (175 sq ft)
Armament:	none

1953

X-Planes Part Two

The US Navy contributed to research flying with the equally experimental Skyrocket series and other record-breakers. The National Advisory Committee on Aeronautics (NACA) became NASA (National Air and Space Administration), to better reflect its work at the edges of the atmosphere and beyond. While one branch of NASA worked towards the Moon landings with ballistic rockets, Edwards AFB saw the limits of wingborne flight expanded to the threshold of space by the X-15.

Douglas D-558-1 Skystreak

Douglas designed the Skystreak and then the Skyrocket in response to a requirement for high-speed research aircraft. The first Skystreak flew in 1947, and broke the world speed record in August of that year. The supersonic D-558-II Skyrocket had a swept wing and fuselage that contained the pilot's jettisonable compartment, turbojet, rocket engine, landing gear and fuel.

SPECIFICATIONS	
Country of origin:	United States
Type:	swept-wing research aircraft
Powerplant:	one 13.61kN (3,059lb) thrust Westinghouse J34-W-22 plus one 27.2 kN (6117lb) thrust Reaction Motors XLR-8 rocket motor
Performance:	maximum speed (turbojet only) 941km/h (583mph); (mixed power) 1159km/h (718mph); (rocket power only) 2012km/h (1247mph)
Weights:	Maximum take-off 6925kg (15,267lb) (turbojet) (mixed powerplant) 7171kg (15,800lb)
Dimensions:	span 7.62m (25ft); length 13.79m (45ft); height 3.51m (11ft) wing area 16.26 sq m (125 sq ft)
Armament:	none

Ryan X-14B

An experimental aircraft, the X-14 constantly evolved, being powered by three different engines throughout its long life. As a VTOL research aircraft capable of hovering, weight and balance was of immense importance. The fuel tanks were external and underwing, keeping them close to the centre of gravity, and the ejector seat was excluded for weight considerations.

SPECIFICATIONS	
Country of origin:	United States
Type:	VTOL research aircraft
Powerplant:	two 13.4kN (3015lb) thrust General Electric J85-GE-19 non-afterburning turbojets, fitted late in the X-14 programme
Performance:	maximum speed 277km/h (172mph); range 480km (300 miles) service ceiling 5500m (18000ft)
Weights:	empty 1437kg (3160lb); maximum take-off weight 1934kg (4255lb)
Dimensions:	span 10.3m (33ft. 9in); length 7.92m (26ft); height 2.68m (8ft 9in); wing area 16.68 sq m (179 sq ft)
Armament:	none

X-PLANES TIMELINE

 1947    1957    1959

North American X-15

After Chuck Yeager piloted the Bell X-1 beyond Mach 1 in 1947, a line of rocket-powered record-breakers followed, climaxing in the North American X-15. A sleek black rocket with tiny wings, the X-15 flew higher and faster than anything before or since. Most of the 199 powered missions between 1960 and 1968 probed the limits of possibility, smashing all previous records in the process.

SPECIFICATIONS

Country of origin:	United States
Type:	single-seat hyper-velocity rocket-powered research aircraft
Powerplant:	one 313kN (70,4000lb) thrust Thiokol (Reaction Motors) XLR99-RM-2 single-chamber throttleable liquid-propellant rocket engine
Performance:	maximum speed 7297km/h (4534mph); maximum altitude 10,7960m (354,000ft); time to height 140 sec from launch at 15,000m (49,212ft) to 10,0000m (320,000ft); range 450km (280 miles)
Weights:	loaded 25,460kg (56,000lb)
Dimensions:	span 6.81m (22ft 4in); length 15.47m (50ft 9in); height 3.96m (12ft 11in); wing area 18.58 sq m (200 sq ft)
Armament:	none

Northrop X-24

To withstand the frictional heating that occurs during re-entry to the Earth's atmosphere, a blunt-nosed, wingless, lifting body was designed. A forerunner of today's Space Shuttle, the X-24 was taken to altitude under the wing of an NB-52B, making its first gliding flight in April 1969. Twenty-eight powered flights were completed before the aircraft was modified to become the X-24B.

SPECIFICATIONS

Country of origin:	United States
Type:	lifting body aircraft for research into reusable spacecraft approach patterns
Powerplant:	one 43.64kN (9820lb) thrust Thiokol XLR-RM-13 four-chamber regeneratively cooled rocket engine, plus two 2.22kN (500lb) thrust hydrogen-peroxide rocket engines
Performance:	maximum speed 1873km/h (1161mph); service ceiling 22,595m (74,100ft)
Weights:	maximum 6260kg (13,772lb)
Dimensions:	span 5.8m (19ft) length 11.43m (37ft 6in); height 3.15m (10ft 4in); lifting surface area 30.66 sq m (330 sq ft)
Armament:	none

Grumman X-29

Grumman won a 1981 contract to build X-29 research planes, and managed to slash costs by using parts from many aircraft: F-5 fuselage and nosewheel, F/A-18 Hornet engine and F-16 main undercarriage. The result was more than the sum of its parts. In several years of experiments, the X-29 demonstrated an ability to manoeuvre at angles of attack as high as 67°. The key feature was that the wings were swept forwards rather than back.

SPECIFICATIONS

Country of origin:	United States
Type:	single-seat forward-swept-wing high-agility research aircraft
Powerplant:	one 71.17kN (15,965lb) thrust General Electric F404-GE-400 turbofan
Performance:	maximum speed Mach 1.87 or 1900km/h at 10,000m (1178mph at 33,000ft); range 560km (347 miles); service ceiling 15,300m (50,000ft)
Weights:	empty 6260kg (13,772lb); maximum 8074kg (17,763lb)
Dimensions:	span 8.29m (27ft) length 16.44m (54ft) height 4.26m (14ft) wing area 188.8 sq m (2031 sq ft)
Armament:	none

1973

1984

Shooting Stars

Lockheed's P-80 was the first successful American jet fighter. It was designed in fewer than 180 days around the British Halford H.1 (Goblin) engine, by a Lockheed team led by Clarence 'Kelly' Johnson. Some 1718 were made in many different variants, from reconnaissance platforms to trainers to supersonic interceptors. The prefix was later changed from 'P' (Pursuit) to 'F' (Fighter). The F-80 C-5 was the final production model, with more powerful engines.

F-80C

The Lockheed P-80 first flew in January 1944, and P-80s were flying under combat conditions in Italy a year later. By the time of the Korean War, the aircraft were considered somewhat obsolete, but nonetheless flew 15,000 sorties in the first four months and shot down the first MiG-15 in November 1950, in what is thought to have been the first jet combat.

SPECIFICATIONS	
Country of origin:	United States
Type:	single-engined fighter-bomber
Powerplant:	one 24kN (5400lb) thrust Allison J33-A-35 turbojet engine
Performance:	maximum speed 965km/h (600mph); service ceiling 14,000m (46,000ft); range 1930km (1200 miles)
Weights:	empty 3819kg (8420lb); maximum 7646kg (16,856lb)
Dimensions:	wingspan 11.81m (38ft 9in); length 10.49m (34ft 5in); height 3.43m (11ft 3in); wing area 22.07 sq m (237.6 sq ft)
Armament:	six .5in (12.7mm) machine guns; two 454kg (1000lb) bombs or eight 2.75in rockets

QF-80 Shooting Star

Many surplus F-80s were converted into pilotless drones at the end of their service lives. The Sperry Gyroscope Company undertook many QF-80 conversions, creating an aircraft that could be shot at by air, land and sea weapons systems or used for various test missions.

SPECIFICATIONS	
Country of origin:	United States
Type:	single-seat fighter bomber
Powerplant:	one 24kN (5400lb) Allison J33-A-35 turbojet
Performance:	maximum speed at sea level 966km/h (594mph); service ceiling 14,265m (46,800ft); range 1328km (825 miles)
Weights:	empty 3819kg (8420lb); maximum take-off weight 7646kg (16,856lb)
Dimensions:	wingspan 11.81m (38ft 9in); length 10.49m (34ft 5in); height 3.43m (11ft 3in); wing area 22.07 sq m (237.6 sq ft)
Armament:	none

RF-80A Shooting Star

Originally designated FP-80A, the RF-80A was a modification of Shooting Star fighters into reconnaissance aircraft by removing armament and installing a new camera nose. The 66 converted aircraft were widely used in Korea.

SPECIFICATIONS	
Country of origin:	United States
Type:	single-seat photo reconnaissance
Powerplant:	one 24kN (5400lb) Allison J33-A-35 turbojet
Performance:	maximum speed at sea level 966km/h (594mph); service ceiling 14,265m (46,800ft); range 1328km (825 miles)
Weights:	empty 3819kg (8420lb); maximum take-off weight 7646kg (16,856lb)
Dimensions:	wingspan 11.81m (38ft 9in); length 10.49m (34ft 5in); height 3.43m (11ft 3in); wing area 22.07 sq m (237.6 sq ft)
Armament:	none

T-33A

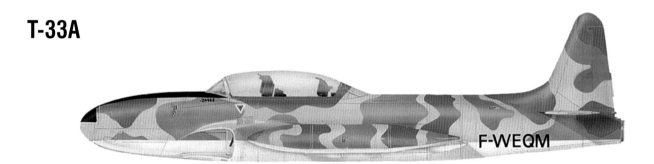

The Lockheed T-33, also named Shooting Star, was the most numerous Western jet trainer of the post-war era, used by nearly 40 nations. This civil-marked ex-Canadian T-33 was refurbished with modern avionics for Bolivia in the 1990s, and still serves in the ground-attack role.

SPECIFICATIONS	
Country of origin:	United States
Type:	two-seat jet trainer
Powerplant:	one 24kN (5400lb) Allison J33-A-35 turbojet
Performance:	maximum speed 879km/h (546mph); service ceiling 14,630m (48,000ft); endurance 3 hours 7 minutes
Weights:	empty 3667kg (8084lb); maximum take-off weight 6551kg (14,442lb)
Dimensions:	wingspan 11.85m (38ft 10.5in); length 11.51m (37ft 10in); height 3.56m (11ft 8in); wing area 21.81 sq m (234.8 sq ft)
Armament:	two .5mm machine guns; wide variety of ordnance in COIN role

F-94 Starfire

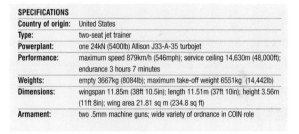

Retaining many of the features of the F-80 and T-33 aircraft from which it was developed, the tandem-seat Starfire was conceived in 1949 as a radar-equipped, all-weather interceptor. The first deliveries began in June 1950. Two improved variants were produced – the F-94B with a blind landing system, and the F-94C, with 24 Mighty Mouse unguided air-to-air rockets in the nose.

SPECIFICATIONS	
Country of origin:	United Kingdom
Type:	tandem-seat all-weather interceptor
Powerplant:	one 26.7kN (6000lb) Allison J33-A-33 turbojet
Performance:	maximum speed at 30,000ft 933km/h (580mph); service ceiling 14,630m (48,000ft); range 1850km (1150 miles)
Weights:	empty 5030kg (11,090lb); maximum take-off weight 7125kg (15,710lb)
Dimensions:	wingspan not including tip tanks 11.85m (38ft 10.5in); length 12.2m (40ft 1in); height 3.89m (12ft 8in); wing area 22.13 sq m (238 sq ft)
Armament:	four .5in machine guns

Navy Jets

Britain's Royal Navy made innovations in naval aviation, including jet operations from carriers, but it was the United States that first put operational jet squadrons on carriers. The greater speeds and slower engine response of jets contributed to terrible accident rates during carrier operations. Further British developments included angled carrier decks, which allowed aircraft to miss arrestor wires without threatening others parked forward, and the advanced mirror landing system.

McDonnell F4H-1 Phantom II

In 1942, the Bureau of Aeronautics entrusted McDonnell with the task of designing and building the two prototypes of what would become the US Navy's first carrier-based, turbojet-powered, single-seat fighter. The resulting prototypes were low-wing monoplanes with retractable landing gear, with power provided by two turbojets buried in the wing roots. After first flying in January 1945, the aircraft became the first US jet to be launched and recovered from a carrier.

SPECIFICATIONS	
Country of origin:	United States
Type:	carrier-based fighter
Powerplant:	two 7.1kN (1600lb) Westinghouse J30-WE-20 turbojets
Performance:	maximum cruising speed 771km/h (479mph); service ceiling 12,525m (41,100ft); combat range 1118km (695 miles)
Weights:	empty 3031kg (6683lb); maximum take-off weight 5459kg (12,035lb)
Dimensions:	wingspan 12.42m (40ft 9in); length 11.35m (37ft 3in); height 4.32m (14ft 2in); wing area 24.64 sq m (276 sq ft)
Armament:	four .5in machine guns

Grumman F9F-2 Panther

The Grumman Panther was the first truly successful American carrier-based jet. Nearly 1400 were built for the US Navy, Marines and Argentina. Panthers were the main naval strike aircraft in Korea, where the F9F-2 illustrated flew with VF-781 aboard USS *Oriskany* in 1952.

SPECIFICATIONS	
Country of origin:	United States
Type:	single-engined carrier-based jet fighter-bomber
Powerplant:	one 26.5kN (5950lb) thrust Pratt & Whitney J42-P-6/P-8 turbojet engine
Performance:	maximum speed 925 km/h (575 mph); range 2100km (1300 miles); service ceiling 13,600m (44,600ft)
Weights:	empty 4220kg (9303lb); maximum 7462kg (16,450lb)
Dimensions:	span 11.6m (38ft); length 11.3m (37ft 5in); height 3.8m (11ft 4in); wing area 23 sq m (250 sq ft)
Armament:	four 20mm M2 cannon; up to 910kg (2000lb) bombs, six 5in (127mm) rockets

McDonnell F2H-2 Banshee

SPECIFICATIONS	
Country of origin:	United States
Type:	carrier-based all-weather fighter
Powerplant:	one 14.5kN (3,250lb) Westinghouse J34-WE-34 turbojet
Performance:	maximum cruising speed 933km/h (580mph); service ceiling 14,205m (46,600ft); combat range 1883km (1170 miles)
Weights:	empty 5980kg (13,183lb); maximum take-off weight 11,437kg (25,214lb)
Dimensions:	wingspan 12.73m (41ft 9in); length 14.68m (48ft 2in); height 4.42m (14ft 6in); wing area 27.31 sq m (294 sq ft)
Armament:	four 20mm cannon; underwing racks with provision for two 227kg (500lb) or four 113kg (250lb) bombs

The success of the FH-1 Phantom in US Navy and Marine Corps service meant that it was almost inevitable that McDonnell would be asked to submit a design to succeed the Phantom in service. The first F2H-1 aircraft was delivered to the Navy in August 1948, and was followed by seven sub-variants. The F2H-2 was the second production version, with wingtip fuel tanks. Production total was 56.

North American AJ-2 Savage

SPECIFICATIONS	
Country of origin:	United States
Type:	mixed-powerplant carrier-based bomber
Powerplant:	two 1864kW (2500hp) Pratt & Whitney R-2800-48 piston engines and one 20.46kN (4600lb) thrust Allison J33-A-19 turbo-jet engine
Performance:	maximum speed 758km/h (471mph); range 2623km (1630 miles); service ceiling 12,192m (40,000ft)
Weights:	empty 12,500kg (27,558lb); maximum 23,973kg (52,852lb)
Dimensions:	span 22.91m (75ft 2in); length 19.22m (63ft 1in); height 6.52m (21ft 5in); wing area 78 sq m (836 sq ft)
Armament:	one 3856kg (8500lb) Mk VI nuclear bomb

The AJ Savage was designed to carry a single large atomic bomb from carriers. Its two piston engines were supplemented by a turbojet in the fuselage to give a higher dash speed over the target. It was not a great success as a bomber, and most Savages were converted into tankers.

North American FJ-3M Fury

SPECIFICATIONS	
Country of origin:	United States
Type:	single-seat fighter-bomber
Powerplant:	one 34.7kN (7800lb) Wright J65-W-2 turbojet
Performance:	maximum speed at sea level 1091km/h (678mph); service ceiling 16,640m (54,600ft); range 1344km (835 miles)
Weights:	empty 5051kg (11,125lb); maximum loaded 9350kg (20,611lb)
Dimensions:	wingspan 11.3m (37ft 1in); length 11.43m (37ft 6in); height 4.47m (14ft 8.75in); wing area 27.76 sq m (288 sq ft)
Armament:	six .5 Colt-Browning M-3 with 267 rpg, underwing hardpoints for two tanks or two stores of 454kg (1000lb), plus eight rockets

Both Army and Navy contracts were awarded to North American in 1944 for a jet fighter. The FJ-1 Fury was unremarkable and the FJ-2 was a navalized version of the land-based F-86E Sabre, with folding wings, catapult hitches and arrestor gear. They were superseded by the FJ-3, which had a more powerful engine, a deeper fuselage, a new canopy and increased weapon load.

The Immortal Dakota

First flown in December 1935, the Douglas Sleeper Transport, or DC-3, went on to become the most produced transport aircraft in history. The vast majority were built for military use as C-47s, C-49s, C-53s and other designations, usually known by their British name, Dakota. So many 'Daks' were available as surplus in 1945 that they hampered post-war development of new airliners and light military transports. Turboprop conversions are still used by air forces in Africa and South America.

Dakota III

Among the many roles of the C-47 was to drop supplies to partisans and resistance groups. This Dakota III, equivalent to the C-47A, was based at Araxos, Greece, and used by No 267 Squadron RAF to drop supplies over Romania, Albania and Yugoslavia in 1944.

SPECIFICATIONS

Country of origin:	United States
Type:	(C-47) two/three-seat transport with accommodation for 28 troops, or 14 litters plus three attendants or 10,000lb (4536kg) of freight
Powerplant:	two 895kW (1200hp) Pratt & Whitney R-1830-92 14-cylinder two-row radial engines
Performance:	maximum speed 370km/h (230mph); service ceiling 7315m (24,000ft); range 2575km (1600 miles)
Weights:	empty 8103kg (17,865lb); maximum take-off weight 14,061kg (31,000lb)
Dimensions:	span 28.9m (95ft); length 19.63m (64ft 5.5in); height 5.2m (16ft 11in)
Armament:	none

Lisunov Li-2

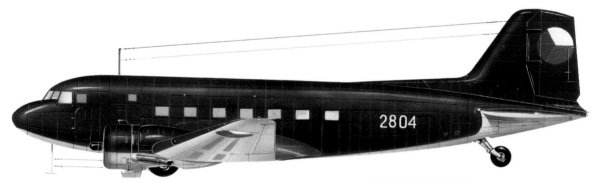

The Li-2 was a licence-built Russian version of the DC-3 with more than 1200 changes incorporated, notably relocation of the passenger door to the starboard side, a new freight door and Shvetsov engines. More than 6000 Li-2s were built from 1938 to 1952, some being used as bombers in wartime.

SPECIFICATIONS

Country of origin:	United States
Type:	twin-engined military transportt
Powerplant:	two 736kW (1000hp) Shvetsov ASh-62IR radial piston engines
Performance:	maximum speed 300km/h (186mph); service ceiling 7315m (24,000ft); range 2500km (1550 miles)
Weights:	empty 7750kg (17,485lb); loaded 10,700kg (23,589lb)
Dimensions:	span 28.9m (95ft); length 19.63m (64ft 5.5in); height 5.2m (16ft 11in)
Armament:	(some versions): three 7.62mm ShKAS and one 12.7mm UBK machine guns; up to 2000kg (908kg) of bombs

Dakota IV

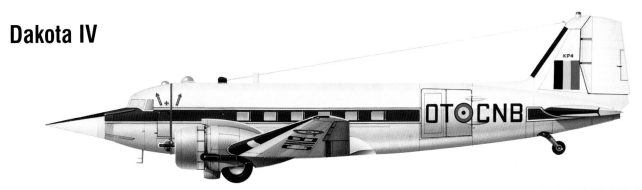

SPECIFICATIONS	
Country of origin:	United States
Type:	twin-engined navigation trainer
Powerplant:	two 895kW (1200hp) Pratt & Whitney R-1830-90C radial engines
Performance:	maximum speed 370km/h (230mph); service ceiling 7315m (24,000ft); range 2575km (1600 miles)
Weights:	empty 8103kg (17,865lb); maximum take-off 14,061kg (31,000lb)
Dimensions:	span 28.9m (95ft); length unknown; height 5.2m (16ft 11in)
Armament:	none

Belgium operated various C-47s and Dakotas from 1944 until 1976. This unusual example was one of two BAF C-47Bs fitted with the radar of the F-104G to train pilots in navigating the Starfighter. They were nicknamed 'Pinocchio' and used for a short time in the late 1960s.

Dakota

SPECIFICATIONS	
Country of origin:	United States
Type:	(C-47) two/three-seat transport with accommodation for 28 troops, or 14 litters plus three attendants or 10,000lb (4536kg) of freight
Powerplant:	two 895kW (1200hp) Pratt & Whitney R-1830-90C radial engines
Performance:	maximum speed 370km/h (230mph); service ceiling 7315m (24,000ft); range 2575km (1600 miles)
Weights:	empty 8103kg (17,865lb); maximum take-off 14,061kg (31,000lb)
Dimensions:	span 28.9m (95ft); length 19.63m (64ft 5.5in); height 5.2m (16ft 11in)
Armament:	none

The Dakota Mk IV was the RAF equivalent of the C-47B, which varied in having supercharged engines for better high-altitude performance. South Africa has used Dakotas since the 1940s. All the SAAF's remaining Dakotas have been given PT-67 turboprop engines and serve with No 35 Squadron.

LC-47 Skiplane

SPECIFICATIONS	
Country of origin:	United States
Type:	(C-47) two/three-seat transport with accommodation for 28 troops, or 14 litters plus three attendants or 10,000lb (4536kg) of freight
Powerplant:	two 895kW (1200hp) Pratt & Whitney R-1830-92 14-cylinder two-row radial engines
Performance:	maximum speed 370km/h (230mph); service ceiling 7315m (24,000ft); range 2575km (1600 miles)
Weights:	empty 8103kg (17,865lb); maximum take-off 14,061kg (31,000lb)
Dimensions:	span 28.9m (95ft); length unknown; height 5.2m (16ft 11in)
Armament:	none

Several nations modified C-47s with skis for use in polar exploration. The US Navy's Operation Deep Freeze made the first landings at the South Pole with LC-47s in 1956. Argentina maintained C-47 skiplanes for supporting its Antarctic bases until 1983.

Suez Crisis

In 1956, Egypt's President Nasser nationalized the Suez Canal against the wishes of Britain and France, who undertook an operation to reclaim the Canal Zone that October. The action involved one of the first mass helicopter assaults in history and a large parachute landing. Egyptian airfields were bombed by carrier- and land-based aircraft, neutralizing air opposition to the landings. Although a military victory, the Suez Crisis was regarded as a political failure for Britain.

De Havilland Venom FB.4

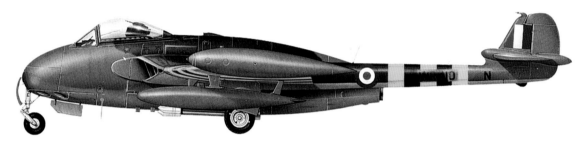

Aircraft operating in what the British called Operation Musketeer were painted with distinctive black and yellow 'Suez stripes' to distinguish them from Egyptian aircraft, as seen on this Venom FB.4 of one of the RAF squadrons on Cyprus during Musketeer.

SPECIFICATIONS	
Country of origin:	United Kingdom
Type:	single-seat fighter bomber
Powerplant:	one 22.9kN (5150lb) de Havilland Ghost 105 turbojet
Performance:	maximum speed 1030km/h (640mph); service ceiling 14,630m (48,000ft); range with drop tanks 1730km (1075 miles)
Weights:	empty 4174kg (9202lb); maximum loaded 6945kg (15,310lb)
Dimensions:	wingspan (over tip tanks) 12.7m (41ft 8in); length 9.71m (31ft 10in); height 1.88m (6ft 2in); wing area 25.99 sq m (279.75 sq ft)
Armament:	four 20mm Hispano cannon with 150 rounds, two wing pylons capable of carrying either two 454kg (1000lb) bombs or two drop tanks; or eight 27.2kg (60lb) rocket projectiles carried on centre-section launchers

English Electric Canberra B.2

RAF Canberras were based on Cyprus and Malta, and began strikes on Egyptian airfields on the night of 31 October 1956. Within five days of attacks, the Egyptian Air Force was effectively destroyed. As well as B.2 bombers, PR.3 reconnaissance variants took pre- and post-strike photos.

SPECIFICATIONS	
Country of origin:	United Kingdom
Type:	two-seat interdictor aircraft
Powerplant:	two 28.9kN (6500lb) Rolls Royce Avon Mk 101 turbojets
Performance:	maximum speed 917km/h (570mph); service ceiling 14,630m (48,000ft); range 4274km (2656 miles)
Weights:	empty approx. 11,790kg (26,000lb); max. take-off 24,925kg (54,950lb)
Dimensions:	wingspan 29.49m (63ft 11in); length 19.96m (65ft 6in); height 4.78m (15ft 8in); wing area 97.08 sq m (1045 sq ft)
Armament:	internal bomb bay with provision for up to 2727kg (6000lb) of bombs, plus an additional 909kg (2000lb) of underwing pylons

Republic F-84F Thunderstreak

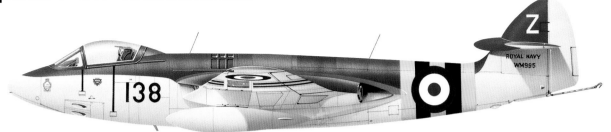

France contributed carrier-based Corsairs, and Dassault Mystères and F-84F Thunderstreaks on Cyprus. F-84s were also based in Israel to prevent an Egyptian counterattack. A large number of Egyptian tanks were destroyed by the French jets, as well as Il-28 bombers on the ground.

SPECIFICATIONS	
Country of origin:	United States
Type:	single-seat fighter bomber
Powerplant:	one 32kN (7220lb) Wright J65-W-3 turbojet
Performance:	maximum speed 1118km/h (695mph); service ceiling 14,020kg (46,000ft); combat radius with drop tanks 1304km (810 miles)
Weights:	empty 6273kg (13,830lb); maximum take-off 12,701kg (28,000lb)
Dimensions:	wingspan 10.24m (33ft 7.25in); length 13.23m (43ft 4.75in); height 4.39m (14ft 4.75in); wing area 30.19 sq m (325 sq ft)
Armament:	six .5in Browning M3 machine-guns, external hardpoints with provision for up to 2722kg (6000lb) of stores

Gloster Meteor NF.11

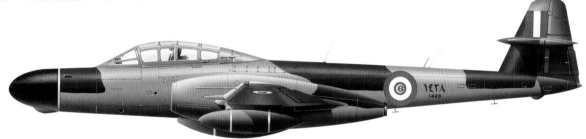

The Royal Egyptian Air Force had mostly Soviet-designed equipment supplied by Czechoslovakia, but also six Meteor night fighters bought from Britain in 1955. Although one pursued an RAF Canberra, which evaded, they claimed no victories during the crisis.

SPECIFICATIONS	
Country of origin:	United Kingdom
Type:	two-seat night fighter
Powerplant:	Two 16kN (3600lb) Rolls-Royce Derwent 8 turbojets
Performance:	maximum speed at 10,000m (33,000ft) 931m/h (579mph); service ceiling 12,192m (40,000ft); range 1580km (980 miles)
Weights:	empty 5400kg (11,900lb); loaded 9979kg (22,000lb)
Dimensions:	wingspan 13.1m (43ft); length 14.78m (48ft 6in); height 4.22m (13ft 10in)
Armament:	four 20mm Hispano cannon

Hawker Sea Hawk FB.Mk.3

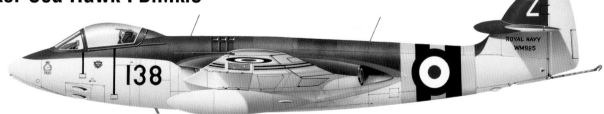

Six squadrons of Sea Hawks, flying from the carriers HMS *Eagle*, *Albion* and *Bulwark*, attacked Egyptian airfields by daylight and provided close air support for the helicopter and seaborne landings with their cannon and rockets.

SPECIFICATIONS	
Country of origin:	United Kingdom
Type:	single-seat carrier-based fighter-bomber
Powerplant:	one 24kN (5000lb) Rolls-Royce Nene turbojet
Performance:	maximum speed at sea level 958km/h (599mph); or 939km/h (587mph) at height; service ceiling 13,560m (44,500ft); standard range 1191km (740 miles)
Weights:	empty 9720lb; maximum take-off 7355kg (16,200lb)
Dimensions:	wingspan 11.89m (39ft); length 12.09m (39ft 8in); height 2.64m (8ft 8in); wing area 25.83sq m (278sq ft)
Armament:	four 20mm Hispano cannon in nose, underwing hardpoints for two 227kg (500lb) bombs

Fleet Air Arm in the 1950s

The British Royal Navy's Fleet Air Arm was still a large organization in the 1950s, operating over 30 squadrons ashore and afloat. Most of these used piston-engined aircraft, but jets and helicopters were arriving by 1954. FAA squadrons saw action in Korea and at Suez, and acquitted themselves well, but the RN sometimes struggled to get its share of the defence budget. By 1959, however, new fleet carriers such as HMS *Hermes* and supersonic fighters and strike aircraft were entering service.

Skyraider AEW.1

The US supplied Britain with Skyraider airborne early warning (AEW) aircraft as part of its assistance programme to NATO nations. Fitted with APS-20 radar in a ventral dome, this Skyraider AEW.1 flew with No 849 Squadron's A Flight on HMS *Eagle* during the Suez Crisis.

SPECIFICATIONS	
Country of origin:	United Kingdom
Type:	carrier-based early warning aircraft
Powerplant:	one 2013kW (2700hp) Pratt & Whitney R-3350 radial piston engine
Performance:	maximum speed unknown; range unknown; service ceiling unknown
Weights:	unknown
Dimensions:	span 15.25m (50ft); length 11.84m (38ft 10in); height 4.78m (15ft 8in); wing area 37.19 sq m (400.31 sq ft)
Armament:	none

Fairey Firefly AS.5

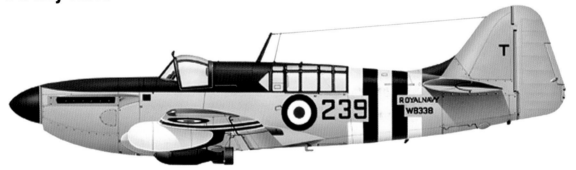

The Fairey Firefly was in production from 1941 to 1955, and was produced in over 25 sub-types. The AS.5 was intended as an anti-submarine strike aircraft, but also saw duties in the ground-attack and fighter roles. This AS.5 was with No 810 Squadron on HMS *Theseus* off Korea in 1950 .

SPECIFICATIONS	
Country of origin:	United Kingdom
Type:	carrier-based fighter/anti-submarine aircraft
Powerplant:	one 1678kW (2250hp) Rolls-Royce Griffon 74 V-12 piston engine
Performance:	maximum speed 618km/h (386mph); range 2092km (1300 miles); service ceiling : 9450m (31,000ft)
Weights:	empty 4388kg (9674lb); maximum 7301kg (16,096lb)
Dimensions:	span 12.55m (41ft 2n); length 8.51m (37ft 11in); height 4.37m (14ft 4in); wing area 30.66 sq m (330 sq ft)
Armament:	four 20mm Hispano cannon; up to 908kg (2000lb) of bombs or 16 27kg (60lb) rockets

Blackburn Firebrand IV

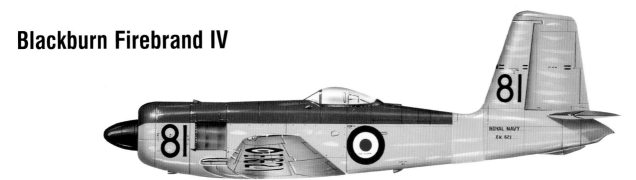

Conceived in 1939, the Firebrand heavy torpedo-carrying fighter was ready for service just too late for the war. Due to its many teething and operational problems, including lack of speed (particularly with a torpedo), only two frontline squadrons were equipped with Firebrands.

SPECIFICATIONS

Country of origin:	United Kingdom
Type:	carrier-based fighter/torpedo bomber
Powerplant:	one 1865kW (2500hp) Bristol Centaurus IX radial piston engine
Performance:	maximum speed 560km/h (350 mph); range 200 km (1250 miles); service ceiling 10,363m (34,000ft)
Weights:	empty 5150kg (11,357lb); maximum 7360kg (16,227lb)
Dimensions:	span 15.62m (51ft 4in); length 12m (39ft 1in); height 4.08m (13ft 3in); wing area 35.44 sq m (381.5 sq ft)
Armament:	four 20mm Hispano Mk II cannon; one 840kg (1850lb) torpedo or 908kg (2000lb) of bombs

Hawker Sea Fury FB.2

Derived from the Tempest Mk II, the Sea Fury was one of the fastest and best post-war piston-engined fighters. Canada, Australia and the Netherlands also flew carrier-based Sea Furies, and land-based versions without folding wings or arrestor hooks were exported to a number of nations.

SPECIFICATIONS

Country of origin:	United Kingdom
Type:	single-engined carrier-based fighter-bomber
Powerplant:	one 1850kW (2480hp) Bristol Centaurus XVIIC radial piston engine
Performance:	maximum speed 740 km/h (460 mph); range 1127km (700 miles); service ceiling 10,900m (35,800ft)
Weights:	empty 4190kg (9240lb); maximum 5670kg (12,500lb)
Dimensions:	span 11.7m (38ft 4in); length 10.6m (34ft 8in); height 4.9m (16ft 1in); wing area 26 sq m (280 sq ft)
Armament:	four 20mm Hispano Mk V cannon; up to 908kg (2000lb) of bombs or 12 3in rockets

Hawker Sea Hawk FGA.4

Although the design of the bifurcated jet pipe caused some concern among defence staff when the prototype P.1040 was first unveiled, the Sea Hawk has a well-earned reputation as a reliable, good-handling fighter. It remained in service with the FAA until 1960. In 1959, the Indian Navy ordered 24 aircraft similar to the Mk 6. Some were new-build and the rest were refurbished ex-RN Mk 6s.

SPECIFICATIONS

Country of origin:	United Kingdom
Type:	single-seat carrier based fighter-bomber
Powerplant:	one 24kN (5400lb) Rolls-Royce Nene 103 turbojet
Performance:	max speed 969km/h (602mph); service ceiling 13,565m (44,500ft); combat radius (clean) 370km (230 miles)
Weights:	empty 4409kg (9720lb); maximum take-off weight 7348kg (16,200lb)
Dimensions:	wingspan 11.89m (39ft); length 12.09m (39ft 8in);height 2.64m (8ft 8in); wing area 25.83 sq m (278 sq ft)
Armament:	four 20mm Hispano cannon; plus provision for four 227kg (500lb) bombs, or two 227kg (500lb) bombs and 20 3in or 16 5in rockets

Vampires and Venoms

De Havilland's compact twin-boomed Vampire was not the most sophisticated or highest-performing jet fighter of the late 1940s, and became comparatively less so over time. Nevertheless, it was enjoyable to fly, simple to maintain, and cheap to operate, and was widely exported. The Venom was a conservative development of the Vampire and as such it was not competitive as a fighter, but it filled a useful niche as a ground-attack platform.

Vampire FB.5

No 112 Squadron was famous for the exploits of its sharksmouth-decorated P-40s in North Africa. A similar marking was sported by its Vampire FB.5s, which operated in the day-fighter role as part of RAF Germany from 1951 to 1956, before replacement by Sabres.

SPECIFICATIONS	
Country of origin:	United Kingdom/Switzerland
Type:	single-seat fighter-bomber
Powerplant:	one 13.8kN (3100lb) thrust de Havilland Goblin 2 turbojet engine
Performance:	maximum speed 883km/h (548mph); service ceiling 13,410m (44,000ft); range with drop tanks 2253km (1400 miles)
Weights:	empty 3266kg (7200lb); loaded with drop tanks 5600kg (12,290lb)
Dimensions:	wingspan 11.6m (38ft); length 9.37m (30ft 9in); height 2.69m (8ft 10in); wing area 24.32 sq m (262 sq ft)
Armament:	four 20mm Hispano cannon with 150 rounds, wing pylons capable of carrying either two 227kg (500lb) bombs or 60lb rocket projectiles

Vampire FB.9

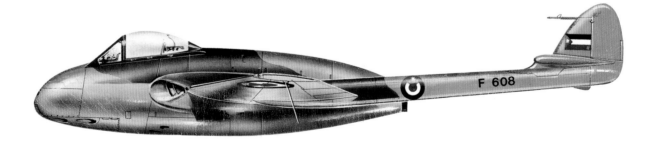

King Abdullah of Jordan was very impressed with RAF Vampires demonstrated in his country, and selected them in 1951 as the first equipment of the new Royal Jordanian Air Force. A mix of FB.9s, FB.52s and T.11s served with the RJAF. The single-seaters were retired in 1967.

SPECIFICATIONS	
Country of origin:	United Kingdom/Switzerland
Type:	single-seat fighter-bomber
Powerplant:	one 14.9kN (3350lb) thrust De Havilland Goblin 3 turbojet engine
Performance:	maximum speed 883km/h (548mph); service ceiling 13,410m (44,000ft); range with drop tanks 2253km (1400 miles)
Weights:	empty 3266kg (7200lb); loaded with drop tanks 5600kg (12,290lb)
Dimensions:	wingspan 11.6m (38ft); length 9.37m (30ft 9in); height 2.69m (8ft 10in); wing area 24.32 sq m (262 sq ft)
Armament:	four 20mm Hispano cannon with 150 rounds, wing pylons capable of carrying either two 227kg (500lb) bombs or 60lb rocket projectiles

Vampire T.11

The success of the two-seat night-fighter version of the Vampire led to the development of a trainer. The nose radar was removed and full dual flight controls were added to the pressurized cockpit. In 1956, the T.11 became the standard jet trainer of the Royal Air Force. The production run totalled 731, with export deliveries to 19 countries.

SPECIFICATIONS	
Country of origin:	United Kingdom
Type:	two-seat basic trainer
Powerplant:	one 15.6kN (3500lb) de Havilland Goblin 35 turbojet
Performance:	maximum speed 885km/h (549mph); service ceiling 12,200m (40,000ft); range on internal fuel 1370km (853 miles)
Weights:	empty 3347kg (7380lb); loaded (clean) 5060kg (11,150lb)
Dimensions:	wingspan 11.6m (38ft); length 10.55m (34ft 7in);height 1.86m (6ft 2in); wing area 24.32 sq m (262 sq ft)
Armament:	two 20mm Hispano cannon

Venom FB.1

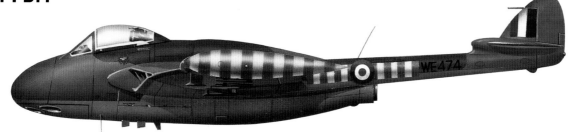

Outwardly similar to the Vampire except for its thinner wing with swept leading edges and wingtip tanks, the Venom also introduced the more powerful Ghost engine and had considerably better performance. The FB.1 entered service with RAF Germany in 1954.

SPECIFICATIONS	
Country of origin:	United Kingdom
Type:	single-seat fighter bomber
Powerplant:	one 21.6kN (4850lb) thrust de Havilland Ghost 103 turbojet engine
Performance:	maximum speed 1030km/h (640mph); service ceiling 14,630m (48,000ft); range with drop tanks 1730km (1075 miles)
Weights:	empty 4174kg (9202lb); maximum loaded 6945kg (15,310lb)
Dimensions:	wingspan (over tip tanks) 12.7m (41ft 8in); length 9.71m (31ft 10in); height 1.88m (6ft 2in); wing area 25.99 sq m (279.75 sq ft)
Armament:	four 20mm Hispano cannon with 150 rounds, two wing pylons capable of carrying either two 454kg (1000lb) bombs or two drop tanks; or eight 27.2kg (60lb) rocket projectiles

Venom FB.50

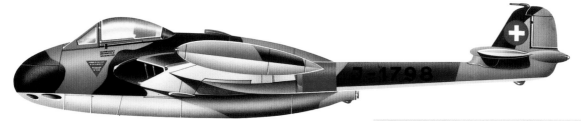

Switzerland has been one of the most enthusiastic of de Havilland's export customers, where they were built under licence. The FB.1, of which 100 were completed, was adopted in 1952 as a successor to the Vampire. These aircraft had long service careers and the final aircraft were not retired until 1983, albeit with substantially altered systems and structures.

SPECIFICATIONS	
Country of origin:	United Kingdom/Switzerland
Type:	single-seat tactical reconnaissance with secondary attack capability
Powerplant:	one 21.6kN (4850lb) de Havilland Ghost 103 turbojet
Performance:	maximum speed 1030km/h (640mph); service ceiling 13,720m (45,000ft); range with drop tanks 1730km (1075 miles)
Weights:	empty 3674kg (8100lb); maximum loaded 6945kg (15,310lb)
Dimensions:	wingspan (over tip tanks) 12.7m (41ft 8in); length 9.71m (31ft 10in); height 1.88m (6ft 2in); wing area 25.99 sq m (279.75 sq ft)
Armament:	four 20mm Hispano cannon with 150 rounds, either two 454kg (1000lb) bombs, or two drop tanks, or eight 27.2kg (60lb) rocket projectiles

French Jets of the 1950s

The French aircraft industry began its post-war recovery by completing unfinished German aircraft left in its factories, then by buying and licence-producing British equipment. Soon reorganized into regional groupings, French manufacturers competed to produce ever-more exotic jet, rocket and ramjet-powered aircraft. The Dassault concern emerged as dominant, creating a family of fighters and attack jets that formed the backbone of L'Armée de l'Air and Aéronavale from the mid-1950s.

De Havilland Vampire (SNCASE Mistral)

France acquired British-built Vampire 5s before the Société Nationale de Constructions Aéronautiques de Sud-Est, or SNCASE, began production. SNCASE produced several versions, including the SE.535 Mistral, with a Rolls-Royce Nene engine that substantially improved performance.

SPECIFICATIONS	
Country of origin:	United Kingdom
Type:	single-seat fighter-bomber
Powerplant:	one 13.8kN (3100lb) thrust De Havilland Goblin 2 turbojet engine
Performance:	maximum speed 883km/h (548mph); service ceiling 13,410m (44,000ft); range with drop tanks 2253km (1400 miles)
Weights:	empty 3266kg (7200lb); loaded with drop tanks 5600kg (12,290lb)
Dimensions:	wingspan 11.6m (38ft); length 9.37m (30ft 9in); height 2.69m (8ft 10in); wing area 24.32 sq m (262 sq ft)
Armament:	four 20mm Hispano cannon with 150 rounds, wing pylons capable of carrying either two 227kg (500lb) bombs or 60lb rocket projectiles

Sud-Ouest Aquilon 203

The Aéronavale adopted the De Havilland Sea Venom as a carrier-based night fighter, most of which were built in France as the SNCASE Aquilon. The Aquilon 203 version had an American radar that partly occupied the cockpit, forcing removal of the second seat.

SPECIFICATIONS	
Country of origin:	France/United Kingdom
Type:	single-seat carrier-based fighter
Powerplant:	one 23.4kN (5150lb) de Havilland Ghost 48 turbojet
Performance:	maximum speed 1030km/h (640mph); service ceiling 14,630m (48,000ft); range with drop tanks 1730km (1075 miles)
Weights:	empty 4174kg (9202lb); maximum loaded 6945kg (15,310lb)
Dimensions:	wingspan (over tip tanks) 12.7m (41ft 8in); length 10.38m (32ft 4in); height 1.88m (6ft 2in); wing area 25.99 sq m (279.75 sq ft)
Armament:	four 20mm Hispano 404 cannon with 150 rpg, two wing pylons for Nord 5103 (AA.20) air-to-air missiles

MD.450 Ouragon

First of the jet fighters produced by Marcel Dassault, the MD.450 Ouragan (Hurricane) entered service with L'Armée de l'Air in 1952. This Ouragan wears the colours of the Patrouille de France aerobatic team, which used the type as its first French-made equipment in 1954–57.

SPECIFICATIONS	
Country of origin:	France
Type:	single-seat fighter/ground attack aircraft
Powerplant:	one 22.5kN (5070lb) Hispano-Suiza Nene 104B turbojet
Performance:	maximum speed 940km/h (584mph); service ceiling 15,000m (49,210ft); range 1000km (620 miles)
Weights:	empty 4150kg (9150lb); maximum take-off 7600kg (17,416lb)
Dimensions:	wingspan over tip tanks 13.2m (43ft 2in); length 10.74m (35ft 3in); height 4.15m (13ft 7in); wing area 23.8sq m (256.18sq ft)
Armament:	four 20mm Hispano 404 cannon; underwing hardpoints for two 434kg (1000lb) bombs, or 16 105mm rockets, or eight rockets and two 458 litre (101 Imp gal) napalm tanks

Dassault Mystère IVA

The US Air Force tested the prototype in September 1952, and placed an off shore contract for 225 of the production aircraft in April 1953. Export orders were won from Israel and India, in addition to the aircraft supplied to the Armée de l'Air. The French aircraft saw action during the Suez conflict, while there were also many sales of the aircraft to the United States, Israel and India.

SPECIFICATIONS	
Country of origin:	France
Type:	single-seat fighter bomber
Powerplant:	one 27.9kN (6280lb) Hispano Suiza Tay 250A turbojet; or 3500kg (7716lb) Hispano Suiza Verdon 350 turbojet
Performance:	maximum speed 1120km/h (696mph); service ceiling 13,750m (45,000ft); range 1320km (820 miles)
Weights:	empty 5875kg (11,514lb); loaded 9500kg (20,950lb
Dimensions:	wingspan 11.1m (36ft 5.75in); length 12.9m (42ft 2in); height 4.4m (14ft 5in)
Armament:	two 30mm DEFA 551 cannon with 150 rounds, four underwing hardpoints with provision for up to 907kg (2000lb) of stores, including tanks, rockets, or bombs

SO.4050 Vautour IIB

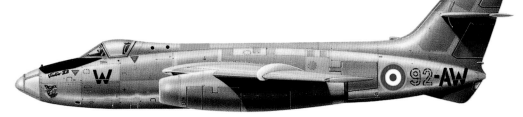

In mid-March 1951, Sud-Ouest flew the prototype of an advanced high-performance twin-jet bomber, designated the SO.4000. From this developed the SO.4050, with swept-wing surfaces and engines mounted in nacelles beneath the wing. Reworked as a two-seat bomber, with a glazed bomb-aiming position in the nose, the aircraft was designated SO.4050-3, first flying in 1954.

SPECIFICATIONS	
Country of origin:	France
Type:	two-seat medium bomber
Powerplant:	two 24.3kN (7716lb) SNECMA Atar 101E-3 turbojets
Performance:	maximum speed 1105km/h (687mph); service ceiling more than 15000m (49,210ft)
Weights:	empty 10,000kg; maximum take-off weight 20,000kg (44,092lb)
Dimensions:	wingspan 15.09m (49ft 6in); length 15.57m (51ft 1in); height 4.5m (14ft 9in)
Armament:	internal bomb bay with provision for up to 10 bombs, underwing pylons for two bombs up to 450kg (992lb), or two drop tanks

Reconnaissance Bombers

With the falling of the 'Iron Curtain' around the Soviet Union and its client states soon after World War II, the activities of the USSR became invisible to the West. The need arose for long-range reconnaissance aircraft, which regularly forayed into Eastern Bloc airspace until the USSR completed its air defences. Converted bombers gave way to specialized aircraft able to fly above fighters and missiles, or look deep inside denied territory using powerful oblique cameras and radars.

Boeing RB-29A Superfortress

Designated F-13s and F-13As before 1948, 117 B-29s and B-29As were modified to carry a suite of six large cameras for photo work over Japan and the Far East. Several RB-29s were shot down by Soviet fighters in 1949–52.

SPECIFICATIONS	
Country of origin:	United States
Type:	four-engined reconnaissance aircraft
Powerplant:	four 1641kW (2200hp) R-3350-57 radial piston engines
Performance:	maximum speed 576km/h (358mph); climb to 6095m (20,000ft) in 38 minutes; service ceiling 9710m (31,850ft); range 9382km (5830 miles)
Weights:	empty 31,816kg (70,140lb); maximum take-off 56,246kg (124,000lb)
Dimensions:	span 43.05m (141ft 2.75in); length 30.18m (99ft); height 9.02m (29ft 7in)
Armament:	one 20mm cannon and six .5in MGs (in tail, each of two dorsal and two ventral barbettes), internal bomb load of 9072kg (20000lb)

Martin P4M-1 Mercator

US Naval Aviation's contribution to surveillance of the Soviet Union in the early 1950s included the P4M-1 Mercator. These modified patrol planes were based in the Philippines, Japan and Morocco for electronic surveillance, or 'ferret' missions, of Soviet radar and radio signals.

SPECIFICATIONS	
Country of origin:	United States
Type:	land-based signals intelligence aircraft
Powerplant:	two 2420kW (3250hp) Pratt & Whitney R-4360 radial piston engines and two 20kN (4600lb) thrust Allison J33-A-23 turbojet engines
Performance:	max speed 660km/h (410 mph); service ceiling 10,500m (34,600 ft); range 4570km (2,840 miles)
Weights:	empty 22,016kg (48,536lb); loaded 40,088kg (88,378lb)
Dimensions:	span 34.7m (114ft); length 26m (85ft 2in); height 8m (26ft 1in); wing area 122 sq m (1311 sq ft)
Armament:	four 20mm cannon, two .5in (12.7mm) MGs; 5400kg (12,000lb) bombs

North American B-45A Tornado

The USAF's first jet bomber, the B-45 Tornado had a fairly short career in its original role, but was developed into the RB-45C with capacity for up to 12 cameras. As well as USAF operations, one RAF squadron flew secret reconnaissance missions over Russia using borrowed RB-45s.

SPECIFICATIONS	
Country of origin:	United States
Type:	four-engined jet bomber
Powerplant:	four 25kN (5200lb) thrust General Electric J47-GE-13 turbojet engines
Performance:	maximum speed 920km/h (570mph); range 1600Km (1000 miles); service ceiling 14,100m (46,400ft)
Weights:	empty 20,726kg (45,694lb); maximum 50,000kg (110,000lb)
Dimensions:	span 27.1m (89ft); length 22.9m (75ft 4in); height 7.7m (25ft 2in); wing area 105 sq m (1125 sq ft)
Armament:	two .5in (12.7mm) machine guns; up to 9997kg (22,000lb) bombs

Boeing RB-47H Stratojet

First bought by the USAAF in October 1945, the jet bomber Model 450 was at its peak in the mid 1950s, with hundreds converted for specialist roles. Thirty-two RB-47H models were made for electronic reconnaissance missions, with the bomb bay converted to accommodate equipment and three EW officers.

SPECIFICATIONS	
Country of origin:	United States
Type:	strategic reconnaissance aircraft
Powerplant:	six 32kN (7200lb) General Electric J47-GE-25 turbojets
Performance:	maximum speed at 4970m (16,300ft) 975km/h (606mph); service ceiling 12,345m (40,500ft); range 6437km (4,000 miles)
Weights:	empty 36,630kg (80,756lb); maximum take-off 89,893kg (198,180lb)
Dimensions:	wingspan 35.36m (116ft); length 33.48m (109ft 10in); height 8.51m (27ft 11in); wing area 132.66 sq m (1428 sq ft)
Armament:	two remotely controlled 20mm cannon in tail

North American RA-5C Vigilante

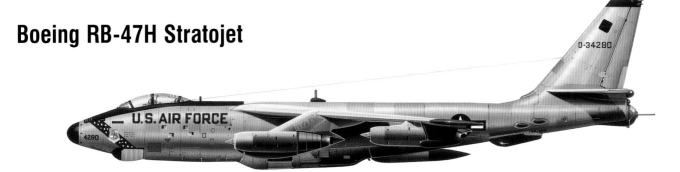

The RA-5C flew in prototype in June 1962. Fifty-five new aircraft were built and all but four of the A-5A Vigilantes were converted to this reconnaissance version. Integrated into the aircraft were all the improvements in range and aerodynamic design that had been developed for the abandoned A-5B project.

SPECIFICATIONS	
Country of origin:	United States
Type:	carrier-based long-range reconnaissance aircraft
Powerplant:	two 79.4kN (17,860lb) General Electric J79-GE-10 turbojets
Performance:	maximum speed at altitude 2230km/h (1385mph); service ceiling 20,400m (67,000ft); range with drop tanks 5150km (3200 miles)
Weights:	empty 17,009kg (37,498lb); maximum loaded 36,285kg (80,000lb)
Dimensions:	wingspan 16.15m (53ft); length 23.11m (75ft 10in); height 5.92m (19ft 5in); wing area 70.05 sq m (754 sq ft)

Soviet Interceptors

The Soviet Union put great store on interceptor aircraft for defence of the Motherland. These normally sacrificed manoeuvrability and pilot view for speed and climb performance. The Soviet approach to interceptors emphasized control by ground stations. Positive ground control at all times up to missile launch took the place of flying skill or initiative. The USSR exported this doctrine to most of the nations it supplied fighters to during the Cold War years.

Mikoyan-Gurevich MiG-19S 'Farmer'

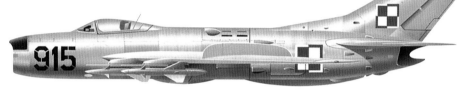

With the unveiling of the MiG-19, the Mikoyan-Gurevich bureau established itself at the forefront of the world's fighter design teams. The first flew in September 1953. With afterburning engines, the MiG-19 became the first supersonic engines in Soviet service. Steadily improved versions culminated in the MiG-19PM, with pylons for four beam-rider air-to-air missiles.

SPECIFICATIONS

Country of origin:	USSR
Type:	single-seat all-weather interceptor
Powerplant:	two 31.9kN (7165lb) Klimov RD-9B turbojets
Performance:	maximum speed at 9080m (20,000ft) 1480km/h (920mph); service ceiling 17,900m (58,725ft); maximum range at high altitude with two drop tanks 2200km (1367 miles)
Weights:	empty 5760kg (12,698lb); maximum take-off weight 9500kg (20,944lb)
Dimensions:	wingspan 9m (29ft 6.5in); length 13.58m (44ft 7in); height 4.02m (13ft 2.25in); wing area 25 sq m (269.11 sq ft)
Armament:	underwing pylons for four AA-1 Alkali air-to-air-missiles, or AA-2 Atoll

Yakovlev Yak-28P 'Firebar'

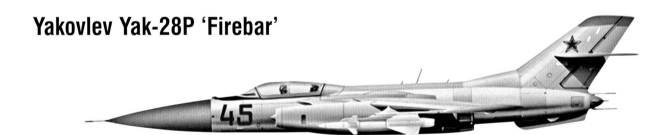

The Yak-28P had a similar configuration to the earlier Yak-25/26 family, but had a high shoulder-set wing with the leading edge extended further forward, a taller fin and rudder, revised powerplant in different underwing nacelles and different nosecone. Designed in the late 1950s, it was produced in tactical attack, reconnaissance, electronic countermeasures and trainer versions.

SPECIFICATIONS

Country of origin:	USSR
Type:	two-seat all-weather interceptor
Powerplant:	two 66.8kN (13,669lb) Tumanskii R-11 turbojets
Performance:	maximum speed 1180km/h (733mph); service ceiling 16,000m (52,495ft); maximum combat radius 925km (575 miles)
Weights:	maximum take-off 19,000kg (41,890lb)
Dimensions:	wingspan 12.95m (42ft 6in); length (long-nose late production) 23m (75ft 7.5in); height 3.95m (12ft 11.5in); wing area 37.6 sq m (404.74 sq ft)
Armament:	four underwing pylons for two AA-2 'Atoll', AA-2-2 ('Advanced Atoll') or AA-3 ('Anab') air-to-air missiles

INTERCEPTORS TIMELINE

 1953　　 1962　　 1967

Sukhoi Su-15 'Flagon'

The Su-15 was developed to a requirement for a successor to the Sukhoi Su-11 and strongly resembles that aircraft in the wings and tail. The 'Flagon A' entered IA-PVO Strany service in 1967, and 1500 Sukhoi 15s in all versions are estimated to have been built. All these aircraft served with Soviet air arms, since the aircraft was never made available for export.

SPECIFICATIONS

Country of origin:	USSR
Type:	single-seat all-weather interceptor
Powerplant:	two 60.8kN (13,668lb) Tumanskii R-11F2S-300 turbojets
Performance:	maximum speed above 11,000m (36,090ft) approximately 2230km/h (1386mph); service ceiling 20,000m (65,615ft); combat radius 725km (450 miles)
Weights:	empty (estimated) 11,000kg (24,250lb); maximum take-off 18,000kg (39,680lb)
Dimensions:	wingspan 8.61m (28ft 3in); length 21.33m (70ft); height 5.1m (16ft 8.5in); wing area 36 sq m (387.5 sq ft)
Armament:	four external pylons for two R8M medium-range air-to-air missiles ouboard and two AA-8 'Aphid' short-range AAMs inboard, plus two under-fuselage pylons for 23mm UPK-23 cannon pods or drop tanks

Mikoyan-Gurevich MiG-25P 'Foxbat-A'

Reports of the development of a long-range, high-speed strategic bomber in the US in the late 1950s (the B-70 Valkyrie) prompted the Soviet authorities to prioritize the development of an interceptor to match it. The prototypes blazed a trail of world records in 1965–67, and when the MiG-25P entered service in 1970 it far outclassed any Western aircraft in terms of speed and height.

SPECIFICATIONS

Country of origin:	USSR
Type:	single-seat interceptor
Powerplant:	two 100kN (22,487lb) Tumanskii R-15B-300 turbojets
Performance:	maximum speed at altitude about 2974km/h (1848mph); service ceiling over 24,385m (80,000ft); combat radius 1130km (702 miles)
Weights:	empty 20,000kg (44,092lb); maximum take-off 37,425kg (82,508lb)
Dimensions:	wingspan 14.02m (45ft 11.75in); length 23.82m (78ft 1.75in); height 6.10m (20ft 0.5in); wing area 61.40 sq m (660.9 sq ft)
Armament:	external pylons for four air-to-air missiles in the form of either two each of the IR- and radar-homing AA-6 'Acrid', or two AA-7 'Apex' and two AA-8 'Aphid' weapons

Mikoyan-Gurevich MiG-31 'Foxhound-A'

The MiG-31 was developed during the 1970s from the impressive MiG-25 'Foxbat' to counter the threat from low-flying cruise missiles and bombers. In fact, the new aircraft was a vast improvement over its older stablemate, with tandem seat cockpit, IR search and tracking sensor, and the Zaslon 'Flash Dance' pulse-Doppler radar providing fire-and-forget engagement capability.

SPECIFICATIONS

Country of origin:	USSR
Type:	two-seat all weather interceptor and ECM aircraft
Powerplant:	two 151.9kN (34,171lb) Soloviev D-30F6 turbofans
Performance:	maximum speed 3000km/h (1865mph); service ceiling 20,600m (67,600ft); combat radius 1400km (840 miles)
Weights:	empty 21,825kg (48,415lb); max take-off 46,200kg (101,850lb)
Dimensions:	wingspan 13.46m (44ft 2in); length 22.68m (74ft 5.25in); height 6.15m (20ft 2.25in); wing area 61.6 sq m (663 sq ft)
Armament:	one 23mm cannon, provision for missiles, ECM pods or drop tanks

1975

MiG-21 'Fishbed'

Eclipsed only by the MiG-15, the Mikoyan MiG-21 'Fishbed' is the most numerous jet fighter ever produced, with an estimated 11,000 built in Russia, Czechoslovakia, India and China, many of the latter unlicensed copies made after the Sino-Soviet split. The first, unsophisticated, MiG-21F models with simple ranging radars entered service in 1959. Continuous development saw armament options increased and various spines and bulges added to house fuel, avionics and electronic equipment.

MiG-21 'Fishbed'

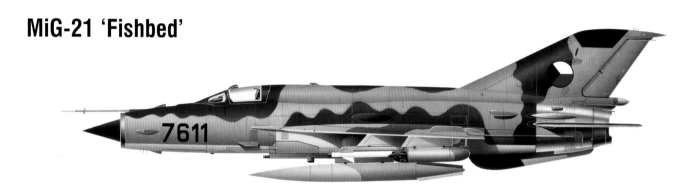

Czech aircraft maker Aero Vodochody began licence production of the initial MiG-21F-13 as the S-106 in 1960. They completed 194 of them, but the aircraft shown is a later Russian-built MiG-21MF. The Czech Republic replaced its last MiG-21s in 2006 with Saab Gripens.

SPECIFICATIONS	
Country of origin:	USSR
Type:	single-seat all-weather multi role fighter
Powerplant:	one 60.8kN (13,668lb) thrust Tumanskii R-13-300 afterburning turbojet
Performance:	maximum speed above 11,000m (36,090ft) 2229km/h (1385mph); service ceiling 17,500m (57,400ft); range on internal fuel 1160km (721 miles)
Weights:	empty 5200kg (11,464lb); maximum take-off 10,400kg (22,925lb)
Dimensions:	wingspan 7.15m (23ft 5.5in); length (including probe) 15.76m (51ft 8.5in); height 4.1m (13ft 5.5in); wing area 23 sq m (247.58 sq ft)
Armament:	one 23mm cannon, provision for about 1500kg (3307kg) of stores, including air-to-air missiles, rocket pods, napalm tanks, or drop tanks

MiG-21PF 'Fishbed-D'

This Indian Air Force MiG-21PFL is depicted wearing an improvised 'tiger' camouflage scheme at around the time of the 1971 Indo-Pakistan War. It carries AA-2 'Atol' air-to-air missiles and a centreline GSh-9 30mm cannon pod.

SPECIFICATIONS	
Country of origin:	USSR
Type:	single-seat all-weather multi role fighter
Powerplant:	one 60.8kN (13,668lb) thrust Tumanskii afterburning turbojet
Performance:	max speed 2050km/h (1300mph); service ceiling 17,000m (57,750ft); range 1800km (1118 miles)
Weights:	max loaded 9400kg (20,723lb)
Dimensions:	wingspan 7.15m (23ft 5.5in); length (including probe) 15.76m (51ft 8.5in); height 4.1m (13ft 5.5in); wing area 23 sq m (247.58 sq ft)
Armament:	one 23mm cannon, provision for about 1500kg (3307kg) of stores, including air-to-air missiles, rocket pods, napalm tanks, or drop tanks

MiG-21PFMA 'Fishbed'

The MiG-21 was supplied to approximately 55 international operators past and present, not counting Chinese variants. Poland had several hundred 'Fishbeds' in service, including the MiG-21PF.

SPECIFICATIONS	
Country of origin:	USSR
Type:	single-seat all-weather multi role fighter
Powerplant:	one 60.8kN (13,668lb) thrust Tumanskii R-11F2S-300 afterburning turbojet
Performance:	maximum speed above 11,000m (36,090ft) 2229km/h (1385mph); service ceiling 17,500m (57,400ft); range on internal fuel 1160km (721 miles)
Weights:	empty 5200kg (11,464lb); maximum take-off 10,400kg (22,925lb)
Dimensions:	wingspan 7.15m (23ft 5.5in); length (including probe) 15.76m (51ft 8.5in); height 4.1m (13ft 5.5in); wing area 23 sq m (247.58 sq ft)
Armament:	one 23mm cannon,provision for about 1500kg (3307kg) of stores, including air-to-air missiles, rocket pods, napalm tanks or drop tanks

MiG-21U 'Mongol'

Aside from the airframe modifications necessary to accommodate the instructor, the 21U is similar in configuration to the initial major production version, the 21F. The first prototype is reported to have flown in 1960. Variations from the single-seater include a one-piece forward airbrake, repositioning of the pilot boom, and adoption of larger mainwheels first introduced on the MiG-21PF.

SPECIFICATIONS	
Country of origin:	USSR
Type:	two-seat trainer
Powerplant:	one 5950kg (13,118lb) Tumanskii R-11F2S-300 turbojet
Performance:	maximum speed 2145km/h (1333mph); service ceiling 17,500m (57,400ft); range 1160km (721 miles)
Weights:	not released
Dimensions:	wingspan 7.15m (23ft 5.5in); length (including probe) 15.76m (51ft 8.5in); height 4.1m (13ft 5.5in); wing area 23 sq m (247.58 sq ft)
Armament:	six 7.92mm (.3in) MGs; 1000kg (2205lb) bomb load

Chengdu F-7

China and Russia's initial cooperation on MiG-21 development ended when relations soured in 1962. Chinese manufacturers Shenyang, then Chengdu carried on with production of unlicensed models as the Jiang-7 (J-7) into the 1990s. China supplied J-7s (under the export designation F-7) to a dozen nations, mainly in Africa.

SPECIFICATIONS	
Country of origin:	USSR
Type:	single-seat all-weather multi role fighter
Powerplant:	one 66.7kN (14,815lb) thrust Liyang Wopen-13F afterburning turbojet
Performance:	max speed 2229km/h (1385mph); service ceiling 17,500m (57,400ft); range 1160km (721 miles)
Weights:	empty 5200kg (11,464lb); maximum take-off 10,400kg (22,925lb)
Dimensions:	wingspan 7.15m (23ft 5.5in); length (including probe) 15.76m (51ft 8.5in); height 4.1m (13ft 5.5in); wing area 23 sq m (247.58 sq ft)
Armament:	one 23mm cannon,provision for about 1500kg (3307kg) of stores, including air-to-air missiles, rocket pods, napalm tanks, or drop tanks

Flying Boxcars

From the late 1940s, Western air forces started to introduce some of the first purpose-designed military transport aircraft. The Fairchild C-82 Packet began a fashion for twin-boomed transports with capacious fuselages that could be loaded via an integral ramp at the rear. A Boxcar could lift a light tank, armoured car or artillery gun and roll it straight off at a forward airstrip, or drop large numbers of paratroopers.

Fairchild R4Q-1 Boxcar

The C-82 Packet was inadequate for some military needs and the design was soon revised into the C-119 Flying Boxcar, of which nearly 1200 were built for the US and export. The US Marine Corps operated 140 Boxcars, including 41 R4Q-1s like the one illustrated here in the markings of VMR-253.

SPECIFICATIONS	
Country of origin:	United States
Type:	twin-engined military airlifter
Powerplant:	two 2535kW (3400hp) Wright R-3350-36W piston engines
Performance:	maximum speed 402km/h (250mph); range 3219 km (2000 miles); service ceiling 7300m (23,950ft)
Weights:	empty 18,136kg (39,983lb); maximum 33,747kg (74,700lb)
Dimensions:	span 33.3m (109ft 3in); length 26.37m (86ft 6in); height 8m (26ft 3in); wing area 134.43 sq m (1447 sq ft)
Armament:	none

Fairchild C-119G Packet

The C-119G was used by India from the early 1960s until the mid-1980s. Indian C-119s were modified with an auxiliary jet engine on top for boost in 'hot and high' operations. This was a Bristol Orpheus, rather than the Westinghouse J34 jet pack used on US versions.

SPECIFICATIONS	
Country of origin:	United States
Type:	twin-engined military airlifter (C-119G Indian)
Powerplant:	two 2610kW (3500hp) Wright R-3350-85 piston engines and one 22kN (4850lb) thrust Bristol Orpheus turbojet
Performance:	maximum speed 470km/h (292mph); range 3669km (2280 miles); service ceiling 7300m (23,950ft)
Weights:	empty 18,136kg (39,983lb); maximum 33,747kg (74,700lb)
Dimensions:	span 33.3m (109ft 3in); length 26.37m (86ft 6in); height 8m (26ft 3in); wing area 134.43 sq m (1447 sq ft)
Armament:	none

FLYING BOXCARS TIMELINE

1944 1947  1949

Blackburn Beverley C.1

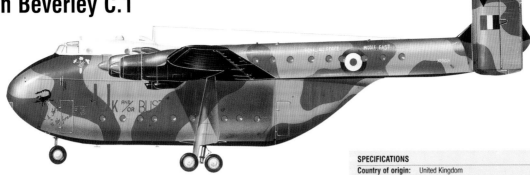

The lumbering Beverley was used mainly to service British garrisons in the Middle East and Far East. It could carry 94 troops (some of them seated in the tail booms) or various vehicles. It could drop 70 paratroopers or up to 11,340kg (25,000lb) of supplies and operate from rough airstrips.

SPECIFICATIONS	
Country of origin:	United Kingdom
Type:	twin-engined military airlifter
Powerplant:	four 2125kW (2850hp) Bristol Centaurus 173 radial piston engines
Performance:	maximum speed 383km/h (238mph); range 5938km (3690 miles); service ceiling 4875m (16,000ft)
Weights:	35,940kg (79,234lb); maximum 64,864kg (143,000lb)
Dimensions:	span 49.38m (162ft); length 30.3m (99ft 5in); height 11.81m (38ft 9in); wing area 271 sq m (2916 sq ft)
Armament:	none

Nord 2501D Noratlas

First flown in 1949, the Nord Noratlas was slow to get into service but became an important European tactical transport built in both France and Germany. This Noratlas was one of many supplied from Luftwaffe stocks to African countries, and served with the Niger National Flight.

SPECIFICATIONS	
Country of origin:	Germany
Type:	twin-engined military transport
Powerplant:	two 1520kW (2040lb) Bristol Hercules 738/739 radial engines
Performance:	maximum speed 582km/h (362mph); range 2500km (1550 miles); service ceiling 7100m (23,300ft)
Weights:	13,075kg (28,825lb); maximum 22,000kg (48,500lb)
Dimensions:	span 32.5m (106ft 8in); length 21.96m (72ft 1in); height 6m (19ft 8in); wing area 101.2 sq m (1089 sq ft)
Armament:	none

Armstrong Whitworth Argosy C.1

The RAF bought 59 Argosy airlifters from 1962. Known as the 'Whistling Wheelbarrow' for its high-pitched Dart turboprop engines, the Argosy could carry 69 troops or light vehicles. The civilian version had a clamshell door in the nose, but the Argosy C.1 had this sealed and a weather radar in the nose.

SPECIFICATIONS	
Country of origin:	United Kingdom
Type:	four-engined military transport aircraft
Powerplant:	four 1820kW (2440hp) Rolls-Royce Dart RDa.8 Mk 10 turboprop engines
Performance:	maximum speed 433km/h (269mph); range 5230km (3250 miles); service ceiling 5500m (18,000ft)
Weights:	empty 4360kg (10,200lb); maximum 46,700kg (103,000lb)
Dimensions:	span 35.05m (115ft); length 27.18m (45ft 3in); height 8.96m (29ft 3in); wing area 135.5 sq m (1458 sq ft)
Armament:	none

1950

1959

Grumman Carrier Twins

Grumman has had a presence on almost every US carrier since the 1930s. No less important than its fighter/attack aircraft are its twin-engined support aircraft, which used common components to build a variety of specialized models for different roles. The S2F Tracker ASW aircraft spawned the Tracer AEW aircraft and the Trader transport. The E-2 Hawkeye AEW aircraft and the C-2 Greyhound transport have both served for 45 years.

S-2F Tracker

The S2F Tracker, or 'Stoof', was the US Navy's primary anti-submarine warfare (ASW) platform from the 1950s to the 1970s. It was also sold to several nations for carrier and land-based use, including Australia, Canada, Argentina and Brazil. Civilian versions are in use as fire bombers.

SPECIFICATIONS	
Country of origin:	United States
Type:	twin-engined carrier-based anti-submarine aircraft
Powerplant:	two 1135kW (1525hp) Wright R-1820-82 radial piston engines
Performance:	maximum speed 438km/h (272mph); range 1558km (968 miles); service ceiling 6949m (22,800ft)
Weights:	empty 7871kg (17,357lb); maximum 11,069kg (24,408lb)
Dimensions:	span 21m (69ft 8in); length 12.8m (42ft); height 4.9m (16ft 3in); wing area 45 sq m (485 sq ft)
Armament:	torpedoes, rockets, depth charges or one Mk 47 or Mk 101 nuclear depth bomb

US-2A Tracker

The US-2A was an S-2 with anti-submarine gear and weapons stripped out and replaced with seats or cargo space for utility duties. It could also tow targets. Japan acquired 47 Trackers for land-based use and converted a number into target tugs.

SPECIFICATIONS	
Country of origin:	United States
Type:	twin-engined carrier-based anti-submarine aircraft
Powerplant:	two 1135kW (1525hp) Wright R-1820-82 radial piston engines
Performance:	maximum speed 438km/h (272mph); range 1558km (968 miles); service ceiling 6949m (22,800ft)
Weights:	empty 7871kg (17,357lb); maximum 11,069kg (24,408lb)
Dimensions:	span 21m (69ft 8in); length 12.8m (42ft); height 4.9m (16ft 3in); wing area 45 sq m (485 sq ft)
Armament:	none

GRUMMAN TWINS TIMELINE
1952   1960

S-2T Tracker

No real fixed-wing replacement exists for the Tracker, particularly for use on smaller carriers. Argentina, Brazil and Taiwan chose to modernize their aircraft in the 1980s. US firm Tracor fitted new turboprop engines and ASW equipment to create the S-2T Turbo Tracker.

SPECIFICATIONS	
Country of origin:	United Kingdom
Type:	twin-engined carrier-based anti-submarine aircraft
Powerplant:	two 1141kW (1530hp) Garrett TPE331-15AW turboprop engines
Performance:	maximum speed 500 km/h (311 mph); range 1558km (968 miles); service ceiling 6949m (22,800ft)
Weights:	unknown
Dimensions:	span 21m (69ft 8in); length 12.8m (42ft); height 4.9m (16ft 3in); wing area 45 sq m (485 sq ft)
Armament:	torpedoes, rockets, bombs or depth charges

C-2A Greyhound

In service since 1966, the C-2 Greyhound is used in the carrier onboard delivery (or COD) role, transferring passengers, mail and urgent supplies such as aircraft engines from shore bases to carriers. It shares the wings, engines, landing gear and tail fins with the E-2 Hawkeye.

SPECIFICATIONS	
Country of origin:	United States
Type:	twin-engined carrier-based cargo/passenger aircraft
Powerplant:	one 3400kW (4800hp) Allison T56-A-425 turboprop engines
Performance:	maximum speed 553km/h (343mph); range 2400km (1496 miles); service ceiling 10,210m (33,500ft)
Weights:	empty 15,310kg (33,746lb); maximum kg (lb)
Dimensions:	span 24.6m (80ft 7in); length 17.3m (56ft 10in); height 4.85m (15ft 11in); wing area 65 sq m (700 sq ft)
Armament:	none

E-2 Hawkeye

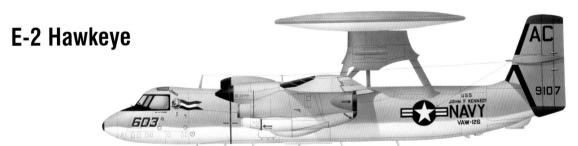

Replacing the E-1 Tracer, a derivative of the S-2 with a fixed radar housing on its back, the E-2 Hawkeye featured a rotating radar dish, or rotodome, mounted on a pylon. The Hawkeye was used to extend the radar range of the carrier battlegroup and direct fighters to intercept air threats.

SPECIFICATIONS	
Country of origin:	United States
Type:	twin-engined carrier-based early warning aircraft (E-2C)
Powerplant:	one 3800kW (5100hp) Allison T56-A-427 turboprop engines
Performance:	maximum speed 604km/h (375mph); range 2583km (1605 miles); service ceiling 10,210m (33,500ft)
Weights:	empty 15,310kg (33,746lb); maximum 24,655kg (60,000lb)
Dimensions:	span 24.6m (80ft 7in); length 17.56m (57ft 7in); height 5.58m (18ft 4in); wing area 65 sq m (700 sq ft)
Armament:	none

1964

1989

Strategic Air Command

At its peak, the USAF's Strategic Air Command (SAC) had several thousand bombers and tankers as well as strategic reconnaissance aircraft and ballistic missiles. It even had its own fighter aircraft and transports. Under General Curtiss LeMay, SAC maintained an around-the-clock airborne alert of bombers ready to wreak destruction on the Soviet Union on the receipt of coded signals from the White House, an eventuality that never came to pass.

Convair B-36J Peacemaker

The extraordinary Convair B-36 had no fewer than 10 engines: four piston engines and six jets. It was designed to carry some of the extremely large atomic and hydrogen bombs of the time, but also had the capacity to drop up to 80 conventional bombs.

SPECIFICATIONS	
Country of origin:	United States
Type:	ten-engined strategic bomber
Powerplant:	six 2500kW (3800hp) Pratt & Whitney R-4360-53 radial and four 23kN (5200lb) thrust General Electric J47-GE-19 turbojet engines
Performance:	maximum speed 685 km/h (420 mph); range 10,945km (6800 miles); service ceiling 15,000m (48,000ft)
Weights:	empty 77,580kg (171,035lb); maximum 186,000kg (410,000lb)
Dimensions:	span 70.1m (230ft); length 49.40m (162ft 1in); height 14.25m (46ft 9in); wing area 443.3 sq m (4772 sq ft)
Armament:	16 20mm cannon; up to 39,010kg (86,000lb) of bombs

B-47E Stratojet

The B-47 was SAC's first all-jet bomber. Creating a large, high-performance, swept-wing jet with podded engines was a considerable challenge, but allowed a thinner wing than used on contemporary Soviet and British bombers. More than 1800 B-47s were built.

SPECIFICATIONS	
Country of origin:	United States
Type:	six-engined strategic bomber
Powerplant:	six 32.1kN (7200lb) thrust General Electric J47-GE-25 turbojet engines
Performance:	maximum speed 901km/h (560mph); range 5636km (3500 miles); service ceiling 11,978m (39,300ft)
Weights:	empty 35,867kg (79,074lb); maximum 102,512kg (226,000lb)
Dimensions:	span 35.36m (116ft); length 32.6m (107ft 1in); height 8.5m (28ft); wing area 132.7 sq m (1428 sq ft)
Armament:	two 20mm M2 cannon; up to 11,000kg (25,000lb) of conventional or nuclear bombs

 **STRATEGIC COMMAND TIMELINE**  1947   1952    1956

B-52D Stratofortress

The B-52 has been in continuous service with Strategic Air Command in one form or another since 1955. Development of this remarkable warhorse, which started life as a turboprop-powered project, began in 1945. The aircraft had been designed to carry stand-off nuclear weapons, but in 1964 a rebuilding programme allowed it to carry 105 'iron bombs'.

SPECIFICATIONS	
Country of origin:	United States
Type:	long-range strategic bomber
Powerplant:	eight 44.5kN (10,000lb) Pratt & Whitney J57 turbojets
Performance:	max speed at 7315m (24,000ft) 1014km/h (630mph): service ceiling 13,720–16,765m (45,000–55,000ft); range 9978km (6200 miles)
Weights:	empty 77,200–87,100kg (171,000–193,000lb); loaded 204,120kg (450,000lb)
Dimensions:	wingspan 56.4m (185ft); length 48m (157ft 7in);height 14.75m (48ft 3in); wing area 371.60 sq m (4000 sq ft)
Armament:	remotely controlled tail mounting with four .5in MGs; internal bomb capacity 12,247kg (27,000lb) to 31,750kg (70,000lb)

KC-135A Stratotanker

SAC's fuel-thirsty jet bombers required an equally large fleet of tanker aircraft to support their patrols. The KC-135 was derived from the same prototype that parented the 707 airliner, and over 800 were built, the majority of them as KC-135As, illustrated.

SPECIFICATIONS	
Country of origin:	United States
Type:	four-engined aerial tanker
Powerplant:	four 244.7kN (55,000lb) Pratt & Whitney J57-59W thrust turbojet engines
Performance:	cruising speed 853km/h (530mph); range 4627km (2875 miles); service ceiling 10,980m (36,000ft)
Weights:	empty 44,665kg (98,465lb); maximum 134,720kg (29,000lb)
Dimensions:	wingspan 39.88m (130ft 10in); length 41.53m (136ft 3in); height 12.7m (41ft 8in); wing area 226.03 sq m (2,433 sq ft)
Armament:	none

Convair B-58 Hustler

The B-58 was the first supersonic bomber and the first to reach Mach 2. It was the first aircraft constructed mainly from a stainless-steel honeycomb sandwich, the first to have a slim body and fat payload pod so that when the load was dropped, the aircraft became slimmer and lighter. The first flight was made on 11 November 1956, and development continued for almost three years.

SPECIFICATIONS	
Country of origin:	United States
Type:	three-seat supersonic bomber
Powerplant:	four 69.3kN (15,600lb) General Electric J79-5B turbojets
Performance:	maximum speed 2125km/h (1385mph); service ceiling 19,500m (64,000ft); range on internal fuel 8248km (5125 miles)
Weights:	empty 25,200kg (55,560lb); maximum take-off 73,930kg (163,000lb)
Dimensions:	wingspan 17.31m (56ft 10in); length 29.5m (96ft 9in); height 9.6m (31ft 5in); wing area 145.32 sq m (1542 sq ft)
Armament:	one 20mm T171 Vulcan rotary cannon in radar-aimed tail barbette, nuclear or conventional weapons in disposable underfuselage pod

Dragon Lady: Lockheed U-2

The U-2 spyplane was initiated in the early 1950s with funding by the Central Intelligence Agency (CIA). The U-2 was designed by the 'Skunk Works' secret research division of Lockheed, led by 'Kelly' Johnson. The U-2 initially operated under the cover of a high-altitude research aircraft programme until CIA pilot Gary Powers was shot down on 1 May 1960 over Sverdlovsk. Later versions of the 'Dragon Lady' remain in service today.

U-2A

Under Project Aquatone, wearing civil registrations, the CIA's U-2s conducted reconnaissance overflights of the Soviet Union from forward bases in Turkey, Pakistan and Norway. They also flew over Cuba during the 1962 Missile Crisis and other hotspots until 1974. N803X was a U-2A.

SPECIFICATIONS	
Country of origin:	United States
Type:	high-altitude spyplane
Powerplant:	one 48.93kN (11,000lb) thrust Pratt & Whitney J75-P-37A turbojet engine
Performance:	maximum speed 795km/h (494mph); range 3542km (2200 miles); service ceiling 16,763m (55,000ft)
Weights:	empty 5306kg (11,700lb); maximum 9523kg (21,000lb)
Dimensions:	span 24.3m (80ft); length 15.1m (49ft 7in); height 3.9m (13ft); wing area 52.49 sq m (565 sq ft)
Armament:	none

U-2C

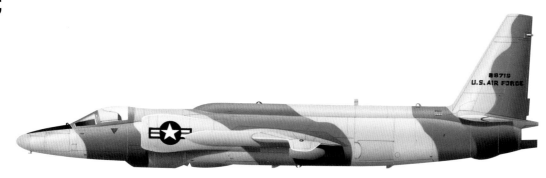

With a more powerful version of the J75 engine, the U-2C had a much higher altitude, putting it out of the range of most fighters and missiles. As extra insurance, it had an exhaust deflector beneath the tailpipe to mask the engine heat signature from infrared sensors.

SPECIFICATIONS	
Country of origin:	United States
Type:	high-altitude spyplane
Powerplant:	one 75.62kN (17,000lb) thrust Pratt & Whitney J75-P-13 turbojet engine
Performance:	maximum speed 850km/h (530mph); range 4830km (2610 miles)); service ceiling 25,930m (85,000ft)
Weights:	empty 5306kg (11,700lb); maximum 9523kg (21,000lb)
Dimensions:	span 24.3m (80ft); length 15.1m (49ft 7in); height 3.9m (13ft); wing area 52.49 sq m (565 sq ft)
Armament:	none

U-2CT

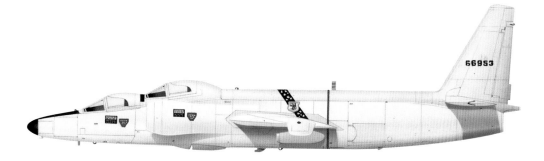

SPECIFICATIONS	
Country of origin:	United States
Type:	high-altitude spyplane
Powerplant:	one 75.62kN (17,000lb) thrust Pratt & Whitney J75-P-13 turbojet engine
Performance:	maximum speed 850km/h (530mph); range 4830km (2610 miles); service ceiling 25,930m (85,000ft)
Weights:	unknown
Dimensions:	span 24.3m (80ft); length 15.1m (49ft 7in); height 3.9m (13ft); wing area 52.49 sq m (565 sq ft)
Armament:	none

Designed along the principles of a glider, the U-2 was tricky to handle at high altitude and on landing. A number were lost in crashes with new pilots, so two U-2Cs were converted to U-2CT trainers with a second, raised cockpit. Only two of this version were built.

U-2D

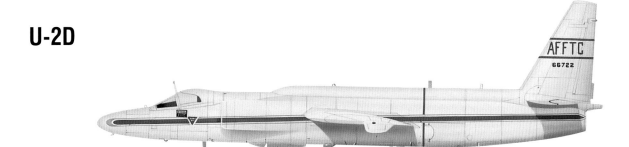

SPECIFICATIONS	
Country of origin:	United States
Type:	high-altitude spyplane
Powerplant:	one 48.93kN (11,000lb) thrust Pratt & Whitney J75-P-37A turbojet engine
Performance:	maximum speed 795km/h (494mph); range 3542km (2200 miles); service ceiling unknown
Weights:	unknown
Dimensions:	span 24.3m (80ft); length 15.1m (49ft 7in); height 3.9m (13ft); wing area 52.49 sq m (565 sq ft)
Armament:	none

The U-2D was another two-seat version, although intended for operational use rather than training. Under Project Low Card, an optical spectrometer was fitted in a housing behind the cockpit. It was used to search for the plume of an ICBM launch. An operator was seated in the former camera bay.

U-2R

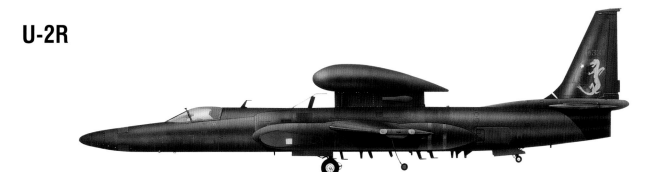

SPECIFICATIONS	
Country of origin:	United States
Type:	single-seat high-altitude reconnaissance aircraft
Powerplant:	one 75.6kN (17,000lb) Pratt & Whitney J75-P-13B turbojet
Performance:	maximum cruising speed at more than 21,335m (70,000ft); operational ceiling 27,430m (90,000ft); maximum range 10,050km (6250 miles)
Weights:	empty 7031kg (15,500lb); maximum take-off weight 18,733kg (41,300lb)
Dimensions:	wingspan 31.39m (103ft); length 19.13m (62ft 9in); height 4.88m (16ft); wing area 92.9 sq m (1000 sq ft)
Armament:	none

The U-2R, first flown in 1967, is significantly larger and more capable than the original aircraft. A distinguishing feature of these aircraft is the addition of a large instrumentation 'superpod' under each wing. It was designed for standoff tactical reconnaissance in Europe.

Dassault Mirage III/5

Dassault's delta-winged Mirage III series began as the experimental Delta Mystère in 1955 and evolved into one of the most combat-proven supersonic fighters ever built. The first model, the Mirage IIIC interceptor, was improved as the Mirage IIIE, which had ground-attack capability and even more sales success. The Mirages 5 and 50 were dedicated export versions sold widely in Africa, the Middle East and South America. Further derivatives were produced by foreign users.

Dassault Mirage IIIC

The Mirage IIIC entered service in 1961, beginning over 25 years of service. The last Armée de l'Air unit to use them was EC 3/10 'Vexin', based at Djibouti-Ambouli until 1988. Contrasting with most of its unpainted metal home-based brethren, the African-based IIICs wore desert camouflage.

SPECIFICATIONS	
Country of origin:	France
Type:	single-engined interceptor fighter
Powerplant:	one 58.72kN (13,200lb) thrust SNECMA Atar 09B-3 afterburning turbojet engine and one 16.46kN (3700lb) thrust auxiliary SEFR 841 rocket motor
Performance:	maximum speed 2350km/h (1460mph); service ceiling 17,000m (55,755 ft); range 2012km (1250 miles)
Weights:	empty 6142kg (13,540lb); maximum 11,676kg (25,740lb)
Dimensions:	span 8.26m (27ft 2in); length 14.91m (48ft 10in); height 4.6m (14ft 10in); wing area 34.84 sq m (375 sq ft)
Armament:	two 30mm DEFA cannon; one Matra R.511 or R.530 AAM, up to 2295kg (5060lb) of bombs

Dassault Mirage IIIO

Australia considered purchasing a Mirage version powered by the Rolls-Royce Avon, but eventually chose the standard Atar engine for its IIIOs, which were generally similar to the IIIE model. This RAAF Mirage was with 77 Squadron, RAF, when based at Butterworth in Malaysia.

SPECIFICATIONS	
Country of origin:	France
Type:	single-engined interceptor fighter
Powerplant:	one 62.63kN (14,080lb) thrust SNECMA Atar 9B3 afterburning turbojet
Performance:	maximum speed 2350km/h (1460mph); range 1006km (625 miles); service ceiling 18,105m (59,400ft)
Weights:	empty 7035kg (15,510lb); maximum 13,671kg (30,140lb)
Dimensions:	span 8.26m (27ft 2in); length 14.91m (48ft 10in); height 4.6m (14ft 10in); wing area 34.84 sq m (375 sq ft)
Armament:	two 30mm DEFA 552A cannon; various AAMs, up to 2295kg (10,725lb) of bombs

Dassault Mirage IIIR

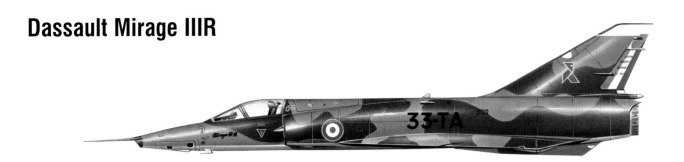

A reconnaissance version of the Mirage IIIE entered service in 1963 as the Mirage IIIR, replacing Republic RF-84F Thunderflashes in French service. This example served with EC 3/33 'Moselle' at Strasbourg-Entzheim. Export models were sold to South Africa, Switzerland, Abu Dhabi and Pakistan.

SPECIFICATIONS	
Country of origin:	France
Type:	single-engined reconnaissance aircraft
Powerplant:	one 58.72kN (13,200lb) thrust SNECMA Atar 09C afterburning turbojet engine
Performance:	maximum speed 1390km/h (864mph); range 1304km (810 miles); service ceiling 17,045m (55,921ft)
Weights:	empty 6608kg (14,569lb); maximum 13,718kg (30,242lb)
Dimensions:	span 8.26m (27ft 2in); length 15.54m (51ft); height 4.6m (14ft 10in); wing area 34.84 sq m (375 sq ft)
Armament:	none

Dassault Mirage 5M

In 1977, Zaire ordered 14 Mirage 5Ms, but took delivery of only eight. They served with 211 Escadrille of the Force Aérienne Zairoise at Kamina. The Mirage 5 was optimized for ground attack with more weapons pylons and a simpler radar system.

SPECIFICATIONS	
Country of origin:	France
Type:	single-engined fighter-bomber
Powerplant:	one 58.72kN (13,200lb) thrust SNECMA Atar 09C afterburning turbojet engine
Performance:	maximum speed 2350km/h (1460mph); range 1307km (812 miles); service ceiling 16,093m (52,800ft)
Weights:	empty 6586kg (14,520lb); maximum 13,671kg (30,140lb)
Dimensions:	span 8.26m (27ft 2in); length 15.65m (51ft 4in); height 2.87m (14ft 10in); wing area 34.84 sq m (375 sq ft)
Armament:	two 30mm DEFA 552A cannon; various AAMs, up to 3991kg (8800lb) of bombs

Dassault Mirage 5SDE

Saudi Arabia purchased about 30 Mirage 5s in 1972 on behalf of Egypt for diplomatic reasons. Although designated Mirage 5SDEs, they were essentially the same as Mirage IIIEs. Too late to participate in the Yom Kippur War with Israel, they saw combat in a short conflict with Libya in 1977.

SPECIFICATIONS	
Country of origin:	France
Type:	single-engined interceptor fighter
Powerplant:	one 62.63kN (14,080lb) thrust SNECMA Atar 9B3 afterburning turbojet
Performance:	maximum speed 2350km/h (1460mph); range 1006km (625 miles); service ceiling 18,105m (59,400ft)
Weights:	empty 7035kg (15,510lb); maximum 13,671kg (30,140lb)
Dimensions:	span 8.26m (27ft 2in); length 14.91m (48ft 10in); height 4.6m (14ft 10in); wing area 34.84 sq m (375 sq ft)
Armament:	two 30mm DEFA 552A cannon; various AAMs, up to 2295kg (10,725lb) of bombs

Mirage Modified

Denied the delivery of 50 Mirage 5Js that it had ordered and paid for, the Israelis sought to acquire plans of the Mirage and build it themselves. Secretly helped by Dassault, Israel Aircraft Industries was set up to produce a version called the *Nesher* (Eagle), which flew in 1969. The *Kfir* (Lion Cub), with the US J79 engine and canard foreplanes, followed. More recently, Israel has assisted South Africa with its Cheetah and Chile with the Pantera.

IAI Kfir

The original Mirage IIIC actually owes much of its inception to the close ties between Dassault and Israel. During the Six-Day War of 5–10 June 1967, this aircraft performed magnificently. Later, Israel Aircraft Industries set about devising an improved version of the Mirage III. The company adapted the airframe to take a General Electric J79 turbojet, under a programme dubbed Black Curtain. Some of these aircraft participated in the 1973 Yom Kippur War.

SPECIFICATIONS	
Country of origin:	Israel
Type:	single-seat interceptor
Powerplant:	one 79.6kN (17,900lb) General Electric J79-J1E turbojet
Performance:	maximum speed above 11,000m (36,090ft) 2445km/h (1520mph); service ceiling 17,680m (58,000ft); combat radius as interceptor 346km (215 miles)
Weights:	empty 7285kg (16,090lb); maximum take-off weight 16,200kg (35,715lb)
Dimensions:	wingspan 8.22m (26ft 11.5in); length 15.65m (51ft 4.25in); height 4.55m (14ft 11.25in); wing area 34.8 sq m (374.6 sq ft)
Armament:	one IAI (DEFA) 30mm cannon; nine external hardpoints with provision for up to 5775kg (12,732lb) of stores; for interception duties AIM-9 Sidewinder air-to-air missiles, or indigenously produced AAMs such as the Shafrir or Python

IAI Kfir C1 (F-21A)

The Kfir represented a significant improvement over the Mirage III. The installation of the J79 engine necessitated a redesign of the fuselage and the addition of a ram-cooling inlet ahead of the fin. The shorter engine resulted in a shorter rear fuselage, but the nose was lengthened to hold a comprehensive avionics suite.

SPECIFICATIONS	
Country of origin:	Israel
Type:	single-seat interceptor/ground attack aircraft
Powerplant:	one 79.6kN (17,900lb) General Electric J79-J1E turbojet
Performance:	maximum speed 2445km/h (1520mph); combat radius as interceptor 346km (215 miles)
Weights:	empty 7285kg (16,090lb); maximum take-off 16,200kg (35,715lb)
Dimensions:	wingspan 8.22m (26ft 11.5in); length 15.65m (51ft 4.25in); height 4.55m (14ft 11.25in); wing area 34.8 sq m (374.6 sq ft)
Armament:	one IAI (DEFA) 30mm cannon; provision for 5775kg (12,732lb) of bombs, rockets, napalm tanks and missiles

IAI Kfir TC2

The Kfir TC2 two-seat trainer first flew in 1982. It retained all the operational avionics of the C1, but had less fuel capacity. The long nose was angled down so as to not hamper the pilot's view during landing. Some TC2s were exported and the survivors were modified to TC7 standard.

SPECIFICATIONS	
Country of origin:	Israel
Type:	single-seat interceptor
Powerplant:	one 79.6kN (17,900lb) General Electric J79-J1E turbojet
Performance:	maximum speed above 11,000m (36,090ft) 2445km/h (1520mph); service ceiling 17,680m (58,000ft); combat radius as interceptor 346km (215 miles)
Weights:	unknown
Dimensions:	wingspan 8.22m (26ft 11.5in); length 16.15m (53ft); height 4.55m (14ft 11.25in); wing area 34.8 sq m (374.60 sq ft)
Armament:	one 30mm cannon; provision for up to 5775kg (12,732lb) of stores; for interception duties AIM-9 Sidewinder air-to-air missiles, or Shafrir or Python AAMs

Atlas Cheetah D

The Atlas Cheetah is, in fact, the South African answer to an international arms embargo imposed on the country in 1977, which prevented the SAAF from importing a replacement for its ageing fleet of Mirage IIIs. The programme involved replacing nearly 50 per cent of the airframe. Production aircraft are modified from both single-seaters and twin seaters.

SPECIFICATIONS	
Country of origin:	South Africa
Type:	one/two-seat combat and training aircraft
Powerplant:	one 70.6kN (15,873lb) SNECMA Atar 9K-50 turbojet
Performance:	maximum speed above 12,000m (39,370ft) 2337 km/h (1452mph); service ceiling 17,000m (55,775ft)
Weights:	not revealed
Dimensions:	wingspan 8.22m (26ft 11.5in); length 15.4m (50ft 6.5in); height 4.25m (13ft 11.5in); wing area 35 sq m (376.75sq ft)
Armament:	two 30mm DEFA cannon, Armscor V3B and V3C Kukri air-to-air missiles, provision for external stores such as cluster bombs, laser designator pods, and rockets

Dassault Mirage 50C (Pantera)

Chile purchased 17 Mirage 50s, including three two-seat 50DC models in 1982–3. Local firm ENAER began upgrading them as the *Pantera* (Panther) with Israeli help soon afterwards. The modernization package includes canard foreplanes and the ability to use a range of Israeli precison weapons.

SPECIFICATIONS	
Country of origin:	France
Type:	single-engined fighter-bomber
Powerplant:	one 70.5kN (15,850lb) thrust SNECMA Atar 09K-50 afterburning turbojet engine
Performance:	maximum speed at high altitude 2350km/h (1460mph); service ceiling 18,105m (59,400ft); range 1408km (875 miles)
Weights:	empty 7136kg (15,730lb); maximum take-off 13,671kg (30,140lb)
Dimensions:	span 8.26m (27ft 2in); length 15.65m (51ft 4in); height 2.87m (14ft 10in); wing area 34.84 sq m (375 sq ft)
Armament:	two 30mm DEFA 552A cannon; various AAMs, up to 3991kg (8800lb) of bombs

Indo-Pakistani Wars

Partitioned at the time of independence in 1947, India and Pakistan fought major wars in 1965 and 1971, and have been involved in low-intensity conflict over the territory of Kashmir ever since. Air power played a vital role in the two major wars, and there were numerous air combats between Indian Air Force (IAF) and Pakistan Air Force (PAF) fighters, which were among the first battles involving supersonic aircraft.

North American F-86F Sabre

Pakistan's Sabre pilots made claims for 19 IAF aircraft in 1965, the majority of them Hunters. Fifteen of these claims match Indian losses. In 1971, they lost 28 Sabres to various causes. Pakistan received 120 Sabres, including Canadair Sabre Mk.6s (illustrated).

SPECIFICATIONS	
Country of origin:	United States/Canada
Type:	(CL-13B Sabre Mk. 6) single-engined jet fighter
Powerplant:	one 32.36kN (7275lb) thrust Avro Orenda Mark 14 turbojet engine
Performance:	maximum speed 965km/h (600mph); combat radius 530km (329 miles); service ceiling 14,600m (48,000ft)
Weights:	empty 4816 kg (10,500 lb); maximum 6628 kg (14,613 lb)
Dimensions:	span 11.58m (39ft); length 11.4m (37ft 6in); height 4.4m (14ft 8in); wing area 28.06 sq m (302 sq ft)
Armament:	six .5in (12.7mm) machine guns

Shenyang F-6 (MiG-19 'Farmer')

Pakistan had three squadrons of Shenyang F-6As (MiG-19s) in its inventory by 1971. Unusually for a non-Western type, they were equipped with AIM-9 Sidewinder missiles. In 1971, four F-6s were lost, one of them in air combat, but they claimed five Indian jets in return.

SPECIFICATIONS	
Country of origin:	USSR
Type:	single-seat all-weather interceptor
Powerplant:	two 31.9kN (7165lb) Klimov RD-9B turbojets
Performance:	max speed 1480km/h (920mph); service ceiling 17,900m (58,725ft); range 2200km (1367 miles)
Weights:	empty 5760kg (12,698lb); maximum take-off weight 9500kg (20,944lb)
Dimensions:	wingspan 9m (29ft 6.5in); length 13.58m (44ft 7in); height 4.02m (13ft 2.25in); wing area 25 sq m (269.11 sq ft)
Armament:	underwing pylons for four AA-1 Alkali air-to-air-missiles, or AA-2 Atoll

Hawker Hunter F.56

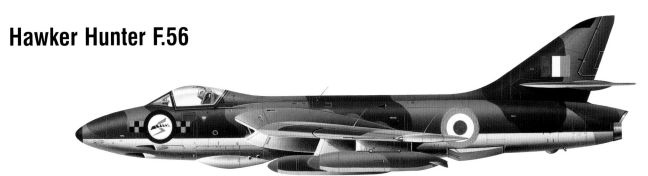

Hunters were the most numerous combat aircraft in the IAF inventory in 1965, and equipped six squadrons in each war. Able to carry bombs or rockets as well as its heavy cannon, it was a powerful ground-attack platform. In one, 1971 battle Hunters were credited with destroying a Pakistani tank division.

SPECIFICATIONS	
Country of origin:	United Kingdom
Type:	single-seat fighter
Powerplant:	one 45.13kN (10,145lb) thrust Rolls-Royce Avon 207 turbojet engine
Performance:	maximum speed at sea level 1144km/h (710mph); service ceiling 15,240m (50,000ft); range on internal fuel 689km (490 miles)
Weights:	empty 6405kg (14,122lb) maximum 17,750kg (24,600lb)
Dimensions:	wingspan 10.26m (33ft 8in); length 13.98m (45ft 10.5in);height 4.02m (13ft 2in); wing area 32.42 sq m (349 sq ft)
Armament:	four 30mm Aden Cannon; up to 2722kg (6000lb) of bombs or rockets

Hawker Sea Hawk FB.Mk 3

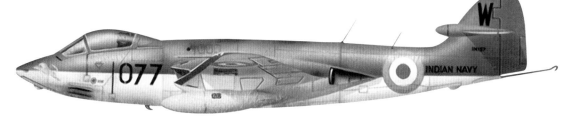

India bought Sea Hawks from the United Kingdom and Germany in 1960 and used them in both wars. They flew from shore bases in 1965 and from the carrier INS *Vikrant* in 1971. Their most notable mission in 1971 was an attack on the port of Chittagong and the Pakistani shipping there.

SPECIFICATIONS	
Country of origin:	United Kingdom
Type:	single-seat carrier based fighter-bomber
Powerplant:	one 24kN (5400lb) Rolls-Royce Nene 103 turbojet
Performance:	maximum speed at sea level 969km/h (602mph); service ceiling 13,565m (44,500ft); combat radius (clean) 370km (230 miles)
Weights:	empty 4409kg (9720lb); maximum take-off weight 7348kg (16,200lb)
Dimensions:	wingspan 11.89m (39ft); length 12.09m (39ft 8in); height 2.64m (8ft 8in); wing area 25.83 sq m (278 sq ft)
Armament:	four 20mm Hispano cannon; plus underwing hardpoints with provision for four 227kg (500lb) bombs, or two 227kg (500lb) bombs and 20 three-inch or 16 five-inch rockets

English Electric Canberra B.66

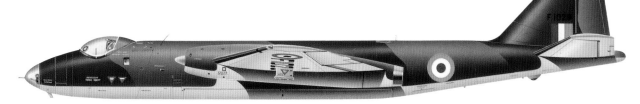

India ordered 80 Canberras in 1957 and acquired more in later years, including 10 refurbished B(I).66 models as illustrated. In 1965, Indian Canberras bombed Pakistan's air bases by night, but also lost some of their number on the ground to PAF attacks.

SPECIFICATIONS	
Country of origin:	United Kingdom
Type:	twin-engined jet bomber
Powerplant:	two 33.23kN (7490lb) thrust turbojet engine Avon R.A.7 Mk,109 turbojet engines
Performance:	maximum speed 933km/h (580mph); range 5440km (3380 miles); service ceiling 15,000m (48,000ft)
Weights:	9820kg (21,650lb); maximum 24,948kg (55,000lb)
Dimensions:	span 19.51m (65ft 6in); length 19.96m (65ft 6in); height 4.77m (15ft 8in); wing area 88.19 sq m (960 sq ft)
Armament:	four 20mm cannon; two rocket pods or up to 2772kg (6000lb) of bombs

Lockheed F-104 Starfighter

The 'missile with a man in it' was one of many names for the Lockheed Starfighter. With its needle-like fuselage and tiny wings, the F-104 had exceptional speed and climb performance, but was not noted for its dogfight manoeuvrability. The US Air Force used it as an interceptor for a fairly short period, but in the so-called 'sale of the century', it was sold to seven European nations, who used it in the fighter and strike roles.

Lockheed F-104C Starfighter

The F-104 was dispatched to Vietnam in 1965, but was not a great success in the escort fighter and fighter-bomber roles. This F-104C of the 8th TFW was based at Udorn, Thailand, in 1966. It is fitted with a fixed refuelling probe to extend its range for low-level operations.

SPECIFICATIONS	
Country of origin:	United States
Type:	single-seat multi-mission strike fighter
Powerplant:	one 70.29kN (15,800lb) thrust General Electric J79-GE-7A afterburning turbojet engine
Performance:	maximum speed at 15,240m (50,000ft) 1845km/h (1146mph); service ceiling 15,240m (50,000ft); range 1740km (1081 miles)
Weights:	maximum 12,634kg (27,853lb)
Dimensions:	wingspan (excluding missiles) 6.36m (21ft 9in); length 16.66m (54ft 8in); height 4.09m (13ft 5in); wing area 18.22 sq m (196.10sq ft)
Armament:	one 20mm cannon, provision for AIM-9 Sidewinder on fuselage, under wings or on tips, and up to 908kg (2000lb) of bombs

Lockheed TF-104G Starfighter

West Germany undertook most initial training of their F-104 pilots in Arizona, using the two-seat TF-104G. A total of 220 examples of this combat-capable version were produced. Operating Starfighters at low level in European weather proved hazardous, and the Luftwaffe lost more than 200 F-104s.

SPECIFICATIONS	
Country of origin:	United States
Type:	single-seat multi-mission strike fighter
Powerplant:	one 69.4kN (15,600lb) General Electric J79-GE-11A turbojet
Performance:	max speed 1845km/h (1146mph); service ceiling 15,240m (50,000ft); range 1740km (1081 miles)
Weight:	empty 6348kg (13,995lb); maximum take-off 13,170kg (29,035lb)
Dimensions:	wingspan (excluding missiles) 6.36m (21ft 9in); length unreleased; height 4.09m (13ft 5in); wing area 18.22 sq m (196.10 sq ft)
Armament:	Provision for AIM-9 Sidewinder on fuselage, under wings or on tips, and/or stores up to a maximum of 1814kg (4000lb)

Lockheed F-104G Starfighter

The F-104G was designed for Germany, but was also exported to several nations, including the Republic of China, which used it from 1960 to 1998. Taiwanese F-104s destroyed two PLAAF J-6s in a skirmish over the Taiwan Straits in January 1967.

SPECIFICATIONS	
Country of origin:	United States
Type:	single-seat multi-mission strike fighter
Powerplant:	one 69.4kN (15,600lb) General Electric J79-GE-11A turbojet engine
Performance:	maximum speed at 15,240m (50,000ft) 1845km/h (1146mph); service ceiling 15,240m (50,000ft); range 1740km (1081 miles)
Weights:	empty 6348kg (13,995lb); maximum take-off 13,170kg (29,035lb)
Dimensions:	wingspan (excluding missiles) 6.36m (21ft 9in); length 16.66m (54ft 8in); height 4.09m (13ft 5in); wing area 18.22 sq m (196.1 sq ft)
Armament:	one 20mm cannon, provision for AIM-9 Sidewinder on fuselage, under wings or on tips, and up to 1814kg (4000lb) stores

Lockheed CF-104G Starfighter

Denmark bought new F-104Gs from Lockheed in 1962 and added further ex-Canadian CF-104s in 1972. They frequently intercepted Soviet aircraft over the Baltic Sea. The RDAF retired its Starfighters in 1985, replacing them with F-16s.

SPECIFICATIONS	
Country of origin:	United States
Type:	single-seat multi-mission strike fighter
Powerplant:	one 69.4kN (15,600lb) General Electric J79-GE-11A turbojet engine
Performance:	maximum speed at 15,240m (50,000ft) 1845km/h (1146mph); service ceiling 15,240m (50,000ft); range 1740km (1081 miles)
Weights:	empty 6348kg (13,995lb); maximum take-off 13,170kg (29,035lb)
Dimensions:	wingspan (excluding missiles) 6.36m (21ft 9in); length 16.66m (54ft 8in); height 4.09m (13ft 5in); wing area 18.22 sq m (196.10 sq ft)
Armament:	one 20mm M61A1 Vulcan cannon; AIM-9B/N Sidewinder AAMs; 2.75in (70mm) rocket pods

Aeritalia/Lockheed F-104 ASA Starfighter

Italy built nearly 250 F-104S Starfighters for itself and Turkey. The S designation denoted the ability to fire AIM-7 Sparrow missiles. The F-104 ASA (Aggiornamento Sistemi d'Arma) upgrade added a new radar and missiles in the 1990s. Italy retired the last military Starfighters in 2004.

SPECIFICATIONS	
Country of origin:	Italy
Type:	single-seat multi-mission strike fighter
Powerplant:	one 79.6kN (17,900lb) thrust General Electric J79-GE-19 afterburning turbojet engine
Performance:	maximum speed 2330km/h (1450mph); service ceiling 17,680m (58,000ft); range 2920km (1815 miles)
Weights:	empty 6760kg (14,900lb), maximum 14,060kg (31,000lb)
Dimensions:	wingspan (excluding missiles) 6.36m (21ft 9in); length 16.66m (54ft 8in); height 4.09m (13ft 5in); wing area 18.22 sq m (196.10 sq ft)
Armament:	one 20mm M61A1 Vulcan cannon; AIM-9L Sidewinder, AIM-7 Sparrow or Selenia Aspide AAMs

Six-Day War

Following a long period of tension between Israel and its neighbours, Israel launched air attacks against Egypt on 5 June 1967, destroying most of the Egyptian Air Force on the ground. Iraqi and Syrian aircraft counterattacked, but most of their aircraft were lost in air combat or return raids by the Israeli Air Force. Israeli air losses were light, and within two days the Arab air forces had ceased to be a factor.

Sud Aviation SO.4050 Vautour

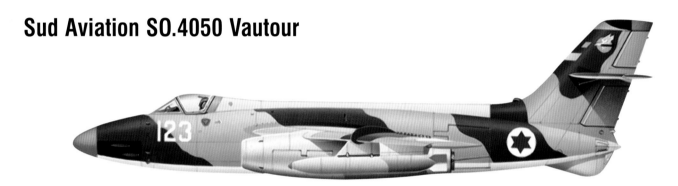

The Vautour IIA was a dedicated ground-attack version, equipped with heavy cannon as well as rockets and bombs. The IDF/AF's 110 Squadron operated a mix of IIA attackers and IIB bombers, while 119 Squadron flew IIN night fighters. Four Vautours were lost in the Six-Day War.

SPECIFICATIONS	
Country of origin:	France
Type:	two-seat medium bomber
Powerplant:	two 34.3kN (7716lb) SNECMA Atar 101E-3 turbojets
Performance:	maximum speed 1105km/h (687mph); service ceiling more than 15000m (49,210ft); range 5400km (3375 miles)
Weight:	maximum 21,000kg (46,300lb)
Dimensions:	wingspan 15.09m (49ft 6in); length 15.57m (51ft 1in); height 4.5m (14ft 9in)
Armament:	four 30mm DEFA cannon; pack containing 116 68mm (2.7in) rockets; up to 4400kg (9700lb) of bombs

Dassault Mystère IVA

Three squadrons of Mystère IVAs led the Israeli attack on Egypt. Once the Egyptian airfields had been neutralized, they turned to supporting ground forces in the Sinai. They were also involved in the controversial attack on the American spy ship USS *Liberty*.

SPECIFICATIONS	
Country of origin:	France
Type:	single-seat fighter bomber
Powerplant:	one 27.9kN (6,280lb) Hispano Suiza Tay 250A turbojet; or 3500kg (7716lb) Hispano Suiza Verdon 350 turbojet
Performance:	maximum speed 1120km/h (696mph); service ceiling 13,750m (45,000ft); range 1320km (820 miles)
Weights:	empty 5875kg (11,514lb); loaded 9500kg (20,950lb)
Dimensions:	span 11.1m (36ft 5.75in); length 12.9m (42ft 2in); height 4.4m (14ft 5in)
Armament:	two 30mm cannon with 150 rounds, provision for up to 907kg (2000lb) of stores, including tanks, rockets or bombs

Dassault Mirage IIICJ

The most important IDF/AF fighter of the Six-Day War was the Mirage IIICJ Shahak (Heavens), which scored 56 aerial victories against the various Arab air forces. This aircraft served with 117 'First Jet' Squadron, which claimed 11 kills in 1967.

SPECIFICATIONS	
Country of origin:	France
Type:	single-engined interceptor fighter
Powerplant:	one 58.72kN (13,200lb) thrust SNECMA Atar 09B-3 afterburning turbojet engine and one 16.46kN (3700lb) thrust auxiliary SEFR 841 rocket motor
Performance:	maximum speed 2350km/h (1460mph); service ceiling 17,000m (55,755 ft); range 2012km (1250 miles)
Weights:	empty 6142kg (13,540lb); maximum 11,676kg (25,740lb)
Dimensions:	span 8.26m (27ft 2in); length 14.91m (48ft 10in); height 4.6m (14ft 10in); wing area 34.84 sq m (375 sq ft)
Armament:	two 30mm DEFA cannon; one Matra R.511 or R.530 AAM, up to 2295kg (5060lb) of bombs

Mikoyan-Gurevich MiG-17 'Fresco'

Egypt had four operational squadrons and a training unit of MiG-17s in 1967. Syria and Iraq also committed theirs to the fighting and lost a number in air combat. In all, the Arab air forces lost 89 MiG-15s and -17s, 90 per cent of them on the ground.

SPECIFICATIONS	
Country of origin:	USSR
Type:	single-seat fighter
Powerplant:	one 33kN (7,452lb) Klimov VK-1F turbojet
Performance:	maximum speed 1145km/h (711mph); service ceiling 16,600m (54,560ft); range at height with slipper tanks 1470km (913 miles)
Weights:	empty 4100kg (9040lb); maximum loaded 600kg (14,770lb)
Dimensions:	wingspan 9.45m (31ft); length 11.05m (36ft 3.75in); height 3.35m (11ft); wing area 20.6 sq m (221.74sq ft)
Armament:	one 37mm N-37 cannon and two 23mm NS-23 cannon, plus up to 500kg (1102lb) of mixed stores on underwing pylons

Mikoyan-Gurevich MiG-21 MF 'Fishbed'

Egypt lost an estimated 90 MiG-21s in the initial air attacks of July 1967. In the subsequent days, they were able to claim five Israeli aircraft destroyed and several more damaged. The combined Arab air forces had bought 235 MiG-21s but had many fewer operational in 1967.

SPECIFICATIONS	
Country of origin:	USSR
Type:	single-seat all-weather multi role fighter
Powerplant:	one 60.8kN (14,550lb) thrust Tumanskii R-13-300 afterburning turbojet
Performance:	maximum speed 2229km/h (1385mph); service ceiling 17,500m (57,400ft); range on internal fuel 1160km (721 miles)
Weights:	empty 5200kg (11,464lb); maximum take-off 10,400kg (22,925lb)
Dimensions:	wingspan 7.15m (23ft 5.5in); length (including probe) 15.76m (51ft 8.5in); height 4.1m (13ft 5.5in); wing area 23 sq m (247.58 sq ft)
Armament:	one 23mm cannon, provision for about 1500kg (3307lb) of stores, including air-to-air missiles, rocket pods, napalm tanks, or drop tanks

Yom Kippur War

On the Jewish holiday of Yom Kippur in October 1973, Syrian and Egyptian forces crossed Israel's borders. The initial days of fighting were the most desperate for Israel and the IDF/AF. Surface-to-air missiles played a much greater part in this war, causing most of Israel's losses. An American airlift of weapons, including aircraft and spare parts, is credited as a factor in preventing Israel's defeat.

Dassault Super Mystère B.2

Known as the 'Sambad', the Super Mystère B.2 was Israel's first supersonic fighter. By early 1973, the IDF/AF had upgraded its Super Mystère B.2s with the J52 engine of the Skyhawk, creating the *Sa'ar* (Tempest), which was used mainly on ground-attack missions.

SPECIFICATIONS	
Country of origin:	France
Type:	single-seat fighter bomber
Powerplant:	one 43.7kN (9833lb) SNECMA Atar 101 G-2/-3 turbojet
Performance:	maximum speed 1195km/h (743mph); service ceiling 17,000m (55,775ft); range 870km (540 miles)
Weights:	empty 6932kg (15,282lb); maximum take-off 10,000kg (22,046lb)
Dimensions:	wingspan 10.52m (34ft 6in); length 14.13m (46ft 4.25in); height 4.55m (14ft 11in); wing area 35 sq m (376.75 sq ft)
Armament:	two 30mm cannon, internal launcher for 35 68mm rockets, provision for up to 907kg (2000lb) of stores, including tanks, rockets or bombs

Douglas A-4N Skyhawk

Over 360 A-4 Skyhawks were delivered to Israel, where they were known as the *Ayit* (Vulture). Thirty examples of the A-4N, designed to Israel's specifications, had been delivered by October 1973. Over 50 A-4s of various sub-types were lost in 1973, mainly to SAMs.

SPECIFICATIONS	
Country of origin:	United States
Type:	single-engined fighter-bomber
Powerplant:	one 49.82kN (11,200lb) thrust Pratt & Whitney J52-P408 turbojet engine
Performance:	maximum speed 1038km/h (645mph); range 1090km (680 miles); service ceiling 11,795m (38,698ft)
Weights:	empty 4747kg (10,465lb); maximum 11,115kg (24,504lb)
Dimensions:	span 8.38m (27ft 6in); length 12.22m (40ft 2in); height 4.57m (15ft); wing area 24.15 sq m (260 sq ft)
Armament:	two 30mm DEFA 534 cannon

McDonnell Douglas F-4E Phantom II

The successes of the Israeli Defence Force/Air Force during the 1973 Yom Kippur War helped to seal the Phantom's reputation as the finest combat aircraft of its generation. Israel purchased 204 F-4Es during the early 1970s, and they remained in front-line operation for many years. Modifications included adoption of the indigenously produced Elta EL/M-2021 multi-mode radar.

SPECIFICATIONS	
Country of origin:	United States
Type:	two-seat all-weather fighter/attack aircraft
Powerplant:	two 79.6kN (17,900lb) General Electric J79-GE-17 turbojets
Performance:	maximum speed 2390km/h (1485mph); service ceiling 19,685m (60,000ft); range 817km (1750 miles)
Weights:	empty 12,700kg (28,000lb); maximum take-off 26,308kg (58,000lb)
Dimensions:	span 11.7m (38ft 5in); length 17.76m (58ft 3in); height 4.96m (16ft 3in); wing area 49.24 sq m (530 sq ft)
Armament:	one 20mm M61A1 Vulcan cannon and four AIM-7 Sparrow recessed under fuselage or other weapons up to 1370kg (3020lb) on centreline pylon; four wing pylons for two AIM-7, or four AIM-9

Mikoyan-Gurevich MiG-17F 'Fresco'

Syrian 'Frescoes' suffered at the hands of Israel's fighters in October 1973, particularly against the Mirages. One Syrian pilot made a claim for an F-4E, but otherwise their contribution was limited. By this time, the MiG-21 had become the predominant type in the Syrian AF inventory.

SPECIFICATIONS	
Country of origin:	USSR
Type:	single-seat fighter
Powerplant:	one 33.1kN (7452lb) Klimov VK-1F turbojet
Performance:	maximum speed 1145km/h (711mph); service ceiling 16,600m (54,560ft); range at height 1470km (913 miles)
Weights:	empty 4100kg (9040lb); maximum loaded 600kg (14,770lb)
Dimensions:	wingspan 9.45m (31ft); length 11.05m (36ft 3.75in); height 3.35m (11ft); wing area 20.6 sq m (221.74 sq ft)
Armament:	one 37mm N-37 cannon and two 23mm NS-23 cannon, plus up to 500kg (1102lb) of mixed stores on underwing pylons

Sukhoi Su-7BM 'Fitter-A'

The Su-7 'Fitter' was supplied to Syria, Iraq and Egypt (illustrated) before 1973. Although fast and with a good warload, the Su-7 had short range and an unreliable afterburner. Many were lost to IDF/AF fighters, although they inflicted considerable damage on Israeli ground forces.

SPECIFICATIONS	
Country of origin:	USSR
Type:	single-seat ground attack fighter
Powerplant:	one 110.3kN (24,802lb) Lyul'ka AL-21F-3 turbojet
Performance:	maximum speed approximately 2220km/h (1380mph); service ceiling 15,200m (49,865ft); combat radius 675km (419 miles)
Weights:	empty 9500kg (20,944lb); maximum take-off 19,500kg (42,990lb)
Dimensions:	wingspan 13.8m (45ft 3in) spread and 10m (32ft 10in) swept; length 18.75m (61ft 6in); height 5m (16ft 5in); wing area 40 sq m (430 sq ft)
Armament:	two 30mm cannon; provision for up to 4250kg (9370lb) of stores, including nuclear weapons, missiles, bombs and napalm tanks

McDonnell Douglas F-4 Phantom

The F-4 Phantom II was built to a US Navy requirement, but was quickly adopted by the USAF in a rare example for the 1950s of joint procurement of a weapons system. Able to carry a heavy ground attack load as well as eight air-to-air missiles, the F-4 also proved a hit on the export market. Phantoms were supplied to 10 nations. Production in the United States and Japan totalled 5195.

F4H-1 Phantom II

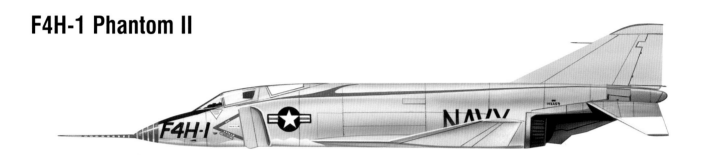

The Phantom II first appeared as the F4H-1F in the pre-1962 US Navy designation system. The Phantom made its maiden flight in May 1957 and the pre-production F4H-1s set a string of records for closed-circuit and point-to-point speed, and for climb to altitude.

SPECIFICATIONS	
Country of origin:	United States
Type:	(F4H-1F) twin-engined two-seat carrier-based fighter
Powerplant:	two 71.84kN (16,150lb) thrust General Electric J79-GE-2 turbojet engines
Performance:	maximum speed unknown; range unknown; service ceiling unknown
Weights:	unknown
Dimensions:	span 11.6m (38ft 4in); length 17.7m (58ft 4in); height 4.9m (16ft 3in); wing area 49.2 sq m (530 sq ft)
Armament:	four AIM-7 Sparrow under fuselage, provision for two AIM-7 or four AIM-9 Sidewinder; provision for 20mm M-61 cannon, and tanks and bombs to a weight of 6219kg (13,500lb)

F-4C Phantom II

The USAF adopted the Phantom in 1960, initially as the F-110A, but later redesignated F-4C. The first production model F-4s had larger radomes and raised rear canopies compared to the F4H-1. This F-4C served with the Michigan Air National Guard in the 1980s.

SPECIFICATIONS	
Country of origin:	United States
Type:	two seat all-weather fighter/attack aircraft
Powerplant:	two 75.6kN (17,000lb) General Electric J79-GE-15 turbojets
Performance:	maximum speed 2414km/h (1500mph); service ceiling 18,300m (60,000ft); range on internal fuel tanks 2817km (1750 miles)
Weights:	empty 12,700kg (28,000lb); maximum take-off 26,308kg (58,000lb)
Dimensions:	span 11.7m (38ft 5in); length 17.76m (58ft 3in); height 4.96m (16ft 3in); wing area 49.24 sq m (530 sq ft)
Armament:	four AIM-7 Sparrow; two wing pylons for two AIM-7, or four AIM-9 Sidewinder, provision for 20mm M-61 cannon; provision for bombs or other stores to a maximum weight of 6219kg (13,500lb)

F-4S Phantom II

One of the lesser known of the F-4 variants, the F-4S was a development of the F-4J models constructed in small numbers for the US Navy. The F-4J had the AWG-10 pulse-doppler radar, drooping ailerons, slatted tail and J79-GE-10 engines. Also incorporated was an automatic carrier landing system. Production of carrier-based Phantoms lasted for a remarkable 17 years.

SPECIFICATIONS	
Country of origin:	United States
Type:	two-seat all-weather fighter/attack carrier-borne aircraft
Powerplant:	two 79.6kN (17,900lb) General Electric J79-GE-10 turbojets
Performance:	maximum speed at high altitude 2414km/h (1500mph); service ceiling over 18,300m (60,000ft); range 2817km (1750 miles)
Weights:	empty 12,700kg (28,000lb); maximum take-off 26,308kg (58,000lb)
Dimensions:	span 11.7m (38ft 5in); length 17.76m (58ft 3in); height 4.96m (16ft 3in); wing area 49.24 sq m (530 sq ft)
Armament:	four AIM-7 Sparrow; two wing pylons for two AIM-7, or four AIM-9 Sidewinder, provision for 20mm cannon in external centreline pod; four wing pylons for tanks, bombs or other stores to a maximum weight of 6219kg (13,500lb)

Phantom FGR.2

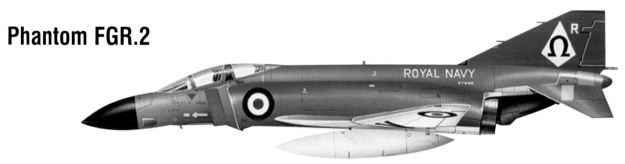

The United Kingdom bought its own model of Phantom for the RAF and FAA. The FG.1 for the Navy and FGR.2 (Air Force, illustrated) had Rolls-Royce Spey engines, which required larger intakes and other airframe changes. When the aircraft carrier *Ark Royal* retired, its Phantoms went to the RAF.

SPECIFICATIONS	
Country of origin:	United States
Type:	two-seat all-weather fighter/attack carrier-borne aircraft
Powerplant:	two 91.2kN (20,515lb) Rolls-Royce Spey 202 turbofans
Performance:	maximum speed 2230km/h (1386mph); service ceiling over 18,300m (60,000ft); range on internal fuel 2817km (1750 miles)
Weights:	empty 12,700kg (28,000lb); maximum take-off 26,308kg (58,000lb)
Dimensions:	span 11.7m (38ft 5in); length 17.55m (57ft 7in); height 4.96m (16ft 3in); wing area 49.24 sq m (530sq ft)
Armament:	four AIM-7 Sparrow recessed under fuselage; two wing pylons for two AIM-7, or four AIM-9 Sidewinder, provision for 20mm cannon; pylons for stores to a maximum weight of 7257kg (16,000lb)

RF-4EJ Phantom II

The Phantom proved easily adaptable into a high-speed tactical reconnaissance aircraft. The RF-4B (Marines) and RF-4C (USAF) preceded the RF-4E export version. RF-4Es were used by Germany, Iran, Greece, Turkey and Japan, whose version (illustrated) was the RF-4EJ.

SPECIFICATIONS	
Country of origin:	United States
Type:	two-seat tactical reconnaissance aircraft
Powerplant:	two 79.6kN (17900lb) thrust General Electric J79-GE-17 afterburning turbojet engines
Performance:	maximum speed at 14,630m (48,000ft) 2390km/h (1485mph); service ceiling 18,900m (62,000ft); range 800km (500 miles)
Weights:	empty 13,768kg (30,328lb); maximum loaded 24,766kg (54,600lb)
Dimensions:	wingspan 11.7m (38ft 5in); length 18m (59ft); height 4.96m (16ft 3in); wing area 49.24 sq m (530 sq ft)
Armament:	none

Vietnam War: FACs and COIN

The Vietnam War began as a relatively low-level counter-insurgency (COIN) operation and grew to involve almost every US weapons system short of nuclear arms. In the South, it was a war of defending villages and military outposts, and interdicting supply routes from the North. Slow but agile prop-driven aircraft provided Forward Air Control (FAC) for fast jets that were vital for the close air support of troops.

Cessna O-2 Skymaster

The Cessna Model 337's unusual push-and-pull engine configuration gave it twin-engined power with single-engined drag and handling characteristics. As the O-2A, it made an effective FAC platform. This one was based at Nakhom Phanom, Thailand, in 1970.

SPECIFICATIONS	
Country of origin:	United States
Type:	(O-2A) twin-engined Forward Air Control Aircraft
Powerplant:	two 157kW (210hp) Continental IO-360C flat-6 piston engines
Performance:	maximum speed 322km/h (200mph)); range 2132KM (1325 miles); service ceiling 5940m (18,000ft)
Weights:	empty 1292kg (2848lb); loaded 2448kg (5400lb)
Dimensions:	span 11.63m (38ft 2in); length 9.07m (29ft 8in); height 2.79m (9ft 2in); wing area 18.8 sq m (202.5 sq ft)
Armament:	rocket pods for target marking

North American OV-10A Bronco

The purpose-built North American (later Rockwell) OV-10 Bronco replaced the O-2 with the USAF, but also served with the Navy and Marines as an FAC and light-attack aircraft. This OV-10A was assigned to the USMC's VMO-4 squadron at Quang Tri, Republic of Vietnam.

SPECIFICATIONS	
Country of origin:	United States
Type:	twin-engined Forward Air Control Aircraft
Powerplant:	two 533kW (715hp) Garrett T76-G-410/412 turboprop engines
Performance:	maximum speed 452km/h (281mph); service ceiling 7315m (24,000ft); range 358km (576 miles)
Weights:	empty 3127kg (6893lb); maximum 6552kg (14,444lb)
Dimensions:	span 12.19m (40ft); length 12.67m (41ft 7in); height 4.62m (15ft 2in); wing area 64.57 sq m (695 sq ft)
Armament:	four 7.62mm M60C machine-guns; pods for 70mm (2.75in) or 125mm (5in) rockets; up to 125kg (500lb) of bombs

On Mark B-26K Counter Invader

SPECIFICATIONS	
Country of origin:	United States
Type:	Twin-engined attack aircraft
Powerplant:	two 1864kW (2500hp) Pratt & Whitney R-2800-52W radial piston engines
Performance:	maximum speed 520 km/h (323 mph); service ceiling 8717m (28,600ft); range 2382km (1480 miles)
Weights:	empty 11,399kg (25,130lb); maximum 17,804kg (39,250lb)
Dimensions:	span 21.79m (71ft 6in); length 15.71m (51ft 7in); height 5.79m (19ft); wing area 50.17 sq m (540 sq ft)
Armament:	14 .5in (12.7mm) machine guns; up to 5443kg (12,000 lb) bombs

The On Mark Corporation converted Douglas B-26B and C Invaders into the B-26K Counter Invader for the USAF's Air Commando units in Vietnam. The structure was strengthened and wingtip fuel tanks added. They flew mainly night-interdiction missions over Vietnam and Laos.

Northrop F-5A Freedom Fighter

The USAF made relatively little use of the F-5, but sent a unit to Bien Hoa, Vietnam in late 1965 under an evaluation programme called 'Skoshi Tiger'. The results were mixed, but helped sell the F-5 as a light fighter and ground attacker to South Vietnam and many other Asian nations.

SPECIFICATIONS	
Country of origin:	United States
Type:	light tactical fighter
Powerplant:	two 18.1kN (4080lb) General Electric J85-GE-13 turbojets
Performance:	maximum speed at 10,975m (36,000ft) 1487km/h (924mph); service ceiling 15,390m (50,500ft); combat radius with maximum warload 314km (195 miles)
Weights:	empty 3667kg (8085lb); maximum take-off 9374kg (20,667lb)
Dimensions:	wingspan 7.7m (25ft 3in); length 14.38m (47ft 2in); height 4.01m (13ft 2in); wing area 15.79 sq m (170sq ft)
Armament:	two 20mm M39 cannon with 280rpg; provision for 1996kg (4400lb) of stores (missiles, bombs, cluster bombs, rocket launcher pods)

North American F-100F Super Sabre

SPECIFICATIONS	
Country of origin:	United States
Type:	single-seat fighter-bomber
Powerplant:	one 75.6kN (17,000lb) Pratt & Whitney J57-P-21A turbojet
Performance:	maximum speed at 10,670m (35,000ft) 1390km/h (864mph); service ceiling 14,020m (46,000ft); range with inernal fuel 966km (600 miles)
Weights:	maximum 17,745kg (39,122lb)
Dimensions:	wingspan 11.82m (38ft 9.5in); length 15.2m (50ft); height 4.95m (16ft 3in); wing area 35.77 sq m (385 sq ft)
Armament:	two 20mm Pontiac M39 cannon; up to 3402kg (7500lb) of rockets, bombs or cannon pods

The two-seat F-100F Super Sabre was used in a variety of roles in Vietnam, including close air support, anti-radar 'Wild Weasel' missions and as a fast FAC, able to reach a battlefield quickly and precisely mark defended targets for attack aircraft.

Vietnam War: Naval Air Power

From August 1964, the aircraft carriers on 'Yankee Station' off the coast of North Vietnam launched daily strike packages against military, industrial and transport targets. Increasingly sophisticated defences, including MiGs, SAMs and radar-controlled anti-aircraft guns of various calibres, took a heavy toll on carrier-based aircraft, with 530 aircraft lost and 620 aviators killed, missing or made prisoner.

Douglas A-4F Skyhawk

During its long career, the Skyhawk has proved to be one of the most versatile combat aircraft ever built, disproving those who argued that the small, lightweight machine would be outclassed by bigger, heavier aircraft. The aircraft pictured is an A-4F, the final attack version for the US Navy, distinguished by the dorsal hump carrying additional avionics and the J52-P-8A engine.

SPECIFICATIONS	
Country of origin:	United States
Type:	single-seat attack bomber
Powerplant:	one 41.3kN (9300lb) J52-8A turbojet
Performance:	maximum speed 1078km/h (670mph); service ceiling 14,935m (49,000ft); range with 4000lb load 1480km (920 miles)
Weights:	empty 4809kg (10,602lb); maximum take-off 12,437kg (27,420lb)
Dimensions:	wingspan 8.38m (27ft 6in); length excluding probe 12.22m (40ft 1.5in); height 4.66m (15ft 3in); wing area 24.15 sq m (260 sq ft)
Armament:	two 20mm Mk 12 cannon with 200rpg; five external hardpoints with provision for 3720kg (8200lb) of stores, including AGM-12 Bullpup air-to-surface missiles, AGM-45 Shrike anti-radar missiles, bombs, cluster bombs, dispenser weapons, rocket-launcher pods, cannon pods, drop tanks and ECM pods

McDonnell Douglas F-4G Phantom II

The Phantom was the Navy's principal fighter of the war. The F-4G illustrated here in an experimental camouflage scheme, was a version of the F-4B with an automatic carrier landing system. This version made one cruise with VF-213 on the USS *Kittyhawk*.

SPECIFICATIONS	
Country of origin:	United States
Type:	two-seat EW/radar-surpression aircraft
Powerplant:	two 54.2kN (17,000lb) thrust General Electric J79-GE-8A afterburning turbojet engines
Performance:	maximum speed at high altitude 2390km/h (1485mph); service ceiling over 18,975m (62,250ft); range 958km (595 miles)
Weights:	empty 13,300kg (29,321lb); maximum take-off 28,300kg (62,390lb)
Dimensions:	span 11.7m (38ft 5in); length 19.2m (63ft); height 5.02m (16ft 5.5in); wing area 49.24 sq m (530 sq ft)
Armament:	two AIM-7 Sparrow; wing pylons for radar suppression weapons

Douglas EKA-3 Skywarrior

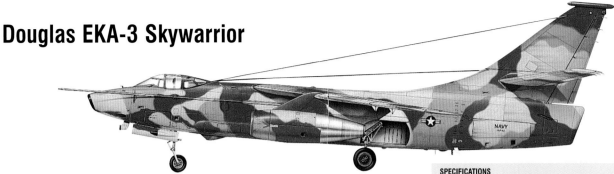

The A3 Skywarrior is notable as the first carrier-based strategic nuclear bomber, designed to be operated from the deck of the Forrestal class of carriers that came into service in 1948. Both the outer wings and tail were designed to fold hydraulically and thus minimize the space occupied by the aircraft on deck. Deliveries began in March 1956 to the US Navy's VH-1 attack squadron. Later variants saw much service in Vietnam as Elint and ECM platforms.

SPECIFICATIONS	
Country of origin:	United States
Type:	carrier-based strategic bomber
Powerplant:	two 55.1kN (12,400lb) Pratt & Whitney turbojets
Performance:	maximum speed 982km/h (610mph); service ceiling 13,110m (43,000ft); range with maximum fuel 3220km (2000 miles)
Weights:	empty 17,875kg (39,409lb); maximum take-off 37,195kg (82,000lb)
Dimensions:	wing span 22.1m (72ft 6in); length 23.3m (76ft 4in); height 7.16m (23ft 6in); wing area 75.43 sq m (812 sq ft)
Armament:	two remotely controlled 20mm cannon in tail turret, plus provision for 5443kg (12,000lb) of conventional or nuclear weapons in internal bomb bay

Vought A-7B Corsair II

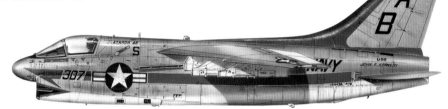

The A-7 entered combat with the Navy in Southeast Asia in December 1967, and replaced the A-4 with most of the light-attack squadrons by 1975. It brought higher performance and a sophisticated radar to the mission. This A-7B is in the markings of VA-46 'Clansmen', operating off the *John F. Kennedy*.

SPECIFICATIONS	
Country of origin:	United States
Type:	single-seat attack aircraft
Powerplant:	one 54.2kN (12,190lb) thrust Pratt & Whitney TF30-P-8 turbofan engine
Performance:	maximum speed at low-level 1123km/h (698mph); combat range with typical weapon load 1150km (4100 miles)
Weights:	empty 8972kg (19,781lb); maximum take-off 19,050kg (42,000lb)
Dimensions:	wingspan 11.8m (38ft 9in); length 14.06m (46ft 1.5in); height 4.9m (16ft 0.75in); wing area 34.84 sq m (375 sq ft)
Armament:	two 20mm Colt Mk 12 cannon; up to 6804kg (15,000lb) of bombs, air-to-surface missiles or other stores

Grumman A-6E Intruder

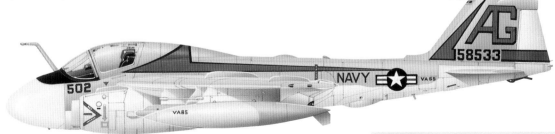

Entering service with the US Navy in February 1963, the Intruder was specifically planned for first pass blind attack on point surface targets at night or in any weather conditions. It was designed to be subsonic and is powered by two straight turbojets. Despite its considerable gross weight, the Intruder has excellent slow-flying qualities with full-span slats and flaps.

SPECIFICATIONS	
Country of origin:	United States
Type:	two-seat carrierborne and landbased all-weather strike aircraft
Powerplant:	two 41.3kN (9300lb) Pratt & Whitney J52-P-8A turbojets
Performance:	maximum speed at sea level 1043km/h (648mph); service ceiling 14,480m (47,500ft); range 1627km (1011 miles)
Weights:	empty 12,132kg (26,746lb); maximum take-off 26,581kg (58,600lb) for carrier launch or 27,397kg (60,400lb) for field take-off
Dimensions:	wingspan 16.15m (53ft); length 16.69; height 4.93m (16ft 2in); wing area 49.13 sq m (528.9 sq ft)
Armament:	five external hardpoints with provision for up to 8165kg (18,000lb) of stores, including nuclear weapons, bombs, missiles, and drop tanks

Vietnam War: Air Force Air Power

The US Air Force committed thousands of aircraft to Vietnam, from light observation types to strategic bombers. South Vietnam's airfields and airspace were so crowded that much of the effort had to be launched from Thailand or Guam. B-52 raids on Hanoi in 1972 helped bring the North to the negotiating table, but the millions of pounds of bombs dropped in the jungle did little to alter the final outcome.

Fairchild AC-119K Stinger

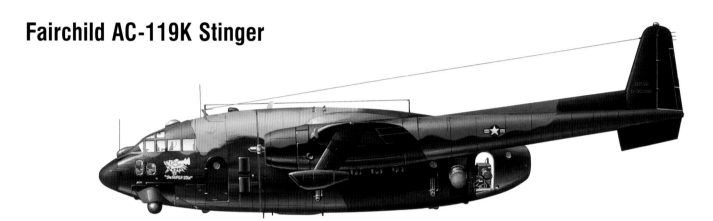

The gunship aircraft with an array of side-facing weapons was a concept originated by the USAF in Vietnam. Following the AC-47 'Spooky' was the AC-119G Shadow and AC-119K Stinger (illustrated). The Shadow was armed with four Miniguns and the Stinger had two Vulcan cannon.

SPECIFICATIONS	
Country of origin:	United States
Type:	Twin-engined gunship
Powerplant:	two 2610kW (3500hp) Wright R-3350-85 radial piston engines
Performance:	maximum speed 335km/h (210 mph); range 3219km (2000 miles); service ceiling 7300m (23,950ft)
Weights:	empty 18,200kg (40,125lb); maximum 28,100kg (62,000lb)
Dimensions:	span 33.3m (109ft 3in); length 26.37m (86ft 6in); height 8m (26ft 3in); wing area 134.43 sq m (1447 sq ft)
Armament:	two 20mm M61 Vulcan cannon

Lockheed AC-130 Spectre

The definitive gunship is the AC-130, introduced into Vietnam in September 1967 and still in use in modernized form today. The AC-130A Spectre was used to hunt for night movements on the Ho Chi Minh Trail supply routes into the South. It also provided fire support for US bases under insurgent attack.

SPECIFICATIONS	
Country of origin:	United States
Type:	(AC-130A) four-engined gunship
Powerplant:	four 3661kW (4910hp) Allison T56-A-15 turboprop engines
Performance:	maximum speed 480km/h (300mph); range 4070km (2530 miles); service ceiling unknown
Weights:	empty unknown; maximum 69,750kg (155,000lb)
Dimensions:	span 40.4m (132ft 7in); length 29.8m (97ft 9in); height 11.7m (38ft 6in); wing area 162.2 sq m (1745.5 sq ft)
Armament:	four 7.62mm GAU-2/A Miniguns and four 20mm Vulcan cannon

Boeing B-52D

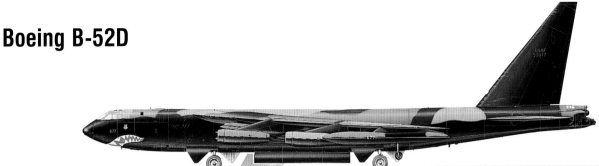

In Vietnam, the USAF found itself using strategic bombers designed for nuclear war to drop conventional bombs against suspected insurgents in thick jungle. These 'Arc Light' missions reportedly had a large psychological effect but did relatively little physical damage to the enemy. This B-52D of the 43rd Bomb Wing was based in Guam in 1972.

SPECIFICATIONS	
Country of origin:	United States
Type:	long-range strategic bomber
Powerplant:	eight 44.5kN (10,000lb) Pratt & Whitney J57 turbojets
Performance:	maximum speed at 7315m (24,000ft) 1014km/h (630mph): service ceiling 13,720–16,765m (45,000–55,000ft); standard range with maximum load 9978km (6200 miles)
Weights:	empty 77,200–87,100kg (171,000–193,000lb); loaded 204,120kg (450,000lb)
Dimensions:	wingspan 56.4m (185ft); length 48m (157ft 7in); height 14.75m (48ft 3in); wing area 371.6 sq m (4000 sq ft)
Armament:	remotely controlled tail mounting with four .5in machine guns; normal internal bomb capacity 12,247kg (27,000lb) including all SAC special weapons; 108 Mk 82 (500-pound) bombs internally and on underwing pylons

Douglas A-1H Skyraider

The outwardly anachronistic Skyraider was valued in Vietnam for its heavy weapons load and long loiter time over the target area. These attributes were most needed when covering the scene of a rescue operation, until the downed aircrew were aboard helicopters and on their way to safety.

SPECIFICATIONS	
Country of origin:	United States
Type:	single-engined attack aircraft
Powerplant:	one 2013kW (2700hp) Pratt & Whitney R-3350-26WA radial piston engine
Performance:	maximum speed 520km/h (320mph); range 2115km (1315mph); service ceiling 8660m (28,500ft)
Weights:	empty 5430kg (11,970lb); maximum 11,340kg (25,000lb)
Dimensions:	span 15.25m (50ft); length 11.84m (38ft 10in); height 4.78m (15ft 8in); wing area 37.19 sq m (400.31 sq ft)
Armament:	four 20mm cannon; up to 3600kg (8000lb) of bombs, rockets, or other stores

General Dynamics F-111

The variable geometry F-111 suffered a difficult gestation, earning it the unwelcome nickname Aardvark. It was developed to meet a bold Department of Defense edict for a common type of fighter to meet all future tactical needs of the US armed forces, and the first of 117 F-111s were eventually delivered into service in 1967. The Royal Australian Air Force bought the F-111C, the only export success for the aircraft.

SPECIFICATIONS	
Country of origin:	United States
Type:	two-seat multi-purpose attack aircraft
Powerplant:	two 11,1.6kN (25,100lb) Pratt & Whitney TF-30-P100
Performance:	maximum speed at optimum altitude 2655km/h (1650mph); service ceiling above 17,985m (59,000ft); range 4707km (2925 miles)
Weights:	empty 21,398kg (47,175lb); maximum take-off 45,359kg (100,000lb)
Dimensions:	wingspan unswept 19.2m (63ft); swept 9.74m (32ft 11.5in); length 22.4m (73ft 6in); height 5.22m (17ft 1.5in); wing area 48.77 sq m (525 sq ft) unswept
Armament:	one 20mm cannon and one 340kg (750lb) B43 bomb, or two B43 bombs in internal bay, provision for 14,290kg (31,000lb) of stores

Vietnam War: MiGs and Thuds

One of the most fiercely fought battles of the air war was that between the F-105 Thunderchief ('Thud') bombers and the North Vietnamese fighters defending the key industrial targets. A mountainous feature pointing towards Hanoi became known as 'Thud Ridge' after the F-105s that used its cover and fell there in large numbers. The North's MiGs claimed 22 F-105s up to 1970, when they were withdrawn.

Republic F-105B Thunderchief

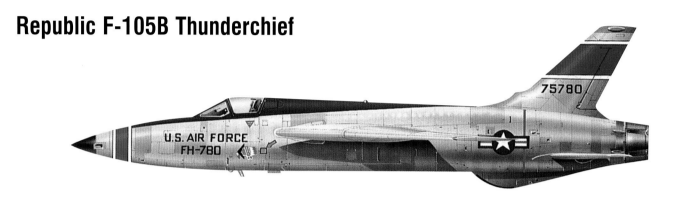

The primary mission of Republic's replacement for the F-84F Thunderstreak was the delivery of nuclear and conventional weapons in all weathers, at high speeds and over long ranges. The production F-105B entered service in August 1958 with the USAF's 335th Tactical Fighter Squadron, three years later than planned. Seventy-five were completed before the aircraft was superseded by the F-105D.

SPECIFICATIONS	
Country of origin:	United States
Type:	single-seat fighter-bomber
Powerplant:	one 104.5kN (23,500lb) Pratt & Whitney J75 turbojet
Performance:	maximum speed 2018km/h (1254mph); service ceiling 15,850m (52,000ft); combat radius with weapon load 370km (230 miles)
Weights:	empty 12,474kg (27,500lb); maximum take-off 18,144kg (40,000lb)
Dimensions:	wingspan 10.65m (34ft 11.25in); length 19.58m (64ft 3in); height 5.99m (19ft 8in); wing area 35.8 sq m (385 sq ft)
Armament:	one 20mm M61 cannon with 1029 rounds; internal bay with provision for up to 3629kg (8000lb) of bombs; five external pylons for additional load of 2722kg (6000lb)

Republic F-105F Thunderchief

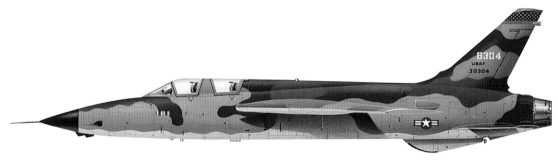

In 1962, the USAF ordered 143 two-seat F-105F trainers. The aircraft were equipped with dual controls and full operational equipment. To incorporate the tandem cockpit, the fuselage was lengthened slightly. It was originally intended to use the aircraft for training and transition training, but the pressures of US involvement in the Vietnam conflict created an urgent requirement for these high-performance fighter-bombers, and many were used operationally in theatre.

SPECIFICATIONS	
Country of origin:	United States
Type:	two-seat operational trainer
Powerplant:	one 108.9kN (24,500lb) Pratt & Whitney J75-19W turbojet
Performance:	maximum speed 2382km/h (1480mph); service ceiling 15,850m (52,000ft); combat radius with 16 750lb bombs 370km (230 miles)
Weights:	empty 12,890kg (28,393lb); maximum take-off 24,516kg (54,000lb)
Dimensions:	wingspan 10.65m (34ft 11.25in); length 21.21m (69ft 7.5in); height 6.15m (20ft 2in); wing area 35.8sq m (385sq ft)
Armament:	one 20mm M61 cannon with 1029 rounds; provision for up to 3629kg (8000lb) of bombs; pylons for additional load of 2722kg (6000lb)

Mikoyan-Gurevich MiG-17 'Fresco'

The North Vietnamese Air Force (NVAF) formed its first fighter unit, No 921 'Sao Do' (Red Star) Regiment, in 1964. It scored its first confirmed victories in April 1965 against F-105Ds. Most MiG-17 kills were scored with its 23mm and 37mm cannon.

SPECIFICATIONS	
Country of origin:	USSR
Type:	single-seat fighter
Powerplant:	one 33.1kN (7452lb) Klimov VK-1F turbojet
Performance:	maximum speed at 3000m (9840ft) 1145km/h (711mph); service ceiling 16,600m (54,560ft); range 1470km (913 miles)
Weights:	empty 4100kg (9040lb); maximum loaded 600kg (14,770lb)
Dimensions:	wingspan 9.45m (31ft); length 11.05m (36ft 3.75in); height 3.35m (11ft); wing area 20.6msq m (221.74sq ft)
Armament:	one 37mm N-37 cannon and two 23mm NS-23 cannon, plus up to 500kg (1102lb) of mixed stores on underwing pylons

Mikoyan-Gurevich MiG-19S 'Farmer'

The MiG-19, or Shenyang J-6, entered NVAF service in 1969 with the 925th Regiment. The small, agile MiGs proved hard to counter, particularly when US rules of engagement dictated their pilots get close enough to positively identify them, thus negating their medium-range missiles.

SPECIFICATIONS	
Country of origin:	USSR
Type:	single-seat all-weather interceptor
Powerplant:	two 31.9kN (7165lb) Klimov RD-9B turbojets
Performance:	maximum speed at 9080m (20,000ft) 1480km/h (920mph); service ceiling 17,900m (58,725ft); maximum range at high altitude with two drop tanks 2200km (1367 miles)
Weights:	empty 5760kg (12,698lb); maximum take-off weight 9500kg (20,944lb)
Dimensions:	wingspan 9m (29ft 6.5in); length 13.58m (44ft 7in); height 4.02m (13ft 2.25in); wing area 25 sq m (269.11 sq ft)
Armament:	underwing pylons for four AA-1 Alkali air-to-air-missiles, or AA-2 Atoll

Mikoyan-Gurevich MiG-21MF 'Fishbed'

The top five aces of the Vietnam War all flew MiG-21s, which entered the war in 1965. Nguyen Van Coc was the leading MiG-21 pilot, with seven USAF and USN aircraft and two unmanned aerial vehicles destroyed between April 1967 and December 1968.

SPECIFICATIONS	
Country of origin:	USSR
Type:	single-seat all-weather multi role fighter
Powerplant:	one 60.8kN (14,550lb) thrust Tumanskii R-13-300 afterburning turbojet
Performance:	maximum speed above 11,000m (36,090ft) 2229km/h (1385mph); service ceiling 17,500m (57,400ft); range on internal fuel 1160km (721 miles)
Weights:	empty 5200kg (11,464lb); maximum take-off weight 10,400kg (22,925lb)
Dimensions:	wingspan 7.15m (23ft 5.5in); length (including probe) 15.76m (51ft 8.5in); height 4.1m (13ft 5.5in); wing area 23sq m (247.58sq ft)
Armament:	one 23mm twin-barrell cannon in underbelly pack, four underwing pylons with provision for about 1500kg (3307kg) of stores

Lockheed P-3 Orion

Derived from the L-188 Electra airliner, the P-3 Orion has become the most widely used maritime patrol aircraft in the world. Designed primarily for anti-submarine work, the basic Orion can also undertake anti-shipping, search-and-rescue and overland reconnaissance missions. Specialized variants are used for airborne radar surveillance, electronic intelligence-gathering and scientific survey work.

P-3A Orion

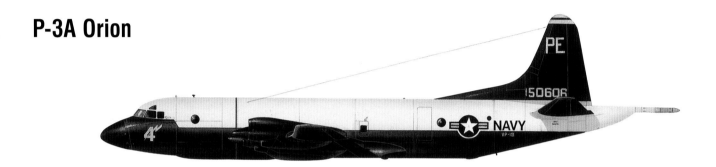

The P-3A entered service with the US Navy in 1962. In total, 157 of this model were built, all for domestic use. In 1975, patrol squadron VP-19 (illustrated) became the first to receive the P-3C with a revised internal layout, much-improved computers and navigation equipment.

SPECIFICATIONS	
Country of origin:	United States
Type:	four-engined maritime patrol aircraft
Powerplant:	four 3356kW (4500hp) Allison T56-A10W turboprop engines
Performance:	maximum speed 766km/h (476mph); range 4075km (2533 miles); service ceiling 8625m (28,300ft)
Weights:	empty 27,216kg (60,000lb); maximum 60,780kg (134,000lb)
Dimensions:	span 30.37m (99ft 8in); length 35.61m (116ft 9in); height 10.27m (33ft 8in); wing area 120.8 sq m (1300 sq ft)
Armament:	up to 9070kg (20,000lb) of ordnance, including bombs, mines and torpedoes

P-3B Orion

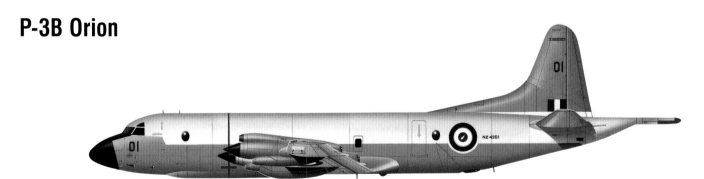

Since 1966, the Royal New Zealand Air Force has been an Orion operator. Its five P-3Bs were joined by an ex-Australian example in the 1980s, and all were updated to P-3K standard with avionics equivalent to the P-3C. Several structural upgrades have further extended their operational life.

SPECIFICATIONS	
Country of origin:	United States
Type:	four-engined maritime patrol aircraft
Powerplant:	four 3700kW (4600hp) Allison T56-A-14 turboprop engines
Performance:	maximum speed 766km/h (476mph); range 4075km (2533 miles); service ceiling 8625m (28,300ft)
Weights:	empty 27,216kg (60,000lb); maximum 60,780kg (134,000lb)
Dimensions:	span 30.37m (99ft 8in); length 35.61m (116ft 9in); height 10.27m (33ft 8in); wing area 120.8 sq m (1300 sq ft)
Armament:	up to 9070kg (20,000lb) of ordnance, including bombs, mines and torpedoes

EP-3E Aries II

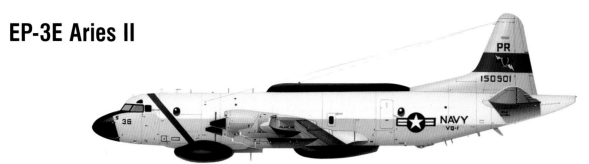

SPECIFICATIONS	
Country of origin:	United States
Type:	four-engined maritime patrol aircraft
Powerplant:	four 3356kW (4500hp) Allison T56-A10W turboprop engines
Performance:	maximum speed 766km/h (476mph); range 4075km (2533 miles); service ceiling 8625m (28,300ft)
Weights:	empty 27,216kg (60,000lb); maximum 60,780kg (134,000lb)
Dimensions:	span 30.37m (99ft 8in); length 32.3m (105ft 11in); height 10.44m (34ft 3in); wing area 120.8 sq m (1300 sq ft)
Armament:	none

Based on the P-3A, the EP-3E has all its ASW mission equipment replaced with systems for antennas to gather electronic intelligence. This EP-3E Aries II served with VQ-1 'World Watchers', which gained worldwide attention in April 2001 when one of its aircraft was forced to land in China.

RP-3A Orion

SPECIFICATIONS	
Country of origin:	United States
Type:	four-engined maritime patrol aircraft
Powerplant:	four 3356kW (4500hp) Allison T56-A10W turboprop engines
Performance:	maximum speed 766km/h (476mph); range 4075km (2533 miles); service ceiling 8625m (28,300ft)
Weights:	empty 27,216kg (60,000lb); maximum 60,780kg (134,000lb)
Dimensions:	span 30.37m (99ft 8in); length 35.61m (116ft 9in); height 10.27m (33ft 8in); wing area 120.8 sq m (1300 sq ft)
Armament:	none

'El Coyote' was a modified P-3A used by the US Navy Oceanographic Office for Project Seascan, which measured sea temperatures, currents and salinity around the globe. This data had application for the tracking of submarines, as well as general environmental research.

P-3 Orion AEW&C

SPECIFICATIONS	
Country of origin:	United States
Type:	airborne warning and control aircraft
Powerplant:	four 3700kW (4600hp) Allison T56-A-14 turboprop engines
Performance:	maximum speed unknown; range unknown; service ceiling 8625m (28,300ft)
Weights:	unknown
Dimensions:	span 30.37m (99ft 8in); length 35.61m (116ft 9in); height 10.27m (33ft 8in); wing area 120.8 sq m (1300 sq ft)
Armament:	none

Developed as a private venture by Lockheed, the P-3 AEW&C (airborne early warning and control) aircraft was offered to countries unable to afford the E-3 Sentry. The only customer was the US Customs Service, which uses the 'Dome' to hunt drug-running boats and aircraft in the Caribbean.

Vertical Take-off

The certainty of fixed airfields being put out of action in the first hours of any major war led to efforts throughout the 1960s to create a viable vertical take-off and landing (VTOL) aircraft that could operate from positions such as forest clearings close to the battlefield. Most concepts performed poorly with the available thrust, but the P.1127 formed the basis of the Harrier, which has served the RAF since 1969.

Ryan XV-5A

The XV-5 was developed for the US Army as a potential battlefield surveillance platform. The power system used two engines driving three fans to provide lift and pitch control. The first flight was made in May 1964, and the first vertical flight was achieved in July, but the prototype was destroyed in a 1965 accident. The army's test programme encompassed 338 flights up to 1967.

SPECIFICATIONS

Country of origin:	United States
Type:	Single-seat fighter
Powerplant:	two 11.79kN (2650lb-thrust) General Electric J85-GE-5 turbojet engines
Performance:	maximum speed 804km/h (498mph); range unknown; service ceiling 12,200m (40,028ft)
Weights:	loaded 5580kg (12,302lb)
Dimensions:	span 9.09m (29ft 10in); length 13.56m (44ft 6in); height 4.5m (14ft 9in)
Armament:	eight 7.7mm (.303in) Browning MGs

VFW-Fokker VAK-191B

A West German-Dutch collaboration, the VAK 191B V/STOL was a reconnaissance-strike aircraft with a fairly conventional swept-wing monoplane configuration design. The first of three prototype aircraft flew in 1971, but the small wing hindered short take-off and landing and the project was terminated in the mid-1970s.

SPECIFICATIONS

Country of origin:	Germany/Holland
Type:	experimental V/STOL aircraft
Powerplant:	two Rolls-Royce R.B 162-81 lift jets and one Rolls-Royce/MTU R.B 193-12 vectored/thrust turbofan for forward propulsion.
Performance:	maximum speed (est) 1046km/h (650 mph); service ceiling (est) 15,250m (50,000ft); range with maximum fuel after vertical take-off 500km (311 miles)
Weights:	maximum vertical take-off 8000kg (17,625lb)
Dimensions:	wingspan 6.16m (20ft); length 13m (42ft 0.5in); height 4m (13ft)
Armament:	none

VERTICAL TAKE-OFF TIMELINE

 1960

 1964

Yakovlev Yak-38 'Forger-A'

Apart from the Harrier, the Yak-38 was the only operational jet VTOL aircraft in the world, albeit a far less capable one. Operational service began in 1976. Unlike the Harrier, the Yak-38 used two fixed turbojets mounted in tandem behind the cockpit for lift, with auxiliary inlets on the top of the fuselage. These were augmented by a third vectoring thrust unit in the rear fuselage.

SPECIFICATIONS	
Country of origin:	USSR (CIS)
Type:	V/STOL carrier-based fighter-bomber
Powerplant:	two 29.9kN (6724lb) Rybinsk RD-36-35VFR lift turbojets; one 6950kg (15,322lb) Tumanskii R-27V-300 vectored-thrust turbojet
Performance:	maximum speed at high altitude 1009km/h (627mph); service ceiling 12,000m (39,370ft); combat range on hi-lo-hi mission with maximum weapon load 370km (230 miles)
Weights:	empty 7485kg (16,502lb); maximum take-off weight 11,700kg (25,795lb)
Dimensions:	wingspan 7.32m (24ft); length 15.5m (50ft 10in); height 4.37m (14ft 4in); wing area 18.5 sq m (199.14sq ft)
Armament:	four external hardpoints with provision for 2000kg (4409lb) of stores, including missiles, bombs, pods and drop tanks

Hawker Siddeley P.1127

The P.1127, the first of what would become the Harrier family, was flown in November 1960. A great deal of test flying in conventional mode and ground tests preceded the first full VTOL flight in September 1961. Five P.1127s were built, one of which made the first vertical carrier landing in 1963.

SPECIFICATIONS	
Country of origin:	United Kingdom
Type:	Experimental VTOL aircraft
Powerplant:	one 67kW (15,000lb) thrust Bristol Siddeley Pegasus 3 vectored-thrust turbofan engine
Performance:	maximum speed 878km/h (545mph); range unknown; service ceiling unknown
Weights:	empty 4500kg (10,000lb); maximum 17,000kg (7700lb)
Dimensions:	span 6.99m (22ft 11in); length 12.95m (42ft 6in); height 3.28m (10ft 9in); wing area 18.68 sq m (201 sq ft)
Armament:	none

Hawker Siddeley Kestrel FGA.1

The success of the experimental P.1127 led to the Kestrel for operational evaluation. A tri-national test unit consisting of the United Kingdom, West Germany and the United States (Army and Navy), called the Tri-partite Evaluation Squadron, flew the nine Kestrels on simulated missions in 1964–65.

SPECIFICATIONS	
Country of origin:	United Kingdom
Type:	Experimental VTOL aircraft
Powerplant:	one 51.2kN (11,500lb) thrust Bristol Siddeley Pegasus 6 vectored-thrust turbofan engine
Performance:	maximum speed 878km/h (545mph); range unknown; service ceiling unknown
Weights:	empty 4500kg (10,000lb); maximum 17,000kg (7700lb)
Dimensions:	span 6.99m (22ft 11in); length 12.95m (42ft 6in); height 3.28m (10ft 9in); wing area 18.68 sq m (201 sq ft)
Armament:	none

1971

First-Generation Harriers

No 1 Squadron RAF introduced the first VTOL fighters to service in 1969. The aircraft soon attracted the attention of the US Marine Corps and an order for 110 AV-8As was made in 1971. Later, Spain and Thailand purchased AV-8As for use off their small carriers. The two-seat versions were produced to introduce pilots to the quirks of VTOL flying, and helped reduce the number of accidents suffered during hovering flight.

AV-8A Harrier

The US AV-8A was equivalent to the RAF's Harrier GR.1s with a few changes, such as AIM-9 Sidewinder capability. The Marines operated AV-8s from their amphibious carriers and shore bases in the close air-support role. The AV-8C designation was given to 47 rebuilt AV-8As.

SPECIFICATIONS	
Country of origin:	United Kingdom
Type:	V/STOL close support and reconnaissance aircraft
Powerplant:	one 91.2kN (20,500lb) thrust Rolls-Royce Pegasus 10 vectored-thrust turbofan engine
Performance:	maximum speed at low altitude over 1186km/h (737mph); service ceiling over 15,240m (50,000ft); range with one inflight refuelling 5560 km (3455 miles)
Weights:	basic operating empty 5579kg (12,300lb); maximum take-off weight 11,340kg (25,000lb)
Dimensions:	wingspan 7.7m (25ft 3in); length 13.87m (45ft 6in); height 3.45m (11ft 4in); wing area 18.68 sq m (201.1 sq ft)
Armament:	maximum of 2268kg (5000lb) of stores on underfuselage and underwing points; one 30mm Aden gun or similar gun, with 150 rounds, rockets, bombs

Harrier GR.3

The GR.3 Harrier is essentially the same as the GR.1, but with a retrofitted 9753kg (21,500lb) Rolls-Royce Pegasus 103 turbofan. Standard equipment on the GR.3 included inflight refuelling equipment, head-up display and a laser rangefinder. From 1970, the aircraft equipped one RAF squadron in the United Kingdom and three in Germany.

SPECIFICATIONS	
Country of origin:	United Kingdom
Type:	V/STOL close support and reconnaissance aircraft
Powerplant:	one 95.6kN (21,500lb) Rolls-Royce Pegasus vectored thrust turbofan
Performance:	maximum speed over 1186km/h (737mph); service ceiling over 15,240m (50,000ft); range with one inflight refuelling 5560km (3455 miles)
Weights:	empty 5579kg (12,300lb); maximum take-off weight 11,340kg (25,000lb)
Dimensions:	wingspan 7.7m (25ft 3in); length 13.87m (45ft 6in); height 3.45m (11ft 4in); wing area 18.68 sq m (201.1sq ft)
Armament:	maximum of 2268kg (5000lb) of stores; one 30mm Aden gun or similar gun, with 150 rounds, rockets, bombs

Harrier T.4

The Harrier GR.1 for the RAF was followed by the T.2 conversion trainer. When the GR.3 was introduced, surviving T.2s were modified to T.4s by adding the laser rangefinder in the nose and the GR.3's other avionics. Twenty-five T.4s were built or converted from T.2s.

SPECIFICATIONS	
Country of origin:	United Kingdom
Type:	V/STOL close support and reconnaissance aircraft
Powerplant:	one 95.6kN (21,500lb) Rolls-Royce Pegasus vectored thrust turbofan
Performance:	maximum speed over 1186km/h (737mph); service ceiling over 15,240m (50,000ft); range with one inflight refuelling 5560km (3455 miles)
Weights:	empty 5579kg (12,300lb); maximum take-off weight 11,340kg (25,000lb)
Dimensions:	wingspan 7.7m (25ft 3in); length 13.87m (45ft 6in); height 3.45m (11ft 4in); wing area 18.68 sq m (201.1 sq ft)
Armament:	maximum of 2268kg (5000lb) of stores; one 30mm Aden gun or similar gun, with 150 rounds, rockets, bombs

AV-8S Matador

Spain's navy bought 12 early Harriers from the United States to operate from their World War II-era escort carrier *Dédalo* in 1976. These were known locally as AV-8S Matadors. Two were TAV-8S trainers. The Spanish later bought AV-8B Harrier IIs and sold its remaining AV-8Ss on to Thailand.

SPECIFICATIONS	
Country of origin:	United Kingdom
Type:	V/STOL close support and reconnaissance aircraft
Powerplant:	one 91.2kN (20,500lb) thrust Rolls-Royce Pegasus 11 vectored-thrust turbofan engine
Performance:	maximum speed over 1186km/h (737mph); service ceiling over 15,240m (50,000ft); range with one inflight refuelling 5560km (3455 miles)
Weights:	empty 5579kg (12,300lb); maximum take-off weight 11,340kg (25,000lb)
Dimensions:	wingspan 7.7m (25ft 3in); length 13.87m (45ft 6in); height 3.45m (11ft 4in); wing area 18.68 sq m (201.1sq ft)
Armament:	maximum of 2268kg (5000lb) of stores; one 30mm Aden gun or similar gun, with 150 rounds, rockets, bombs

Sea Harrier FRS.Mk 1

The Sea Harrier FRS.1 was ordered to equip the three Royal Navy 'through-deck cruisers' in the fighter, anti-submarine and surface-attack roles. Installing the Blue Fox radar meant lengthening the nose, and the cockpit was raised to accommodate a more substantial avionics suite and to afford the pilot a better all-round view. The aircraft proved an important asset during the Falklands War.

SPECIFICATIONS	
Country of origin:	United Kingdom
Type:	shipborne multi-role combat aircraft
Powerplant:	one 95.6kN (21,500lb) Rolls-Royce Pegasus vectored thrust turbofan
Performance:	maximum speed 1110km/h (690mph); service ceiling 15,545m (51,000ft); intercept radius 740km (460 miles)
Weights:	empty 5942kg (13,100lb); maximum take-off weight 11,884kg (26,200lb)
Dimensions:	wingspan 7.7m (25ft 3in); length 14.5m (47ft 7in); height 3.71m (12ft 2in); wing area 18.68sq m (201.1sq ft)
Armament:	two 30mm cannon, provision for AIM-9 Sidewinder or Matra Magic air-to-air missiles, and two Harpoon or Sea Eagle anti-shipping missiles, up to a total of 3629kg (8000lb) bombs

Last of the Flying Boats

For nations with significant sea areas to protect, large flying boats and amphibians continued to play a military role long after World War II. Patrol of sea lanes, anti-submarine warfare, mine-laying and combat search-and-rescue were all duties suited to aircraft flying low over water. Even today, Japan possesses a small fleet of Shin Meiwa amphibians, and Beriev has a jet flying boat in production, mainly for use as a firefighting aircraft.

Martin P5M Marlin

The Marlin was a post-war replacement for the Mariner. The US Navy used them throughout the Vietnam War to catch boats from the North supplying the Viet Cong. France leased 10 P5Ms in 1959 for use by the Aéronavale in West Africa.

SPECIFICATIONS	
Country of origin:	United States
Type:	(PFM-2) twin-engined flying boat
Powerplant:	two 2570kW (3450hp) Wright R-3350-32WA radial piston engines
Performance:	maximum speed 404km/h (251mph); range 3300km (2050 miles); service ceiling 7300m (24,000ft)
Weights:	empty 22,900kg (50,485lb); maximum 38,600kg (85,000lb)
Dimensions:	span 35.7m (117ft 2in); length 30.7m (100ft 7in); height 100m (32ft 9in); wing area 130.1 sq m (1406 sq ft)
Armament:	up to 8000lb of bombs, mines or torpedoes or one nuclear depth charge

Beriev Be-10 'Mallow'

Given the Nato reporting name 'Mallow', the Be-10 was one of a few jet-engined flying-boat types that were built in small numbers in the 1940s and 1950s. The Be-10 was displayed in public in 1961 and broke several records in its class, but did not enter large-scale service.

SPECIFICATIONS	
Country of origin:	USSR
Type:	twin-engined jet flying boat
Powerplant:	two 71.2kN (16,000lb) thrust Lyulka AL-7PB turbojet engines
Performance:	maximum speed 910km/h (565mph); service ceiling 12,500m (41,010ft); range 3150km (1957 miles)
Weights:	empty 27,600kg (60,900lb); maximum 48,500kg (106,900lb)
Dimensions:	span 28.6m (93ft 10in); length 31.45m (103ft 2in); height 10.7m (35ft 1in); wing area 130 sq m (1400 sq ft)
Armament:	four 23mm AM-23 cannon; up to 1360kg (3000lb) of bombs, torpedoes or mines

FLYING BOATS TIMELINE   1937    1948    1956

Beriev Be-12 'Mail'

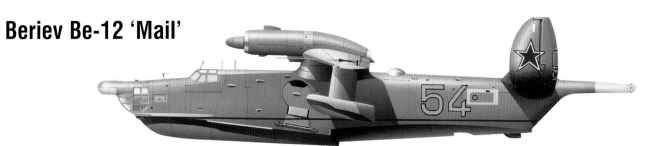

The Be-12 'Mail' amphibian was regarded as more worthy of development than the 'Mallow'. Derived from the piston-engined Be-6, it first flew in 1960 and was frequently encountered by Western pilots on patrol over the oceans of the world. A handful are still in Russian service.

SPECIFICATIONS	
Country of origin:	USSR
Type:	twin-engined flying boat
Powerplant:	two 3864kW (5180hp) Ivchenko Progress AI-20D turboprop engines
Performance:	maximum speed 530km/h (330mph); range 3300km (2100 miles); service ceiling 8000m (26,247ft)
Weights:	empty 24,000kg (52,800lb); maximum 36,000kg (79,200lb)
Dimensions:	span 29.84m (97ft 11in); length 30.11m (98ft 9in); height 7.94m (26ft 1in); wing area 99 sq m (1065 sq ft)
Armament:	1500kg (3300lb) of bombs, depth-charges or torpedoes

Short Sunderland

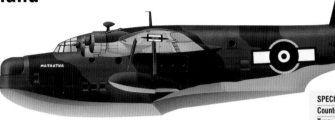

The RNZAF used four Sunderland IIIs in wartime, and bought a further 16 in the early 1950s for patrol of New Zealand and the Pacific Islands. The last examples served with No 5 Squadron until fully replaced by P-3B Orions in 1967.

SPECIFICATIONS	
Country of origin:	United Kingdom
Type:	(Sunderland Mk I) 10-seat maritime reconnaissance flying boat
Powerplant:	four 753kW (1010hp) Bristol Pegasus XXII nine-cylinder single-row radial engines
Performance:	maximum speed 336km/h (209mph); service ceiling 4570m (15,000ft); range 4023km (2500 miles)
Weights:	empty 13,875kg (30,589lb); maximum take-off weight 22,226kg (49,000lb)
Dimensions:	span 34.38m (112ft 9.5in); length 26.0m (85ft 3.5in); height 10.52m (34ft 6in)
Armament:	eight .303in machine guns in bow turret, in tail turret, in each beam position; internal bomb, depth charge and mine load of 907kg (2000lb)

Shin Meiwa PS-1

A successor to the wartime Kawanishi company, Shin Meiwa of Japan designed the PS-1 flying boat for the Japanese Maritime Self Defence Force in the late 1960s. The US-1A is an air-sea rescue variant with a retractable landing gear, and is still in service in small numbers.

SPECIFICATIONS	
Country of origin:	Japan
Type:	four-engined flying boat
Powerplant:	four 2250kW (3017hp) General Electric T-64-IHI-10J turboprop engines
Performance:	maximum speed 545km/h (339mph); range 4700km (2921 miles); service ceiling 9000m (29,550ft)
Weights:	empty 26,300kg (57,982lb); maximum 43,000kg (94,799lb)
Dimensions:	span 33.1m (108ft 7n); length 33.5m (109ft 11in); height 9.7m (31ft 10in); wing area 135.8 sq m (1462 sq ft)
Armament:	bombs, torpedoes or depth charges

1960

1967

Convair Deltas

In 1948, Convair flew the world's first delta-wing aircraft, the XF-92A, which was part of a programme intended to lead to a supersonic fighter. This was terminated, but the US Air Force later issued a specification for an extremely advanced all-weather interceptor to carry the Hughes MX-1179 electronic control system. This effectively made the carrier aircraft subordinate to its avionics, a radical concept in the early 1950s. Convair was awarded the contract in September 1961.

F-102 Delta Dagger

Early flight trials of the F-102 prototype were disappointing, but once the design was right, 875 were delivered. In the search mode, the pilot flew with two control columns – the left-hand one was used to adjust the sweep angle and range of the radar.

SPECIFICATIONS	
Country of origin:	United States
Type:	supersonic all-weather single-seat fighter-interceptor
Powerplant:	one 76.5kN (17,200lb) Pratt & Whitney J57-P-23 turbojet
Performance:	maximum speed at 10,970m (36,000ft) 1328km/h (825mph); service ceiling 16,460m (54,000ft); range 2172km (1350 miles)
Weights:	empty 8630kg (19,050lb); maximum take-off weight 14,288kg (31,500lb)
Dimensions:	wingspan 11.62m (38ft 1.5in); length 20.84m (68ft 4.5in); height 6.46m (21ft 2.5in); wing area 61.45 sq m (661.5 sq ft)
Armament:	two AIM-26/26A Falcon missiles, or one AIM-26/26A plus two AIM-4A Falcons, or one AIM-26/26A plus two AIM-4C/Ds, or six AIM-4As, or six AIM-4C/Ds, some aircraft fitted with 12 2.75in folding-fin rockets

F-102 Delta Dagger

The only export customers for the Delta Dagger were Greece and Turkey. In 1974, when the countries fought over Cyprus, the two sides' F-102s did not endure any decisive engagements with each other. Each side had retired its 'Deuces' by 1980.

SPECIFICATIONS	
Country of origin:	United States
Type:	supersonic all-weather single-seat fighter-interceptor
Powerplant:	one 76.5kN (17,200lb) Pratt & Whitney J57-P-23 turbojet
Performance:	maximum speed at 10,970m (36,000ft) 1328km/h (825mph); service ceiling 16,460m (54,000ft); range 2172km (1350 miles)
Weights:	empty 8630kg (19,050lb); maximum take-off weight 14,288kg (31,500lb)
Dimensions:	wingspan 11.62m (38ft 1.5in); length 20.84m (68ft 4.5in); height 6.46m (21ft 2.5in); wing area 61.45 sq m (661.5 sq ft)
Armament:	Various combinations of AIM missiles, some aircraft fitted with 12 2.75in folding-fin rockets

TF-102 Delta Dagger

The two-seat TF-102A was unusual for a trainer version of a fighter in having a side-by-side seating arrangement. Although it retained the weapons capabilities of the F-102A, its performance was reduced. TF-102s were used for some missions in Vietnam, including as B-52 escorts.

SPECIFICATIONS	
Country of origin:	United States
Type:	supersonic all-weather single-seat fighter-interceptor
Powerplant:	one 76.5kN (17,200lb) Pratt & Whitney J57-P-23 turbojet
Performance:	maximum speed at 10,970m (36,000ft) 1328km/h (825mph); service ceiling 16,460m (54,000ft); range 2172km (1350 miles)
Weights:	empty 8630kg (19,050lb); maximum take-off weight 14,288kg (31,500lb)
Dimensions:	wingspan 11.62m (38ft 1.5in); length 20.84m (68ft 4.5in); height 6.46m (21ft 2.5in)
Armament:	two AIM-26/26A Falcon missiles, or one AIM-26/26A plus two AIM-4A Falcons, or one AIM-26/26A plus two AIM-4C/Ds, or six AIM-4As, or six AIM-4C/Ds, some aircraft fitted with 12 2.75in folding-fin rockets

F-106A Delta Dart

Although the F-102 was designed to carry the Hughes ECS, the avionics were then delivered in time and so were rescheduled for the F-106 programme. This was delayed by engine problems, and flight tests proved disappointing. The aircraft eventually entered service in October 1959 and remained active in updated versions until 1988.

SPECIFICATIONS	
Country of origin:	United States
Type:	supersonic all-weather single-seat fighter-interceptor
Powerplant:	one 76.5kN (17,200lb) Pratt & Whitney J57-P-23 turbojet
Performance:	maximum speed at 10,970m (36,000ft) 1328km/h (825mph); service ceiling 16,460m (54,000ft); range 2172km (1350 miles)
Weights:	empty 8630kg (19,050lb); maximum take-off weight 14,288kg (31,500lb)
Dimensions:	wingspan 11.62m (38ft 1.5in); length 20.84m (68ft 4.5in); height 6.46m (21ft 2.5in); wing area 61.45 sq m (661.5 sq ft)
Armament:	Various combinations of AIM missiles, some aircraft fitted with 12 2.75in folding-fin rockets

F-106B Delta Dart

Unlike the TF-102, the trainer version of the Delta Dart, the F-106B – which was also combat capable – had its two seats arranged in tandem. Each F-106 unit, including two in the California Air National Guard, had a two-seater assigned.

SPECIFICATIONS	
Country of origin:	United States
Type:	supersonic all-weather single-seat fighter-interceptor
Powerplant:	one 76.5kN (17,200lb) Pratt & Whitney J57-P-23 turbojet
Performance:	maximum speed at 10,970m (36,000ft) 1328km/h (825mph); service ceiling 16,460m (54,000ft); range 2172km (1350 miles)
Weights:	empty 8630kg (19,050lb); maximum take-off weight 14,288kg (31,500lb)
Dimensions:	wingspan 11.62m (38ft 1.5in); length 20.84m (68ft 4.5in); height 6.46m (21ft 2.5in); wing area 61.45 sq m (661.5 sq ft)
Armament:	Various combinations of AIM missiles, some aircraft fitted with 12 2.75in folding-fin rockets

Soviet Bombers

The Soviet Union's Long Range Aviation (Dalnaya Aviatsiya) force evolved from using Soviet copies of the B-29 Superfortress, and by the early 1960s it had become a powerful force of jet and turboprop nuclear-armed bombers. The Tupolev Design Bureau's 'Bear', 'Badger' and 'Blinder' bombers formed the backbone of the force. Unlike Strategic Air Command, Long Range Aviation did not mount airborne patrols and had far fewer tankers, relying on staging bases in the Arctic instead.

Ilyushin Il-28 'Beagle'

First appearing in prototype form as early as 1948, the Il-28 afforded Eastern Bloc armed forces the same degree of flexibility and duration of service as the Canberra did for Britain. The prototype was powered by two Soviet-built turbojets developed directly from the Rolls-Royce Nene, supplied by the British government in a fit of contrition.

SPECIFICATIONS	
Country of origin:	USSR
Type:	three seat bomber and ground attack/dual control trainer/torpedo carrier
Powerplant:	two 58.1kN (13,062lb) Klimov VK-1 turbojets
Performance:	maximum speed 902km/h (560mph); service ceiling 12,300m (40,355ft); range 2180km (1355 miles); with bomb load 1100km (684 miles)
Weights:	empty 12890kg (28,418lb); maximum take-off weight 21,200kg (46,738lb)
Dimensions:	wingspan 21.45m (70ft 4.5in); length 17.65m (57ft 10.75in); height 6.7m (21ft 11.8in); wing area 60.8 sq m (654.47 sq ft)
Armament:	four 23mm NR-23 cannon; internal bomb capacity up to 1000kg (2205lb), maximum bomb capacity 3000kg (6614lb); torpedo version had provision for two 400mm light torpedoes

Myasishchev M-4 'Bison C'

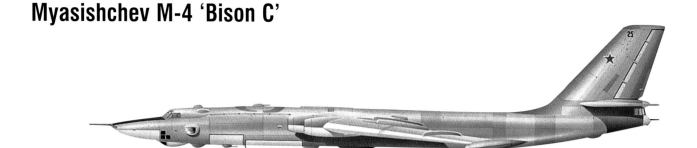

The M-4 was produced in some numbers as the 'Bison-A' strategic bomber, before being adapted for long-range strategic reconnaissance and ECM duties. In the 'Bison-C' sub-type, a large search radar was fitted inside a lengthened and modified nose. The 'C' model was most frequently encountered on high- and low-level missions over the Arctic, and the Atlantic and Pacific oceans.

SPECIFICATIONS	
Country of origin:	USSR
Type:	multi-role reconnaissance bomber
Powerplant:	four 127.4kN (28,660lb) Soloviev D-15 turbojets
Performance:	maximum speed 900km/h (560mph); service ceiling 15,000m (49,200ft); range 11,000km (6835 miles)
Weights:	empty 80,000kg (176,400lb); loaded 170,000kg (375,000lb)
Dimensions:	wing span 50.48m (165ft 7.5in); length 47.2m (154ft 10in); height 14.1m (46ft); wing area 309 sq m (3,326.16s q ft)
Armament:	six 23mm cannon in two forward turrets and tail turret; internal bay with provision over 4500kg (10,000lb) of stores

Tupolev Tu-22R 'Blinder-C'

SPECIFICATIONS	
Country of origin:	USSR
Type:	long-range maritime reconnaissance/patrol aircraft
Powerplant:	two (estimated) 117.6kN (26,455lb) Koliesov VD-7 turbojets
Performance:	maximum speed 1487km/h (924mph); service ceiling 18,300m (60,040ft); combat radius with internal fuel 3100km (1926 miles)
Weights:	empty 40,000kg (88,185lb); maximum take-off 84,000kg (185,188lb)
Dimensions:	wingspan 23.75m (77ft 11in); length 40.53m (132ft 11.75in); height 10.67m (35ft); wing area 162 sq m (1722.28 sq ft)
Armament:	one 23mm NR-23 two-barrel cannon in radar-controlled tail barbette; internal weapons bay with provision for 12,000kg (26,455lb) of stores, including nuclear weapons and free-fall bombs, or one AS-4 carried semi-recessed under the fuselage

The Tu-22 was designed in the late 1950s as a replacement for the Tu-16, which was effectively rendered obsolete by a new generation of Western interceptors and missile systems. The Tu-22 'Blinder' was designed to penetrate hostile airspace at high speed and high altitude. The 'Blinder-C' was a dedicated maritime reconnaissance version with cameras and sensors in the weapons bay.

Tupolev Tu-16R 'Badger-K'

SPECIFICATIONS	
Country of origin:	USSR
Type:	medium bomber
Powerplant:	two 13.1kN (20.944lb) Mikulin RD-3M turbojets
Performance:	maximum speed at 6000m (19,685ft) 960km/h (597mph); service ceiling 15,000m (49,200ft); combat range with maximum weapon load 4800km (2983 miles)
Weights:	empty 40,300kg (88,846lb); maximum take-off 75,800kg (167,110lb)
Dimensions:	wingspan 32.99m (108ft 3in); length 36.5m (120ft); height 10.36m (34ft 2in); wing area 164.65 sq m (1772.3 sq ft)
Armament:	one forward and one rear ventral barbette each with two 23mm NR-23 cannon; two 23mm NR-23 cannon in radar-controlled tail position

The Tu-16R was a maritime/electronic reconnaissance version of the Tupolev medium bomber. 'Badger-E' had provision for a photoreconnaissance pallet in the weapons bay and passive Elint capability. 'Badger-F' was similar, but usually carried underwing ESM (Electronic Signal Monitoring) pods. Badger-K was based on Badger-F, but had enhanced Elint capability.

Tupolev Tu-95 'Bear'

SPECIFICATIONS	
Country of origin:	USSR
Type:	four-engined turboprop bomber
Powerplant:	four 11,000kW (14,800hp) Kuznetsov NK-12MV turboprop engines
Performance:	maximum speed 920km/h (575mph); range 15,000km (9400 miles); service ceiling 12,000m (39,000ft)
Weights:	empty 90,000kg (198,000lb); maximum 188,000kg (414,500lb)
Dimensions:	span 51.1m (167ft 8in); length 49.5m (162ft 5in); height 12.12m (39ft 9in); wing area 310 sq m (3330 sq ft)
Armament:	two 23mm AM-23 cannon; up to 15,000kg (33,000lb) of bombs or anti-surface or anti-shipping missiles

The Tu-95 'Bear' was unique in being a swept-wing turboprop bomber. Although slower than its counterparts, it had enormous range. Entering service in 1956, it remains in use by Russia. Later versions were equipped to carry variety of cruise missiles.

Fleet Air Arm

With the arrival of new fleet carriers like HMS *Hermes* and *Ark Royal*, and supersonic fighters and attack aircraft, the Fleet Air Arm was able to project airpower and deploy nuclear weapons over large parts of the world. Technologically, however, its aircraft were falling behind those of the United States, and the total number deployed was dropping due to budgetary pressures. Conventional fixed-wing naval aviation was abandoned in 1978 with the retirement of the *Ark Royal*.

Supermarine Scimitar F.1

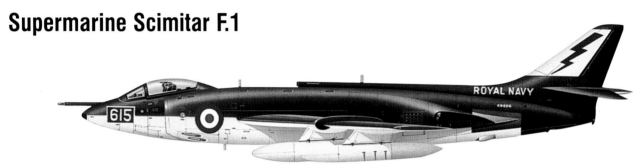

The Scimitar had an extremely protracted gestation period. The first prototype, the Supermarine 508, was a thin, straight-winged design with a butterfly tail. Production aircraft were delivered from August 1957. A total of 76 were built, providing the Fleet Air Arm with a capable low-level supersonic attacker until the Scimitar was superseded by the Buccaneer in 1969.

SPECIFICATIONS	
Country of origin:	United Kingdom
Type:	single-seat carrier-based multi-role aircraft
Powerplant:	two 50kN (11,250lb) Rolls-Royce Avon 202 turbojets
Performance:	maximum speed 1143km/h (710mph); service ceiling 15,240m (50,000ft); range, clean at height 966km (600 miles)
Weights:	empty 9525kg (21,000lb); maximum take-off weight 15,513kg (34,200lb)
Dimensions:	wingspan 11.33m (37ft 2in); length 16.87m (55ft 4in); height 4.65m (15ft 3in); wing area 45.06 sq m (485 sq ft)
Armament:	four 30mm Aden cannon, four 454kg (1000lb) bombs or four Bullpup air-to-ground missiles, or four sidewinder air-to-air missiles, or drop tanks

De Havilland Sea Vixen FAW.2

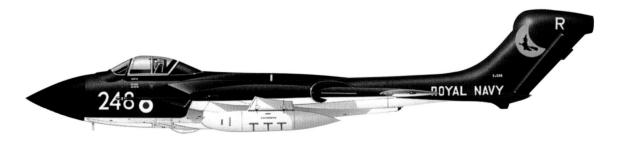

The Sea Vixen, like many of the aircraft operated by the Royal Navy, was originally designed to a 1946 RAF requirement for a land-based, all-weather interceptor. Mk 1s featured a hinged and pointed radome, power-folding wings and hydraulically steerable nosewheel. The FAW.2 had increased fuel capacity and provision for four Red Top missiles.

SPECIFICATIONS	
Country of origin:	United Kingdom
Type:	two-seat all-weather strike fighter
Powerplant:	two 49.9kN (11,230lb) Rolls-Royce Avon 208 turbojets
Perfomance:	maximum speed 1110km/h (690mph); service ceiling 21,790m (48,000ft); range about 965.6km (600 miles) (FAW 1) and 1287.5km (800 miles) (FAW 2)
Weights:	empty weight about 22,000lb; maximum take-off 18,858kg (41,575lb)
Dimensions:	wingspan 15.54m (51ft); length 17.02 m (55ft 7in); height 3.28 m (10ft 9in); wing area 60.2 sq m (648 sq ft)
Armament:	four Red Top air-to-air missiles (FAW 2); on outer pylons 1000lb bombs, Bullpup air-to-surface missiles or equivalent stores

Fairey Gannet AS.1

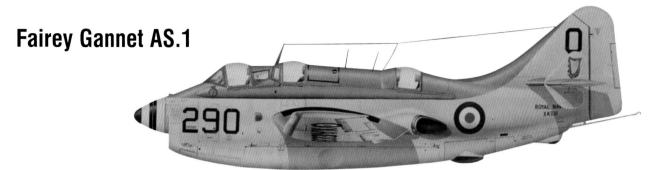

SPECIFICATIONS

Country of origin:	United Kingdom
Type:	carrier-based anti-submarine aircraft
Powerplant:	one 2200kW (2950hp) Double Mamba 100 turboprop engine
Performance:	maximum speed 499km/h (310mph); range 1111km (690 miles); service ceiling 7620m (25,000ft)
Weights:	empty 6835kg (15,069lb); maximum 8890kg (19,600lb)
Dimensions:	span 16.54m (54ft 4in); length 13.11m (43ft); height 4.18m (13ft 9in); wing area 44.9 sq m (483 sq ft)
Armament:	up to 908kg (2000lb) of torpedoes, mines, bombs or depth charges

The Gannet AS.1 three-seat anti-submarine aircraft was the first of a family of variants that included early-warning, transport, trainer and electronic-warfare aircraft. The Double Mamba turboprop was essentially two coupled engines and drove counter-rotating propellers.

Blackburn Buccaneer S.2

SPECIFICATIONS

Country of origin:	United Kingdom
Type:	two-seat attack aircraft
Powerplant:	two 50.4kN (11,255lb) Rolls-Royce RB.168 Spey Mk 101 turbofans
Performance:	maximum speed at 61m (200ft) 1040km/h (646mph); service ceiling over 12,190m (40,000ft); combat range with typical weapons load 3701km (2300 miles)
Weights:	empty 13,608kg (30,000lb); maximum take-off 28,123kg (62,000lb)
Dimensions:	wingspan 13.41m (44ft); length 19.33m (63ft 5in); height 4.97m (16ft 3in); wing area 47.82 sq m (514.7 sq ft)
Armament:	four 454kg (1000lb) bombs, fuel tank or reconnaissance pack, provision for 5443kg (12,000lb) of bombs or missiles

The Buccaneer was the first aircraft to be designed specifically for carrierborne strike operations at below radar level. The S.1 was marginal on power, but the greatly improved S.2 was a reliable and formidable aircraft. The first 84 were ordered by the Royal Navy, and after giving good service most were transferred to the Royal Air Force from 1969.

McDonnell Douglas Phantom FG.1

SPECIFICATIONS

Country of origin:	United States
Type:	two-seat all-weather fighter/attack carrier-borne aircraft
Powerplant:	two 91.2kN (20,515lb) Rolls-Royce Spey 202 turbofans
Performance:	maximum speed 2230km/h (1386mph); service ceiling over 18,300m (60,000ft); range with no weapon load 2817km (1750 miles)
Weights:	empty 12,700kg (28,000lb); maximum take-off 26,308kg (58,000lb)
Dimensions:	span 11.7m (38ft 5in); length 17.55m (57ft 7in); height 4.96m (16ft 3in); wing area 49.24 sq m (530 sq ft)
Armament:	four AIM-7 Sparrow; provision for 20mm M61A1 cannon; wing pylons for stores to a maximum weight of 7257kg (16,000lb)

The Royal Navy's decision to buy the Phantom was governed by a requirement that the aircraft be equipped with British-built engines. To this end, an Anglicized version of the F-4J was produced, powered by two Rolls-Royce Spey turbofans; fitting these engines necessitated widening the fuselage. Twenty-eight aircraft were delivered to the Navy from 1964, and a further 20 to the Royal Air Force.

F-5 Freedom Fighter/Tiger II

Northrop developed a lightweight combat aircraft under the designation N-156 in the late 1950s. The USAF used relatively few, but adopted a derivative as the T-38 Talon trainer. As the F-5 Freedom Fighter and the improved F-5E Tiger II, however, the design was a big export hit, used by 35 countries – most of whom still operate the aircraft today. Supersonic but simple, the F-5 was a good combat plane, but could also act as an adversary or aggressor in training missions.

T-38 Talon

The highly successful T-38 trainer aircraft was derived from a requirement issued by the US Government in the mid-1950s for a lightweight fighter to supply to friendly nations under the Military Assistance Program. Service began with the USAF in March 1961. The T-38 was used by the US Air Force Thunderbirds display team between 1974 and 1981.

SPECIFICATIONS	
Country of origin:	United States
Type:	two-seat supersonic basic trainer
Powerplant:	two 17.1kN (3850lb) General Electric J85-GE-5 turbojets
Performance:	maximum speed at 10,975m (36,000ft) 1381km/h (858mph); service ceiling 16,340m (53,600ft); range with internal fuel 1759km (1093 miles)
Weights:	empty 3254kg (7174lb); maximum take-off weight 5361kg (11,820lb)
Dimensions:	wingspan 7.7m (25ft 3in); length 14.14m (46ft 4.5in); height 3.92m (12ft 10.5in); wing area 15.79 sq m (170 sq ft)
Armament:	none

F-5A Freedom Fighter

The F-5A was a largely privately funded project by Northrup. In October 1962, the US Department of Defense decided to buy the aircraft in large numbers to supply friendly countries on advantageous terms. More than 1000 were supplied to Iran, Taiwan, Greece, South Korea, Phillipines, Turkey, Ethiopia, Morocco, Norway, Thailand, Libya and South Vietnam.

SPECIFICATIONS	
Country of origin:	United States
Type:	light tactical fighter
Powerplant:	two 18.1kN (4080lb) General Electric J85-GE-13 turbojets
Performance:	maximum speed at 10,975m (36,000ft) 1487km/h (924mph); service ceiling 15,390m (50,500ft); combat radius 314km (195 miles)
Weights:	empty 3667kg (8085lb); maximum take-off weight 9374kg (20,667lb)
Dimensions:	wingspan 7.7m (25ft 3in); length 14.38m (47ft 2in); height 4.01m (13ft 2in); wing area 15.79 sq m (170 sq ft)
Armament:	two 20mm M39 cannon; provision for 1996kg (4400lb) of stores on external pylons, including missiles, bombs, rocket launcher pods

F-5B Freedom Fighter

SPECIFICATIONS	
Country of origin:	United States
Type:	light tactical fighter
Powerplant:	two 18.1kN (4080lb) General Electric J85-GE-13 turbojets
Performance:	maximum speed at 10,975m (36,000ft) 1487km/h (924mph); service ceiling 15,390m (50,500ft); combat radius 314km (195 miles)
Weights:	empty 3667kg (8085lb); maximum 8936kg (19,700lb)
Dimensions:	wingspan 7.7m (25ft 3in); length 14.14 m (46 ft 5 in); height 4.01m (13ft 2in); wing area 15.79 sq m (170 sq ft)
Armament:	provision for 1996kg (4400lb) of stores on external pylons, including air-to-air missiles, bombs, cluster bombs, rocket launcher pods

The two-seat F-5B is close in appearance to the T-38A, but is heavier, combat-capable and shares the F-5A's wing, braking parachute and other features. Over 200 were built, mainly for export. The example shown is from the Netherlands Air Force's 313 Squadron.

F-5E Tiger II

SPECIFICATIONS	
Country of origin:	United States
Type:	light tactical fighter
Powerplant:	two 22.2kN (5000lb) General Electric J85-GE-21B turbojets
Performance:	maximum speed at 10,975m (36,000ft) 1741km/h (1082mph); service ceiling 15,790m (51,800ft); combat radius 306km (190 miles)
Weights:	empty 4410kg (9723lb); maximum take-off weight 11,214kg (24,722lb)
Dimensions:	wingspan 8.13m (26ft 8in); length 14.45m (47ft 4.75in); height 4.07m (13ft 4.25in); wing area 17.28 sq m (186 sq ft)
Armament:	two 20mm cannon; two air-to-air missiles, five external pylons with provision for 3175kg (7000lb) of stores, including missiles, bombs, ECM pods, cluster bombs, rocket launcher pods and drop tanks

The F-5E Tiger II won a US industry competition in November 1970 for a follow-on International Fighter Aircraft to replace the F-5A. The improved aircraft was equipped with more powerful powerplants, extending nosegear to improve short field performance, extra fuel in a longer fuselage, new inlet ducts, widened fuselage and wing, root extensions and manoeuvring flaps. Deliveries began in 1972. The US Air Force still operates the aircraft for aggressor training.

RF-5E Tigereye

SPECIFICATIONS	
Country of origin:	United States
Type:	light tactical reconnaissance fighter
Powerplant:	two 22.2kN (5000lb) General Electric J85-GE-21B turbojets
Performance:	maximum speed at 10,975m (36,000ft) 1741km/h (1082mph); service ceiling 15,390m (50,500ft); combat radius 463km (288 miles)
Weights:	empty 4423kg (9750lb); maximum take-off weight 11,192kg (24,765lb)
Dimensions:	wingspan 8.13m (26ft 8in); length 14.65m (48ft 0.75in); height 4.07m (13ft 4.25in); wing area 17.28 sq m (186 sq ft)
Armament:	one 20mm cannon; two air-to-air missiles, five external pylons with provision for 3175kg (7000lb) of stores, including air-to-surface missiles

The RF-5E was a reconnaissance version of the F-5E Tiger, the improved version of the Freedom Fighter. The export success of this aircraft led to the development of a specialized tactical reconnaissance version, which first appeared at the Paris Air Show in 1978. Externally, the RF-5E is similar to the fighter, except for an extended 'chisel' nose housing camera equipment.

Maritime Patrol

Land-based maritime patrol aircraft have tended to be either converted airliner designs (such as the P-3 Orion and Il-38 'May') or purpose-built types like the Shackleton and Neptune. Advantages of the former include pressurized fuselages and greater internal space. Low-level flight over water causes stress on airframes and subjects them to salt corrosion, so maritime patrol aircraft need more frequent inspections and may require rebuilding to maintain their structural strength and to replace outdated avionics several times in their careers.

Avro Shackleton MR.2

Often said to have been derived from the Avro Lancaster, the Shackleton patrol aircraft owed more to the Lincoln, with which it shared wings, engines, tail surfaces and landing gear. Deliveries began in April 1951. The MR (maritime reconnaissance) Mk 2 had a longer fuselage, with the radar moved from the nose to a ventral 'dustbin' position, and a turret with two 20mm (.79in) cannon in the nose, rather than tail guns.

SPECIFICATIONS	
Country of origin:	United Kingdom
Type:	long-range maritime patrol aircraft
Powerplant:	four 1831kW (2455hp) Rolls-Royce Griffon 57A V-12 piston engines
Performance:	maximum speed 500km/h (311mph); service ceiling 6400m (21,000ft); range 5440km (3380 miles)
Weight:	39010kg (86,000lb) loaded
Dimensions:	wing span 36.58m (120ft); length 26.59m (87ft 3in); height 5.1m (16ft 9in)
Armament:	two Hispano No. 1 Mk 5 20mm (.79in) cannon in nose turret; up to 4536kg (10,000lb)

Kawasaki P-2J Neptune

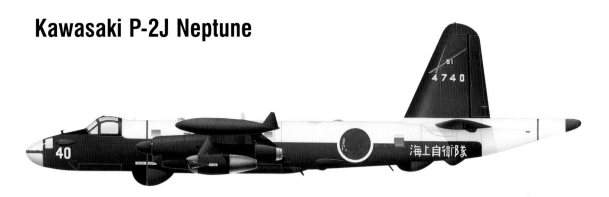

SPECIFICATIONS	
Country of origin:	Japan
Type:	four-engined maritime patrol aircraft
Powerplant:	two 2125kW (2850hp) General Electric T64-IHI-10 turboprop and two 13.7kN (3085kg) thrust IHI-JE turbojet engines
Performance:	maximum speed 1650km/h (403mph); service ceiling unknown; range 5633km (3500 miles)
Weights:	empty 19,278 kg (42,500 lb); maximum 34,020 kg (75,000 lb)
Dimensions:	span 30.9m (101ft 4in); length 27.9m (91ft 8in); height 8.9m (29ft 1in); wing area 93 sq m (1,000 sq ft)
Armament:	up to 16 5in rockets and up to 3628kg (8000lb) of bombs, depth charges or torpedoes

The last examples of the Lockheed Neptune series were the 89 produced by Kawasaki in Japan as the P-2J with turboprop main engines. The original piston-engined Neptunes served with many nations, including the United States, Netherlands, United Kingdom, France, Australia, Canada and Japan.

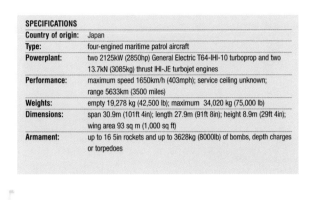

Ilyushin Il-38 'May'

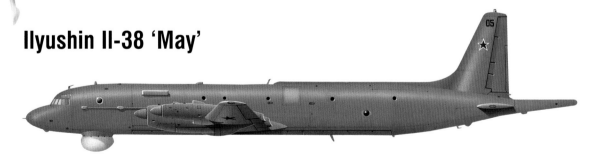

Like the P-3, the Il-38 had its origins as an airliner. The fuselage of the Il-18 'Coot' was stretched and ASW equipment fitted, including a Magnetic Anomaly Detector in a tail boom to create the Il-38 in 1967. About a quarter of the 176 built still serve in Russia, and India bought five.

SPECIFICATIONS	
Country of origin:	USSR
Type:	four-engined maritime patrol aircraft
Powerplant:	3170kW (4250hp) Progress AI-20M turboprop engines
Performance:	maximum speed 650km/h (406mph); service ceiling 10,000m (32,800ft); range 9500km (5937 miles)
Weights:	empty 33,700kg (74,140lb); maximum 63,500kg (139,700lb)
Dimensions:	span 37.42m (122ft 9in); length 39.6m (129ft 11in); height 10.16m (33ft 4in); wing area 140 sq m (1506 sq ft)
Armament:	up to 5000kg (11,000lb) of depth-charges, torpedoes or missiles

Falklands: Argentine Navy

When Argentina invaded the Falkland Islands in April 1982, it did not expect the United Kingdom to dispatch a task force to recover the islands. The Argentine Navy was equipped with a conventional aircraft carrier and the islands were in range of land-based patrol aircraft, as well as air-refuelled aircraft equipped with anti-ship weapons such as the Exocet missile, which inflicted considerable damage.

Lockheed L-188PF Electra

The Lockheed Electras of the Argentine Navy were used as blockade-running transports between the mainland and Port Stanley on the Falklands. These flights were made at night and at low level. They also flew patrol missions using their weather radar to search for British ships.

SPECIFICATIONS	
Country of origin:	United States
Type:	four-engined transport
Powerplant:	one four 2796kW (3750hp) Allison 501D-13 turboprop engines
Performance:	maximum speed 652km/h (405mph); range 3541km (2200 miles); service ceiling 28,400ft (9500m)
Weights:	empty 27,895kg (61,500lb); maximum 52,664kg (116,000lb)
Dimensions:	span 30.18m (99m); length 31.81m (104ft 6in); height 10m (32ft 10in); wing area 120.8 sq m (1300 sq ft)
Armament:	none

Lockheed SP-2H Neptune

The Argentina Navy's Escuadrilla de Exploracion operated two SP-2H Neptunes in 1982. The aircraft illustrated was used to make radar searches for the task force, and guided the Super Etendards that struck HMS *Sheffield* with Exocets on 4 May 1982.

SPECIFICATIONS	
Country of origin:	United States
Type:	four-engined maritime patrol aircraft
Powerplant:	two 2759kW (3700hp) Wright R-3350-32W Cyclone radial and two 13.7kN (3085kg) thrust Westinghouse J-34-WE-36 turbojet engines
Performance:	maximum speed 586km/h (364mph); range 3540km (2200 miles); service ceiling 6827m (22,400ft)
Weights:	empty 49,935lb (22,650kg); maximum 79,895lb (35,240kg)
Dimensions:	span 31.65m (103ft 10in); length 27.9m (91ft 8in); height 8.9m (29ft 4in); wing area 93 sq m (1000 sq ft)
Armament:	up to 4540kg (10,000lb) of bombs, mines or torpedoes

Grumman S-2E Tracker

SPECIFICATIONS	
Country of origin:	United States
Type:	twin-engined carrier-based anti-submarine aircraft
Powerplant:	two 1135kW (1525hp) Wright R-1820-82WA radial piston engines
Performance:	maximum speed 438km/h (272mph); range 1558km (968 miles); service ceiling 6949m (22,800ft)
Weights:	empty 8505kg (18,750lb); maximum 13,222kg (29,150lb)
Dimensions:	span 21m (69ft 8in); length 12.8m (42ft); height 4.9m (16ft 3in); wing area 45 sq m (485 sq ft)
Armament:	torpedoes, rockets, depth charges

Based on the carrier *25 de Mayo*, the S-2E Trackers of the Escuadrilla Antisubmarina located the British fleet on 2 May but lost it again before a strike by the carrier's Skyhawks could be launched. They also carried out attacks against suspected submarines.

McDonnell Douglas A-4Q Skyhawk

SPECIFICATIONS	
Country of origin:	United States
Type:	single-seat attack bomber
Powerplant:	one 34.7kN (7800lb) J65-W-16A turbojet
Performance:	maximum speed 1078km/h (670mph); service ceiling 14,935m (49,000ft); range with 4000lb load 1480km (920 miles)
Weights:	empty 4809kg (10,602lb); maximum take-off weight 12,437kg (27,420lb)
Dimensions:	wingspan 8.38m (27ft 6in); length excluding probe 12.22m (40ft 1.5in); height 4.66m (15ft 3in); wing area 24.15 sq m (260 sq ft)
Armament:	two 20mm Mk 12 cannon; five external hardpoints with provision for 2268kg (5000lb) of stores, including air-to-surface missiles, bombs, rocket-launcher pods, cannon pods, drop tanks and ECM pods

Argentina has been one of the largest users of the Skyhawk, acquiring many ex-US Navy aircraft. During the late 1960s, it acquired 66 A-4B aircraft, which were refurbished and redesignated A-4P (air force) and A-4Q (navy). During the Falklands conflict, these were used extensively in attacks on British shipping, and despite suffering heavy losses at the hands of the Royal Navy Sea Harrier pilots, Argentine pilots inflicted some damage on the British fleet at San Carlos.

Dassault Super Etendard

SPECIFICATIONS	
Country of origin:	France
Type:	single-seat carrierborne strike/attack and interceptor aircraft
Powerplant:	one 49kN (11,023lb) SNECMA Atar 8K-50 turbojet
Performance:	maximum speed 1180km/h (733mph); service ceiling 13,700m (44,950ft); combat radius 850km (528 miles)
Weights:	empty 6500kg (14,330lb); maximum take-off 12,000kg (26,455lb)
Dimensions:	wingspan 9.6m (31ft 6in); length 14.31m (46ft 11.2in); height 3.86m (12ft 8in); wing area 28.4sq m (305.7sq ft)
Armament:	two 30mm cannon, provision for up to 2100kg (4630lb) of stores, including nuclear weapons and Exocet air-to-surface missiles

Dassault's super Etendard has a substantially redesigned structure, a more efficient engine, inertial navigation system and other upgraded avionics. The first prototype flew on 3 October 1975; deliveries to the Aeronavale began in June 1978. Fourteen Super Etendards were used by Argentina to great effect against British shipping during the Falklands War.

Falklands: Argentine Air Force

The few airfields on the Falklands were not capable of operating combat aircraft beyond the light Aermacchi MB.339 and Pucara attack aircraft. The Fuerza Aerea Argentina had to fly most of its missions from the mainland at the extremes of the range of its fighter-bombers. Only one pass at a target was usually possible, and there was no time for dogfighting over the islands.

Dassault Mirage IIIEA

Responding to an Armée de l'Air light-interceptor specification of 1952, Dassault found the Mirage's initial powerplant insufficient and produced a larger, heavier and more powerful aircraft, the Mirage III. In October 1958, a pre-production Mirage IIIA-01 became the first West European fighter to attain Mach 2 in level flight. The longer and heavier IIIE was developed for a ground-attack role, with the Atar 9C turbojet and increased internal fuel.

SPECIFICATIONS	
Country of origin:	France
Type:	single-seat day visual fighter bomber
Powerplant:	one 60.8kN (13,668lb) SNECMA Atar 9C turbojet
Performance:	maximum speed at sea level 1390km/h (883mph); service ceiling 17,000m (55,755ft); combat radius at low level with 907kg (2000lb) load 1200km (745 miles)
Weights:	empty 7050kg (15,540lb); loaded 13,500kg (27,760lb)
Dimensions:	wingspan 8.22m (26ft 11.875in); length 16.5m (56ft); height 4.5m (14ft 9in); wing area 35 sq m (376.7 sq ft)
Armament:	two 30mm DEFA 552A cannon with 125rpg; three external pylons with provision for up to 3000kg (6612lb) of stores, including bombs, rockets, and gun pods

McDonnell Douglas A-4P Skyhawk

The McDonnell Douglas A-4P (later A-4B) had a strengthened rear fuselage, inflight refuelling equipment, provision for the Martin Bullpup air-to-surface missile, navigation and bombing computer, and the J65-W-16A turbojet. In total, 542 aircraft were built for the US Navy and US Marine Corps, 66 of which were rebuilt in the late 1960s for the Argentine Air Force and Navy as the A-4P. The A-4P was used extensively during the Falklands War.

SPECIFICATIONS	
Country of origin:	United States
Type:	single-seat attack bomber
Powerplant:	one 34.7kN (7800lb) J65-W-16A turbojet
Performance:	maximum speed 1078km/h (670mph); service ceiling 14,935m (49,000ft); range with 4000lb load 1480km (920 miles)
Weights:	empty 4809kg (10,602lb); maximum take-off weight 12,437kg (27,420lb)
Dimensions:	wingspan 8.38m (27ft 6in); length excluding probe 12.22m (40ft 1.5in); height 4.66m (15ft 3in); wing area 24.15 sq m (260 sq ft)
Armament:	two 20mm Mk 12 cannon with 200rpg; five external hardpoints with provision for 2268kg (5000lb) of stores

Canberra B.2

Most of the 10 Canberras in service with the FAA's Grupo 2 de Bombardeo were deployed to Trelew Air Base for attacks against British troops on the islands. They also bombed a civilian tanker in error. Two were shot down, one by a Sea Harrier and another by a Sea Dart fired from HMS *Exeter*.

SPECIFICATIONS

Country of origin:	United Kingdom
Type:	two-seat interdictor aircraft
Powerplant:	two 28.9kN (6500lb) Rolls Royce Avon Mk 101 turbojets
Performance:	maximum speed at 12,192m (40,000ft) 917km/h (570mph); service ceiling 14,630m (48,000ft); range 4274km (2656 miles)
Weights:	empty not published approx 11,790kg (26,000lb); maximum take-off weight 24,925kg (54,950lb)
Dimensions:	wingspan 29.49m (63ft 11in); length 19.96m (65ft 6in); height 4.78m (15ft 8in); wing area 97.08 sq m (1045 sq ft)
Armament:	internal bomb bay with provision for up to 2727kg (6000lb) of bombs, plus an additional 909kg (2000lb) of underwing pylons

FMA IA-58 Pucara

The Fábrica Militar de Aviones (FMA) Pucara was an indigenous counter-insurgency aircraft. Most of those deployed to the islands were destroyed in a Special Air Services raid. A-515 illustrated was captured intact and evaluated in the United Kingdom.

SPECIFICATIONS

Country of origin:	United Kingdom
Type:	twin-engined light attack aircraft
Powerplant:	two 729kW (978hp) Turbomeca Astazou XVIG turboprop engines
Performance:	maximum speed 500km/h (310mph); range 3710km (2305 miles); service ceiling 10,000m (31,800ft)
Weights:	empty 4020kg (8862lb); maximum 6800kg (14,991lb)
Dimensions:	span 14.5m (47ft 6in); length 14.25m (46ft 9in); height 5.36m (17ft 7in); wing area 30.3 sq m (326 sq ft)
Armament:	two 20mm Hispano-Suiza HS.804 cannon and four 7.62mm FM M2-20 machine guns; up to 1500kg (3300lb) of bombs or rockets

C-130E Hercules

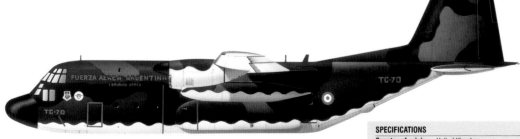

The C-130s of the FAA's Grupo 1 de Transporte Aereo Escuadron 1 flew transport missions to the islands, conducted aerial refuelling of Skyhawks and Super Etendards, and were even used as bombers with weapons racks under the wings. One was shot down on a reconnaissance mission by a Sea Harrier.

SPECIFICATIONS

Country of origin:	United Kingdom
Type:	four-engined transport/tanker
Powerplant:	four 3021kW (4050hp) Allison T56-A-7A turboprop engines
Performance:	maximum speed 547km/h (340mph); range 3896km (2420 miles); service ceiling 7010m (23,000ft)
Weights:	empty 72,892lb (33,057kg); maximum 79,375kg (175,000lb)
Dimensions:	span 40.4m (132ft 7in); length 29.8m (97ft 9in); height 11.7m (38ft 6in); wing area 162.2 sq m (1745.5 sq ft)
Armament:	(as bomber) 12 500lb bombs on Multiple Ejector Racks

Falklands: British Forces

British fixed-wing airpower in the South Atlantic was mostly restricted to two small aircraft carriers and their Sea Harriers and Harrier GR.3s. The Exocet threat kept the ships to the east of the Falklands, restricting the ability to mount continuous patrols over the islands. The Avro Vulcan made its only combat missions here, flying from Ascension Island to bomb Stanley Airfield and attack radars on the Falklands.

Sea Harrier FRS.1

The Fleet Air Arm's Sea Harriers were assigned to No 809 Squadron on HMS *Invincible* and No 899 Squadron on *Hermes*. This example from the former unit was flown by Flight Lieutenant Dave Morgan when he shot down two Argentine Air Force A-4B Skyhawks over Choiseul Sound on 8 June 1982.

SPECIFICATIONS	
Country of origin:	United Kingdom
Type:	shipborne multi-role combat aircraft
Powerplant:	one 95.6kN (21,500lb) Rolls-Royce Pegasus Mk.104 vectored thrust turbofan
Performance:	maximum speed at sea level 1110km/h (690mph) with maximum AAM load; service ceiling 15,545m (51,000ft); intercept radius 740km (460 miles) on high level mission with full combat reserve
Weights:	empty 5942kg (13,100lb); maximum take-off 11,884kg (26,200lb)
Dimensions:	wingspan 7.7m (25ft 3in); length 14.5m (47ft 7in); height 3.71m (12ft 2in); wing area 18.68sq m (201.1sq ft)
Armament:	two 30mm Aden cannon, provision for AIM-9 Sidewinder air-to-air missiles, and two anti-shipping missiles, up to a total of 3629kg (8000lb)

Sea Harrier FRS.1

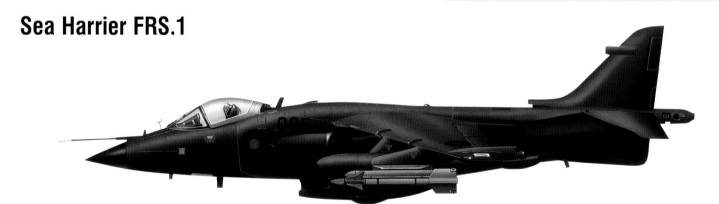

Sea Harrier XZ453 of No 899 Squadron damaged a Mirage III on 1 May 1982 over West Falkland with a sidewinder missile. The Argentine fighter was shot down by Argentine anti-aircraft guns while trying to make an emergency landing at Port Stanley. Sea Harriers destroyed 21 enemy aircraft in 1982.

SPECIFICATIONS	
Country of origin:	United Kingdom
Type:	shipborne multi-role combat aircraft
Powerplant:	one 95.6kN (21,500lb) Rolls-Royce Pegasus vectored thrust turbofan
Performance:	maximum speed at sea level 1110km/h (690mph) with maximum AAM load; service ceiling 15,545m (51,000ft); intercept radius 740km (460 miles) on high level mission with full combat reserve
Weights:	empty 5942kg (13,100lb); maximum take-off weight 11,884kg (26,200lb)
Dimensions:	wingspan 7.7m (25ft 3in); length 14.5m (47ft 7in); height 3.71m (12ft 2in); wing area 18.68 sq m (201.1 sq ft)
Armament:	two 30mm Aden cannon, provision for AIM-9 Sidewinder air-to-air missiles, and two anti-shipping missiles, up to a total of 3629kg (8000lb)

BAe Nimrod MR.2P

Hawker Siddeley began the design of the Nimrod in 1964, using the Comet 4C airliner as the basis for a new aircraft to replace the Avro Shackelton in the maritime patrol and anti-submarine warfare roles. Nimrods were very active during the Falklands War; inflight refuelling equipment was hastily added to a number of aircraft to allow them to operate from Ascension Island.

SPECIFICATIONS	
Country of origin:	United States
Type:	maritime patrol and anti-submarine warfare aircraft
Powerplant:	four 54kN (12,140lb) Rolls Royce Spey Mk 250 turbofans
Performance:	maximum speed 925km/h (575mph); service ceiling 12,800m (42,000ft); range on internal fuel 9262km (5,755 miles)
Weights:	empty 39,010kg (86,000lb); maximum take-off 87,090kg (192,000lb)
Dimensions:	wingspan 35m (114ft 10in); length 39.34m (129ft 1in); height 9.08m (29ft 9.5in); wing area 197.04 sq m (2,121 sq ft)
Armament:	internal bay with provision for 6123kg (13,500lb) of stores, including nine torpedoes and/or depth charges; underwing pylons for Harpoon anti-ship missiles or pairs of Sidewinder air-to-air missiles

Lockheed C-130K Hercules C.1

During the war, the RAF rapidly modified six C-130s with refuelling probes to extend their range. Flying from Ascension Island, Hercules made supply drops to the task force in mid-ocean. Several were later modified to refuel other aircraft, and were redesignated C.1Ks.

SPECIFICATIONS	
Country of origin:	United Kingdom
Type:	four-engined transport/tanker
Powerplant:	four 3021kW (4050hp) Allison T56-A-7A turboprop engines
Performance:	maximum speed 547km/h (340mph); range 3896km (2420 miles); service ceiling 7010m (23,000ft)
Weights:	empty 72,892lb (33,057kg); maximum 79,375kg (175,000lb)
Dimensions:	span 40.4m (132ft 7in); length 29.8m (97ft 9in); height 11.7m (38ft 6in); wing area 162.2 sq m (1745.5 sq ft)
Armament:	none

Avro Vulcan B.2

This Vulcan B.2a of No 101 Squadron is depicted in the late low-visibility colour scheme. The matt paint is paler than previous schemes, and Type B (two-colour) roundels and fin flash are also shown. The B.2A was optimized for low-level penetration missions. Vulcan B.2 XM607 of the Waddington Wing flew the first epic 'Black Buck' raid, flying from Ascension Island in mid-Atlantic with multiple aerial refuellings to bomb Stanley airfield. These raids convinced Argentina to keep back Mirage fighters to protect Buenos Aires.

SPECIFICATIONS	
Country of origin:	United Kingdom
Type:	low-level strategic bomber
Powerplant:	four 88.9kN (20,000lb) Olympus Mk.301 turbojets
Performance:	maximum speed 1038km/h (645mph) at high altitude; service ceiling 19,810m (65,000ft); range with normal bomb load about 7403km/h (4600 miles)
Weights:	maximum take-off weight 113,398kg (250,000lb)
Dimensions:	wingspan 33.83m (111ft); length 30.45m (99ft 11in); height 8.28m (27ft 2in); wing area 368.26 sq m (3,964 sq ft)
Armament:	internal weapon bay for up to 21,454kg (47,198lb) bombs

Spyplanes

Gathering intelligence on an enemy's disposition and intentions has now become more a matter of monitoring emissions across the radio spectrum than traditional observation and photography. The role of modern 'spyplanes' is grouped under the banner ISTAR (Intelligence, Surveillance, Target Acquisition and Reconnaissance), which includes photoreconnaissance, electronic intelligence gathering (Elint), signals intelligence (Sigint) and communications intelligence (Comint).

Boeing RC-135V

Although derived from the Boeing 707, the RC-135V bears little physical relation to the civilian aircraft. The RC-135V was the tenth of 12 variants, which have been tasked with electronic surveillance since the mid-1960s. As well as the cheek antennae fairings and sidewards-looking airborne radar (SLAR), the modified aircraft were fitted with a thimble nose and under-fuselage blade aerials.

SPECIFICATIONS	
Country of origin:	United States
Type:	electronic reconnaissance aircraft
Powerplant:	four 80kN (18,000lb) Pratt & Whitney TF33-P-9 turbojets
Performance:	maximum speed at 7620m (25,000ft) 991km/h (616mph); service ceiling 12,375m (40,600ft); range 4305km (2675 miles)
Weights:	empty 46,403kg (102,300lb) maximum take-off weight 124,965g (275,500lb)
Dimensions:	wingspan 39.88m (130ft 10in); length 41.53m (136ft 3in); height 12.7m (41ft 8in); wing area 226.03 sq m (2,433 sq ft)
Armament:	six 7.92mm (.3in) MGs; 1000kg (2205lb) bomb load

Lockheed SR-71A Blackbird

Deliveries of the SR-71 began in 1966, but it has the looks and performance of an aircraft of the twenty-first century. It was designed as a strategic reconnaissance aircraft to succeed the U-2. Although detailed design work began in 1959, the US Government did not formally acknowledge the existence of the SR-71 until 1964.

SPECIFICATIONS	
Country of origin:	United States
Type:	strategic reconnaissance aircraft
Powerplant:	two 144.5kN (32,500lb) Pratt & Whitney JT11D-20B bleed-turbojets
Performance:	maximum speed at 24,385m (80,000ft) more than 3219km/h (2000mph); ceiling in excess of 24,385m (80,000ft); standard range 4800km (2983 miles)
Weights:	empty 27,216kg (60,000lb); maximum take-off 77,111kg (170,000lb)
Dimensions:	wingspan 16.94m (55ft 7in); length 32.74m (107ft 5in); height 5.64m (18ft 6in); wing area 167.22 sq m (1800 sq ft)
Armament:	none

Lockheed TR-1A

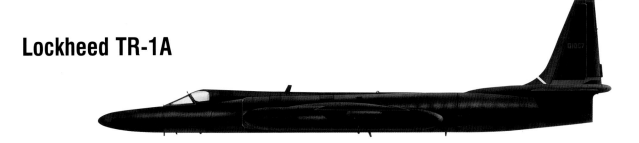

SPECIFICATIONS	
Country of origin:	United States
Type:	single-seat high-altitude reconnaissance aircraft
Powerplant:	one 75.6kN (17,000lb) Pratt & Whitney J75-P-13B turbojet
Performance:	maximum cruising speed at more than 21,335m (70,000ft); operational ceiling 27,430m (90,000ft); maximum range 10,050km (6250 miles)
Weights:	empty 7031kg (15,500lb); maximum take-off weight 18,733kg (41,300lb)
Dimensions:	wingspan 31.39m (103ft); length 19.13m (62ft 9in); height 4.88m (16ft); wing area 92.9 sq m (1000 sq ft)
Armament:	none

The first U-2s were deployed in England and Germany in 1956. Official reports announced that the glider-like aircraft were used for atmospheric research, when in fact they were overflying communist territory on reconnaissance missions. In 1978, the production line was reopened, and the first of 25 TR-1A aircraft followed. The TR-1A's primary role is that of tactical surveillance.

Beech RC-12D

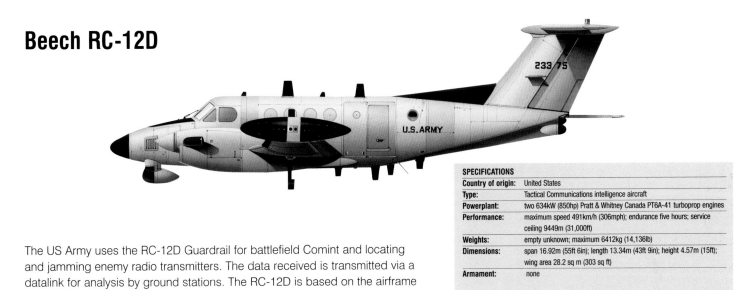

SPECIFICATIONS	
Country of origin:	United States
Type:	Tactical Communications intelligence aircraft
Powerplant:	two 634kW (850hp) Pratt & Whitney Canada PT6A-41 turboprop engines
Performance:	maximum speed 491km/h (306mph); endurance five hours; service ceiling 9449m (31,000ft)
Weights:	empty unknown; maximum 6412kg (14,136lb)
Dimensions:	span 16.92m (55ft 6in); length 13.34m (43ft 9in); height 4.57m (15ft); wing area 28.2 sq m (303 sq ft)
Armament:	none

The US Army uses the RC-12D Guardrail for battlefield Comint and locating and jamming enemy radio transmitters. The data received is transmitted via a datalink for analysis by ground stations. The RC-12D is based on the airframe of the civilian Beech Super King Air.

BAe Nimrod R.1

SPECIFICATIONS	
Country of origin:	United Kingdom
Type:	electronic reconnaissance aircraft
Powerplant:	four 54.09kN (12,160lb thrust) Rolls-Royce Spey turbofans
Performance:	Maximum speed: 923km/h (575mph); operational ceiling 13,411m (44,000ft); maximum range 9,265km (5,755 miles)
Weights:	empty 39,009kg (86,000lb); maximum take-off 87,090kg (192,000lb)
Dimensions:	wingspan 35.0m (114ft 10in); length 38.65m (126ft 9in); height 9.14m (31ft); wing area 197.05m (2,121 sq ft)
Armament:	none

The RAF's Nimrod fleet includes three specialized and secretive R.1 models serving with No 51 Squadron. With a similar role to the RC-135V, they are filled with sensors, recorders and language specialists. Communications such as mobile phone calls can be intercepted, monitored and analyzed in real time.

Heavy Lifters

For strategic airlift and some tactical missions, jet aircraft replaced 1950s-style propeller-driven transports in many of the world's larger air forces. Powerful high-bypass turbofans made possible super-heavy aircraft like the C-5 Galaxy (and the 747, which had its origins in the same competition). Ramp loading allowed vehicles as large as main battle tanks to be carried by air, and refuelling equipment gave the range to deploy whole infantry brigades anywhere in the world within hours.

Lockheed C-141B StarLifter

Designed in the early 1960s, the StarLifter was the most numerous of Military Airlift Command's strategic transport aircraft. The aircraft were delivered between April 1965 and February 1968. All 270 surviving C-141As were converted in the late 1970s to C-141B standard by stretching the fuselage by 7.11m (23ft 4in). The aircraft saw service in Vietnam, Grenada and in the 1991 Gulf War, before being retired in 2006.

SPECIFICATIONS	
Country of origin:	United States
Type:	heavy strategic transport
Powerplant:	four 93.4kN (21,000lb) Pratt & Whitney TF33-7 turbofans
Performance:	maximum speed 912km/h (567mph); range with maximum payload 4723km (2935 miles)
Weights:	empty 67,186kg (148,120lb); maximum take-off weight 155,582kg (343,000lb)
Dimensions:	wingspan 48.74m (159ft 11in); length 51.29m (168ft 3.5in); height 11.96m (39ft 3in); wing area 299.88 sq m (3228 sq ft)
Armament:	none

Lockheed C-5 Galaxy

For a time during the early 1970s, the giant C-5 Galaxy reigned as the world's largest aircraft, although it has now been overtaken by the Antonov An-225. Despite its huge size, the Galaxy can operate from rough airstrips. To this end, it has a high flotation landing gear with 28 wheels. The aircraft can carry complete missile systems and M1 Abrams tanks.

SPECIFICATIONS	
Country of origin:	United States
Type:	heavy strategic transport
Powerplant:	(C5A) four 82.3kN (41,000lb) General Electric TF39-1turbofans
Performance:	maximum speed 919km/h (571mph); service ceiling at 272,910kg (615,000lb) 10,360m (34,000ft); range with maximum payload 100,228kg (220,967lb) 6033km (3749 miles)
Weights:	empty 147,528kg (325,244lb); maximum take-off weight 348,810kg (769,000lb)
Dimensions:	wingspan 67.88m (222ft 8.5in); length 75.54m (247ft 10in); height 19.85m (65ft 1.5in); wing area 575.98 sq m (6200 sq ft)
Armament:	none

HEAVY LIFTERS TIMELINE

 1963

 1968

 1970

Kawasaki C-1A

The C-1 was designed specifically to replace the Curtiss C-46 Commando transport aircraft in service in Japan. The first flight was made in November 1970; flight testing and evaluation led to a production order for 11 in 1972. The C-1 was designed with a short range suitable only for flights within Japan, in line with Japan's strict self-defence policy.

SPECIFICATIONS	
Country of origin:	Japan
Type:	short-range transport
Powerplant:	two 64.5kN (14,500lb) Mitsubishi (Pratt & Whitney) JT8-M-9 turbofans
Performance:	maximum speed at 7620m (25,000ft) 806km/h (501mph); service ceiling 11,580m (38,000ft); range 1300km (808 miles) with 7900kg (17,417lb) payload
Weights:	empty 23320kg (51,412lb); maximum take-off weight 45,000kg (99,208lb)
Dimensions:	wingspan 30.6m (100ft 4.75in); length 30.5m (100ft 4in); height 10m (32ft 9.3in); wing area 102.5 sq m (1297.09 sq ft)
Armament:	none

Lockheed TriStar K Mk 1

Since March 1986, the Royal Air Force has operated a converted version of the Lockheed Tristar jetliner as its primary tanker aircraft. Six of the 500 series aircraft were adapted for inflight refuelling operations. Four of the aircraft retained a commercial cabin configuration to allow passengers to be carried. The two other aircraft were fitted with a large cargo door on the port side.

SPECIFICATIONS	
Country of origin:	United Kingdom/United States
Type:	long-range strategic transport and inflight refuelling tanker
Powerplant:	three 222.3kN(50,000lb) Rolls-Royce RB.211-524B turbofans
Performance:	maximum cruising speed 964km/h (599mph) at 10,670m (35,000ft); service ceiling 13,105m (43,000ft); range on internal fuel with maximum payload 7783km (4836 miles)
Weights:	empty 110,163kg (242,684lb); maximum take-off weight 244,944kg (540,000lb)
Dimensions:	wingspan 50.09m (164ft 4in); length 50.05m (164ft 2.5in); height 16.87m (55ft 4in); wing area 329.96 sq m (3541 sq ft)
Armament:	none

Ilyushin Il-76 'Candid'

The Il-76 'Candid' (NATO reporting name) was first seen in the West at the 1971 Paris Air Salon. With a high cruising speed and intercontinental range, it was designed as a capable freighter that could carry large indivisible loads and operate from relatively poor and partially prepared airstrips. Aeroflot was the first operator, while India operates a fleet of 24.

SPECIFICATIONS	
Country of origin:	USSR (now CIS)
Type:	heavy freight transport
Powerplant:	four 117.6kN (26,455lb) Soloviev D-30KP-1 turbofans
Performance:	maximum speed at 11,000m (36,090ft) 850km/h (528mph); maximum cruising altitude 12,000m (39,370ft); range with 40,000kg (88,185lb) payload 5000km (3107 miles)
Weights:	empty about 75,000kg (165,347lb); maximum take-off weight 170,000kg (374,786lb)
Dimensions:	wingspan 50.5m (165ft 8.2in); length 46.59m (152ft 10.25in); height 14.76m (48ft 5in); wing area 300 sq m (3229.28 sq ft)
Armament:	provision for two 23mm cannon in tail

1971

Douglas A-4 Skyhawk

First flown in 1954 as a light bomber able to carry a single nuclear weapon, the A4D (later A-4) Skyhawk went on to be one of the longest-serving US Navy aircraft, finally retiring in 2003. Production for the United States and export also lasted a record time – 27 years – and the 'Bantam Bomber' was sold to eight nations, either new or second-hand. The Skyhawk remains in service with Argentina, Brazil, Israel, Singapore and several military contractors.

A-4C Skyhawk

The A-4C was the first model to be equipped with a fixed refuelling probe, and had an improved weapons delivery system compared to its predecessors. The 'Charlie' was used extensively in Vietnam, this example serving with VA-144 'Roadrunners' aboard the USS *Kitty Hawk*.

SPECIFICATIONS	
Country of origin:	United States
Type:	single-seat attack bomber
Powerplant:	one 34.7kN (7800lb) J65-W-16A turbojet
Performance:	maximum speed 1078km/h (670mph); service ceiling 14,935m (49,000ft); range with 4000lb load 1480km (920 miles)
Weights:	empty 4809kg (10,602lb); maximum take-off weight 12,437kg (27,420lb)
Dimensions:	wingspan 8.38m (27ft 6in); length excluding probe 12.22m (40ft 1.5in); height 4.66m (15ft 3in); wing area 24.15 sq m (260 sq ft)
Armament:	two 20mm Mk 12 cannon; provision for 2268kg (5000lb) of stores, including air-to-surface missiles, bombs, cluster bombs, dispenser weapons, rocket-launcher pods, cannon pods, drop tanks and ECM pods

A-4G Skyhawk

Australia purchased a version of the A-4F for use on its ex-British carrier HMAS *Melbourne*. The A-4Gs were supplemented by ex-USN A-4Fs and the survivors sold on to New Zealand when *Melbourne* was retired, supplementing that country's own fleet of A-4Ks.

SPECIFICATIONS	
Country of origin:	United States
Type:	single-seat attack bomber
Powerplant:	one 41.3kN (9300lb) J52-8A turbojet
Performance:	maximum speed 1078km/h (670mph); service ceiling 14,935m (49,000ft); range with 4000lb load 1480km (920 miles)
Weights:	empty 4809kg (10,602lb); maximum take-off weight 12,437kg (27,420lb)
Dimensions:	wingspan 8.38m (27ft 6in); length excluding probe 12.22m (40ft 1.5in); height 4.66m (15ft 3in); wing area 24.15 sq m (260 sq ft)
Armament:	two 20mm Mk 12 cannon; provision for 3720kg (8200lb) of stores, including AIM-9G Sidewinder AAMs, rocket-launcher pods and ECM pods

Douglas A-4M Skyhawk

The A-4M was a much-improved version for the US Marines, with an enlarged canopy, larger engine and revised avionics, including electronic counter measures (ECM) and laser-designation equipment. Some surplus A-4Ms were supplied to Argentina in the 1990s.

SPECIFICATIONS

Country of origin:	United States
Type:	single-seat attack bomber
Powerplant:	one 49.82kN (11,500lb) thrust Pratt & Whitney J52-P408 turbojet engine
Performance:	maximum speed 1083km/h (673mph); service ceiling 14,935m (49,000ft); range 3310km (2200 miles)
Weights:	empty 4809kg (10,602lb); maximum take-off weight 12,437kg (27,420lb)
Dimensions:	wingspan 8.38m (27ft 6in); length excluding probe 12.22m (40ft 1.5in); height 4.66m (15ft 3in); wing area 24.15 sq m (260 sq ft)
Armament:	two 20mm Mk 12 cannon; provision for 3720kg (8200lb) of stores, including AIM-9G Sidewinder AAMs, rocket-launcher pods and ECM pods

A-4PTM Skyhawk

Malaysia bought 40 ex-US Skyhawks in the mid-1980s and had Grumman update them from A-4C standard with modern avionics. The new designation was A-4PTM, which stands for *Persekutan Tanah Melayu*, or Federation of Malay States, although is sometimes said to mean 'Peculiar to Malaysia'.

SPECIFICATIONS

Country of origin:	United States
Type:	single-seat attack bomber
Powerplant:	one 34.7kN (7800lb) J65-W-16A turbojet
Performance:	maximum speed 1078km/h (670mph); service ceiling 14,935m (49,000ft); range with 4000lb load 1480km (920 miles)
Weights:	empty 4809kg (10,602lb); maximum take-off weight 12,437kg (27,420lb)
Dimensions:	wingspan 8.38m (27ft 6in); length excluding probe 12.22m (40ft 1.5in); height 4.66m (15ft 3in); wing area 24.15 sq m (260 sq ft)
Armament:	two 20mm Mk 12 cannon; provision for 2268kg (5000lb) of stores, including air-to-surface missiles, bombs, cluster bombs, drop tanks

TA-4J Skyhawk

Few people believed designer Ed Heinemann when he said he could build a jet attack bomber for the Navy at half the specified weight of 13,600kg (30,000lb). But ultimately his aircraft stayed in production for over 20 years, in a multiplicity of different versions. The TA-4J was a variant built for the US Navy, with the fuselage lengthened by .8m (2.5ft) to accommodate the instructor's tandem cockpit.

SPECIFICATIONS

Country of origin:	United States
Type:	two-seat carrier trainer
Powerplant:	one 37.8kN (8500lb) J52-P-6 turbojet
Performance:	maximum speed 1084km/h (675mph); service ceiling 14,935m (49,000ft); range 1287km (800 miles)
Weights:	empty 4809kg (10,602lb); maximum take-off weight 11,113kg (24,500lb)
Dimensions:	wingspan 8.38m (27ft 6in); length excluding probe 12.98m (42ft 7.25in); height 4.66m (15ft 3in); wing area 24.15 sq m (260 sq ft)
Armament:	one 20mm cannon

The Mighty Hercules

Lockheed's C-130 Hercules has been in production for over 50 years, with around 3000 aircraft built. It has become the standard military transport of the West, with few major nations not possessing any 'Herks'. The C-130 has been produced in versions for many tasks, including tankers, gunships, ski-planes and rescue variants. The C-130J, with new engines, propellers and electronics, is slowly emulating the export success of its predecessors.

C-130B Hercules

The C-130B entered service in 1959 and a number are still in use with air forces including South Africa, Turkey and Romania. It was the first model to have auxiliary fuel tanks under the wings, a feature of all subsequent Hercules prior to the C-130J.

SPECIFICATIONS	
Country of origin:	United States
Type:	four-engined transport aircraft
Powerplant:	four 3021kW (4050hp) Allison T56-A-7 turboprop engines
Performance:	maximum speed 547km/h (340mph); range 3896km (2420 miles); service ceiling 7010m (23,000ft)
Weights:	empty (34,686kg); maximum 79,375kg (175,000lb)
Dimensions:	span 40.4m (132ft 7in); length 29.8m (97ft 9in); height 11.7m (38ft 6in); wing area 162.2 sq m (1745.5 sq ft)
Armament:	none

EC-130E Hercules

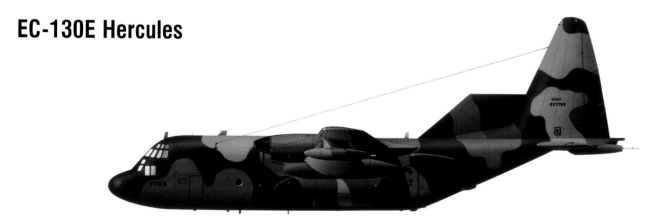

Known as a 'flying broadcast station', the EC-130E Commando Solo is fitted with powerful transmitters to send programming to TV viewers and radio listeners in enemy territory during a conflict. These broadcasts can be used to influence public opinion or counter the enemy's own propaganda.

SPECIFICATIONS	
Country of origin:	United States
Type:	Psychological operations aircraft
Powerplant:	four 3660kW (4910hp) Allison T56-A-15 turboprop engines
Performance:	maximum speed 547km/h (340mph); range 3896km (2420 miles); service ceiling 7010m (23,000ft)
Weights:	empty unknown; maximum 70,306kg (155,000lb)
Dimensions:	span 40.4m (132ft 7in); length 29.8m (97ft 9in); height 11.7m (38ft 6in); wing area 162.2 sq m (1745.5 sq ft)
Armament:	none

EC-130Q Hercules

The EC-130Q was a version for the Navy's TACAMO (TAke Charge And Move Out) mission, which involved communication with submerged ballistic-missile submarines. The aircraft was fitted with a Very Low Frequency (VLF) radio transmitter and long trailing-wire antenna.

SPECIFICATIONS	
Country of origin:	United States
Type:	Communications relay aircraft
Powerplant:	four 3660kW (4910hp) Allison T56-A-15 turboprop engines
Performance:	maximum speed 547km/h (340mph); range 3896km (2420 miles); service ceiling 7010m (23,000ft)
Weights:	empty 72,892 lb (33,057 kg); maximum 79,375 kg (175,000 lb)
Dimensions:	span unknown; length 29.8m (97ft 9in); height 11.7m (38ft 6in); wing area 162.2 sq m (1745.5 sq ft)
Armament:	none

KC-130F Hercules

Originally introduced as the GV-1 in the pre-1962 designation system, the KC-130F became the US Navy and Marines' primary transport and tactical refuelling aircraft. The underwing fuel tanks were replaced with pods containing a hose reel and drogue. The 'Blue Angels' aerobatic team use KC-130Fs as support aircraft.

SPECIFICATIONS	
Country of origin:	United States
Type:	tanker/transport aircraft
Powerplant:	four 3660kW (4910hp) Allison T56-A-15 turboprop engines
Performance:	maximum speed 604km/h (374mph); range 3896km (2420 miles); service ceiling 10,058m (33,000ft)
Weights:	empty 72,892lb (33,057kg); maximum 70,306kg (155,000lb)
Dimensions:	span 40.4m (132ft 7in); length 29.8m (97ft 9in); height 11.7m (38ft 6in); wing area 162.2 sq m (1745.5 sq ft)
Armament:	none

WC-130H Hercules

The 'Hurricane Hunters' of the USAF's 53rd Weather Reconnaissance Squadron flew the WC-130H Hercules over the Atlantic and the Gulf of Mexico to detect hurricanes and gather data to predict their direction and strength. The unit was one of the first to get C-130J models.

SPECIFICATIONS	
Country of origin:	Germany
Type:	weather reconnaissance aircraft
Powerplant:	four 3660kW (4910hp) Allison T56-A-15 turboprop engines
Performance:	maximum speed 547km/h (340mph); range 3896km (2420 miles); service ceiling 10,058m (33,000ft)
Weights:	empty 72,892lb (33,057kg); maximum 79,375kg (175,000lb)
Dimensions:	span 40.4m (132ft 7in); length 29.8m (97ft 9in); height 11.7m (38ft 6in); wing area 162.2 sq m (1745.5 sq ft)
Armament:	(as bomber) 5670kg (12,500lb) bombs on Multiple Ejector Racks

One-offs

The exciting pace of development of aviation in the post-war years left many aircraft by the wayside. Some were technological dead-ends, such as rocket-powered interceptors. Others were too costly and ambitious. Two promising programmes, the Canadian Arrow and the British TSR.2, fell victim to the then-fashionable theory that missiles would make manned combat aircraft obsolete. In these cases, the national aerospace industries suffered and only American aircraft companies benefited.

Republic XF-91 Thunderceptor

The XF-91 was a bold attempt in 1946 to produce a high-altitude interceptor to the USAAF. Republic introduced unusual features such as a variable-incidence inverse tapered wing, with tandem-wheel main gears at the tips and the twin powerplant. The fairing for a Reaction Motors XLR-11-RM-9 rocket motor, visible under the tail, could be used to augment top speed for short periods.

SPECIFICATIONS

Country of origin:	United States
Type:	experimental high-altitude interceptor
Powerplant:	one General Electric J47-GE-3 turbojet; Reaction Motors XLR-11-RM-9 rocket motor
Performance:	maximum speed attained 1812km/h (1126mph); ceiling (approximately) 15,250m (50,000ft)
Weights:	unknown
Dimensions:	unknown
Armament:	none

Saunders Roe SR.53

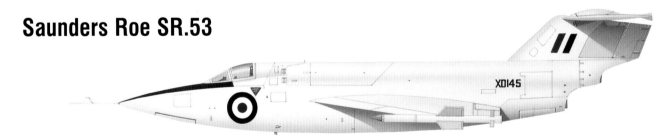

The SR.53 was intended as a pure rocket-powered interceptor, but a small turbojet was added to allow it to land under power after it had made its interception. One of the two SR.53s built crashed in 1958, but by then the UK Government had decided to cancel almost all manned fighter programmes.

SPECIFICATIONS

Country of origin:	United Kingdom
Type:	experimental mixed-power interceptor
Powerplant:	one 7.3kN (1640lb) thrust Armstrong Siddeley Viper turbojet engine and one 35.6kN (8008lb) thrust Spectre Rocket engine
Performance:	maximum speed Mach 2.2; endurance: 7 minutes at full power; service ceiling 20,000m (65,600ft)
Weights:	loaded 8363kg (18,400lb)
Dimensions:	span 7.65m (25ft 1in); length 13.71m (10ft 5in); height 3.3m (10ft 10in); wing area 25.45 sq m (274 sq ft)
Armament:	two Firestreak or Blue Jay AAMs

ONE-OFFS TIMELINE

1949

1957

Myasishchev M-50 'Bounder'

Vladimir M. Myasishchev's design for the M-50 was extremely advanced and was considered a significant potential threat when details of its capabilities first became known. Only ever built in prototype form, it featured a shoulder-mounted cropped delta wing, coupled with a conventional tail unit and all-swept surfaces. The fuselage was pressurized and incorporated a large weapons bay.

SPECIFICATIONS	
Country of origin:	USSR
Type:	prototype supersonic strategic bomber
Powerplant:	four wing-mounted 128.3kN (28,860lb) Soloviev D-15 turbojets
Performance:	(estimated) maximum speed at altitude 1950km/h (1,212mph)
Weights:	not released
Dimensions:	not released
Armament:	probably at least one cannon; internal bomb bay carrying stand-off nuclear weapons

Avro Arrow

The story of the Arrow bears a startling resemblance to that of the BAC TSR.2. Both projects showed great promise during the early stages of development in the mid-1950s, and both were destroyed by the decisions of politicians convinced that the days of the manned interceptor were numbered. The design incorporated a huge, high-set delta wing.

SPECIFICATIONS	
Country of origin:	Canada
Type:	two-seat all-weather long range supersonic interceptor
Powerplant:	two 104.5kN (23,500lb) Pratt and Whitney J75-P-3 turbojets
Performance:	Mach 2.3 recorded during tests
Weights:	empty 22,244kg (49,040lb); average take-off weight during trials 25,855kg (57,000lb)
Dimensions:	wingspan 15.24m (50ft); length 23.72m (77ft 9.75in); height 6.48m (21ft 3in); wing area 113.8 sq m (1225 sq ft)
Armament:	eight Sparrow air-to-air missiles in internal bay

BAC TSR.2

Conceived as a replacement for the English Electric Canberra, the cancellation of the TSR.2 programme was widely regarded within the aviation industry as the greatest disaster to befall the post-war British aviation industry. In retrospect, it is clear that much of the pioneering research carried out by the project team was of great benefit during the development of Concorde.

SPECIFICATIONS	
Country of origin:	United Kingdom
Type:	two-seat strike/reconnaissance aircraft
Powerplant:	two 136.1kN (30,610lb) thrust Bristol Siddeley Olympus 320 turbojets
Performance:	maximum speed at altitude 2390km/h (1485mph); operating ceiling 16,460m (54,000ft); range at low level 1287km (800 miles)
Weights:	average 36,287kg (80,000lb); maximum 43,545kg (96,000lb)
Dimensions:	wingspan 11.28m (37ft); length 27.13m (89ft); height 7.32m (24ft); wing area 65.03 sq m (700 sq ft)
Armament:	(planned) up to 2722kg (6000lb) of conventional or nuclear weapons internally; four underwing pylons for up to 1814kg (4000lb) of weapons

1958

1964

SAAB: Part 1

Neutral Sweden was surrounded by warring nations in 1939–45. Without modern aircraft, it had no way of preventing incursions across its borders or into its airspace. State aircraft maker Saab (Svenska Aeroplan Aktiebolaget), which had previously built aircraft under licence, created its first original design, the B 17, in 1940. It was followed by more innovative designs, including aircraft firsts: ejection seats; conversion of piston-engines to jet power; and, a first for Europe, swept-wing craft.

B 17

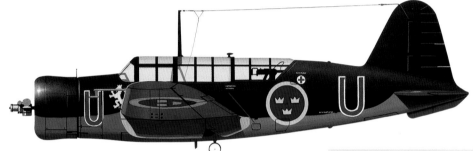

Saab hired American engineers to help it produce its first all-new design, the B 17, and the result bore more than a passing resemblance to the Curtiss Helldiver. The B 17 was built in dive-bomber and level-bomber variants and a dedicated photoreconnaissance version.

SPECIFICATIONS	
Country of origin:	Sweden
Type:	single-engined dive bomber
Powerplant:	one 882-kW (1,183-hp) Pratt and Whitney R-1830-S1C3G Twin Wasp radial piston engine
Performance:	maximum speed 435 km/h (270 mph)); range 1800km (1118 miles); service ceiling 8700m (28,543ft)
Weights:	empty 2600kg (5732lb); maximum 3605kg (7948lb)
Dimensions:	span 13.7m (45ft); length 9.8m (32ft 1in); height 4m (13ft 2in); wing area 28.5 sq m (307 sq ft)
Armament:	three 8mm machine guns, up to 500kg (1102lb) of bombs

91 Safir

The Safir was one of Saab's biggest export successes, selling to operators in over 20 countries. Sweden used it as its primary military trainer for many years, and Austria bought 24 in the mid-1960s, using them as primary trainers and navigation trainers.

SPECIFICATIONS	
Country of origin:	Sweden
Type:	two-seat trainer
Powerplant:	one 134-kW (180-hp) Avco Lycoming O-360-A1A piston engine
Performance:	maximum speed 266km/h (165mph); range 1000km (621 miles); service ceiling 5000m (16,400ft)
Weights:	empty 710kg (1565lb); maximum 1205kg (2657lb)
Dimensions:	span 10.6m (34ft 9in); length 7.95m (26ft 1in); height 2.2m (7ft 3in); wing area 13.6 sq m (146 sq ft)
Armament:	none

SAAB TIMELINE

1940

1943

1945

J 21

Inspired by the P-38 Lightning, but with a single pusher engine, the J 21 was one of the most unusual fighters to fly during the war years. It was equipped with an ejection seat so the pilot could avoid hitting the propeller if forced to bail out.

SPECIFICATIONS	
Country of origin:	Sweden
Type:	single-engined fighter-bomber
Powerplant:	one 1100kW (1475hp) Daimler-Benz DB 605B piston engine
Performance:	maximum speed 640 km/h (400 mph); range 1500km (930 miles); service ceiling 10,200m (33,450ft)
Weights:	empty 3350kg (7165lb); maximum 9730kg (4415lb)
Dimensions:	span 11.61m (38ft 1in); length 22.2m (38ft 1in); height 4m (13ft 2in); wing area 22.2 sq m (239 sq ft)
Armament:	one 20mm cannon and four 13.2mm machine-guns

J 29 Tunnan

The Tunnan (Barrel) was only the third swept-wing jet fighter to fly after the F-86 and MiG-15. Sweden took them on the only Flygvapnet (Air Force) combat deployment to date, flying ground-attack missions in support of UN operations in the Congo in 1961.

SPECIFICATIONS	
Country of origin:	Sweden
Type:	single-engined fighter
Powerplant:	27kN (6072.7lb) thrust Volvo RM 2B (de Havilland Ghost) afterburning turbojet engine
Performance:	maximum speed 1060km/h (659mph); range 1100km (684 miles); service ceiling 15,700m (51,000ft)
Weights:	empty 4845kg (10,680lb); maximum 8375kg (18,465lb)
Dimensions:	span 11m (36ft 1in); length 10.1m (33ft 2in); height 3.8m (12ft 6in); wing area 24 sq m (258 sq ft)
Armament:	four 20mm cannon, two AIM-9B Sidewinder AAMs

J 32B Lansen

Designed to replace the Saab 18 light-bomber, the Type 32 was a large, all-swept machine of outstanding quality, designed and developed ahead of similar aircraft elsewhere in Western Europe. Entering service in 1953, the Type 32 served well into the 1990s as aggressor aircraft, target tugs and trials aircraft. The J 32B pictured had S6 radar fire control for lead/pursuit interception.

SPECIFICATIONS	
Country of origin:	Sweden
Type:	all-weather and night fighter
Powerplant:	one 67.5kN (15,190lb) Svenska Flygmotor (Rolls-Royce Avon) RM6A
Performance:	maximum speed 1114km/h (692mph); service ceiling 16,013m (52,500ft); range with external fuel 3220km (2000 miles)
Weights:	empty 7990kg (17,600lb); maximum loaded 13,529kg (29,800lb)
Dimensions:	wingspan 13m (42ft 7.75in); length 14.5m (47ft 6.75in); height 4.65m (15ft 3in); wing area 37.4 sq m (402.58 sq ft)
Armament:	four 30mm Aden M/55 cannon; four Rb324 (Sidewinder) air-to-air missiles or FFAR (Folding Fin Air-launched Rocket) pods

1948

1952

SAAB: Part Two

Since World War II, Saab has built most of Sweden's combat aircraft and trainers, continuing its innovation with the double-delta Draken (Dragon), the canard-wing Viggen (Thunderbolt) and the fly-by-wire Gripen (Griffin). Politics prevented fighter export sales to most countries likely to go to war with them, but more recently Saab has sold the Gripen to non-traditional customers.

MFI-15

A light utility aircraft and trainer, the civilian Saab MFI-15 Safari and military MFI-17 Supporter have been used by a number of air forces, including Norway, one of whose aircraft is shown. Pakistan has produced a version known locally as the Mushshak for its primary training needs.

SPECIFICATIONS

Country of origin:	Sweden
Type:	utility aircraft/trainer
Powerplant:	one 149kW (200hp) Avco Lycoming IO-360-A1B6 piston engine
Performance:	maximum speed 235km/h (146mph); range unknown; service ceiling 4100m (13,450 ft)
Weights:	empty 690kg (1521 lb); maximum 1200kg (2646 lb)
Dimensions:	span 8.85m (29ft); length 7m (23ft); height 2.6m (8ft 6in); wing area 11.9 sq m (129 sq ft)
Armament:	none

J 35F Draken

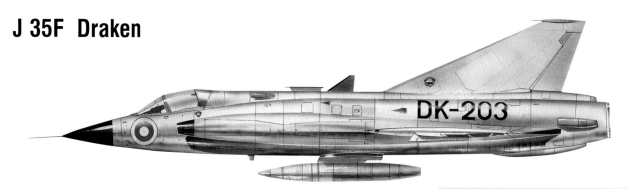

The Draken was designed to a demanding specification for a single-seat interceptor that could operate from short air strips, had rapid time-to-height performance and supersonic performance. The 'double-delta' wing is an ingenious method of arranging items one behind the other to allow a long aircraft a small frontal area and correspondingly high aerodynamic efficiency.

SPECIFICATIONS

Country of origin:	Sweden
Type:	single-seat all-weather interceptor
Powerplant:	one 76.1kN (17,110lb) Svenska Flygmotor RM6C turbojet
Performance:	maximum speed 2125km/h (1320mph); service ceiling 20,000m (65,000ft); range with maximum fuel 3250km (2020 miles)
Weights:	empty 7425kg (16,369lb); maximum take-off weight 16,000kg (35,274lb)
Dimensions:	wingspan 9.4m (30ft 10in); length 15.4m (50ft 4in); height 3.9m (12ft 9in); wing area 49.2 sq m (526.6 sq ft)
Armament:	one 30mm Aden M/55 cannon, air-to-air missiles, or up to 4082kg (9000lb) of bombs on attack mission

SAAB TIMELINE

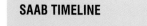 1955  1961 1963

105/Sk 60

SPECIFICATIONS

Country of origin:	Sweden
Type:	training/liason aircraft with secondary attack capability
Powerplant:	two 73kN (1640lb) Turbomeca Aubisque turbofans
Performance:	maximum speed at 6095m (20,000ft) 770km/h (480mph); service ceiling 13,500m (44,290ft); range 1400km (870 miles)
Weights:	empty 2510kg (5534lb); maximum take-off weight 4050kg (8929lb)
Dimensions:	wingspan 9.5m (31ft 2in); length 10.5m (34ft 5.375in); height 2.7m (8ft 10.25in); wing area 16.3 sq m (175.46 sq ft)
Armament:	six external hardpoints with provision for up to 700kg (1543lb) of stores, including two Saab Rb05 air-to-surface missiles, or two 30mm cannon pods, or 12 135mm rockets, or bombs, cluster bombs and rocket launcher pods

Having established its reputation with the Draken, Saab extended its range by developing the privately funded 105. This aircraft is a swept shoulder-wing monoplane with side-by-side cabin accommodation for either two or four crew. The first prototype flew in June 1963, and after successful evaluation by the Swedish Air Force, orders were placed for 150 production aircraft.

SF 37 Viggen

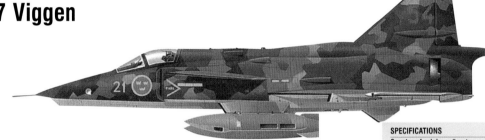

The SF37 was a dedicated single-seat reconnaissance version intended to replace the S 35E in service with the Swedish air force. The first prototype flew in May 1973. Production aircraft were distinguished by a chisel nose containing seven cameras, which are often supplemented by surveillance pods on the shoulder hardpoints.

SPECIFICATIONS

Country of origin:	Sweden
Type:	single-seat all-weather attack aircraft
Powerplant:	one 115.7kN (26,015lb) Volvo Flygmotor RM8 turbofan
Performance:	maximum speed at high altitude 2124km/h (1320mph); service ceiling 18,290m (60,000ft); combat radius 1000km (621 miles)
Weights:	empty 11,800kg (26,015lb); maximum take-off weight 20,500kg (45,194lb)
Dimensions:	wingspan 10.6m (34ft 9.25in); length 16.3m (53ft 5.75in); height 5.6m (18ft 4.5in); wing area 46 sq m (495.16 sq ft)
Armament:	seven external hardpoints with provision for 6000kg (13,228lb) of stores, including cannon pods, rocket pods, missiles and bombs

JAS 39 Gripen

Saab has produced another excellent lightweight fighter in the form of the Gripen. It was conceived during the late 1970s as a replacement for the AJ, SH, SF and JA versions of the Saab 37 Viggen, and the configuration follows Saab's convention with an aft-mounted delta and swept-canard foreplanes. The flying surfaces are controlled via a fly-by-wire system.

SPECIFICATIONS

Country of origin:	Sweden
Type:	single-seat all-weather fighter, attack and reconnaissance aircraft
Powerplant:	one 80.5kN (18,100lb) Volvo Flygmotor RM12 turbofan
Performance:	maximum speed more than Mach 2; range on hi-lo-hi mission with external armament 3250km (2020 miles)
Weights:	empty 6622kg (14,600lb); maximum take-off weight 12,473kg (27,500lb)
Dimensions:	wingspan 8m (26ft 3in); length 14.1m (46ft 3in); height 4.7m (15ft 5in)
Armament:	one 27mm Mauser BK27 cannon, provision for air-to-air missiles, air-to-surface missiles, anti-ship missiles, bombs, cluster bombs, rocket-launcher pods, reconnaissance pods, drop tanks and ECM pods

1967

1988

THE MODERN ERA

Military aircraft have matured to become 'systems platforms' as much as simply a means of taking weapons to the enemy.

Since the early 1990s, the previous generations of warplanes have been swept aside by aircraft with fly-by-wire control systems, data-linked sensors and the ability to travel at supersonic speeds. Composite materials such as carbon fibre make up a large part of aircraft structures. The increasing cost of such sophisticated warplanes has led to fierce competition by manufacturers for scarce orders.

Left: The Eurofighter Typhoon is an example of multinational cooperation to produce a fighter for the differing needs of four air forces.

Vought A-7 and F-8

The Vought Company (as Chance-Vought) had created the classic F4U Corsair during World War II, but stumbled in the early post-war years. It redeemed itself with the record-breaking F8U (F-8) Crusader, which became the US Navy's primary fighter and served with great distinction in Vietnam. The company reorganized as Ling-Temco Vought (LTV) in the 1960s. Its last aircraft, the A-7 Corsair II, successfully used the F-8's configuration for a compact attack aircraft.

Vought F-8D Crusader

In 1955, Vought began the development of a totally new Crusader. Designated XF8U-3 Crusader III, the aircraft was rejected in favour of the Phantom II. Vought steadily improved the aircraft, the most potent version being the F-8D, with J57-P-20 turbojet, extra fuel and new radar for a specially produced radar-homing AIM-9C Sidewinder air-to-air missile. A total of 152 F-8Ds were produced.

SPECIFICATIONS	
Country of origin:	United States
Type:	single-seat carrier-based fighter
Powerplant:	one 80kN (18,000lb) Pratt & Whitney J57-P-20 turbojet
Performance:	maximum speed at 12,192m (40,000ft) 1975km/h (1227mph); service ceiling about 17,983m (59,000ft); combat radius 966km (600 miles)
Weights:	empty 9038kg (19,925lb); maximum take-off weight 15,422g (34,000lb)
Dimensions:	wingspan 10.72m (35ft 2in); length 16.61m (54ft 6in); height 4.8m (15ft 9in)
Armament:	four 20mm Colt Mk 12 cannon with 144rpg, up to four Motorola AIM-9C Sidewinder air-to-air missiles; or two AGM-12A or AGM-12B Bullpup air-to-surface missiles

Vought RF-8G Crusader

The Crusader made a useful high-speed reconnaissance aircraft, and the RF-8A provided vital intelligence during the Cuban Missile Crisis and the Vietnam War. The RF-8G was rebuilt from older A models and became the last version in US service, finally retired from reserve units in 1987. It could carry four cameras in a fuselage bay, but no armament.

SPECIFICATIONS	
Country of origin:	United States
Type:	carrier-based reconnaissance aircraft
Powerplant:	one 80.1kN (18,000lb) thrust Pratt & Whitney J57-P-22 afterburning turbojet engine
Performance:	maximum speed at 12,192m (40,000ft) 1975km/h (1227mph); service ceiling about 17,983m (59,000ft); combat radius 966km (600 miles)
Weights:	empty 9038kg (19,925lb); maximum take-off weight 15,422g (34,000lb)
Dimensions:	wingspan 10.72m (35ft 2in); length 16.61m (54ft 6in); height 4.8m (15ft 9in)
Armament:	none

Vought F-8E(N) Crusader

Vought sold a version of the F-8E to the French Aéronavale, even though the carriers *Foch* and *Clemenceau* were thought too small for such aircraft. To create the F-8E (FN), Vought redesigned the wing and tail to provide greater lift and to improve low-speed handling. The first FN flew in June 1964, and in 1991, nearly 25 years after entering service, *Clemenceau's* aircraft were involved in the first Gulf War.

SPECIFICATIONS	
Country of origin:	United States
Type:	single-seat carrier-borne interceptor and attack aircraft
Powerplant:	one 80kN (18,000lb) Pratt & Whitney J57-P-20A turbojet
Performance:	maximum speed at 10,975m (36,000ft) 1827km/h (1135mph); service ceiling 17,680m (58,000ft); combat radius 966km (600 miles)
Dimensions:	wingspan 10.87m (35ft 8in); length 16.61m (54ft 6in); height 4.8m (15ft 9in); wing area 32.51sq m (350sq ft)
Weights:	empty 9038kg (19,925lb); maximum take-off weight 15,420kg (34,000lb)
Armament:	four 20mm M39 cannon; provision for up to 2268kg (5000lb) of stores, including two Matra R530 air-to-air missiles or eight 5in rockets

Vought A-7D Corsair II

Though derived from the F-8 Crusader, the Corsair is a totally different aircraft. By restricting performance to high subsonic speed, it was possible to reduce structural weight, and correspondingly the range increased and weapon load multiplied by nearly four times. The first flight was made in September 1965. During the Vietnam War, more than 90,000 Corsair missions were flown.

SPECIFICATIONS	
Country of origin:	United States
Type:	single-seat attack aircraft
Powerplant:	one 63.4kN (14,250lb) Allison TF41-1 (Rolls-Royce Spey) turbofan
Performance:	maximum speed at low-level 1123km/h (698mph); combat range with typical weapon load 1150km (4100 miles)
Weights:	empty 8972kg (19,781lb); maximum take-off weight 19,050kg (42,000lb)
Dimensions:	wingspan 11.8m (38ft 9in); length 14.06m (46ft 1.5in); height 4.9m (16ft 0.75in); wing area 34.84sq m (375sq ft)
Armament:	one 20mm M61 Vulcan, provision for up to 6804kg (15,000lb) of stores, including bombs, napalm tanks, air-to-surface missiles and drop tanks

Vought A-7H Corsair II

A number of nations expressed interest in the Vought A-7 at an early stage in the programme, but the first foreign nation to take delivery of the fighter was Greece. The A-7H aircraft are used in both ground-attack and air-defence roles, and may be equipped with AIM-9L Sidewinder.

SPECIFICATIONS	
Country of origin:	United States
Type:	single-seat tactical fighter
Powerplant:	one 66.7kN (15,000lb) Allison TF-41-A-400 turbofan
Performance:	maximum speed at sea level 1112km/h (691mph); service ceiling 15,545m (51,000ft); range with typical load 1127km (700 miles)
Weights:	empty 8841kg (19,490lb); maximum take-off weight 19,051kg (42,000lb)
Dimensions:	wingspan 11.81m (38ft 9in); length 14.06m (46ft 1in); height 4.9m (16ft); wing area 34.84 sq m (375 sq ft)
Armament:	one 20-mm M61A1 multi-barrelled cannon; eight external pylons with provision for up to 6804kg (15,000lb) of stores, including bombs, cluster bombs, rocket pods and/or air-to-air missiles

Fouga Magister

One of the most successful and widely used trainer aircraft, the Magister was conceived and designed by Castello and Mauboussin for Fouga in 1950. It was the first purpose-built jet trainer. Despite the unusual butterfly-type tail, it proved a delight to fly. Total production of this and the version fitted with an arrestor hook (CM.75 Zephyr) was 437. In 1967, the Magister saw action with the Israeli Air Force during the Six-Day War.

CM.170 Magister

After prolonged testing, the Magister was put into production for L'Armée de l'Air. When Fouga was absorbed into the Potez company in 1958, Potez continued to produce a number of variants for international customers. Pictured is a version that flew with the 'Patrouille de France', the mount of the French national aerobatic team. The team now uses the Dassault/Dornier Alpha jet.

SPECIFICATIONS	
Country of origin:	France
Type:	two-seat trainer and light attack aircraft
Powerplant:	two 4kN (882lb) Turbomeca Marbore IIA turbojets
Performance:	maximum speed at 9150m (30,000ft) 715km/h (444mph); service ceiling 11,000m (36,090ft); range 925km (575 miles)
Weights:	empty equipped 2150kg (4740lb); maximum takeoff 3200kg (7055lb)
Dimensions:	over tip tanks 12.12m (39ft 10in); length 10.06m (33ft); height 2.8m (9ft 2in); wing area 17.3 sq m (186.1sq ft)
Armament:	two 7.5mm (.295in) or 7.62mm machine guns; rockets, bombs or Nord AS.11 missiles on underwing pylons

CM.170 Magister

Lebanon acquired Magisters in the 1960s and used them mainly as trainers. Their only combat operations were against the Palestine Liberation Organization (PLO) in refugee camps within Lebanon in 1973. Armed with 12.7mm machine guns, they attacked fortifications inside the camps.

SPECIFICATIONS	
Country of origin:	France
Type:	two-seat trainer and light attack aircraft
Powerplant:	two 4kN (882lb) Turbomeca Marbore IIA turbojets
Performance:	maximum speed at 9150m (30,000ft) 715km/h (444mph); service ceiling 11,000m (36,090ft); range 925km (575 miles)
Weights:	empty equipped 2150kg (4740lb); maximum takeoff 3200kg (7055lb)
Dimensions:	over tip tanks 12.12m (39ft 10in); length 10.06m (33ft); height 2.8m (9ft 2in); wing area 17.3 sq m (186.1sq ft)
Armament:	two 7.5mm (.295in) or 7.62mm machine guns; rockets, bombs or Nord AS.11 missiles on underwing pylons

CM.170 Magister

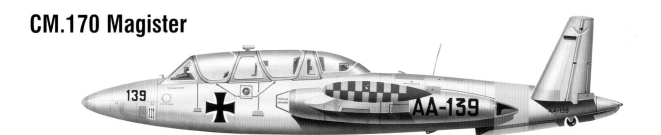

The Luftwaffe bought 40 Magisters, and Heinkel-Messerschmitt built 244 more under licence for use by the Luftwaffe and Marineflieger. This one belonged to the flight leader's school Flugzeug Fuhrerschule A, at Landsberg. The school had an aerobatic team called *Das Magister Team*.

SPECIFICATIONS	
Country of origin:	France
Type:	two-seat trainer and light attack aircraft
Powerplant:	two 4kN (882lb) Turbomeca Marbore IIA turbojets
Performance:	maximum speed at 9150m (30,000ft) 715km/h (444mph); service ceiling 11,000m (36,090ft); range 925km (575 miles)
Weights:	empty equipped 2150kg (4740lb); maximum takeoff 3200kg (7055lb)
Dimensions:	over tip tanks 12.12m (39ft 10in); length 10.06m (33ft); height 2.8m (9ft 2in); wing area 17.3 sq m (186.1sq ft)
Armament:	two 7.5mm (.295in) or 7.62mm machine guns; rockets, bombs or Nord AS.11 missiles on underwing pylons

CM.170 Magister

The Belgian Air Force aerobatic team *Les Diables Rouges* (Red Devils) flew the Magister from 1965 until 1977. In the 1990s and 2000s, the BAF revived the memory of the team with solo displays of a Magister dressed in *Les Diables Rouges* colours.

SPECIFICATIONS	
Country of origin:	France
Type:	two-seat trainer and light attack aircraft
Powerplant:	two 4kN (882lb) Turbomeca Marbore IIA turbojets
Performance:	maximum speed at 9150m (30,000ft) 715km/h (444mph); service ceiling 11,000m (36,090ft); range 925km (575 miles)
Weights:	empty equipped 2150kg (4740lb); maximum takeoff 3200kg (7055lb)
Dimensions:	over tip tanks 12.12m (39ft 10in); length 10.06m (33ft); height 2.8m (9ft 2in); wing area 17.3 sq m (186.1sq ft)
Armament:	two 7.5mm (.295in) or 7.62mm machine guns; rockets, bombs or Nord AS.11 missiles on underwing pylons

CM.170 Magister

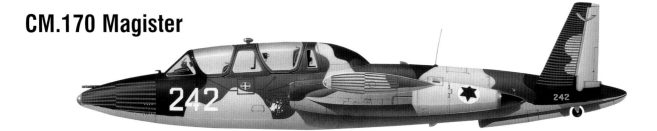

Israel has used the Magister since 1960 as a trainer and light-attack aircraft. Many were lost in attacks against Arab armour in 1967. Local industry upgraded 87 from 1980 as the *Tzukit* (Thrush or Merlin) and they remain in service, although they are due for replacement by the Beech Texan II turboprop.

SPECIFICATIONS	
Country of origin:	France
Type:	two-seat trainer and light attack aircraft
Powerplant:	two 4.7kN (1055lb) thrust Turbomeca Marboré IV turbojet engines
Performance:	maximum speed at 9150m (30,000ft) 715km/h (444mph); service ceiling 11,000m (36,090ft); range 925km (575 miles)
Weights:	empty equipped 2150kg (4740lb); maximum takeoff 3200kg (7055lb)
Dimensions:	over tip tanks 12.12m (39ft 10in); length 10.06m (33ft); height 2.8m (9ft 2in); wing area 17.3 sq m (186.1sq ft)
Armament:	two 7.5mm (.295in) or 7.62mm machine guns; rockets, bombs or Nord AS.11 missiles on underwing pylons

Panavia Tornado

The Tornado was the result of a 1960s requirement for a strike and reconnaissance aircraft capable of carrying a heavy and varied weapons load and of penetrating Warsaw Pact defensive systems by day and night, at low level and in all weathers. To develop and build the aircraft, a consortium of European companies (primarily British, West German and Italian) was formed under the name of Panavia.

Tornado F.Mk 3

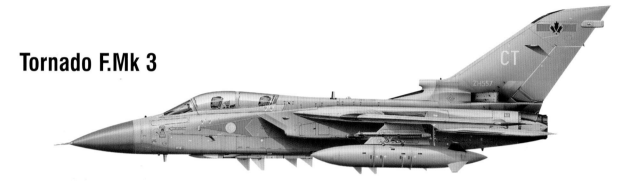

In the late 1960s, the RAF saw the need to replace its McDonnell Douglas Phantom II and BAe Lighting interceptors, and ordered the development of the Tornado ADV (Air Defence Variant), a dedicated air-defence aircraft with all-weather capability, based on the same airframe as the GR.1 ground-attack aircraft. Structural changes include a lengthened nose for the Foxhunter radar. The ADV was given the designations F.Mk 2 and F.Mk 3 in RAF service.

SPECIFICATIONS	
Country of origin:	Germany/Italy/United Kingdom
Type:	all-weather air defence aircraft
Powerplant:	two 73.5kN (16,520lb) Turbo-Union RB.199-34R Mk 104 turbofans
Performance:	maximum speed above 11,000m (36,090ft) 2337km/h (1452mph); operational ceiling about 21,335m (70,000ft); intercept radius more than 1853km (1150 miles)
Weights:	empty 14,501kg (31,970lb); maximum take-off 27,987kg (61,700lb)
Dimensions:	wingspan 13.91m (45ft 7.75in) spread and 8.6m (28ft 2.5in) swept; length 18.68m (61ft 3in); height 5.95m (19ft 6.25in); wing area 26.6 sq m (286.3 sq ft)
Armament:	two 27mm IWKA-Mauser cannon with 180rpg, six external hardpoints with provision for up to 5806kg (12,800lb) of stores, including Sky Flash medium-range air-to-air missiles, AIM-9L Sidewinder short range air-to-air missiles and drop tanks

Tornado GR.1

SPECIFICATIONS	
Country of origin:	United Kingdom/West Germany/Italy
Type:	tactical reconnaissance aircraft
Powerplant:	two 71.5kN (16,075lb) Turbo-Union RB.199-34R Mk 103 turbofans
Performance:	maximum speed 2337km/h (1452mph); service ceiling 15,240m (50,000ft); combat radius 1390km (864 miles)
Weights:	27,216kg (60,000lb) loaded
Dimensions:	wing span 13.91m (45ft 7in) spread and 8.6m (28ft 2.5in) swept; length: 16.72m (54ft 10in); height 5.95m (19ft 6.25in)
Armament:	up to 9000kg (19,840lb) of stores; Vinten Linescan infrared sensors and TIALD (Thermal Imaging and Laser Designator)

Tornado IDS

Italy's share in the Tornado programme comprised 100 Tornado IDS (interdictor/ strike) variants, equivalent to the RAF's GR.1. They later converted 15 to Tornado ECR (electronic combat and reconnaissance) standard, with the ability to launch HARM anti-radar missiles. A mid-life upgrade programme is underway for 80 Italian Tornadoes.

SPECIFICATIONS	
Country of origin:	United Kingdom/West Germany/Italy
Type:	multi-role combat aircraft
Powerplant:	two 71.5kN (16,075lb) Turbo-Union RB.199-34R Mk 103 turbofans
Performance:	maximum speed above 11,000m (36,090ft) 2337km/h (1452mph); service ceiling 15,240m (50,000ft); combat radius with weapon load on hi-lo-hi mission 1390km (864 miles)
Weights:	empty 14,091kg (31,065lb); maximum take-off 27,216kg (60,000lb)
Dimensions:	wingspan 13.91m (45ft 7in) spread; length 16.72m (54ft 10in); height 5.95m (19ft 6.25in); wing area 26.6 sq m (286.3 sq ft)
Armament:	two 27mm IWKA-Mauser cannon with 180rpg, seven external hard-points with provision for up to 9000kg (19,840lb) of stores, including ALARM anti-radiation missiles, air-to-air, air-to-surface and anti-ship missiles, conventional and guided bombs, cluster bombs, ECM pods and drop tanks TIALD (Thermal Imaging and Laser Designator)

The first Tornado GR.1s were delivered in July 1980. The RAF took delivery of 229 GR.1 strike aircraft, the Luftwaffe 212, the German Naval Air Arm 112, and the Aeronautica Militare Italiana (Italian Air Force) 100. RAF and Italian Tornados saw action in the 1991 Gulf War.

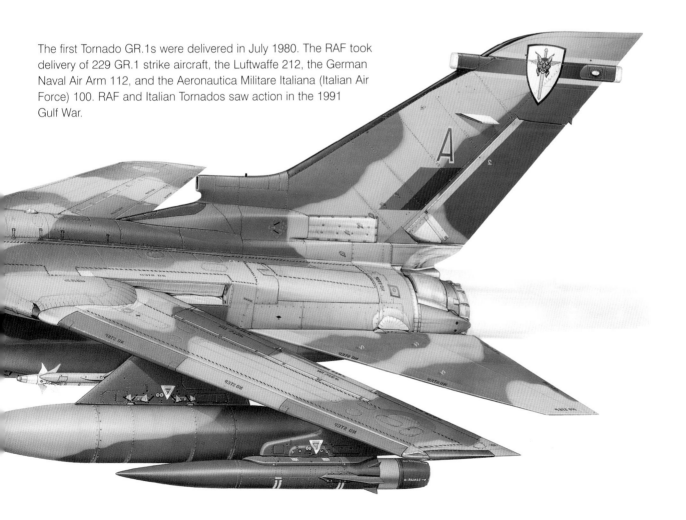

SEPECAT Jaguar

Developed jointly by BAC in Britain and Dassault-Breguet in France (Societé Européenne de Production de l'Avion Ecole de Combat at Appui Tactique), to meet a joint requirement of L'Armée de l'Air and the Royal Air Force, the Jaguar emerged as a far more powerful and effective aircraft than originally envisaged. It was planned as a light trainer and close-support machine, but as a single-seat tactical support aircraft, it formed the backbone of the French tactical nuclear strike force.

Jaguar A

The Jaguar A first flew in March 1969 and when service deliveries began in 1973, 160 aircraft were produced. Power was provided by a turbofan developed jointly from the Rolls-Royce RB.172 by Rolls-Royce and Turbomeca.

SPECIFICATIONS

Country of origin:	France and United Kingdom
Type:	single-seat tactical support and strike aircraft
Powerplant:	two 32.5kN (7305lb) Rolls-Royce/Turbomeca Adour Mk 102 turbofans
Performance:	maximum speed at 11,000m (36,090ft) 1593km/h (990mph); combat radius on lo-lo-lo mission with internal fuel 557km (357 miles)
Weights:	empty 7000kg (15,432lb); maximum take-off weight 15,500kg (34,172lb)
Dimensions:	wingspan 8.69m (28ft 6in); length 16.83m (55ft 2.5in); height 4.89m (16ft 0.5in); wing area 24 sq m (258.34 sq ft)
Armament:	two 30mm DEFA cannon; provision for 4536kg (10,000lb) of stores, including tactical nuclear weapon or conventional loads, ASMs, drop tanks and rocket-launcher pods, and a reconnaissance pod

Jaguar GR.1

The RAF bought 165 single-seat Jaguar GR.1s from 1973, and they served with nine frontline squadrons over the years, including No 14 (illustrated), which operated in the strike role from RAF Bruggen in Germany. The Jaguar went through several upgrades before the last GR.3 models were retired in 2007.

SPECIFICATIONS

Country of origin:	France and United Kingdom
Type:	single-seat tactical support and strike aircraft
Powerplant:	two 32.5kN (7305lb) Rolls-Royce/Turbomeca Adour Mk 102 turbofans
Performance:	maximum speed at 11,000m (36,090ft) 1593km/h (990mph); combat radius on lo-lo-lo mission with internal fuel 557km (357 miles)
Weights:	empty 7000kg (15,432lb); maximum take-off weight 15,500kg (34,172lb)
Dimensions:	wingspan 8.69m (28ft 6in); length 16.83m (55ft 2.5in); height 4.89m (16ft 0.5in); wing area 24 sq m (258.34 sq ft)
Armament:	two 30mm DEFA cannon; provision for 4536kg (10,000lb) of stores, including a nuclear weapon or conventional loads

Jaguar International

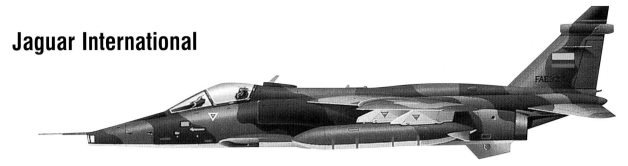

The outstanding versatility of the Jaguar encouraged the Anglo-French SEPECAT company to develop a version for the export market, though by the mid-1990s only 169 had been ordered by four nations. The first Jaguar International took to the air in August 1976. The aircraft was optimized for anti-shipping, air-defence, ground-attack and reconnaissance roles. This example was used by Ecuador.

SPECIFICATIONS	
Country of origin:	France and United Kingdom
Type:	single-seat tactical support and strike aircraft
Powerplant:	two 37.3kN (8400lb) Rolls-Royce/Turbomeca Adour Mk 811 turbofans
Performance:	maximum speed at 11,000m (36,090ft) 1699km/h (1056mph); combat radius on lo-lo-lo mission with internal fuel 537km (334 miles)
Weights:	empty 7700kg (16,976lb); maximum take-off weight 15,700kg (34,613lb)
Dimensions:	wingspan 8.69m (28ft 6in); length 16.83m (55ft 2.5in); height 4.89m (16ft 0.5in); wing area 24.18 sq m (260.28 sq ft)
Armament:	two 30mm Aden Mk.4 cannon; provision for 4763kg (10,500lb) of stores, including air-to-air missiles, anti-ship missiles, laser-guided or conventional bombs, napalm tanks, drop tanks and ECM pods

Jaguar T.2

The RAF version of the Jaguar E has the service designation Jaguar T.2. It retains full operational capability and is equipped to the same standard as the GR.1. The RAF received 38 T.2s, three more than originally planned. Updated aircraft are T.2A.

SPECIFICATIONS	
Country of origin:	France and United Kingdom
Type:	single-seat tactical support and strike aircraft
Powerplant:	two 37.3kN (8040lb) Rolls-Royce/Turbomeca Adour Mk 104 turbofans
Performance:	maximum speed at 11,000m (36,090ft) 1593km/h (990mph); combat radius on lo-lo-lo mission with internal fuel 557km (357 miles)
Weights:	empty 7000kg (15,432lb); maximum take-off weight 15,500kg (34,172lb)
Dimensions:	wingspan 8.69m (28ft 6in); length 16.83m (55ft 2.5in); height 4.89m (16ft 0.5in); wing area 24 sq m (258.34 sq ft)
Armament:	two 30mm DEFA cannon; provision for 4536kg (10,000lb) of stores, including one tactical nuclear weapon or conventional loads

Jaguar IM (Shamsher)

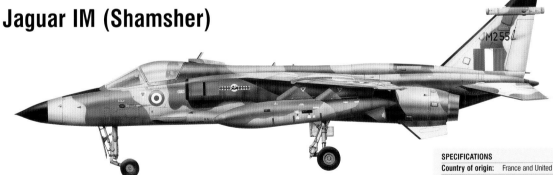

Although most other users have retired their Jaguars, Hindustan Aeronautics Limited (HAL) continues to produce the Jaguar or Shamsher (Sword of Justice) for the Indian Air Force. A unique Indian variant is the Jaguar IM maritime strike aircraft, with an Agave radar and Sea Eagle missile capability.

SPECIFICATIONS	
Country of origin:	France and United Kingdom
Type:	single-seat maritime attack aircraft
Powerplant:	two 37.3kN (8400lb) thrust Rolls-Royce/Turbomeca RT172-58 Adour Mk.811 afterburning turbofan engines
Performance:	maximum speed at 11,000m (36,090ft) 1699km/h (1056mph); combat radius on lo-lo-lo mission with internal fuel 537km (334 miles)
Weights:	empty 7700kg (16,976lb); maximum take-off weight 15,700kg (34,613lb)
Dimensions:	wingspan 8.69m (28ft 6in); length unknown; height 4.89m (16ft 0.5in); wing area 24.18 sq m (260.28 sq ft)
Armament:	two 30mm Aden Mk.4 cannon; provision for 4763kg (10,500lb) of stores

Grumman Intruder and Prowler

Selected from 11 competing designs in December 1957, the Intruder was specifically planned for first-pass blind-attack on point surface targets at night or in any weather conditions. The Intruder first came into service with the US Navy in February 1963; during the Vietnam War, the A-6A worked round-the-clock on precision bombing missions that no other aircraft was capable of undertaking until the introduction of the F-111.

A-6 Intruder

The A-6 was introduced in Vietnam and saw its last combat action over Iraq and Kuwait in 1991. This A-6E of VMA-533 was deployed to Bahrain for Operation Desert Storm in 1991. It is shown here carrying 227kg (500lb) Mk 82 bombs on underwing and centreline multiple ejector racks.

SPECIFICATIONS	
Country of origin:	United States
Type:	two-seat carrierborne and landbased all-weather strike aircraft
Powerplant:	two 41.4kN (9300lb) Pratt & Whitney J52-P-8A turbojets
Performance:	maximum speed at sea level 1043km/h (648mph); service ceiling 14,480m (47,500ft); range 1627km (1011 miles)
Weights:	empty 12,132kg (26,746lb); maximum take-off weight 26,581kg (58,600lb)
Dimensions:	wingspan 16.15m (53ft); length 16.69; height 4.93m (16ft 2in); wing area 49.13 sq m (528.9 sq ft)
Armament:	five external hardpoints with provision for up to 8165kg (18,000lb) of stores, including nuclear weapons, conventional and guided bombs, air-to-surface missiles and drop tanks

EA-6A Intruder

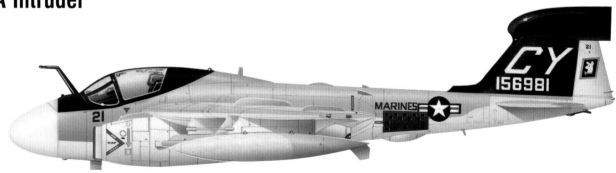

The EA-6A was a replacement for the elderly EF-10 Sky Knight electronic warfare aircraft. EA-6As were sent to Southeast Asia to deal with the increasing sophistication of North Vietnam's air-defence network. Able to jam and confuse radar, they had a rarely used capability to fire anti-radar Shrike missiles.

SPECIFICATIONS	
Country of origin:	United States
Type:	electronic warfare aircraft
Powerplant:	two 41.4kN (9300lb) Pratt & Whitney J52-P-8A turbojets
Performance:	maximum speed at sea level 1043km/h (648mph); service ceiling 14,480m (47,500ft); range 1627km (1011 miles)
Weights:	empty 12,132kg (26,746lb); maximum take-off weight 26,581kg (58,600lb)
Dimensions:	wingspan 16.15m (53ft); length 16.69; height unknown; wing area 49.13 sq m (528.9 sq ft)
Armament:	AGM-45 Shrike anti-radiation missiles

A-6E Intruder

The original A-6A model was replaced by the A-6E, with a new digital computer and other electronic improvements, from 1971. Later A-6Es had an undernose turret called TRAM (Target Recognition Attack Multi-sensor), which included an infrared sensor and a laser designator, which allowed the use of more precision weapons.

SPECIFICATIONS	
Country of origin:	United States
Type:	two-seat carrierborne and landbased all-weather strike aircraft
Powerplant:	two 41.4kN (9300lb) Pratt & Whitney J52-P-8A turbojets
Performance:	maximum speed at sea level 1043km/h (648mph); service ceiling 14,480m (47,500ft); range 1627km (1011 miles)
Weights:	empty 12,132kg (26,746lb); maximum take-off weight 26,581kg (58,600lb)
Dimensions:	wingspan 16.15m (53ft); length 16.69; height 4.93m (16ft 2in); wing area 49.13 sq m (528.9 sq ft)
Armament:	five external hardpoints with provision for up to 8165kg (18,000lb) of stores, including nuclear weapons, conventional and guided bombs, air-to-surface missiles and drop tanks

KA-6D Prowler

The KA-6D was a conversion of the A-6A modified to refuel carrier-based aircraft. Bombing equipment was removed and a hose-drum unit fitted in the fuselage. The weapons pylons were used to carry additional fuel tanks. This KA-6D also carries a 'buddy' refuelling pod on the centreline.

SPECIFICATIONS	
Country of origin:	United States
Type:	electronic countermeasures platform
Powerplant:	two 49.8kN (11,200lb) Pratt & Whitney J52-P-408 turbojets
Performance:	maximum speed at sea level 982km/h (610mph); service ceiling 11,580m (38,000ft); combat range with full external fuel 1769km (1099 miles)
Weights:	empty 14,588kg (32,162lb); maximum take-off weight 29,484kg (65,000lb)
Dimensions:	wingspan 16.15m (53ft); length 18.24m (59ft 10in); height 4.95m (16ft 3in); wing area 49.13 sq m (528.9 sq ft)
Armament:	none on early models, retrofitted with external hardpoints for four or six AGM-88 HARM air-to-surface anti-radar missiles

EA-6B Prowler

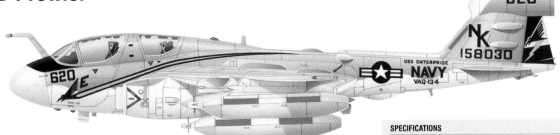

The US Navy rarely undertakes a strike mission without the protection offered by the EA-6 ECM. This aircraft was developed from the successful A-6 Intruder family. The cockpit provides seating for the pilot and three electronic warfare officers, who control the most sophisticated and advanced ECM equipment ever fitted to a tactical aircraft, including the ALQ-99 tactical jamming system.

SPECIFICATIONS	
Country of origin:	United States
Type:	electronic countermeasures platform
Powerplant:	two 49.8kN (11,200lb) Pratt & Whitney J52-P-408 turbojets
Performance:	maximum speed at sea level 982km/h (610mph); service ceiling 11,580m (38,000ft); combat range 1769km (1099 miles)
Weights:	empty 14,588kg (32,162lb); maximum take-off weight 29,484kg (65,000lb)
Dimensions:	wingspan 16.15m (53ft); length 18.24m (59ft 10in); height 4.95m (16ft 3in); wing area 49.13 sq m (528.9 sq ft)
Armament:	none on early models, retrofitted with external hardpoints for four or six AGM-88 HARM air-to-surface anti-radar missiles

USA vs Libya

Libya and the United States of America fought several actions in the 1980s over Libya's claim to parts of the Mediterranean Sea and its support for terrorism. These included the Gulf of Sidra Incident in 1981, which saw US Navy F-14s destroy Libyan Su-22s; and Operation El Dorado Canyon in 1986, which followed a terrorist attack in a Berlin nightclub targeted at American servicemen. The US blamed Libya, and launched an attack on targets in Tripoli and Benghazi on 15 April 1986.

Grumman F-14A Tomcat

While asserting the right to navigate in international waters, patrols from the carrier USS *Nimitz* encountered Libyan Arab Republic Air Force (LARAF) fighters on several occasions in August 1981. Responding to a Libyan missile launch, F-14As from VF-41 'Black Aces' destroyed two LARAF Su-22 'Fitters' with AIM-9 Sidewinders.

SPECIFICATIONS	
Country of origin:	United States
Type:	two-seat carrierborne fleet defence fighter
Powerplant:	two 92.9kN (20,900lb) Pratt & Whitney TF30-P-412A turbofans
Performance:	maximum speed at high altitude 2517km/h (1564mph); service ceiling 17,070m (56,000ft); range about 3220km (2000 miles)
Weights:	empty 18,191kg (40,104lb); maximum take-off 33,724kg (74,349lb)
Dimensions:	wingspan 19.55m (64ft 1.5in) unswept; 11.65m (38ft 2.5in) swept; length 19.1m (62ft 8in); height 4.88m (16ft); wing area 52.49sq m (565sq ft)
Armament:	one 20mm M61A1 Vulcan rotary cannon with 675 rounds; external pylons for a combination of AIM-7 Sparrow medium range air-to-air missiles, AIM-9 medium range air-to-air missiles, and AIM-54 Phoenix long range air-to-air missiles

General Dynamics F-111F

The main strike of El Dorado Canyon was launched from the UK by F-111s, including F-111Fs of the 48th Tactical Fighter Wing at Lakenheath (illustrated). One F-111F and crew was lost on the raid, having probably hit the sea while flying at low level.

SPECIFICATIONS	
Country of origin:	United States
Type:	two-seat attack aircraft
Powerplant:	111.7kN (25,100lb) thrust Pratt & Whitney TF30-P-100 afterburning turbojet engines
Performance:	maximum speed 2334km/h (1,452 mph); range 5851km (3634 miles); service ceiling 18,287m (60,000ft)
Weights:	empty 20,943kg (46,172lb); maximum 44,875kg (98,950lb)
Dimensions:	span 19.2m (63ft); length 22.4m (73ft 6in); height 5.2m (17ft 2in); wing area 61 sq m (657 sq ft)
Armament:	up to 11,250kg (25,000lb) of bombs, rockets, missiles or fuel tanks

Mikoyan-Gurevich MiG-23 'Flogger-E'

Libya and a number of other Arab countries purchased a much-simplified export version of the MiG-23M 'Flogger-B', designated MiG-23 'Flogger-E'. The aircraft retains the same basic airframe as its predecessor, but is powered by the 98kN (22,046lb) Tumanskii R-27F2M-300 turbojet.

SPECIFICATIONS

Country of origin:	USSR
Type:	single-seat air combat fighter
Powerplant:	one 98kN (22,046lb) Tumanskii R-27F2M-300 turbojet
Performance:	maximum speed at altitude about 2445km/h (1520mph); service ceiling over 18,290m (60,000ft); combat radius 966km (600 miles)
Weights:	empty 10,400kg (22,932lb); maximum loaded 18,145kg (40,000lb)
Dimensions:	wingspan 13.97m (45ft 10in) spread and 7.78m (25ft 6.25in) swept; length (including probe) 16.71m (54ft 10in); height 4.82m (15ft 9.75in); wing area 37.25 sq m (402 sq ft) spread
Armament:	one 23mm GSh-23L cannon, six external hardpoints with provision for up to 3000kg (6614lb) of stores, including AA-2 Atoll air-to-air missiles, cannon pods, rocket launcher pods, large calibre rockets and bombs

Mikoyan-Gurevich MiG-25P 'Foxbat-A'

Designed as an interceptor to meet the challenge of the planned US B-70 long-range, high-speed strategic bomber in the late 1950s, the MiG-25 far outclassed any Western aircraft in terms of speed and height when it finally entered service in the early 1970s (and long after the B-70 programme was cancelled). This aircraft is also operated by Libya, Algeria, India, Iraq and Syria.

SPECIFICATIONS

Country of origin:	USSR
Type:	single-seat interceptor
Powerplant:	two 100kN (22,487lb) Tumanskii R-15B-300 turbojets
Performance:	maximum speed at altitude about 2974km/h (1848mph); service ceiling over 24,385m (80,000ft); combat radius 1130km (702 miles)
Weights:	empty 20,000kg (44,092lb); maximum take-off 37,425kg (82,508lb)
Dimensions:	wingspan 14.02m (45ft 11.75in); length 23.82m (78ft 1.75in); height 6.1m (20ft 0.5in); wing area 61.4 sq m (660.9 sq ft)
Armament:	external pylons for four air-to-air missiles in the form of either two each of the IR- and radar-homing AA-6 'Acrid', or two AA-7 'Apex' and two AA-8 'Aphid' weapons

Ilyushin Il-76MD 'Candid'

F-111Fs and A-6E Intruders attacked several Libyan airfields in August 1986, destroying about 14 MiG-23s on the ground and up to five Il-76 'Candid' freighters belonging to the LARAF and state-owned airlines. One of them was this aircraft, Il-76MD 5A-DZZ of Libyan Arab Airlines.

SPECIFICATIONS

Country of origin:	USSR
Type:	heavy freight transport
Powerplant:	four 117.6kN (26,455lb) Soloviev D-30KP-1 turbofans
Performance:	maximum speed at 11,000m (36,090ft) 850km/h (528mph); maximum cruising altitude 12,000m (39,370ft); range 5000km (3107 miles)
Weights:	empty about 75,000kg (165,347lb); maximum take-off weight 170,000kg (374,786lb)
Dimensions:	wingspan 50.5m (165ft 8.2in); length 46.59m (152ft 10.25in); height 14.76m (48ft 5in); wing area 300 sq m (3229.28 sq ft)
Armament:	provision for two 23mm cannon in tail

Airborne Early Warning

Experience in the Pacific in World War II showed the need for airborne radars that could detect attackers beyond the radar range of surface ships. Carrier-based airborne early warning (AEW) aircraft were soon joined by land-based radar 'pickets'. The mission evolved to encompass the control of strike aircraft and fighters on offensive operations, as well as a degree of overwater and overland surveillance.

Avro Shackleton AEW.2

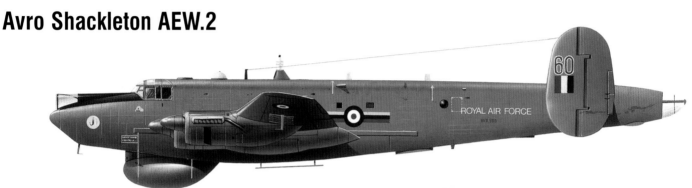

The Shackleton AEW.2 was created from the MR.2 patrol aircraft to provide AEW coverage for the Royal Navy, which was phasing out the carrier-based Gannet, as well as for the RAF. Its radar was the Gannet's 1940s-vintage APS-20, and the 'Shack' was slow, low-flying and noisy. It lasted in service until 1990.

SPECIFICATIONS

Country of origin:	United Kingdom
Type:	8–10 crew long-range maritime patrol aircraft
Powerplant:	four 1831kW (2455hp) Rolls-Royce Griffon 57A V-12 piston engines
Performance:	max speed 500km/h (311mph); service ceiling 6400m (21,000ft); range 5440km (3380 miles)
Weights:	39010kg (86,000lb) loaded
Dimensions:	wing span 36.58m (120ft); length 26.59m (87ft 3in); height 5.1m (16ft 9in)
Armament:	none

Grumman E-2C Hawkeye

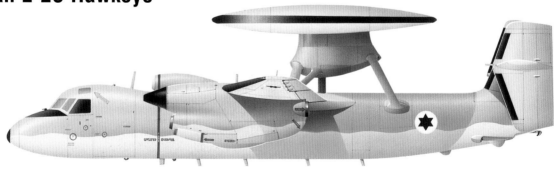

Israel was one of several operators without aircraft carriers to acquire the E-2C Hawkeye to patrol its airspace. Others included Singapore, Egypt and Taiwan. The IDF/AF Hawkeyes were retired in the 1990s, and three of the four purchased were later sold to the Mexican Navy.

SPECIFICATIONS

Country of origin:	United States
Type:	twin-engined carrier-based early warning aircraft (E-2C)
Powerplant:	one 3800kW (5100hp) Allison T56-A-427 turboprop engines
Performance:	maximum speed 604km/h (375mph); range 2583km (1605 miles); service ceiling 10,210m (33,500ft)
Weights:	empty 15,310kg (33,746lb); maximum 24,655kg (60,000lb)
Dimensions:	span 24.6m (80ft 7in); length 17.56m (57ft 7in); height 5.58m (18ft 4in); wing area 65 sq m (700 sq ft)
Armament:	none

Hawker Siddeley Nimrod AEW.3

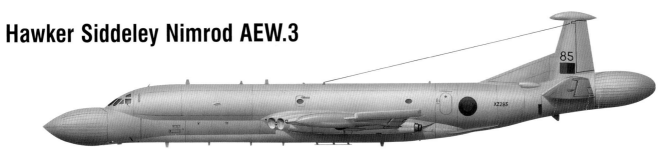

The Nimrod AEW.3 was an attempt to replace the Shackleton with a jet aircraft fitted with modern multi-mode radars. It proved very difficult to coordinate the pictures from the nose and tail radars, and the project went way over budget. It was cancelled and the RAF bought E-3 Sentries.

SPECIFICATIONS	
Country of origin:	United Kingdom
Type:	maritime patrol and anti-submarine warfare aircraft
Powerplant:	four 54kN (12,140lb) Rolls Royce Spey Mk 250 turbofans
Performance:	maximum speed 925km/h (575mph); service ceiling 12,800m (42,000ft); range on internal fuel 9262km (5,755 miles)
Weights:	maximum take-off weight 85,185kg (187,800lb)
Dimensions:	wingspan 35m (114ft 10in) excluding wingtip ESM pods; length 41.97m (37 ft 9 in); height 9.08m (29ft 9.5in); wing area 197.04 sq m (2121 sq ft)
Armament:	none

Boeing E-3A Sentry

The Boeing E-3 Sentry introduced the term AWACS to common use, and became the platform of choice for the United States, Saudi Arabia, the United Kingdom, France and NATO. The airframe is based on that of the Boeing 707. The Westinghouse APY-1 radar in its giant rotodome can detect targets up to 650km (400 miles) away.

SPECIFICATIONS	
Country of origin:	Germany
Type:	Airborne Warning and Control System platform
Powerplant:	four 93-kN (21,000-lb) thrust Pratt & Whitney TF33-PW-100A turbofan engines
Performance:	maximum speed 855km/h (530mph); service ceiling 12,500m (41,000ft); range 7400km (4598 miles)
Weights:	empty 73,480kg (162,000lb); maximum 147, 400kg (325,000lb)
Dimensions:	span 44.42m (145ft 9in); length 46.61m (152ft 11in); height 12.6m (41ft 4in); wing area 3050 sq m (283 sq ft)
Armament:	none

Beriev A-50 'Mainstay'

Based on a stretched Ilyushin Il-76, the A-50 was developed by Beriev as the Soviet counterpart to the E-3. Known to NATO as the 'Mainstay', it entered service in 1989 and about 40 were produced. A programme to cooperate with China on an improved variant was halted, but India has ordered the type.

SPECIFICATIONS	
Country of origin:	Germany
Type:	AWACS aircraft
Powerplant:	four 157kN (35,200lb) thrust Aviadvigatel PS-90A turbofan engines
Performance:	maximum speed 750km/h (466mph); service ceiling 10,000m (32,800ft); range 7500km (4660 miles)
Weights:	loaded 190,000kg (418,880lb)
Dimensions:	span 50.5m (165ft 8in); length 46.59m (152ft 10in); height 14.76m (48ft 5in); wing area 300 sq m (3228 sq ft)
Armament:	none

MiGs: Fagot, Fresco and Farmer

The first generation of Mikoyan-Gurevich MiG jet fighters—the MiG-15 'Fagot', MiG-17 'Fresco' and MiG-19 'Farmer'—filled the inventories of the Soviet Union and its allies for four decades. Even today, some Russian-built examples can be found in African and Asian air forces. Chinese derivatives are more common, with Pakistan and North Korea being particular bastions of the last Shenyang J-6s and Nanchang Q-5s, both descendants of the MiG-19 of 1955.

MiG-15bis 'Fagot' (S-103)

Czechoslovakia built the 'Fagot' under licence as the Avia S.102 (MiG-15) and S.103 (MiG-15bis). Single-seat MiG-15s were also produced in large numbers in Poland as the Lim-1 and Lim-2. Czech MiG-15s served the country's air force from 1951 until 1983.

SPECIFICATIONS	
Country of origin:	USSR
Type:	single-seat fighter
Powerplant:	one 26.5kN (5952lb) Klimov VK-1 turbojet
Performance:	maximum speed 1100km/h (684mph); service ceiling 15,545m (51,000ft); range at height with slipper tanks 1424km (885 miles)
Weights:	empty 4000kg (8820lb); maximum loaded 5700kg (12,566lb)
Dimensions:	wingspan 10.08m (33ft 0.75in); length 11.05m (36ft 3.75in); height 3.4m (11ft 1.75in); wing area 20.6 sq m (221.74 sq ft)
Armament:	one 37mm N-37 cannon and two 23mm NS-23 cannon, plus up to 500kg (1102lb) of mixed stores on underwing pylons

MiG-15UTI 'Midget'

There was no Soviet-built two-seat version of the MiG-17 or -19, but the MiG-15UTI 'Midget' served as the advanced trainer for thousands of pilots who went on to fly all models of MiG jet. Egypt was one of over 20 countries to operate the MiG-15 UTI.

SPECIFICATIONS	
Country of origin:	USSR
Type:	single-engined jet trainer
Powerplant:	one 26.5kN (5952lb) thrust Klimov RD-45FA turbojet engine
Performance:	maximum speed 1015km/h (631mph); service ceiling 15,545m (51,000ft); range 1054km (655 miles)
Weights:	empty 3724kg (8208lb); maximum loaded 5700kg (12,566lb)
Dimensions:	wingspan 10.08m (33ft 0.75in); length 11.05m (36ft 3.75in); height 3.7m (12ft 1.7in); wing area 20.6 sq m (221.74 sq ft)
Armament:	two 23mm NS-23 cannon

MiG-17 'Fresco'

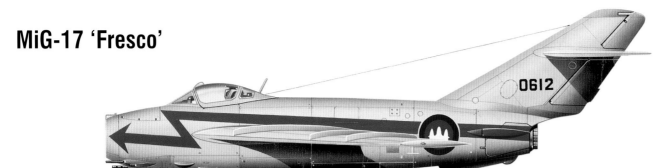

Although outwardly similar to the MiG-15, the -17 was in fact a completely different aircraft. The design began in 1949, its most important aspect being the new wing. Along with reduced thickness, a different section and platform, and three fences, this resulted in much-improved handling at high speed. Deliveries commenced in 1952; total production was more than 5000.

SPECIFICATIONS	
Country of origin:	USSR
Type:	single-seat fighter
Powerplant:	one 33.1kN (7452lb) Klimov VK-1F turbojet
Performance:	maximum speed at 3000m (9,840ft) 1145km/h (711mph); service ceiling 16,600m (54,560ft); range 1470km (913 miles)
Weights:	empty 4100kg (9040lb); maximum loaded 600kg (14,770lb)
Dimensions:	wingspan 9.45m (31ft); length 11.05m (36ft 3.75in); height 3.35m (11ft); wing area 20.6 sq m (221.74 sq ft)
Armament:	one 37mm N-37 cannon and two 23mm NS-23 cannon, plus up to 500kg (1102lb) of mixed stores on underwing pylons

MiG-17PF 'Fresco-D'

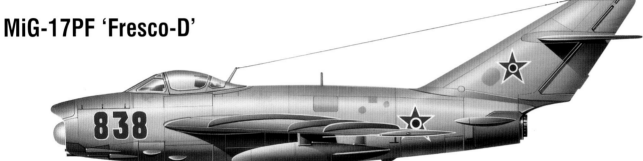

The MiG-17PF 'Fresco-D' was a night-fighter development with the RP-1 Izumrud or 'Scan Odd' radar mounted in the upper lip of the intake. The later MiG-17PFU could carry radar-guided missiles, but the PF was armed with cannon and bombs or unguided rockets only.

SPECIFICATIONS	
Country of origin:	USSR
Type:	single-seat all-weather interceptor
Powerplant:	one 33.1kN (7452lb) thrust Klimov VK-1F afterburning turbojet
Performance:	maximum speed at 9080m (20,000ft) 1480km/h (920mph); service ceiling 17,900m (58,725ft); maximum range 2200km (1367 miles)
Weights:	empty 4182kg (9212lb); maximum 6350kg (14,000lb)
Dimensions:	wingspan 9m (29ft 6.5in); length 11.68m (38ft 4in); height 4.02m (13ft 2.25in); wing area 25 sq m (269.11 sq ft)
Armament:	three 23mm NS-23 cannon; up to 500kg (1102lb) of bombs or rockets

MiG-19 'Farmer'

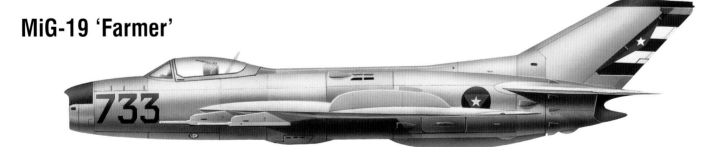

With the MiG-19, the Mikoyan-Gurevich bureau established itself at the forefront of the world's fighter design teams. It was first flown in September 1953, and steadily improved versions culminated in the MiG-19PM, with guns removed and pylons for four early beam-rider air-to-air missiles. In the late 1990s, some aircraft remained in service with training units.

SPECIFICATIONS	
Country of origin:	USSR
Type:	single-seat all-weather interceptor
Powerplant:	two 31.9kN (7165lb) Klimov RD-9B turbojets
Performance:	maximum speed at 9080m (20,000ft) 1480km/h (920mph); service ceiling 17,900m (58,725ft); maximum range at high altitude with two drop tanks 2200km (1367 miles)
Weights:	empty 5760kg (12,698lb); maximum take-off weight 9500kg (20,944lb)
Dimensions:	wingspan 9m (29ft 6.5in); length 13.58m (44ft 7in); height 4.02m (13ft 2.25in); wing area 25 sq m (269.11 sq ft)
Armament:	underwing pylons for four AA-1 Alkali air-to-air-missiles, or AA-2 Atoll

Sukhoi Fitters

Less well-known in the West than MiG, the Sukhoi Design Bureau produced interceptors such as the Su-9 and Su-15, which were rarely seen outside the Soviet Union, and the 'Fitter' series, which was widely exported. The simple Su-7 with a fixed, swept wing was followed by the Su-17 (designated Su-20 for export) with variable-geometry ('swing') wings and the Su-22M with improved avionics and more fuel. Poland and Vietnam are among the few remaining Su-22 users.

Su-7BM 'Fitter-A'

Planned as a fighter to intercept the USAF's North American F-100 and F-101, the large swept-wing Sukhoi fighter in fact became the standard tactical fighter-bomber of the Soviet air forces. The Su-7B was ordered into production in 1958, and in a variety of sub-variants became the standard Soviet Bloc attack aircraft. Thousands were supplied to all Warsaw Pact nations, among other countries.

SPECIFICATIONS	
Country of origin:	USSR
Type:	ground-attack fighter
Powerplant:	one 88.2kN (19,842lb) Lyulka AL-7F turbojet
Performance:	maximum speed at 11,000m (36,090ft) approximately 1700km/h (1056mph); service ceiling 15,150m (49,700ft); typical combat radius 320km (199 miles)
Weights:	empty 8620kg (19,000lb); maximum take-off weight 13,500kg (29,750lb)
Dimensions:	wingspan 8.93m (29ft 3.5in); length 17.37m (57ft); height 4.7m (15ft 5in)
Armament:	two 30mm NR-30 cannon; four external pylons for two 750kg (1653lb) and two 500kg (1102lb) bombs, but with two tanks on fuselage pylons, total external weapon load is reduced to 1000kg (2205lb)

Su-7BMK 'Fitter-A'

The Su-7BMK was a version built largely for export between 1968 and 1971. Some served with the Soviet Air Force's Frontal Aviation arm, including the one illustrated, which was on the strength of a unit in the Trans-Baikal Military District in 1978.

SPECIFICATIONS	
Country of origin:	USSR
Type:	ground-attack fighter
Powerplant:	one 88.2kN (19,842lb) Lyulka AL-7F turbojet
Performance:	max speed at 11,000m (36,090ft) approximately 1700km/h (1056mph); service ceiling 15,150m (49,700ft); combat radius 320km (199 miles)
Weights:	empty 8620kg (19,000lb); maximum take-off weight 13,500kg (29,750lb)
Dimensions:	span 8.93m (29ft 3.5in); length 17.37m (57ft); height 4.7m (15ft 5in)
Armament:	two 30mm NR-30 cannon; four external pylons for two 750kg (1653lb) and two 500kg (1102lb) bombs, but with two tanks on fuselage pylons, total external weapon load is reduced to 1000kg (2205lb)

Su-7UM 'Moujik-A'

Known as 'Moujik' to NATO, the Su-7UM was the two-seat transition trainer version of the Fitter-A, used by most operators, including Egypt. The installation of a second seat reduced the fuel capacity, and a periscope was needed by the instructor to have a forward view.

SPECIFICATIONS	
Country of origin:	USSR
Type:	ground-attack fighter
Powerplant:	one 94.1kN (21,164lb) thrust Lyulka AL-7F-1-250 afterburning turbojet engine
Performance:	max speed at 11,000m (36,090ft) approximately 1700km/h (1056mph); service ceiling 16,992m (55,760ft); range 1000km (621 miles)
Weights:	empty 8620kg (19,000lb); maximum take-off weight 13,500kg (29,750lb)
Dimensions:	span 8.93m (29ft 3.5in); length 17.37m (57ft); height 4.7m (15ft 5in)
Armament:	two 30mm NR-30 cannon; four external pylons for two 750kg (1653lb) and two 500kg (1102lb) bombs, but with two tanks on fuselage pylons, total external weapon load is reduced to 1000kg (2205lb)

Su-17M-4 'Fitter-K'

The Su-71G prototype with a variable-geometry wing was first flown in 1966. The new aircraft was found to have far superior performance than even the most developed Su-7, especially for short-field operations. Entering service in 1971, the ultimate development of the aircraft was the Su-17M-4, distinguishable by an airscoop for the cooling system on the leading edge of the tailfin root.

SPECIFICATIONS	
Country of origin:	USSR
Type:	single-seat ground-attack fighter
Powerplant:	one 110.3kN (24,802lb) Lyul'ka AL-21F-3 turbojet
Performance:	max speed approximately 2220km/h (1380mph); service ceiling 15,200m (49,865ft); combat radius 675km (419 miles)
Weights:	empty 9500kg (20,944lb); maximum take-off weight 19,500kg (42,990lb)
Dimensions:	wingspan 13.8m (45ft 3in) spread and 10m (32ft 10in) swept; length 18.75m (61ft 6in); height 5m (16ft 5in); wing area 40 sq m (430 sq ft)
Armament:	two 30mm NR-30 cannon; nine external pylons with provision for up to 4250kg (9370lb) of stores, including tactical nuclear weapons

Su-20 'Fitter-C'

The first version of the variable-geometry wing Sukhoi Su-17 ground-attack aircraft made available for export was designated Su-20. Poland was the only country to receive the full-standard Fitter-C, but a reduced-equipment version was operated by Afghanistan, Algeria, Angola, Egypt, Iraq, North Korea and Vietnam.

SPECIFICATIONS	
Country of origin:	USSR
Type:	single-seat ground-attack fighter
Powerplant:	one 110.3kN (24,802lb) Lyul'ka AL-21F-3 turbojet
Performance:	max speed approx 2220km/h (1380mph); service ceiling 15,200m (49,865ft); combat radius load 675km (419 miles)
Weights:	empty 9500kg (20,944lb); maximum take-off weight 19,500kg (42,990lb)
Dimensions:	span 13.8m (45ft 3in) spread, 10m (32ft 10in) swept; length 18.75m (61ft 6in); height 5m (16ft 5in); wing area 40 sq m (430 sq ft)
Armament:	two 30mm NR-30 cannon; nine external pylons with provision for up to 4250kg (9370lb) of stores, including tactical nuclear weapons

McDonnell F-15 Eagle

To succeed the F-4 Phantom in US service, McDonnell Douglas produced the F-15 Eagle. Since its inception, this aircraft has assumed the crown as the world's greatest air-superiority fighter, although it has now been superseded by later F-15C and -B variants in US service. The first prototype of the F-15A, a single-seat, twin-turbofan, swept-wing aircraft, flew in July 1972. Impressive flying characteristics became immediately apparent during flight testing.

F-15A Eagle

The F-15's powerful Pratt & Whitney engines and extensive use of titanium in construction (more than 20 per cent of the airframe weight of production aircraft) enabled high sustained speeds (Mach 2.5 plus) at high altitude. Deliveries began in November 1974 and production continued until 1979, with 385 built.

SPECIFICATIONS	
Country of origin:	United States
Type:	single-seat air superiority fighter with secondary strike/attack role
Powerplant:	two 106kN (23,810lb) Pratt & Whitney F100-PW-100 turbofans
Performance:	maximum speed at high altitude 2655km/h (1650mph); initial climb rate over 15,240m (50,000ft)/min; ceiling 30,500m (100,000ft); range on internal fuel 1930km (1200 miles)
Weights:	empty 12,700kg (28,000lb); with maximum load 25,424kg (56,000lb)
Dimensions:	span 13.05m (42ft 9.75in); length 19.43in (63ft 9in); height 5.63m (18ft 5in); wing area 56.48 sq m (608 sq ft)
Armament:	one 20mm M61A1 cannon, pylons with provision for up to 7620kg (16,800lb) of stores

F-15B Eagle

The F-15 SMTD (Short take-off and Maneuver Technology Demonstrator) was a modification of an F-15B to test canard foreplanes, thrust-vectoring engines and advanced pilot-interface systems. Most aspects were not continued, but the thrust-vectoring research was useful to the F-22 programme.

SPECIFICATIONS	
Country of origin:	United States
Type:	Technology demonstrator
Powerplant:	two 106kN (23,810lb) thrust Pratt & Whitney F100-PW-229 IPE afterburning turbofan engines
Performance:	maximum speed unknown; service ceiling unknown; range unknown
Weights:	unknown
Dimensions:	span 13.05m (42ft 9.75in); length 19.43in (63ft 9in); height 5.63m (18ft 5in); wing area 56.48 sq m (608 sq ft)
Armament:	none

F-15A Eagle

The F-15A was supplied to Air Defense Command to replace its F-106 interceptors during the 1980s. One unit was the 5th Fighter Interceptor Squadron 'Spittin' Kittens' at Minot, North Dakota. The 5th FIS used the Eagle for only a few years, disbanding in 1988.

SPECIFICATIONS	
Country of origin:	United States
Type:	single-seat fighter and strike aircraft
Powerplant:	two 71.1kN (16,000lb) General Electric F404-GE-400 turbofans
Performance:	maximum speed at 12,190m (40,000ft) 1912km/h (1183mph); combat ceiling 15,240m (50,000ft); combat radius 1065km (662 miles)
Weights:	empty 10,455kg (23,050lb); maximum take-off 25,401kg (56,000lb)
Dimensions:	wingspan 11.43m (37ft 6in); length 17.07m (56ft); height 4.66m (15ft 3.5in); wing area 37.16 sq m (400 sq ft)
Armament:	one 20mm M61A1 Vulcan rotary cannon; nine hardpoints with provision for up to 7711kg (17,000kg) of stores

F-15J Eagle

By the late 1970s, the USAF had accepted the increasing tactical necessity for an interceptor that could provide top cover during long-range strike missions. Consequently, the F-15A was upgraded to the F-15C. The most obvious change is the provision for two low-drag conformal fuel tanks (CFTs). When built under license to Japan, the F-15C was designated the F-15J.

SPECIFICATIONS	
Country of origin:	United States/Japan
Type:	single-seat strike/attack aircraft and air superiority fighter
Powerplant:	two 105.7kN (23,770lb) Pratt & Whitney F100-PW-220 turbofans
Performance:	maximum speed at high altitude 2655km/h (1650mph); service ceiling 30,500m (100,000ft); range 5745km (3570 miles)
Weights:	empty 12,793kg (23,770lb); maximum take-off 30,844kg (68,000lb)
Dimensions:	wingspan 13.05m (42ft 9.75in); length 19.43in (63ft 9in); height 5.63m (18ft 5in); wing area 56.48 sq m (608 sq ft)
Armament:	one 20mm M61A1 cannon, provision for up to 10,705kg (23,600lb) of stores, including missiles, bombs, tanks, pods and rockets

F-15B Strike Eagle

In 1980, under a private-venture programme called 'Strike Eagle', McDonnell Douglas converted an F-15B to a demonstrator of an advanced two-seat strike aircraft. It competed in the Dual-Role Fighter contest and was selected over the F-16XL. The production version became the F-15E.

SPECIFICATIONS	
Country of origin:	United States
Type:	Two seat strike aircraft demonstrator
Powerplant:	two 105.9kN (23,810lb) Pratt & Whitney F100-PW-229 turbofans
Performance:	max speed at high altitude 2655km/h (1650mph); service ceiling 30,500m (100,000ft); range with fuel tanks 5745km (3570 miles)
Weights:	empty 14,379kg (31,700lb); maximum take-off 36,741kg (81,000lb)
Dimensions:	wingspan 13.05m (42ft 9.75in); length 19.43in (63ft 9in); height 5.63m (18ft 5in); wing area 56.48sq m (608sq ft)
Armament:	one 20mm M61A1 cannon; provision for up to 11,100kg (24,500lb) of stores, air-to-air missiles and conventional and guided bombs

Second-Generation Harriers

The AV-8B version of the Harrier was developed for the US Marine Corps, which had a requirement for a single-seat, close-support aircraft to supersede the AV-8A Harriers in service from the mid-1970s. The design resulted from a collaboration between the two companies, which had individually sought to improve on the Harrier design. The first of four full-scale development aircraft was flown on 5 November 1981 and entered service with the Marine Corps in January 1985.

McDonnell Douglas AV-8B Harrier II

The AV-8B was the first of the second-generation Harriers to enter service, replacing AV-8As and A-4M Skyhawks in the Marines' light-attack squadrons. Early AV-8Bs like this VMA-331 'Bumblebees' aircraft had day-attack capability only, with no radar or laser systems.

SPECIFICATIONS	
Country of origin:	United States and United Kingdom
Type:	V/STOL close-support aircraft
Powerplant:	one 105.8kN (23,800lb) Rolls-Royce Pegasus vectored thrust turbofan
Performance:	maximum speed at sea level 1065km/h (661mph); service ceiling more than 15,240m (50,000ft); combat radius with 2722kg (6000lb) bombload 277km (172 miles)
Weights:	empty 5936kg (13,086lb); maximum take-off weight 14,061kg (31,000lb)
Dimensions:	wingspan 9.25m (30ft 4in); length 14.12m (46ft 4in); height 3.55m (11ft 7.75in); wing area 21.37 sq m (230 sq ft)
Armament:	one 25mm GAU-12U cannon, six external hardpoints with provision for up to 7711kg (17,000lb) (Short take-off) or 3175kg (7000lb) (Vertical take-off) of stores

McDonnell Douglas TAV-8B Harrier

Built in small numbers for the USMC, Italy and Spain, the TAV-8B retained the attack capability of the AV-8B, but has rarely – if ever – been used on operations. The TAV-8B also served as the basis for the Harrier T.10 for the RAF.

SPECIFICATIONS	
Country of origin:	United States and United Kingdom
Type:	V/STOL close-support aircraft
Powerplant:	one 95.4kN (21,450lb) thrust Rolls-Royce F402-RR-406 Pegasus vectored-thrust turbofan engine
Performance:	maximum speed at sea level 1065km/h (661mph); service ceiling more than 15,240m (50,000ft); combat radius with 2722kg (6000lb) bombload 277km (172 miles)
Weights:	empty 6450kg (14,233lb); maximum 14,058kg (31,000lb)
Dimensions:	span 9.2m (30ft 4in); length 15.3m (50ft 3in); height 3.5m (11ft 7in); wing area 22.1 sq m (239 sq ft)
Armament:	none

British Aerospace Harrier GR.5

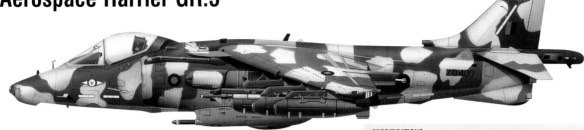

First of the 'big wing' Harriers for the Royal Air Force, the GR.5 was something of an interim model, delayed for technical and budgetary reasons. Most were converted into GR.7s, with FLIR systems and night-vision goggle capability.

SPECIFICATIONS	
Country of origin:	United Kingdom and United States
Type:	V/STOL close-support aircraft
Powerplant:	one 95.4kN (21,450lb) thrust Rolls-Royce Pegasus 11-21/Mk. 105 vectored-thrust turbofan engine
Performance:	max speed 1065km/h (661mph); service ceiling more than 15,240m (50,000ft); combat radius 277km (172 miles)
Weights:	empty 7050kg (15,542lb); maximum take-off weight 14,061kg (31,000lb)
Dimensions:	wingspan 9.25m (30ft 4in); length 14.36m (47ft 1.5in); height 3.55m (11ft 7.75in); wing area 21.37 sq m (230 sq ft)
Armament:	two 25mm Aden cannon; provision for up to 4082kg (9000lb) (Short take-off) or 3175kg (7000lb) (Vertical take-off) of stores

British Aerospace Sea Harrier FRS Mk 2

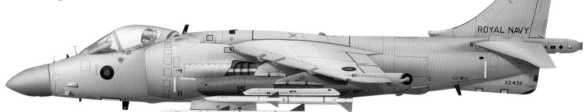

In 1985, BAe began modernizing the fleet of FRS Mk 1s. The primary aim was to give the Sea Harrier the ability to engage beyond-visual-range targets with the AIM-120 AMRAAM medium-range air-to-air missile. The most obvious difference is the shape of the forward fuselage, which accommodates the Ferranti Blue Vixen pulse-Doppler track-while-scan radar. Deliveries commenced in 1992.

SPECIFICATIONS	
Country of origin:	United Kingdom
Type:	shipborne multi-role combat aircraft
Powerplant:	one 95.6kN (21,500lb) Rolls-Royce Pegasus vectored thrust turbofan
Performance:	maximum speed 1185km/h (736mph); service ceiling 15,545m (51,000ft); intercept radius 185km (115 miles) on hi-hi-hi CAP with 90 minuted loiter on station
Weights:	empty 5942kg (13,100lb); maximum take-off weight 11,884kg (26,200lb)
Dimensions:	wingspan 7.7m (25ft 3in); length 14.17m (46ft 6in); height 3.71m (12ft 2in); wing area 18.68 sq m (201.1 sq ft)
Armament:	two 25mm Aden cannon, provision for missiles, up to a total of 3629kg 8000lb) rockets, pods and drop tanks

British Aerospace Harrier GR.7

The GR.7 became the definitive Harrier II for the RAF. They have been used over the Balkans, Iraq and Afghanistan, and fly from RN carriers as part of Joint Force Harrier. Conversion with new avionics and structural improvements has created the GR.9, able to carry a wider range of precision weapons.

SPECIFICATIONS	
Country of origin:	United Kingdom and United States
Type:	V/STOL close-support aircraft
Powerplant:	one 96.7kN (21,750lb) Rolls-Royce Pegasus vectored-thrust turbofan
Performance:	max speed 1065km/h (661mph); service ceiling more than 15,240m (50,000ft); combat radius 277km (172 miles)
Weights:	empty 7050kg (15,542lb); maximum take-off weight 14,061kg (31,000lb)
Dimensions:	wingspan 9.25m (30ft 4in); length 14.36m (47ft 1.5in); height 3.55m (11ft 7.75in); wing area 21.37 sq m (230 sq ft)
Armament:	provision for up to 4082kg (9000lb) (Short take-off) or 3175kg (7000lb) (Vertical take-off) of stores

MiG-23/27 'Flogger'

The MiG-23 and related MiG-27 ground-attack aircraft superseded the MiG-21 as primary equipment for the Soviet tactical air forces and Voyska PVO home-defence interceptor force. The aircraft is still flown by all the former Warsaw Pact air forces, though it is now a little long in the tooth when compared to European and American aircraft. Most MiG-23MFs serve in the fighter role, and are configured for high performance with modest weapons loads.

MiG-23MF 'Flogger-B'

This aircraft served with the Czech Air Force and has the designation MiG-23MF. This was the major production version from 1978, with improved radar and an infrared sensor pod. The ventral fin folds prior to landing.

SPECIFICATIONS	
Country of origin:	USSR
Type:	single-seat air combat fighter
Powerplant:	one 98kN (22,046lb) Rumanskii R-27F2M-300
Performance:	max speed about 2445km/h (1520mph); service ceiling over 18,290m (60,000ft); combat radius on hi-lo-hi mission 966km (600 miles)
Weights:	empty 10,400kg (22,932lb); maximum loaded 18,145kg (40,000lb)
Dimensions:	wingspan 13.97m (45ft 10in) spread and 7.78m (25ft 6.25in) swept; length 16.71m (54ft 10in); height 4.82m (15ft 9.75in); wing area 37.25 sq m (402 sq ft) spread
Armament:	one 23mm GSh-23L cannon, underwing pylons for AA-3 Anab, AA-7 Apex, and/or AA-8 Aphid air-to-air missiles

MiG-23M 'Flogger-B'

By 1975, several hundred MiG-23s, including the attack and trainer versions, had been delivered to Warsaw Pact air forces. Production continued until the mid-1980s; by far the largest operator was the Soviet Union. The engine – one of the most powerful to be fitted to a combat aircraft – gives good short-field performance and high top speed.

SPECIFICATIONS	
Country of origin:	USSR
Type:	single-seat air combat fighter
Powerplant:	one 100kN (22,485lb) Khachaturov R-29-300 turbojet
Performance:	max speed about 2445km/h (1520mph); service ceiling over 18,290m (60,000ft); combat radius on hi-lo-hi mission 966km (600 miles)
Weights:	empty 10,400kg (22,932lb); maximum loaded 18,145kg (40,000lb)
Dimensions:	span 13.97m (45ft 10in) spread and 7.78m (25ft 6.25in) swept; length 16.71m (54ft 10in); height 4.82m (15ft 9.75in); wing area 37.25 sq m (402 sq ft) spread
Armament:	one 23mm GSh-23L cannon, underwing pylons for air-to-air missiles

MiG-23UB 'Flogger-C'

A two-seat version of the MiG-23 was produced for conversion training. The second cockpit, for the instructor, is to the rear of the standard cockpit. The seat is slightly raised and is provided with a retractable periscopic sight to give a more comprehensive forward view.

SPECIFICATIONS

Country of origin:	USSR
Type:	two-seat conversion trainer
Powerplant:	one 98kN (22,046lb) Tumanskii R-27F2M-300 turbojet
Performance:	max speed at altitude about 2445km/h (1520mph); service ceiling over 18,290m (60,000ft); operational radius about 966km(600 miles)
Weights:	empty 11,000kg (24,200lb); maximum loaded 18,145kg (40,000lb)
Dimensions:	wingspan 13.97m (45ft 10in) spread and 7.78m (25ft 6.25in) swept; length 16.71m (54ft 10in); height 4.82m (15ft 9.75in); wing area 37.25 sq m (402 sq ft) (spread)
Armament:	one 23mm GSh-23L cannon; provision for up to 3000kg (6614lb) of stores, including air-to-air missiles, pods and bombs

MiG-23BN 'Flogger F'

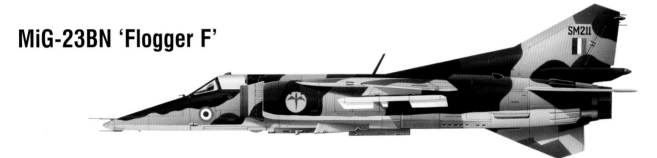

The MiG-23BN/BM 'Flogger-F' are basically fighter-bomber versions of the MiG-23 for the export market. The aircraft have similar nose shape, the same laser rangefinder, raised seat, cockpit external armour plate, and low-pressure tyres of the Soviet air forces' MiG-27 'Flogger-D', but retain the powerplant, variable geometry intakes and cannon armament of the MiG-23MF 'Flogger B'.

SPECIFICATIONS

Country of origin:	USSR
Type:	single-seat fighter bomber
Powerplant:	one 98kN (22,046lb) Tumanskii R-27F2M-300 turbojet
Performance:	max speed about 2445km/h (1520mph); service ceiling over 18,290m (60,000ft); combat radius on hi-lo-hi mission 966km (600 miles)
Weights:	empty 10,400kg (22,932lb); maximum loaded 18,145kg (40,000lb)
Dimensions:	span 13.97m (45ft 10in) spread, 7.78m (25ft 6.25in) swept; length 16.71m (54ft 10in); height 4.82m (15ft 9.75in); wing area 37.25 sq m (402 sq ft) spread
Armament:	one 23mm GSh-23L cannon, provision for 3000kg (6614lb) of stores

MiG-27 'Flogger-J'

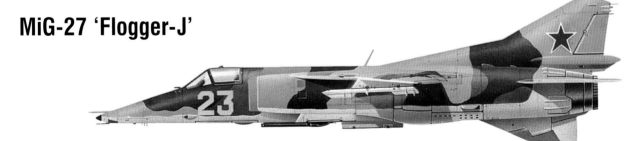

The MiG-27 was a highly developed version of the MiG-23. The aircraft was designed from the outset as a dedicated ground-attack aircraft and is optimized for operations over the battlefield. The most obvious difference is the nose, which was designed to give the pilot an enhanced view of the ground during approaches. The aircraft began to enter service in the late 1970s.

SPECIFICATIONS

Country of origin:	USSR
Type:	single-seat ground attack aircraft
Powerplant:	one 103.4kN (23,353lb) Tumanskii R-29B-300 turbojet
Performance:	max speed 1885km/h (1170mph); service ceiling over 14,000m (45,900ft); combat radius on lo-lo-lo mission 540km (335 miles)
Weights:	empty 11,908kg (26,252lb); maximum loaded 20,300kg (44,750lb)
Dimensions:	span 13.97m (45ft 10in) spread, 7.78m (25ft 6.25in) swept; length 17.07m (56ft 0.75in); height 5m (16ft 5in); wing area 37.35 sq m (402 sq ft) spread
Armament:	one 23mm cannon, provision for up to 4000kg (8818lb) of stores

War over Lebanon

In June 1982, Israel launched an invasion of southern Lebanon to destroy Palestinian terrorist bases there. Syria became involved and large air battles were fought over the Bekaa, Lebanon's central valley. By this time, Israel had replaced the majority of its equipment of French origin with the latest aircraft from the United States, and Syria's aircraft were at best half a generation behind. It is estimated that 86 Syrian aircraft were destroyed for no Israeli losses in aerial combat.

General Dynamics F-16A Fighter

Israel's first 75 F-16s were delivered from 1980. Even before the Lebanon War, they destroyed four Syrian aircraft in skirmishes. In 1982, they claimed 44 Syrian jets and also destroyed numerous radar and SAM sites while acting in the 'Wild Weasel' role.

SPECIFICATIONS

Country of origin:	United States
Type:	single-seat air combat and ground-attack fighter
Powerplant:	either one 105.7kN (23,770lb) Pratt & Whitney F100-PW-200 or one 128.9kN (28,984lb) General Electric F110-GE-100 turbofan
Performance:	maximum speed 2142km/h (1320mph); service ceiling above 15,240m (50,000ft); operational radius 925km (525 miles)
Weights:	empty 7070kg (15,586lb); maximum take-off weight 16,057kg (35,400lb)
Dimensions:	span 9.45m (31ft); length 15.09m (49ft 6in); height 5.09m (16ft 8in); wing area 27.87 sq m (300 sq ft)
Armament:	one General Electric M61A1 20mm multi-barrelled cannon, wingtip missile stations; provision for up to 9276kg (20,450lb) of stores

McDonnell Douglas F-15 Eagle

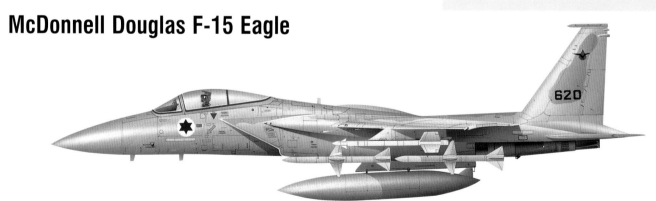

The first Israeli F-15s arrived in 1976, having been acquired as a counter to Syrian (and Soviet) MiG-25 incursions into Israel's airspace. In Operation Peace for Galilee, the 1982 invasion, they scored around 40 kills, mainly with Sidewinder and Python 3 short-range missiles.

SPECIFICATIONS

Country of origin:	United States
Type:	single-seat air superiority fighter with secondary strike/attack role
Powerplant:	two 105.9kN (23,810lb) Pratt & Whitney F100-PW-100 turbofans
Performance:	max speed at high altitude 2655km/h (1650mph); service ceiling 30,500m (100,000ft); range on internal fuel 1930km (1200 miles)
Weights:	empty 12,700kg (28,000lb); with maximum load 25,424kg (56,000lb)
Dimensions:	span 13.05m (42ft 9.75in); length 19.43in (63ft 9in); height 5.63m (18ft 5in); wing area 56.48 sq m (608 sq ft)
Armament:	one 20mm M61A1 cannon, provision for up to 7620kg (16,800lb) of stores, including air-to-air missiles, conventional and guided bombs

Mikoyan-Gurevich MiG-23MS 'Flogger-E'

SPECIFICATIONS	
Country of origin:	USSR
Type:	single-seat air combat fighter
Powerplant:	one 98kN (22,046lb) Tumanskii R-27F2M-300 turbojet
Performance:	max speed about 2445km/h (1520mph); service ceiling over 18,290m (60,000ft); combat radius on hi-lo-hi mission 966km (600 miles)
Weights:	empty 10,400kg (22,932lb); maximum loaded 18,145kg (40,000lb)
Dimensions:	span 13.97m (45ft 10in) spread, 7.78m (25ft 6.25in) swept; length 16.71m (54ft 10in); height 4.82m (15ft 9.75in); wing area 37.25 sq m (402 sq ft) spread
Armament:	one 23mm GSh-23L cannon with 200 rounds, provision for up to 3000kg (6614lb) of stores

Syria's most important fighter in 1982 was the MiG-23. Against the Mirage or Phantom, it was a comparable opponent, but its missiles were the 1960s-era AA-2 'Atoll'. In combat with the F-15 and F-16, armed with modern all-aspect missiles, the Syrian MiG pilots had little chance.

Mikoyan-Gurevich MiG-23BN 'Flogger-F'

SPECIFICATIONS	
Country of origin:	USSR
Type:	single-seat fighter bomber
Powerplant:	one 98kN (22,046lb) Tumanskii R-27F2M-300 turbojet
Performance:	max speed about 2445km/h (1520mph); service ceiling over 18,290m (60,000ft); combat radius on hi-lo-hi mission 966km (600 miles)
Weights:	empty 10,400kg (22,932lb); maximum loaded 18,145kg (40,000lb)
Dimensions:	span 13.97m (45ft 10in) spread, 7.78m (25ft 6.25in) swept; length 16.71m (54ft 10in); height 4.82m (15ft 9.75in); wing area 37.25 sq m (402 sq ft) spread
Armament:	one 23mm GSh-23L cannon, provision for 3000kg (6614lb) of stores

The Syrians also flew the export model of the MiG-27, the MiG-23BN 'Flogger-F'. This had considerably poorer ECM systems than the versions in Soviet service. Israeli air-to-air victories in 1982 include a dozen MiG-23BNs amongst the various 'Floggers' claimed destroyed.

Hawker Hunter F.70

SPECIFICATIONS	
Country of origin:	United Kingdom
Type:	single-seat fighter
Powerplant:	one 45.13kN (10,145lb) thrust Rolls-Royce Avon 207 turbojet engine
Performance:	max speed 1144km/h (710mph); service ceiling 15,240m (50,000ft); range on internal fuel 689km (490 miles)
Weights:	empty 6405kg (14,122lb) maximum 17,750kg (24,600lb)
Dimensions:	span 10.26m (33ft 8in); length 13.98m (45ft 10.5in); height 4.02m (13ft 2in); wing area 32.42 sq m (349 sq ft)
Armament:	four 30mm Aden Cannon; up to 2722kg (6000lb) of bombs or rockets; AIM-9 Sidewinder AAMs or AGM-65 ASMs

Lebanon received 19 Hunters over a period of nearly 20 years. Although they fought with Israeli fighters in 1967 and were active in 1982–83, there were no combats in this period. After years of dormancy, Lebanon restored several of its Hunters to airworthy status in 2008.

Desert Storm: Iraq and Kuwait

Having fought a long and inconclusive war with Iran, Iraqi forces under Saddam Hussein invaded neighbouring Kuwait in August 1990. With a strength on paper of 550 frontline aircraft, Iraq had the sixth largest air force in the world, including some of the latest Soviet designs. Its many air bases were protected by Western-built hardened shelters, and its air-defence system was well integrated. However, Iraq's pilots were poorly trained and their officer corps weakened by Saddam's purges.

Mikoyan-Gurevich MiG-21PF 'Fishbed'

An estimated 204 MiG-21s were in the Iraqi inventory in 1990, making them the most numerous combat aircraft type facing the US-led coalition. They and their pilots were optimized for point defence under strict ground control, and were ineffective when faced by jamming and destruction of control centres.

SPECIFICATIONS	
Country of origin:	USSR
Type:	single-seat all-weather multi role fighter
Powerplant:	one 73.5kN (16,535lb) Tumanskii R-25 turbojets
Performance:	max speed 2229km/h (1385mph); service ceiling 17,500m (57,400ft); range on internal fuel 1160km (721 miles)
Weights:	empty 5200kg (11,464lb); maximum take-off 10,400kg (22,925lb)
Dimensions:	wingspan 7.15m (23ft 5.5in); length (including probe) 15.76m (51ft 8.5in); height 4.1m (13ft 5.5in); wing area 23 sq m (247.58 sq ft)
Armament:	one 23mm GSh-23 twin-barrell cannon, provision for about 1500kg (3307kg) of stores, including air-to-air missiles, rocket pods, drop tanks

Dassault Mirage F1 CK

Both Iraq and Kuwait were users of the Mirage F1 in 1990. Kuwait's Mirage F1CKs were less sophisticated and less numerous than Iraq's F1EQ models. At least two KAF Mirages were destroyed on the ground during the Iraqi invasion and others captured. The remainder fled to Saudi Arabia and took a limited part in the effort to recapture the country under the 'Free Kuwait Air Force' banner.

SPECIFICATIONS	
Country of origin:	France
Type:	single-seat multi-mission fighter attack aircraft
Powerplant:	one 100kN (15,873lb) SNECMA Atar 9K-50 turbojet
Performance:	max speed at high altitude 2350km/h (1460mph); service ceiling 20,000m (65,615ft); range with maximum load 900km (560 miles)
Weights:	empty 7400kg (16,314lb); maximum take-off 15,200kg (33,510lb)
Dimensions:	wingspan 8.4m (27ft 7in); length 15m (49ft 2.25in); height 4.5m (14ft 9in); wing area 25sq m (269 sq ft) spread
Armament:	two 30mm 553 DEFA cannon with 135 rpg, five external pylons with provision for up to 6300kg (13,889lb) of stores; AIM-9 Sidewinder and Matra 530 air-to-air missiles

Mikoyan-Gurevich MiG-23BN

SPECIFICATIONS	
Country of origin:	USSR
Type:	single-seat fighter bomber
Powerplant:	one 98kN (22,046lb) Tumanskii R-27F2M-300 turbojet
Performance:	max speed about 2445km/h (1520mph); service ceiling over 18,290m (60,000ft); combat radius on hi-lo-hi mission 966km (600 miles)
Weights:	empty 10,400kg (22,932lb); maximum loaded 18,145kg (40,000lb)
Dimensions:	span 13.97m (45ft 10in) spread, 7.78m (25ft 6.25in) swept; length 16.71m (54ft 10in); height 4.82m (15ft 9.75in); wing area 37.25 sq m (402 sq ft) spread
Armament:	one 23mm GSh-23L cannon, provision for up to 3000kg (6614lb) of stores, including air-to-air missiles, AS-7 Kerry air-to-surface missiles, cannon pods, rocket launcher pods, large calibre rockets and bombs

About 70 MiG-23BNs were delivered to Iraq in the mid-1980s and some were later fitted with Mirage F.1-style refuelling probes. Four MiG-23BNs were among the 150 Iraqi aircraft that fled to Iran to escape destruction by coalition air forces near the end of the war.

Mikoyan-Gurevich MiG-29

SPECIFICATIONS	
Country of origin:	USSR
Type:	single-seat air-superiority fighter with secondary ground attack capability
Powerplant:	two 81.4kN (18,298lb) Sarkisov RD-33 turbofans
Performance:	max speed 2443km/h (1518mph); service ceiling 17,000m (55,775ft); range with internal fuel 1500km (932 miles)
Weights:	empty 10,900kg (24,030lb); maximum take-off 18,500kg (40,785lb)
Dimensions:	wingspan 11.36m (37ft 3.75in); length (including probe) 17.32m (56ft 10in); height 7.78m (25ft 6.25in); wing area 35.2 sq m (378.9 sq ft)
Armament:	one 30mm GSh-30 cannon, provision for up to 4500kg (9921lb) of stores

Although Iraq had ordered over 130 MiG-29s by 1990, only about two squadrons' worth were in service before the invasion of Kuwait. They failed to score against the Kuwait Air Force, and although regarded as the main air threat to coalition forces, were no more effective in 1991.

McDonnell Douglas A-4KU Skyhawk

SPECIFICATIONS	
Country of origin:	United States
Type:	single-seat attack bomber
Powerplant:	one 49.82kN (11,500lb) thrust Pratt & Whitney J52-P408 turbojet engine
Performance:	maximum speed 1083km/h (673mph); service ceiling 14,935m (49,000ft); range with 4000lb load 3310 km (2200 miles)
Weights:	empty 4809kg (10,602lb); maximum take-off 12,437kg (27,420lb)
Dimensions:	wingspan 8.38m (27ft 6in); length (excluding probe) 12.22m (40ft 1.5in); height 4.66m (15ft 3in); wing area 24.15 sq m (260 sq ft)
Armament:	two 20mm Mk 12 cannon with 200rpg; five external hardpoints with provision for 3720kg (8200lb) of stores

Kuwait's A-4KU Skyhawks are said to have destroyed several Iraqi helicopters during the initial invasion. When their base was shelled, they relocated to a highway strip and continued attacks, before retreating to Saudi Arabia and flying as the 'Free Kuwait Air Force'.

Desert Storm: Coalition Air Forces

Within days of the invasion, the first elements of an international coalition were sent to air bases in the region. The largest non-US contributor was the United Kingdom, but combat aircraft from France, Italy, Canada, Saudi Arabia, Bahrain, Qatar and exiled Kuwaiti units took part in Operation Desert Shield, which became Desert Storm when the air campaign began in January 1991. The RAF's Operation Granby was the largest air component, incorporating bombers, fighters and other aircraft.

Panavia Tornado GR.1

Based at Tabuk, Saudi Arabia, Tornado GR.1 'MiG Eater' flew 40 missions and destroyed a MiG-29 on the ground. The RAF lost six Tornados in combat during the initial low-level attack missions. They then mainly switched to striking bridges and hunting for mobile 'Scud' missile launchers.

SPECIFICATIONS

Country of origin:	Germany/Italy/United Kingdom
Type:	multi-role combat aircraft
Powerplant:	two 71.5kN (16,075lb) Turbo-Union RB.199-34R Mk 103 turbofans
Performance:	max speed above 11,000m (36,090ft) 2337km/h (1452mph); service ceiling 15,240m (50,000ft); combat radius with weapon load on hi-lo-hi mission 1390km (864 miles)
Weights:	empty 14,091kg (31,065lb); maximum take-off 27,216kg (60,000lb)
Dimensions:	wingspan 13.91m (45ft 7in) spread and 8.6m (28ft 2.5in) swept; length 16.72m (54ft 10in); height 5.95m (19ft 6.25in); wing area 26.6 sq m (286.3 sq ft)
Armament:	two 27mm IWKA-Mauser cannon with 180rpg, seven external hardpoints with provision for up to 9000kg (19,840lb) of stores, including nuclear and JP233 runway denial weapon, ALARM anti-radiation missiles, air-to-air, air-to-surface and anti-ship missiles, conventional and guided bombs, cluster bombs, ECM pods and drop tanks

SEPECAT Jaguar GR.1A

The RAF's Gulf War Jaguars were fitted with overwing Sidewinder pylons for self-defence, although they never encountered an enemy fighter in the air. GR.1A 'Sadman' flew 47 missions over Iraq from its base at Muharraq, on the island of Bahrain.

SPECIFICATIONS

Country of origin:	France and United Kingdom
Type:	single-seat tactical support and strike aircraft
Powerplant:	two 32.5kN (7305lb) Rolls-Royce/Turbomeca Adour Mk 102 turbofans
Performance:	maximum speed at 11,000m (36,090ft) 1593km/h (990mph); combat radius on lo-lo-lo mission with internal fuel 557km (357 miles)
Weights:	empty 7000kg (15,432lb); maximum take-off 15,500kg (34,172lb)
Dimensions:	wingspan 8.69m (28ft 6in); length 16.83m (55ft 2.5in); height 4.89m (16ft 0.5in); wing area 24 sq m (258.34 sq ft)
Armament:	two 30mm DEFA cannon with 150rpg; five external hardpoints with provision for 4536kg (10,000lb) of stores, including one tactical nuclear weapon, eight 454kg (1000lb) bombs

Hawker Siddeley Buccaneer S.2B

Buccaneers from RAF Lossiemouth were dispatched to provide laser designation for the RAF's Tornadoes once the latter switched to medium-level operations. Later in the conflict, they carried out their own bombing missions. This Buccaneer bore the names 'Lynn', 'Glenfiddich' and 'Jaws'.

SPECIFICATIONS	
Country of origin:	United Kingdom
Type:	two-seat attack aircraft
Powerplant:	two 50kN (11,255lb) Rolls Royce RB.168 Spey Mk 101 turbofans
Performance:	max speed 1040km/h (646mph); service ceiling over 12,190m (40,000ft); combat range 3701km (2300 miles)
Weights:	empty 13,608kg (30,000lb); maximum take-off 28,123kg (62,000lb)
Dimensions:	wingspan 13.41 (44ft); length 19.33m (63ft 5in); height 4.97m (16ft 3in); wing area 47.82 sq m (514.7 sq ft)
Armament:	four 454kg (1000lb) bombs, fuel tank, or reconnaissance pack on inside of rotary bomb door, four underwing pylons with provision for up to 5443kg (12,000lb) of bombs or missiles, including Harpoon and Sea Eagle anti-shipping missiles, and Martel anti-radar missiles

Dassault Mirage 2000C

Under the codename Operation Daguet, France provided 12 Mirage 2000Cs to help in the defence of Saudi Arabia. France also sent Mirage F.1s and Jaguar As to participate, plus transports, helicopters and a considerable ground component.

SPECIFICATIONS	
Country of origin:	France
Type:	single-seat air-superiority and attack fighter
Powerplant:	one 97kN (21,834lb) SNECMA M53-P2 turbofan
Performance:	max speed 2338km/h (1453mph); service ceiling 18,000m (59,055ft); range with 1000kg (2205lb) load 1480km (920 miles)
Weights:	empty 7500kg (16,534lb); maximum take-off 17,000kg (37,480lb)
Dimensions:	wingspan 9.13m (29ft 11.5in); length 14.36m (47ft 1.25in); height 5.2m (17ft 0.75in); wing area 41 sq m (441.3 sq ft)
Armament:	two DEFA 554 cannon; nine external pylons with provision for up to 6300kg of stores, including air-to-air missiles, rocket launcher pods, and various attack loads, including 1000lb bombs

McDonnell Douglas F-15C Eagle

The only non-American fighter kill of the war was scored by Saudi F-15C pilot Captain al-Shamrani of No 13 Squadron RSAF, who used AIM-9L Sidewinders to destroy two Iraqi Mirage F.1EQs that were heading to launch an Exocet attack on coalition warships.

SPECIFICATIONS	
Country of origin:	United States
Type:	single-seat air-superiority fighter with secondary strike/attack role
Powerplant:	two 101kN (23,830lb) thrust Pratt & Whitney F100-PW-220 afterburning turbofan engines
Performance:	maximum speed at high altitude 2655km/h (1650mph); service ceiling 19,812m (65,000ft); range 5552km (3450 miles)
Weights:	empty 12,247kg (27,000lb); maximum 29,937kg (66,000lb)
Armament:	one 20mm M61A1 cannon with 960 rounds, external pylons with provision for up to 10,705kg (23,600lb) of stores

Desert Storm: US Air Power

The vast bulk of missions against Iraq in 1991 were flown by US Air Force, Marine Corps and Navy aircraft. Over 12,600 strike sorties were flown against fixed strategic targets alone, and many more against battlefield targets and in support of these missions. Air supremacy was won quite quickly, and tactical airpower weakened or neutralized much of the Iraqi Army, but few – if any – SS-1 'Scud' mobile missile launchers were put out of action, and they continued to be fired throughout the war.

McDonnell Douglas F-15C MSIP

The F-15C was the dominant fighter of the war, credited with destroying 33 Iraqi Air Force and Army aircraft in flight. This aircraft of the 33rd Tactical Fighter Wing destroyed three of them, including a MiG-23 with an AIM-9 Sparrow missile.

SPECIFICATIONS	
Country of origin:	USA
Type:	single-seat air superiority fighter with secondary strike/attack role
Powerplant:	two Pratt and Whitney F100-PW-220 turbofans
Performance:	maximum speed at high altitude 2655km/h (1650mph); initial climb rate over 15,240m (50,000ft)/min; ceiling 30,500m (100,000ft); range 5745km (3570 miles)
Weights:	empty 12,700kg (28,000lb); maximum take-off 30,844kg (68,000lb)
Dimensions:	wingspan 13.05m (42ft 9in); length 19.43m (63ft 9in); height 5.63m (18ft 5in); wing area 56.48sq m (608sq ft)
Armament:	one 20mm M61A1 cannon with 960 rounds, external pylons with provision for up to 7620kg (16,800lb) of stores, for example four AIM-7 Sparrow air-to-air missiles and four AIM-9 Sidewinder AAMs: when configured for attack role conventional and guided bombs, rockets, air-to-air surface missiles; tanks and/or ECM pods.

Fairchild Republic A-10A

The Fairchild Republic A-10A grew out of the US Air Force's A-X programme, begun in 1967, to produce a highly battleproof, heavily armed close air-support aircraft to replace the A-1 Skyraider. The A-10A is dominated by the huge GAU-8/A cannon, but the range of weaponry that it can carry is devastating. This was proved during actions against Iraqi armour the 1991 Gulf War.

SPECIFICATIONS	
Country of origin:	United States
Type:	single-seat close support aircraft
Powerplant:	two 40.3kN (9065lb) General Electric TF34-GE-100 turbofans
Performance:	max speed 706km/h (439mph); combar radius 402km (250 miles) for a 2-hour loiter with 18 Mk82 bombs plus 750 rounds cannon ammunition
Weights:	empty 11,321kg (24,959lb); maximum take-off 22,680kg (50,000lb)
Dimensions:	wingspan 17.53m (57ft 6in); length 16.26m (53ft 4in); height 4.47m (14ft 8in); wing area 47.01 sq m (506 sq ft)
Armament:	one 30mm GAU-8/A rotary cannon with capacity for 1350 rounds of ammunition, eleven hardpoints with provision for up to 7528kg (16,000lb) of disposable stores

Northrop Grumman E-8A J-STARS

SPECIFICATIONS	
Country of origin:	United States
Type:	four-engined surveillance aircraft
Powerplant:	four 85.5kN (19,200lb) thrust TF33-102C turbofan engines
Performance:	max speed 945km/h (587mph); endurance nine hours; service ceiling: 12,802 m (42,000 ft)
Weights:	empty 77,564kg (171,000lb); maximum 152,409kg (336,000lb)
Dimensions:	span 44.4m (145ft 9in); length 46.6m (152ft 11in); height 13m (42ft 6in)
Armament:	none

An all-new technology deployed to the Gulf was the Joint Surveillance Target Attack Radar System (J-STARS), which allowed constant monitoring of ground movements in real time. The two E-8A development aircraft, still under testing, were rushed to the region, where they provided invaluable intelligence.

McDonnell Douglas F/A-18D

SPECIFICATIONS	
Country of origin:	United States
Type:	tandem-seat conversion trainer with combat capability
Powerplant:	two 71.1kN (16,000lb) General Electric F404-GE-400 turbofans
Performance:	maximum speed at 12,190m (40,000ft) 1912km/h (1183mph); combat ceiling about 15,240m (50,000ft); combat radius 1020km (634 miles) on attack mission
Weights:	empty 10,455kg (23,050lb); maximum take-off 25,401kg (56,000lb)
Dimensions:	wingspan 11.43m (37ft 6in); length 17.07m (56ft); height 4.66m (15ft 3.5in); wing area 37.16 sq m (400 sq ft)
Armament:	one 20mm M61A1 Vulcan six-barrell rotary cannon with 570 rounds, nine external hardpoints with provision for up to 7711kg (17,000lb) of stores

Desert Storm marked the combat debut of the F/A-18 Hornet. The type proved its ability to switch between fighter and bomber roles in the same mission. On the first day of the war, Navy Hornets destroyed two Iraqi MiG-21s and lost one of their number to a MiG-25. This is an F/A-18D of VMFA(AW)-121.

McDonnell Douglas-BAe AV-8B Harrier

SPECIFICATIONS	
Country of origin:	United States and United Kingdom
Type:	V/STOL close-support aircraft
Powerplant:	one 105.8kN (23,800lb) Rolls Royce F402-RR-408 Pegasus vectored thrust turbofan
Performance:	max speed 1065km/h (661mph); service ceiling more than 15,240m (50,000ft); combat radius 277km (172 miles)
Weights:	empty 5936kg (13,086lb); maximum take-off 14,061kg (31,000lb)
Dimensions:	wingspan 9.25m (30ft 4in); length 14.12m (46ft 4in); height 3.55m (11ft 7.75in); wing area 21.37 sq m (230 sq ft)
Armament:	one 25mm GAU-12U cannon; provision for up to 7711kg (17,000lb) (short take-off) or 3175kg (7000lb) (vertical take-off) of stores

VMA-311's AV-8B Harrier IIs operated from King Abdul Aziz air base in Saudi Arabia and from austere forward operating locations in the desert. The Harriers provided effective close air support but proved vulnerable to IR-guided missiles due to their large underside heat signature.

Grumman F-14 Tomcat

The F-14 was developed largely because of the failure of the F-111B fleet-fighter programme, yet has not enjoyed a trouble-free service life itself. Continuing problems led to escalating maintenance costs and a relatively high accident rate. Despite these problems, the Tomcat is widely regarded as the finest interceptor flying anywhere in the world. The F-14 succeeded the F-4 as the premier fleet-defence fighter. A total of 478 F-14As were supplied to the US Navy.

F-14A Tomcat

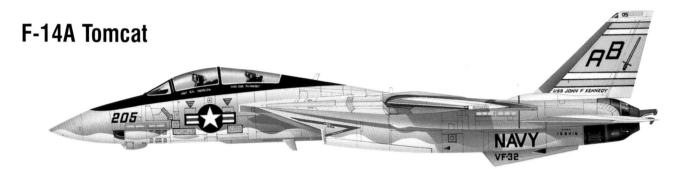

VF-32 'Swordsmen' was the first Atlantic Fleet squadron to form up with the Tomcat, making its first operational cruise in June 1975 on the USS *John F. Kennedy*. From the 1970s until the late 1980s, F-14s were mostly painted in gloss grey and white with colourful unit markings.

SPECIFICATIONS	
Country of origin:	United States
Type:	two-seat carrierborne fleet defence fighter
Powerplant:	two 92.9kN (20,900lb) Pratt & Whitney TF30-P-412A turbofans
Performance:	maximum speed at high altitude 2517km/h (1564mph); service ceiling 17,070m (56,000ft); range about 3220km (2000 miles)
Weights:	empty 18,191kg (40,104lb); maximum take-off 33,724kg (74,349lb)
Dimensions:	wingspan 19.55m (64ft 1.5in) unswept; 11.65m (38ft 2.5in) swept; length 19.1m (62ft 8in); height 4.88m (16ft); wing area 52.49 sq m (565 sq ft)
Armament:	one 20mm M61A1 Vulcan rotary cannon with 675 rounds; external pylons for a combination of AIM-7 Sparrow medium range air-to-air missiles, AIM-9 medium range air-to-air missiles, and AIM-54 Phoenix long range air-to-air missiles

F-14A Tomcat

In the 1980s, it was realized that brightly painted aircraft were more visible to infrared and other sensors, as well as to the naked eye. F-14 pilot C. J. Heatly and artist Keith Ferris were behind several experimental camouflage schemes, including this one, seen on an F-14A of VF-1.

SPECIFICATIONS	
Country of origin:	United States
Type:	two-seat carrierborne fleet defence fighter
Powerplant:	two 92.9kN (20,900lb) Pratt & Whitney TF30-P-412A turbofans
Performance:	maximum speed at high altitude 2517km/h (1564mph); service ceiling 17,070m (56,000ft); range about 3220km (2000 miles)
Weights:	empty 18,191kg (40,104lb); maximum take-off 33,724kg (74,349lb)
Dimensions:	wingspan 19.55m (64ft 1.5in) unswept; 11.65m (38ft 2.5in) swept; length 19.1m (62ft 8in); height 4.88m (16ft); wing area 52.49 sq m (565 sq ft)
Armament:	one 20mm M61A1 Vulcan rotary cannon with 675 rounds; external pylons for a combination of medium and long range air-to-air missiles

F-14A Tomcat

The only export customer for the Tomcat was the Imperial Iranian Air Force, which received 79 of 80 F-14As ordered before the Islamic revolution in 1979. Despite US sanctions, the Islamic Republic of Iran Air Force managed to keep about two dozen F-14s in service into the 2000s.

SPECIFICATIONS	
Country of origin:	United States
Type:	two-seat carrierborne fleet defence fighter
Powerplant:	two 92.9kN (20,900lb) Pratt & Whitney TF30-P-412A turbofans
Performance:	maximum speed at high altitude 2517km/h (1564mph); service ceiling 17,070m (56,000ft); range about 3220km (2000 miles)
Weights:	empty 18,191kg (40,104lb); maximum take-off 33,724kg (74,349lb)
Dimensions:	wingspan 19.55m (64ft 1.5in) unswept; 11.65m (38ft 2.5in) swept; length 19.1m (62ft 8in); height 4.88m (16ft); wing area 52.49 sq m (565 sq ft)
Armament:	one 20mm M61A1 Vulcan rotary cannon with 675 rounds; external pylons for a combination of AIM-7 Sparrow medium range air-to-air missiles, AIM-9 medium range air-to-air missiles, and AIM-54 Phoenix long range air-to-air missiles

F-14B Tomcat

The F-14B introduced the more powerful and less trouble-prone F110 engine, Martin-Baker ejection seats and other improvements. This F-14B of VF-74 'Bedevilers' illustrates the toned-down all-over grey colour schemes that became prevalent during the 1990s.

SPECIFICATIONS	
Country of origin:	United States
Type:	two-seat carrierborne fleet defence fighter
Powerplant:	two 120kN (27,000lb) General Electric F110-GE-400 turbofans
Performance:	maximum speed at high altitude 1988km/h (1241mph); service ceiling 16,150m (53,000ft); range about 1994km (1239 miles) with full weapon load
Weights:	empty 18,951kg (41,780lb); maximum 33,724kg (74,349lb)
Dimensions:	span 19.55m (64ft 1.5in) unswept; 11.65m (38ft 2.5in) swept; length 19.1m (62ft 8in); height 4.88m (16ft); wing area 52.49 sq m (565 sq ft)
Armament:	one 20mm M61A1 Vulcan rotary cannon with 675 rounds; external pylons for a combination of medium and long range air-to-air missiles

F-14D Tomcat

In 1984, it was decided to develop an interim improved version of the F-14 with General Electric F110-GE-400, designated the F-14A (Plus). Thirty-two aircraft were converted and later designated F-14B. The F-14D project suffered a seemingly endless round of cancellations and reinstatements prior to the funding of 37 new-build aircraft and 18 rebuilds from F-14As.

SPECIFICATIONS	
Country of origin:	United States
Type:	two-seat carrierborne fleet defence fighter
Powerplant:	two 120kN (27,000lb) General Electric F110-GE-400 turbofans
Performance:	max speed 1988km/h (1241mph); service ceiling 16,150m (53,000ft); range about 1994km (1239 miles) with full weapon load
Weights:	empty 18,951kg (41,780lb); maximum take-off 33,724kg (74,349lb)
Dimensions:	span 19.55m (64ft 1.5in) unswept; 11.65m (38ft 2.5in) swept; length 19.1m (62ft 8in); height 4.88m (16ft); wing area 52.49 sq m (565 sq ft)
Armament:	one 20mm M61A1 Vulcan rotary cannon with 675 rounds; external pylons for a combination of AIM-7 Sparrow medium range air-to-air missiles, AIM-9 medium range air-to-air missiles, and AIM-54A/B/C Phoenix long range air-to-air missiles

Afghan Wars

Throughout its history, Afghanistan has been in an almost constant state of war, either against outsiders or as a result of civil conflict. From 1979 to 1989, the Soviet Union attempted to exert its influence, launching an invasion to support the Communist government in Kabul. Over the following decade, various groups, many of them covertly backed by the United States, fought to expel Soviet forces. The USSR used many types of tactical aircraft and even strategic bombers.

MiG-17 'Fresco-C'

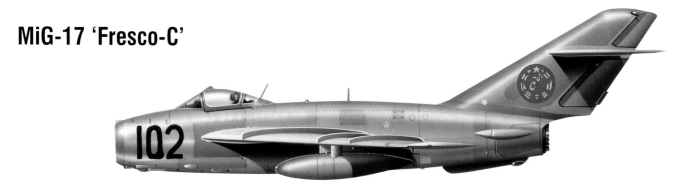

The Afghan Air Force was equipped with a variety of mostly Soviet-built types, including around 100 MiG-17s delivered from 1957. By 1985, they had an estimated 50 remaining. By mid-2001, what was left of the Air Force inventory was split amongst the Taliban and various Afghan factions.

SPECIFICATIONS	
Country of origin:	USSR
Type:	single-seat fighter
Powerplant:	one 33kN (7,452lb) Klimov VK-1F turbojet
Performance:	maximum speed at 3000m (9,840ft) 1145km/h (711mph); service ceiling 16,600m (54,560ft); range at height with slipper tanks 1470km (913 miles)
Weights:	empty 4100kg (9040lb); maximum loaded 600kg (14,770lb)
Dimensions:	wingspan 9.45m (31ft); length 11.05m (36ft 3.75in); height 3.35m (11ft); wing area 20.6 sq m (221.74 sq ft)
Armament:	one 37mm N-37 cannon and two 23mm NS-23 cannon, plus up to 500kg (1102lb) of mixed stores on underwing pylons

Sukhoi Su-25 'Frogfoot'

The prototype 'Frogfoot' first flew in 1975, and production of the single-seat close-support Su-25K (often compared to the Fairchild A-10 Thunderbolt II) began in 1978. A nose-mounted laser rangefinder and marked target seeker reportedly allows bombing accuracy to within 5m (16.4ft) over a stand-off range of 20km (12.5 miles). A trial unit was deployed to Afghanistan as early as 1980.

SPECIFICATIONS	
Country of origin:	USSR
Type:	single-seat close-support aircraft
Powerplant:	two 44.1kN (9921lb) Tumanskii R-195 turbojets
Performance:	maximum speed at sea level 975km/h (606mph); service ceiling 7000m (22,965ft); combat radius on lo-lo-lo mission 750km (466 miles)
Weights:	empty 9500kg (20,950lb); maximum take-off 17,600kg (38,800lb)
Dimensions:	wingspan 14.36m (47ft 1.5in); length 15.53m (50ft 11.5in); height 4.8m (15ft 9in); wing area 33.7 sq m (362.75 sq ft)
Armament:	one 30mm GSh-30-2 cannon with 250 rounds; eight external pylons with provision for up to 4400kg (9700lb) of stores, including AAMs, ASMs, ARMs, anti-tank missiles, guided bombs, cluster bombs

Mikoyan-Gurevich MiG-23MLD 'Flogger-K'

This MiG-23MLD was the commander's aircraft of the 120th Fighter Regiment, which deployed to Bagram in Afghanistan in 1986. The 'Floggers' were mainly used to escort Su-22 bombers on missions close to the Pakistan border. The white stars on the nose mark combat missions flown.

SPECIFICATIONS	
Country of origin:	USSR
Type:	single-seat air combat fighter
Powerplant:	one 100kN (22,485lb) Khachaturov R-29-300 turbojet
Performance:	maximum speed at altitude about 2445km/h (1520mph); service ceiling over 18,290m (60,000ft); combat radius on hi-lo-hi mission 966km (600 miles)
Weights:	empty 10,400kg (22,932lb); maximum loaded 18,145kg (40,000lb)
Dimensions:	wingspan 13.97m (45ft 10in) spread and 7.78m (25ft 6.25in) swept; length (including probe) 16.71m (54ft 10in); height 4.82m (15ft 9.75in); wing area 37.25 sq m (402 sq ft) spread
Armament:	one 23mm GSh-23L cannon, underwing pylons for AA-3 Anab, AA-7 Apex, and/or AA-8 Aphid air-to-air missiles

Tupolev Tu-22PD 'Blinder-E'

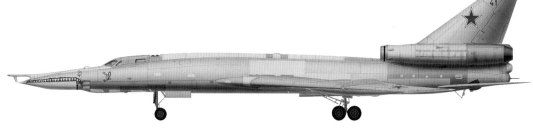

Used as a jammer and Elint aircraft, the Tu-22PD was used as an escort for the TU-22M-3 'Backfire' bombers used occasionally in Afghanistan, such as during the siege of Khost in 1987. Operating close to the Pakistan border, the 'Blinders' helped protect the 'Backfires' from interception.

SPECIFICATIONS	
Country of origin:	USSR
Type:	electronic warfare aircraft
Powerplant:	two 161.9kN (36,376lb) thrust RD-7M2 afterburning turbojet engines
Performance:	maximum speed 1487km/h (924mph); service ceiling 18,300m (60,040ft); combat radius with internal fuel 3100km (1926 miles)
Weights:	empty 40,000kg (88,185lb); maximum take-off 84,000kg (185,188lb)
Dimensions:	wingspan 23.75m (77ft 11in); length 40.53m (132ft 11.75in); height 10.67m (35ft); wing area 162 sq m (1722.28 sq ft)
Armament:	one 23mm NR-23 two-barrel cannon

General Dynamics F-16A

This F-16A, flown by Squadron Leader Hameed Qadri of the Pakistan Air Force, destroyed two Soviet Su-22M-3s in an engagement over the border area in May 1986. A friendly-fire incident in April 1987 saw a Pakistani pilot accidentally shoot down his wingman over Afghanistan.

SPECIFICATIONS	
Country of origin:	United States
Type:	single-seat air combat and ground attack fighter
Powerplant:	either one 105.7kN (23,770lb) Pratt & Whitney F100-PW-200 or one 128.9kN (28,984lb) General Electric F110-GE-100 turbofan
Performance:	maximum speed 2142km/h (1320mph); service ceiling above 15,240m (50,000ft); operational radius 925km (525 miles)
Weights:	empty 7070kg (15,586lb); maximum take-off 16,057kg (35,400lb)
Dimensions:	wingspan 9.45m (31ft); length 15.09m (49ft 6in); height 5.09m (16ft 8in); wing area 27.87 sq m (300 sq ft)
Armament:	one 20mm multi-barrelled cannon, wingtip missile stations; seven external hardpoints with provision for up to 9276kg (20,450lb) of stores

Stealth Attack Aircraft

The F-117 is probably the most important aircraft to enter service in the past two decades. It is likely that the secretive programme of stealth technology began in the wake of a number of radar-guided missile attacks on US-built F-4s during the 1973 Yom Kippur War. Delivered by Lockheed in 1982, Nighthawks really hit the headlines in the 1991 Gulf War, when pilots penetrated Iraqi air space undetected and delivered useful quantities of ordnance with pinpoint accuracy.

Lockheed F-117A Nighthawk

Both Lockheed and Northrop submitted proposals for the Experimental Stealth Technology requirement issued by the Department of Defense, with Lockheed's proposal being selected in 1977. The F-117 has been used several times in war. Its first mission was during the United States invasion of Panama in 1989. During that invasion two F-117A Nighthawks dropped two bombs on Rio Hato airfield. The F-117A can employ a variety of weapons and is equipped with sophisticated navigation and attack systems integrated into a state-of-the-art digital avionics suite that increases mission effectiveness and reduces pilot workload.

SPECIFICATIONS	
Country of origin:	United States
Type:	single-seat stealth attack aircraft
Powerplant:	two 48kN (10,800lb) General Electric F404-GE-F1D2 turbofans
Performance:	maximum speed about Mach 1 at high altitude; combat radius about 1112km (691 miles) with maximum payload
Weights:	empty about 13,608kg (30,000lb); maximum take-off 23,814kg (52,500lb)
Dimensions:	wingspan 13.2m (43ft 4in); length 20.08m (65ft 11in); height 3.78m (12ft 5in); wing area about 105.9 sq m (1140 sq ft)
Armament:	provision for 2268kg (5000lb) of stores on rotary dispenser in weapon bay; including the AGM-88 HARM anti-radiation missile; AGM-65 Maverick ASM, GBU-19 and GBU-27 optronically guided bombs, BLU-109 laser-guided bomb, and B61 free-fall nuclear bomb

Lockheed XST 'Have Blue'

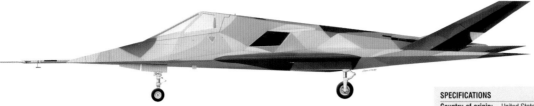

First flown secretly in December 1977 under the codename 'Have Blue', the Lockheed XST proved the aerodynamic shape intended for the F-117, although there were numerous differences, including the inwardly canted tailfins. Both prototypes crashed during testing.

SPECIFICATIONS	
Country of origin:	United States
Type:	stealth aircraft prototype
Powerplant:	two 12.4kN (2800lb) thrust General Electric CJ610 turbofan engines
Performance:	max speed unknown; range unknown; service ceiling unknown
Weights:	loaded 5440kg (11,993lb)
Dimensions:	span 6.86m (22ft 6in); length 11.58m (38ft 0in); height 2.29m (7ft 6in); wing area unknown
Armament:	none

Lockheed F-117A Nighthawk

Known as 'Spell Bound' during Operation Desert Storm, this F-117A flew eight or nine combat missions, the lowest number of those Nighthawks deployed. F-117s also saw action over Panama, Kosovo and Iraq in 2003. They were retired from USAF service in 2008.

SPECIFICATIONS	
Country of origin:	United States
Type:	single-seat stealth attack aircraft
Powerplant:	two 48kN (10,800lb) General Electric F404-GE-F1D2 turbofans
Performance:	maximum speed about Mach 1 at high altitude: combat radius about 1112km (691 miles) with maximum payload
Weights:	empty about 13,608kg (30,000lb); max take-off 23,814kg (52,500lb)
Dimensions:	wingspan 13.2m (43ft 4in); length 20.08m (65ft 11in); height 3.78m (12ft 5in); wing area about 105.9 sq m (1140 sq ft)
Armament:	provision for 2268kg (5000lb) of stores on rotary dispenser in weapon bay; including B61 free-fall nuclear bomb

Warsaw Pact

By the late 1980s, the air forces of the Warsaw Pact, including the 16th Air Army, part of the Soviet Group of Forces in Germany, had largely re-equipped with the latest tactical aircraft. Each of the main types in NATO and United States Air Forces Europe had its equivalent on the other side of the Iron Curtain. Only the Su-27 was kept back for defence of the Motherland. After the edifice crumbled in 1989, the Soviets began to withdraw, leaving a legacy of air bases and aircraft.

Mikoyan-Gurevich MiG-21MF 'Fishbed-J'

The Air Force of the German Democratic Republic was given the best versions of the Soviet aircraft rather than the downgraded models available to other WarPac air arms. This MiG-21MF was with JG 8 at Marxwalde in 1985, a unit that disbanded in September 1990.

SPECIFICATIONS	
Country of origin:	USSR
Type:	single-seat all-weather multi role fighter
Powerplant:	one 60.8kN (14,550lb) thrust Tumanskii R-13-300 afterburning turbojet
Performance:	maximum speed 2229km/h (1385mph); service ceiling 17,500m (57,400ft); range on internal fuel 1160km (721 miles)
Weights:	empty 5200kg (11,464lb); maximum take-off 10,400kg (22,925lb)
Dimensions:	wingspan 7.15m (23ft 5.5in); length (including probe) 15.76m (51ft 8.5in); height 4.1m (13ft 5.5in); wing area 23 sq m (247.58 sq ft)
Armament:	one 23mm GSh-23 twin-barrell cannon in underbelly pack, four underwing pylons with provision for 1500kg (3307kg) of stores

Sukhoi SU-17M-4 'Fitter K'

Among the last Russian Air Force aircraft in Germany were the Su-17M-4s of the 20th Fighter-Bomber Regiment at Gross Dölln (Templin), which finally packed up and left in April 1994. This machine carries AS-14 'Kedge' anti-radar missiles under the fuselage.

SPECIFICATIONS	
Country of origin:	USSR
Type:	single-seat ground-attack fighter
Powerplant:	one 110.3kN (24,802lb) Lyul'ka AL-21F-3 turbojet
Performance:	max speed approximately 2220km/h (1380mph); service ceiling 15,200m (49,865ft); combat radius 675km (419 miles)
Weights:	empty 9,500kg (20,944lb); maximum take-off 19,500kg (42,990lb)
Dimensions:	wingspan 13.8m (45ft 3in) spread and 10m (32ft 10in) swept; length 18.75m (61ft 6in); height 5m (16ft 5in); wing area 40 sq m (430 sq ft)
Armament:	two 30mm NR-30 cannon; nine external pylons with provision for up to 4250kg (9370lb) of stores, including tactical nuclear weapons

Mikoyan-Gurevich MiG-23 BN 'Flogger-H'

The unified German Luftwaffe retained most of the former GDR's equipment for only a short time. Most of the older MiGs were retired quickly, but some, such as this MiG-23BN, were used by test unit WTD-61 for evaluation against Western types.

SPECIFICATIONS	
Country of origin:	USSR
Type:	single-seat fighter bomber
Powerplant:	one 98kN (22,046lb) Tumanskii R-27F2M-300 turbojet
Performance:	maximum speed about 2445km/h (1520mph); service ceiling over 18,290m (60,000ft); combat radius on hi-lo-hi 966km (600 miles)
Weights:	empty 10,400kg (22,932lb); maximum loaded 18,145kg (40,000lb)
Dimensions:	wingspan 13.97m (45ft 10in) spread and 7.78m (25ft 6.25in) swept; length (including probe) 16.71m (54ft 10in); height 4.82m (15ft 9.75in); wing area 37.25 sq m (402 sq ft) spread
Armament:	one 23mm GSh-23L cannon with 200 rounds, six external hardpoints with provision for up to 3000kg (6614lb) of stores, including AA-2 Atoll air-to-air missiles, AS-7 Kerry air-to-surface missiles, cannon pods, rocket launcher pods, large calibre rockets and bombs

Mikoyan-Gurevich MiG-29 'Fulcrum A'

Following the break-up of the Soviet Union, the Czechoslovak Air Force was greatly reduced in size. The splitting of the country into Czech and Slovak Republics saw the one unit of MiG-29s transferred to the new Slovak AF. The nine aircraft have since been modernized and supplemented by others.

SPECIFICATIONS	
Country of origin:	USSR
Type:	single-seat air-superiority fighter with secondary ground attack capability
Powerplant:	two 81.4kN (18,298lb) Sarkisov RD-33 turbofans
Performance:	max speed above 11000m (36,090ft) 2443km/h (1518mph); service ceiling 17,000m (55,775ft); range with internal fuel 1500km (932 miles)
Weights:	empty 10,900kg (24,030lb); maximum take-off 18,500kg (40,785lb)
Dimensions:	wingspan 11.36m (37ft 3.75in); length (including probe) 17.32m (56ft 10in); height 7.78m (25ft 6.25in); wing area 35.2 sq m (378.9 sq ft)
Armament:	one 30mm GSh-30 cannon with 150 rounds, eight external hardpoints with provision for up to 4500kg (9921lb) of stores, including infrared- or radar-guided air-to-air missiles

Sukhoi Su-24MR 'Fencer-E'

The 'Fencer E' is a version of the Su-24 strike and attack aircraft, designed for tactical reconnaissance. Approximately 65 Su-24MRs have been constructed with internal and external podded sensors of various types. Some of these sensors can transmit data to ground-based receivers for real-time surveillance. Service deliveries began in 1985.

SPECIFICATIONS	
Country of origin:	USSR
Type:	two-seat maritime reconnaissance aircraft
Powerplant:	two 110.3kN (24,802lb) Lyul'ka AL-21F-3A turbojets
Performance:	maximum speed above 11,000m (36,090ft) approximately 2316km/h (1,439mph); service ceiling 17,500m (57,415ft); combat radius on hi-lo-hi mission with 3000kg (6614lb) load 1050km (650 miles)
Weights:	empty 19,00kg (41,888lb); maximum take-off 39,700kg (87,520lb)
Dimensions:	span 17.63m (57ft 10in) spread, 10.36m (34ft) swept; length 24.53m (80ft 5.75in); height 4.97m (16ft 0.75in); wing area 42 sq m (452.1 sq ft)
Armament:	(in secondary strike role) nine external pylons with provision for up to 8000kg (17,635lb) of stores, which may include air-to-air missiles

F-16 Fighting Falcon

The F-16 was undoubtedly one of the most important fighter aircraft of the twentieth century. It started fairly inauspiciously as a technology demonstrator to see to what degree it would be possible to build a useful fighter that was significantly smaller and cheaper than the F-15 Eagle. Interest from a number of America's NATO allies led to a revision of the programme and it was announced that the US Air Force would buy 650. General Dynamics' first production aircraft was flown in August 1978.

F-16A

The 8th Tactical Fighter Wing based at Kunsan in Korea was the first unit outside the United States to be equipped with F-16s, when it exchanged its last F-4s for Fighting Falcons in May 1981. This F-16A wears the codes and emblem of the 8th TFW, known as the 'Wolf Pack'.

SPECIFICATIONS	
Country of origin:	United States
Type:	single-seat air combat and ground attack fighter
Powerplant:	either one 105.7kN (23,770lb) Pratt & Whitney F100-PW-200 or one 128.9kN (28,984lb) General Electric F110-GE-100 turbofan
Performance:	maximum speed 2142km/h (1320mph); service ceiling above 15,240m (50,000ft); operational radius 925km (525 miles)
Weights:	empty 7070kg (15,586lb); maximum take-off 16,057kg (35,400lb)
Dimensions:	wingspan 9.45m (31ft); length 15.09m (49ft 6in); height 5.09m (16ft 8in); wing area 27.87 sq m (300 sq ft)
Armament:	one General Electric M61A1 20mm multi-barrelled cannon, wingtip missile stations; seven external hardpoints with provision for up to 9276kg (20,450lb) of stores

F-16/79

The F-16/79 was an attempt to produce a less-sophisticated variant for the export market. An improved version of the J 79 engine, as used in the F-104 and F-4, was installed in two F-16s for demonstration purposes. The J 79 required heavy heat shielding and produced less thrust, and no one bought the F-16/79.

SPECIFICATIONS	
Country of origin:	United States
Type:	single-seat air combat and ground attack fighter
Powerplant:	one 80.1kN (18,000lb) thrust General Electric J79-GE-17X afterburning turbojet engine
Performance:	Mach 2; service ceiling above 15,240m (50,000ft); radius 925km (525 miles)
Weights:	empty 7730kg (17,042lb); maximum 17,010kg (37,500lb)
Dimensions:	wingspan 9.45m (31ft); length 15.09m (49ft 6in); height 5.09m (16ft 8in); wing area 27.87 sq m (300 sq ft)
Armament:	one General Electric M61A1 20mm multi-barrelled cannon, wingtip missile stations; provision for up to 9276kg (20,450lb) of stores

F-16N

To replace older F-5s and A-4s in the adversary role, the US Navy acquired a batch of 26 F-16Ns and two-seat TF-16Ns in the late 1980s. Armament was removed and the wing was strengthened for use in regular air-combat training. This F-16N served with VF-43 at NAS Oceana, Virginia.

SPECIFICATIONS

Country of origin:	United States
Type:	single-engined adversary fighter
Powerplant:	one 76.3kN (17,155lb) thrust General Electric F110-GE-100 afterburning turbofan engine
Performance:	maximum speed 2142km/h (1320mph); service ceiling above 15,240m (50,000ft); operational radius 925km (525 miles)
Weights:	unknown
Dimensions:	wingspan 9.45m (31ft); length 15.09m (49ft 6in); height 5.09m (16ft 8in); wing area 27.87 sq m (300 sq ft)
Armament:	none

F-16A Block 15 ADF

The F-16 ADF is a version optimized for air-defence interception with a modified radar, improved IFF equipment and a searchlight for identifying intruders at night. Most were supplied to Air National Guard units such as Puerto Rico's 198th Fighter Squadron.

SPECIFICATIONS

Country of origin:	United States
Type:	Air Defence Fighter
Powerplant:	one 105.7kN (23,770lb) thrust Pratt & Whitney F100-PW-220 afterburning turbofan engine
Performance:	maximum speed 2142km/h (1320mph); service ceiling 16,764m (55,000ft); range 3862km (2400 miles)
Weights:	empty 7387kg (16,285lb); maximum 17,010kg (37,500lb)
Dimensions:	wingspan 9.45m (31ft); length 15.09m (49ft 6in); height 5.09m (16ft 8in); wing area 27.87 sq m (300 sq ft)
Armament:	One 20mm M61A1 Vulcan cannon; AIM-9 Sidewinder and AIM-7 Sparrow or AIM-120 AMRAAM air-to-air missiles

F-16C Block 50D

The F-16C became the major production version after 1984. The Block 50/52 appeared in late 1990, offered with Pratt & Whitney F100 (Block 50) or General Electric F110 (Block 52) engines. One customer for many of the F-16C sub-variants has been Greece, one of whose Block 50s is illustrated.

SPECIFICATIONS

Country of origin:	United States
Type:	single-seat air combat and ground attack fighter
Powerplant:	one 126.7kN (28,500lb) thrust Pratt & Whitney F100-PW-229 afterburning turbofan engine
Performance:	maximum speed 2177km/h (1353mph); service ceiling 15,240m (49,000ft); range 3862km (2400 miles)
Weights:	empty 8273kg (18,238lb); maximum 19,187kg (42,300lb)
Dimensions:	wingspan 9.45m (31ft); length 15.09m (49ft 6in); height 5.09m (16ft 8in); wing area 27.87 sq m (300 sq ft)
Armament:	one General Electric M61A1 20mm multi-barrelled cannon, wingtip missile stations; seven external hardpoints with provision for up to 9276kg (20,450lb) of stores

Balkan Air Wars

The state of Yugoslavia was broken into separate nations by a series of wars from 1991 to 1999. Aircraft in Federal Yugoslav armouries and air bases was appropriated by the various factions. Air power was mostly limited to sporadic ground-attack operations. Despite atrocities committed by most participants, the West was slow to take action. In 1993, a no-fly zone over Bosnia was imposed by NATO, in which four J-21s of the Republika Srpska Air Force were later shot down by USAF F-16s.

SOKO G-2A Galeb

In 1948, SOKO began licensed production of foreign designs before embarking on the design and construction of the G-2A Galeb trainer in 1957. This is a conventional low-wing monoplane of all-metal construction, retractable tricycle undercarriage and turbojet power. The crew are accommodated in tandem seats in a heated and air-conditioned cockpit.

SPECIFICATIONS	
Country of origin:	Yugoslavia
Type:	basic trainer
Powerplant:	one 11.1kN (2500lb) Rolls-Royce Viper 11 Mk 226 turbojet
Performance:	maximum speed at 6000m (19,685ft) 730km/h (454mph); service ceiling 12,000m (39,370ft); range with maximum standard fuel 1240km (771 miles)
Weights:	empty 2620kg (5776lb); maximum take-off weight 4300kg (9480lb)
Dimensions:	wingspan 9.73m (31ft 11in); length 10.34m (33ft 11in); height 3.28m (10ft 9in); wing area 19.43 sq m (209.15 sq ft)
Armament:	two 12.7mm machine guns with 80rpg; underwing racks for 150kg (331lb) bomblet containers, 100kg (220lb) bombs, 127mm rockets, and 55mm rocket-launcher pods

SOKO J-21 Jastreb

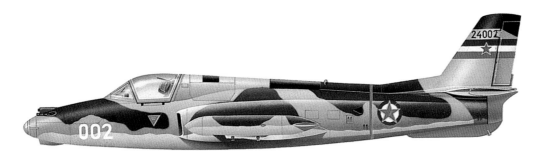

It was a relatively simple process for SOKO designers to convert the G-2A Galeb into a single-seat, light-attack aircraft. To improve weapons-carrying ability, an uprated version of the Viper engine was introduced, but apart from some local airframe strengthening, uprated wing hardpoints and the installation of a braking parachute, little was changed.

SPECIFICATIONS	
Country of origin:	Yugoslavia
Type:	single-seat light attack aircraft
Powerplant:	one 13.3kN (3000lb) Rolls-Royce Viper Mk 531 turbojet
Performance:	max speed 820km/h (510mph); service ceiling 12,000m (39,370ft); combat radius with standard fuel 1520km (944 miles)
Weights:	empty 2820kg (6217lb); maximum take-off weight 5100kg (11,244lb)
Dimensions:	wingspan 11.68m (38ft 3.75in); length 10.88m (38ft 8.25in); height 3.64m (11ft 11.25in); wing area 19.43 sq m (209.15 sq ft)
Armament:	three 12.7mm machine guns with 135 rpg; inboard hardpoints with provision for 500kg (1102lb) of stores

UTVA 75

Another indigenous Yugoslav type that found itself in various hands after the break-up of the country, the UTVA-75 was a trainer with a light secondary ground-attack capability. Many were camouflaged and used as such by Croatia. The survivors serve as trainers in the modern Croatian Air Force.

SPECIFICATIONS	
Country of origin:	Yugoslavia
Type:	trainer/light-attack aircraft
Powerplant:	one 134kW (180hp) Lycoming IO-360-B1F 4 cylinder flat piston engine
Performance:	maximum speed 215km/h (134mph); range 800km (500 miles); service ceiling 4000m (13,100ft)
Weights:	empty 685kg (1510lb); maximum 970kg (2135lb)
Armament:	mountings for machine-gun pods, two-round rocket launchers or 200kg (441lb) of bombs
Dimensions:	span 9.73m (31ft 11in); length 7.11m (23ft 4in); height 3.15m (10ft 4in); wing area 14.63 sq m (158 sq ft)
Armament:	none

Mikoyan-Gurevich MiG-21-bis 'Fishbed'

Yugoslavia operated a large number of MiG-21s before 1991, including MiG-21bis, MF and PFM models, but their reliability fell to a very low level during the civil wars. With the loss of many MiG-29s in 1999 and the poor condition of the survivors, the MiG-21 again became Serbia's main fighter.

SPECIFICATIONS	
Country of origin:	USSR
Type:	single-seat all-weather multi role fighter
Powerplant:	one 73.5kN (16,535lb) Tumanskii R-25 turbojets
Performance:	max speed 2229km/h (1385mph); service ceiling 17,500m (57,400ft); range on internal fuel 1160km (721 miles)
Weights:	empty 5200kg (11,464lb); maximum take-off weight 10,400kg (22,925lb)
Dimensions:	wingspan 7.15m (23ft 5.5in); length (including probe) 15.76m (51ft 8.5in); height 4.1m (13ft 5.5in); wing area 23 sq m (247.58 sq ft)
Armament:	one 23mm GSh-23 twin-barrell cannon in underbelly pack, provision for about 1500kg (3307kg) of stores

Mikoyan-Gurevich MiG-29B 'Fulcrum'

Serbia's MiG-29s made only about a dozen sorties in the Kosovo War in 1999. Six 'Fulcrums' were shot down, two of them by USAF 493rd Fighter Squadron F-15 pilot Jeffery Hwang, including the MiG-29A illustrated. A MiG-29 shot down by a Dutch F-16 was the first non-US NATO victory.

SPECIFICATIONS	
Country of origin:	USSR
Type:	single-seat air-superiority fighter with secondary ground attack capability
Powerplant:	two 81.4kN (18,298lb) Sarkisov RD-33 turbofans
Performance:	maximum speed above 11000m (36,090ft) 2443km/h (1518mph); service ceiling 17,000m (55,775ft); range with internal fuel 1500km (932 miles)
Weights:	empty 10,900kg (24,030lb); maximum take-off 18,500kg (40,785lb)
Dimensions:	wingspan 11.36m (37ft 3.75in); length (including probe) 17.32m (56ft 10in); height 7.78m (25ft 6.25in); wing area 35.2sq m (378.9sq ft)
Armament:	one 30mm GSh-30 cannon with 150 rounds, eight external hardpoints with provision for up to 4500kg (9921lb) of stores

Balkan Air Wars: NATO

NATO's first military action was to shoot down Bosnian Serb aircraft in 1994 under Operation Deny Flight. In April 1995, Operation Deliberate Force targeted the Army of Republika Srpska to prevent further massacres, but the major action was Operation Allied Force in 1999, which ended the conflict over Kosovo.

BAe Sea Harrier FA.2

Flying from Royal Navy carriers in the Adriatic, FAA Sea Harriers enforced the no-fly zone and provided close air support for UN troops. One Sea Harrier FRS.1 was shot down by a Serbian SAM in 1994, but this is a later FA.2, flying from HMS *Illustrious* during 'Allied Force' in 1999.

SPECIFICATIONS	
Country of origin:	United Kingdom
Type:	shipborne multi-role combat aircraft
Powerplant:	one 95.6kN (21,500lb) Rolls-Royce Pegasus Mk 106 vectored thrust turbofan
Performance:	maximum speed at sea level with maximum AAM load 1185km/h (736mph); service ceiling 15,545m (51,000ft); intercept radius 185km (115 miles) on hi-hi-hi CAP with 90 minuted loiter on station
Weights:	empty 5942kg (13,100lb); maximum take-off weight 11,884kg (26,200lb)
Dimensions:	wingspan 7.7m (25ft 3in); length 14.17m (46ft 6in); height 3.71m (12ft 2in); wing area 18.68 sq m (201.1 sq ft)
Armament:	two 25mm Aden cannon with 150 rounds, five external pylons with provision for AIM-9 Sidewinder, AIM-120 AMRAAM, and two Harpoon or Sea Eagle anti-shipping missiles, up to a total of 3629kg (8000lb)

BAe/McDonnell Douglas Harrier GR.7

RAF Harrier GR.7s saw their first active combat during Allied Force, although their LGB-dropping missions were initially hampered by cloud and bad weather. This led to a switch to conventional 'dumb' munitions such as BL-755 cluster bombs and eventually to the development of British GPS-guided bombs.

SPECIFICATIONS	
Country of origin:	United Kingdom/United States
Type:	V/STOL close-support aircraft
Powerplant:	one 96.7kN (21,750lb) Rolls-Royce Mk 105 Pegasus vectored-thrust turbofan
Performance:	max speed 1065km/h (661mph); service ceiling more than 15,240m (50,000ft); combat radius 277km (172 miles)
Weights:	empty 7050kg (15,542lb); maximum take-off weight 14,061kg (31,000lb)
Dimensions:	wingspan 9.25m (30ft 4in); length 14.36m (47ft 1.5in); height 3.55m (11ft 7.75in); wing area 21.37 sq m (230 sq ft)
Armament:	two 25mm Aden cannon with 100rpg; six external hardpoints with provision for up to 4082kg (9000lb) (short take-off) or 3175kg (7000lb) (vertical take-off) of stores

McDonnell Douglas CF-18A Hornet

Canada contributed CF-18A Hornets to Allied Force with a unit designated Task Force Aviano. The CAF Hornets were able to fly in night and bad weather, and could strike with laser-guided bombs aided by Nighthawk targeting pods. Spanish Air Force, USN and USMC Hornets also took part.

SPECIFICATIONS	
Country of origin:	United States
Type:	single-seat multi-mission fighter
Powerplant:	two 71.1kN (16,000lb) General Electric F404-GE-400 turbofans
Performance:	maximum speed at 12,190m (40,000ft) 1912km/h (1183mph); combat ceiling about 15,240m (50,000ft); combat radius 740km (460 miles) on escort mission or 1065km (662 miles) in attack role
Weights:	empty 10,455kg (23,050lb); maximum take-off 25,401kg (56,000lb)
Dimensions:	wingspan 11.43m (37ft 6in); length 17.07m (56ft); height 4.66m (15ft 3.5in); wing area 37.16 sq m (400 sq ft)
Armament:	one 20mm M61A1 Vulcan six-barrel rotary cannon with 570 rounds, nine external hardpoints with provision for up to 7711kg (17,000lb) of stores

Boeing E-3D Sentry AEW.1

During Allied intervention over the Balkans, E-3 Sentries from the United States, NATO and the RAF were vital in guiding fighters to interceptions, controlling rescue missions and warning of enemy air activity. The E-3Ds of the RAF's Nos 8 and 23 Squadrons assisted in several successful fighter engagements.

SPECIFICATIONS	
Country of origin:	United States
Type:	Airborne Warning and Control System platform
Powerplant:	four 106.8kN (24,000lb) thrust CFM56-2A-3 turbofan engines
Performance:	maximum speed 852km/h (529mph); range 3200km (1988 miles); service ceiling 10,668m (35,000ft)
Weight:	loaded 147,000kg (324,000lb)
Dimensions:	span 44.98m (147ft 7in); length 46.68m (153ft); height 12.6m (41ft 4in); wing area 3050 sq m (283 sq ft)
Armament:	none

Northrop Grumman B-2A

The B-2A Spirit 'stealth bomber' made its combat debut over Kosovo, Serbia and Montenegro in March 1999. Flying non-stop missions of up to 44 hours from Whiteman AFB, Missouri, the B-2s flew the longest-duration bombing raids in history and employed GPS-guided bombs for the first time.

SPECIFICATIONS	
Country of origin:	United States
Type:	strategic bomber and missile-launch platform
Powerplant:	four 84.5kN (19,000lb) General Electric F118-GE-110 turbofans
Performance:	maximum speed at high altitude 764km/h (475mph); service ceiling 15,240m (50,000ft); range on high level mission with standard fuel and 16,919kg (37,300lb) warload 11,675km (7255 miles)
Weights:	empty 45,360kg (100,000lb); max take-off 181,437kg (400,000lb)
Dimensions:	wingspan 52.43m (172ft); length 21.03m (69ft); height 5.18m (17ft); wing area more than 464.5 sq m (5000 sq ft)
Armament:	two internal bomb bays, provision for up to 22,680kg (50,000lb) of stores; each bay can carry 16 1.1 megaton thermonuclear free-fall bombs, 22 680kg (1500lb) bombs, or 80 227kg (500lb) free-fall bombs

Sukhoi Fencer and Frogfoot

In the 1980s, Soviet forces began to field more modern fighter, ground-attack and strike aircraft equivalent to those in the West. The Sukhoi Su-24 'Fencer' swing-wing bomber matched the F-111, and the Su-25 'Frogfoot' was a heavily armoured close air-support platform along the same lines as the A-10. Both types were widely exported, or left in the hands of former Soviet Republics, and have seen combat in Iraq, Chechnya, Georgia and other post Cold-War hotspots.

Su-25 'Frogfoot-A'

The single-seat Su-25 became fully operational in 1984, serving extensively in Afghanistan. As a testament to the longevity of the type, the Republic of Macedonia Air Force used Su-25s in their fight against Albanian insurgents in 2001, and in 2008 Georgia and Russia were both reported to be employing the Su-25 in South Ossetia.

SPECIFICATIONS	
Country of origin:	USSR
Type:	single-seat close-support aircraft
Powerplant:	two 44.1kN (9921lb) Tumanskii R-195 turbojets
Performance:	max speed 975km/h (606mph); service ceiling 7000m (22,965ft); combat radius on lo-lo-lo mission 750km (466 miles)
Weights:	empty 9500kg (20,950lb); maximum take-off weight 17,600kg (38,800lb)
Dimensions:	wingspan 14.36m (47ft 1.5in); length 15.53m (50ft 11.5in); height 4.8m (15ft 9in); wing area 33.7 sq m (362.75 sq ft)
Armament:	one 30mm GSh-30-2 cannon with 250 rounds; eight external pylons with provision for up to 4400kg (9700lb) of stores

Su-25K 'Frogfoot-A'

The Su-25K was an export variant of the basic 'Frogfoot' built from the mid-1980s. The Czechoslovak Air Force had 36 Su-25Ks at the time of the 'Velvet Divorce' between the Czech and Slovak republics in 1992–93. The Czech Air Force retained 24 of them but retired the type from service in 2000.

SPECIFICATIONS	
Country of origin:	USSR
Type:	single-seat close-support aircraft
Powerplant:	two 44.1kN (9921lb) Tumanskii R-195 turbojets
Performance:	max speed 975km/h (606mph); service ceiling 7000m (22,965ft); combat radius on lo-lo-lo mission 750km (466 miles)
Weights:	empty 9500kg (20,950lb); maximum take-off 17,600kg (38,800lb)
Dimensions:	wingspan 14.36m (47ft 1.5in); length 15.53m (50ft 11.5in); height 4.8m (15ft 9in); wing area 33.7 sq m (362.75 sq ft)
Armament:	one 30mm GSh-30-2 cannon with 250 rounds; eight external pylons with provision for up to 4400kg (9700lb) of stores

Su-25UTG 'Frogfoot B'

The Su-25UB 'Frogfoot-B' two-seat trainer has a longer forward fuselage to accommodate a second cockpit. Production of a navalized version, the Su-25UTG, began in the late 1980s with strengthened undercarriage and arrestor gear. The aircraft pictured passed to the Ukrainian Air Force after the dissolution of the Soviet Union.

SPECIFICATIONS	
Country of origin:	USSR
Type:	two-seat carrier-training aircraft
Powerplant:	two 44.1kN (9921lb) Tumanskii R-195 turbojets
Performance:	maximum speed at sea level 950km/h (590mph); service ceiling 10,000m (32,810ft); combat radius on lo-lo-lo mission with 4400kg (9700lb) load 4000km (248 miles)
Weights:	empty 9500kg (20,950lb); maximum take-off 17,600kg (38,800lb)
Dimensions:	wingspan 14.36m (47ft 1.5in); length 15.53m (50ft 11.5in); height 4.8m (15ft 9in); wing area 33.7 sq m (362.75 sq ft)
Armament:	one 30mm GSh-30-2 cannon with 250 rounds; eight external pylons with provision for up to 4400kg (9700lb) of stores

Su-24 'Fencer-B'

The 'Fencer-B' was a variant of the initial-production Su-24, identified by its brake parachute housing and revised shape around the rear fuselage. This example probably served with a Guards regiment based at Osla in Poland in the early 1990s.

SPECIFICATIONS	
Country of origin:	USSR
Type:	two-seat strike and attack aircraft
Powerplant:	two 110.3kN (24,802lb) Lyul'ka AL-21F-3A turbojets
Performance:	max speed approximately 2316km/h (1439mph); service ceiling 17,500m (57,415ft); combat radius 1050km (650 miles)
Weights:	empty 19,000kg (41,888lb); maximum take-off 39,700kg (87,520lb)
Dimensions:	span 17.63m (57ft 10in) spread, 10.36m (34ft) swept; length 24.53m (80ft 5in); height 4.97m (16ft 0.75in); wing area 42 sq m (452.1 sq ft)
Armament:	one 23mm GSh-23-6 six-barrelled cannon; nine external pylons with provision for up to 8000kg (17,635lb) of stores

Su-24M 'Fencer-D'

In 1965, the Soviet government prompted Sukhoi to begin designing a new Soviet variable-geometry attack aircraft comparable in performance to the F-111. One of the requirements was the ability to penetrate radar defences at very low level and at supersonic speeds. Service deliveries of the 'Fencer A' began in 1974, with the improved 'Fencer D' (Su-24M) entering service in 1986.

SPECIFICATIONS	
Country of origin:	USSR
Type:	two-seat strike and attack aircraft
Powerplant:	two 110.3kN (24,802lb) Lyul'ka AL-21F-3A turbojets
Performance:	max speed approximately 2316km/h (1439mph); service ceiling 17,500m (57,415ft); combat radius 1050km (650 miles)
Weights:	empty 19,000kg (41,888lb); maximum take-off 39,700kg (87,520lb)
Dimensions:	span 17.63m (57ft 10in) spread, 10.36m (34ft) swept; length 24.53m (80ft 5in); height 4.97m (16ft 0.75in); wing area 42 sq m (452.1 sq ft)
Armament:	one 23mm GSh-23-6 six-barrelled cannon; nine external pylons with provision for up to 8000kg (17,635lb) of stores

SEAD and Jamming

Suppression of Enemy Air Defences (SEAD) is a role that evolved from World War II-era electronic jamming and 'Wild Weasel' missions in Vietnam. It is defined by NATO as 'that activity which neutralizes, temporarily degrades or destroys enemy air defences by destructive and/or disruptive means'. This can be in the form of either a 'soft-kill' method such as jamming or spoofing radars, or by 'hard-kill' anti-radiation missiles or other ordnance.

Grumman EA-6B Prowler

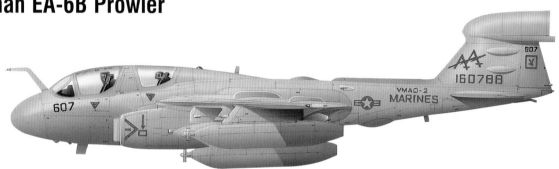

The Prowler was unarmed until the Improved Capability II (ICAP II) upgrade in the 1980s, which allowed it to carry the AGM-88 high-speed anti-radiation missile (HARM). This missile can reach a radar before it has time to shut down or use inbuilt memory to strike a target that has stopped emitting.

SPECIFICATIONS	
Country of origin:	United States
Type:	electronic countermeasures platform
Powerplant:	two 49.8kN (11,200lb) Pratt & Whitney J52-P-408 turbojets
Performance:	max speed at sea level 982km/h (610mph); service ceiling 11,580m (38,000ft); combat range with full external fuel 1769km (1099 miles)
Weights:	empty 14,588kg (32,162lb); maximum take-off 29,484kg (65,000lb)
Dimensions:	wingspan 16.15m (53ft); length 18.24m (59ft 10in); height 4.95m (16ft 3in); wing area 49.13 sq m (528.9 sq ft)
Armament:	none on early models, retrofitted with external hardpoints for four or six AGM-88 HARM air-to-surface anti-radar missiles

Mikoyan-Gurevich MiG-25BM 'Foxbat F'

Russia's SEAD aircraft have included unmodified Su-25s and variants of the MiG-25 'Foxbat'. The MiG-25BM 'Foxbat-F' was based on the airframe of the MiG-25RB reconnaissance model. Its normal armament for the SEAD role was the Raduga Kh-58 (AS-11 'Kilter') anti-radiation missiles.

SPECIFICATIONS	
Country of origin:	USSR
Type:	SEAD aircraft
Powerplant:	two 109.8kN (24,691lb) Tumanskii R-15BD-300 turbojets
Performance:	maximum speed at altitude about 3339km/h (2112mph); service ceiling 27,000m (88,585ft); operational radius 900km (559 miles)
Weights:	empty 19,600kg (43,211lb); maximum take-off 33,400kg (73,634lb)
Dimensions:	wingspan 13.42m (44ft 0.75in); length 23.82m (78ft 1.75in); height 6.1m (20ft 0.5in); wing area not disclosed
Armament:	four Raduga Kh-58 (AS-11 'Kilter') anti-radiation missiles

Grumman (General Dynamics) EF-111A

The biggest threat to US aircraft in Vietnam proved to be ground-based radar-guided missiles, supplied by the USSR to NVA forces. A development programme was begun and Grumman's adapted F-111A entered service in 1981, its most recognizable feature being the fin-tip pod that houses the jamming system's receiver and antenna.

SPECIFICATIONS	
Country of origin:	United States
Type:	two-seat ECM tactical jamming aircraft
Powerplant:	two 82.3kN (18,500lb) Pratt & Whitney TF-30-P3 turbofans
Performance:	maximum speed at optimum altitude 2272km/h (1412mph); service ceiling above 13,715m (45,000ft); range with internal fuel 1495km (929 miles)
Weights:	empty 25,072kg (55,275lb); maximum take-off 40,346kg (88,948lb)
Dimensions:	wingspan unswept 19.2m (63ft); swept 9.74m (32ft 11.5in); length 23.16m (76ft); height 6.1m (20ft); wing area 48.77 sq m (525 sq ft) unswept

McDonnell Douglas F-4G 'Phantom II'

The F-4G was designed and built specifically for the radar-suppression role in the wake of significant USAF losses to Soviet-supplied SA-2 'Guideline' SAMs over Vietnam. By 1972, about 12 F-4C 'Wild Weasels' had been introduced to service. The F-4G was the result of a much more extensive modification programme, and was produced by modifying F-4Es.

SPECIFICATIONS	
Country of origin:	United States
Type:	two-seat EW/radar-suppression aircraft
Powerplant:	two 79.6kN (17,900lb) General Electric J79-GE-17 turbojets
Performance:	maximum speed at high altitude 2390km/h (1485mph); service ceiling over 18,975m (62,250ft); range on internal fuel with weapon load 958km (595 miles)
Weights:	empty 13,300kg (29,321lb); maximum take-off weight 28,300kg (62,390lb)
Dimensions:	span 11.7m (38ft 5in); length 19.2m (63ft); height 5.02m (16ft 5.5in); wing area 49.24 sq m (530 sq ft)
Armament:	two AIM-7 Sparrow recessed under rear fuselage; wing pylons for radar suppression weapons such as AGM-45 Shrike, AGM-78 Standard or AGM-88 HARM anti-radiation missiles

Tornado ECR

Germany and Italy collaborated on the Tornado ECR electronic combat and reconnaissance version of the standard ground attack Tornado IDS. The Luftwaffe accepted 35 ECRs equipped with an emitter locator and armed with the AGM-88 HARM anti-radar missile.

SPECIFICATIONS	
Country of origin:	Germany, Italy and UK
Type:	multi-role combat aircraft
Powerplant:	two 7292kg (16,075lb) Turbo-Union RB.199-34r Mk 103 turbofans
Performance:	maximum speed above 11,000m (36,090ft) 2337km/h (1452mph); service ceiling 15,240m (50,000ft); combat radius wuth weapon load on hi-lo-mission 1390km (864 miles)
Weights:	empty 14091kg (31,065lb); maximum loaded 27,216kg (60,000lb)
Dimensions:	wingspan 13.91m (45ft 7in) spread and 8.6m (28ft 2.5in) swept; length 16.72m (54ft 10in); height 5.95m (19ft 6.25in); wing area 26.6 sq m (286.3 sq ft)
Armament:	two 27mm IWKA-Mauser cannon with 180 rpg, seven external hard points with provision for up to 9000kg (19,840lb) of stores; including AGM-88 HARM anti-radar missile

Dassault Mirage 2000

Early research and experience had shown that the delta-wing configuration carried some notable disadvantages, not least a lack of low-speed manoeuvrability. With the development of fly-by-wire technology during the late 1960s and early 1970s, it was possible for airframe designers to overcome some of these problems, when coupled with advances in aerodynamics. The 2000C was designed by Dassault to be a single-seat interceptor to replace the F.1.

Mirage 2000-01

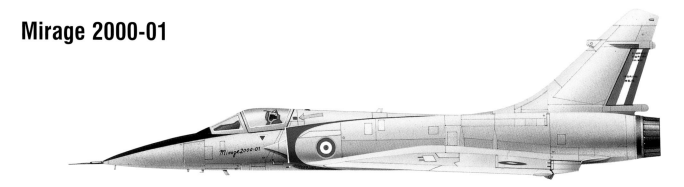

First flown in March 1978, the Mirage 2000 built on the success of the delta-winged Mirage III and IV with the addition of fly-by-wire controls. Four prototypes were built, all of them single-seaters. The test programme was quick by later standards and the first production aircraft flew in 1982.

SPECIFICATIONS	
Country of origin:	France
Type:	single-seat air-superiority and attack fighter
Powerplant:	one 83.36kN (18,839lb) thrust SNECMA M53-2 afterburning turbofan engine
Performance:	maximum speed at high altitude 2338km/h (1453mph); service ceiling 18,000m (59,055ft); range 1480km (920 miles)
Weights:	empty 7500kg (16,534lb); maximum take-off weight 17,000kg (37,480lb)
Dimensions:	wingspan 9.13m (29ft 11.5in); length 14.36m (47ft 1.25in); height 5.2m (17ft 0.75in); wing area 41 sq m (441.3 sq ft)
Armament:	two DEFA 554 cannon with 125rpg; nine external pylons with provision for up to 6300kg of stores, including R.530 air-to-air missiles, AS.30 or A.30L missiles, rocket launcher pods

Mirage 2000C

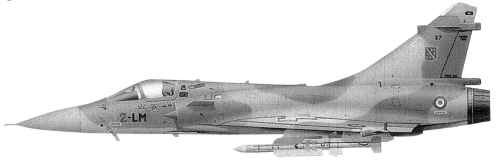

The 2000C was adopted by the French Government in December 1975 as the primary combat aircraft of the French air force, and was developed initially under contract as an interceptor and air-superiority fighter. Deliveries to L'Armée de l'Air began in July 1984: early production examples were fitted with the SNEMCA M53-5; aircraft built after that date have the more powerful M53-P2.

SPECIFICATIONS	
Country of origin:	France
Type:	single-seat air-superiority and attack fighter
Powerplant:	one 97.1kN (21,834lb) SNECMA M53-P2 turbofan
Performance:	maximum speed at high altitude 2338km/h (1453mph); service ceiling 18,000m (59,055ft); range 1480km (920 miles)
Weights:	empty 7500kg (16,534lb); maximum take-off weight 17,000kg (37,480lb)
Dimensions:	wingspan 9.13m (29ft 11.5in); length 14.36m (47ft 1.25in); height 5.2m (17ft 0.75in); wing area 41 sq m (441.3 sq ft)
Armament:	two DEFA 554 cannon with 125rpg; nine external pylons with provision for up to 6300kg of stores, including R.530 air-to-air missiles, AS.30 or A.30L missiles, rocket launcher pods

Mirage 2000P

Peru was the first Latin-American export customer for the Mirage 2000, buying 10 Mirage 2000Ps and two 2000DP two-seaters, although it had originally ordered 26 in total. The export-standard radar allowed a smaller range of weapons options than was available for aircraft of L'Armée de l'Air.

SPECIFICATIONS	
Country of origin:	France
Type:	single-seat air-superiority and attack fighter
Powerplant:	one 97.1kN (21,834lb) SNECMA M53-P2 turbofan
Performance:	maximum speed at high altitude 2338km/h (1,453mph); service ceiling 18,000m (59,055ft); range with 1000kg (2205lb) load 1,480km (920 miles)
Weights:	empty 7500kg (16,534lb); maximum take-off weight 17,000kg (37,480lb)
Dimensions:	wingspan 9.13m (29ft 11.5in); length 14.36m (47ft 1.25in); height 5.2m (17ft 0.75in); wing area 41 sq m (441.3 sq ft)
Armament:	two DEFA 554 cannon with 125rpg; nine external pylons with provision for up to 6300kg of stores, including R.530 air-to-air missiles, AS.30 or A.30L missiles, rocket launcher pods, and various attack loads, including 1000lb bombs. For air defence weapon training, the Cubic Corpn AIS (airborne instrumentation subsystem)

Mirage 2000B

Because of the complexity of the third-generation Mirage 2000, the French air force decided to pursue a programme of development for a two-seat trainer to run concurrently with the single-seat 2000C. The fifth Mirage 2000 prototype was flown in this format as the 2000B in October 1980. Production aircraft are distinguished by a slightly longer fuselage.

SPECIFICATIONS	
Country of origin:	France
Type:	dual-seat jet trainer with operational capability
Powerplant:	one 97.1kN (21,834lb) SNECMA M53-P2 turbofan
Performance:	maximum speed 2338km/h (1453mph); service ceiling 18,000m (59,055ft); range with two 1700 litre (374 Imp gal) drop tanks 1850km (1150miles)
Weights:	empty 7600kg (16,755lb); maximum take-off weight 17,000kg (37,480lb)
Dimensions:	wingspan 9.13m (29ft 11.5in); length 14.55m (47ft 9in); height 5.15m (16ft 10.75in); wing area 41 sq m (441.3 sq ft)
Armament:	seven external pylons with provision for R.530 air-to-air missiles, AS.30 or A.30L missiles and 1000lb bombs

Mirage 2000N

The Mirage 2000N is France's primary nuclear-strike aircraft. Although also capable of conventional attack, its main armament is the Mach-2 ASMP (*Air-Sol Moyenne Portée*) missile with a range of about 250km (155 miles) from high altitude, and a nuclear yield of 150 or 300 kilotons.

SPECIFICATIONS	
Country of origin:	France
Type:	single-seat strike aircraft
Powerplant:	one 97.1kN (21,834lb) SNECMA M53-P2 turbofan
Performance:	maximum speed at high altitude 2338km/h (1453mph); service ceiling 18,000m (59,055ft); range with two 1700 litre (374 Imp gal) drop tanks 1850km (1150 miles)
Weights:	empty 7600kg (16,755lb); maximum take-off weight 17,000kg (37,480lb)
Dimensions:	wingspan 9.13m (29ft 11.5in); length 14.55m (47ft 9in); height 5.15m (16ft 10.75in); wing area 41 sq m (441.3 sq ft)
Armament:	one ASMP stand off nuclear missile, seven external pylons with provision for air-to-air missiles and various attack loads, including 1000lb bombs

A-10 Thunderbolt II

The Fairchild Republic A-10A grew out of the US Air Force's A-X programme, begun in 1967, to produce a highly battleproof, heavily armed, close air-support aircraft to replace the A-1 Skyraider. In December 1970, three companies were chosen to build prototypes for evaluation, and Fairchild's YA-10A emerged as the winner in January 1973. The A-10A is dominated by the huge GAU-8/A cannon, but the range of weaponry that it can carry is devastating, as demonstrated during the 1991 Gulf War.

Fairchild-Republic YA-10A Thunderbolt II

The YA-10A won a competitive fly-off against the Northrop YA-9A in 1973, and went on to a period of evaluation for the USAF. Because the GAU-8 cannon was not ready, the two prototypes (this is the second) were armed with the M61 Vulcan used by most other USAF tactical aircraft.

SPECIFICATIONS	
Country of origin:	United States
Type:	prototype close air support aircraft
Powerplant:	two 40.3kN (9065lb) General Electric TF34-GE-100 turbofans
Performance:	maximum speed at sea level 706km/h (439mph); combat radius 402km (250 miles)
Weights:	unknown
Dimensions:	wingspan 17.53m (57ft 6in); length 16.26m (53ft 4in); height 4.47m (14ft 8in); wing area 47.01 sq m (506 sq ft)
Armament:	one 20mm M61A1 Vulcan cannon

Fairchild-Republic A-10A Thunderbolt II

With its intended role being low-level tank-hunting in regions such as Western Europe and Korea, the question of a suitable camouflage scheme for the A-10 became important. This is one pattern trialled during the USAF/Army Joint Attack Weapons Systems (JAWS) tests in 1977.

SPECIFICATIONS	
Country of origin:	United States
Type:	single-seat close support aircraft
Powerplant:	two 40.3kN (9065lb) General Electric TF34-GE-100 turbofans
Performance:	maximum speed at sea level 706km/h (439mph); combat radius 402km (250 miles)
Weights:	empty 11,321kg (24,959lb); maximum take-off 22,680kg (50,000lb)
Dimensions:	wingspan 17.53m (57ft 6in); length 16.26m (53ft 4in); height 4.47m (14ft 8in); wing area 47.01 sq m (506 sq ft)
Armament:	one 30mm rotary cannon with 1350 rounds, 11 hardpoints with provision for up to 7528kg (16,000lb) of disposable stores

Fairchild-Republic A-10A N/AW Thunderbolt II

SPECIFICATIONS	
Country of origin:	United States
Type:	two-seat night/adverse weather attack aircraft
Powerplant:	two 40.3kN (9065lb) General Electric TF34-GE-100 turbofans
Performance:	maximum speed at sea level 706km/h (439mph); combat radius 402km (250 miles) for a 2-hour loiter with 18 Mk82 bombs plus 750 rounds cannon ammunition
Weights:	empty 11,321kg (24,959lb); maximum take-off 22,680kg (50,000lb)
Dimensions:	wingspan 17.53m (57ft 6in); length 16.26m (53ft 4in); height unknown; wing area 47.01 sq m (506 sq ft)
Armament:	one 30mm GAU-8/A rotary cannon with capacity for 1350 rounds of ammunition, eleven hardpoints with provision for up to 7528kg (16,000lb) of disposable stores; weapons include conventional bombs, incendiary bombs, Rockeye cluster bombs

The simple A-10A had no avionics for night or bad-weather flying. The first production A-10A was converted with a second seat, a podded weather radar and other avionics to create the A-10A N/AW (Night/Adverse Weather). A proposed A-10B based on this design was ordered but later cancelled.

Fairchild-Republic A-10A Thunderbolt II

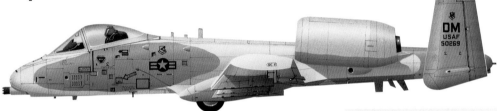

SPECIFICATIONS	
Country of origin:	United States
Type:	single-seat close support aircraft
Powerplant:	two 40.3kN (9065lb) General Electric TF34-GE-100 turbofans
Performance:	maximum speed at sea level 706km/h (439mph); combat radius 402km (250 miles) for a 2-hour loiter with 18 Mk82 bombs plus 750 rounds cannon ammunition
Weights:	empty 11,321kg (24,959lb); maximum take-off 22,680kg (50,000lb)
Dimensions:	wingspan 17.53m (57ft 6in); length 16.26m (53ft 4in); height 4.47m (14ft 8in); wing area 47.01 sq m (506 sq ft)
Armament:	one 30mm GAU-8/A rotary cannon with capacity for 1350 rounds of ammunition, 11 hardpoints with provision for up to 7528kg (16,000lb) of disposable stores

Although A-10s were fielded for many years in the 'European One' or 'lizard' colour scheme, this gave way in time to light greys similar to that of other USAF tactical aircraft. This A-10 is seen in an earlier grey/grey camouflage that saw limited use with the 355th TFW at Davis Monthan AFB, Arizona.

Fairchild-Republic OA-10A

SPECIFICATIONS	
Country of origin:	United States
Type:	single-seat close support aircraft
Powerplant:	two 40.3kN (9065lb) General Electric TF34-GE-100 turbofans
Performance:	maximum speed at sea level 706km/h (439mph); combat radius 402km (250 miles) loaded
Weights:	empty 11,321kg (24,959lb); maximum take-off 22,680kg (50,000lb)
Dimensions:	wingspan 17.53m (57ft 6in); length 16.26m (53ft 4in); height 4.47m (14ft 8in); wing area 47.01 sq m (506 sq ft)
Armament:	one 30mm GAU-8/A rotary cannon with capacity for 1350 rounds of ammunition, 11 hardpoints with provision for up to 7528kg (16,000lb) of stores, pods for 70mm (2.75in) target-making rockets

Conflict over the role of the Air Force versus the Army in providing close air support nearly caused the A-10's retirement several times. As part of this debate, several A-10 units, including that of the Pennsylvania ANG, were given the FAC role and their aircraft renamed OA-1As, despite being unchanged.

General Dynamics F-111

The variable-geometry General Dynamics F-111 suffered a difficult gestation, earning it the unwelcome nickname 'Aardvark'. Developed to meet a bold Department of Defense edict that a common type of fighter should be developed to meet all future tactical needs of the US armed forces, the F-111 seemed at the outset both a success and a great failure. After a troubled development process, the first of 117 aircraft, designated F-111As, were eventually delivered in 1967.

F-111A/TACT

The F-111A suffered several accidents and mysterious disappearances in Vietnam, but eventually overcame most of its numerous teething troubles. Under the Transonic Aircraft Technology (TACT) and other programmes, NASA tested this F-111 with new 'supercritical' wing sections.

SPECIFICATIONS	
Country of origin:	United States
Type:	two-seat attack aircraft
Powerplant:	two 82.29kN (18,500lb) thrust Pratt & Whitney TF30-P-3 afterburning turbofan engines
Performance:	maximum speed 2338km/h (1453mph); range 5094km (3165 miles); service ceiling 17,678m (58,000ft)
Weights:	empty 20,943kg (46,172lb); maximum 44,838kg (98,850lb)
Dimensions:	span 19.2m (63ft); length 22.4m (73ft 6in); height 5.33m (17ft 6in); wing area 48.77 sq m (525 sq ft)
Armament:	one 20mm M61A1 Vulcan rotary cannon; up to 13,608kg (30,000lb) of bombs, missiles or fuel tanks

FB-111A

Strategic Air Command adopted its own model of the F-111 as a replacement for the B-58 Hustler and some B-52s. With a longer wing and more powerful engines, the FB-111 could carry six AGM-69 Short-Range Attack Missiles (SRAMs) under the wings and in its internal bomb bay.

SPECIFICATIONS	
Country of origin:	United States
Type:	two-seat attack aircraft
Powerplant:	two 90.52kN (20,350lb) thrust Pratt & Whitney TF30-P-7 afterburning turbofan engines
Performance:	maximum speed 2338km/h (1453mph); range 7702km (4786 miles); service ceiling 15,320m (50,263ft)
Weights:	empty 21,763kg (47,980lb); maximum 54,091kg (119,250lb)
Dimensions:	span 21.34m (70ft); length 22.4m (73ft 6in); height 5.33m (17ft 6in); wing area 51.1 sq m (550 sq ft)
Armament:	six Boeing AGM-69 SRAM nuclear missiles; up to 17,010kg (37,500lb) of bombs, missiles or fuel tanks

F-111E

The F-111E was an improved F-111A with more efficient intakes and better navigation and electronic-warfare equipment. All the Es were allocated to the 20th TFW at Upper Heyford, England. They had less precision-bombing capability than the F-111F, but were used against Libya in 1986.

SPECIFICATIONS	
Country of origin:	United States
Type:	two-seat attack aircraft
Powerplant:	two 90.52kN (20,350lb) thrust Pratt & Whitney TF30-P-7 afterburning turbofan engines
Performance:	maximum speed 2338km/h (1453mph); range 7702km (4786 miles); service ceiling 15,320m (50,263ft)
Weights:	empty 21,763kg (47,980lb); maximum 54,091kg (119,250lb)
Dimensions:	span 21.34m (70ft); length 22.4m (73ft 6in); height 5.33m (17ft 6in); wing area 51.1 sq m (550 sq ft)
Armament:	six Boeing AGM-69 SRAM nuclear missiles; up to 17,010kg (37,500lb) of bombs, missiles or fuel tanks

F-111C

Australia was the only export customer for the F-111, acquiring 24 F-111Fs in the 1970s and later adding F-111Gs to the fleet. The F-111C had the longer wings of the FB-111 and the ability to use weapons such as the Harpoon anti-shipping missile. They are the last F-111s remaining in service.

SPECIFICATIONS	
Country of origin:	United States
Type:	two-seat attack aircraft
Powerplant:	two 92.70kN (20,840lb) thrust Pratt & Whitney TF30-P-109RA afterburning turbofan engines
Performance:	maximum speed 2338km/h (1453mph); range 7702km (4786 miles); service ceiling 15,320m (50,263ft)
Weights:	empty 20,943kg (46,172lb); maximum 41,414kg (91,300lb)
Dimensions:	span 21.34m (70ft); length 22.4m (73ft 6in); height 5.33m (17ft 6in); wing area 51.1 sq m (550 sq ft)
Armament:	up to 13,608kg (30,000lb) of bombs or missiles, including AGM-84 Harpoon anti-ship and AGM-88 HARM anti-radiation missiles

F-111G

The FB-111 was retired from SAC as the B-1B Lancer came into service. A number were modified with increased conventional weapons capability and new intakes. Redesignated as F-111Gs, they served with the 27th TFW at Cannon AFB, New Mexico.

SPECIFICATIONS	
Country of origin:	United States
Type:	two-seat attack aircraft
Powerplant:	two 90.52kN (20,350lb) thrust Pratt & Whitney TF30-P-7 afterburning turbofan engines
Performance:	maximum speed 2338km/h (1453mph); range 7702km (4786 miles); service ceiling 15,320m (50,263ft)
Weights:	empty 21,763kg (47,980lb); maximum 54,091kg (119,250lb)
Dimensions:	span 21.34m (70ft); length 22.40m (73ft 6in); height 5.33m (17ft 6in); wing area 51.1 sq m (550 sq ft)
Armament:	six Boeing AGM-69 SRAM nuclear missiles; up to 17,010kg (37,500lb) of bombs, missiles or fuel tanks

Tactical Transports

The market for tactical transport aircraft able to move troops and equipment around within a region or combat theatre, and to operate from short runways there, is one largely ignored by US manufacturers but enthusiastically taken up elsewhere. Turboprop or turbofan engines, multiwheel landing gears and high-lift wings, as well as other devices, allow operation from austere strips in 'hot-and-high' conditions, where C-130s and larger aircraft cannot go or struggle to carry a useful load.

Aeritalia G.222

The Aeritalia (now Alenia) G.222 has a wide fuselage and particularly good short take-off performance. The Italian Air Force bought nearly 50, but new examples were exported in small numbers. The C-27J Spartan, based on the G.222 with C-130J technology, has had some notable sales successes.

SPECIFICATIONS	
Country of origin:	Italy
Type:	twin-engined tactical transport
Powerplant:	two 2535kW (3400hp) General Electric T64-GE-P4D turboprop engines
Performance:	maximum speed 540km/h (336mph); range 4685km (2910 miles); service ceiling 7620m (25,000ft)
Weights:	empty 11,940kg (26,320lb); maximum 31,800kg (70,107lb)
Dimensions:	span 28.7m (94ft 2in); length 22.7m (74ft 6in); height 9.8m (32ft 2in); wing area 82 sq m (893 sq ft)
Armament:	none

CASA 212 Aviocar

Able to take off in as little as 400m (1312ft), the CASA 212 Aviocar was particularly popular with African and Latin-American air forces. In the Middle East, Saudi Arabia and Jordan were customers. The Royal Jordanian Air Force bought four 212-100s in the mid-1970s, one of which is shown.

SPECIFICATIONS	
Country of origin:	Spain
Type:	twin-engined tactical transport
Powerplant:	two 671kW (900hp) Garrett TPE331-10R-513C turboprop engines
Performance:	maximum speed 370km/h (230mph); range 2680km (1665 miles); service ceiling 7925m (26,000ft)
Weights:	empty 4400kg (9700lb); maximum 8000kg (17,637lb)
Dimensions:	span 20.28m (66ft 7in); length 15.18m (49ft 9in); height 6.6m (21ft 8in); wing area 41 sq m (441 sq ft)
Armament:	none

Antonov An-72 'Coaler'

The design of the An-72 'Coaler' is optimized for STOL capability, with a variety of high-lift features to permit short-field operation. The most noticeable of these is the positioning of the twin powerplants, at a position high up and well forward on the wing. When the inboard flaps are deployed, the engine exhaust is deflected over them, producing greatly increased lift.

SPECIFICATIONS

Country of origin:	USSR (Ukraine)
Type:	STOL transport
Powerplant:	two 63.7kN (14,330lb) Zaporozhye/Lotarev D-36 turbofans
Performance:	maximum speed 705km/h (438mph) at 10,000m (32,810ft); service ceiling 11,800m (38,715ft); range 800km (497 miles) with maximum payload
Weights:	empty 19,050kg (41,997lb); maximum take-off weight 34,500kg (76,059lb)
Dimensions:	wingspan 31.89m (104ft 7.5in); length 28.07m (92ft 1in); height 8.65m (28ft 4.5in); wing area 98.62 sq m (1062 sq ft)
Armament:	none

Transall C.160

Built by the Franco-German Transport Allianz consortium over a 20-year period, the Transall C-160 became the main airlifter for L'Armée de l'Air and the Luftwaffe . Other military users were Turkey and South Africa, and total production numbered over 200 aircraft.

SPECIFICATIONS

Country of origin:	France and Germany
Type:	twin-engined transport
Powerplant:	two 4225kW (5565hp) Rolls-Royce Tyne 22 turboprops engines
Performance:	maximum speed 513km/h (319mph); range 1850km (1150 miles); service ceiling 8230m (30,000ft)
Weights:	empty 30,000kg (62,700lb); maximum 46,000kg (103,400lb)
Dimensions:	span 40m (131ft 3in); length 32.4m (106ft 4in); height 12.36m (38ft 3in); wing area 160 sq m (1721 sq ft)
Armament:	none

Airtech CN-235

CASA of Spain and IPTN in Indonesia joined forces under the Airtech name in the early 1980s to produce the CN-235 military airlifter and civil airliner. The Saudi Air Force Royal Flight is one user, operating four CN-235M-10 models. The CN-235 spawned the larger CN-295, which also remains in production.

SPECIFICATIONS

Country of origin:	Spain and Indonesia
Type:	twin-engined transport
Powerplant:	two 1395-kW (1,750-hp) General Electric CT7C turboprop engines
Performance:	maximum speed 509km/h (317mph); range 5003km (3108 miles); service ceiling 9145m (30,000ft)
Weights:	empty 9800kg (21,605lb); maximum 15,100kg (33,290lb)
Dimensions:	span 25.81m (84ft 8in); length 21.4m (70ft 3in); height 8.18m (26ft 10in); wing area 59.1 sq m (636 sq ft)
Armament:	none

British Aerospace Hawk

The Hawk has been one of the truly outstanding successes of the British aerospace industry in the past three decades. Much of this success is due to the exceptional service life of the airframe, low maintenance requirements, the relatively inexpensive purchase price when originally offered for export, large optional payload, and its ability to operate in the medium range attack and air-superiority role for a fraction of the cost of more powerful types. The first operational aircraft were delivered in 1976.

BAe Hawk T.Mk 1

The Royal Air Force aerobatic team, the 'Red Arrows', flew its first season with the Hawk T.Mk 1 in 1980, replacing the Folland Gnat. The team uses nine Hawks, modified with tanks and piping able to make trails of red, white and blue smoke to enhance the display.

SPECIFICATIONS

Country of origin:	United Kingdom
Type:	two-seat basic and advanced jet trainer
Powerplant:	one 23.1kN (5200lb) Rolls Royce/Turbomeca Adour Mk 151 turbofan
Performance:	maximum speed 1038km/h (645mph); service ceiling 15,240m (50,000ft); endurance 4 hours
Weights:	empty 3647kg (8040lb); maximum take-off weight 7750kg (17,085lb)
Dimensions:	wingspan 9.39m (30ft 9.75in); length 11.17m (36ft 7.75in); height 3.99m (13ft 1.75in); wing area 16.69 sq m (179.64sq ft)
Armament:	none

BAe Hawk T.Mk 1A

The RAF also operates the T.Mk 1 for weapons instruction. The T.Mk 1A has three pylons; the central one is normally occupied by a 30mm (1.2in) Aden cannon, the two underwing pylons can be fitted with a wide combination of weapons, including Matra rocket pods. This aircraft is carrying a centreline drop tank and rocket pods for weapons training.

SPECIFICATIONS

Country of origin:	United Kingdom
Type:	two-seat weapons training aircraft
Powerplant:	one 23.1kN (5200lb) Rolls-Royce/Turbomeca Adour Mk 151 turbofan
Performance:	maximum speed 1038km/h (645mph); service ceiling 15,240m (50,000ft); endurance 4 hours
Weights:	empty 3647kg (8040lb); maximum take-off weight 7750kg (17,085lb)
Dimensions:	wingspan 9.39m (30ft 9.75in); length 11.17m (36ft 7.75in); height 3.99m (13ft 1.75in); wing area 16.69 sq m (179.64 sq ft)
Armament:	underfuselage/wing hardpoints with provision for up to 2567kg (5660lb) of stores, wingtip mounted air-to-air missiles

BAe Hawk T.52

SPECIFICATIONS	
Country of origin:	United Kingdom
Type:	two-seat weapons training aircraft
Powerplant:	one 23.1kN (5200lb) Rolls-Royce/Turbomeca Adour Mk 151 turbofan
Performance:	maximum speed 1038km/h (645mph); service ceiling 15,240m (50,000ft); endurance 4 hours
Weights:	empty 3647kg (8040lb); maximum take-off weight 7750kg (17,085lb)
Dimensions:	wingspan 9.39m (30ft 9.75in); length 11.17m (36ft 7.75in); height 3.99m (13ft 1.75in); wing area 16.69 sq m (179.64 sq ft)
Armament:	underfuselage/wing hardpoints with provision for up to 2567kg (5660lb) of stores, wingtip mounted air-to-air missiles

The Hawk is the most successful British combat aircraft export of recent years, with sales to 15 countries, including Indonesia. The Indonesians eventually bought a total of 20 Hawk T.53s in four batches and later added further Hawk 100 and 200 ground-attack models.

BAe Hawk T.51

SPECIFICATIONS	
Country of origin:	United Kingdom
Type:	two-seat weapons training aircraft
Powerplant:	one 23.1kN (5200lb) Rolls-Royce/Turbomeca Adour Mk 151 turbofan
Performance:	maximum speed 1038km/h (645mph); service ceiling 15,240m (50,000ft); endurance 4 hours
Weights:	empty 3647kg (8040lb); maximum take-off weight 7750kg (17,085lb)
Dimensions:	wingspan 9.39m (30ft 9.75in); length 11.17m (36ft 7.75in); height 3.99m (13ft 1.75in); wing area 16.69 sq m (179.64 sq ft)
Armament:	one 12.7mm (.5in) VKT machine-gun pod and two R-60 (AA-8 'Aphid' IR-homing AAMs

Finland was the Hawk's first export customer, buying 48 T.51s, the majority of which were built under licence by Valmet. As well as use as advanced trainers, they had a secondary air-defence role, armed with a machine-gun pod and two R-60 air-to-air missiles.

McDonnell Douglas T-45A Goshawk

SPECIFICATIONS	
Country of origin:	United States
Type:	tandem-seat carrier-equipped naval pilot trainer
Powerplant:	one 26kN (5845lb) Rolls Royce/Turbomeca F-405-RR-401 turbofan
Performance:	maximum speed at 2440m (8000ft) 997km/h (620mph); service ceiling 12,875m (42,250ft); range on internal fuel 1850km (1150 miles)
Weights:	empty 4263kg (9399lb); maximum take-off weight 5787kg (12,758lb)
Dimensions:	wingspan 9.39m (30ft 9.75in); length 11.97m (39ft 3.125in); height 4.27m (14ft); wing area 16.69 sq m (179.6 sq ft)
Armament:	none

The Goshawk is a development of the highly successful BAe (HS) Hawk trainer for the US Navy. A joint McDonnell Douglas/BAe venture that entered service in 1990, the aircraft is significantly different from the Hawk, with strong twin-wheel nose gear, strengthened long-stroke main gear legs, an arrestor hook and twin lateral airbrakes.

America's Strategic Bombers

The conclusion of the Cold War saw enormous changes to US strategic air power. In 1991, SAC bombers were taken off 24-hour alert. A drawdown in strategic assets saw the retirement of the B-52G and FB-111 and the purchase of fewer B-2s than planned. The B-1B later lost its nuclear role. The heavy bombers, however, found new roles in the 'War on Terror'. With GPS-guided weapons, the former nuclear bombers have conducted close air-support missions in Iraq and Afghanistan.

Boeing B-52G

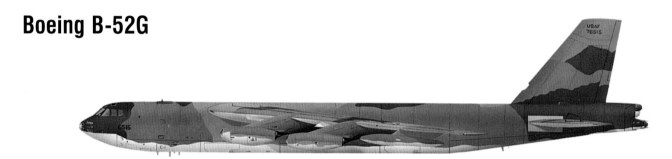

The B-52G introduced a host of significant improvements, including a wet wing that housed far more fuel, more powerful turbojets, a shortened fin of increased chord, and a remote-controlled rear turret. It was first flown in October 1958, and a total of 193 B-52G models were built, the last in 1960. Some 173 of these were later converted to carry 12 Boeing AGM-86B Air Launched Cruise Missiles.

SPECIFICATIONS	
Country of origin:	United States
Type:	long-range strategic bomber
Powerplant:	eight 61.1kN (13,750lb) Pratt & Whitney J57-P-43W turbojets
Performance:	maximum speed 1014km/h (630mph): service ceiling 16,765m (55,000ft); standard range with maximum load 13,680km (8500 miles)
Weights:	empty 77,200–87,100kg (171,000–193,000lb); loaded 221,500kg (448,000lb)
Dimensions:	wingspan 56.4m (185ft); length 48m (157ft 7in); height 12.4m (40ft 8in); wing area 371.6 sq m (4000 sq ft)
Armament:	remotely controlled tail mounting with four .5in machine guns; normal internal bomb capacity 12,247kg (27,000lb), including all SAC special weapons; external pylons for two Hound Dog missiles

Boeing B-52H

The turbofan-engined Boeing B-52H became the only version in service when the B-52G was retired in 1992. The main visual difference was a 20mm (.8in) cannon in the tail rather than four machine guns, although this was later removed. B-52Hs have served in every recent major conflict.

SPECIFICATIONS	
Country of origin:	United States
Type:	long-range strategic bomber
Powerplant:	four 76kN (17,000lb) Pratt & Whitney thrust turbofan engines
Performance:	maximum speed at 7315m (24,000ft) 1014km/h (630mph): service ceiling 16,765m (55,000ft); range 13,680km (8500 miles)
Weights:	185,000lb (83,250kg); loaded 221,500kg (448,000lb)
Dimensions:	wingspan 56.4m (185ft); length 48.5m (159ft 4in); height 12.4m (40ft 8in); wing area 371.60 sq m (4000 sq ft)
Armament:	remotely controlled tail mounting with one 20mm M61A1 Vulcan cannon (later removed); up to 31,500kg (70,000lb) of bombs, mines or air-to-surface missiles

Rockwell B-1A

SPECIFICATIONS	
Country of origin:	United States
Type:	four-engined strategic bomber prototype
Powerplant:	four 136.9kN (30,618lb) thrust General Electric F101-GE-101 afterburning turbofan engines
Performance:	maximum speed 2351km/h (1458mph); range 9915km (6085 miles); service ceiling 12,000m (39,360ft)
Weights:	maximum 176,810kg (388,982lb)
Dimensions:	span (unswept) 41.67m (136ft 8in); length 45.78m (150ft 2in); height 10.24m (33ft 7in); wing area 191 sq m (1950 sq ft)
Armament:	up to 52,160kg (114,752lb) of conventional or nuclear bombs, AGM-69A SRAMs or AGM-86 air-launched cruise missiles

The B-1A was intended to replace the B-52 in SAC. It was designed as a Mach 2 high-altitude bomber armed with bombs or short-range missiles. Doubts about its abilitiy to survive this approach, and the increasing cost, caused its cancellation in 1977, although two B-1As flew on as test aircraft.

Rockwell B-1B

SPECIFICATIONS	
Country of origin:	United States
Type:	long-range multi-role strategic bomber
Powerplant:	four 136.9kN (30,780lb) General Electric F101-GE-102 turbofans
Performance:	maximum speed at high altitude 1328km/h (825mph); service ceiling 15,240m (50,000ft); range on internal fuel 12,000km (7455 miles)
Weights:	empty 87,090kg (192,000lb); maximum take-off 216,634kg (477,000lb)
Dimensions:	wingspan 41.67m (136ft 8.5in) unswept, 23.84m (78ft 2.5in) swept; length 44.81m (147ft); height 10.36m (34ft); wing area 181.16 sq m (1950 sq ft)
Armament:	three internal bays with provision for up to 34,019kg (75,000lb) of weapons, plus eight underfuselage stations with a capacity of 26,762kg (59,000lb)

In the early days after its service entry in 1985, several B-1B aircraft were lost after engine failures. Very low-level penetration missions are dependent on state-of-the-art avionics, including a satellite communications link, Doppler radar altimeter, forward-looking and terrain-following radars, and a defensive suite weighing over a ton.

Northrop B-2

SPECIFICATIONS	
Country of origin:	United States
Type:	strategic bomber and missile-launch platform
Powerplant:	four 84.5kN (19,000lb) General Electric F118-GE-110 turbofans
Performance:	max speed 764km/h (475mph); service ceiling 15,240m (50,000ft); range on high-level mission loaded 11,675km (7255 miles)
Weights:	empty 45,360kg (100,000lb); maximum take-off 181,437kg (400,000lb)
Dimensions:	wingspan 52.43m (172ft); length 21.03m (69ft); height 5.18m (17ft); wing area more than 464.50 sq m (5,000 sq ft)
Armament:	two internal bomb bays each carrying one eight-round Boeing Rotary launcher for a total of 16 1.1 megaton B83 thermonuclear free-fall bombs

Since 1978, the B-2 has been developed to a US Air Force requirement for a strategic penetration bomber to complement and replace the Rockwell B-1 Lancer and the Boeing B-52 Stratofortress. The B-2's radar reflectivity is very low because of smooth blended surfaces and the use of radiation-absorbent materials. This image shows the first B-2A, Spirit of America.

China

The People's Liberation Army Air Force (PLAAF) has almost exclusively been equipped with aircraft of Soviet origin since its formation in 1949. When relations broke down between the two powers in 1960, Chinese state aircraft factories kept producing the same designs, in many cases long after production had ended in Russia. China supplied many fighters to Pakistan, North Korea and other nations. Today, China assembles Russian as well as indigenous designs.

Shenyang FT-6

The Shenyang FT-6 was the Chinese-produced version of the MiG-19UTI advanced trainer. Known as the JJ-6 in China, it replaced the FT-5 (JJ-5) in service with Egypt and Pakistan. Egypt's FT-6s served with 20 and 21 Squadrons of the EAF's 221 fighter ground-attack brigade.

SPECIFICATIONS	
Country of origin:	China
Type:	two-seat conversion trainer
Powerplant:	two 36.78kN (8267lb) Liming Wopen-6A (Tumansky RD-9B) afterburning turbojet engines
Performance:	maximum speed 1540km/h (957mph); service ceiling 17,900m (58,725ft); range with internal fuel 1390km (864 miles)
Weights:	empty 5760kg (12,699lb); maximum take-off weight 10,000kg (22,046lb)
Dimensions:	wingspan 9.2m (30ft 2.25in); length (without probe) 13.3m (43ft 8in); height 3.88m (12ft 8.75in); wing area 25 sq m (269.11 sq ft)
Armament:	one 30mm NR-30 cannon, four external hardpoints with provision for up to 500kg (1102lb) of stores

Harbin H-5

The Harbin Aircraft Manufacturing Corporation began as an aircraft-repair plant but went on to produce thousands of the H-5 (H standing for *Hongzha* or bomber), from 1965 to 1984. The H-5 was a reverse-engineered Il-28 'Beagle' and served past 2000 in China. The last user is probably North Korea.

SPECIFICATIONS	
Country of origin:	USSR
Type:	three-seat bomber & ground attack/dual control trainer/torpedo carrier
Powerplant:	two 26.3kN (5952lb) Klimov VK-1 turbojets
Performance:	maximum speed 902 km/h (560mph); service ceiling 12,300m (40,355ft); range 2180km (1355 miles); with bomb load 1100km (684 miles)
Weights:	empty 12890kg (28,418lb); maximum take-off weight 21,200kg (46,738lb)
Dimensions:	wingspan 21.45sq m (70ft 4.5in); length 17.65m (57ft 10.75in); height 6.7m (21ft 11.8in); wing area 60.8 sq m (654.47 sq ft)
Armament:	four 23mm NR-23 cannon (in nose and tail turret); internal bomb capacity of up to 1000kg (2205lb), maximum bomb capacity 3000kg (6614lb); torpedo version had provision for two 400mm light torpedoes

Shenyang J-6

When Sino-Soviet relations cooled in 1960, locally manufactured components were used to assemble Mikoyan-Gurevich MiG-19Ss. The Chinese-built MiG-19S was designated J-6 and entered service in mid-1962, becoming its standard day fighter. Production numbered in the thousands.

SPECIFICATIONS	
Country of origin:	China
Type:	single-seat day fighter
Powerplant:	two 31.9kN (7165lb) Shenyang WP-6 turbojets
Performance:	maximum speed 1540km/h (957mph); service ceiling 17,900m (58,725ft); range with internal fuel 1390km (864 miles)
Weights:	empty 5760kg (12,699lb); maximum take-off 10,000kg (22,046lb)
Dimensions:	wingspan 9.2m (30ft 2.25in); length 14.9m (48ft 10.5in); height 3.88m (12ft 8.75in); wing area 25 sq m (269.11 sq ft)
Armament:	three 30mm NR-30 cannon; four external hardpoints with provision for up to 500kg (1102lb) of stores, including air-to-air missiles, 250kg bombs, 55mm rocket-launcher pods, 212mm rockets or drop tanks

Shenyang F-6

Pakistan was a major user of the F-6 (Chinese J-6), and they were extensively used in the 1971 war with India, acquitting themselves well against the IAF's Su-7s and Hunters. This example served with No 11 Squadron, Pakistan Air Force, in around 1970.

SPECIFICATIONS	
Country of origin:	China
Type:	single-seat day fighter
Powerplant:	two 31.9kN (7165lb) Shenyang WP-6 turbojets
Performance:	maximum speed 1540km/h (957mph); service ceiling 17,900m (58,725ft); range with internal fuel 1390km (864 miles)
Weights:	empty 5760kg (12,699lb); maximum take-off 10,000kg (22,046lb)
Dimensions:	wingspan 9.2m (30ft 2.25in); length 14.9m (48ft 10.5in); height 3.88m (12ft 8.75in); wing area 25 sq m (269.11 sq ft)
Armament:	three 30mm NR-30 cannon; four external hardpoints with provision for up to 500kg (1102lb) of stores, including air-to-air missiles, 250kg bombs, 55mm rocket-launcher pods, 212mm rockets or drop tanks

Chengdu F-7P Airguard

The Pakistan Air Force operates many Chengdu F-7s – Chinese-produced MiG-21s – and made technical contributions to the F-7M, a modernized version. It also commissioned the F-7P Airguard with new radar and weapons. F-7Ps are being further upgraded with an Italian radar.

SPECIFICATIONS	
Country of origin:	China
Type:	single-engined fighter
Powerplant:	one 59.8kN (13,448lb) thrust Liyang afterburning turbojet engine
Performance:	maximum speed 2175km/h (1350mph); range 1740km (1081 miles); service ceiling 18,200m (59,720ft)
Weights:	empty (5275kg (11,629lb); loaded 7531kg (16,603lb)
Dimensions:	span 7.15m (23ft 6in); length 13.95m (45ft 9in); height 4.11m (13ft 6in); wing area 23 sq m (248 sq ft)
Armament:	two 30mm Type 30-1 cannon; pods for 57mm or 90mm rockets; up to 1300kg (2866lb) of bombs

Eurofighter Typhoon

In May 1988, an agreement was signed between the United Kingdom, West Germany and Italy to develop the Eurofighter. Spain joined in November of that year. The aircraft was designed ostensibly for the air-to-air role, with secondary air-to-surface capability. With its canard design and fly-by-wire control system, the aircraft is supremely manoeuvrable and has achieved considerable export success, with examples in service with Austria and Saudi Arabia as well as the four partner nations.

Typhoon T.1

The two-seat Typhoon has the same combat capability as the single-seater. This Typhoon T.1 of No. 29 Squadron, RAF is depicted dropping a Paveway IV laser/GPS-guided bomb. It is fitted with a PIRATE (Passive InfraRed Airborne Tracking Equipment) sensor forward of the cockpit.

SPECIFICATIONS	
Country of origin:	Germany/Italy/Spain/United Kingdom
Type:	twin-seat fighter/trainer
Powerplant:	two 90kN (20,250lb) Eurojet EJ200 turbofans
Performance:	maximum speed at 11,000m (36,090ft) 2125km/h (1321mph); combat radius about 463 and 556km
Weights:	empty 10,000 kg (22,044 lb); maximum take-off weight 23,000 kg (50,705 lb)
Dimensions:	wingspan 10.5m (34ft 5.5in); length 16.0m (52 ft 6 in); height 4m (13ft 1.5in); wing area 52.4 sq m (564.05 sq ft)
Armament:	one 27mm Mauser cannon; thirteen fuselage hardpoints for a wide variety of stores

Eurofighter Typhoon DA-2

The first British Typhoon was the second development aircraft DA-2. Flown initially with Turbo-Union RB.119 engines, it later received the Eurojet EJ 200 engines intended for the production aircraft. The Royal Air Force plans to acquire 232 Typhoons in three main tranches.

SPECIFICATIONS	
Country of origin:	Germany/Italy/Spain/United Kingdom
Type:	multi-role fighter
Powerplant:	two 9185kg (20,250lb) Eurojet EJ200 turbofans
Performance:	maximum speed at 11,000m (36,090ft) 2125km/h (1321mph); combat radius about 463 and 556km
Weights:	empty 9750kg (21,495lb); maximum take-off weight 21,000kg (46,297lb)
Dimensions:	wingspan 10.5m (34ft 5.5in); length 14.5m (47ft 4in); height 4m (13ft 1.5in); wing area 52.4 sq m (564.05 sq ft)
Armament:	one 27mm Mauser cannon; thirteen fuselage hardpoints for a wide variety of stores

BAe EAP

The BAe EAP (Experimental Aircraft Prototype) was built to test concepts for the proposed European Fighter Aircraft (EFA), which later became the Typhoon. It incorporated many parts from the Tornado, including its engines and tailfin. Nearly 200 test flights were made from 1986.

SPECIFICATIONS	
Country of origin:	United Kingdom
Type:	experimental aircraft prototype
Powerplant:	two 71.3kN (16,000lb) thrust Turbo-Union RB199-104 turbofan engines
Performance:	maximum speed 2414km/h (1500mph); range unknown; service ceiling unknown
Weights:	empty 9935kg (21,900lb); maximum 18,145kg (40,000lb)
Dimensions:	span 10.5m (34ft 5in); length 16.8m (55ft 1in); height 5.8m (19ft); wing area 50 sq m (538 sq ft)
Armament:	none

MiG-29 'Fulcrum'

In 1972, the Soviet Air Force began seeking a replacement for the MiG-21, -23, Sukhoi Su-15, and -17 fleets then in service. The MiG bureau submitted the winning entry, and flight testing of the new fighter – designated 'Ram L' (later 'Fulcrum') by Western intelligence – began in October 1977. First deliveries of the aircraft were made to Soviet Frontal Aviation units in 1983 and the type became operational in 1985. More than 600 of the first production model, the 'Fulcrum-A', were delivered.

Mikoyan-Gurevich MiG-29 'Fulcrum-A'

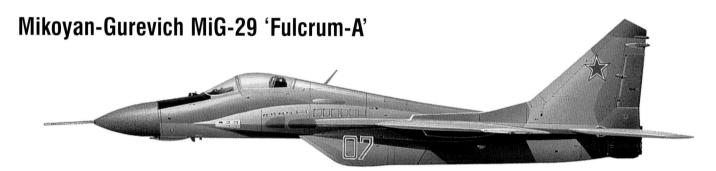

The MiG-29 was first seen clearly in the West when a squadron from Kubinka Air Base, including the aircraft illustrated, visited Finland's Kuopio-Rissala Air Base in July 1986. Many assumptions about Soviet aircraft, including poor build quality, were dispelled. The first MiG-29s visited Farnborough in 1988.

SPECIFICATIONS	
Country of origin:	USSR
Type:	single-seat air-superiority fighter with secondary ground-attack capability
Powerplant:	two 81.4kN (18,298lb) Sarkisov RD-33 turbofans
Performance:	maximum speed 2443km/h (1518mph); service ceiling 17,000m (55,775ft); range with internal fuel 1500km (932 miles)
Weights:	empty 10,900kg (24,030lb); maximum take-off 18,500kg (40,785lb)
Dimensions:	wingspan 11.36m (37ft 3.75in); length (including probe) 17.32m (56ft 10in); height 7.78m (25ft 6.25in); wing area 35.2 sq m (378.9 sq ft)
Armament:	one 30mm GSh-30 cannon with 150 rounds, eight external hardpoints with provision for up to 4500kg (9921lb) of stores

Mikoyan-Gurevich MiG-29UB 'Fulcrum-B'

Although capable of carrying the same weapons load as the single-seat MiG-29, the MiG-29UB's offensive capacity is limited by its lack of radar. The infrared search-and-track (IRST) sensor was retained, allowing cueing of short-range missiles. Romania has now retired its 'Fulcrums'.

SPECIFICATIONS	
Country of origin:	USSR
Type:	single-seat air-superiority fighter with secondary ground-attack capability
Powerplant:	two 81.4kN (18,298lb) Sarkisov RD-33 turbofans
Performance:	maximum speed 2232km/h (1387mph); service ceiling 17,762m (58,275ft); range 1835km (1140 miles)
Weights:	empty 15,300kg (33,731lb); maximum 19,700kg (43,431lb)
Dimensions:	wingspan 11.36m (37ft 3.75in); length 17.42m (57ft 1in); height 7.78m (25ft 6.25in); wing area 35.2 sq m (378.9 sq ft)
Armament:	one 30mm GSh-30 cannon with 150 rounds, eight external hardpoints with provision for up to 4500kg (9921lb) of stores

Mikoyan-Gurevich MiG-29 'Fulcrum-A'

Iran received anything from 24 to 40 MiG-29s from the Soviet Union, and may also have integrated a number of Iraqi aircraft into its inventory that fled in 1991. Only two squadrons are known to be equipped with them, the 11th Fighter Squadron at Tehran-Mehrabad and the 23rd at Tabriz.

SPECIFICATIONS	
Country of origin:	USSR
Type:	single-seat air-superiority fighter with secondary ground-attack capability
Powerplant:	two 81.4kN (18,298lb) Sarkisov RD-33 turbofans
Performance:	maximum speed 2443km/h (1518mph); service ceiling 17,000m (55,775ft); range with internal fuel 1500km (932 miles)
Weights:	empty 10,900kg (24,030lb); maximum take-off 18,500kg (40,785lb)
Dimensions:	wingspan 11.36m (37ft 3.75in); length (including probe) 17.32m (56ft 10in); height 7.78m (25ft 6.25in); wing area 35.2 sq m (378.9 sq ft)
Armament:	one 30mm GSh-30 cannon with 150 rounds, eight external hardpoints with provision for up to 4500kg (9921lb) of stores

Mikoyan-Gurevich MiG-29M 'Fulcrum D'

Work commenced on advanced versions of the MiG-29 at the end of the 1970s, with attention paid to improving its range and versatility. One of the most significant changes was the incorporation of an advanced analogue fly-by-wire control system. Physical appearance is similar, although the MiG-29M has an extended chord tailplane and a recontoured dorsal fairing.

SPECIFICATIONS	
Country of origin:	USSR
Type:	single-seat air-superiority fighter with secondary ground-attack capability
Powerplant:	two 92.1kN (20,725lb) Sarkisov RD-33K turbofans
Performance:	max speed 2300km/h (1430mph); service ceiling 17,000m (55,775ft); range with internal fuel 1500km (932 miles)
Weights:	empty 10,900kg (24,030lb); maximum take-off 18,500kg (40,785lb)
Dimensions:	wingspan 11.36m (37ft 3.75in); length (including probe) 17.32m (56ft 10in); height 7.78m (25ft 6.25in); wing area 35.2 sq m (378.9 sq ft)
Armament:	one 30mm GSh-30 cannon with 150 rounds, six external hardpoints with provision for up to 3000kg (6614lb) of stores

Mikoyan-Gurevich MiG-29K

The carrier-capable MiG-29K was tested in the early 1990s, but development stalled due to financial issues. This aircraft made the first landing of a conventional fixed-wing aircraft on a Soviet carrier in September 1990. A modernized version of the MiG-29K has been sold to India.

SPECIFICATIONS	
Country of origin:	USSR
Type:	single-seat air-superiority fighter with secondary ground-attack capability
Powerplant:	two 92.1kN (20,725lb) Sarkisov RD-33K turbofans
Performance:	maximum speed above 11000m (36,090ft) 2300km/h (1430mph); service ceiling 17,000m (55,775ft); range 2900km (1802 miles)
Weights:	maximum 22,400kg (49,340lb)
Dimensions:	span 12m (39ft 4in); length 17.27m (56ft 8in); height 4.73m (15ft 6in); wing area 41.6 sq m (448 sq ft)
Armament:	one 30mm GSh-30 cannon with 150 rounds, six external hardpoints with provision for up to 3000kg (6614lb) of stores

India

The modern Indian Air Force (Bharatiya Vayu Sena) has always chosen its combat aircraft from a variety of international suppliers, in keeping with India's non-aligned status. Until recently, the United States has made little headway in India, and Russia, the United Kingdom, France and various European consortiums have provided most equipment. Hindustan Aeronautics Ltd (HAL) has long assembled foreign designs and built some indigenous trainers, but it is now designing combat aircraft locally.

Hawker Siddeley/HAL 748M

The Hawker Siddeley (BAe) 748 was just one of the many types produced under licence by HAL, which built 69 aircraft beginning in 1964. About half are still in service for communication and transport training duties. One was tested as an AEW platform with a large rotodome on a dorsal mount.

SPECIFICATIONS	
Country of origin:	United Kingdom and India
Type:	twin-engined military transport
Powerplant:	two1700kW (2280hp) Rolls-Royce Dart RDa 7 Mk 536-2 turboprop engines
Performance:	maximum speed 452km/h (281mph); range 2630km (1645 miles); service ceiling 7620m (25,000ft)
Weights:	empty 11,671kg (25,730lb); maximum 29,092kg (46,500lb)
Dimensions:	span 31.23m (102ft 6in); length 20.42m (67ft); height 7.57m (24ft 10in); wing area 77 sq m (829 sq ft)
Armament:	none

Ilyushin Il-76TD Gajaraj 'Candid'

Known as the *Gajaraj* (King Elephant), the Il-76 is India's main heavy airlifter, with nearly 30 in service. As well as aircraft bought from the Soviet Union in the mid-1980s, a further six Il-78 tanker versions were obtained second-hand from Uzbekistan after 2001.

SPECIFICATIONS	
Country of origin:	USSR (now CIS)
Type:	heavy freight transport
Powerplant:	four 117.6kN (26,455lb) Soloviev D-30KP-1 turbofans
Performance:	maximum speed 850km/h (528mph); maximum cruising altitude 12,000m (39,370ft); range 5000km (3107 miles)
Weights:	empty about 75,000kg (165,347lb); maximum take-off weight 170,000kg (374,786lb)
Dimensions:	wingspan 50.5m (165ft 8.2in); length 46.59m (152ft 10.25in); height 14.76m (48ft 5in); wing area 300 sq m (3229.28 sq ft)
Armament:	provision for two 23mm cannon in tail

Mikoyan-Gurevich MiG-21FL 'Fishbed E'

The MiG-21FL was the first major variant of the 'Fishbed' to enter Indian service and was flown by 10 squadrons. The MiG-21 remains in IAF service with the MiG-21bis 'Bison', an upgraded variant with a modernized cockpit, improved radar warning systems and beyond visual range missiles.

SPECIFICATIONS	
Country of origin:	USSR
Type:	single-seat all-weather multi role fighter
Powerplant:	one 73.5kN (16,535lb) Tumanskii R-25 turbojets
Performance:	maximum speed above 11,000m (36,090ft) 2229km/h (1385mph); service ceiling 17,500m (57,400ft); range 1160km (721 miles)
Weights:	empty 5200kg (11,464lb); maximum take-off weight 10,400kg (22,925lb)
Dimensions:	wingspan 7.15m (23ft 5.5in); length (including probe) 15.76m (51ft 8.5in); height 4.1m (13ft 5.5in); wing area 23 sq m (247.58 sq ft)
Armament:	one 23mm GSh-23 twin-barrell cannon in underbelly pack, four underwing pylons with provision for about 1500kg (3307kg) of stores

SEPECAT Jaguar

This Jaguar IS (Indian Single-seater), of No 5 Squadron 'The Tuskers', was one of 35 supplied as pattern aircraft from the United Kingdom before local production by HAL began. At least 95 Jaguars in strike, maritime-attack and trainer variants have been built in India.

SPECIFICATIONS	
Country of origin:	France and United Kingdom
Type:	single-seat tactical support and strike aircraft
Powerplant:	one 56.4kN (12,676lb) thrust Tumansky R-11 afterburning turbojet engine
Performance:	maximum speed at 11,000m (36,090ft) 1699km/h (1056mph); combat radius on lo-lo-lo mission with internal fuel 537km (334 miles)
Weights:	empty 7700kg (16,976lb); maximum take-off weight 15,700kg (34,613lb)
Dimensions:	wingspan 8.69m (28ft 6in); length 16.83m (55ft 2.5in); height 4.89m (16ft 0.5in); wing area 24.18 sq m (260.28 sq ft)
Armament:	two 30mm Aden Mk.4 cannon with 150rpg; seven external hardpoints with provision for 4763kg (10,500lb) of stores

Dassault Mirage 2000H Vajra

Export contracts for the agile and capable 2000C were plentiful, and by 1990 Dassault had received orders from Abu Dhabi, Egypt, Greece, India and Peru. The Indian aircraft pictured is one of 40 ordered in October 1982 that carry the designation 2000H. Final delivery was made in September 1984. Vajra means 'Thunder'. A follow-on order for a further nine aircraft was made in March 1986.

SPECIFICATIONS	
Country of origin:	France
Type:	single-seat air-superiority and attack fighter
Powerplant:	one 97.1kN (21,834lb) SNECMA M53-P2 turbofan
Performance:	maximum speed 2338km/h (1453mph); service ceiling 18,000m (59,055ft); range with 1000kg (2205lb) load 1480km (920 miles)
Weights:	empty 7500kg (16,534lb); maximum take-off weight 17,000kg (37,480lb)
Dimensions:	wingspan 9.13m (29ft 11.5in); length 14.36m (47ft 1.25in); height 5.2m (17ft 0.75in); wing area 41 sq m (441.3 sq ft)
Armament:	two DEFA 554 cannon with 125rpg; nine external pylons with provision for up to 6300kg of stores

Dassault Rafale

The Rafale has been designed and built to replace the fleet of SEPECAT Jaguars with L'Armée de l'Air, and to form part of the new French nuclear-carrier force's air wing. The first flight took place on 4 July 1986. The airframe is largely constructed of composite materials, with a fly-by-wire control system. Early flight trials were particularly encouraging, with the aircraft achieving Mach 1.8 on only its second flight. Original production orders have been cut since the end of the Cold War.

Rafale M

Rafale is produced in three versions: the Rafale C single-seat, multi-role aircraft for the French air force; the two-seat Rafale B; and the navalized Rafale M, a production version of which is shown here.

SPECIFICATIONS	
Country of origin:	France
Type:	two-seat multi-role combat aircraft
Powerplant:	two 73kN (16,424lb) SNECMA M88-2 turbofans
Performance:	max speed 2130km/h (1324mph); service ceiling classified; combat radius 1854km (1152 miles)
Weights:	19,500kg (42,990lb) loaded
Dimensions:	wing span 10.9m (35ft 9in); length 15.3m (50ft 2in); height 5.34m (17ft 6in)
Armament:	one 30mm DEFA 791B cannon, up to 6000kg (13,228lb) of external stores

Dassault Rafale A

SPECIFICATIONS

Country of origin:	France
Type:	prototype combat aircraft
Powerplant:	two 72.96kN (16,402lb) thrust SNECMA M88-2 afterburning turbofan engines
Performance:	maximum speed 2125km/h (1321mph); range unknown; service ceiling unknown
Weights:	empty 9500kg (20,944lb); maximum 20,000kg (44,092lb)
Dimensions:	span 11.2m (36ft 9in); length 15.8m (51ft 10in); height unknown; wing area 47 sq m (506 sq ft)
Armament:	none

Under the Avion de Combat Experimental (ACX) programme, Dassault built the Rafale A demonstrator, which at the time met French air force and navy requirements for lighter aircraft better than the Eurofighter 2000. The Rafale A was slightly larger than the production Rafale models.

Although both L'Armée de l'Air and the French navy considered the Eurofighter to replace the SEPECAT Jaguar, the smaller and lighter Rafale was chosen. This is a Rafale-M navalized fighter.

Rafale M

SPECIFICATIONS

Country of origin:	France
Type:	carrier-based multi-role combat aircraft
Powerplant:	two 73kN (16,424lb) SNECMA M88-2 turbofans
Performance:	maximum speed at high altitude 2130km/h (1324mph); combat radius air-to-air mission 1853km (1152 miles)
Weights:	empty equipped 9800kg; maximum take-off weight 19,500kg (42,990lb)
Dimensions:	wingspan 10.9m (35ft 9.175in); length 15.3m (50ft 2.5in); height 5.34m (17ft 6.25in); wing area 46 sq m (495.1 sq ft)
Armament:	one 30mm DEFA 791B cannon, 14 external hardpoints with provision for up to 6000kg (13,228lb) of stores

Tiltrotors

From the early 1950s, aircraft manufacturers sought to overcome the speed and range limitations of helicopters by creating hybrid aircraft that could switch between hovering and wingborne flight. Various concepts were tested over the years, including tilt-wings, tilt-props and tilt-fans. The best of these was the tiltrotor, which used fixed wings and tilting engine nacelles to turn propellers into rotors, and vice versa.

Dornier Do 29

The 1950s and 1960s saw an explosion of research into vertical and short take-off and landing aircraft in Germany. The smallest and lightest was the Dornier Do 29, derived from the Do 27. The Do 29, which first flew in December 1958, replaced the Do 27's single nose-mounted engine with two pusher turboprops that could be tilted downwards as much as 90°.

SPECIFICATIONS

Country of origin:	Germany
Type:	single-seat V/STOL aircraft
Powerplant:	two 201kW (270hp) Lycoming GO-480-B1A6 six-cylinder piston engines
Performance:	cruising speed 290km/h (180mph); service ceiling unknown
Weights:	maximum 2500kg (5511lb)
Dimensions:	wingspan 13.2m (43ft 4in); length 9.5m (31ft 2in); height unknown
Armament:	none

Canadair CL-84-1

Canada's Dynavert was a private-venture attempt to create a tilt-wing tactical transport and gunship for the export market. The CL-84 began hovering trials in May 1965 and was well advanced in its test programme when it crashed two years later. Improvements and further trials were made, but the Canadian military showed little interest in the project and development ceased.

SPECIFICATIONS

Country of origin:	Canada
Type:	tilt-wing tactical transport plane and gunship
Powerplant:	two 1118kW (1500hp) Lycoming LTC1K-4A turboprop engines
Performance:	maximum speed 517km/h (321mph); service ceiling unknown
Weights:	maximum 6577kg (14,500lb)
Dimensions:	span 10.56m (34ft 8in); length 16.34m (53ft 8in); height (wing horizontal) 4.34m (14ft 3in)
Armament:	none

TILTROTORS TIMELINE

 1958
 1965
 1977

Bell XV-15

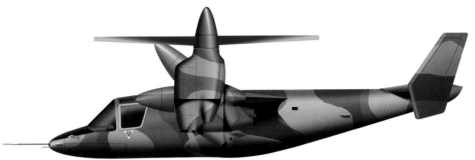

To prove its concept of tilting rotors, Bell produced the XV-15 in 1977. A relatively simple craft, its successful testing paved the way for the V-22. The XV-15 also led to the Bell-Agusta BA.609 of similar size, which is being offered for civil and military use, including potentially as a V-22 escort.

SPECIFICATIONS	
Country of origin:	United States
Type:	Tiltrotor demonstrator
Powerplant:	two 1156kW (1550hp) Avco Lycoming LTC1K-4K turboshaft engines
Performance:	maximum speed 557km/h (350mph); range 825km (515 miles); service ceiling 8840m (29,500ft)
Weights:	empty 4574kg (10,083lb); maximum 6009kg (13,248lb)
Dimensions:	span 17.42m (57ft 2in); length 12.83m (42ft 1in); height 3.86m (12ft 8in); rotor diameter 7.62m (25ft)
Armament:	none

Bell/Boeing V-22 Osprey

Turning the tiltrotor concept into a useful military aircraft took much longer and was much costlier than anticipated. Its complex systems and unusual flight characteristics contributed to several accidents. This is the second Full-Scale Development (FSD) aircraft, which first flew in August 1989.

SPECIFICATIONS	
Country of origin:	United States
Type:	Tiltrotor transport prototype
Powerplant:	two 4586kW (6150hp) Allison T406-AO-400 turboshaft engines
Performance:	maximum speed 584km/h (363mph); range 3892km (2418 miles); service ceiling 7925m (26,000ft)
Weights:	empty 14,433kg (31,820lb); maximum 21,546kg (47,500lb)
Dimensions:	span 25.55m (84ft 6in); length 17.47m (57ft 4in); height 6.63m (21ft 9in); rotor diameter 11.58m (38ft)
Armament:	none

Bell/Boeing MV-22 Osprey

The Osprey is in service with the US Marines as the MV-22B assault transport (illustrated) and the USAF as the CV-22 for special-forces use. The much modified production aircraft first saw operational service in Iraq in 2008 with the Marines, proving superior to helicopters for most missions.

SPECIFICATIONS	
Country of origin:	United States
Type:	Tiltrotor transport
Powerplant:	Powerplant: two 4586kW (6150hp) Rolls-Royce AE1107C turboshaft engines
Performance:	maximum speed 584km/h (363mph); range 3892km (2418 miles); service ceiling 7925m (26,000ft)
Weights:	empty 14,433kg (31,820lb); maximum 23,495kg (52,600lb)
Dimensions:	span 25.55m (84ft 6in); length 17.47m (57ft 4in); height 6.73m (22ft 1in); rotor diameter 11.58m (38ft)
Armament:	one 7.62mm M240 machine gun on rear ramp

1989

2002

From Cobra to Super Hornet

The F/A-18 Hornet was originated by Northrop, developed and manufactured by McDonnell Douglas, and is now a Boeing product. Along the way, it has evolved from a lightweight fighter into a replacement for the F-14 Tomcat, A-6 Intruder and F-4 Phantom with the Navy and Marine Corps. The F/A-18A to D 'Legacy' Hornets had considerable export success, which the FA-18E/F 'Super Bug' looks likely to emulate.

Northrop YF-17

The YF-17 competed in a 'fly-off' evaluation for the USAF's Lightweight Fighter competition in the mid-1970s. The contest was won by the YF-16, but Northrop collaborated with McDonnell Douglas on a production version that became the substantially different F/A-18 Hornet.

SPECIFICATIONS	
Country of origin:	United States
Type:	twin-engined fighter prototype
Powerplant:	two 64.08kN (14,414lb) thrust General Electric YJ101-GE-100 turbojet engines
Performance:	maximum speed 2124km/h (1316mph); range 4500km (2790 miles); service ceiling 18,288m (59,800ft)
Weights:	empty 9527kg (20,960lb); maximum 13,894kg (30,567lb)
Dimensions:	span 10.67m (35ft); length 16.92m (55ft 6in); height 4.42m (14ft 6in); wing area 32.51 sq m (350 sq ft)
Armament:	one 20mm M61A1 Vulcan cannon; two AIM-9 Sidewinder AAMs

McDonnell Douglas F/A-18A Hornet

Although the Hornet was originally to have been produced in both fighter and attack versions, service aircraft are easily adapted to either role. Deliveries to the US Navy began in May 1980 and were completed in 1987.

SPECIFICATIONS	
Country of origin:	United States
Type:	single-seat fighter and strike aircraft
Powerplant:	two 71.1kN (16,000lb) General Electric F404-GE-400 turbofans
Performance:	maximum speed at 12,190m (40,000ft) 1912km/h (1183mph); combat ceiling 15,240m (50,000ft); combat radius 1065km (662 miles)
Weights:	empty 10,455kg (23,050lb); maximum take-off 25,401kg (56,000lb)
Dimensions:	wingspan 11.43m (37ft 6in); length 17.07m (56ft); height 4.66m (15ft 3.5in); wing area 37.16 sq m (400 sq ft)
Armament:	one 20mm M61A1 Vulcan rotary cannon; nine external hardpoints with provision for up to 7711kg (17,000kg) of stores

COBRA/SUPER HORNET TIMELINE  1974  1978  1979

McDonnell Douglas F/A-18B Hornet

The combat-capable, tandem-seat trainer Hornet is designated F/A-18B. The aircraft is produced with the same navigation/attack systems as the single-seat variant, although internal fuel capacity has been reduced due to the inclusion of a second seat under a longer canopy. Performance is similar to the single-seat variant, with the exception of range.

SPECIFICATIONS	
Country of origin:	United States
Type:	tandem-seat conversion trainer with combat capability
Powerplant:	two 71.1kN (16,000lb) General Electric F404-GE-400 turbofans
Performance:	maximum speed at 12,190m (40,000ft) 1912km/h (1183mph); combat ceiling about 15,240m (50,000ft); combat radius 1020km (634 miles) on attack mission
Weights:	empty 10,455kg (23,050lb); maximum take-off 25,401kg (56,000lb)
Dimensions:	wingspan 11.43m (37ft 6in); length 17.07m (56ft); height 4.66m (15ft 3.5in); wing area 37.16 sq m (400 sq ft)
Armament:	one 20mm M61A1 Vulcan rotary cannon with 570 rounds; nine external hardpoints with provision for up to 7711kg (17,000kg) of stores

McDonnell Douglas F/A-18C Hornet

The F/A-18A was updated in the late 1980s with new radar and avionics, and the ability to carry new weapons such as the AMRAAM missile. After the Gulf War, Kuwait took delivery of F/A-18Cs to replace its A-4KU Skyhawks. Other F/A-18C operators include Switzerland and Finland.

SPECIFICATIONS	
Country of origin:	United States
Type:	twin-engined fighter/attack aircraft
Powerplant:	two 79.2kN (17,750lb) thrust General Electric F404-GE-402 turbofan engines
Performance:	maximum speed 1915km/h (1190mph); service ceiling 15,000m (50,000ft); combat radius 1065km (662 miles)
Weights:	empty 11,200kg (24,700lb); maximum 23,400kg (51,500lb)
Dimensions:	wingspan 11.43m (37ft 6in); length 17.07m (56ft); height 4.66m (15ft 3.5in); wing area 37.16 sq m (400 sq ft)
Armament:	one 20mm M61A1 Vulcan six-barrel rotary cannon with 570 rounds, nine external hardpoints with provision for up to 7711kg (17,000lb) of stores

Boeing F/A-18E Super Hornet

The Super Hornet, built in single-seat F/A-18E and two-seat F/A-18F versions, has very little in common with its forebears except overall configuration. As well as fighter and attack missions, the F/A-18E can be used as a tanker aircraft with a centreline 'buddy' refuelling pod.

SPECIFICATIONS	
Country of origin:	United States
Type:	carrier-based single-seat fighter/attack aircraft
Powerplant:	two 97.90kN (22,000lb) thrust General Electric F414-GE-400 afterburning turbofan engines
Performance:	maximum speed 1190 km/h (1190mph); combat radius 722km (449 miles); service ceiling 15,000m (50,000ft)
Weights:	empty 13,900kg (30,600lb); maximum 29,900kg (66,000lb)
Dimensions:	span 13.62m (60ft 1in); length 13.62m (44ft 9in); height 4.88m (16ft); wing area 46.45 sq m (500 sq ft)
Armament:	one 20mm M61A1 Vulcan cannon; 11 external hardpoints for up to 8050kg (17,750lb) of stores

1987

1995

Japan

Japan's post-war constitution prohibits the establishment of armed forces, but nonetheless, the nation maintains air, ground and maritime 'self-defence forces' that are amongst the most powerful in Asia. Although forbidden to export weapons systems, Japan's aviation industry produces indigenously designed trainers, transports, patrol aircraft and some combat aircraft for its own needs. Japan has also manufactured American-designed fighters, from the F-86 Sabre to the F-15 Eagle.

McDonnell Douglas F-4EJ Kai Phantom

The EJ is a licence-built air-defence version of the Phantom F-4E. The original F-4E(J) model was built by McDonnell Douglas, and the remainder under licence by Mitsubishi with Kawasaki as a subcontractor. The last was delivered in May 1981. The original batch of 45 was then updated to F-4EJ Kai standard with improved weapon and avionics systems such as digital displays.

SPECIFICATIONS

Country of origin:	United States
Type:	two-seat all-weather fighter/attack aircraft
Powerplant:	two 79.6kN (17,900lb) General Electric J79-GE-17 turbojets
Performance:	maximum speed 2390km/h (1485mph); service ceiling 19,685m (60,000ft); range on internal fuel with no weapon load 2817km (1750 miles)
Weights:	empty 12,700kg (28,000lb); maximum take-off 26,308kg (58,000lb)
Dimensions:	span 11.7m (38ft 5in); length 17.76m (58ft 3in); height 4.96m (16ft 3in); wing area 49.24 sq m (530 sq ft)
Armament:	one 20mm M61A1 Vulcan cannon and four AIM-7 Sparrow recessed under fuselage or other weapons up to 1370kg (3020lb) on centreline pylon; four wing pylons for stores to a maximum weight of 5888kg (12,980lb)

McDonnell Douglas F-15DJ Eagle

The F-15DJ is the two-seat version of the F-15C (the upgraded version of the F-15A and the principal production version) for the Japanese Air Self-Defence Force. This aircraft is configured to carry conformal fuel tanks that fit flush with the fuselage, leaving all store hardpoints available for the carriage of weapons. Twelve were delivered.

SPECIFICATIONS

Country of origin:	United States
Type:	twin-seat air superiority fighter trainer with secondary strike/attack role
Powerplant:	two 105.4kN (23,700lb) Pratt & Whitney F100-PW-220 turbofans
Performance:	maximum speed at high altitude 2655km/h (1650mph); ceiling 30,500m (100,000ft); range on internal fuel 4631km (2878 miles)
Weights:	empty 13,336kg (29,400lb); maximum take-off 30,844kg (68,000lb)
Dimensions:	wingspan 13.05m (42ft 9.75in); length 19.43in (63ft 9in); height 5.63m (18ft 5in); wing area 56.48 sq m (608 sq ft)
Armament:	one 20mm M61A1 cannon with 960 rounds, external pylons with provision for up to 10,705kg (23,600lb) of stores

JAPAN TIMELINE

 1975  1984  1985

Kawasaki EC-1

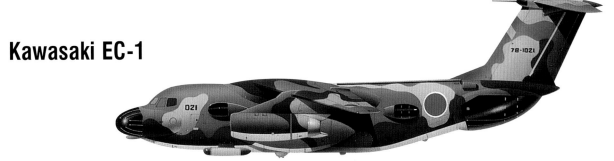

SPECIFICATIONS	
Country of origin:	Japan
Type:	ECM trainer aircraft
Powerplant:	two 64.5kN (14,500lb) Mitsubishi (Pratt & Whitney) JT8-M-9 turbofans
Performance:	maximum speed at 7620m (25,000ft) 806km/h (501mph); service ceiling 11,580m (38,000ft); range 1300km (808 miles) with 7900kg (17,417lb) payload
Weights:	empty 23320kg (51,412lb); maximum take-off weight 45,000kg (99,208lb)
Dimensions:	wingspan 30.6m (100ft 4.75in); length 30.5m (100ft 4in); height 10m (32ft 9.3in); wing area 102.5 sq m (1297.09 sq ft)
Armament:	none

First flying in 1970, the C-1 was designed specifically to replace the Curtiss C-46 Commando transport aircraft in service with the Japanese Air Self-Defence Force. This aircraft differs from standard models by distinctive radomes on the nose and tail, an ALQ-5 ECM system and antennae beneath the fuselage.

Kawasaki T-4

SPECIFICATIONS	
Country of origin:	Japan
Type:	twin-engined trainer
Powerplant:	two 32.56kN (7320lb) Ishikawajima-Harima F3-IHI-30 turbofan engines
Performance:	max speed 1038km/h (645mph); range 1668km (1036 miles); service ceiling 14,815m (48,606 ft)
Weights:	empty 3790kg (8356lb); maximum 7500kg (16,535lb)
Dimensions:	span 9.94 m (32 ft 7 in); length 13m (42 ft 8 in); height 4.6 m (15 ft 1 in); wing area 21 sq m (226 sq ft)
Armament:	two hardpoints for training bombs or rocket launchers

The Kawasaki T-4 replaced the elderly Lockheed T-33 and Fuji T-1 in service in the training role with the Japan Air Self-Defence Force. Most of the airframe is built by Fuji, with the nose section and final assembly the responsibility of Kawasaki. The JASDF's 'Blue Impulse' team flies the T-4.

Mitsubishi XF-2B

SPECIFICATIONS	
Country of origin:	Japan and United States
Type:	single-engined fighter prototype
Powerplant:	one 131.7kN (29,607lb) thrust General Electric F110-GE-129 turbofan
Performance:	maximum speed 2125km/h (1321mph); combat radius 834km (518 miles); service ceiling 20,000m (65,555ft)
Weights:	empty 9527kg (21,000lb); maximum 22,000kg (48,500lb)
Dimensions:	span 11.13m (36ft 6in); length 15.52m (50ft 11in); height 4.69m (15ft 5in); wing area 34.84 sq m (375 sq ft)
Armament:	up to 9000kg (19,840lb) of stores, including Mitsubishi AAM-3 air-to-air missiles and ASM-2 anti-ship missiles

Japan's requirement for a replacement for the Mitsubishi F-1 anti-ship attack aircraft led to a collaboration with General Dynamics to develop a version of the F-16, to be produced in Japan. The resulting F-2 was larger and heavier, and considerably more expensive, leading to a reduction in planned numbers.

1988

1995

Foxbat and Foxhound

The Mikoyan-Gurevich MiG-25 caused a sensation in the West with its Mach 3 performance, which was unmatched by any other production combat aircraft. As an interceptor and reconnaissance aircraft, it was not noted for its manoeuvrability, but its speed and altitude made it invulnerable to most contemporary weapons systems. The MiG-31 was an all-new aircraft, designed along the same lines but with two seats and a 'look-down shoot-down' capability.

Mikoyan-Gurevich MiG-25 'Foxbat'

It was designed to counter the planned B-70 bomber, but when the BO-70 programme was cancelled, the MiG-25 'Foxbat' was left in search of a role. It entered service in 1970 as an interceptor, its role now defined as being capable of countering all air targets in all weather conditions.

Mikoyan-Gurevich MiG-25R 'Foxbat'

The reconnaissance version of the 'Foxbat', the MiG-25R provided the Indian Air Force with a strategic reconnaissance capability, using two powerful cameras and SLAR radar. Known as the Garuda in IAF service, they saw the majority of their service with No 102 Squadron 'Trisonics'.

SPECIFICATIONS	
Country of origin:	USSR
Type:	single-seat reconnaissance aircraft
Powerplant:	two 109.8kN (24,691lb) Tumanskii R-15BD-300 turbojets
Performance:	maximum speed at altitude about 3339km/h (2112mph); service ceiling 27,000m (88,585ft); operational radius 900km (559 miles)
Weights:	empty 19,600kg (43,211lb); maximum take-off weight 33,400kg (73,634lb)
Dimensions:	wingspan 13.42m (44ft 0.75in); length 23.82m (78ft 1.75in); height 6.10m (20ft 0.5in); wing area not disclosed
Armament:	six external pylons for six 500kg (1102lb) bombs

SPECIFICATIONS	
Country of origin:	USSR
Type:	interceptor
Powerplant:	two 100kN (22,487lb) thrust Tumanskii R-15B-300 turbojets
Performance:	maximum speed 2974km/h (1848mph); range 1130km (702 miles); service ceiling 24,383m (80,000ft)
Weights:	loaded 37,425kg (82,508lb)
Dimensions:	span 14.02m (45ft 11in); length 23.82m (78ft 1in); height 6.1m (20ft)
Armament:	four underwing pylons for various combinations of air-to-air missiles

Mikoyan-Gurevich MiG-31 'Foxhound A'

The MiG-31 was developed during the 1970s from the impressive MiG-25 'Foxbat' to counter the threat from low-flying cruise missiles and bombers. The MiG-31 was a vast improvement over the 'Foxbat', with tandem seat cockpit, IR search and tracking sensor, and the Zaslon 'Flash Dance' pulse-Doppler radar providing genuine fire-and-forget engagement capability against multiple targets flying at lower altitudes.

SPECIFICATIONS	
Country of origin:	USSR
Type:	two-seat all weather interceptor and ECM aircraft
Powerplant:	two 151.9kN (34,171lb) Soloviev D-30F6 turbofans
Performance:	maximum speed at 17,500m (57,400ft) 3000km/h (1865mph); service ceiling 20,600m (67,600ft); combat radius 1400km (840 miles)
Weights:	empty 21,825kg (48,415lb); maximum take-off weight 46,200kg (101,850lb)
Dimensions:	wingspan 13.46m (44ft 2in); length 22.68m (74ft 5.25in); height 6.15m (20ft 2.25in); wing area 61.6 sq m (663 sq ft)
Armament:	one 23mm GSh-23-6 cannon with 260 rounds, eight external hardpoints with provision for air-to-air missiles, ECM pods or drop tanks

Sweden

Neutral Sweden has long practised self-reliance in most fields of defence procurement, to include not only locally designed combat aircraft, but the development of radars, datalinks, missiles and systems. Where components such as engines have been sourced from abroad, Swedish engineers have worked to improve them. Despite post-Cold War cutbacks, the Swedish Air Force (Flygvapent) remains one of the best-equipped and technologically advanced in Europe.

Saab A 32A Lansen N

The Lansen first flew in 1952 and has had a very long career, with a couple of examples still in use in the radiological detection role. They were used mainly as ground attack aircraft, but also as reconnaissance aircraft, radar jammers and as airborne testbeds. This particular example was heavily modified to test the Ericsson PS 37 radar for the VIggen.

SPECIFICATIONS	
Country of origin:	Sweden
Type:	all-weather and night fighter
Powerplant:	one 67.5kN (15,190lb) Svenska Flygmotor (Rolls-Royce Avon) RM6A
Performance:	maximum speed 1114km/h (692mph); service ceiling 16,013m (52,500ft); range with external fuel 3220km (2000 miles)
Weights:	unknown
Dimensions:	wingspan 13m (42ft 7.75in); length unknown; height 4.65m (15ft 3in); wing area 37.4 sq m (402.58 sq ft)
Armament:	four 30mm Aden M/55 cannon; four Rb324 (Sidewinder) air-to-air missiles or FFAR (Folding Fin Air-launched Rocket) pods

Saab JA 37 Viggen

The interceptor version of the Viggen, and an integral part of the System 37 series, was the single-seat JA 37. Externally, the aircraft closely resembles the attack AJ 37, although the fin is slightly taller and the interceptor has four elevon actuators under the wing instead of three as on other versions. Production of the JA 37 totalled 149 aircraft, with the last delivered in June 1990.

SPECIFICATIONS	
Country of origin:	Sweden
Type:	single-seat all-weather interceptor aircraft with secondary attack capability
Powerplant:	one 125kN (28,109lb) Volvo Flygmotor RM8B turbofan
Performance:	maximum speed at high altitude 2124km/h (1320mph); service ceiling 18,290m (60,000ft); combat radius on lo-lo-lo mission with external armament 500km (311 miles)
Weights:	empty 15,000kg (33,060lb); maximum take-off 20,500kg (45,194lb)
Dimensions:	wingspan 10.6m (34ft 9.25in); length 16.3m (53ft 5.75in); height 5.9m (19ft 4.25in); wing area 46 sq m (495.16 sq ft)
Armament:	one 30mm Oerlikon KCA cannon with 150 rounds; six external hardpoints with provision for 6000kg (13,228lb) of stores

SWEDEN TIMELINE

1953

1973

1978

Saab Sk 37 Viggen

The two-seat conversion trainer of the Viggen, the SK 37, had an unusual seating arrangement, with a second cockpit and canopy for the instructor. Periscopes were built into the framing to allow a forward view. The last Viggens in service were SK 37E 'Eriks' used for electronic-warfare training.

SPECIFICATIONS	
Country of origin:	Sweden
Type:	two-seat conversion trainer
Powerplant:	one 115.7kN (26,015lb) Volvo Flygmotor RM8 turbofan
Performance:	maximum speed at high altitude 2124km/h (1320mph); service ceiling 18,290m (60,000ft); range unknown
Weights:	empty 11,800kg (26,015lb); maximum take-off 20,500kg (45,194lb)
Dimensions:	wingspan 10.6m (34ft 9.25in); length 16.3m (53ft 5.75in); height 5.16m (18ft 9in); wing area 46 sq m (495.16 sq ft)
Armament:	none

North American Sabreliner TP 86

SPECIFICATIONS	
Country of origin:	United States
Type:	twin-engined avionics testbed
Powerplant:	two 14.7kN (3307lb) Pratt & Whitney JT12A-8 turbojet engines
Performance:	maximum speed 885km/h (550mph); range 4020km (2500mph); service ceiling 12,200m (40,000ft)
Weights:	empty 4199kg (9257lb); maximum 8500kg (lb)
Dimensions:	span 13.61 m (44ft 8in); length 13.76m (45ft 1in); height 4.88m (16ft); wing area 31.79 sq m (342 sq ft)
Armament:	none

Saab JAS 39A Gripen

The JAS 39 Gripen has now replaced the Viggen in Flygvapnet service. This JAS 39A wears the markings of Flygflotilj 7 at Såtenäs, the first unit to be equipped with the Gripen. Although just over 200 were ordered, Sweden is reducing its fighter force to 100 improved JAS 39C/D versions.

SPECIFICATIONS	
Country of origin:	Sweden
Type:	single-seat all-weather fighter, attack and reconnaissance aircraft
Powerplant:	one 80.5kN (18,100lb) Volvo Flygmotor RM12 turbofan
Performance:	maximum speed more than Mach 2; range on hi-lo-hi mission with external armament 3250km (2020 miles)
Weights:	empty 6622kg (14,600lb); maximum take-off 12,473kg (27,500lb)
Dimensions:	wingspan 8m (26ft 3in); length 14.1m (46ft 3in); height 4.7m (15ft 5in)
Armament:	one 27mm Mauser BK27 cannon with 90 rounds, six external hardpoints with provision for Rb71 Sky Flash and Rb24 Sidewinder air-to-air missiles, Maverick air-to-surface missiles, Rb15F anti-ship missiles, bombs, cluster bombs, rocket-launcher pods, reconnaissance pods, drop tanks and ECM pods

1981

1988

F-22 Raptor

Designed in collaboration between Lockheed and Boeing, the YF-22 won a fly-off against Northrop and McDonnell Douglas's YF-23. The production F-22A Raptor is touted as an 'air-dominance' fighter, able to outperform all current and anticipated opponents. Modern technology allows greater stealth than the F-117 without the faceted shape. The powerful engines allow the Raptor to 'supercruise', or remain supersonic without using afterburner. The engine nozzles are moveable, allowing their use to help manoeuvre the aircraft in pitch and roll.

Lockheed Martin F-22A

The first F-22A Raptor development aircraft flew in 1997 and underwent testing at Edwards Air Force Base. The first squadron was declared operational in 2007. Plans for a force of 383 Raptors were scaled back to 187 due to the 137 million-dollar cost per aircraft.

SPECIFICATIONS	
Country of origin:	United States
Type:	Stealth fighter
Powerplant:	two 160kN (35,000lb) thrust Pratt & Whitney F119-PW-100 thrust-vectoring afterburning turbofan engines
Performance:	maximum speed 2410km/h (1500mph); service ceiling 15,524m (50,000ft); combat radius 2977km (1850 miles)
Weights:	empty 19,700kg (43,340lb); maximum take-off 38,000kg (83,500lb)
Dimensions:	wingspan 13.6m (44ft 6in); length 18.9m (62ft 1in); height 5.1m (16ft 8in 8in); wing area 78.04 m2 (840 sq ft)
Armament:	one 20mm M61A2 Vulcan cannon; internal weapons bays for two AIM-9 Sidewinder and six AIM-120 ASRAAM air-to-air missiles

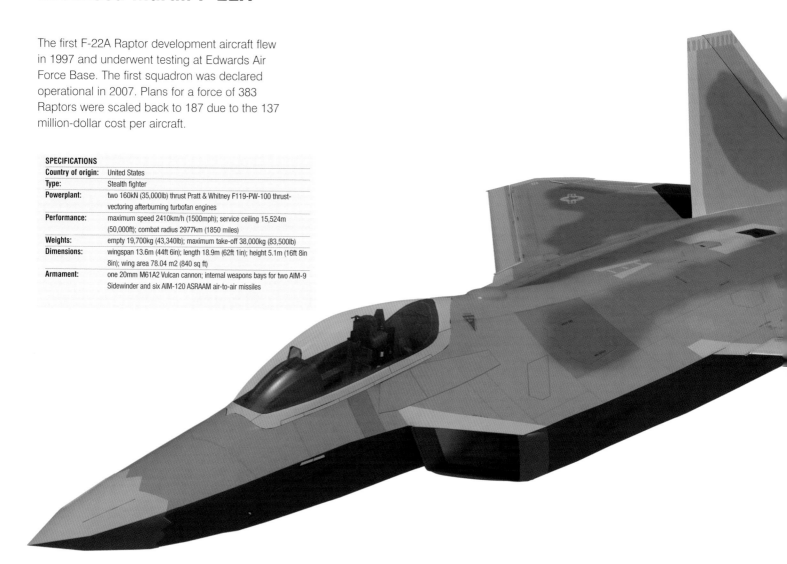

Northrop YF-23A

The Northrop design incorporated many of the stealth features seen on the B-2 Spirit bomber, and the first of two prototype aircraft – dubbed the 'Grey Ghost' – flew in August 1990. However, after a successful flight-testing programme involving both YF-23A prototypes (designated PAV-1 and -2), the aircraft was rejected in favour of the Lockheed YF-22. The two Northrop aircraft were subsequently placed in secure storage at Edwards Air Force Base. It is interesting to compare Northrop's approach to stealth with Lockheed's F-117 Nighthawk.

SPECIFICATIONS

Country of origin:	United States
Type:	single-seat tactical fighter
Powerplant:	one aircraft with two 155.6kN (35,000lb) Pratt & Whitney YF119-PW-100 turbofans; one with General Electric YF120-GE-100 turbofans
Performance:	maximum speed approximately Mach 2; service ceiling 19,812m (65,000ft); range on internal fuel 1200km (750 miles)
Weights:	empty 16,783kg (37,000lb); combat take-off 29,030kg (64,000lb)
Dimensions:	wingspan 13.2m (43ft 7in); length 20.5m (67ft 4in); height 4.2m (13ft 10in); wing area 87.8 sq m (945.07 sq ft)
Armament:	(planned) one 20mm M61 cannon, internal bay for AIM-9 Sidewinder air-to-air missiles and AIM-120 AMRAAMS, 'Have Dash 2' AAMs and 'Have Slick' air-to-surface missiles

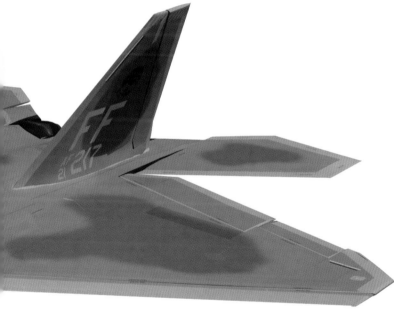

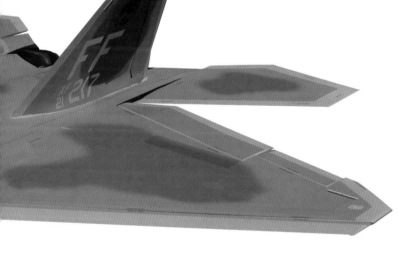

Lockheed Martin YF-22 Raptor

The first F-22A Raptor development aircraft flew in 1997 and underwent testing at Edwards Air Force Base. The first squadron was declared operational in 2007. Plans for a force of 383 Raptors were scaled back to 187 due to the cost – $137 million per aircraft.

SPECIFICATIONS

Country of origin:	United States
Type:	Stealth fighter
Powerplant:	two 155.6kN (35,000lb) thrust Pratt & Whitney F119-PW-100 thrust-vectoring afterburning turbofan engines
Performance:	maximum speed 2410km/h (1500mph); range 2977km (1850 miles); service ceiling 15,524m (50,000ft)
Weights:	empty 19,700kg (43,340lb); maximum 38,000kg (83,500lb)
Dimensions:	span 13.6m (44ft 6in); length 18.9m (62ft 1in); height 5.1m (16ft 8in); wing area 78.04 sq m (840 sq ft)
Armament:	one 20mm M61A2 Vulcan cannon; internal weapons bays for two AIM-9 Sidewinder and six AIM-120 ASRAAM air-to-air missiles

Sukhoi 'Flankers'

Development of the Su-27 began in the mid-1970s, with the aim of producing a combat aircraft for Soviet forces comparable to the McDonnell Douglas F-15 Eagle. Given this seemingly daunting design brief, Sukhoi proceeded with impressive haste, and by the end of May 1977 the prototype Su-27 had flown. Development from prototype stage was somewhat longer and involved some fundamental design changes, necessitated by poor structural strength, flutter and excessive weight.

Su-27 T-10-1 'Flanker-A'

The prototype of the Su-27 series, the T-10-1 first flew in May 1977. It suffered from excessive drag, a weak structure and other problems. Even before the second crash among the four prototypes, it was deemed inferior to the F-15, and a total redesign was ordered.

SPECIFICATIONS	
Country of origin:	USSR
Type:	Prototype twin-engined fighter
Powerplant:	two 106kN (24,000lb) thrust Lyul'ka AL-21FZAI afterburning turbofan engines
Performance:	maximum speed unknown; range unknown; service ceiling unknown
Weights:	unknown
Dimensions:	unknown
Armament:	unknown

Su-27UB 'Flanker-C'

It was not until 1980 that full-scale production of the Su-27 began, and service entry started in 1984. The aircraft represents a significant advance over previous generations of Soviet aircraft. The Su-27UB 'Flanker-C', the first variant produced, was a tandem-seat trainer.

SPECIFICATIONS	
Country of origin:	USSR
Type:	tandem-seat operational conversion trainer
Powerplant:	two 122.5kN (27,557lb) Lyul'ka AL-31M turbofans
Performance:	maximum speed 2150km/h (1335mph); service ceiling 17,500m (57,400ft); combat radius 1500km (930 miles)
Weights:	maximum take-offweight 30,000kg (66,138lb)
Dimensions:	wingspan 14.7m (48ft 2.75in); length 21.94m (71ft 11.5in); height 6.36m (20ft 10.25in); wing area 46.5 sq m (500 sq ft)
Armament:	one 30mm GSh-3101 cannon with 149 rounds; 10 external hardpoints with provision for 6000kg (13,228kg) of stores

SUKHOI 'FLANKERS' TIMELINE

 1977

 1985

 1988

Su-33/Su-27K 'Flanker-D'

Experiments with Su-27s modified for carrier operations began as early as 1982, leading to what NATO calls the Su-27K 'Flanker-D' and Sukhoi calls the Su-33, with folding wings and a strengthened landing gear. The 1st Squadron of the Russian Navy occasionally flies them from the carrier *Admiral Kuznetsov*.

SPECIFICATIONS	
Country of origin:	USSR
Type:	twin-engined carrier-based fighter
Powerplant:	two 130.4kN (29,321lb) thrust Lyul'ka AL-31K afterburning turbofan engines
Performance:	maximum speed 2300km/h (1429mph); range 1864 miles (3000km); service ceiling 17,000m (55,750ft)
Weights:	empty 18,400kg (40,600lb); maximum 33,000kg (72,753lb)
Dimensions:	span 14.7m (48ft 3in); length 21.15m (69ft 5in); height 5.85m (19ft 2in); wing area 67.8 sq m (730 sq ft)
Armament:	one 30mm GSh-301 cannon; 12 hardpoints for up to 6500kg (14,330lb) of bombs, air-to-surface missiles, rockets or air-to-air missiles

Su-27IB/Su-34 'Fullback'

Known variously during its development as the Su-27IB and the Su-32FN, the Su-34 'Fullback' has been chosen as Russia's future strike aircraft and is slowly entering squadron service. The side-by-side cockpit has provision for a foldaway galley and toilet to improve crew comfort on long-range missions.

SPECIFICATIONS	
Country of origin:	United States
Type:	twin-engined attack aircraft
Powerplant:	two 137.2kN (30,845lb) thrust Lyul'ka AL-35F afterburning turbofans
Performance:	maximum speed 1900km/h (1180mph); range 4000km (2490 miles); service ceiling 15,000m (49,200ft)
Weights:	empty 22,000kg (48,502lb); maximum 45,100kg (99,425lb)
Dimensions:	span 14.7m (48ft 3in); length 23.34m (72ft 2in); height 6.09m (19ft 5in); wing area 62 sq m (666 sq ft)
Armament:	one SPPU-22 23-mm six-barrelled cannon with 140 rounds; 10 hardpoints for up to 8000kg (17,630lb) of stores

Su-35 (Su-27M)

One of the ongoing developments of the Su-27 is the single-seat Su-35 all-weather air-superiority fighter (derived from the 'Flanker-B'). This aircraft, which has similar powerplant and configuration to the Su-27, is an attempt to provide a second-generation Su-27 with improved agility and operational capability. It first flew in 1988.

SPECIFICATIONS	
Country of origin:	USSR
Type:	single-seat all-weather air superiority fighter
Powerplant:	two 122.5kN (27,557lb) Lyul'ka AL-31M turbofans
Performance:	maximum speed at high altitude 2500km/h (1500mph); service ceiling 18,000m (59,055ft); combat radius 1500km (930 miles)
Weights:	maximum take-off weight 30,000kg (66,138lb)
Dimensions:	wingspan 14.7m (48ft 2.75in); length 21.94m (71ft 11.5in); height 6.36m (20ft 10.25in); wing area 46.5 sq m (500 sq ft)
Armament:	one 30mm GSh-3101 cannon with 149 rounds; 10 external hardpoints with provision for 6000kg (13,228kg) of stores

1990

1994

Glossary

AAM: Air-to-Air Missile

ADP: Automatic Data Processing

ADV: Air Defence Variant (of the Tornado)

Aeronautics: the science of travel through the Earth's atmosphere

Aeroplane (Airplane): powered heavier-than-air craft supported in flight by fixed wings

AEW: Airborne Early Warning

Afterburning (reheat): method of increasing the thrust of a gas turbine aircraft engine by injecting additional fuel into the hot exhaust duct between the engine and the tailpipe, where it ignites to provide a short-term increase of power

Aileron: an aerofoil used for causing an aircraft to roll around its longitudinal axis, usually fitted near the wingtips. Ailerons are controlled by use of the pilot's control column

ALARM: Air-Launched Anti-Radiation Missile

All-Up Weight: the total weight of an aircraft in operating condition. Normal maximum AUW is the maximum at which an aircraft is permitted to fly within normal design restrictions, while overload weight is the maximum AUW at which an aircraft is permitted to fly subject to ultimate flying restrictions

Altimeter: instrument that measures altitude, or height above sea level

AMRAAM: Advanced Medium-Range Air-to-Air Missile

Angle of Attack: the angle between the wing (airfoil) and the airflow relative to it

Aspect Ratio: the ratio of wing span to chord

ASV: Air to Surface Vessel – airborne detection radar for locating ships and submarines

ASW: Anti-Submarine Warfare

ATF: Advanced Tactical Fighter

Autogiro: heavier-than-air craft which supports itself in the air by means of a rotary wing (rotor), forward propulsion being provided by a conventional engine

Automatic Pilot (Autopilot): automatic device that keeps an aircraft flying on a set course at a set speed and altitude

AWACS: Airborne Warning and Control System

Basic Weight: the tare weight of an aircraft plus the specified operational load

Bf: abbreviation for Bayerische Flugzeugwerke (Bavariant Aircraft Factories)

CAP: Combat Air Patrol

Centre of Gravity: point in a body through which the sum of the weights of all its parts passes. A body suspended from this point is said to be in a state of equilibrium

Centre of Pressure: point through which the lifting force of a wing acts

Charged Particle Beam: a stream of charged atomic particles of intense energy, focused on a target

Chord: cross-section of a wing from leading edge to trailing edge

Circular Error Probable (CEP): A measure of the accuracy attributable to ballistic missiles, bombs and shells. It is the radius of a circle into which 50 per cent of the missiles aimed at the centre of the circle are expected to fall.

Clutter: a term used in radar parlance to describe reflected echoes on a cathode ray tube caused by the ground, sea or bad weather

Convertiplane: vertical take-off and landing craft with wing-mounted rotors that act as helicopter rotors for take-off, then tilt to act as conventional propellers for forward flight

Delta Wing: aircraft shaped like the Greek letter delta

Disposable Load: the weight of crew and consumable load (fuel, missiles etc.)

Electronic Combat Reconnaissance (ECR): a variant of the Panavia Tornado optimized for electronic warfare

Electronic Countermeasures (ECM): systems designed to confuse and disrupt enemy radar equipment

Electronic Counter-Countermeasures (ECCM): measures taken to reduce the effectiveness of ECM by improving the resistance of radar equipment to jamming

Elevator: a horizontal control surface used to control the upward or downward inclination of an aircraft in flight. Elevators are usually hinged to the trailing edge of the tailplane

ELF: Extremely Low Frequency. A radio frequency used for communication with submarines

ELINT: Electronic Intelligence. Information gathered through monitoring enemy electronic transmissions by specially equipped aircraft, ships or satellites

Empty Equipped (also known as Tare Weight): the weight of an aircraft equipped to a minimum scale, i.e. with all equipment plus the weight of coolant in the engines, radiators and associated systems, and residual fuel in tanks, engines and associated systems

EW: Electronic Warfare

FAC: Forward Air Controller. A battlefront observer who directs strike aircraft on to their targets near the front line

FAE: Fuel-Air Explosive. A weapon that disperses fuel into the atmosphere in the form of an aerosol cloud. The cloud is ignited to produce intense heat and heat effects

FGA: Fighter Ground Attack

FLIR: Forward-Looking Infra-Red. Heat-sensing equipment fitted in an aircraft that scans the path ahead to detect heat from objects such as vehicle engines

FRS: Fighter Reconnaissance Strike

Gas turbine: engine in which burning fuel supplies hot gas to spin a turbine

Geodetic construction: a 'basket weave' system of aircraft construction producing a self-stabilizing framework in which loads in any direction are automatically equalized by forces in the intersecting set of frames, producing high strength for low weight

GPS: Global Positioning System. A system of navigational satellites

GR: General Reconnaissance

Helicopter: powered aircraft that achieves both lift and propulsion by means of a rotary wing (rotor)

HOTAS: Hands on Throttle and Stick. A system whereby the pilot exercises full control over his aircraft in combat without the need to remove his hands from the throttle and control column to operate weapons selection switches or other controls

HUD: Head-Up Display. A system in which essential information is projected on to a cockpit windscreen so that the pilot has no need to look down at his instrument panel

IFF: Identification Friend or Foe. An electronic pulse emitted by an aircraft to identify it as friendly on a radar screen

INS: Inertial Navigation System. An on-board guidance system that steers an aircraft or missile over a pre-determined course by measuring factors such as the distance travelled and reference to 'waypoints' (landmarks) en route

Interdiction: Deep air strikes into enemy areas to sever communications with the battlefield

IR: Infra-Red

Jet propulsion: method of propulsion in which an object is propelled in one direction by a jet, or stream of gases, moving in the other

JSTARS: Joint Surveillance and Target Attack Radar System. An airborne command and control system that directs air and ground forces in battle

Jumo: abbreviation for Junkers Motorenwerke (Junkers Engine Works)

Kiloton: Nuclear weapon yield, one kiloton (kT) being roughly equivalent to 1000 tons of TNT

Laminar Flow: airflow passes over an aircraft's wing in layers, the first of which, the boundary layer, remains stationary while successive layers progressively accelerate; this is known as laminar flow. The smoother the wing surface, and the more efficient its design, the smoother the airflow

LAMPS: Light Airborne Multi-Purpose System. Anti-submarine helicopter equipment, comprising search radar, sonobuoys and other detection equipment

Landing Weight: the AUW of an aircraft at the moment of landing

Lantirn: Low-Altitude Navigation and Targeting Infra-Red for Night. An infra-red system fitted to the F-15E Strike Eagle that combines heat sensing with terrain-following radar to enable the pilot to view the ground ahead of the aircraft during low-level night operations. The information is projected on the pilot's head-up display

LWR: Laser Warning Radar. Equipment fitted to an aircraft that warns the pilot if he is being tracked by a missile-guiding radar beam

Mach: named after the Austrian Professor Ernst Mach, a Mach number is the ratio of the speed of an aircraft or missile to the local speed of sound. At sea level, Mach One (1.0M) is approximately 1226 km/h (762mph), decreasing to about 1062 km/h (660mph) at 30,000 feet. An aircraft or missile travelling faster than Mach One is said to be supersonic. Mach numbers are dependent on variations in atmospheric temperature and pressure and are registered on a Machmeter in the aircraft's cockpit

MAD: Magnetic Anomaly Detection. The passage of a large body of metal, such as a submarine, through the earth's magnetic field, causes disturbances which can be detected by special equipment, usually housed in an extended tail boom, in an anti-submarine warfare aircraft

Maximum Landing Weight: the maximum AUW, due to design or operational limitations, at which an aircraft is permitted to land

Maximum Take-Off Weight: the maximum AUW, due to design or operational limitations, at which an aircraft is permitted to take off

Megaton: Thermonuclear weapon yield, one megaton (mT) being roughly equal to 1,000,000 tons of TNT

MG: Machine gun (Maschinengewehr in German, hence MG 15)

Microlight: very light aircraft with a small engine; a powered hang-glider

Mk: mark (of aircraft)

MK: Maschinenkanone (automatic cannon, e.g. MK.108)

Muzzle Velocity: the speed at which a bullet or shell leaves a gun barrel

NATO: North Atlantic Treaty Organization

NBC: Nuclear, Chemical and Biological (warfare)

NVG: Night Vision Goggles. Specially designed goggles that enhance a pilot's ability to see at night

OBOGS: On-Board Oxygen Generating System. A system that generates oxygen, avoiding the need to rely on pre-charged oxygen bottles and extending the time a pilot can stay airborne during long transit flights over the ocean, for example

Operational Load: The weight of equipment necessarily carried by an aircraft for a particular role

Payload: the weight of passengers and/or cargo

Phased-Array Radar: A warning radar system using many small aerials spread over a large flat area, rather than a rotating scanner. The advantage of this system is that it can track hundreds of targets simultaneously, electronically directing its beam from target to target in microseconds (millionths of a second)

PLSS: Precision Location Strike System. A battlefield surveillance system installed in the Lockheed TR-1 that detects the movement of enemy forces and directs air and ground attacks against them

Pulse-Doppler Radar: a type of airborne interception radar that picks out fast-moving targets from background clutter by measuring the change in frequency of a series of pulses bounced off the targets. This is based on the well-known Doppler Effect, an apparent change in the frequency of waves when the source emitting them has a relative velocity towards or away from an observer. The MiG-29's noted tail-slide manoeuvre is a tactical move designed to break the lock of a pulse-Dopper radar

Ramjet: simple form of jet engine which is accelerated to high speed causing air to be forced into the combustion chamber, into which fuel is sprayed and then ignited. The Pulse Jet engine, used in the V-1 flying bomb, is a form of ramjet

Rudder: movable vertical surface or surfaces forming part of the tail unit, by which the yawing of an aircraft is controlled

RWR: Radar Warning Receiver. A device mounted on an aircraft that warns the pilot if he is being tracked by an enemy missile guidance or intercept radar

SAM: Surface-to-Air Missile

SHF: Super High Frequency (radio waves)

SIGINT: Signals Intelligence. Information on enemy intentions gathered by monitoring electronic transmissions from his command, control and communications network

SLAM: Stand-off Land Attack Missile – a missile that can be air-launched many miles from its target

SLAR: Side-Looking Airborne Radar. A type of radar that provides a continuous radar map of the ground on either side of the aircraft carrying the equipment

Sound Barrier: popular name for the concept that the speed of sound (see Mach) constitutes a limit to to flight through the atmosphere to all aircraft except those specially designed to penetrate it. The cone-shaped shock wave created by an aircraft breaking the 'barrier' produces a 'sonic boom' when it passes over the ground

Spin: a spin is the result of yawing or rolling an aeroplane at the point of a stall

SRAM: Short-range Attack Missile

Stall: condition that occurs when the smooth flow of the air over an aircraft's wing changes to a turbulent flow and the lift decreases to the point where control is lost

Stealth Technology: technology applied to aircraft or fighting vehicles to reduce their radar signatures. Examples of stealth aircraft are the Lockheed F-117 and the Northrop B-2

STOVL: Short Take-off, Vertical Landing

Stuka: abbreviation of Sturzkampfflugzeug (literally Diving Battle Aircraft)

TADS: Target Acquisition/Designation System. A laser sighting system fitted to the AH-64 Apache attack helicopter

Take-Off Weight: the AUW of an aircraft at the moment of take-off

Thermal Imager: Equipment fitted to an aircraft or fighting vehicle which typically comprises a telescope to collect and focus infra-red energy emitted by objects on a battlefield, a mechanism to scan the scene across an array of heat-sensitive detectors, and a processor to turn the signals from these detectors into a 'thermal image' displayed on a TV screen

TIALD: Thermal Imaging/Airborne Laser Designator. Equipment fitted to the Panavia Tornado IDS enabling it to locate and attack precision targets at night

Turbofan engine: type of jet engine fitted with a very large front fan that not only sends air into the engine for combustion but also around the engine to produce additional thrust. This results in faster and more fuel-efficient propulsion

Turbojet engine: jet engine that derives its thrust from a stream of hot exhaust gases

Turboprop engine: jet engine that derives its thrust partly from a jet of exhaust gases, but mainly from a propeller powered by a turbine in the jet exhaust

Variable-Geometry Wing: a type of wing whose angle of sweep can be altered to suit a particular flight profile. Popularly called a Swing Wing

VHF: Very High Frequency

VLF: Very Low Frequency

V/STOL: Vertical/Short Take-off and Landing

Wild Weasel: code name applied to specialized combat aircraft tasked with defence suppression

Window: strips of tinfoil cut to the wavelengths of enemy radars and scattered from attacking aircraft to confuse enemy defences. Also known as 'chaff'

Yaw: the action of turning an aircraft in the air around its normal (vertical) axis by use of the rudder. An aircraft is said to yaw when the fore-and-aft axis turns to port or starboard, out of the line of flight

Aircraft Index

General Index

Picture Credits